ENCYCLOPEDIA OF AMERICAN BUSINESS

Revised Edition

VOLUME I

GENERAL EDITOR

W. DAVIS FOLSOM

ASSOCIATE EDITOR

STACIA N. VANDYNE

☑ Facts On File
An Infobase Learning Company

Encyclopedia of American Business, Revised Edition

Facts On File, Inc.
An imprint of Infobase Learning
132 West 31st Street
New York NY 10001

Library of Congress Cataloging-in-Publication Data

Encyclopedia of American business / general editor, W. Davis Folsom ; associate editor, Stacia N. VanDyne.—Rev. ed.
   p. cm.
  Includes bibliographical references and index.
  ISBN 978-0-8160-8112-7 (hc : alk. paper) 1. United States—Commerce—Encyclopedias. 2. Business—United States—Encyclopedias. 3. Finance—United States—Encyclopedias. 4. Industries—United States—Encyclopedias. I. Folsom, W. Davis. II. VanDyne, Stacia N.
  HF3021.E53 2011
338.097303—dc22
                                        2010028372

Facts On File books are available at special discounts when purchased in bulk quantities for businesses, associations, institutions, or sales promotions. Please call our Special Sales Department in New York at (212) 967-8800 or (800) 322-8755.

You can find Facts On File on the World Wide Web at http://www.infobaselearning.com

Excerpts included herewith have been reprinted by permission of the copyright holders; the author has made every effort to contact copyright holders. The publisher will be glad to rectify, in future editions, any errors or omissions brought to its notice.

Text design by Erika K. Arroyo
Illustrations by Patricia Meschino
Composition by Hermitage Publishing Services
Cover printed by Yurchak Printing, Inc., Landisville, Pa.
Book printed and bound by Yurchak Printing, Inc., Landisville, Pa.
Date printed: June 2011
Printed in the United States of America

10 9 8 7 6 5 4 3 2 1

This book is printed on acid-free paper.

CONTENTS

LIST OF ENTRIES

INTRODUCTION

The *Encyclopedia of American Business* is designed to assist students and other individuals in understanding the complex world of American business. The United States's economy, at more than $14 trillion in 2010, is the largest economy in the world. The many organizations, institutions, government agencies, laws, and business concepts that make up the U.S. economic system create a complex and confusing, yet exciting, business environment. The goal in creating this encyclopedia is to provide readers with a resource to help them understand the many facets of American business. With the focus on American business, this encyclopedia provides useful insight for businesspeople around the world learning about the U.S. system.

Two major resources were used in determining which topics to include in the encyclopedia. The first was the *Wall Street Journal,* the quintessential U.S. business newspaper. Issues, concepts, laws, and institutions discussed in the *Journal* were a major source of topics for this book. The second was "principles" texts used in beginning management, marketing, economics, finance, and accounting courses. Principles texts introduce students to concepts, laws, and institutions that make up the world of business. The goal is to provide short summaries of these topics as a resource for students and individuals learning about American business.

I would like to thank many individuals who assisted with this project, including Dr. Tao Jin; Dr. Kendra Albright; Dr. Robert Williams; Professor Megan Fox; Melissa Hudson; Judy Mims; Vera Basilone; Tom Odom; our Facts On File editor, Owen Lancer; and the many contributing authors who assisted this effort. Thanks also to the University of South Carolina Beaufort for the support and resources used in creating this work.

This book is dedicated to the many "teachers," family, and friends who have influenced and enriched my life, including Myrtle and Morris Folsom; Ralph, Ellen, Roger, and Herb Folsom; Kathy and Brad Folsom; Dr. A. Robert Koch, Dr. Alpha Chang, Bertie Nelson "The Pro" Butts, Kathie Turick Robie, Jerry and Faye Rosenthal, Phil and Marilyn Ray, Bert and Lucille Keller, Helen Reece, Dr. Robert Botsch, Dr. Jim Snyder, and Dr. Mack Tennyson.

A special thanks to Stacia VanDyne for her careful and insightful editing.

INTRODUCTION TO THE
SECOND EDITION

So much has changed since the publication of the first edition. Corporate giants including General Motors, Federal National Mortgage Association, and Merrill Lynch retreated from the center stage of American business. American financial markets, once a dominant force in the world, panicked and froze. A recession, deeper than any since the 1930s, threw our business system into a myriad of crises.

Understanding our economic system became a concern for all Americans. The second edition includes added emphasis on financial markets, instruments, and regulatory authorities. New entries, including subprime mortgages, multiple listing services, consumer economics, and investment fraud, are all designed to add to consumers' understanding of their role and rights in the business of America.

LIST OF CONTRIBUTORS

ROBERT AMERSON, MLIS, University of South Carolina

RACHEL ARCHANGEL, University of South Carolina Beaufort

DONNA BEALES, Librarian CME Coordinator, Lowell General Hospital

JENNIFER BELL, University of South Carolina

PATTY BERGIN, MLS, Simmons College

ANDREW BLATCHFORD, University of South Carolina

BILL BOLAND, MLIS, University of South Carolina

DR. CAROL SEARS BOTSCH, Professor, University of South Carolina Aiken

DR. ROBERT BOTSCH, Professor, University of South Carolina Aiken

BETH M. BRACCIA, MLS, Simmons College

JANET HADWIN BRACKETT, MLIS, University of Maine, Farmington

JILL BRIGGS, University of South Carolina Beaufort

LAURA W. CARTER, Reference Librarian, Clark County Library

WANDA CARTER, MLIS, University of South Carolina

KAREN M. CIMINO, University of South Carolina Beaufort

TERRYE CONROY, MLIS, University of South Carolina

DR. ELIZABETH L. CRALLEY, American University

ROSA L. CUMMINGS, MLIS, University of South Carolina

JOAN CUNNINGHAM, MLS, Simmons College

JILLANDA DELAHUNTY, University of South Carolina Beaufort

MARY DOW, University of South Carolina

MARGARET C. DUNLAP, MLIS, University of South Carolina

MARY ELIZABETH DUNLAP, MLIS, University of South Carolina

KAREN BRICKMAN EMMONS, MLIS, University of South Carolina

MEGAN D. FENNESSY, MLS, Simmons College

RICHARD FITZGERALD, MD, SC Ethics Commission

RALPH FOLSOM, JD, Professor, University of San Diego Law School

LEAH KNINDE FRAZIER-GASKINS, University of South Carolina Beaufort

LISA VINCENT GAGNON, Librarian, Simmons College

KRISTEN GAUDES, MLS, Simmons College

ABBEY GEHMAN, MLIS, University of South Carolina

JEREMIAH GLENN, University of South Carolina Beaufort

STEPHANIE GODLEY, Reference Librarian, Nixon Peabody LLP

KAREN S. GROVES, MLIS, University of South Carolina

GAYATRI GUPTA, University of San Diego Law School

CINDY L. HALSEY, MLIS, University of South Carolina

R. JOSEPH HAROLD, University of South Carolina Beaufort

MELISSA HUDSON, University of South Carolina Beaufort

LINDSAY INGRAM, University of South Carolina Beaufort

KIMBERLY JEFFERS, University of South Carolina Beaufort

LINDA TRANT JOHNSON, MLIS, University of South Carolina

KRISTI KOHL, MLIS, Louisiana State University

AARON S. JONES, Librarian, Simmons College

ALISON KAISER JONES, MLS, Simmons College

JOI PATRICE JONES, MLIS, University of South Carolina

ANDREW KEARNS, MLIS, University of South Carolina

JENNIFER A. KESSLER, MLS, Simmons College

JOSEPH F. KLEIN, Librarian, University of South Carolina

JENNIFER KOENIG, MLIS, Louisiana State University

JENNIFER R. LAND, MLIS, University of South Carolina

JEMMA LASSETER, MPA, Valdosta State University

JAMES A. LAMEE, MLIS, University of South Carolina

MARK LANE, MLIS, University of South Carolina

GREG LAVERGNE, MLIS, Louisiana State University

CRISSY D. LEWIS, University of South Carolina

THOMAS LIDE, MLIS, University of South Carolina

GEOFF LOCICERO, MLIS, University of South Carolina

RICK LOCKETT, A.G. Edwards and Sons

MELISSA LUMA, University of South Carolina Beaufort

LAURIE MAC WHINNIE, MLIS, University of South Carolina

THOMAS MADDEN, MLS, Simmons College

PAULA MALONEY, MLS, Simmons College

ADRIENNE MATHEUS, University of South Carolina

KATHERINE L. MAY, MSW, MLS, Newton, Massachusetts

TARA LYNN McDONALD, MLS, Simmons College

JENNIFER McGEORGE, MLS, Simmons College

DR. LEANNE McGRATH, Professor, University of South Carolina Aiken

DR. LINDA BRADLEY McKEE, Professor, College of Charleston

CAROLYN McKELVEY, MLS, Simmons College

DR. JERRY MERWIN, Assistant Professor, Valdosta State University

JEREMY MICKELSON, University of South Carolina Beaufort

APRIL MILLER, MLIS, University of South Carolina

KAREN MILLER, MLIS, University of South Carolina

JULIE MILO, MLIS, University of South Carolina

JUDY MIMS, Instructor, University of South Carolina Beaufort

BRANDY MIRE, MLIS, Louisiana State University

MICHELLE MITCHELL, MLIS, University of South Carolina

SUSAN SOURA-MORT, MLS, Simmons College

MAUREN MURRAY, MLS, Simmons College

BETH MYERS, MLIS, University of South Carolina

JIM NIX, University of South Carolina Beaufort

LINDA HICKEY O'QUINN, MLIS, University of South Carolina

LOURDES OWENS, University of South Carolina Beaufort

MEG PARK, MLIS, University of South Carolina

AMANDA RANNSDEN, MLIS, University of South Carolina

KATRINA V. REILING, MLS, Simmons College

JERRY ROSENTHAL, Zip's Business Services

JESSE ROSENTHAL, University of Chicago

DEBORAH J. ROTH, MLS, Simmons College

KRISTIN ROWAN, MLIS, University of South Carolina

DR. HOWARD RUDD, Professor, College of Charleston

RICK PELLETIER, MLIS, University of South Carolina

SUSAN POORBAUGH, MLIS, Medical College of Georgia

JEANNE SAWYER, Sawyer Partnership

ALEXIA SCOTT, University of South Carolina Beaufort

LAURA M. SCOTT, Reference Librarian, Simmons College

SARAH SHEALY, MLIS, University of South Carolina

SUSAN J. SLAGA, MLS, Simmons College

TARA SMITH, MLIS, University of South Carolina

JEREMY SNELL, MLIS, University of South Carolina

DAVID G. SPOOLSTRA, MLS, Simmons College

ALICIA GAIL STOUT, MLIS, Westvaco Corporation

JONATHON R. SULLIVAN, University of South Carolina Beaufort

DR. MACK TENNYSON, Professor, College of Charleston

FRANK UBHAUS, JR., Valdosta State University

ASTA VAICHYS, MLS, Simmons College

GRETCHEN WADE, MLS, Simmons College

AARON WEBSTER, MLIS, Louisiana State University

DANIEL P. WHICKER, University of South Carolina Beaufort

CARRIE WILSON, University of South Carolina Beaufort

DOMINQUE WINN, MLIS, Simmons College

STAN YOCCO, University of South Carolina Beaufort

KATE ANDERSON YOUNG, MLIS, Simmons College

DIANE ZYDLEWSKI, MLS, Simmons College

Special Assistance

Dr. Kendra Albright, University of South Carolina

Professor Megan Fox, Simmons College

Dr. Tao Jin, PhD, Professor, Louisiana State University

Dr. Robert Williams, Professor, University of South Carolina

A

Accounting   See AUDITING; FINANCIAL
ACCOUNTING; MANAGERIAL ACCOUNTING.

Accounting Oversight Board

The Public Company Accounting Oversight Board
(PCAOB) is a five-member board created when
the Sarbanes-Oxley Act was signed into law on
July 30, 2002. The AOB was established to protect
the interests of the investors and the integrity of
financial markets. It was set up in response to the
scandals at Enron, WorldCom, and Andersen as a
means for Congress to assure investors, employees,
and pensioners that the hardships and losses they
had suffered would not be repeated.

The AOB performs the following duties:
registers public accounting firms; establishes
AUDITING, QUALITY CONTROL, ethics, independence, and other standards relating to the preparation of audit reports for issuers; conducts
inspections of accounting firms; conducts investigations and disciplinary proceedings, imposing appropriate sanctions; enforces compliance
with the Sarbanes-Oxley Act and other professional standards; and sets the budget and
manages the operations of the Board and its
staff. The PCAOB is thus given the power to
discipline accountants and issue subpoenas. It
also has authority to amend, modify, repeal,
and reject any standards suggested by the professional groups of accountants and any advi-

sory groups. Some of these relevant groups are:
the FASB (FINANCIAL ACCOUNTING STANDARDS
BOARD), the IASB (International Accounting
Standards Board), the FASAB (Federal Accounting Standards Advisory Board), the GASB (Governmental Accounting Standards Board), and
the AICPA (AMERICAN INSTITUTE OF CERTI-
FIED PUBLIC ACCOUNTANTS). The AOB must
report its standard-setting activity to the SECU-
RITIES AND EXCHANGE COMMISSION annually.
It requires registered public accounting firms
to prepare and maintain files for a period of at
least seven years, to audit work papers and other
information related to an audit report in sufficient detail to support the conclusions reached
in the report.

Members of the board are appointed by the
Securities and Exchange Commission (SEC) in
consultation with the Federal Reserve Chairman
and the Secretary of the Treasury. The Sarbanes-
Oxley Act states that board members must be
"prominent individuals of integrity and reputation who have demonstrated commitment to
the interests of investors and the public, and an
understanding of the responsibilities and nature
of financial disclosure . . . and the obligations of
accountants with respect to the preparation and
issuance of audit reports with respect to such
disclosures." By law, two members of the board
must be or must have been CERTIFIED PUBLIC

ACCOUNTANTS and the three remaining members must not be and cannot have been certified public accountants. Members of the board are appointed for a five-year term during which time they will serve on a full-time basis.

Soon after the Accounting Oversight Board came into existence, controversy arose over the process of selecting board members. The SEC named William Webster, former director of both the FBI and the CIA, as chairman of the board in a divided vote (a 3-2 approval). Criticism mounted after the *New York Times* reported that Webster had warned SEC Chairman Harvey Pitt, but not the entire Commission, before the vote on his nomination that he had recently headed the auditing committee of a company facing FRAUD accusations from investors. Additionally, SEC Commissioner Harvey J. Goldschmid argued that Pitt had initially promised the chairmanship to John Biggs, head of the giant teachers pension fund TIAA-CREF, who had called for tight oversight of the accounting industry. Goldschmid further argued that Pitt had changed his mind under pressure from the industry and Republican lawmakers. There was general consensus among SEC members to open an investigation into the process used to select William Webster and other board members. Webster subsequently resigned his position as chairman.

In 2009 Mark W. Olson, a former member of the Federal Reserve's Board of Governors chaired the PCAOB. Other board members included Daniel L. Goelzer, former general counsel at the SEC; Bill Gradison, a former member of Congress; Steven B. Harris; and Charles D. Niemeier, formerly a senior enforcement official at the SEC. All of the PCAOB board members, except the chair, have served since the creation of the board in 2002.

The Accounting Oversight Board is funded by assessed contributions from publicly traded CORPORATIONS. The Board collects a registration fee and an annual fee from every public accounting firm in amounts that are sufficient to recover the COSTS of processing and reviewing applications and ANNUAL REPORTS.

Further reading

American Institute of Certified Public Accountants. "Summary of Sarbanes-Oxley Act of 2002." American Institute of Certified Public Accountants Web site. Available online. URL: http://www.aicpa.org/info/sarbanes_oxley_summary.htm. Accessed on May 27, 2003. "Statement by SEC Commissioner: New Public Company Accounting Oversight Board by Commissioner Harvey J. Goldschmid," U.S. Securities and Exchange Commission, Open Committee Meeting, October 25, 2002. Accessed on May 27, 2003. URL: www.sec.gov/news/press.html.

—Beth Myers

accounts payable, trade credit
Accounts payable are a part of a firm's current liabilities, debts that must be paid within the short term. The accounts payable are the firm's trade credit. As the firm does business with its suppliers and other firms on a credit basis, accounts payable accrue. Trade credit is a source of CAPITAL for the firm. Using invoices instead of cash, trade credit facilities purchases from suppliers and others; cumbersome cash transactions aren't necessary when firms have good trade credit. When the accounts payable are kept current (i.e., paid on a timely basis), trade credit creates a good reputation for the firm among those with whom it does business.

To encourage the early payment of invoices, most suppliers' invoices contain sales discounts. There are percentages that can be deducted for the early payment of an invoice. A commonly used sales discount found on invoices is "2/10, net 30." This means that 2 percent may be deducted from the invoice if payment is made within 10 days of the invoice date; otherwise the full amount of the invoice is due within 30 days of the invoice date.

Sales discounts apply to short periods of time, usually 10 or 15 days, but when expressed as an annual percentage rate, these discounts are considerable and are powerful incentives for credit customers to pay early. The sales discount of "2/10, net 30" is greater than 36 percent when expressed as an annual percentage rate; "1/15, net 30" is approximately a 24-percent annual percentage rate. Consider a firm with a sizable amount of trade credit, which consistently pays its bills late, not taking advantage of the sales discounts. Such a firm is using its suppliers' money, borrowing it at INTEREST RATES more commonly associated with CREDIT CARDS and finance companies.

accounts receivable

Accounts receivable are part of a firm's ASSETS; they represent monies owed to the firm. (While receivables are assets, payables are liabilities to a firm. Payables are the firm's debt—that is, monies owed by the firm.) An account receivable is created when a firm sells a good or service to a customer on credit (see DEBIT, CREDIT). Rather than receiving an asset in the form of cash, the firm records an asset called an account receivable. The sum of all the monies owed to the firm by its customers collectively is called accounts receivable.

Because accounts receivable are assets, debit entries will increase accounts receivable, and credit entries will decrease accounts receivable. Because of the dual nature of a transaction (an exchange of equal-valued resources between two parties), for every account receivable in a firm's ledger, there is an equal-valued account payable in another firm's ledger.

Every firm that sells on credit will have an INVESTMENT in accounts receivable. The presence of accounts receivable, especially when sizable, creates a cash-flow problem for a firm. A sale was made; the merchandise was sold, but it was not liquidated (cash was not received). Thus, accounts receivable are in reality a pool of idle cash. To offset cash-flow problems, the accounts receivable need to be collected on a timely basis. Firms monitor their investment in accounts receivable by comparing their "days sales outstanding" (DSO) ratio with that of their industry.

A popular way firms attempt to offset cash-flow problems associated with receivables is to offer sales discounts on the invoices sent to their credit customers. Sales discounts are percentages that can be deducted for the early payment of an invoice. A commonly used sales discount found on invoices is "2/10, net 30." This means that 2 percent may be deducted from the invoice if payment is made within 10 days of the invoice date; otherwise, the full amount of the invoice is due within 30 days of the invoice date. These sales discounts apply to short periods of time, usually 10 or 15 days, but when expressed as an annual percentage rate, these discounts are considerable and are powerful incentives for credit customers to pay early.

Because it is impossible to predict with accuracy which customers are good credit risks, it is natural and expected that some of the accounts receivable will ultimately prove to be uncollectible, at which time they will be written off as BAD DEBTS. Bad-debt expense can be minimized by a tightening of a firm's credit policy. However, there is a trade-off: having a tight credit policy means that a firm will sacrifice sales to its marginal credit customers. Periodically a firm may review the status of its accounts receivable using an accounting method known as aging of accounts receivable (see BAD DEBTS, AGING OF ACCOUNTS), where the outstanding balance of each account and its DURATION are determined.

See also ACCOUNTS PAYABLE, TRADE CREDIT.

accrual basis, cash basis

GENERALLY ACCEPTED ACCOUNTING PRINCIPLES (GAAP) require accounting on the accrual basis, as opposed to the cash basis for accounting. In cash-basis accounting, revenues are recorded when the monies are received. Expenses are recognized and recorded only when they are paid. In other words, revenues and expenses are recorded only when there is a movement of cash either into or out of the firm, respectively. The use of cash-basis accounting is found in only a few types of businesses, namely restaurants, medical offices, and legal firms.

Accrual-basis accounting is based upon GAAP, primarily the revenue and matching principles. The revenue principle requires that revenues be recognized and recorded when they are earned; this may not be at the same time that the revenues are received. For example, suppose a firm sells a computer on credit in December 2009, and the customer pays for the purchase in January 2010.

Using the accrual basis, the sale and revenue is recorded when the transaction occurs—that is, in 2009. When payment from the customer is received in the next year, this is an entirely separate transaction and is recorded with the other transactions of the firm for the year 2010. (If cash-basis accounting were used, the firm would not record the computer sale in 2009, although that is when the sale was made. It would record the computer sale in 2010, because that is when the firm received payment for the computer. Transactions in cash-basis accounting are not recorded unless there is either a receipt or payment of money.)

It is impossible for a firm to generate revenue without incurring some sort of expense. When a good is sold, the expense account—COST OF GOODS SOLD—is debited (increased). If a service is performed, labor and/or supplies expense is debited. The matching principle requires that the expenses incurred in the generation of a firm's revenue for a particular time period be recorded (included) in the same time period as the revenues to which they are related. For example, suppose a firm receives its telephone bill in January for its telephone expense that month, and the firm pays that bill two months later, in March. Even though the expense is paid in March, it is a January expense, not a March expense. The matching principle requires the expense to be recorded in January.

It is evident from the examples above that an accurate measurement of a firm's periodic revenues and expenses in only realized with accrual-basis accounting. In the accrual basis, revenues and expenses are recorded when the sale is made and the expense is incurred. Cash-basis accounting ignores the concept of periodicity by recording revenues and expenses only when money changes hands. For this reason, accrual-basis accounting is generally accepted.

achievement motivation

Achievement motivation has to do with how inspired people are to pursue and accomplish their goals. When an individual does accomplish a desired goal, it typically results in a sense of positive self-worth, which contributes to personal and professional growth and development. The motivation to achieve may be affected both by dispositional characteristics, such as individuals' perceptions of their abilities and potential to succeed; and by external forces, such as the promise of rewards for success or threat of punishment for failure.

Some individuals appear to have an intrinsically high level of achievement motivation. These people typically do not require the use of external incentives to prompt them to work towards their goals because they already have the desire to do so. People who are motivated mainly by a high need to achieve will seek out challenging tasks and work hard to succeed at them. People low in the need for achievement tend to pursue very easy tasks, where the chances of success are high; or they choose tasks that are extremely difficult, where no reasonable person could be expected to succeed. Thus when failure occurs, it is not attributed to the person's lack of skills or abilities but to the difficult nature of the task.

In contrast, some individuals are driven primarily by a fear of failure rather than a need to achieve. This fear of failure may lead them to avoid challenging tasks altogether. People who are motivated mainly by this fear will avoid the risks presented by difficult or complex tasks, precisely because they may result in failure. Instead, these individuals tend to prefer easy tasks where, even though the rewards may be small, the chances of success are great. A smaller subset of individuals may be motivated by a fear of success. People who fear success may worry that after succeeding at a challenging task, other people will raise their expectations of them. The pressure of these expectations, coupled with the individual's fear that he or she will be unable to continue success at that level, may lead these individuals to sabotage their own efforts to succeed in the first place. Thus they avoid the potential anxiety and pressure associated with success.

In addition, the nature of any given task may affect an individual's decision to pursue it and how hard that person tries to succeed. Specific tasks may elicit either intrinsic or extrinsic motivation, or both. Intrinsic motivation involves the desire to perform a behavior or task for its own sake, perhaps because the person finds it pleasurable or exciting. Extrinsic motivation involves performing a behavior or task in order to earn external rewards or to avoid punishments. Maximizing intrinsic motivation appears to be very effective for increasing and maintaining the performance of a desired behavior. Therefore employers or supervisors who try to make routine tasks more interesting or exciting may increase the chances that employees will want to work on those tasks.

On the other hand, providing external motivators for a task that is already intrinsically motivating may backfire, inadvertently decreasing the person's intrinsic motivation to perform it. For example, one study found that people who were given money as an external motivator for working on a puzzle found the puzzle to be less interesting than people who were not paid for working on it. Extrinsic rewards may change people's perceptions of how attractive or fun a particular task may be. In other words, once someone receives money for a task, it becomes more like work than like pleasure. In this respect the extrinsic reward may be interpreted as a control device used to entice a person into working on a task that has little intrinsic value.

However, the use of extrinsic rewards can be highly effective under certain conditions, such as when they are used to provide feedback or information concerning a person's performance. For example, when a salesperson receives an unexpected bonus for successful work, he may increase his future efforts, thus leading to improved performance rather than a decreased interest in continuing the task.

Finally, achievement motivation is linked to EMPLOYEE MOTIVATION in the sense that people motivated by a high need to achieve will likely seek out challenging tasks at work and strive to accomplish them. Employees with a high level of achievement motivation can contribute in significant ways to the success of any business.

See also MOTIVATION THEORY; PERFORMANCE APPRAISAL.

Further reading
Baron, Robert A., and Donn Byrne. *Social Psychology.* 11th ed. Boston: Allyn and Bacon, 2006; Myers, David G. *Exploring Psychology.* 7th ed. New York: Worth Publishers, 2007.

—Elizabeth L. Cralley

acquisitions   See MERGERS AND ACQUISITIONS.

activity-based costing
Activity-based costing (ABC) is a cost-accounting tool that attempts to determine the cost of each activity in the production or service process. Traditional cost accounting focuses on accumulating the total cost of the item produced by cost inputs (i.e., salaries, materials, overhead). ABC overcomes the deficiencies in this process by looking at the cost from an activity perspective instead of an inputs perspective. For example, a traditional cost-accounting system may say the painting department had the following COSTS for painting one appliance: direct labor, $20; direct materials, $10; assigned overhead, $20. An activity-based cost system would show the cost by activities: sanding, $5; cleaning, $5; spraying, $25; drying, $10; inspection, $5.

At the heart of this concept is the handling of overhead. Traditional cost accounting incorrectly assigns overhead based on some other cost such as direct labor. This often causes erroneous management data that assigns too much overhead to large jobs and too little to small jobs. It may allocate too much overhead to departments with less machinery and too little overhead to departments with more machinery.

Activity-based accounting tries to address this shortfall by allocating cost based on what it calls "cost drivers." Cost drivers are the items in the business that create overhead. Examples of cost drivers include number of production runs, number of engineering change orders, number of purchase orders, number of vendors, and number of parts. Activity-based costing requires the additional effort needed to determine what cost drivers are producing the overhead, and then it allocates the overhead to the activities based on the driver. This gives a much more accurate total cost calculation.

adaptability screening

Adaptability screening is identifying prospective employees who will be most likely to adjust to a company's work environment. Psychologist Dr. Saul Sells, who developed adaptability screening in the 1950s, emphasized the need to study behavior in its natural setting. In his first adaptability screening research, Dr. Sells tested pilots training for the U.S. Air Force and then assessed their performance in combat during the Korean War. His research became the basis for pilot selection and performance prediction.

Adaptability screening is now used in a wide variety of businesses. Predictive models help managers estimate the needed staffing level, adjusting for sick leave, relief, and physical conditions. Models can also predict which workers will adjust to shift work, changing schedules in factories operating 24 hours a day. By identifying those workers who can adjust to changes in sleep, fatigue, and health, adaptability screening can reduce absenteeism and improve safety and the work environment.

When combined with payroll systems and task load management, the results of adaptability screening can be used to optimize production operations. Screening also reduces training costs through more effective recruitment and retention rates.

See also INDUSTRIAL-ORGANIZATIONAL PSYCHOLOGY.

Further reading

Kaplan, D., and R. L. Venezky. *What Can Employers Assume about the Literacy Skills of GED Students?* Technical Publication of the National Center on Adult Literacy, September 1993; Simpson, D. Dwayne. "Founder and Former Director of IBR: Saul B. Sells," *American Psychologist* (December 1988): 1088.

adjusting entry, trial balance, adjusted trial balance

An adjusting entry is a journal entry made at the end of an accounting period to record accruals that have occurred during that time period. Adjusting entries are common to ACCRUAL BASIS accounting, but they are not found in cash basis accounting. An accrual is an ASSET (other than cash), LIABILITY, equity account, revenue or expense that has accrued within a particular accounting period. In the case of a long-term note receivable, interest income will be earned each accounting period, although the interest income may not be received until the maturation of the note. Interest income will accrue over the life of the note, and it must be recorded as it is earned, not when it is received. In the case of a note payable, interest expense will accrue over time. As interest expense accrues, it must be recorded. The recognition and recording of such accruals is normally done at the end of the accounting period with adjusting entries.

As with most accounting entries, an adjusting entry is a double entry with one account being debited and another account credited. One of the entries will always be an INCOME STATEMENT account (either a revenue account or expense account), and the other entry will be a BALANCE SHEET account (either an asset, liability, or equity account). Because adjusting entries are necessary for the proper application of accrual-basis accounting, cash is never one of the accounts in an adjusting entry.

Frequently a trial balance is performed before the adjusting entries are made. The trial balance, consisting of a debit and a credit column, is a listing of all the ledger accounts with their net debit or net credit balances. The total of all the ledger accounts with debit balances should be equal to the total of all the accounts with credit balances. If the total debits are unequal to the total credits, an accounting error has been made. If there is equality, the trial balance signals the "green light" to proceed to the next step in the accounting cycle, the adjusting entries.

A trial balance constructed after the adjusting entries have been made is called an adjusted trial balance. As such, the adjusted trial balance includes all of the firm's revenue and expense transactions for that accounting period—that is, the cash transactions and the accruals. If the total debits are equal to the total credits, the adjusting trial balance again signals a "green light" to proceed to the next phase of the accounting cycle.

See also DEBIT, CREDIT.

administrative law

Administrative law is all law regarding administrative agencies, including rules, statutes, regulations, and agency and court interpretations of these activities. An administrative agency is any nonjudicial, nonlegislative government entity that creates and administers laws. Major administrative agencies affecting businesses in the United States include the FEDERAL TRADE COMMISSION (FTC), ENVIRONMENTAL PROTECTION AGENCY (EPA) and DEPARTMENT OF LABOR, to name a few.

Administrative agencies can be created by either statutes or executive orders. Most are created by statutes known as organic acts, whereby a legislature recognizes a problem and creates an agency to address the problem. Administrative agencies are often created when

- legislatures and courts do not have the technical expertise to deal with specific issues
- ongoing oversight is needed for the protection of society from harm
- the weak and poor need assistance
- there is need for speed and efficiency in government decision making
- conflicts exist between groups and the judicial system

Some of the more important federal administrative law statutes include

- the Federal Register Act (1935), providing ways for citizens to access up-to-date information about agencies and regulations
- the Administrative Procedure Act (1946), setting requirements for conducting rulemaking and adjudication by agencies
- the FREEDOM OF INFORMATION ACT (FOIA, 1966), requiring agencies to disclose information in their possession to citizens
- the Federal Privacy Act of 1974, preventing agencies from disclosing about individuals without prior written consent

- the Sunshine Act (Government in Sunshine Act of 1976), or open meeting law, requiring agencies to conduct business in open forums
- the Civil Service Reform Act (1978), protecting many, but not all, civilian federal employees involved in WHISTLE-BLOWER complaints

Administrative law also includes sunset provisions, which terminate administrative agencies after a set period of time; and the creation of ombudspersons, agency representatives whose job is to ensure agencies operate for the purpose and benefit they were created.

Further reading

Fisher, Bruce D., and Michael J. Phillips. *The Legal, Ethical and Regulatory Environment of Business.* 8th ed. Cincinnati, Ohio: Cengage/South-Western, 2003.

adoption process

The adoption process is the series of stages through which consumers determine whether or not to become regular purchasers of a PRODUCT. When considering a new product, most consumers go through five stages in the adoption process: awareness, interest, evaluation, trial, and adoption/rejection. Marketers, recognizing which stage in the adoption process consumers are in, adjust their MARKETING STRATEGY to meet consumer needs.

During the awareness stage, potential consumers first learn that a new product exists, but lack complete information about the product. Marketers with new products attempt to create awareness through publicity, promotion, and word-of-mouth referral.

During the interest stage, consumers begin to seek information about new products. Often potential consumers will seek out consumer innovators—people they know who are knowledgeable about specific categories of products. Potential consumers will also request or look for information from the company or objective sources.

During the evaluation stage, consumers will consider the benefits of the product. For consumers in the evaluation stage, marketers attempt to demonstrate the benefits of their product, sometimes emphasizing the superiority of their new product compared to existing products. If the benefits meet the needs of the consumers, they will enter the trial stage. Samples, price discounts, and demonstrations are offered to encourage consumer trials. If the trial stage produces positive results, consumers will adopt the product and use it regularly; if not, it is rejected.

Consumers go through the adoption process for many categories of goods, including routinely purchased convenience goods, shopping goods, and specialty goods. Less time is involved for convenience goods and more time allotted for specialty goods. Consider the purchase of a new snack food (a convenience good). Usually consumers become aware of the existence of the new product through a store display or by being offered samples. Often they will only consider a new snack food when their favorite food is not available. Snack foods are not expensive, so people will try new products, which they will quickly adopt or reject. For specialty products, things people seek out and spend time evaluating before purchase, marketers recognize they will often need to use image ADVERTISING to generate awareness and interest and PERSONAL SELLING to move potential buyers through the evaluation and trial stages.

Further reading

Boone, Louis E., and David Kurtz. *Contemporary Marketing.* 14th ed. Fort Worth: South-Western, 2009.

advertising

Advertising—communication of a product or service through various media—is distinguished from publicity in that it is paid for and from PERSONAL SELLING in that it is nonpersonal and directed toward a group of consumers, the firm's target market. While many people think advertising and personal selling are essentially all there is to marketing, advertising is part of an organization's integrated MARKETING COMMUNICATIONS. Integrated marketing communications is the coordination of all promotional efforts, including advertising, DIRECT MAIL, personal selling, SALES PROMOTION, and PUBLIC RELATIONS. An organization's integrated marketing communications are,

in turn, part of the organization's marketing strategy, including pricing, distribution, and PRODUCT strategies as well as marketing communications.

Advertising in the United States began in the 18th century with craftsmen placing signs outside their dwellings to symbolize their trade. Cobblers used a shoe, gunsmiths used a rifle, and seamstresses used scissors to convey to consumers what product or service they offered. Especially in a market where many consumers were illiterate, symbols told consumers what was available. Even today these symbols can still be seen in company logos and small-town businesses. (Twentieth-century restaurateurs also used pictures of meal combinations to assist illiterate consumers.) Before billboard advertising, firms hired individuals to carry sandwich boards along city streets telling consumers about their products. Early print advertisements included newspaper ads and flyers distributed in markets.

Advertisements typically promote either products or institutions. Product advertisements promote particular products or SERVICES, while institutional advertisements promote ideas; concepts; philosophies; or the goodwill of an industry, firm, or organization. Advertising is used by both for-profit and nonprofit organizations. Major media are required to provide outlets for community-service advertising.

Generally there are three goals in advertising: to inform, persuade, or remind consumers and potential customers. Modern advertisements may consist of a billboard announcing a new business located nearby (inform), a television advertisement trying to convince diners to eat at a particular fast-food restaurant (persuade), or a postcard from the dentist to say a tooth cleaning is due (remind).

One variation of persuasive advertising is comparative advertising: efforts that directly or indirectly promote comparisons with competing products. Companies that are not the dominant firm in the industry often favor this form of advertising, comparing their products to the offerings of the leading firm in the industry. Avis car rentals was one of the early users of comparative advertising with their "We're #2, We Try Harder" campaign. FEDERAL TRADE COMMISSION regulations require advertisers to be able to substantiate claims made in comparative advertisements.

Few consumers realize how much effort and planning goes into advertising campaigns. Marketers start by defining objectives for an advertising effort. TARGET MARKETS are identified, advertising messages and media determined, and the new advertising campaign coordinated with other elements in the organization's marketing strategy.

Often considerable research is used in making advertising decisions. Consumer opinions and reactions are tested, and product features, market conditions, and competitors are all analyzed before executing an advertising campaign. Creative aspects of advertising—including wording, symbols, colors, and use of celebrities—are all carefully analyzed. FOCUS GROUPS are often asked to comment on advertising design before the campaign is implemented.

Print advertisements typically contain four elements: the headline, illustration, body COPY, and signature. The headline is a catchy word or phrase designed to gain attention. The illustration or images combine with the headline to gain interest as well as attention. The body copy serves to inform and then persuade consumers into taking action. The signature includes the company's name, address, and/or TRADEMARK to remind viewers who is sponsoring the advertisement.

Once advertising objectives are defined, tactical plans are developed, including budgets, media choices, and scheduling. Each step is critical to the success of an advertising campaign. A good message conveyed through the right media but at the wrong time will likely fail. For example, Campbell Soup Company once coordinated a radio campaign in the Northeast, scheduling messages with weather reports. The first message said, "Storms are coming, time to stock up on Campbell Soup." When storms arrived, the follow-up message said, "It's cold outside, time to stay warm with a cup of Campbell Soup." The same message delivered in the summertime would have failed.

There are seven media alternatives advertisers can use to convey their message to their target audience: television, radio, newspapers, magazines, direct mail, outdoor, and electronic/interactive. In the 21st century, seismic shifts have occurred in advertising priorities. In general, the use of television and newspaper advertising has declined, direct mail has diminished, outdoor advertising features electronic billboards, and Internet advertising has grown dramatically as marketers better understand the power of interactive media to target and communicate with consumers. Each media alternative has advantages and disadvantages:

	advantages	disadvantages
television	mass coverage, prestige, repetition	expensive, temporary, lack of selectivity, zapping, public distrust
radio	low cost, targeted audience; quickly delivered	short life span; highly fragmented audiences
newspapers	community reputation, ability to refer to	image reproduction, life span
magazines	selectivity, long life, image reproduction	lack of flexibility
direct mail	selectivity, flexibility, personalized message	cost, consumer distrust, mailing list problems
outdoor	quick, visual, link to locations, repetition	brief exposure, environmental concerns, limited message
electronic/ interactive	two-way communication, cost flexibility, consumer-directed demographics	Internet problems, Web viewer acceptance

As portrayed on many television shows, most major advertisers hire advertising agencies to plan and prepare advertising campaigns (automobile manufacturers, the military, and beer companies are the largest spenders in the United States). Advertising agencies live and die with decisions by major clients to take their account to another agency. In today's global marketplace, ad agencies have emerged to become international service providers for their clients.

Further reading

Boone, Louis E., and David L. Kurtz. *Contemporary Marketing.* 10th ed. Fort Worth, Tex.: South-Western, 2009.

affluent society

The term *affluent society* comes from economist John Kenneth Galbraith's 1958 book *The Affluent Society.* Writing during a period when the United States maintained unilateral dominance of the global economy, Galbraith predicted a widening gap between rich and poor which, in turn, would destabilize economic systems. To overcome the disparities between the wealthiest and poorest Americans, Galbraith argued for significant public INVESTMENT in education, transportation, parks, and social needs.

The Affluent Society remains a classic analysis of the conflict between capitalism and society's needs. Using the language and logic of an economist, Galbraith articulated more expanded economic role for government than was generally accepted at that time. His book is credited with influencing such politicians as Bill Clinton and Tony Blair. The affluent society has come to symbolize widespread prosperity, sometimes referring to levels of conspicuous CONSUMPTION associated with the 1980s in the United States.

Further reading

Galbraith, John Kenneth. *The Affluent Society.* Boston: Houghton Mifflin, 1958.

affluenza

A 1997 Public Broadcasting System (PBS) documentary defined affluenza as, "1. The bloated, sluggish and unfulfilled feeling that results from efforts to keep up with the Joneses. 2. An epidemic of stress, overwork, waste and indebtedness caused by dogged pursuit of the AMERICAN DREAM. 3. An unsustainable addiction to economic growth. 4. A television program that could change your life." Produced by John de Graaf and narrated by PBS news reporter Scott Simon, *Affluenza* and its sequel *Escape from Affluenza* challenged long-held American attitudes toward material CONSUMPTION.

Affluenza is not solely an American affliction. British psychologist Oliver James suggests that higher rates of mental disorders are the result of excessive wealth-seeking behavior in consumerist nations. James defines affluenza as "placing a high value on money, possessions, appearances (physical and social) and fame." He contends that societies can control the negative affects of affluenza by pursuing real needs over perceived wants, and by people defining themselves as having value independent of their material possessions.

The first part of the PBS definition suggests that affluenza constitutes a personal set of values and that spending priorities are inculcated in, embraced, or blindly accepted by consumers. As early as 1960, Vance Packard, in *The Hidden Persuaders,* suggested advertisers manipulate consumers, creating and then fulfilling supposed "needs." More recently, Adbusters.org annually challenges North Americans with its "Buy Nothing Day" campaign on the day after Thanksgiving, traditionally the largest retail sales day of the year. The PBS documentaries and adbusters.org are designed to highlight dysfunctional relationships many individuals have with money/wealth.

The second part of the PBS definition, "an epidemic of stress, overwork, waste and indebtedness" addresses the psychological, environmental, and economic consequences of affluenza. In *God Bless You Mr. Rosewater,* author Kurt Vonnegut described the psychological consequences of pursuing the American dream as "fright about not getting enough to eat, about not being able to pay the doctor, about not being able to give your family nice clothes, a safe, cheerful, comfortable place to live, a decent education, and a few good times." The environmental consequences are easily observed in landfills around the country, while the economic effects of affluenza became evident with widespread home foreclosures in many parts of the country during the 2008–09 housing crisis. The "unsustainable addiction to economic growth" has been demonstrated in the collapse of the global financial system and in the global warming impact challenges facing the planet.

Further reading

"Adbusters." Available online. URL: www.adbusters.org. Accessed March 13, 2009; James, Oliver. *Affluenza: How to Be Successful and Stay Sane.* London: Vermilion, 2007; PBS Affluenza Web site. Available online. URL: www.pbs.org/kcts/affluenza. Accessed May 4, 2010.

agency theory

Agency theory is a management and economic theory that attempts to explain relationships and self-interest in business organizations. In agency theory, principals contract with agents to perform tasks for the benefit of the principal. In making the CONTRACT with the agent, the principal delegates authority regarding how a task is to be accomplished, holding the agent responsible for attaining a certain outcome but not dictating the methods used to achieve the outcome.

Typical principal-agent relationships include shareholder-manager and manager-employee relationships. In a shareholder-manager relationship, the SHAREHOLDERS, through their BOARD OF DIRECTORS, set goals and managers allocate the company's RESOURCES to attain the goals. As evidenced in the Enron scandal, management's goals may be in conflict with those of shareholders. In the Enron case, managers manipulated financial arrangements among themselves, profiting significantly but ultimately bankrupting the company and leaving Enron shareholders (and many employees) with nothing.

Agency theory suggests that a system is needed to ensure managers operate in the best interests of the principals they represent. As in the Enron case, AUDITING is one agency cost principals incur in order to monitor the activities of managers. Limits placed by shareholders on the options managers can choose, such as private PARTNERSHIPS with executives, and bonus systems are also used to reduce the conflict of purposes between the self-interests of managers and the interests of shareholders.

Performance-based pay systems are designed to give agents—whether managers reporting to the board of directors of employees reporting to managers—incentives to work for the best interests of the principals. In many instances, these systems fail to attain the desired goal. MIT management professor Robert Gibbons describes three cases where incentive systems failed.

At the H. J. Heinz Company, for example, division managers received bonuses only if earnings increased from the prior year. The managers delivered consistent earnings growth by manipulating the timing of shipments to customers and by prepaying for services not yet received. At Dun & Bradstreet, salespeople earned no commission unless the customer bought a larger subscription to the firm's credit-report services than in the previous year. In 1989, the company faced millions of dollars in lawsuits following charges that its salespeople deceived customers into buying larger subscriptions by fraudulently overstating their historical usage. In 1992, Sears abolished the commission plan in its auto-repair shops, which paid mechanics based on the profits from repairs authorized by customers. Mechanics misled customers into authorizing unnecessary repairs, leading California officials to prepare to close Sears' auto-repair business statewide. In each of these cases, employees took actions to increase their compensation, but these actions were seemingly at the expense of long-run firm value.

Sales managers frequently face principal-agent conflicts. Straight salary systems would deter actions on the part of sales agents that are in conflict with the goals of the sales manager, but straight salary systems do not give salespeople positive work incentives.

Agency theory suggests that businesses operate under conditions of uncertainty and lack of complete information. Given these obstacles, two agency problems arise: the problem of employees not putting forth their maximum effort, referred to as moral hazard; and the problem of agents misrepresenting their ability to do the work for which they are being hired, called adverse selection. As in the situations Gibbons described, tying compensation to performance or profits does not eliminate the problem of conflicting interests between principals and agents. While agency theory illustrates the economic conflicts between groups, few solutions beyond vigilance, on the part of principals, have been proposed.

See also PERFORMANCE APPRAISAL.

Further reading

Gibbons, Robert S., "Agency Theory, Part II: Getting What You Pay for." Available online. URL: web.mit.edu/rgibbons/www/903_1n2.pdf; Kaplan, B., "Transaction Costs vs. Agency Theory." Available online URL: wizrd.ucr.edu/~bkaplan/soc/lib/txcosta.pdf.

aging of accounts   See BAD DEBTS, AGING OF ACCOUNTS.

agricultural support programs

Agriclultural support programs are payments and incentives that subsidize agricultural businesses and growers. These subsidies include price supports, TARIFFS, and deficiency payments. Included in the system are incentives to conserve land and water resources, help stabilize the INCOME of farmers and ranchers, and enable new or disadvantaged farmers to get into the food production business. Agricultural subsidies, both in the United States and elsewhere, are political and highly controversial.

Agriculture is the world's most heavily subsidized trade sector. The WORLD TRADE ORGANIZATION (WTO) estimates that current government subsidies to farmers worldwide amount to $350 billion per year. The EUROPEAN UNION, United States, and Japan, in that order, are the major users of agricultural support programs. Government support and protection of industries has been increasing and all countries have felt the consequences. These programs impact ECONOMIC GROWTH, increase trade friction between nations, increase budget expenditures, and depress COMMODITY MARKETS. High price supports encourage surpluses, which distort global market prices. Restrictive import barriers keep some producers from being able to sell their products in certain markets.

The underlying reason for agricultural subsidies is to make sure there is enough food and fiber on American tables and to ensure that American farmers can produce our food. When the U.S. population was still growing at a fast rate, the focus of the federal government's agricultural policy was on feeding its citizens. Many of the policy elements now in place were essential to accomplishing those goals.

Agricultural policy is political. U.S. government support for agriculture began in the late 1800s but became more structured and institutionalized after the GREAT DEPRESSION. Since the 1930s, agricultural support programs have been reexamined, and roughly every six years major new legislation has been passed. American farmers generally have resisted changes in subsidies and efforts to integrate the production and export market considerations.

The 1985 Farm Bill established the Conservation Reserve Program (CRP), providing incentives that encourage farmers to contract to set aside environmentally sensitive farmland for a period of time, usually 10 years. The Federal Agriculture Improvement and Reform (FAIR) Act (also known as the 1996 Farm Bill and "Freedom to Farm") was the first major attempt to get rid of much of the old structure in farm programs. Farmers had been chafing for years at the controls in place on what they could grow and how much they could produce. Many felt that efficient, productive farmers were penalized, and farmers who were poor managers or not as productive as others were rewarded. There had been major abuses in the system, with large agribusiness CONGLOMERATES getting much of the money intended for small-family farmers. The "Freedom to Farm" bill was intended to solve many of the problems that had been in the system up to that point. Farmers were optimistic about the bill, because it increased their flexibility in making choices about their farm operations by "decoupling" benefits. This meant they were not restricted to certain crops and they could make better use of their land. Because it rewarded land ownership, the 1996 Farm Bill had the unintended consequence of artificially inflating farmland prices.

One of the most unpopular elements of past farm legislation had been deficiency payments to producers, which, in essence, paid the farmer the difference between the commodity's market price and the allowance for it. A major thrust of the 1996 Farm Bill was to get rid of deficiency payments. However, large and well-funded lobbies and growers for some commodities managed to override this action by threatening to prevent passage of the entire bill unless their crops were exempted.

The Farm Security and Rural Investment Act of 2002, also known as the 2002 Farm Bill, reversed the 1996 Farm Bill and increased agricultural spending over the next 10 years by 80 percent, from just over $100 billion to more than $180 billion annually. Federal subsidies for the major program crops will rise by more than 70 percent. Throughout the world this was seen as a major reversal of President George W. Bush's FREE TRADE policy and of the U.S. commitment to reform world agriculture markets. Many predict that this will make negotiations at the next round of WTO talks much more difficult, since agriculture is to be the main focus of negotiations in the future. In 2007 President Bush offered to eliminate U.S. agricultural subsidies if the European Union would do likewise. For a brief period, candid discussions were held about the proposal but agricultural interest groups on both sides of the Atlantic Ocean pressured for maintaining the status quo. In 2008, the United States passed a five-year, nearly $300 billion agricultural bill, continuing the trend of support for the agricultural industry at the expense of consumers, taxpayers, and producers in developing countries.

Further reading
U.S. Department of Agriculture Web site. Available online. URL: http://www.usda.gov; "Food and Agricul-

tural Policy: Taking Stock for the New Century," U.S. Department of Agriculture. Available online. URL: http://www.usda.gov/news/pubs/farmpolicy01/fpindex. htm; 2002 Farm Bill. Available online. URL: http://www.usda.gov/farmbill/; "U.S. Proposal for Global Agricultural Trade Reform." Available online. URL: http://www.fas.usda.gov/itp/wto/.

—Laura Carter

Aid to Families with Dependent Children

The Aid to Families with Dependent Children (AFDC) program was a federal WELFARE program that originated during the GREAT DEPRESSION as part of the 1935 Social Security Act. The SOCIAL SECURITY Act provided funds for the states to help the elderly, the blind, and underprivileged children. The provision to help states provide support for children was contained in Title IV of the act, and participation by any state was voluntary. With the original title "Aid to Dependent Children," the initial purpose of Title IV was to provide financial assistance for disadvantaged dependent children and did not provide assistance for parents or guardians involved in the child's raising. (There was, however, a requirement that the child live with an adult in order to be eligible for aid.) It was not until 1950 that the government began to provide funds to aid in the care of the adults responsible for the children. In 1960 states were allowed to claim federal reimbursement for funds used to aid the child of an unemployed parent *and* the unemployed parent, and in 1962 aid was allowed for a second parent in the family. Hence the name of the program was changed to "Aid to Families with Dependent Children."

Instead of setting apart a fixed amount of money each year to be divided among the states, Congress approved reimbursement of a certain percentage of state expenditures without any limit on the total amount. Originally each state with an approved plan was reimbursed by the Secretary of the Treasury for one-third of its benefit payments, up to maximum federal payment of $6 per month for the first child plus $4 for each additional child. This general plan went through several changes over the years, but the basic method of funding remained the same until the passage of the Temporary Assistance to Needy Families Act (TANF) in 1996.

In 1967 a set of formal rules for the program was published in the *Code of Federal Regulations*. This stated that each state was required to assign a single agency to be in charge of the administration of the program, that the state's program be available in all parts of the state, and that the rules be universally enforced. This prevented local governments from having the power to impose local rules and regulations. The states were also required to "provide an opportunity for anyone to apply for aid, to furnish aid with reasonable promptness to all eligible persons, and to provide the opportunity for a fair hearing to those denied assistance or not given a response within a reasonable period of time."

Eligibility for the program was regulated by the particular state of residence. Each state was required to establish a "standard of need" or maximum amount of INCOME and other resources a family could have and be eligible for assistance. These standards of need varied by the size of the family. Each state determined eligibility by comparing family income to the state's need standard. If the family had gross income that did not exceed 85 percent of the state's need standard, and gross income (less specified deductions) that did not exceed 100 percent of the need standard, then the family was eligible for assistance. All children through the age of 15 were eligible for assistance. Each state had the option of aiding children older than 15 if certain conditions were met. Children aged 16–17 had to be attending school regularly, students aged 18–20 had to be in high school or a course of vocational or technical training, and students aged 18–20 had to be in college or university. In 1981 changes were made that ended a child's eligibility on his or her 18th birthday or, if the state chose, on his 19th if still in high school. Also in 1981, Congress required states to calculate the income of a child's stepparent when figuring a family's needs, income, and resources, and allowed states to claim federal reimbursement for aid to an unborn child in the last trimester of pregnancy.

In 1962, for states that included unemployed parents in the program, Community Work and Training (CWT) programs were established for federally aided recipients age 18 and over. These programs were to pay wages comparable to those present in the community and were required to ensure that appropriate standards of health and safety were followed. In 1964, under Title V of the Economic Opportunity Act, Congress allowed the formation of CWT projects in states that had not yet included the unemployed parents category in their AFDC programs. In 1968, in conjunction with the Department of Health, Education, and Welfare (HEW) and the DEPARTMENT OF LABOR, Work Incentive (WIN) programs were created for certain AFDC recipients; all unemployed fathers had to be referred to the program. In 1971 the government required that all AFDC parents register for work or training with the WIN program (except for mothers of children under age six). Finally, in 1988 WIN was replaced by the Job Opportunities and Basic Skills Training (JOBS) program in a new part IV-F of the Social Security Act. This mandated that states engage most mothers with no children below age three in education, work, or job training.

Originally, in 1935, Congress set the federal share of AFDC payments at 33 percent, up to individual payments of $18 for the first child and $12 for additional children. As stated previously, this comes to a maximum federal share of $6 for the first child. Over the years matching maximums were increased and based on average spending per recipient. In 1956 variable rates were established, providing more generous federal reimbursement for states with lower per capita income. In 1965, with the creation of Medicaid, federal matching for each state dollar spent on the AFDC program was provided. Each state that implemented Medicaid was allowed to use the open-ended matching formula for claiming federal reimbursement of a portion of total AFDC benefits as well. Numbers provided for the years between 1971 and 1996 show that expenditures rose from $6 billion to $24 billion in actual dollars, however, when adjusted for INFLATION, total expenditures increased very slightly. In constant 1996 dollars, the amount spent on benefits actually declined from a high of $26 billion in 1976 to $20.4 billion in 1996 (Office of ASPE Web site, 2001).

Critics of the AFDC argue that the program created a set of incentives that were harmful to the nation's "social fabric." The welfare system was allegedly dehumanizing; encouraged dependency; supported female-headed families, divorce, and unmarried childbearing; and encouraged low levels of work effort among recipients. Supporters argue that the AFDC program helped to reduce poverty and provided work and skill training, in addition to its success in keeping intact poor female-headed families with young children.

On August 22, 1996, President Bill Clinton signed into law the Personal Responsibility and Work Opportunity Reconciliation Act (PRWORA) of 1996 (Public Law 104-193). PRWORA replaced the AFDC program with Temporary Assistance for Needy Families (TANF).

Further reading

Brandon, Peter D. "Did the AFDC Program Succeed in Keeping Mothers and Young Children Living Together?" *Social Service Review* 74, no. 2 (June 2000): 214; Office of the Assistant Secretary for Planning & Evaluation. "Aid to Families with Dependent Children: The Baseline," *Human Services Policy,* June 1998. Available online. URL: aspe.hhs.gov/hsp/AFDC/afdcbase98. htm. Accessed on October 31, 2001; Social Security Administration. *Social Security Bulletin* (Annual 1994 57n SUPP): 114–137.

—April Miller

American Bankers Association

The American Bankers Association (ABA) is an organization representing banking interests at the national level. Created in 1875 to urge for the repeal of taxes on CAPITAL, deposits, and checks, the ABA is a powerful lobbying force in Washington on financial issues. ABA interests have changed with technological advances over the years. In the 19th century ABA efforts focused on banker education and advocacy. One of the early problems was bank robbers. In the 1890s an ABA program paying rewards for the conviction of bank robbers significantly reduced this problem and led to the death of notorious bank criminals, including Butch Cassidy and the Sundance Kid in Bolivia.

As telegraph technology became available, in the early 1900s the ABA created a cipher telegraphic code for use in banking communications. With today's INTERNET technology the ABA supported legislation creating the first Web-based bank in 1995. With the easing of GREAT DEPRESSION-era banking restrictions, the ABA is advocating new legislation expanding banking activities in the areas of INSURANCE and securities. In 1997 *Forbes* rated the ABA as the 12th most influential lobbying group in the country.

Further reading

American Bankers Association Web site. Available online. URL: www.aba.com.

American Bar Association

The American Bar Association (ABA) is the largest and most powerful law organization in the United States. Created in 1878 when 100 lawyers met in Saratoga Springs, New York, the ABA today has more than 370,000 members, including lawyers, judges, court administrators, law teachers, legal assistants, and law librarians. About half of the attorneys in the United States belong to the ABA. The percentage was higher in past decades but declined when ABA positions on major social and legal issues met with disagreement among its members.

The ABA publishes books, pamphlets, and brochures on almost every facet of the law, making it the largest legal publisher in the world. ABA publications are designed for the general public as well as members of the legal profession. The organization is also a major lobbying force in Washington and in state legislatures. ABA committees often create model legislation presented for adoption by legislatures. For example, The Model Business Corporation Act (1950) was drafted by the ABA Committee on Business Corporations.

While the ABA has over 150 committees, subcommittees and task forces, two of the most important functions of the organization are accrediting U.S. law schools and reviewing presidential nominations for judicial appointments. An ABA rating of "not qualified" is a major rebuke of a president's choice for a judgeship. In 2001 President George W. Bush announced he would no longer refer candidates for judicial appointments to the ABA review committee.

Further reading
American Bar Association Web site. Available online. URL: www.abanet.org.

American Customer Satisfaction Index

The American Customer Satisfaction Index (ACSI) is an indicator of changing customer satisfaction with the quality of goods and services available to households in the United States. The ACSI uses a national survey to measure customer satisfaction with over 200 companies and federal government agencies. ACSI conducts more than 50,000 interviews annually with customers of the companies and federal agencies included in the index. The scores for one or two sectors of the U.S. economy are updated quarterly.

For example, in 2009 the updated scores for manufacturing and cable/satellite television were released. Using a 100-point scale, among automobile manufacturers BMW and Toyota Lexus received the highest rating (87), while Jeep (Chrysler) received the lowest rating (76). Among personal computer manufacturers, Apple received the highest rating (85) and H-P the lowest (70). When grouped, automobiles, consumer electronics, and household appliances had the highest average ratings (82, 83, and 80 respectively), while personal computers and Internet news and information had the lowest average ratings (74 and 75). A *Wall Street Journal* writer concluded, "It shows that shoppers are happier with Old Economy products . . . than they are with New Economy [products and services]."

In the last quarter of 2008, the scores for federal agencies were updated (only those agencies that have significant interaction with consumers are included in the survey). Overall the government-wide index was 68.9, significantly lower than the scores for the private sector. Among the federal agencies, Pension Benefit Guaranty Corp. and Natural Resources Conservation Service received the highest rating while the Internal Revenue Service, Federal Aviation Administration and Federal Emergency Management Administration received the lowest ratings among federal agencies.

The ASCI is produced through a partnership consisting of the University of Michigan Business School, the AMERICAN SOCIETY FOR QUALITY, and the CFI Group, a private consulting firm. The University of Michigan's School of Business is well known for its INDEX OF CONSUMER EXPECTATIONS. Like the Index of Consumer Expectations, the ASCI is used to predict CONSUMER BEHAVIOR. ASCI researchers developed an econometric model using the scores to predict customer complaints and CUSTOMER LOYALTY. Marketers know building and retaining relationships with customers is critical to long-term success. The developers of the ACSI have found their index is correlated with changes in the Dow Jones Industrial Average, and that companies rated in the upper half of the index have generated significantly greater shareholder WEALTH than those rated in the lower half of the index.

Further reading
American Customer Satisfaction Index Web site. Available online. URL: www.theacsi.org; Hilsenrath, Jon E., and Joe Flint, "Consumers Find Fault with Products of New Economy," *Wall Street Journal,* 20 August 2001, p. A2.

American depository receipts

American depository receipts (ADRs) are certificates issued by a U.S. bank or brokerage firm, representing foreign shares held by the institution. One ADR may represent one share, a portion of a foreign share, or a bundle of shares of a foreign CORPORATION. ARBITRAGE, the simultaneous buying and selling of like securities in different markets to take advantage of slight price differences, keeps the prices of ADRs and underlying foreign shares essentially equal.

Most ADRs are "sponsored," meaning the corporation provides financial information and other assistance to the institution and may subsidize the administration of the ADRs. Institutions sponsoring ADRs act as custodian for the company issuing the stock and handle DIVIDEND payout, notifications, and processing. Depository receipts are registered with the SECURITIES AND EXCHANGE COMMISSION and trade like any other U.S. security in national exchanges or over-the-counter markets. Generally the foreign company approaches the institution requesting sponsorship. "Unsponsored" ADRs are issued by one or more depository institutions in response to market DEMAND but do not receive assistance from the corporation.

The U.S. financial market is the largest in the world. By selling shares of stock in their companies through ADRs, foreign corporations raise CAPITAL in U.S. markets for their business operations. In 2009 total U.S. market trading in ADRs exceeded $2 trillion, representing shares in over 2,000 companies. The companies with the largest volume of ADR transactions included Teva Pharmaceuticals, America Movil, BP plc, and Petrobras-Petroleo Brasileiro SA.

For investors, ADRs offer a low-cost opportunity to diversify their portfolios. Until the creation of ADRs, it was difficult for individual investors to purchase stocks of foreign companies. But ADRs are subject to a variety of risks: currency risk; the potential for decline in value as a country's currency declines in FOREIGN EXCHANGE markets; political risk, the potential for violence or DEFAULT of a government; and economic risk, the potential for decline in the foreign company's home economy.

See also GLOBAL SHARES.

Further reading
"ADR Trading Tops The $1 Trillion Mark For the First Time," *Wall Street Journal,* 2 January 2001, p. C10.

American dream

The American dream is the aspirations of working-class citizens, parents, and immigrant groups to attain their image of a middle-class STANDARD OF LIVING. Americans and people coming to the United States often desire home ownership, better jobs, education for their children, and perhaps their own business. Most working-class parents express the American dream by desiring that their children do better and have more than they did.

World War II, in which many poor and uneducated American soldiers traveled and interacted with people of different social classes and cultural backgrounds, strengthened their desire for a better standard of living for themselves and their children. Sometimes it was expressed as wanting a "bigger piece of the pie" as payment for their sacrifices during the war. Levittown, a major housing development created to meet the demands of veterans for their own homes, symbolized early images of the American dream. Subsequently, immigrant groups have pursued similar dreams, striving to educate their children and to succeed by standards known as the American dream.

American Federation of Labor and Congress of Industrial Organizations (AFL-CIO)

The American Federation of Labor and Congress of Industrial Organizations (AFL-CIO) is a voluntary league of national labor unions representing over 13 million workers. Its mission is to bring social and economic justice to America's workforce through political and legislative delegation. The AFL-CIO functions primarily to promote fair-trade legislation, affordable health care, quality public education, fair wages substantial enough to support a family, job safety, and retirement benefits including a pension program.

Sixty-four UNIONS make up the AFL-CIO, some of which include the Writers Guild of America, United Farm Workers of America, United American Nurses, Transport Union of America, Seafarers International Union of North America, and Association of Flight Attendants. Delegates elected by their local union govern the AFL-CIO along with an executive council. They meet every two years at a convention where policies are made and goals are set. Officers who run the AFL-CIO operations are elected at the convention every four years. John J. Sweeney, president of the AFL-CIO, was first elected in 1995.

The American labor movement began in the 1820s when skilled workers from various cities formed organizations in order to obtain better pay. National unions were formed in the 1850s when blacksmiths, machinists, printers, carpenters and other skilled laborers began a union organization named the Knights of St. Crispin. Philadelphia garment workers established the Knights of Labor, the first organized labor union to last more than a few years. Its main goals were to do away with the 10-hour workday, abolish child labor, and get equal pay for equal work.

In 1881 wage earners organized the union that became the American Federation of Labor (AFL). Samuel Gompers served as the AFL's president from 1886 to 1894 and from 1896 to 1924 for a total of 37 years. Gompers was not as politically active as other labor leaders had been. He stressed COL-LECTIVE BARGAINING to obtain higher wages and better working conditions. The AFL campaigned to encourage the public to buy goods with the "union label," made by union employees.

Organized labor had many setbacks in the early 1900s, including violent strikes and unfavorable legislation, and union membership declined. The AFL was too conservative for those workers with a more socialist view. The union didn't begin to gain membership again until immigration was restricted with the Immigration Act of 1924. COM-PETITION for jobs decreased and the bargaining power of the work force increased.

The GREAT DEPRESSION forced changes in the AFL. Business leaders were no longer in favor with workers because they could not bring about an end to the depression. Political leaders developed new laws to help the nation's economy. President Franklin Delano Roosevelt's New Deal program guaranteed a MINIMUM WAGE for all workers as well as the right to join unions, but the U.S. Supreme Court ruled it unconstitutional. In 1935 the National Labor Relations Act, also known as the WAGNER ACT, replaced the New Deal program. It established a board with the authority to punish unfair labor practices.

The AFL formed the Committee for Industrial Organization to organize mass-production industries. Union membership quickly grew in the steel, automobile, and rubber industries. Conflicts resulted with the AFL throwing out CIO union members. The Committee for Industrial Organization then changed its name to the Congress of Industrial Organizations and established its own league of unions under the leadership of John L. Lewis.

When the United States entered World War II, labor leaders agreed not to strike for the duration of the war. Wages did not increase during this period, but "fringe benefits" were established. After World War II, unions sought large wage increases through organized strikes, and the economy boomed. The TAFT-HARTLEY ACT in 1947 established government controls over unions. AFL leader George Meany and CIO leader Walter Reuther merged the two leagues in 1955, and they became known as the AFL-CIO.

The league of unions that make up the AFL-CIO has 13 departments, including the Safety and Health Department, the Organizing Department (which assists in the recruitment and training of union organizers), the Civil and Human Rights Department, the Field Mobilization Department (which coordinates a community services sector and mobilizes thousands of members across the nation to support political action), the Corporate Affairs Department (which assists national unions in collective bargaining), and the Legislative Department (which promotes equal pay for women, part-time workers, the minimum wage, public education, SOCIAL SECURITY, and economic policies).

The AFL-CIO goals remain much the same as they were when the AFL first was established:

- unionization of workers
- economic justice
- occupational safety and health
- education
- political lobbying

Civil rights and discrimination in all forms are also priorities of today's AFL-CIO. Through its Committee on Political Education, the AFL-CIO encourages members to vote on Election Day. An international department assists with organized labor in other countries. President John J. Sweeney, was first elected in 1995. The AFL-CIO's mission focuses on building a broader labor movement and stronger political voice.

Further reading

Dark, Taylor E. *The Unions and the Democrats: An Enduring Alliance, Updated Edition.* Ithaca, N.Y.: Cornell University Press, 2001; Mangum, Garth L., *Union Resilience in Troubled Times: The Story of the Operating Engineers, AFL-CIO, 1960–1993.* Armonk, N.Y.: M. E. Sharpe, 1994; Mort, Jo-Ann, ed. *Not Your Father's Union Movement: Inside the AFL-CIO.* New York: Verso, 1998; Tillman, Ray M., and Michael S. Cummings. *The Transformation of U.S. Unions: Voices, Visions, and Strategies from the Grassroots.* Boulder, Colo.: Lynne Rienner Publishers, 1999.

—Cindy L. Halsey

American Industrial Revolution

The American Industrial Revolution (1877–1919) was an era in which the nation was transformed from its agrarian, rural roots to an increasingly urban, mechanized, and innovative power. Marked by the escalating use of machines to perform work, expansion of transportation services and available markets, and the birth of labor UNIONS, the Industrial Revolution shaped the future face of American business.

During this period, deposit banking was born and delivered the funds necessary to bankroll technological improvements in transportation, agriculture, and manufacturing, which provided increased production at reduced COSTS. Profits were reinvested into each sector and paid for future innovations and technological changes. Meanwhile the labor movement was born in an effort to keep workers' needs in balance with big business's power. In all, five pillars evolved to bring about the foundations of U.S. business today.

Banking

CAPITAL fueled the Industrial Revolution. The roots of change in the banking industry were planted by the federal government's search for Civil War financing, which led to the National Banking Act of 1863 and the revised act of 1864. The 1863 act established a uniform national currency of federally chartered bank notes, backed by federal government BONDS to be sold to state banks. The revised act of 1864 created a tax on state bank-issued notes and led to the virtual elimination of state bank notes. However, the currency of national bank notes failed to adequately provide for the growing nation's need for flexible currency. Ten years later, loans in the form of bank notes gave way to deposit banking, in which banks delivered loan proceeds by crediting a depositor's account. Greenbacks, also known as paper money, were first issued as non-gold-backed legal tender in 1862 as part of the federal government's effort to raise money for the Civil War. Greenbacks became a permanent part of U.S. currency with the 1875 Resumption Act as well as 1878 congressional compromise that provided for paper money to be redeemable in gold and limited resumption of silver dollars, as proposed in the Bland-Allison Act. Multiple monetary panics closed the 19th century and led to the 1913 creation of the FEDERAL RESERVE SYSTEM: 12 regional, relatively independent banks to oversee regional monetary needs.

The increasing availability of loans allowed the nation's railroads to expand and add additional tracks between important cities and to invest in better equipment and technology. The expansion served to open new markets for agricultural products and industry, in addition to enhancing further development of the country's natural resources, including gold, silver, pig iron, and coal.

Railroads

America's first transcontinental railroad was completed by the Union and Central Pacific railroads in 1869. The nation boasted of 79,082 miles of railroad in 1877, and with the addition of five cross-country routes and extensive building of secondary and feeder tracks, railroad track mileage tripled to 240,293 miles by 1910. When completed, travel time from New York to Chicago was reduced from almost a month to two days. England's industrial accomplishments heavily influenced America's rail industry. Steel rails, available because of the steel manufacturing improvements by the Bessemer and open-hearth processes in England, were an improvement over the pre–Civil War rails. Steam locomotives (made practical by Englishman George Stephenson), air brakes, and automatic couplers to link cars together lengthened trains and, in turn, increased the tonnage each could carry. Additionally, the introduction of the refrigerated cargo car allowed for the transportation of perishable goods over longer distances. These improvements in technology increased individual freight train cargoes from 20 tons in the 1880s to 80 tons by 1914.

Farmers' dependence on railroads to get products to regional and urban markets led to increasing government regulation and consolidation of the railroad companies.

Agriculture

While the Industrial Revolution signalled America's decreasing reliance on agriculture for its WEALTH, agriculture nevertheless remained prominent. Wheat, cotton, flour, and meat products held the greatest export value for farmers and were the bulk of U.S. exports, which rose in annual value from $590 million in 1877 to $1.37 billion in 1900. Technology again played an important role, as the "sodbuster," designed to break up virgin land, allowed farmers to plant crops on their new western farms, as encouraged by the Homestead Act of 1862. Refrigerated railcars carried perishables from local markets into regional markets and urban areas; fruit and vegetables from the Great Lakes, Florida, and California; dairy products from Michigan, Minnesota, New York, and Wisconsin; cattle to Chicago; and meat products from Chicago. Further mechanization occurred as farmers ploughed earnings into more land and newer equipment in an attempt to increase profitability.

Manufacturing

Improved railroad transportation allowed inexpensive coal delivery, which fueled steam-powered factories and freed factories from waterpower restrictions. As a result, factories spread throughout the Northeast. Manufacturing gained the largest benefit from technology, as business insisted on new processes, machines, products, and distribution methods. New PRODUCTS created new industries, as the period saw the successful installation of the gasoline internal-combustion engine (1893); automobile manufacturing (1900); aircraft production (1903); the electric light, patented by Thomas A. Edison (1890); and the telephone, radio, typewriter, phonograph, and cash register.

As productivity grew, the price of producing goods dropped, and improved mechanization increasingly accelerated the process of America's shift to manufacturing as a source of wealth. In 1860 leading manufacturing industries were, in order of rank, flour and meal, cotton goods, lumber, boots and shoes, and iron founding and machinery. By 1919 technology's influence had altered the top five industries to slaughtering and meatpacking, iron and steel, automobiles, foundry and machine shop products, and cotton goods. That same year the wealth derived from manufacturing was three times that of agriculture's wealth.

As industries grew so did COMPETITION, as many companies operated with varying levels of success and product quality. This situation resulted in overproduction, which led to lower prices and profits. To better control financial outcomes, industries began to operate collectively as TRUSTS. One of the earliest and most famous trusts was John D. Rockefeller's Standard Oil Company (1882), which was created when Rockefeller and associates bought nearly 90 percent of the country's kerosene industry. Similarly, James B. Duke invited competitors to join his American Tobacco Company or watch their markets be taken over by successful American Tobacco ADVERTISING campaigns.

As big business pooled the resources and interests of competing parties, by 1919 it was employing 86 percent of America's wage earners and created 87.7 percent of the value of goods manufactured. Additionally, the annual value of manufactured goods ballooned from $5.4 billion in 1870 to $13 billion in 1899.

Trusts faced opposition by state and federal governments. In 1911, the Supreme Court used the 1890 SHERMAN ANTITRUST ACT to decree Standard Oil and American Tobacco as monopolies, and further ruled the two companies be broken into smaller companies.

Labor

In the face of the overwhelming power of trusts and big business, the labor movement took root as tensions between workers and employers increased. The Knights of Labor was the earliest influential group, founded in 1869 and designed to unify producers' interests. At its height (1884–85), the Knights claimed 700,000 members nationwide and backed successful strikes against the Southwest System, Union Pacific, and Wabash railroads, which prevented a reduction in wages and gained public sympathy. But the union's influence waned after 1886, when only half of 1,600 strikes involving 600,000 workers were successful. Additionally, strife within the union between skilled and unskilled workers weakened the Knights' membership and influence. As the Knights' power declined, the AMERICAN FEDERATION OF LABOR (AFL) gained the mantle of trade union leadership. Organized in 1881, the AFL had 548,000 members by 1900 and focused its efforts on economic gain for the membership, including better hours, wages, and working conditions. While the Knights attempted to meet goals through political influence and education, the AFL used economic means to meet its goals.

Further reading

Cleland, Hugh G., "Industrial Revolution." In *Encyclopedia Americana*, vol. 15, 122–127. Danbury, Conn.: Grolier Inc., 2002; Davis, W. N., Jr., "The Age of Industrial Growth, 1877–1919." In *Encyclopedia Americana*, vol. 27, 745–745r. Danbury, Conn.: Grolier Inc., 2002; Martin, Albro, "Economy from Reconstruction to 1914." In *Encyclopedia of American Economic History: Studies of the Principal Movements and Ideas*, vol. 1, 91–109. New York: Scribner, 1980; "United States of America: Industrialization of the U.S. Economy." In *The*

New Encyclopedia Britannica, vol. 29, 242–243. Chicago: Encyclopaedia Britannica, 2002.

—Katrina Reiling

American Institute of Certified Public Accountants

The American Institute of Certified Public Accountants (AICPA), with over the 350,000 members, is the most prominent national professional association for CPAs (whose profession is the practice of FINANCIAL ACCOUNTING) in the United States.

AICPA qualifies individuals for the practice of public accounting by awarding its professional designation of "certified public accountant" (CPA). CPAs perform financial accounting services for the general public and charge professional fees for rendering them.

In addition to its professional designation activities, AICPA also supports its Accounting Standards Team and publishes the *Journal of Accountancy*, a monthly publication focusing on "the latest news and developments related to the field of accounting." Objectives of the Accounting Standards Team are "to determine Institute technical policies regarding financial accounting and reporting standards, and generally to be the Institute's official spokesperson on these matters; to provide guidance to members of the Institute on financial accounting and reporting issues not otherwise covered in authoritative literature; and to influence the form and content of pronouncements of the FINANCIAL ACCOUNTING STANDARDS BOARD . . . and other bodies that have authority over financial accounting or reporting standards."

Further reading

AICPA Web site. Available online. URL: www.aicpa.org.

American Medical Association

Founded in 1847, the American Medical Association (AMA), the leading organization representing medical doctors in the United States, is a powerful force influencing health-care policy and spending in the country. When first organized, the AMA focused on developing a code of ethics for medical practitioners. Later, in 1883, they established the *Journal of the American Medical Association* (JAMA), a premier medical journal highly quoted and influential among the medical establishment. In the early 20th century the AMA established its medical school accreditation program, controlling quality and growth of the number of physicians in the country.

U.S. health care accounts for over 16 percent of GROSS DOMESTIC PRODUCT annually, significantly more than the amount spent in other industrialized countries in the world. Critics of the AMA argue that the organization represents the interests of the medical industry at the expense of American consumers. Supporters counter that the AMA has a long history of ensuring high-quality medical care in the country. The AMA is a leading POLITICAL ACTION COMMITTEE in Washington.

Further reading
American Medical Association Web site. Available online. URL: www.ama-assn.org.

American Society for Quality
The American Society for Quality (ASQ) is the leading quality-improvement organization in the United States. The ASQ has over 100,000 individual members and over 1,000 corporate sustaining members worldwide. Created in 1946, the organization is an outgrowth of efforts to improve production standards during World War II. Using the methods of Walter Shewhart, the War Production Board—later the American Society for Quality Control (changed to ASQ in 1997)—sponsored courses to train people in QUALITY CONTROL.

The ASQ now offers a variety of quality-control programs, including home study, conferences, certification, and administration of the BALDRIGE AWARD (Malcolm Baldrige National Quality Award). Through its Registrar Accreditation Board, the ASQ assists with the International Standards Organization's ISO 9000 and ISO 14000 accreditation and certification. ASQ training focuses on statistical process control, quality cost management, TOTAL QUALITY MANAGEMENT, failure management, and zero defects.

As stated on the ASQ Web site:

- Quality is not a program; it is an approach to business.
- Quality is a collection of powerful tools and concepts that is proven to work.
- Quality is defined by the customer through his/her satisfaction.
- Quality includes continuous improvement and breakthrough events.
- Quality tools and techniques are applicable in every aspect of the business.
- Quality is aimed at performance excellence; anything less is an improvement opportunity.
- Quality increases customer satisfaction, reduces CYCLE TIME and COSTS, and eliminates errors and rework.
- Quality is not just for businesses. It works in nonprofit organizations like schools, health care and social services, and government agencies.
- Results (performance and financial) are the natural consequence of effective quality management.

Further reading
American Society for Quality Web site. Available online. URL: www.asq.org.

American Stock Exchange
The American Stock Exchange (AMEX), was a self-regulating organization registered with the SECURITIES AND EXCHANGE COMMISSION, and, until it was acquired by the New York Stock Exchange in 2008, was the second largest stock exchange in the United States. The AMEX originated in the late 1700s and was known as the New York Curb Market. In 1921 the curb market moved indoors in lower Manhattan. In the 1940s, after struggling through the depression years, the exchange was renamed the American Stock Exchange.

The NEW YORK STOCK EXCHANGE (NYSE) is the preeminent stock exchange in the country and in the world. The AMEX was much smaller and less prestigious; in the mid-1990s AMEX trading volume was only one-twentieth of NYSE volume. It survived by being less expensive to list companies on the exchange and by introducing new products and services. In the 1950s the AMEX expanded into "satellite markets," began trading in commodities and monetary instruments, and introduced automated trading. In 1975 options trading was initiated, and in 1995 the AMEX, in conjunction with STANDARD & POOR's, began offering Standard and Poor's Depository Receipts, or SPDRs, referred to as "spiders."

SPDRs were the first stock exchange–traded MUTUAL FUNDS. Mutual funds accept funds from investors, sell them shares and use the proceeds to invest in various financial securities ranging from short-term debt instruments to long-term BONDS and stocks. Purchasers of mutual funds own an interest in a pool of stocks or bonds. Owning an interest in a pool of ASSETS reduces investors' risk. Mutual funds are CORPORATIONS that manage and market their securities, charging investors a management fee, usually about 1 percent of the assets. "Load" funds charge investors an up-front fee, anywhere from 1 to 5 percent of the amount invested to purchase shares in the fund. By creating exchange-traded mutual funds, the AMEX allowed investors to buy and sell mutual fund products without having to go through a mutual fund.

In 2008 the American Stock Exchange merged with NYSE Euronext, which operates both the New York Stock Exchange (NYSE) and Euronext securities exchanges. The AMEX, now called the NYSE Amex Equities, trades emerging growth companies, options, and exchange-traded funds.

See also COMMON STOCK, PREFERRED STOCK, TREASURY STOCK.

Further reading
American Stock Exchange Web site. Available online. URL: www.nyse.com/attachment/amex_landing.htm.

Americans with Disabilities Act

Enacted in 1992, the Americans with Disabilities Act (ADA) provides civil rights protections to individuals with disabilities. These rights are similar to those provided by the Equal Rights Act (1964). The ADA guarantees equal opportunity for people with disabilities in public accommodations, EMPLOYMENT, transportation, state and local government services, and telecommunications.

The ADA applies to government agencies and employers with 15 or more employees, protecting "qualified individuals with disabilities." Disabilities include physical or mental impairment that limits one or more life activities. Individuals with nonchronic conditions of short duration are not covered under ADA. Those who are covered must have a substantially limiting and permanent impairment, requiring employers to provide "reasonable accommodation."

"Qualified individuals" is defined by the act as people who meet legitimate skill, experience, education, or other requirements of an employment position and can perform "essential functions" of the position with or without reasonable accommodation. Reasonable accommodation is modification or adjustment to a job or work environment that will enable a qualified applicant or employee with a disability to participate in the application process or perform essential job functions.

The phrase "reasonable accommodation" has been the subject of considerable debate and interpretation. Critics claimed expensive adaptations to facilities for employees and customers would bankrupt small businesses. The act mandated modification of public-accommodation practices requiring provision for products and services such as assistive listening devices, note takers, written materials for people with hearing impairments, and materials in braille. The ADA requires removal of barriers to people with disabilities when removal is "readily achievable" and "easily accomplished without much difficulty or expense." The act has influenced the design of public facilities and fostered a positive change in social attitudes toward people with disabilities.

Further reading
U.S. Department of Justice ADA Web site. Available online. URL: www.ada.gov

amortization

Amortization is an accounting term used in three circumstances. Its most common use refers to the amortization of a loan or MORTGAGE. The series of loan payments associated with a loan or mortgage, along with the amount of each payment going to interest expense and to repayment of the principal, is known as an amortization schedule. Thus, to amortize a loan is to repay (pay off) that loan using a series of ANNUITY payments (payments of equal dollar amounts paid over regular intervals of time).

Another use of the term is associated with long-term, intangible ASSETS. While the systematic transfer of a firm's tangible assets from cost to expense over time is depreciation, the systematic transfer of a firm's intangible assets from cost to expense is amortization. One of the most fundamental of the GENERALLY ACCEPTED ACCOUNTING PRINCIPLES is the matching principle. It requires that a firm's expenses be matched with the revenues generated. Thus, as the intangible assets of a firm generate revenue (or some benefit), a portion of their costs must be amortized—that is, systematically transferred to expense, in this case amortization expense.

Amortization is also encountered in the accounting for non-interest-bearing notes payable. When funds are obtained with a non-interest-bearing note, the proceeds from that note are less than the face value of the note, requiring the creation of an account called Discount on Note Payable, a contra liability. The account Discount on Note Payable is amortized over the life of the note as interest expense accrues on the borrowed funds.

See also DEPRECIATION, DEPLETION, AMORTIZATION.

amortized loan

An amortized loan is one in which the principal and interest are repaid over time via a series of equal payments made over regular intervals of time. Because all the payments are equal in value and are due on the same day of each month over the DURATION of the loan, the stream of payments is considered an ANNUITY. The most common amortized loans are those for car and home purchases.

The payment schedule for an amortized loan typically includes a listing of each payment, indicating how much of each payment goes toward the repayment of principal, how much is interest expense, and the remaining principal. Especially for long-term loans such as 30-year home mortgages, most of each monthly payment for the first couple of years is interest expense, with very little of the payment remaining for the repayment of principal. However, with each successive payment, increasingly less of it is interest expense, leaving more for the repayment of principal. This pattern continues over the life of the loan, and as the end of the loan period approaches, most of each payment goes to the repayment of principal.

The majority of amortized loans are MORTGAGES (secured loans). Mortgages are backed by collateral, pledge ASSETS, titles, or deeds. With auto loans the lender retains title to the automobile until the last payment of the AMORTIZATION schedule is made. With the purchase of real property, the lender holds the deed to the real estate until the mortgage has been fully amortized (paid off).

Many Web sites now offer amortization calculators or tables. For examples, visit www.bankrate.com and click on the link to calculators.

annual report

The annual report is a collection of a firm's FINANCIAL STATEMENTS and other financial information, published yearly. All firms whose stocks are publicly traded are required by the SECURITIES AND EXCHANGE COMMISSION (SEC) to publish annual reports. Annual reports are attractive, well-designed booklets of financial data about a firm. Among the financial statements normally included are INCOME STATEMENTS for the current year and preceding year(s), BALANCE SHEET for the current year and preceding year(s), and cash-flow statements, all in accordance with GENERALLY ACCEPTED ACCOUNTING PRINCIPLES (GAAP). Written reports from the BOARD OF DIRECTORS and key management personnel are always an integral part of the annual report. When the report is distributed within a short time before the stockholders' annual meeting, it also includes election, voting, and PROXY information for the stockholders.

While annual reports are mailed to each stockholder within a firm, the annual report is also very useful to firms, individuals, creditors, and organizations outside of the firm being reported. Because of the SEC requirement that the financial statements be constructed and reported in accordance with GAAP, the comparison of financial statements among firms is possible when they all measure, record, and report accounting data in the same fashion and according to the same rules.

annuity

An annuity is a stream of equal payments (or receipts) of money over regular intervals of time. The most popular annuities are car payments and house payments. In these loans (which are actually MORTGAGES, i.e., secured loans), one makes the same payment on a particular day each month until the principal (the amount borrowed) and the interest expense have been satisfied according to the loan agreement.

Lottery and sweepstakes winners are often paid with an annuity. While the grand prize may be $1 million, it is common for the winner to receive the money over time—for instance, $25,000 a year for 40 years. The sum of the annuity payments over 40 years is $1 million, but the present value of such a payoff, the value of the annuity discounted for the time value of money, is less than $1 million.

Holders of long-term BONDS payable receive annuities in the form of coupon interest payments as stipulated on the face of the bonds for the life of the bonds or until they sell the bonds to another investor.

In a very real sense, retirees who receive SOCIAL SECURITY benefits are annuity recipients, getting a check for a fixed amount from the Social Security Administration each month. Unless a cost-of-living adjustment is made, the monthly payment remains fixed, creating a stream of income payments to retirees that constitute an annuity.

See also COMPOUNDING, FUTURE VALUE.

antitrust law

Antitrust law is the set of legal rules used to help promote COMPETITION in the economy. Antitrust law in the United States is a very distinct subject reflecting American economic history and perspectives. It has been borrowed, with variations, by many other countries around the world. Most U.S. antitrust litigation involves private actions taken for punitive remedies with treble DAMAGES. Thus, unlike other nations in the world, the United States does not rely principally upon public law enforcement in the area of antitrust.

One impact of U.S. antitrust law is its influence on business practices and the terms of business agreements. Most sales representatives' agreements and distributorships are drafted to minimize the risk of antitrust action and treble damages. This is often done by creating "areas of primary sales responsibility," a technique allowing control of an area but approved by the U.S. Supreme Court. Clauses in many distributorship agreements governing exclusive dealing, full-line coverage, purchase agreements, covenants not to compete, resale prices, and termination are written with careful consideration of avoiding antitrust actions. Similarly, joint ventures and licensing agreements are scrutinized for antitrust compliance, and many U.S. companies conduct "compliance reviews" of any business proposal.

The earliest antitrust statutes were created by states in the 1880s, and most adopted antitrust laws in the early 1900s. State antitrust laws typically prohibit TRUSTS (combinations in restraint of trade). The antitrust law of each state applies to activities affecting that state's commerce, including interstate or foreign activities.

Three major statutes govern federal antitrust law: the SHERMAN ANTITRUST ACT of 1890, the CLAYTON ANTITRUST ACT of 1914, and the FEDERAL TRADE COMMISSION Act of 1914. Federal and state antitrust laws are both applicable to most U.S. trade and commerce. Under recent antitrust law, there is very little subject matter covered exclusively by either state or federal law. This means businesses are subject to both state and federal interpretations in antitrust jurisdiction.

Interpretation of federal antitrust laws has varied over time. The Sherman Act initiated antitrust policy, but enforcement was minimal. Using the "rule of reason" standard, the anticompetitive effects of an action must be demonstrated to prove illegality. Just being a MONOPOLY or attempting to monopolize was not in itself illegal. The Clayton Act changed the basis of antitrust law to the "rule per se," where actions that could be considered anti-competitive were considered intrinsically illegal. Under the rule per se, activities attempting to monopolize markets were sufficient to be prosecuted. From 1914 until the Reagan administration (1980–88), rule per se antitrust enforcement was used. The Clinton administration (1992–2000) tightened antitrust enforcement. The George W. Bush administration generally eased antitrust enforcement.

Further reading

Boyes, William, and Michael Melvin. *Microeconomics.* 7th ed. Boston: Houghton Mifflin, 2007; Mallor, Jane P., A. James Barnes, Thomas Bowers, Michael J. Philips, and Arlen W. Langvardt. *Business Law: The Ethical, Global, and E-Commerce Environment.* 14th ed. Boston: McGraw-Hill, 2009.

arbitrage

Arbitrage—the practice of buying a product at a low price in one market and selling it at a higher price in another market—is as old as trade. A basic business maxim is: "Buy low and sell high." Knowledgeable middlemen, knowing the prices of products in different parts of the world, would buy from producers in one region and sell to consumers or merchants in another region. One motivation for the exploration of the New World was the control of land-based trade by merchants in the Middle East. European businesspeople and monarchs knew that new DISTRIBUTION CHANNELS would reduce the power of arbitrageurs.

Arbitrage is based on information. With today's global communications systems, the opportunities for arbitrage are both fewer and greater. In financial markets, arbitrageurs simultaneously buy and sell securities, commodity contracts, and currency contracts in two markets, with profits based on slight differences in prices in the markets. For example, currency exchanges operate in many countries around the world. The major currency markets are in New York (New York Mercantile Exchange—NYMEX) and London. If the U.S. dollar was being traded at a rate of $1.4225 dollars per British pound in New York and $1.4220 in London, an arbitrageur could buy British pounds in London and sell British pounds for U.S. dollars in New York, earning a small PROFIT ($0.0005) on the exchange. Five-hundredths of a penny is not much money, but when trading millions of dollars and British pounds, there is potential for profit. Increased access to global markets increases opportunities for arbitrage but also increases market knowledge, reducing disparities in market prices.

Arbitrage occurs in more than just financial securities and international trade. INTERNET auction sites are helping to bring together buyers and sellers, providing vast amounts of market information and opportunities for businesspeople using this resource. For many years classic cars have sold at a premium in California. Entrepreneurs often purchase cars in other parts of the country, hoping to sell them at a premium in the Golden State. Now automobiles, boats, and all kinds of products are being sold over the Internet.

arbitration

Arbitration is a method of business DISPUTE SETTLEMENT involving neutral "arbitrators." Arbitration is often required under business and consumer contracts and is seen as an alternative to litigation in courts. In most cases courts will honor arbitration clauses in CONTRACTS and refrain from entertaining lawsuits covered by arbitration.

The disputing parties typically choose the arbitrators, often with each side selecting one arbitrator and the two selected arbitrators choosing a third arbitrator. Alternatively, arbitrators may be chosen from an approved list through an "arbitration center," such as the American Arbitration Association or the International Chamber of Commerce in Paris. Together the arbitrators are a "panel." Arbitrators operate under rules of procedure regarding evidence, testimony, and the like that are more informal than court rules. Ultimately the arbitrators will render a decision that is binding upon the disputing parties. The binding nature of arbitration distinguishes it from mediation and conciliation, which is nonbinding. Mediators and conciliators act as "go-betweens," attempting to facilitate resolution of the dispute, not decide it.

The decisions of arbitrators are called "arbitral awards." Such awards are generally enforceable in courts under the U.S. Federal Arbitration Act and internationally, in the many countries like the United States that adhere to the "New York Convention" on judicial enforcement of arbitral awards. The enforceability of business-related arbitral awards around the globe is one of its key attributes.

Further reading
Folsom, Ralph H., Michael Gordon, and John Spanogle. *International Business Transactions in a Nutshell*. 7th ed. Eagan, Minn.: West Group, 2004.

assembly line

An assembly line is a manufacturing system where specialized workers focus on repetitive tasks, adding efficiency to the PRODUCTION of a PRODUCT. An assembly line is likely to be composed of numerous subassembly lines, taking raw materials and making parts and components, which are then used in producing the final product.

The idea behind assembly lines is division and specialization, which was first articulated by Scottish philosopher Adam Smith. Considered the father of modern economics and author of *The Wealth of Nations* (1776), Smith used a pin factory to describe assembly line production:

> One man draws out the wire, another straightens it, a third cuts it, a fourth points it, a fifth grinds it at the top for receiving the head; to make the head requires two or three distinct operation; to put it on is a peculiar business, to whiten the pin is another; it is even a trade by itself to put them into the paper.

As Smith noted, "it is even a trade by itself," suggesting the assembly-line system was an alternative to the existing trade and craft system of production. In the 18th century most goods were produced by craftsmen who worked alone or with apprentices, producing small quantities of specialized products. For example, Paul Revere, before his famous ride, was a silversmith; Benjamin Franklin was a printer. As Smith suggested, specialization and division of labor could be used to increase output.

Assembly-line systems used during the Industrial Revolution in Britain and then during the AMERICAN INDUSTRIAL REVOLUTION dramatically increased manufacturing output, decreasing the cost of production. The most famous American assembly-line system was initiated in 1913 by automobile manufacturer Henry Ford at his Highland Park, Michigan, plant. Within two years, by using conveyor systems to bring materials to workers and dividing tasks, Ford tripled production and reduced labor time per vehicle by 90 percent. This allowed him to reduce car prices, forcing thousands of small-scale automobile manufacturers to leave the industry.

Modern assembly-line production utilizes computerized coordination of materials and subassembly operations to maximize output. Managers at automobile factories know it costs thousands of dollars every minute the assembly line is not moving. Bells and whistles sound, and repairmen and managers run whenever the system stops. Assembly-line systems have added just-in-time (JIT) delivery systems, where suppliers ship parts and components to factories on an as-needed basis, reducing inventory costs for assembly-line manufacturers. Today, assembly-line efficiency is achieved in many organizations. Engineers and production managers constantly look for wasted time and motion, whether producing automobiles or hamburgers.

One of the problems associated with assembly-line production is repetitive stress syndrome. Workers doing the same task repeatedly often develop physical ailments.

Further reading
Miller, Roger LeRoy. *Economics Today*. 18th ed. Boston: Addison Wesley, 2009.

assembly plants

Assembly plants are factories located all over the world that bring together materials and machines to produce PRODUCTS. They are typically located where there is access to large numbers of low-cost workers. MAQUILADORAS, assembly plants located in the northern part of Mexico, take materials and parts produced around the world and produce components and final goods primarily destined for the North American marketplace. The primary manufacturer or a local production management company that agrees to manage PRODUCTION for another firm may own assembly plants.

Textile factories are another typical example of assembly plants. Textile equipment is relatively easily shipped and assembled anywhere in the world. Examination of labels in almost any U.S. clothing store will show that the clothes are made in Mauritius, Mongolia, Mexico, or the Northern Marianas. Entrepreneurs shift assembly-plant textile production based on cheap labor, transportation, and TARIFFS. Changes in international trade laws and regional ECONOMIC CONDITIONS frequently result in new, low-cost centers of assembly-plant production. Often developing countries initially expand their export production based on assembly plants. As market opportunities and workers' skills improve, they move into higher, value-added products for global markets.

assessment center

An assessment center is a tool or a service used in HUMAN RESOURCES management and designed to assist in career choice and development. In large organizations, assessment centers are part of a human resources department and are used to select new personnel, evaluate performance, and assist in internal promotion decisions.

With the advent of INTERNET technology, many on-line self-assessment centers assist workers and students with career path decisions. One on-line service, careers-by design, offers four self-assessment tools. The most widely used tool, the Myers Briggs Type Indicator (MBTI), is used to assist in career change decisions and assess personality type. Personality type assessment can be used to determine the "fit" between an individual and the team or organization they are considering.

The Strong Interest Inventory (SII) is used to assist in career change decisions as well as college major and vocation choice decisions. As the title suggests, the SII measures peoples' interests, which then can be used to predict success and enjoyment in various career options.

The Fundamental Interpersonal Relations Orientation-Behavior (FIRO-B) is used for team building, leadership style, and management development purposes. FIRO-B helps assess individual behavior in work environments. The 16 PF Questionnaire assesses 16 personality factors, which influence management style. The 16 PF Questionnaire is used in corporate selection and career development decisions.

College placement offices and many job placement companies offer self-assessment tools along with résumé services, and interview preparation services.

See also PERFORMANCE APPRAISAL.

Further reading

Assessment Center Web site. Available online. URL: www. careers-by-design.com.

assets

Assets are revenue-generating resources owned by every firm. It is impossible for a firm to earn (generate) revenues without owning and using its assets.

Assets are divided into current assets and long-term assets. Current assets, which are the more liquid assets that a firm owns, have useful lives of one year or less. Examples of current assets are cash, ACCOUNTS RECEIVABLE, merchandise inventory, supplies, various prepaid expenses such as prepaid rent and prepaid insurance, and short-term investments.

Long-term assets are less liquid and have useful lives greater than one year. In other words, their useful lives will span several, if not many, accounting periods, and they are expected to generate revenues for the firm over many accounting periods. There are three classes of long-term assets: man-made assets (such as plant and equipment); natural resources (such as timber tracts, mineral deposits, mines, and oil wells); and intangible assets (legal rights and privileges such a PATENTS, COPYRIGHTS, TRADEMARKS, logos, franchises, and GOODWILL). Assets are increased by debits to those accounts and decreased by credit entries (see DEBIT, CREDIT).

In terms of the accounting equation *assets = liabilities + owners equity,* the assets are the uses of the firm's CAPITAL. The liabilities and owners' EQUITY are the sources of the firm's capital. Thus, the left and right sides of the accounting equation must always be in balance.

Because assets are used in the generation of a firm's revenues, most are transferred to expense over their useful life. While supplies reside in inventory, they are classified as assets (supplies inventory). When those supplies are used, their cost is classified as an expense (supplies expense). Likewise, when machinery is used, it is depreciated. When natural resources are used, they are depleted. When intangible assets help to generate revenue, they are amortized (see AMORTIZATION).

attention, interest, desire, action concept

The attention, interest, desire, action (AIDA) concept, first proposed by E. K. Strong in the 1930s, explains the process that individuals go through when making a purchase decision. The AIDA concept is a tool managers consider when designing their marketing strategies.

Attention, the first step, refers to marketer's efforts to make consumers aware that a firm's PRODUCTS and SERVICES exist. Consumers will not purchase goods or services they do not know about. Whether through SALES PROMOTION, PUBLIC RELATIONS, PERSONAL SELLING, or ADVERTISING, a first goal of marketers is to gain attention. Attention can be gained through simple efforts like a press release or major advertising expenditures like an ad aired during the Super Bowl. For many retail businesses, billboard advertising is used to make consumers aware that their business exists. Sometimes attention messages are designed to inform consumers of a problem; other times, of an opportunity.

The second step, interest, focuses on appealing to the needs and desires of consumers and addresses why they should care about the product or service. Humor and fear appeals are often used to capture consumer interest.

Desire, the third step, convinces consumers of the product's ability to satisfy their needs. Before and after advertising and dramatization of results are often used to increase consumer desire.

Finally, sales presentations, advertisements, and promotions attempt to produce action, hopefully resulting in a sale or at least providing additional opportunities for the marketer to continue a dialogue with the potential consumer. "Pick up your telephone now" and "Ask your doctor or pharmacist" promotional messages are calls to action.

Further reading

Boone, Louis E., and David L. Kurtz. *Contemporary Marketing.* 14th ed. Fort Worth: South-Western, 2009.

attitude, interests, opinions statements

Attitude, interests, opinions (AIO) statements are a type of market research survey designed to learn about consumers' attitudes, interests, and opinions. AIO statements are one method of developing psychographic profiles of market segments. The survey technique involves creating a series of statements with which respondents are asked to agree or disagree.

Market researchers often use AIO research to divide geographic or demographic groups into smaller segments. Different marketing strategies are then developed for each segment based on the groups' attitudes, interests, and opinions. For example, among today's college students aged 18–25 there are "traditionalists," people who have generally accepted the attitudes and opinions of mainstream America. There are also "experimenters," young people who are questioning traditional values and attitudes, exploring new interests, and open to new products and ideas. In addition there are "rejecters," people who are critical about mainstream opinions and values, often looking to subcultures within society. Each of these groups has different needs and wants. If a segment is large enough and has sufficient purchasing power, marketers will develop distinct marketing mixes to appeal to their attitudes, interests, and opinions.

Even within organizations there can be subsegments with different ideas. AIO surveys can be used to define groups with both common and different opinions and concerns. For example, a small church organization faced a typical set of problems: Should it expand services to every Sunday (they were only meeting twice a month), and should they first hire a full-time minister or build a church (they were meeting in a rented facility)? Using AIO statements like the ones below, the church group was able to identify the different "factions" within the organization.

1. The first priority of the church should be to get a full-time minister.

    strongly agree   agree   neutral
    strongly disagree   disagree

2. Meeting twice a month is preferable to me.

    strongly agree   agree   neutral
    strongly disagree   disagree

3. The first priority of the church should be to get our own building.

    strongly agree   agree   neutral
    strongly disagree   disagree

4. Meeting every Sunday is preferable to me.

    strongly agree   agree   neutral
    strongly disagree   disagree

5. The current facility meets the needs for our church.

    strongly agree   agree   neutral
    strongly disagree   disagree

6. Having different ministers/speakers each Sunday is interesting.

    strongly agree   agree   neutral
    strongly disagree   disagree

See also DEMOGRAPHICS; MARKETING STRATEGY.

auditing

Along with bookkeeping, FINANCIAL ACCOUNTING, and MANAGERIAL ACCOUNTING, auditing is one of the branches of accountancy. Auditing—the process of examining the books and records of a business, agency, or organization to determine the accuracy of the accounts contained therein—verifies that the accounting system accurately represents and reports the transactions that have occurred over the past year.

External auditing is performed by accounting firms or by accountants who are not a part of the organization being audited. Fund-raising organizations, charities, and CORPORATIONS publishing their ANNUAL REPORTS regularly use external audits to provide impartial, objective reviews of their accounting systems.

Internal auditing is performed by accountants who are employees of the firm being audited. Internal audits check for conformance to a firm's own policies as well as to accounting standards. Because internal audits are performed by accountants within the firm or organization, such audits are not considered to be as impartial and objective as external audits.

automatic stabilizers (built-in stabilizers)

Automatic or built-in stabilizers are government programs and policies that cushion the impact of a change in spending in the economy. Technically automatic stabilizers reduce the multiplier effect of an autonomous change in spending.

FISCAL POLICY includes taxation and spending decisions by government designed to stimulate the economy during periods of RECESSION and to slow economic activity during periods of peak levels of output. In the United States, personal income taxes are slightly progressive, meaning the marginal tax rate increases as income increases. During periods of peak economic activity, the higher marginal tax rates reduce consumers' disposable INCOME, which in turn slightly reduces their consumption spending. This automatically slows the rate of growth in the economy, and economists suggest it helps reduce the potential for INFLATION.

Similarly, during recessions, when economic output is declining, workers are often laid off or put on temporary furlough. Most workers in the United States are then eligible for UNEMPLOYMENT benefits. These benefits allow workers to maintain some of the spending in the economy they were doing before they lost their job. During the GREAT DEPRESSION, unemployment and WELFARE benefits did not exist. When workers lost their jobs, their income dropped to zero, which in turn dramatically decreased their spending and reduced national income even further. Unemployment benefits and welfare benefits automatically offset some of the lost income and spending during a recession, cushioning its impact by supporting some level of consumer spending.

During periods of extreme economic decline, like the Great Depression, the federal government also engages in discretionary fiscal policy, tax cuts, and/or increases in government spending to stimulate economic activity when there is not sufficient consumer spending or private INVESTMENT. Automatic stabilizers, as the term suggests, occur without direct intervention of government policy makers.

Auto Pact

The United States–Canada Auto Pact (1965), formally entitled the Agreement Concerning Automotive Products between the Government of Canada and the Government of the United States, was a bilateral agreement liberalizing trade in automobiles and original equipment manufacturer (OEM) parts. The Auto Pact was an important precursor to the Canadian-U.S. Free Trade Agreement (CFTA, 1989), which, in turn, was the "blueprint" for the NORTH AMERICAN FREE TRADE AGREEMENT (NAFTA).

Prior to the Auto Pact, Canada used British Commonwealth "content requirements" to impose significant TARIFFS against non-Commonwealth automobiles and parts. The "Big Three" U.S. automakers (DaimlerChrysler, Ford, and General Motors) manufactured cars and parts in Canada on this basis for the small Canadian market. This significantly reduced the ability of U.S. automobile manufacturers' ability to take advantage of economics of scale based on U.S. manufacturing, but it also protected Canada's small manufacturing industry.

During the 1960s, Canadian tariff refunds linked the degree of Canadian content of its automobiles and OEM parts to exports. U.S. manufacturers perceived this as an unfair trade subsidy and filed a complaint seeking the imposition of countervailing duties. With a trade war threatening this important industry, the Auto Pact was negotiated.

Under the Auto Pact, U.S. manufacturers could import on a duty-free basis regardless of origin only if 75 percent of their sales in Canada were manufactured there. In addition, each existing or subsequent automobile manufacturer had to meet "Canadian value-added content requirements," generally 60 percent. Manufacturers meeting these requirements attained Auto Pact status. The result of these requirements was expanded production of automobiles and OEM parts in Canada.

In the Auto Pact, the United States' criteria for duty-free entry were different. The United States required 50-percent American-Canadian content, meaning Canadian vehicles and OEM parts could enter the United States without tariff if 50 percent of their appraised value was of Canadian or American origin (or both). The U.S. standard was based on fears of Japanese or other foreign automobile manufacturers using Canada as a production platform for entry into the U.S. market.

Generally, the Auto Pact was a successful industry-specific, bilateral trade agreement with the United States' largest trading partner. Under CFTA, the 50-percent appraised value was replaced with a 50-percent value based on value of materials plus direct processing costs, a more demanding standard.

Further reading

Folsom, Ralph H., and W. Davis Folsom. *Understanding NAFTA and Its International Business Implications.* New York: Matthew Bender/Irwin, 1996.

B

bad debts, aging of accounts

Bad debts, also known as uncollectible accounts, arise from ACCOUNTS RECEIVABLE that ultimately prove to be bad credit risks. When an account receivable is determined to be uncollectible, it should be written off—that is, removed from the collection of accounts receivable.

Periodically a firm estimates the amount of its bad-debt expense by an aging of its accounts receivable. This requires that the accounts and their outstanding balances be grouped according to their currency (how up-to-date they are): 0–30 days past due, 31–60 days past due, 61–90 days past due, etc. While it varies from firm to firm, there is some length of time overdue beyond which a firm will deem an account to be uncollectible.

An aging of accounts also helps the firm to control the amount of its INVESTMENT in accounts receivable. Accounts receivable, which actually represent an investment of a part of the firm's CAPITAL, are credit sales waiting to be liquidated; the sales have been made, but the cash has not yet been received.

If a firm believes its bad-debt expense is too large, it will tighten its credit policy, thereby decreasing the number of potential customers to whom it will sell on credit. Thus, a credit tightening will decrease revenues from credit sales. A lax credit policy will increase credit sales, but it will simultaneously increase bad-debt expense, illus-

trating the risk/return tradeoff that is prevalent in all business decisions.

bait-and-switch

The FEDERAL TRADE COMMISSION (FTC) defines bait-and-switch, or bait, advertising as an alluring but insincere offer to sell a product or service that the advertiser in truth does not intend, or want, to sell. Its purpose is to switch consumers from buying the advertised merchandise in order to sell them something else, usually at a higher price or on a basis more advantageous to the advertiser. The primary aim of a bait-and-switch advertisement is to get consumers into retail stores and/or obtain leads in identifying persons interested in buying merchandise of the type so advertised. The FTC guide states: "No advertisement containing an offer to sell a product should be published when the offer is not a bona fide effort to sell the advertised product."

The FTC also states regarding the initial offer:

No statement or illustration should be used in any advertisement which creates a false impression of the grade, quality, make, value, currency of model, size, color, usability, or origin of the product offered, or which may otherwise misrepresent the product in such a manner that later, on disclosure of the true facts, the purchaser may be switched from the advertised product to another.

Even though the true facts are subsequently made known to the buyer, the law is violated if the first contact or interview is secured by deception.

Unscrupulous marketers have also been known to discourage consumers, once in the store, from buying the low-priced item. FTC guidelines state:

No act or practice should be engaged in by an advertiser to discourage the purchase of the advertised merchandise as part of a bait scheme to sell other merchandise. Among acts or practices which will be considered in determining if an advertisement is a bona fide offer include:

- The refusal to show, demonstrate, or sell the product offered in accordance with the terms of the offer,
- The disparagement by acts or words of the advertised product or the disparagement of the guarantee, credit terms, availability of service, repairs or parts, or in any other respect, in connection with it,
- The failure to have available at all outlets listed in the advertisement a sufficient quantity of the advertised product to meet reasonably anticipated demands, unless the advertisement clearly and adequately discloses that supply is limited and/or the merchandise is available only at designated outlets,
- The refusal to take orders for the advertised merchandise to be delivered within a reasonable period of time,
- The showing or demonstrating of a product which is defective, unusable or impractical for the purpose represented or implied in the advertisement,
- Use of a sales plan or method of compensation for salesmen or penalizing salesmen, designed to prevent or discourage them from selling the advertised product.

Another bait-and-switch method is called "unselling," in the event of sale of the advertised product with the intent and purpose of selling other merchandise in its stead. Unselling acts include:

- Accepting a deposit for the advertised product, then switching the purchaser to a higher priced product,
- Failure to make delivery of the advertised product within a reasonable time or to make a refund,
- Disparagement by acts or words of the advertised product, or the disparagement of the guarantee, credit terms, availability of service, repairs, or in any other respect, in connection with it,
- The delivery of the advertised product that is defective, unusable, or impractical for the purpose represented or implied in the advertisement.

In addition to retailers, service providers, including realtors, contractors, and lawyers, have been known to lure potential customers with attractive prices and promotions that are unavailable or not appropriate when consumers inquire about them.

Bait-and-switch advertising differs from other common marketing practices such as the use of LOSS LEADERS (offering some products below cost to get customers in the store), cross-selling (selling consumers additional goods or services to go along with their initial purchase), and the use of teasers (initial low prices or interest rates with subsequent increases). Marketers using loss leaders have quantities of the product available at that price. Cross-selling does not use deception to get the initial sale. Marketers using teasers tell consumers how and when the price will change. Bait-and-switch is closest to the marketing practice of upselling, that is, persuading consumers to purchase more expensive models of the product they intended to buy. Upselling involves communicating and convincing consumers of the added value in the more expensive item, while bait-and-switch involves intentional acts of misrepresentation.

Further reading
Federal Trade Commission. "Guides Against Bait Advertising." Available online. URL: www.ftc.gov/bcp/guides/baitads-gd.htm. Accessed on April 26, 2010.

balance of payments
Balance of payments is a summary of a country's economic exchanges with the rest of the world for a given period of time. Typically, countries trade

goods, services, and financial ASSETS. The balance of payments shows whether a country is accruing debits or credits in its trade with other countries. For a country, exports of goods and services and investment INCOME from other countries represent credits against foreigners, while IMPORTS and investment income paid to foreigners are debits. Debits result in demand for FOREIGN EXCHANGE; credits generate supply of foreign exchange. Without offsetting activities, net trade balances influence foreign EXCHANGE RATES.

There are also unilateral transfers, gifts, and retirement pensions sent to and from countries for which there is no exchange of goods or services. Many foreign-born workers in the United States send money back to their families in other countries. For the United States there are more unilateral transfers out of the country than coming into the country.

Balance of payments, by definition, must balance or be equal, but different components of the balance of payments can have net positive or negative balances. The three most important components of a country's balance of payments are the merchandise account, current account, and capital account. The merchandise account records all international transactions involving goods. For decades the United States has run a negative net trade in merchandise. The merchandise account is also called the balance of trade. The current account is the sum of a country's trade in merchandise, services, investment income, and unilateral transfers. While the United States has a negative balance in merchandise trade, it has a positive balance of trade in services, and INVESTMENT income going out of the country is almost equal to investment income coming into the country. The United States has had a current account deficit for many years. In 2008, the U.S. current account was approximately $673 billion.

When a country like the United States has a current-account deficit, three things can occur. First, foreigners can exchange the excess dollars for their own currency. This increases the supply of dollars as well as the DEMAND for other currencies, causing the value of the dollar to fall in world currency markets. A decreasing dollar will make imports more expensive and exports cheaper to foreigners, reducing the current account deficit.

Second, foreigners can use the excess dollars to make DIRECT INVESTMENTS in the United States. For example, during the early 1990s foreign investors bought many visible symbols of Americana, including the Empire State building and the Pebble Beach Resort. In both cases they paid too much for these assets and subsequently sold them at a loss.

Third, foreigners can use the excess dollars to purchase financial assets, stocks, and BONDS in U.S. companies and U.S. TREASURY SECURITIES. These are known as portfolio investments. For decades foreigners have invested heavily in U.S. securities. Foreign investors hold almost 20 percent of U.S. Treasury securities. Alarmists fear this could lead to economic blackmail, where foreigners threaten to pull their funds out of the United States if the federal government does not follow policies they support. But foreigners, not foreign governments, are buying U.S. securities, and foreigners are buying these securities primarily because of the relative safety of financial investments in the United States. To try to undermine the authority of the U.S. government would be counter to their investment objective.

Because foreigners have primarily used excess dollars to purchase U.S. investments and securities, the value of the dollar has remained stable and even increased, and the capital account—net investment in the United States versus outside the country by U.S. investors—has been positive. This means the United States (businesses and the government) is selling more bonds and other financial assets to foreigners than it is purchasing from abroad. The media therefore portrays the United States as a "net debtor" nation. Since 1985 the U.S. net debtor status has grown annually. These financial assets represent claims against future income and output from the United States.

See also DEBIT, CREDIT.

Further reading
Boyes, William, and Michael Melvin. *Macroeconomics.* 7th ed. Boston: Houghton Mifflin, 2007.

balance of trade   See TRADE BALANCE.

balance sheet

The balance sheet is a statement of the financial position and net worth of a firm. Built on the accounting equation *assets = liabilities + owners' equity,* the balance sheet is a two-columned statement with ASSETS listed on the left side and liabilities and owners' EQUITY listed on the right side. Because the right side represents the sources of CAPITAL for the firm and the left side represents the uses of that capital, the two sides of the balance sheet must always be in balance.

On the asset side, current assets are listed at the top, followed by the long-term assets. The bottom of the left side of the balance sheet is called Total Assets.

On the right side of the balance sheet, liabilities—the firm's debt—are listed at the top, followed by the equity. The bottom of the right side of the balance sheet is called Total Liabilities and Equity. The left and right-side totals will be equal in dollar amount.

There is a physical significance to the arrangement of the right side of the balance sheet, with liabilities being listed above and before the firm's equity. This signifies and recognizes that the firm's creditors (represented by liabilities) have a priority to be paid in the event that the firm should have to liquidate (due to insolvency or bankruptcy, for example). The equity owners can receive payment from liquidation only after all the creditors have been paid in full. For this reason, the firm's equity is often referred to as the residual equity.

The idea of residual equity is also evident in the concept of net worth. With a simple transposition of the accounting equation *assets - liabilities = owners' equity,* it is evident that the equity is the firm's net worth. When debts are subtracted from assets, the residual, if any, is the firm's net worth.

Individuals and households can construct balance sheets, just as firms do. This is most useful if one wishes to determine his or her net worth. It should be noted that net worth can be negative when the liabilities (debts) exceed the assets.

If a firm has a negative net worth, it is insolvent or bankrupt. If an individual or household has a negative net worth, the expression "living hand to mouth" describes the situation more aptly.

Baldrige Award

The Baldrige Award—formally known as Malcolm Baldrige National Quality Award—is an annual award designed to recognize quality management. It was created in 1987 and named after former Secretary of Commerce Malcolm Baldrige, who had died in a rodeo accident that year. During the 1980s the United States was perceived as not having products that could compete in world markets. U.S. products, symbolized by U.S. automobiles, were considered to be not "world class." As Secretary of Commerce, Malcolm Baldrige had led efforts to improve quality and productivity in U.S. industries.

The National Institute of Standards and Technology (NIST), part of the Department of Commerce, manages the Baldrige Award, criteria for which include

- leadership
- STRATEGIC PLANNING
- customer and market focus
- information and analysis
- human resource focus
- process management
- business results

Companies submit applications for the award and are evaluated by an independent Board of Examiners. Early recipients of the Baldrige Award have included Motorola Inc., Westinghouse Electric, Xerox, and Milliken & Co. Because of the public recognition associated with the Baldrige Award, some companies hire consultants and spend considerable sums attempting to win this symbol of quality. Winners often use the fact that their company won the award as part of their ADVERTISING efforts.

In 2008 the Baldrige recipients were Cargill Corn Milling (manufacturing), Poudre Valley Health System (health care) and Iredell-Stateville Schools (education).

Winners are expected to share their organization's performance strategies and methods. Some state and local organizations have also created Baldrige Award competitions. The award is in some ways similar to Japan's Deming Award, named after American statistician W. Edwards Deming, who led in the development of TOTAL QUALITY MANAGEMENT (TQM) strategies in Japan during the 1950s and 1960s.

Further reading
Malcolm Baldrige Award Web site. Available online. URL: www.quality.nist.gov.

banking system
A banking system provides financial intermediation, taking deposits from individuals and households with excess cash balances and making LOANS to individuals and businesses wishing to borrow funds for CONSUMPTION or INVESTMENT. Banks also provide safekeeping for depositors' liquid ASSETS. Historically, banking systems evolved from early goldsmiths and silversmiths who provided depository and safekeeping services for merchants and traders. Metalsmiths often charged a fee for storing MONEY and issued a receipt to depositors. These receipts were often exchanged in commerce, becoming currency. Over time the receipts became standardized with respect to value, creating the first paper currency. Recipients could redeem them for gold or silver, but frequently held and used the receipts to make their purchases.

Metalsmiths, observing that not all receipts were redeemed during any time period, realized they could issue more receipts than the amount of gold or silver they had in their vaults. They could, in effect, create money. Money is anything people will accept as a means of payment. Since merchants and consumers had always been able to redeem these receipts for precious metals, they became accepted as money. Metalsmiths began making loans in the form of receipts to traders, accepting a note promising to repay the loan with interest, usually on completion of the trading venture. In the process, metalsmiths were engaging in fractional reserve banking, maintaining less gold or silver in their vaults than the exchange value of the receipts outstanding.

Today banking systems, as early metalsmiths did, create money through fractional reserve banking. Of course, there is the danger that depositors will all demand their money back at the same time. During the GREAT DEPRESSION there were many "runs" on banks, causing over 9,000 banks (more than 40 percent of the banks in the country) to fail during the period from 1930 to 1933.

Because of the risks involved, banking systems in any country are regulated. The first American bank was the Bank of North America, established in Philadelphia in 1782. The bank issued banknotes, convertible into gold or silver coins. Soon commercial banks were established in all major colonial cities, and the early American banks were controversial. Merchants and traders supported their creation as a means of access to credit (previously secured through British sources), but farmers perceived banking as a nonproductive activity and a source of INFLATION in the economy. Also, many colonists had come to North America to escape from their previous experiences with creditors and debtor prisons in Europe.

At the end of the American Revolution, part of the federalist/antifederalist debate concerned the development and control of banking. Federalists won the debate, resulting in the creation of the first central bank, the Bank of the United States, in 1791. Charged to regulate the MONEY SUPPLY in the public's best interests, the Bank of the United States operated both as a commercial bank and as a central bank. Like commercial banks, it took deposits, made loans, and issued banknotes, but it also controlled the amount of banknotes (money) state banks could issue and acted as the banking agent for the federal government. When its officials thought a state bank was extending too much credit, the bank would accumulate a large amount of the state bank's notes and present them for redemption. This decreased that bank's precious metal reserves, forcing the bank to reduce its lending activity or face bank failure. Antifederalists decried this policy, and in 1811 Congress failed to renew the charter of the Bank of the United States.

After a period of inflation, Congress established the Second Bank of the United States during the War of 1812. It operated as the central bank until President Andrew Jackson set out to destroy it, and after a protracted period known as the Bank War, the Second Bank's charter was not renewed in 1836. From this time until the establishment of the Federal Reserve in 1913, the U.S. banking system operated without a central bank. State chartered banks expanded during the period after 1836, but not without problems. Politics and corruption allowed state banks to operate without regulatory supervision, resulting in numerous bank failures and widespread distribution of banknotes of questionable worth; one publication, *The Bank Note Reporter and Counterfeit Detector,* reported the existence of over 1,000 counterfeit banknotes. In addition to counterfeiting problems, without a central bank the money supply varied widely, contributing to inflation and bank panics. States and regions attempted a variety of remedies, including bank reserves holding agreements, bank holdings of state BONDS, and state deposit insurance, but problems persisted.

The federal government's need to finance the Civil War resulted in the creation of a national banking system (the National Bank Act of 1862). (Readers who have seen the classic Civil War film *Gone With the Wind* may recall the South also created its own banking system. Ashley Wilkes patriotically exchanged his gold and silver assets for Confederate currency, but Rhett Butler shrewdly held his precious metals.) National banks were required to purchase bonds issued by the federal government, generating needed resources for the war effort. National banknotes printed by the U.S. Treasury were redeemable at any national bank. In addition to establishing nationally chartered banks and a common currency, the National Bank Act established CAPITAL requirements, placed restrictions on the type and amount of loans that could be made, set up minimum RESERVE REQUIREMENTS, and provided bank supervision by the COMPTROLLER OF THE CURRENCY.

State banks continued to exist, but their banknotes were driven out of existence by the imposition of a 10-percent tax in 1865. In response, state banks replaced banknotes with checks written on bank deposits. As a result, the United States developed a dual banking system, with both state chartered and nationally chartered banks but, until 1913, no central bank. After a series of financial panics that culminated in the panic of 1907, the FEDERAL RESERVE SYSTEM was created to act as the nation's monetary authority, lender of last resort to banks facing liquidity problems, manager of a bank payment system, and supervisor of bank operations.

Even with the creation of the Federal Reserve, the U.S. banking system continued to have problems, resulting in the creation of the FEDERAL DEPOSIT INSURANCE CORPORATION in 1934 and similar deposit insurance protection for other nonbank FINANCIAL INTERMEDIARIES. Historically (much less so today), commercial banks made loans to businesses but not to households. This left a need for other financial intermediaries, leading to the creation of mutual savings banks, SAVINGS AND LOAN ASSOCIATIONS, CREDIT UNIONS, and finance companies, all of which provide home MORTGAGES and consumer credit loans.

Further reading
Kidwell, David S., David W. Blackwell, David A. Whidbee, and Richard L. Peterson. *Financial Institutions, Markets, and Money.* 10th ed. Hoboken, N.J.: John Wiley & Sons, 2008.

Bank of International Settlements
The Bank of International Settlements (BIS) is an international organization supporting cooperation among central banks and other agencies. The bank's mission is to ensure international monetary and financial stability. The BIS functions as:

- a forum for international central bankers,
- a provider of financial services for central banks,
- a center for monetary and economic research,
- an agent or trustee for implementation of international financial agreements.

One of the major activities of the BIS is operating the Financial Stability Institute (FSI). The FSI, created in 1998, provides seminars and information programs training central bank personnel from around the world. In 2009, BIS hosted a conference on "Portfolio and risk management for central banks and sovereign wealth funds." As demonstrated in the CIRCULAR FLOW MODEL of an economic system, monetary flows are needed to facilitate the flow of resources and goods and services. Monetary authorities must provide the needed amount of funds to facilitate exchanges, savings, and INVESTMENT. Excessive or "tight" monetary policies impair economic performance. Financial stability is necessary for sustained ECONOMIC GROWTH. The FSI trains central bank personnel in areas concerning promotion of adequate CAPITAL standards, effective risk management, and transparency (openness) in financial markets. The best-known BIS agreement is the 1988 Basel Capital Accord. (The BIS is headquartered in Basel, Switzerland.) The accord strives for international convergence in the measurement of the adequacy of banks' capital and to establish minimum capital standards.

The BIS was created in 1930 as part of the Young Plan from the Treaty of Versailles ending World War I. The BIS took over responsibility for reparations payments imposed on Germany and was directed to promote cooperation among central banks. Responsibility for war reparations ended with the financial chaos in Germany during the 1930s, focusing BIS efforts toward central bank cooperation. The BIS supported the BRETTON WOODS system, with a gold standard and the dollar as the international reserve currency until the early 1970s, and it managed capital flows during the oil crises in the 1970s. The organization also assisted with the international debt crisis in the 1980s and with financial management associated with GLOBALIZATION in the 1990s.

In addition to providing training and a forum for central bank officials' discussion, the BIS provides banking services, such as reserve management and gold transactions for central banks and international organizations. At various times it has acted as the agent for EXCHANGE RATE agreements among European countries. It also hosts G10 (Group of 10, previously G7) central bank governors meetings. The G10 leaders attempt to coordinate monetary polices to stabilize world ECONOMIC CONDITIONS. The G10 includes Belgium, Canada, France, Germany, Italy, Japan, the Netherlands, Sweden, the United Kingdom, and the United States.

See also BANKING SYSTEM.

Further reading
Bank for International Settlements Web site. Available online. URL: www.bis.org.

Bank of the United States

Most nations have a central bank, such as the Bank of England and Deutsche Bundesbank (Bank of Germany). The United States has, instead, the FEDERAL RESERVE SYSTEM. The key word being *system,* it consists of a series of 12 regional banks, owned and operated by the commercial banks in each geographic area, with central committees, the Board of Governors, and the Federal Open Market Committee (FOMC) coordinating national banking and monetary policies. But the United States twice had a Bank of the United States, first as a new nation, established in 1791, and a Second Bank of the United States chartered in 1816. The history of these banks helps explain creation of the Federal Reserve (1913) and the dual banking system, in which both the federal government and the state governments retain the right to charter commercial banks.

The First Bank of the United States received a 20-year charter beginning in 1791. The bank was established to support the financial management of the newly formed government. The establishment of a central bank was controversial, pitting Thomas Jefferson (anti-Federalist) versus Alexander Hamilton (Federalist). At the end of the American Revolution, only a few banks existed, coins from various European countries were widely used for payment, and scrip issued by states and private businesses was unregulated and used in local transactions. Hamilton proposed creation of a national bank that would establish a mint, act as financial agent for the central government, and address the problem of "Continentals," namely, the scrip issued by the Continental Congress. He suggested an excise tax on whiskey be used to help fund the bank along with the sale of stock, thus making the bank a private company. Jefferson and others opposed creation of the bank, fearing centralization of financial power in the North but also perceiving that the burden of the excise tax would unfairly fall on southerners. Hamilton won the debate and the bank was established in Philadelphia.

In a 1996 speech, then Federal Reserve chairman Alan Greenspan reflected on the evolution of central banking in the United States, saying: "A central bank in a democratic society is a magnet for many of the tensions that such a society confronts. Any institution that can affect the purchasing power of the currency is perceived as potentially affecting the level and distribution of wealth among the participants of that society, hardly an inconsequential issue."

Not surprisingly, the evolution of central banking in this nation has been driven by such concerns. The experiences with paper money during the Revolutionary War were decidedly inauspicious. "Not worth a Continental" was scarcely the epithet one would wish on a medium of exchange. This moved Alexander Hamilton, with some controversy, to press for legislation that established the soundness of the credit of the United States by assuming, and ultimately repaying, the war debts not only of the fledgling federal government, but also of the states. The chartering of the First Bank of the United States proved equally controversial. Although it had few of the functions of a modern central bank, it was nonetheless believed to be a significant threat to states' rights and the Constitution itself.

Although majority controlled by private interests, the bank engaged in actions perceived to shift power to the federal government. Such a shift was thought by many to constitute a fundamental threat to the new democracy, and an essential element of what was feared to be a Hamilton plan to reestablish a powerful ruling aristocracy. The First Bank—and especially its successor, the Second Bank of the United States—endeavored to restrict

state bank credit expansion when it appeared inordinate by gathering bank notes and tendering them for specie. This reduced the reserve base and the ability of the fledgling American banking system to expand credit. The issue of states' rights and concern about the power of the central government reflected the free-wheeling individualism of that time.

The charter of the First Bank of the United States was allowed to expire after its initial term in 1811. In 1816, under President James Madison, a Second Bank of the United States was chartered, also for 20 years. The Second Bank emerged in response to the rise in inflation and a lack of monetary policy during the War of 1812. The Second Bank was similar to the first, combining both public and private funding. Eventually it helped bring monetary stability but renewal of its charter was opposed by Andrew Jackson and others who distrusted the concept of a single powerful financial institution. The Second Bank was a major issue during the election of 1832. Earlier that year, President Andrew Jackson had vetoed the bill to extend the bank's charter, and the election became a referendum on his veto. The outcome was a resounding victory for Jackson and the death knell for the bank. The bank's charter was not renewed.

From 1836 until the creation of the Federal Reserve, no central bank of the United States existed. During the Civil War, the federal government enacted the National Banking Act (1864), chartering banks with a unified currency. State-chartered banks were unaffected by the act, resulting in the dual banking system. The result led to nationally chartered banks supervised by the federal government and state-chartered banks supervised by both state and federal regulators. Finally, after the financial panic of 1907, Congress created the Federal Reserve System (1913). As Alan Greenspan stated in his 1996 speech: "The Federal Reserve System itself also reflects this American preference for dispersal of authority. In 1913 the Congress, fearful of central authority, attempted to create a set of regional central banks. Today the twelve Reserve Banks, with the Board of Governors in Washington, provide the regional representation and authority so dear to the American psyche."

Further reading
Greenspan, Alan. "The Challenge of Central Banking in a Democratic Society." Available online. URL: www.federalreserve.gov/boarddocs/speeches/1996/19961205.htm. Accessed on April 26, 2010.

bankruptcy   See BUSINESS FAILURE; CONSUMER BANKRUPTCY.

barriers to entry

Barriers to entry are restrictions preventing or discouraging new competitors from participating in a market. Barriers to entry most often occur in monopolistic and oligopolistic markets, reducing the number of competing firms and increasing prices and profits for those firms protected by barriers to entry. From a social perspective, barriers to entry generally harm consumers, reducing the number of choices available as well as price COMPETITION. From a business perspective, firms attempt to create and maintain barriers to entry. Economists use the term *rent-seeking* to describe the use of resources by firms on lobbying and influence-buying to acquire MONOPOLY rights from the government, creating a barrier to entry for future entrants. The government, particularly the Antitrust Division of the Justice Department and the FEDERAL TRADE COMMISSION, is responsible for monitoring anticompetitive practices in the United States. Potential competitors evaluate the cost of overcoming existing barriers to entry as part of their marketing strategy decisions.

Barriers to entry arise from a variety of sources.

- Product differentiation: This is any feature or perceived value to consumers that increases BRAND loyalty and reduces consumer consideration of alternatives in the marketplace. Marketers in the United States spend billions of dollars annually promoting the differences in their products, and offering price incentives for repeat and bulk purchases to existing customers.

- ECONOMIES OF SCALE: Products requiring a high initial capital cost, but with low variable costs production, allow existing producers to spread their fixed costs as output expands. Potential competitors are discouraged from entering the market because they cannot start small and later expand as DEMAND grows. Independent retailers such as hardware stores often join in buying franchises in order to obtain the economies of scale in PURCHASING and ADVERTISING of nationally owned competitors.

- Capital requirements: Products or services requiring significant initial INVESTMENT discourage potential competitors. Existing automobile manufacturers, steel producers, and communications companies have spent significant sums creating their enterprises. The investment CAPITAL required for new competitors is a barrier to entry.

- Access to DISTRIBUTION CHANNELS: Often existing firms control access to customers, either through ownership or contractual relationships. Small and new producers frequently have difficulty getting shelf space in retail stores and finding representatives to promote and sell their products through distribution channels.

- Other cost advantages: Through lower rents negotiated in long-term contracts, experience, access to materials, and relationships in the industry, existing companies can often produce at a lower cost than potential competitors, discouraging entry into the marketplace.

- Government policy: LICENSING, PATENTS, safety and pollution standards, and access to distribution create barriers to entry. Patents give a firm a monopoly for a specified period of time. Licenses create costs and tests limiting entry. Many industries seek out government licensing as a way to restrict further entry into their market. Safety and pollution standards increase paperwork and initial costs for would-be competitors. Government restrictions on access to distribution act as a barrier to entry. For example, airline companies fight for government allocation of boarding space at airports around the country.

Information and gaining access to information has traditionally acted as a barrier to entry. Today's global INTERNET technology is changing this and also creating alternative distribution channels, reducing this barrier to entry.

See also OLIGOPOLY.

Further reading
Dwyer, F. Robert, and John F. Tanner Jr. *Business Marketing.* 4th ed. Boston: Irwin McGraw-Hill, 2008; Ruffin, Roy J., and Paul R. Gregory. *Principles of Economics.* 7th ed. Boston: Addison Wesley, 2000.

barriers to trade   See TRADE BARRIERS.

barter
Barter is the exchange of one service or commodity for another without exchanging MONEY. Barter was used by primitive peoples and is still practiced in some parts of the world. A barter economy requires a "coincidence of needs"—that is, a person having something to trade must find another who wants it and has something acceptable to offer in exchange. In a money economy, the owner of a commodity may sell it for money, which is acceptable in payment for goods, thus avoiding the time and effort that would be required to find someone who could make an acceptable trade. The money economy is considered the keystone of modern economic life.

Barter is still active, not only in countries with chronically weak currencies but also in western countries like the United States, where it made something of comeback with the onset of the INTERNET. Another reason for its revival is that barter can be attractive for smaller businesses to save money. For example, a painting contractor could paint the exterior of an auto body shop in exchange for car repairs.

Success in bartering requires finding an agreeable trading partner. Participants must agree on a fair value of the products or services that are being traded. It is best to put all bartering agreements in writing to avoid "he said, she said" kinds of problems. Bartering has become so accepted that even federal and state tax collec-

tors recognize its value. Barter-system deals are included in taxes dollar for dollar, as if the two participants were simply exchanging checks for the amount of their trade.

The Internet has opened a vast array of bartering opportunities. Some sites for consumers to view are barter quest.com, and U-exchange.com.

See also COUNTERTRADE.

Further reading
Goff, Robert. "Swap 'Til You Drop . . . Or Drop Out." *Forbes,* 11 September 2000, p. 62.
                                        —Susan Poorbaugh

beggar-thy-neighbor policy
Beggar-thy-neighbor policies are actions taken by a country to improve the economic situation in the country at the expense of its trade partners. Especially during economic recessions, politicians attempt to reduce UNEMPLOYMENT and increase domestic output by reducing the volume of imported products, thereby increasing demand for domestically made alternatives. Typically, political leaders will enact laws to increase tariffs on imported products or expand nontariff barriers, rules, and regulations that impede the ability of foreign firms to gain access to their market. The classic example of a beggar-thy-neighbor policy was the SMOOT-HAWLEY TARIFF ACT of 1930, which raised tariffs on a wide array of imported products by an average of 60 percent. Within a year, most of the trading partners of the United States enacted similar restrictions on U.S. exports, dramatically curtailing international trade. Most economists believe Smoot-Hawley contributed significantly to the length and depth of the GREAT DEPRESSION.

Another form of beggar-thy-neighbor policy involves competitive devaluation of a country's currency, making imported products more expensive and exports less expensive. It also creates instability in world currency and trade markets, undermining the benefits of trade based on COMPARATIVE ADVANTAGE. First articulated by English economist David Ricardo (1722–1823), the principle of comparative advantage suggests that people and countries should engage in those activities for which their advantage over others is the largest or their disadvantage is the smallest.

In 2009, at the G-20 conference in London, President Barack Obama urged leaders of the other major countries not to regress in adopting beggar-thy-neighbor strategies to address the global recession.

Beggar-thy-neighbor policies are similar to the "tragedy of the commons" problem associated with resources that are not owned privately. For common property resources, no incentive exists for individuals to conserve and maintain the resource for future users. "Tragedy of the commons" is associated with fishing rights and air and water usage in identifying a problem in which individuals can maximize their short-term benefits at the expense of their neighbors but in the process deplete or ruin the resource.

Further reading

U.S. Department of State."Smoot-Hawley Tariff." Available online. URL: future.state.gov/when/timeline/1921_timeline/smoot_tariff.html. Accessed April 6, 2010.

benchmarking

Benchmarking is the process of identifying and learning from the best business practices in a company, an industry, or the world. As stated by C. Jackson Grayson Jr., chairman of the American Productivity and Quality Center, the essence of benchmarking is, "Why reinvent the wheel if I can learn from someone else who has already done it?" The goals of benchmarking typically include cost reductions, quality improvement, and new product or process ideas.

Benchmarking involves a variety of considerations, including processing, legal issues, and limitations. Benchmarking is a structured analysis, starting with identification of the business or process to be benchmarked. In addition to comparing products with the "best in the business," companies also compare processes. For example, Walmart is well known as a leader in inventory management. Many companies, including Amazon (which was sued for hiring away Walmart

inventory management executives), benchmark Walmart as the leading firm in the area of cost control. Similarly, the United States is perceived by many nations as a leader in education. Education management personnel from other countries are often sent to the United States to study and bring back for adoption educational practices used in this country.

Once the product or process to be studied is identified, organizations develop a team to participate in the benchmarking process. Since benchmarking, by definition, is designed to create change, who is involved in the process is an important consideration. Team members must be knowledgeable, be open to new ideas, be able to analyze data, and have influence within the organization.

Once the team is formed, the benchmarking process typically involves data collection. For internal benchmarking, where similar operating units within an organization are compared, internal data is usually available. For example, many national sales organizations are broken down into dozens or hundreds of regional and local offices. Sales, cost per sales, gross margins, and other performance measures can be compared. For competitive benchmarking, where companies compare their performance with direct competitors, data collection can be more difficult. Public data, observation, and surveys are often needed to collect needed information. Quality comparisons are often conducted using reverse engineering, purchasing and dismantling competitors' products in order to assess quality, and production processes.

Using the data collected, the benchmarking team looks for gaps between the company's processes and PRODUCTS and those of the leading unit, firm, or industry. Once gaps are identified, causes are searched for and hopefully identified. This leads to the final step in the process: taking action to change existing practices to match or exceed those of the benchmarked unit or competitor.

As Dean Elmuti et al. suggest, benchmarking can lead to legal issues. Especially in competitive benchmarking, copying the practices or processes of the leading firm in an industry can generate problems associated with PROPRIETARY INFOR-

MATION and INTELLECTUAL PROPERTY. Groups of firms working together to improve industry standards and practices can violate antitrust and unfair trade practices laws.

Benchmarking peaked as a business management process in the 1990s. While many companies used the process to reduce costs and improve quality, benchmarking has its limitations. First, the focus of benchmarking is data. If the numbers are not accurate or do not allow valid comparisons, the process will fail. Also, focusing on data can distract managers from their need to address the desires of customers and needs of employees. With its emphasis on details, benchmarking can misinterpret the organization's "big picture," their reason for existing.

Typical areas of business practices where benchmarking is applied include billing and collection, customer satisfaction, distribution and logistics, employee EMPOWERMENT, equipment maintenance, manufacturing flexibility, marketing, product development, QUALITY CONTROL, supply chain management, and worker training.

Further reading
Elmuti, Dean, Yunus Kathawala, and Scott Lloyd. "The Benchmarking Process: Assessing Its Value and Limitations," *Industrial Management* 39, no. 2 (July–August 1997): 12–19.

benefits   See COMPENSATION AND BENEFITS; EMPLOYEE BENEFITS.

beta coefficient, capital asset pricing model
A beta coefficient is a measure of a stock's volatility relative to the market for all stocks. As an integral component of the theoretical capital ASSET pricing model that is used to determine the required return for a particular stock, beta coefficients are measures of a stock's risk.

The beta coefficient for all stocks collectively is 1, and a stock whose returns move with the market has a beta of 1. Thus, a beta coefficient of 1 indicates average volatility, and stocks with betas of 1 carry the same risk as the STOCK MARKET in general. If a stock's returns are more volatile than the average movements in the stock market, its beta is greater than 1. Stocks whose returns are less volatile than the average movements in the market have betas less than 1. (There are some stocks that are countercyclical, and their betas are negative.) Beta coefficients can be easily obtained for all stocks publicly traded.

The capital asset pricing model (CAPM) is based on risk aversion, the assumption that investors require compensation for assuming risk. CAPM is an equation used to calculate a stock's required return based upon the riskiness of that stock as measured by its beta coefficient:

$$k_s = k_{rf} + (k_m - k_{rf})b_s$$

where k_s is the required return for some individual stock s, k_{rf} is the theoretic return an investor would require in a risk-free world, k_m is the average return for all stocks in the market, and b_s is the beta coefficient of the stock s.

In the model, $(k_m - k_{rf})$—the difference between the average return for all stocks and the risk-free rate of return—is the stock market's average risk premium. The average risk premium is multiplied by a stock's beta coefficient to determine the risk premium associated with that particular stock. For example, when the beta is 1, the stock will have the same risk premium as the market's. When the beta is greater than 1, the stock's risk premium will be greater than the market's average risk premium, and when the beta is less than 1, the stock's risk premium will be less than the market's average risk premium. Thus the CAPM equation indicates that a stock's required return is the sum of the risk-free rate of return and the risk premium for that stock as determined by that stock's beta coefficient.

For example, assume a risk-free rate of return, k_{rf}, of 3 percent and an average return in the stock market, k_m, of 7 percent. Using the CAPM equation, if Stock A has a beta of 1, its required return, k_A, is [3 + (7 - 3)1] = 7 percent. Because Stock A is no more and no less volatile than the stock market in general (indicated by its beta coefficient of 1), the required return for Stock A is the same as the average return in the stock market. If Stock B has a beta of 2, its required return, k_B, is $[3 + (7 - 3)2] = 11$ percent. As indicated by its beta coefficient of 2, Stock B is twice as volatile and twice as risky as the average stock, and higher required return reflects the added riskiness of this stock's returns. If Stock C has a beta of .5, its required return is 5 percent. Stock C is less volatile and less risky, and as a result it has a lower required return.

Better Business Bureau

The Better Business Bureau (BBB) is a private, nonprofit organization with a mission to promote and foster ethical relationships between businesses and the public. The BBB is best known for its complaint service, where dissatisfied consumers contact local BBB offices to resolve disputes with businesses.

Established in 1912, the BBB today has 125 local bureaus and over 380,000 business members nationwide. The national organization is the Council of Better Business Bureaus (CBBB). In 2004 the BBB received over 41 million requests for reports from American consumers. The bureau usually suggests consumers first contact companies directly. If they are not satisfied with the results, the BBB will intercede. The bureau has no power to force businesses to resolve disputes with consumers. Instead, it uses the fear of adverse publicity to pressure businesses to act promptly and ethically.

The major BBB activities include providing

- business reliability reports
- dispute resolution
- truth in advertising
- consumer and business education
- charity review

Business reliability reports provide consumers with information about past complaints involving local companies. Local BBBs collect and disseminate information about unanswered questions and unresolved complaints. For consumers the fact that a company has unresolved disputes registered with the local BBB is a signal that there may be problems. The CBBB plans to reliability report information on-line.

Dispute resolution services include buyer/seller mediation and ARBITRATION services. The BBB provides specialized on-line complaint services for auto-related and moving- and storage-related disputes. In addition it provides a customer assistance program. Along with auto and moving disputes, home-improvement and ordered products receive the greatest number of complaints.

One of the early functions of the BBB was to improve truth in ADVERTISING. False and misleading advertising by a few firms in a market hurts the public perception of all businesses. The BBB's Code of Advertising includes guidelines for ethical use of comparative pricing, savings claims, free offers, credit, distress sales, warranties, disclosures, bait and switch advertising, and even use of asterisks. The use of testimonials, superiority claims, contests, and extra charges, all issues that can lead to misrepresentation of products, are addressed by BBB codes.

A fourth function of the BBB is to provide consumer and business education. Knowledge improves business practices and consumer satisfaction. The CBBB writes and produces numerous alerts and press releases designed to inform businesses and consumers. Many newspapers include consumer-alert columns with information disseminated by the BBB. Recently, with the rapid growth of INTERNET commerce, the BBB established a Code of Online Business Practices for members. The code calls for on-line businesses to post privacy policies, protect user's security, and resolve consumer complaints promptly.

In conjunction with the Philanthropic Advisory Service, the BBB provides information about nonprofit organizations, educating private and corporate donors.

Further reading

Better Business Bureau Web site. Available online. URL: www.bbb.org.

Big Mac Index

The Big Mac Index is a half-serious and half-humorous measure of the relative purchasing power of currencies around the world. First published in *The Economist* in 1986, the index compares the current U.S. dollar price of a McDonald's Big Mac with the price of Big Macs in other countries after converting the price in local currencies to their equivalent in U.S. dollars.

Why is the Big Mac used as a measure of prices? For one it is a relatively standardized product. A 1970s TV commercial described it as "twoallbeef-pattiesspecialsaucelettucecheesepicklesonionsona sesameeseedbun." It is also sold at over 25,000 McDonald's restaurants in 116 countries around the world.

The Big Mac Index is based on PURCHASING POWER PARITY THEORY (PPP), which suggests that EXCHANGE RATES should increase or decrease to make the price of a basket of goods the same in each country. The theory was developed by Swedish economist Gustav Cassel in 1920, who suggested that identical goods should have the same price. PPP theory assumes global trade exists, TRANSACTIONS COSTS are not significant, and goods and services are similar in each country. Since the Big Mac Index includes only one item, it is not representative of prices for consumer goods and services; rather, it is a symbolic measure and quoted regularly in the media. Because prices for Big Macs vary with local economic conditions and what is considered fast food in developed countries is sometimes considered a social status purchase in developing countries, relative prices for Big Macs are best compared among countries with similar levels of INCOME.

As shown in the table below, in January 2009 the U.S. price for a Big Mac was $3.54 while the dollar equivalent price in Switzerland was $5.75, suggesting the Swiss currency was overvalued by approximately 60 percent ($5.75 - $3.54 ÷ $3.54 × 100.) At the other extreme, the dollar equivalent price in South Africa was $1.68, suggesting the South African currency was significantly undervalued ($1.68 - 3.54 ÷ $3.54 × 100 = −53 percent.)

In addition to the Big Mac Index, in 2004, *The Economist* created the Tall Latte Index (Starbucks) and an Australian bank created the iPod index. The *Wall Street Journal* regularly creates charts comparing dollar equivalent cost of hotel rooms,

BIG MAC		
Country	U.S. dollar equivalent Price (Jan.2009)	Implied over/under valuation (%)
United States	$3.54	—
Switzerland	$5.75	63%
Norway	$5.74	62%
Euro areas	$4.50	27%
Brazil	$3.39	−4.0%
China	$1.83	−48%
South Africa	$1.68	−53%

a dozen roses, champagne, and other products around the world.

Further reading
"Sandwiched: The Big Mac Index," *The Economist*, 24 July 2008; "Big Mac Index," *The Economist*, 22 January 2009.

bill of lading
A bill of lading is a document issued by a shipping company to acknowledge that the seller has delivered particular goods to it. Bills of lading are used in both interstate and international shipments. The Federal Bill of Lading Act (1916, formally called the Pomerene Act) governs the transfer and transferability of bills of lading, of which there are two types: a nonnegotiable or "straight" bill of lading; and negotiable bills of lading, known as "white" and "yellow" bills because of the colors of paper on which they are printed. Both types usually represent the seller's CONTRACT with the shipping company, setting the terms and TARIFFS of that contract.

In a nonnegotiable bill of lading, the carrier is obligated to deliver the goods to the designated destination point and is liable for misdelivery of the goods. Nonnegotiable bills of lading are sometimes called "air waybills," "sea waybills," and "freight receipts," depending on the intended method of transportation. Nonnegotiable bills are used when the seller is expecting payment upon delivery, not for payment based on bill-of-lading documentation.

The carrier issues a negotiable bill of lading to a person (consignee) or "order." This allows the person to endorse the bill of lading to "order" delivery of the goods to others. Negotiable bills can be endorsed to third parties, buyers or creditors, allowing the "holder" of the bill to receive the goods at the destination point. The shipping company is liable to the holder of a negotiable bill of lading for misdelivery if it delivers the goods to anyone but the holder. In this way the negotiable bill of lading is similar to a title document conferring ownership of the goods. Negotiable bills of lading are used when sellers are being paid at the time goods are shipped. In international business letters of credit are often used, obligating the buyer's bank to pay the amount of the contract once bills of lading are submitted, usually by the seller's bank to the buyer's bank. The banks use negotiable bills of lading to control title to the goods in their contracts with buyers and sellers. In the United States, negotiable bills of lading are most often used, but some countries only allow the use of nonnegotiable bills of lading.

Further reading

Folsom, Ralph H., and Michael Gordon. *International Business Transactions*. 6th ed. Eagan, Minn.: West Group, 2002.

Black Monday, Tuesday, Thursday

Black Monday, Tuesday, and Thursday refer to days when the U.S. stock market declined significantly. Though mostly associated with the GREAT DEPRESSION, Black Monday can refer to either October 28, 1929, or October 19, 1987. The use of the color *black* to describe these days implies mourning as the stock market died. Alternatively, these days could have been called red Monday, Tuesday, and Thursday as the market both bled and produced "red ink," huge losses that are usually displayed by the use of red colored figures. The impact of these "black" days are all measured by declines in the Dow JONES Industrial Average (DJIA), the most widely quoted, though limited, measure of the U.S. stock market.

What caused each of these market declines is still being debated and is of interest to investors and federal regulators as they attempt to assuage the 2008 financial crisis. Chronologically, Black Thursday occurred first—October 24, 1929. After reaching a five-year peak on September 3, 1929, in the following month the market dropped by 17 percent, recovered about half that amount, and then fell precipitously on Thursday, October 24th. The next day, major banks interceded, directing NEW YORK STOCK EXCHANGE vice president, Richard Whitney to purchase a large block of shares in U.S. Steel and other "blue chip" companies at prices higher than what was being bid in the market. Like the widely reported purchases and loans made by billionaire investment sage Warren Buffett in 2008, these purchases "stemmed the tide" and the stock market closed on a calm note that Friday.

The calm ended abruptly on Black Monday and Black Tuesday (October 28 and 29, 1929) when the market fell by 12 percent each day (12.82% on Monday and 11.73% on Tuesday.) The causes of these declines included fear and speculation as well as weakening fundamentals in the economy. One fear was that President Herbert Hoover would not veto the recently passed SMOOT-HAWLEY TARIFF legislation (which took effect leading to huge increases in tariffs on imported goods and subsequent reciprocal tariffs against U.S. exports) and the concern that this would harm international trade. Speculation played a role in the stock market because, at the time, brokerage firms would let investors put up as little as 10 percent of the face value of stocks they were buying. This allowed investors and speculators to leverage their funds and make larger profits as stock prices rose (much like the use of LEVERAGE by U.S. banks in the 2008 crisis.) Stories from the time describe waiters, waitresses, and shoe-shine boys all borrowing and buying shares based on the latest tip they heard from the powerful Wall Street elite. The problem came when stock prices fell. When the price of stocks declined enough to cancel the initial capital put up by investors, they received "margin calls," requiring them to put up more funds or have their shares involuntarily sold. This increased the supply of shares being sold and further depressed market prices, resulting in the dramatic declines each day.

Economic fundamentals also played a role in the dramatic plunge in stock market prices. Housing prices had peaked several years earlier and were in decline. Similarly, agricultural prices were falling and Dust Bowl problems were forcing farmers to leave their land. Depression-era economist Irving Fisher argued that the predominant factors leading to the Great Depression were excessive use of credit and deflation. He suggested the interaction of nine factors under conditions of debt and deflation drove the economy downward. Fisher's chain of events proceeded as follows:

1. Debt liquidation and distress selling
2. Contraction of the money supply as bank loans are paid off
3. A fall in the level of asset prices
4. A still greater fall in the net worth of businesses, precipitating bankruptcies
5. A fall in profits
6. A reduction in output, in trade, and in employment
7. Pessimism and loss of confidence
8. Hoarding of money
9. A fall in nominal interest rates and a rise in deflation adjusted interest rates

Numerous books have been written about the Great Depression and many are being reread as American households and policy makers attempt to understand and cope with the 2008 crisis.

As stated earlier, Black Monday also refers to October 19, 1987. On that day the DJIA fell by 508 points, or 22.6 percent, the largest one-day drop in U.S. stock market history. The day began with stock markets in Hong Kong and Europe falling precipitously, followed by the decline in the U.S. market. One explanation for the decline is the use of program trading, computerized models that buy and sell large blocks of shares based on changes in prices of related securities and derivatives. This created a "snowball effect" as more and more computer models triggered additional selling. Another

explanation of this second Black Monday was the perception that the market was overvalued and sellers followed the lead of Asian investors and dumped shares. Like earlier black days in the stock market, the causes of this Black Monday are still being debated.

Further reading

Bernanke, Ben. *Essays on the Great Depression*. Princeton, N.J.: Princeton University Press, 2000; Fisher, Irving. "The Debt-Deflation Theory of Great Depressions." *Econometrica* 1 (October 1933): 337–357.

blind trust

A blind trust exists when a beneficiary, the party for whom the benefit of a TRUST exists, turns over control of their ASSETS to a trustee, who is an independent third party, typically a professional money manager. The trustee is given broad discretion over the assets. The trust is "blind" because the beneficiary does not know the exact identity, nature, and extent of their financial interests within the trust's holdings. In other words, the beneficiary will become "blind" to the activity and makeup of the fund. The beneficiary will only receive a report on how the investments are performing, but no details on the actual investments. Blind trusts are typically set up when there is a CONFLICT OF INTEREST involving the beneficiary and the investments held in the trust.

The most common individuals to set up blind trusts are government officials, who arrange their assets this way so that no one can claim they are acting in their own self-interest when performing governmental service. All presidents and first ladies since Jimmy Carter have established blind trusts before taking office, with the exception of Bill and Hillary Clinton, who did not set up theirs until July 1993, and only then because of pressure due to conflict of interest. Without a blind trust, the Clintons were fair game for the media. It was revealed that when Hillary Clinton headed the health reform committee, her personal portfolio held more than $1 million in health stocks, and the portfolio was making money from sales of these health stocks. Soon after the news revelation of this $1 million conflict of interest, the Clintons created a blind trust naming Essex Investment Company, a Boston-based firm, as the trustee.

Ever since the Declaration of Independence, citizens have put their trust in government and have held that public officials should perform their duties in the public's interest and for the public's good. The ethics program within the executive branch of government helps to support this public trust and ensure that officials perform their duties impartially and free of conflicts of interest. The U.S. OFFICE OF GOVERNMENT ETHICS (OGE) was established by the Ethics in Government Act of 1978. This office oversees six major areas, including financial disclosure. Within the financial-disclosure area the OGE supervises the creation and operation of blind trusts and compliance with the Ethics in Government Act of 1978. The act permits two types of blind trusts: a qualified blind trust (QBT) and a qualified diversified trust (QDT). The difference between these two trusts is the level of restriction of the assets within the trust to the beneficiary's conflict of interest. In other words, with the QBT the initial assets may cause the beneficiary to be subject to conflict of interest, but these assets would be subsequently disposed of or valued at less than $1,000. In a QBT the beneficiary is then only blind to the subsequent assets purchased by the trustee. In a QDT the initial assets transferred into the blind trust are subject to more restrictions than the QBT. In other words, the initial assets cannot contain securities that may subject the beneficiary to conflict of interest. Both types of trusts are subject to rules of filing by the OGE and approval of both the actual blind trust and the appointed trustee.

Another example of when a blind trust is a remedy for a potential conflict of interest can be found within the financial industry. In 2000 the SECURITIES AND EXCHANGE COMMISSION (SEC) issued the Regulation FAIR DISCLOSURE (FD) and two new insider-trading rules. The latter rules (10b5-1 and 10b5-2) create insider-trading liability for anyone who may buy or sell stock in a company based on their knowledge of inside company information that has not been announced publicly. In order to comply with these new rules and protect themselves from insider-trading liability, many investment firms have instructed their traders to transfer their personal portfolios into blind trusts. Individuals such as CHIEF EXECUTIVE OFFICERS, company managers, members of a BOARD OF DIRECTORS, or holders of more than 10 percent of a particular company's shares would also establish blind trusts in order to avoid conflict-of-interest and insider-trading liability.

See also INSIDER TRADING.

—Maureen Murray

blue-chip stocks

Blue-chip stocks are COMMON STOCKS of nationally known companies that have a proven record of profitability, increases in stock value, and reputations for being leaders in their respective industries. Blue-chip stocks typically sell at a premium compared to other firms in their industry and usually pay moderate DIVIDEND yields. Blue-chip companies have quality management, products, and services. The term *blue chip* comes from poker, where the blue chip is the highest-valued chip.

International Business Machines (IBM), General Electric, Dow Chemical, DuPont, and until 2009 General Motors are examples of traditional American blue-chip stocks. In recent years dominant firms in the technology industry, such as Microsoft and Intel, have also become known as blue-chip stocks. Ironically, Enron and MCI WorldCom were also considered blue chips. Sometimes business media refer to the Dow Jones Industrial Average (DJIA) as the blue-chip average. The DJIA, initially an index of manufacturing company stocks, has been reconfigured in recent years to reflect the growing importance of service and technology companies in the U.S. economy. Now the DJIA includes dominant firms from many nonmanufacturing U.S. industries, including McDonalds (fast food), Wal-Mart (discount retailing), and American Express (credit). AT&T, once the most widely held stock in the United States, has lost its blue-chip status to some investors.

Blue-chip stock is also an internationally used term. In Australia companies such as Australian

Gas and Light, Amcor, National Australian Bank, Rio Tinto, and Qantas are known as blue-chip stocks.

In January 2009, *Wall Street Journal* writer Karen Blumenthal asked, "Are there any blue-chip stocks left?" With the decline and demise of so many respected U.S. companies, including General Motors, Citigroup, and AIG, it was a valid question. Blumenthal then provides four "chips" for identifying blue-chip companies in a time of financial crisis. First, "cash chips" or cash flow: Firms that have sufficient incoming revenue to cover their bills, and invest in new products and technology will survive economic hard times. Related to cash flow, companies that increase their dividends are confident about their future. Second, she defines "macro chips" as companies that have the ability to adapt to changing macroeconomic conditions. Management leadership, a difficult quality to assess, separates blue-chip companies from the rest of their industry. Third, "brand chips," what marketers refer to as brand equity, creates a competitive advantage through loyal customers who continue to purchase firms' products while their incomes are declining. During recessions, consumers typically purchase more generic or store-brand products, reducing their consumption of name brand products. Fourth, the writer identifies "big chips," suggesting that larger companies are more likely to survive and prosper than smaller firms. Blumenthal also notes that the initial government bailouts were targeted for companies considered "too big to fail." Of course, Lehman Brothers chairman Richard Fuld thought his firm was in that category, only to find out otherwise. The changing definition of what are "blue-chip" companies suggests investors cannot simply invest in blue chips and forget about them.

Further reading

Blumenthal, Karen. "Identifying the Blue-Chips, Post-Meltdown," *Wall Street Journal,* 14 January 2009, p. D1.

blue-collar

The term *blue-collar* refers to workers who traditionally wear blue work uniforms, including ASSEMBLY LINE and other laborers. Laborers typically wear dark-colored clothing because it does not show dirt or sweat as easily as lighter colors. Blue-collar contrasts to WHITE-COLLAR professionals, administrators, and office workers. Blue-collar is often used to describe specific locations, groups, or products.

One news story described efforts to redevelop Warren, Michigan, a blue-collar city, "with its plethora of factories and industrial buildings and endless concrete ribbons that carry traffic." Blue-collar groups are stereotypically portrayed as hard-working people with relatively little education and minimal aesthetic tastes, and blue-collar products appeal to this market segment. Blue-collar workers are more likely to be unionized and working in manufacturing rather than in service industries. A blue-collar recession would be a decline in the manufacturing sector of the economy.

Further reading

Shine, Kim North. "General Motors Plans to Help Redevelop Downtown Warren, Mich.," *Detroit Free Press,* 16 May 2001.

blue laws

Blue laws are legislation regulating activities associated with the Sabbath (Sunday). In the Bible, the Sabbath, or holy day, is a day of rest. Blue laws got their name from 17th-century laws in Connecticut, which were written on blue paper. Some of the early laws included:

- No one shall cross a river on the Sabbath but authorized clergymen.
- No one shall travel, cook victuals, make beds, sweep houses, cut hair, or shave on the Sabbath Day.
- No one shall kiss his or her children on the Sabbath or feasting days.
- The Sabbath Day shall begin at sunset on Saturday.

Most blue laws have been eliminated based on questions of their constitutionality, economics, and practicality. Constitutional challenges are usually based on the First Amendment, which states, "Congress shall make no laws respecting the establishment of religion."

Economic realities and lost sales and tax revenues have also pressured governments into repealing blue laws. Some southern states, particularly South Carolina, retain blue-law restrictions. Title 53, Chapter 1, Section 53-1-40 of the State of South Carolina Code of Laws reads in part: "On the first day of the week, commonly called Sunday, it shall be unlawful for any person to engage in worldly work, labor, business of his ordinary calling or the selling or ordering to sell publicly or privately or by telephone, at retail or at wholesale to the consumer any goods, wares or merchandise or to employ others to engage in work, labor or business or selling or offering to sell any goods, wares or merchandise, excepting work of necessity or charity." The act does allow the Sunday sale of tobacco, motor fuels, novelties, souvenirs, undergarments, and the operation of public eating places, funeral homes, and cemeteries.

Most Americans never encounter blue laws. Those who do are usually shocked or bemused to find they cannot purchase liquor in some southern states on Sundays. In South Carolina, counties can vote to overrule blue laws, and in most regions of the state where tourism is a significant source of INCOME, blue laws have been repealed or modified.

Further reading
Sunday Blue Laws, www.sundaybluelaws.org/index.html. Accessed on June 2, 2009.

board of directors

A company's board of directors makes its strategic decisions, including hiring and terminating executives, directing company policy, and considering proposals from outside investors or other companies to purchase or be purchased by the company. In the United States, a CORPORATION must have a board of directors elected by its SHAREHOLDERS, whose best interests the board of directors is charged to represent. (Many nonprofit organizations also have boards of directors providing similar functions to the organization but without responsibility to shareholders.)

A typical corporate board of directors creates at least three oversight committees: nominating, compensation, and audit. The nominating committee selects new candidates to be reviewed for positions on the board. The compensation committee determines the executive' pay. The audit committee reviews reports from independent audit firms and internal audits. In addition, some boards of directors create a finance committee to oversee CAPITAL investment decisions.

A board of directors can be large or small. Most corporate management specialists recommend that boards contain no more than 10 members. Larger boards allow for greater diversity but also slow decision making. Historically most U.S. corporate board of directors did not aggressively assert the interests of shareholders but instead generally accepted the recommendations of management. In the 1990s critics, especially giant pension-fund managers TIAA-CREF and CALPERS, challenged the status-quo "rubber stamping" by corporate boards. In 2009 the Obama administration pressured major companies receiving government bailouts to replace many members of corporate boards.

The Council of Institutional Investors (CII), created in 1985, developed a set of standards for board accountability and has acted as a "watch dog" group that oversees practices by boards. The CII developed a detailed set of recommendations, including core policies, general principles (shareholder rights, shareholder meeting rights, board accountability, and director and management compensation for board of directors), and positions.

Core Policies

1. Confidential ballots counted by independent tabulators should elect all directors annually.
2. At least two-thirds of a corporation's directors should be independent. A director is deemed independent if his or her only non-trivial professional, familial or financial connection to the corporation, its chairman, CEO or any other executive officer is his or her directorship.
3. A corporation should disclose information necessary for shareholders to determine whether each director qualifies as independent.

4. Companies should have audit, nominating and compensation committees. All members of these committees should be independent. The board (rather than the CEO) should appoint committee chairs and members. Committees should have the opportunity to select their own service providers.

5. A majority vote of common shares outstanding should be required to approve major corporate decisions concerning the sale or pledge of corporate assets, which would have a material effect on shareholder value.

General Principles

A. Shareholder Voting Rights

1. Each share of COMMON STOCK, regardless of class, should have one vote. Corporations should not have classes of common stock with disparate voting rights.

2. Shareholders should be allowed to vote on unrelated issues individually. Individual voting issues, particularly those amending a company's charter, BYLAWS, or anti-takeover provisions, should not be bundled.

3. A majority vote of common shares outstanding should be sufficient to amend company bylaws or take other action requiring or receiving a shareholder vote.

4. Broker non-votes and abstentions should be counted only for purposes of a quorum.

5. A majority vote of common shares outstanding should be required to approve major corporate decisions including:

   a. the corporation's acquiring, other than by TENDER OFFER to all shareholders, 5 percent or more of its common shares at above-market prices;

   b. provisions commonly known as shareholder rights plans, or poison pills;

   c. abridging or limiting the rights of common shares;

   d. permitting or granting any executive or employee of the corporation upon termination of EMPLOYMENT, any amount in excess of two times that person's average annual compensation for the previous three years; and

   e. provisions resulting in the issuance of debt to a degree that would excessively LEVERAGE the company and imperil the long-term viability of the corporation.

6. Shareholders should have the opportunity to vote on all equity-based compensation plans that include any director or executive officer of the company.

B. Shareholder Meeting Rights

1. Corporations should make shareholders' expense and convenience primary criteria when selecting the time and location of shareholder meetings.

2. Appropriate notice of shareholder meetings, including notice concerning any change in meeting date, time, place or shareholder action, should be given to shareholders in a manner and within time frames that will ensure that shareholders have a reasonable opportunity to exercise their franchise.

3. All directors should attend the annual shareholders' meeting and be available, when requested by the chair, to answer shareholder questions.

4. Polls should remain open at shareholder meetings until all agenda items have been discussed and shareholders have had an opportunity to ask and receive answers to questions concerning them.

5. Companies should not adjourn a meeting for the purpose of soliciting more votes to enable management to prevail on a voting item.

6. Companies should hold shareholder meetings by remote communication (so-called electronic or "cyber" meetings) only as a supplement to traditional in-person shareholder meetings, not as a substitute.

7. Shareholders' rights to call a special meeting or act by written consent should not be eliminated or abridged without the approval of the shareholders.

8. Corporations should not deny shareholders the right to call a special meeting if such a right is guaranteed or permitted by state law and the corporation's articles of INCORPORATION.

C. Board Accountability to Shareholders

1. Corporations and/or states should not give former directors who have left office (so-called "continuing directors") the power to take action on behalf of the corporation.
2. Boards should review the performance and qualifications of any director from whom at least 10 percent of the votes cast are withheld.
3. Boards should take actions recommended in shareholder proposals that receive a majority of votes cast for and against.
4. Directors should respond to communications from shareholders and should seek shareholder views on important governance, management and performance matters.
5. Companies should disclose individual director attendance figures for board and committee meetings.

D. Director and Management Compensation

1. Annual approval of at least a majority of a corporation's independent directors should be required for the CEO's compensation, including any bonus, severance, equity-based, and/or extraordinary payment.
2. Absent unusual and compelling circumstances, all directors should own company common stock, in addition to any OPTIONS and unvested shares granted by the company.
3. Directors should be compensated only in cash or stock, with the majority of the compensation in stock.
4. Boards should award CHIEF EXECUTIVE OFFICERS no more than one form of equity-based compensation.
5. Unless submitted to shareholders for approval, no "underwater" options should be re-priced or replaced, and no discount options should be awarded. (Underwater means option prices below the current market price of the company's stock.)
6. Change-in-control provisions in compensation plans and compensation agreements should be "double-triggered," stipulating that compensation is payable only (1) after a control change actually takes place and (2) if a covered executive's job is terminated as a result of the control change.
7. Companies should disclose in the annual PROXY statement whether they have rescinded and re-granted options exercised by executive officers during the prior year or if executive officers have hedged (by buying puts and selling calls or employing other risk-minimizing techniques) shares awarded as stock-based incentive or acquired through options granted by the company.

Council of Institutional Investors Positions

A. Board Shareholder Accountability

1. Shareholders' right to vote is inviolate and should not be abridged.
2. CORPORATE GOVERNANCE structures and practices should protect and enhance accountability to, and equal financial treatment of, shareholders.
3. Shareholders should have meaningful ability to participate in the major fundamental decisions that affect corporate viability.
4. Shareholders should have meaningful opportunities to suggest or nominate director candidates.
5. Shareholders should have meaningful opportunities to suggest processes and criteria for director selection and evaluation.
6. Directors should own a meaningful position in company common stock, appropriate to their personal circumstances.
7. Absent compelling and stated reasons, directors who attend fewer than 75 percent of board and board-committee meetings for two consecutive years should not be renominated.
8. Boards should evaluate themselves and their individual members on a regular basis.

B. Board Size and Service

1. A board should neither be too small to maintain the needed expertise and independence, nor too large to be efficiently functional. Absent compelling, unusual circumstances, a board should have no fewer than 5 and no more than 15 members.

2. Companies should set and publish guidelines specifying on how many other boards their directors may serve. Absent unusual or specified circumstances, directors with full-time jobs should not serve on more than two other boards.

C. Board Meetings and Operations

1. Directors should be provided meaningful information in a timely manner prior to board meetings. Directors should be allowed reasonable access to management to discuss board issues.
2. Directors should be allowed to place items on board agendas.
3. Directors should receive training from independent sources on their fiduciary responsibilities and liabilities.
4. The board should hold regularly scheduled executive sessions without the CEO or staff present.
5. If the CEO is chairman, a contact director should be specified for directors wishing to discuss issues or add agenda items that are not appropriately or best forwarded to the chair/CEO.
6. The board should approve and maintain a CEO succession plan.

D. Compensation

Pay for directors and managers should be indexed to peer or market groups, absent unusual and specified reasons for not doing so.

An important issue in governance of a board of directors is whether the board member is independent or not. The CII defines an independent director as someone whose only nontrivial professional, familial, or financial connection to the corporation, its chairman, CEO, or any other executive officer is his or her directorship. The CII's position on independent directors is based on the problems of conflicts of interest for board members who are also managers; and interlocking directorships, where board members represent the interests of shareholders for different corporations.

Further reading
Council of Institutional Investors Web site. Available online. URL: www.cii.org.

bond market See STOCK MARKET, BOND MARKET.

bonds

Bonds are long-term debt instruments used by both the private and public sectors to raise funds. They are liabilities for the issuer and can be excellent INVESTMENT opportunities. In the private sector, corporate bonds are most common. In the public sector there are Treasury bonds and U.S. Savings Bonds issued by the federal government and municipal bonds issued by local governments and municipalities.

With the exception of bonds issued by the federal government, all bonds have some risk of DEFAULT. Moody's and Standard and Poor are the two major firms that rate bonds, both public and private sector, according to their default risk. Both organizations use two broad classifications of risk. Those bonds with ratings of "BBB" or "Baa" and higher are termed *investment grade* or *investment quality* bonds. These are the bonds with minimal default risk. Bonds with ratings less than BBB or Baa are termed speculations because of their considerable risk of default. The more common name for these speculative bonds is *junk bonds*.

All bonds have a maturity date and a face value, the amount that is paid to the bondholder on the maturity date. Most bonds, especially corporate bonds, also have a coupon-interest rate. The interest that a coupon bond pays is determined by multiplying the coupon-interest rate by the face value of the bond. Bonds may pay coupon interest annually, semiannually, or quarterly, depending on what is stipulated on the face of the bond.

The object of the bond issuer who is trying to raise CAPITAL is to get as much money for each bond as is possible while at the same time trying to minimize the interest expense associated with the bond. To accomplish this, the issuer sets the coupon-interest rate at the going rate of interest in the market at the time the bonds are issued. This helps to ensure that the bonds will sell "at par"—that is, for their face value. (If one looks in the newspaper at the reporting for the bond exchanges, one notices that there are many bonds outstanding, all with different coupon-interest rates. This is because there are bonds issued every day, and the various coupon-interest rates reflect the going rates of interest when the bonds were issued.)

A bond with a coupon-interest rate lower than the going rate of interest in the market, ceteris paribus (other things being equal), will not be viewed as an attractive INVESTMENT. Why should one purchase this bond when most any other investment in the market will yield a higher return? In order for the return on this bond to be more attractive, investors would only be willing to buy this bond at a discount (i.e., below its face value). This would add a CAPITAL GAIN to the bond's comparatively low interest yield. (At maturity, a bond will pay its face value, regardless of what was initially paid for it.) Thus, for organizations in need of funds, it makes no sense to issue bonds with coupon rates that are lower than current market rates.

A bond with a coupon-interest rate higher than the going rate of interest in the market, ceteris paribus, will be viewed as a very attractive investment. Investors will clamor to purchase such a bond, causing it to sell at a premium, or for more than its face value. Organizations in need of funds will not offer such high coupon-interest rates because this increases the interest expense they must pay on the borrowed funds.

Coupon-interest rates are also determined, in part, by default risk. Rational investors are risk-averse, and they demand to be compensated for assuming risk. Thus the higher the degree of default risk, the higher the bond's coupon interest rate, ceteris paribus.

Occasionally, a firm finds that it needs to raise funds during a period of high interest rates in the economy. In order for the bonds it issues to sell at par, the coupon-interest rate will be set at the current market interest rate. However, the bonds will most probably be callable. A CALLABLE BOND is one that will be called in by the issuer for redemption before the bond reaches it maturity date. The call period is normally stated on the face of the bond, and investors who own callable bonds expect not to be able to hold such an attractive

bond until its maturity. The call provision allows firms to escape the costly interest expense of the high coupon-interest rates by allowing the bonds to remain outstanding only until their call dates. Often firms will use the funds obtained from newer, lower coupon-interest rate bonds to call in and redeem their callable bonds.

Some bonds are convertible bonds, which may be converted to shares of COMMON STOCK (as a fixed price) at the option of the bondholder. Because they offer the potential for a capital gain when the stocks are eventually sold, convertible bonds normally carry lower coupon-interest rates than bonds that are not convertible.

Some bonds have no coupon-interest rates. These are known as zero-coupon (or deep discount) bonds. When issued, they always sell at a discount. The return from investing in such bonds is a capital gain, because the face value received at maturity is more than the purchase price of the bond. Treasury bills and U.S. Savings Bonds are examples of zero-coupon bonds issued by the federal government.

Bonds may be secured or unsecured. Secured bonds have collateral or pledged ASSETS backing them, minimizing their risk. Unsecured bonds have no such backing and are known as debentures. Ceteris paribus, secured bonds are less risky than debentures and, thus, offer lower interest yields than debentures.

Local governments and municipalities often sell bonds to finance INFRASTRUCTURE and to build schools. The interest earned on a municipal bond, called a muni, is exempt from federal taxation. Because the interest earnings on munis are not federally taxable, this allows local and municipal governments to issue their bonds at lower coupon-interest rates than other similar bonds, with the savings accruing to the local taxpayers.

The largest issuer of bonds is the federal government, selling Treasury securities and savings bonds. When there is a budget deficit, the federal government is forced to make up the shortfall by borrowing from the private sector. It does this by selling Treasury securities: Treasury bills with maturities up to one year; Treasury notes with one to five-year maturities; and Treasury bonds with five to thirty years. With the national debt at approximately $12 trillion, this is roughly the amount of money the federal government has borrowed (bonds outstanding) as a result of spending in excess of tax revenues in past years.

See also BRADY BONDS; STOCK MARKET, BOND MARKET.

book value (carrying value)

Book (or carrying) value is an accounting term that usually refers to a net amount, the remainder after a subtraction has occurred. Book values are commonly encountered in the accounting for ASSETS and liabilities.

For example, assume a firm has ACCOUNTS RECEIVABLE in the amount of $300,000. The related contra-asset account, Allowance for BAD DEBTS, has a balance of $25,000. The asset account has a debit balance, the contra-asset account has a credit balance, and the difference between the two is a net debit balance of $275,000. Because not all of the accounts receivable will prove collectible, the net realizable value of the firm's accounts receivable is $275,000, and this is the book, or carrying, value of the accounts receivable. Paying homage to the principle of conservatism (one of the GENERALLY ACCEPTED ACCOUNTING PRINCIPLES), the accounts receivable are being "carried" at $275,000, the amount that is more likely to be collected than the amount of $300,000 actually owed to the firm.

Assume Machine No. 3 has a cost of $900,000. The related contra-asset account, Accumulated Depreciation, has a credit balance of $350,000. The difference between the two amounts is a net debit balance of $550,000. This is the book (carrying) value of Machine No. 3.

For another example, assume a firm borrows money with a non-interest-bearing note payable. With such notes the interest rate is implicit, and the proceeds of the note are less than its face value. When the borrower records this LIABILITY as a note payable, a contra-liability account, Discount on Note Payable, is also established to record the difference between the face value of the note payable and the proceeds received from issuing the note. This will allow the book, or carrying, value of the note payable to be equal to the proceeds received from issuing the note.

See also DEBIT, CREDIT.

Border Environmental Cooperation Commission

The Border Environmental Cooperation Commission (BECC), a binational organization created in 1993 as a side agreement to the NORTH AMERICAN FREE TRADE AGREEMENT (NAFTA), helps states, localities, and the private sector develop and find financing for environment INFRASTRUCTURE projects along the U.S.-Mexico border. The BECC, which identifies, evaluates, and certifies affordable environment projects with the goal of improving the quality of life for citizens along the border, is an outgrowth of ideas put forth by UCLA urban planning professor Raul Hinjosa and others. The idea for the BECC was adopted by the Bush Administration in 1992 and superseded the 1983 Agreement on Cooperation for the Protection and Improvement of the Environment on the Border Area (the 1983 La Paz Agreement).

The Commission maintains offices in both El Paso, Texas, and Ciudad Juarez, Mexico, and is directed by a 10-member BOARD OF DIRECTORS, with five board members from each country. The Director of the U.S. Environmental Protection Agency is an ex officio member of the BECC board. Decisions of the board are based on a majority vote, thus requiring support from members representing both countries. A major role of the BECC is certifying projects for financing by the NORTH AMERICAN DEVELOPMENT BANK (NAD Bank). By 2007 the BECC had certified 135 projects, mostly water-treatment and municipal solid-waste projects.

Many U.S.-Mexico border problems stem from rapid growth of the MAQUILADORAS in Mexico. After the PESO CRISIS (1994–95), the reduced cost of Mexican labor for international firms and NAFTA increased access to the U.S. market and overwhelmed an already weak infrastructure.

Further reading
Folsom, Ralph H., and W. Davis Folsom. *NAFTA Law and Business.* The Hague: Kluwer Law International, 1998; BECC Web site. Available online. www.cocef.org.

boycotts

Boycotts are organized attempts to influence a company, organization, or government through refusal to patronize a business or other group. Boycotts are frequently used to affect business practices. Sometimes boycotts are organized to challenge labor or environmental issues; other times they are used to sway social practices or policies.

In the United States, possibly the most famous boycott was organized by the United Farm Workers (UFW). During the 1960s, 1970s, and 1980s, led by charismatic UFW President César Chávez, the UFW asked American consumers to not purchase table grapes, claiming unfair labor practices and poor working conditions by grape farmers. By 1975 an estimated 17 million Americans had stopped buying grapes. In another agricultural boycott, the UFW used a DIRECT MAIL campaign asking consumers to boycott Lucky Supermarkets because they were buying nonunion lettuce. The campaign targeted ethnic neighborhoods, areas with high agricultural EMPLOYMENT, and liberal, middle and high-income groups. After nine months Lucky agreed to stop buying nonunion lettuce but claimed the decision had nothing to do with the boycott.

Peace and environmental groups have often attempted to use boycotts to influence government policy. In 1990 Neighbor to Neighbor initiated a boycott of Folgers coffee, a Proctor and Gamble product, accusing P&G of prolonging the El Salvadoran civil war by buying Salvadoran coffee beans. The campaign brought attention to the plight of El Salvadorans but was actively opposed by the Bush administration. (The war ended when the Clinton administration withdrew financial support for the El Salvadoran military.) Similarly, American and other activists have long supported a boycott of Burma (now called Myanmar) because of its military rule and abuse of human rights. In 1995

U.S. environmental groups organized a short-lived protest of French products in reaction to France's nuclear tests in the South Pacific.

Boycotts are also used to influence social and political policies. The Boston Tea Party was one of America's first boycotts. Similarly, one of the hallmarks of the civil rights era was the 1950s boycott of buses in Montgomery, Alabama. The boycott of South Africa in the 1980s displayed the power of economic sanctions to influence social policies. As one author states, "Boycott. It's not blackmail. It's not censorship. What it is is capitalism. A boycott, after all, is merely a way to vote with our wallets."

In 1994 the National Organization of Women organized a boycott against orange juice when the Florida Citrus Commission decided to advertise on conservative Rush Limbaugh's talk show. Limbaugh supporters countered by increasing their purchases of orange juice. In 1996 Jesse Jackson threatened a boycott of Texaco stores in an effort to pressure Texaco to settle a racial discrimination suit. The next year Southern Baptists attempted to dissuade the Disney corporation from its gay-friendly employment policies by declaring a boycott against the company. In 1999 the NAACP organized a boycott of tourism in South Carolina because the state continued to fly the Confederate flag over its state capitol. The National Collegiate Athletic Association (NCAA) joined the boycott, refusing to bring collegiate athletic events to the state. Removal of the flag from the capital to a place on the capital grounds appeased some groups.

Further reading
Kalisher, Jesse. "Art of Noise (Impact of Boycotts)," *Brandweek* 39, no. 18 (4 May 1998): 66.

Bracero program

The Bracero program, officially named the Mexican Farm Labor Program, was a guest-worker program created during World War II to provide agricultural labor for farmers in the United States. During the war, millions of Americans left the country to fight in both the European and Pacific theaters, leaving a huge labor shortage. Mexican workers had a history of migrating north for work during the summer and fall and then returning home in winter. The Bracero program legalized the entry of Mexican workers into the United States. Jointly operated by the Departments of Justice, State, and Labor, the program constituted a formal agreement between the U.S. and Mexican governments. The provisions of the agreement included:

- It is understood that Mexicans contracting to work in the United States shall not be engaged in any military service.
- The worker shall be paid in full the salary agreed upon, from which no deduction shall be made in any amount for any of the concepts mentioned in the above sub-paragraph.
- The employer or contractor shall issue a bond or constitute a deposit in cash in the Bank of Workers, or in the absence of same, in the Bank of Mexico, to the entire satisfaction of the respective labor authorities, for a sum equal to repatriation costs of the worker and his family, and those originated by transportation to point of origin.
- Mexicans entering the United States under this understanding shall not be employed to displace other workers, or for the purpose of reducing rates of pay previously established.
- Contracts will be made between the employer and the worker under the supervision of the Mexican Government. (Contracts must be written in Spanish.)
- All transportation and living expenses from the place of origin to destination, and return, as well as expenses incurred in the fulfillment of any requirements of a migratory nature shall be met by the Employer.
- Wages to be paid the worker shall be the same as those paid for similar work to other agricultural laborers under the same conditions within the same area, in the respective regions of destination. Piece rates shall be so set as to enable the worker of average ability to earn the prevailing wage. In any case wages for piece work or hourly work will not be less than 30 cents per hour.

- There shall be considered illegal any collection by reason of commission or for any other concept demanded of the worker.
- Workers domiciled in the migratory labor camps or at any other place of employment under this understanding shall be free to obtain articles for their personal consumption, or that of their families, wherever it is most convenient for them.
- The Mexican workers will be furnished without cost to them with hygienic lodgings, adequate to the physical conditions of the region of a type used by a common laborer of the region and the medical and sanitary services enjoyed also without cost to them will be identical with those furnished to the other agricultural workers in the regions where they may lend their services.
- Groups of workers admitted under this understanding shall elect their own representatives to deal with the Employer, but it is understood that all such representatives shall be working members of the group.
- The Mexican Consuls, assisted by the Mexican Labor Inspectors, recognized as such by the Employer will take all possible measures of protection in the interest of the Mexican workers in all questions affecting them, within their corresponding jurisdiction, and will have free access to the places of work of the Mexican workers. The Employer will observe that the sub-employer grants all facilities to the Mexican Government for the compliance of all the clauses in this contract.
- The respective agencies of the Government of the United States shall be responsible for the safekeeping of the sums contributed by the Mexican workers toward the formation of their Rural Savings Fund, until such sums are transferred to the Wells Fargo Bank and Union Trust Company of San Francisco for the account of the Bank of Mexico, S.A., which will transfer such amounts to the Mexican Agricultural Credit Bank. This last shall assume responsibility for the deposit, for the safekeeping and for the application, or in the absence of these, for the return of such amounts.

By the end of the war, more than 50,000 Mexican agricultural laborers were working in the United States (a brief program for railroad workers also existed that ended in 1945). Participation declined from 1946 through 1948, but rose rapidly in the 1950s, reaching a peak of 445,000 guest workers in 1956. The program was terminated in 1964 following criticism of exploitation of workers and human rights abuses. One Department of Labor official described the Bracero program as "legalized slavery." Labor unions led by Farm Workers Union leaders César Chávez and Dolores Huerta captured the support of American consumers with their call to boycott products sold by companies using nonunion, and thus implicitly exploited, farm labor.

While the language of the agreement protected the rights of workers, during the war enforcement was not a high priority, and afterward powerful agribusiness interests held greater influence than did labor advocates. Workers signed contracts in English without knowing what they were agreeing to. Housing and sanitation conditions were often unsafe or unsanitary. Access to stores or products other than what was sold through the employer was often limited, leaving workers continually in debt to their employers. Lawsuits filed later to collect workers' savings in the Rural Savings Fund were dismissed.

In the 2008 presidential election, at the outset considerable interest was raised and debate arose regarding the issue of illegal immigration. Opponents argued that these workers were taking jobs away from Americans. Others suggested that, by being illegal, these workers were easily exploited by employers and therefore a way to legal entry was needed. Some argued for the return of the Bracero program. However, as economic conditions worsened, addressing the problem of illegal immigrants became a low priority.

Further reading
University of California-Berkeley. Center for Latin American Studies. Available online. URL: clas.berkeley. edu/Outreach/education/migrations2003/index.html. Accessed on April 27, 2010; The Official Bracero Agree-ment. Available online. URL: are.berkeley.edu/APMP/pubs/agworkvisa/braceroagreemt42.html. Accessed on April 27, 2010.

Brady bonds
Brady bonds are debt instruments issued by governments and private lenders in developing countries as a means of restructuring their debt. Named after Nicholas Brady, secretary of the Treasury during the George H. W. Bush administration, these BONDS were first issued by the Mexican government as part of a plan to repackage loans made to Mexico during the 1980s. Many governments in developing countries had borrowed billions of dollars but were not able to pay back the loans. Poor INVESTMENT management and corruption led governments into situations where they owed significant amounts to foreign lenders and had few productive ASSETS to use or tax to pay off the loans. Just the interest due on the loans represented a significant portion of most governments' budgets. Known as "debt overhang," these payments prevented governments from making new investments in education, INFRASTRUCTURE, and resource development needed to generate ECONOMIC DEVELOPMENT.

Under Nicholas Brady, a pool of funds from the United States, WORLD BANK, and INTERNATIONAL MONETARY FUND (IMF) was used to guarantee new bonds issued by the developing country government. The new bonds offered to lenders reduced the amount of debt owed and stretched payments over a longer period of time. This lowered the payments of the debtor country, allowing its government greater financial resources to be used in economic development plans. An alternative procedure provided no debt reduction but lower INTEREST RATES on the new debt than that paid for the old debt in return for guarantees of payment of the principal with the proceeds from long-term bonds provided by the United States and other developed countries. To lenders who faced DEFAULT by the borrowing country, the new debt plans, backed by the funds coordinated by Nicholas Brady, were better than default and more secure than direct loans to the borrowing government.

Brady plan restructurings were used in many developing countries in the late 1980s and early 1990s. As world ECONOMIC CONDITIONS improved, some countries, particularly Mexico, paid off their Brady bonds. On the other hand, in 1999 Ecuador became the first government to default on its bonds.

Once issued, Brady bonds became part of international financial debt instruments. A few MUTUAL FUNDS specialized in purchasing Brady bonds of various countries at deep discounts, hoping to profit from the eventual payoff of these high-risk bonds. These investors recognize the biggest concern associated with these bonds is political risk. The Brady plan was an outgrowth of an earlier strategy proposed by then-Secretary of Treasury James Baker, which emphasized economic reforms as a condition for new lending to developing countries.

Further reading

Appleyard, Dennis R., and Alfred J. Field, Jr. *International Economics.* 6th ed. Homewood, Ill.: McGraw-Hill, 2007.

brain drain

Brain drain is a popular term for the movement of individuals with knowledge and technical skills from one country to another. While brain drain is a global phenomenon, it is particularly associated with the inflow of people to the United States. In the United States, businesses regularly apply for H1-B visas allowing primarily workers with specialized technical skills to enter and work here. In 2009 the limit under H1-B visas was 65,000 people annually. In past years, applications for these visas by U.S. companies were quickly filled, but, after the recession of 2008–09, fewer firms were bringing in foreign expertise and, for the first time in decades, the quota was not filled.

In economic terms, brain drain is the loss of human capital. In simple production function relationships, output depends on human, natural, and capital resources and the level of development of technology. Countries losing human capital limit their potential output and, more important, their potential growth in output.

In addition to work visas, general immigration can, in part, create brain drain. Historically, discrimination, violence, political and religious freedoms, and economic opportunity contributed to explaining why people leave their home country. When China resumed control over Hong Kong in 1997, a major exodus of skilled workers from Hong Kong ensued. Canada, in particular, offered entry to doctors, nurses, and other individuals with technical or business skills. Similarly, in the 1960s and 1970s, many Indian doctors entered the United States looking for economic opportunities. Changes in the NORTH AMERICAN FREE TRADE AGREEMENT (NAFTA) led to the movement of physicians, attorneys, architects, and other "brains" from Canada to the United States. In arguing that the government paid for their education, Cuba charges physicians and other educated citizens a tax to leave the country.

In the 21st century, post 9/11 changes in U.S. immigration laws have reduced and, in some cases, reversed the brain drain. The Homeland Security Act has restricted student visas into the United States. For decades, foreign students flocked to the United States on student visas and then found ways to stay, either through H1-B visas or marriage to Americans. According to a 2004 *New York Times* article, the National Science Foundation reported,

A minor exodus also hit one of the hidden strengths of American science: vast ranks of bright foreigners. In a significant shift of demographics, they began to leave in what experts call a reverse brain drain. After peaking in the mid-1990's, the number of doctoral students from China, India and Taiwan with plans to stay in the United States began to fall by the hundreds, according to the foundation. These declines are important, analysts say, because new scientific knowledge is an engine of the American economy and technical innovation, its influence evident in everything from potent drugs to fast computer chips.

Further reading

Broad, William J. "US Is Losing Its Dominance in the Sciences," *New York Times,* 3 May 2004. Available online. URL: www.commondreams.org/headlines04/0503-03.htm. Accessed on April 26, 2010.

brands, brand names

Brands are names, terms, designs, signs, symbols or some combination that identify a firm's PRODUCTS. Brands facilitate easy recognition of a company's products and increase consumer loyalty through repeat purchase. According to MARKET RESEARCH, consumers' brand loyalty goes through three stages: recognition, preference, and insistence.

A marketer's first objective is to gain brand recognition—that is, consumer knowledge of a company's brand. In ADVERTISING, marketers typically have three objectives: to inform, persuade, and remind consumers about the company's products. Brand recognition is consistent with informing customers about a brand. Gaining brand recognition in a national market like the United States is expensive. With a large geographic area, over 300 million people, and tremendous COMPETITION from other firms, marketers have to work hard to gain brand recognition. One option used by several small firms is advertising during the Super Bowl, the most widely watched television event in the United States. Super Bowl advertising is very expensive, but several small firms have successfully used it as a way to gain national brand recognition.

Brand preference is the stage where consumers select a particular brand over competing offerings. Typically brand preference is based on past experiences with a firm's products. In many categories of consumer products, customers tend to be very brand-loyal. Often brand loyalty is based on what peoples' parents purchased. For decades Sears's strongest MARKETING STRATEGY was brand preference and insistence based on consumers' past experiences with their tools and appliances.

Brand insistence is brand loyalty to the point where consumers refuse alternatives and seek out brands they most desire. Airlines and, more recently, hotel chains have successfully built brand loyalty through frequent-flyer/stay programs.

There are four types of brands: manufacturers, private, family, and individual. Manufacturers' brands, also called national brands, are those owned by the manufacturer. General Motors, Kodak, and Coca-Cola are all examples of national brands. Manufacturers protect and support their brands, often using price competition with private brands and cooperative advertising and promotion with retailers to maintain and expand brand loyalty.

Private brands are brand names created and marketed by WHOLESALERS and retailers. For example, Sears owns the Kenmore, Craftsman, and DieHard brand names. Sears contracts with manufacturers to make products to be sold under these private names. Traditionally manufacturers dominated brand marketing, but since World War II, retailers have greatly increased their control of DISTRIBUTION CHANNELS and have used this market power to expand their use of private brands.

A family brand is a single brand name used to identify a group of related products. For example, Johnson & Johnson offers a variety of product lines all under one brand name. Many companies market a variety of individual brands. Proctor and Gamble's Tide is one of the longest-lasting individual brand names in cleaning products, and Crest Toothpaste is a leading brand in health products.

As previously noted, the goal of brands and brand names is to increase consumer loyalty. Marketers refer to this as gaining brand equity, which means DEMAND for a firm's product is less elastic. Loyal consumers are more likely to continue to purchase a product even when the price is raised. Brand equity makes it infinitely easier for a firm to introduce new products, since most consumers who have had a positive experience with a company's products are more likely to try new product offerings from that firm.

Marketers know developing effective brand equity is difficult and usually expensive. New brand names generally should be easy to pronounce, recognize, and remember. A brand name should also be consistent with the image a company wants to convey: status, safety, or confidence. TRADEMARKS are brands and brand names owned by a company.

Further reading

Boone, Louis E., and David L. Kurtz. *Contemporary Marketing.* 14th ed. Fort Worth: South-Western, 2009.

break-even analysis

Break-even analysis is a tool used by managers to estimate either the quantity they need to sell at a given price to cover all costs or the price they must charge to cover all costs for a given quantity of output. Break-even analysis is often used when managers are considering new INVESTMENTS or new PRODUCTS.

Break-even quantity (BEQ) is estimated using the formula $BEQ = FC \div (P - AVC)$, where FC is total fixed costs, P is price per unit, and AVC is average variable cost per unit. Break-even analysis assumes a manager can estimate:

- the initial fixed costs (equipment, buildings, licenses; any cost that is required to get started but does not change with the level of output),
- the average variable cost (materials, labor, energy) in the range of output being considered.

If these costs can be estimated, a manager can then determine how many units must be sold at various prices to break even. For example, if FC is $1000 and AVC is $10, then at:

P = $20, BEQ = 100
P = $30, BEQ = 50
P = $40, BEQ = 33.3

Break-even analysis allows a manager to create a hypothetical DEMAND curve. Using the information from the BEQ analysis, managers then determine whether they think they can sell at least that quantity at a given price. Managers may then employ sales forecasting techniques to compare the results of BEQ analysis with potential market demand.

In the above formula, $P - AVC$ is often called the contribution margin. For each unit produced and sold, the difference between price and the average variable cost (if the difference is negative, the product should not be produced) contributes to "covering" fixed costs, and when all fixed costs are covered, ultimately contributes to profit.

Break-even price (BEP) is estimated using the formula $BEP = (FC \div Q) + AVC$, which says that the BEP equals average total cost. Using this same

example above, if FC are $1000 and AVC is $10 then at:

Q = 50, BEP = $30
Q = 100, BEP = $20
Q = 200, BEP = $15

Managers can use BEP analysis to answer the question, "If we produce and sell 100 units, what price do we have to get in order to at least break even?"

Retail store managers frequently use break-even analysis when considering new products. In RETAILING, firms often "keystone" products—that is, price their products at twice the cost to the store. If a manager orders 100 spring shirts at $10 each and prices them at $20 each, then they must sell at least 50 shirts to break even.

Another way to use break-even analysis is when considering ADVERTISING options. If a magazine ad costs $500, the product advertised sells for $10, and the average variable cost is $5, then the advertisement would need to generate 100 additional sales to break even.

Further reading

Dwyer, F. Robert, and John F. Tanner, Jr. *Business Marketing*. 4th ed. McGraw-Hill, 2008.

Bretton Woods

Bretton Woods, a small town in New Hampshire, was the host, in July 1944, for a major economic summit that has since transformed international economic relations. In economic discussions, the phrase "ever since Bretton Woods" means ever since the creation of the INTERNATIONAL MONETARY FUND (IMF) and International Bank for Reconstruction and Development (IBRD, also called the WORLD BANK), which were created at the Bretton Woods conference at the Mount Washington Hotel.

Planning for the conference began in 1942 in the midst of World War II. Most world leaders agreed that weaknesses in the fixed EXCHANGE RATE system had contributed to the global depression and the rise of fascism. In response to the depression, governments expanded spending on public goods. But under the gold standard, where each country's currency was convertible to a specified amount of gold, government spending could over-stimulate an economy and result in a BALANCE OF PAYMENTS crisis. Over-stimulation led to increased IMPORTS and to price increases for export PRODUCTS. This resulted in a larger trade deficit and balance-of-payments problem. The gold standard, which was in effect during this time, required a country to send gold to trading partners, decreasing the country's MONEY SUPPLY. This constricted growth in the economy through higher INTEREST RATES. What was needed was an international monetary system that would allow domestic Keynesian economic stimulation without creating a monetary crisis.

British and American political and economic leaders proposed changes in the international monetary system. The British—led by John Maynard Keynes, by then the most widely acclaimed economist in the world—proposed a system with an international agency and a new currency, "bancors." Bancors would replace gold and U.S. dollars as the basic reserve currency for all national banks.

The British, and most of the 45 participating nations at Bretton Woods, recognized that the United States would be one of the few economically strong countries after World War II and would have a significant trade surplus with the rest of the world. Keynes proposed increasing the value of the dollar as a means of reducing the impending trade surplus and stimulating exports from war-torn countries. U.S. negotiators, led by Treasury Secretary Henry M. Morgenthau and Harry Dexter White, proposed that the trade deficit countries would have to devalue their currencies and/or cut government spending in order to balance international trade.

At Bretton Woods, the American proposal won out, resulting in the creation of the IMF. The IMF would assist countries with short-term problems in their international debt problems Funds for IMF operations were created by subscription. The United States, being the largest subscriber, became the dominating force in the organization.

Discussions over the creation of the World Bank were less controversial. While the IMF would minimize short-term trade problems, an organization was needed to provide long-term CAPITAL for INVESTMENT, particularly in developing countries. As envisioned, the World Bank would finance redevelopment of European economies and expand into assistance for other areas of the world. Like the IMF, the World Bank was established with funds by subscription, and the United States was the largest contributor. As planned, it would primarily guarantee loans made by private banks, thus stimulating investment in financially viable projects. The United States became the major source of funding for postwar European redevelopment.

Over time the World Bank became a leading source of funds for ECONOMIC DEVELOPMENT as well as a symbol of U.S. dominance in international economic affairs. The IMF, while initially created to support government deficit spending, later became the international "watchdog" against excessive government spending. The IMF continues to provide short-term international finance assistance but with stringent requirements. Countries in need of IMF assistance are often required to reduce spending and raise interest rates in order to put their financial affairs in order. This is usually accepted begrudgingly, adding to developing countries' disdain for the power of the United States and other industrialized countries over their economic affairs.

Further reading
Geisst, Charles. *The Encyclopedia of American Business History.* New York: Facts On File, 2004.

bribery
The crime of bribery is the offer or gift of money, goods, or anything of value in order to influence federal, state, or local public officials in the discharge of their duties. Bribery of foreign government officials may violate the federal FOREIGN CORRUPT PRACTICES ACT. Commercial bribery in the business world is an unfair trade practice.

Bribery is as old as civilization. One Egyptian pharaoh ruled that any priest or official taking a bribe was subject to the death penalty. One of the most widely reported bribery scandals involved International Olympic Committee officials accepting multimillion-dollar payments in exchange for their vote on locating the Winter 2002 Olympic Games.

Bribery is known by many names. It is called *dash* in West Africa, *la bustarella* (the little envelope) in Italy, *rishvat* in India, and *grease* in the United States.

The OFFICE OF GOVERNMENT ETHICS (OGE) proscribes government officials from taking anything of value from individuals or organizations affected by their government duties. Under the RACKETEER INFLUENCED CORRUPT ORGANIZATION ACT, predicate offenses that can be used to establish a pattern of FRAUD (and thus prosecution under the act) include bribery.

For businesses or government, detecting bribery is difficult, but a variety of "red flags" can be used to raise concern and investigation, including

- employee spending that surpasses INCOME
- unusually friendly relationships between an employee and an outside contractor
- employees who "stretch" or ignore standard operating procedures
- employees who repeatedly rationalize deficiencies on the part of suppliers
- employees who are under pressure due to external needs (family-member illness, drug or alcohol dependency, or gambling)

In 1999 the ORGANIZATION FOR ECONOMIC COOPERATION AND DEVELOPMENT (OECD) created a 17-article antibribery convention, which states:

Each Party shall take such measures as may be necessary to establish that it is a criminal offence under its law for any person intentionally to offer, promise or give any undue pecuniary or other advantage, whether directly or through intermediaries, to a foreign public official, for that official or for third party, in order that the official act or refrain from acting in relation to the performance of official duties, in order to obtain or retain business or other improper advantage in the conduct of international business.

Transparency International (TI), an organization that monitors international bribery, focuses on increasing awareness and providing information to individuals and institutions. TI has established an "Integrity Pact" for bidders and procures in government purchasing, creating a binding agreement among parties to conduct business in an ethical and legal manner. The organization also publishes a bribery index, rating countries on how likely bribes are paid to gain business. In 2007 Paraguay and Peru were rated as having the most corrupt judicial systems, while Singapore and Denmark were least likely. The United States ranked in the middle.

Further reading
Organization for Economic Cooperation and Development Web site. Available online. URL: www.oecd.org; Podgor, Ellen S., and Jerold H. Israel. *White Collar Crime in a Nutshell.* 2d ed. Eagan, Minn.: West Group, 1997; Transparency International Web site. Available online. URL: www.transparency.org.

Buddhist economics
Buddhist economics is the study of maximizing well-being while minimizing CONSUMPTION. This goal of Buddhist economics seems contradictory to modern Western economics, where increased consumption is perceived as analogous to improved well-being.

The German-born British economist E. F. Schumacher popularized Buddhist economics in the 1970s. In his classic book *Small Is Beautiful: Economics As If People Mattered* (1973), Schumacher challenged standard assumptions of modern economic systems regarding labor, consumption, technology, peace, and the environment.

Labor, in the modern Western economic perspective, is a necessary evil. For an employer, labor is a cost to be minimized for workers, a sacrifice of one's energy and time. Employers would prefer output and INCOME without incurring the cost of labor, and workers would prefer the benefits of output and income without having to work. Labor, in the Buddhist economic perspective is necessary for the development of character and for overcoming ego. Work should be organized to benefit the needs of workers to develop their potential.

Consumption in the modern Western economic perspective, represents a better quality of life and therefore increased consumption is a major goal. According to Buddhists, consumption should support the goal of maximizing contentment. Attachment to WEALTH and desire for material goods are seen as causes of suffering, reducing contentment.

Technology, in the modern Western economic perspective, is seen as a source of increasing productivity. Improvements in technology are viewed as positive contributions to economic systems. Technology, in the Buddhist economic perspective, should enhance the natural capabilities and skills of workers. (Schumacher, a critic of blindly exporting industrial technology to developing countries, established the Intermediate Technology Development Group (1966).)

Peace, in the modern Western economic perspective, includes maintaining or increasing control over the resources needed to preserve a country's STANDARD OF LIVING. Resource conflicts arise as countries compete for control. Peace, in the Buddhist economic perspective, is enhanced through conservation and local control of resources.

The environment, in the modern Western economic perspective, is primarily a collection of resources to be used in maximizing production. Natural systems are perceived as constraints on ECONOMIC GROWTH. The environment, in the Buddhist economic perspective, is the natural system within which economic systems operate. Buddhist economics distinguishes between renewable and nonrenewable resources, emphasizing use of the first and using the latter sparingly. Exploitation of the environment is perceived as an act of violence.

Further reading
Schumacher, E. F. *Small Is Beautiful: Economics As If People Mattered.* New York: HarperCollins, 1973; Schumacher Society Web site. Available online. URL: www.schumachersociety.org.

budget, personal
A personal budget is a finance tool used to understand, allocate, and manage household INCOME and expenditures. Personal budgeting provides insights into how income is currently being spent and how it can be used to set priorities and establish personal financial goals. Surprisingly, most Americans do not use personal budgeting and therefore can make only educated guesses regarding where their monthly income is going. Personal finance software, online bill paying, and newer budgeting Web sites such as www.mint.com, www.betterbudgeting.com, and free budgeting templates on Google are facilitating and expanding the use of personal budgeting.

Numerous variations in the design of personal budgets exist but typically they include three sections; income, mandatory expenditures, and discretionary expenditures. For most households, income includes wages, salaries, and bonuses. Some households also receive alimony, child support, interest and dividend income, rents, and royalties; however, for most Americans their take home paycheck represents the vast majority of their income.

Mandatory expenditures are consumers' "must pay" bills. Mandatory expenditures begin with MASLOW's physiological and safety "needs," including food, water, shelter, and security. Must pay bills typically include mortgage payment or rent, basic food and medicine costs, heat, electric and water expenses, taxes, and, for most Americans, car payments. Commuting costs, telephone bills, childcare expenses, school supplies, clothing, and health insurance usually constitute a second level of mandatory expenditures. Payments for past expenditures, including credit card debt and student and other personal loans, are usually part of consumers' mandatory expenditures. Many Americans consider cable and Internet services necessities in addition to personal care, prepared food, and entertainment costs. Of course, one person's necessity can be another person's luxury.

For decades, Americans have regularly traded in three- or four-year-old cars, considering a new car and a monthly car payment as a mandatory expense. Economic recessions often force consumers to redefine what are priority and nonpriority expenditures. Discretionary expenditures typically include movies, dining out, travel, expensive clothing, jewelry, and other luxury purchases.

A simple monthly budget might include:

Net income: _____

Housing expenses: _____	Insurances: _____
Basic food costs: _____	auto _____
Automobile expenses: _____	life _____
Debt repayment: _____	health _____
Clothing: _____	Entertainment/travel: ____
School/childcare: _____	Savings/investment: _____

As stated earlier, a first use of personal budgets is to understand where household income is being spent. The U.S. DEPARTMENT OF LABOR provides an annual "Consumer Expenditures" report, allowing Americans to compare their expenditure patterns with others. A second use is to establish priorities, determining which expenditures provide greater benefit than others. Jerrod Mundis and others recommend that households create spending plans rather than budgets. With a spending plan in place, when consumers consider whether or not to increase their spending in one category, they also consider what categories to cut or reduce spending allocations. As Mundis states: "Budgets constrain and limit you. Plans give you choices and options. Budgets are fixed. Plans are flexible. Budgets lead to penny-pinching and deprivation. Plans encourage action and increase." The difference may only be psychological but the concept of using a plan or budget to prioritize spending is an effective personal finance tool.

Personal budgeting can also be used to establish goals; get out of debt, eliminate the car payment, establish a contingency fund, eliminate fees and charges, and save for retirement are all typical personal financial goals. Unfortunately, most Americans rarely achieve such goals. In the "Secret History of the Credit Card Industry" Frontline reporters documented practices by the credit industry designed to encourage spending and indebtedness. Consumers who pay off their bill each month are referred to as "deadbeats." In 2007, the average American household owed over $8,000 in credit card debt, yet almost 25 percent had no credit cards and 30 percent paid off their credit card purchases monthly, suggesting most Americans are managing their debt but some are overdosed with indebtedness.

Another use of personal budgeting is to reduce unnecessary expenses. A 2007 study showed that major banks receive over half of their income from fees and penalties charged to consumers. One "bounced" check can trigger $50 to $100 in fees and penalties. Personal budgeting can help consumers avoid fees and set up contingency funds to protect against unexpected expenses and to back up checking and credit card accounts to avoid overdraft charges. Most financial counselors recommend a contingency fund of at least three months' spending, and, with the recession in 2008, many were recommending at least six months' worth of contingency funds to protect against layoffs and sudden declines in income. By helping consumers prioritize and establish goals, personal budgeting gives individuals greater control over their lives, improves the quality of life, and reduces personal stress.

Further reading
Mundis, Jerrold. *How to Get Out of Debt. Stay Out of Debt & Live Prosperously.* New York: Bantam Books, 1988; PBS. "The Secret History of the Credit Card Industry." Frontline Report, 23 November 2004. Available online. URL: www.pbs.org/wgbh/pages/frontline/shows/credit/. Accessed on March 3, 2010; U.S. Department of Labor. Consumer Expenditures 2007. Available online. URL: www.bls.gov/news.release/cesan.nr0.htm. Accessed on March 3, 2010.

budgeting, capital budgeting
Budgeting is the process of developing budgets, or financial plans that project a firm's inflows and outflows for a future time period. Often budgeting

results in the construction of pro forma statements, namely the budgeted INCOME STATEMENT and the budgeted BALANCE SHEET. Pro forma, as a matter of form, statements have generally accepted formats but are based on projections. A budgeted (pro forma) income statement is one that reflects projections rather than being based on prior transactions; thus it represents expectations rather than actual data. Likewise, a budgeted (pro forma) balance sheet is one that is constructed using projections rather than actual data. Pro-forma statements are important tools used in planning and decision-making. In banking, pro forma statements are commonly used as the basis for making loans of VENTURE CAPITAL and loans to new businesses.

Capital budgeting is the planning for a firm's fixed ASSETS in particular. How a firm decides to use its capital is the most important of all managerial decisions, and since fixed assets represent the majority of most firms' assets, capital budgeting is the most crucial of all budgeting activities.

While there are infinite uses for a firm's capital, its sources are limited, and capital budgeting determines its best uses. Payback period, net present value (NPV), and internal rate of return (IRR) are three capital-budgeting tools commonly used to determine a firm's most profitable INVESTMENT opportunities.

Payback period, the first capital budgeting tool to be developed, is the expected number of years required for a firm to recoup its original investment in a fixed asset or project. The decision rule when using payback is that shorter payback periods are preferable over longer ones. For example, suppose Project A requires an investment of $10,000 and will generate cash inflows of $3,000 per year for the next five years. Assuming that these inflows are evenly distributed over the next five years, the payback period for Project A is $10,000/$3,000 = 3.33 years. Suppose Project Z costs $10,000 and will generate cash inflows of $2,000 per year for the next 10 years. The payback period for Project Z is $10,000/$2,000 = 5 years. If payback is used to rank these two projects, Project A is the preferred investment opportunity because of its shorter payback period.

There are two major shortcomings of payback period as a capital-budgeting tool. Only the inflows required to recoup the original investment are considered; the inflows occurring after the payback period are ignored. For Project A above, returns continue for an additional 1.67 years beyond the payback period, but they aren't considered. For Project Z, returns continue for another five years beyond the payback period. Payback is particularly flawed when used to evaluate investment opportunities where the returns are slow for the first couple of years, but become significant in later years.

An even more serious flaw is that payback is not a discounted cash flow technique; it ignores the time value of money. In Project Z, for example, the $2,000 received in Year 5 is viewed as just as valuable as the $2000 received in Year 1. Depending on the DISCOUNT RATE (cost of capital for the firm) used to determine the present value of the cash inflows, Project Z may, in reality, be a more profitable investment. This makes payback period a crude tool for evaluating and ranking profitable investment opportunities.

To incorporate the time value of money in capital budgeting, NPV and IRR were developed. These are discounted cash-flow techniques and are more valid tools for decision making than payback period.

NPV is the present value of a project's future cash inflows minus the initial cash outflow (original investment) required. The decision rule is to accept the project if its NPV is positive but reject if it is negative. If projects are not mutually exclusive, those with greater NPVs are ranked more preferable than those with lower NPVs. Suppose a project's NPV is +$50,000. The present value of the project's inflows are $50,000 greater than its initial cost, and this net return accrues to the firm's owners.

IRR, also a discounted cash-flow technique, is similar to NPV except that, while NPV is expressed in dollars, IRR is expressed in percentages. IRR is the discount rate that equates the present value of a project's expected inflows and its cost. The decision rule to follow when using IRR is to accept projects where the IRR is greater than the firm's cost of capital and reject those opportunities where the IRR is less than the firm's cost of capital. For example, if a project's IRR is 20 percent for a firm whose cost of capital is also 20 percent, undertaking and investing in the project will add nothing to the firm's PROFITS; the project's return exactly offsets the cost of the investment in the project. Thus the cost of capital is a "threshold" which must be exceeded when using IRR as a capital budgeting tool. If projects are not mutually exclusive, projects with higher IRRs are ranked more preferable than those with lower IRRs, and projects whose IRR is less than the firm's cost of capital are rejected.

See also FEDERAL BUDGETING; ZERO-BASE BUDGETING.

built-in stabilizers   See AUTOMATIC STABILIZERS.

Bureau of Economic Analysis

The Bureau of Economic Analysis (BEA) is an agency within the Department of Commerce that produces U.S. economic statistics. Each month the BEA estimates GROSS DOMESTIC PRODUCT (GDP); gross domestic income; and industry, regional, and international economic statistics. To make important policy, INVESTMENT, and spending decisions, government officials, business managers, and individuals use economic estimates produced by the BEA.

GDP and other important measures are usually first announced as press releases and widely quoted in the business media. GDP estimates are first released as a preliminary estimate followed by a first and second revision as more data become available. Financial markets watch GDP statistics closely, and analysts watch growth (or lack thereof) in the industries in which they are involved. Regional economic statistics provide estimates of personal INCOME, population, and EMPLOYMENT by state. International economic statistics include BALANCE OF PAYMENTS figures, U.S. DIRECT INVESTMENT abroad, and foreign direct investment in the United States.

The BEA's monthly journal, *Survey of Current Business,* presents detailed estimates, analyses, research, and methodology used by the agency to measure economic activity in the U.S. economy.

Further reading

Bureau of Economic Analysis Web site. Available online. URL: www.bea.gov.

Bureau of Labor Statistics

The Bureau of Labor Statistics (BLS), part of the DEPARTMENT OF LABOR, is the principal agency providing labor statistics in the United States. The most important BLS statistics generated each month are the CONSUMER PRICE INDEX (CPI), the UNEMPLOYMENT rate, and the PRODUCER PRICE INDEX (PPI). The CPI is the most widely used and quoted measure of INFLATION. Changes in the unemployment rate are a major indicator of strength or weakness in the economy. The PPI measures prices received by producers and is a leading indicator of future price changes for consumers. In addition, the BLS measures productivity; average hourly earnings; demographic characteristics of the LABOR FORCE; and wages, earnings, and benefits by area, occupation, and industry.

BLS statistics are available through the *Occupational Outlook Handbook* and other publications.

Further reading

Bureau of Labor Statistics Web site. Available online. URL: www.bls.gov.

Bureau of Land Management

The Bureau of Land Management (BLM), an agency in the Department of Interior, manages over 264 million acres of public land primarily in 12 western states and Alaska. In addition, the BLM manages 300 million acres of below-ground mineral rights throughout the country. (Ownership of land is considered ownership of a "bundle of rights" to the land. Often, in areas of the United States where there are mineral deposits [oil, gas, gold, silver, etc.], developers and homeowners purchase surface rights, while other individuals or businesses own the right to extract subsurface minerals, which has led to conflicts.)

The BLM states its mission is "to sustain the health, diversity and productivity of the public lands for the use and enjoyment of present and future generations." On public lands the agency manages a wide variety of resources and their uses, including energy and mineral extraction, timber, forage, wild horse and burro populations, wildlife habitats, and archaeological and historical sites.

The BLM's roots go back to the Land Ordinance of 1785 and the Northwest Ordinance of 1787, laws that provided for surveys and settlement of land beyond the original 13 colonies. In 1812 Congress established the General Land Office to oversee disposition of federal lands. Homesteading Laws and the Mining Law of 1872 expanded federal efforts to establish settlements in western territories.

By the end of the 19th century, with the creation of the first national parks, forests, and wildlife refuges, Congress withdrew these lands from settlement and also initiated a change in policy goals for public lands toward resource use. Acts in the early 20th century authorized mineral leasing, cattle grazing, and timberland management. In 1946 the Grazing Service was merged with the General Land Office to form the BLM, which operated under more than 2,000 laws, often in conflict with each other, until 1976. That year the Federal Land Policy and Management Act (FLPMA) was enacted, and Congress defined the BLM's role as "management of public lands and their various resource values so that they are utilized in the combination that will best meet the present and future needs of the American people."

While directed to achieve "multiple use management," the BLM remains a controversial federal agency. Traditional users of public lands, including grazing, timber, and mining interests, are often in conflict with increasing public calls for conservation, environmental management, and recreation. Supporters of the BLM point to the many conservation and environmental management actions taken by the bureau, while critics point to status quo practices subsidizing private development of public resources.

Further reading
Bureau of Land Management Web site. Available online. URL: www.blm.gov.

business and the U.S. Constitution

The parameters established by the U.S. Constitution affect business and commerce through federalism, judicial interpretation, and politics. Federalism is the relationship (division) of powers between the national government and state governments and, along with separation of powers and checks and balances, forms the foundation of the Constitution. Judicial interpretation resolves conflicting constitutional issues between national and state authority over business, namely through the COMMERCE CLAUSE (Article 1, Section 8), which gives Congress the power to regulate commerce among states. The policies of Franklin Delano Roosevelt's New Deal in the 1930s and of Lyndon B. Johnson's Great Society in the 1960s are examples of extending national authority over business and commerce. Former Presidents Richard M. Nixon (1969–73) and George H. W. Bush (1989–93) supported transferring power from the national government back to state authority through the appointment of Supreme Court justices committed to limiting national power.

Although the theories of federalism provide a means of ensuring a federal system of government, politics ultimately determine the division of power between the national government and state governments. The two fundamental models of federalism are dual federalism and cooperative federalism. Dual federalism holds that the powers of the national government are fixed and limited and that all rights not explicitly conferred to the national government are reserved to the states. This model was appropriate for American society (business and commerce) from 1789 to 1933. The GREAT DEPRESSION, however, required a more cooperative relationship between the states and the national government in dealing with the social and economic deprivation of that era.

Cooperative federalism theory states that there is no discernment between state and national powers; their functions and responsibilities are intermingled. This model relies on the elastic clause of Article 1, Section 8 that gives Congress the power to "make laws which are necessary and proper for carrying into Execution the foregoing powers" and confines the Tenth Amendment to specific limitations not given to the national government. Cooperative efforts between the states and national government that influenced business and commerce in the 20th century have now shifted the power back to the states in the 21st century, limiting the national government's scope.

Since the 1960s the federal government's use of categorical and block grants has become prevalent as a means of shaping its relationships with state governments. Categorical grants are conditionally given for specific purposes; they increase national government power and reduce state government's power, because states must relinquish the freedom to set their own standards in order to receive financial assistance. Block grants are given for general purposes and allow greater flexibility in state spending, therefore increasing state powers and reducing national power. Greater discretionary state spending may also increase business enterprise with additional financial assistance available to businesses that work in cooperation with state agencies. Since the late 1960s, presidents have revised categorical and block grants in order to return business and commerce regulation to the states. Furthermore, the courts' interpretation of policies and society's social and economic welfare influence the continued shifting of business regulation and responsibilities.

Further reading
Baradate, L. P. "The Principles of the Constitution." In *Understanding American Democracy,* 20–44. New York: HarperCollins Publishers, 1992; Janda, K., J. Berry, and J. Goldman. "Federalism." In *The Challenge of Democracy.* 7th ed., 95–123. Boston: Houghton-Mifflin, 2002.
—Frank Ubraus and Jerry Merwin

business cycles
Business cycles are the patterns of increase and decreases in GROSS DOMESTIC PRODUCT (GDP) that occur in an economy. Most countries' economies have tended to grow over time, but within the trend of overall growth there have been periods of expansion, peaks, contractions, and troughs, followed again by expansion. The movement of an economy through periods of expansion and contraction is called a business cycle.

In the United States the longest period of economic expansion began with a trough in the first quarter of 1991 and continued until 2001. Since 1929 there have been 13 RECESSIONS, or periods of economic contraction. During the 1930 election, President Herbert Hoover claimed the country was not in a recession, just a mild depression. Since then a severe and prolonged recession has been called a depression. The longest period of recession in U.S. history, the GREAT DEPRESSION, lasted from 1929 to 1934. One saying suggested the distinction between a recession and a depression was that "in a recession your neighbor is unemployed; in a depression, you are too!"

During the Great Depression, GDP declined by one-third and UNEMPLOYMENT rose to 25 percent. Economists continue to analyze and debate the causes of the Great Depression and the causes of business cycles. Changes from economic expansion to contraction are caused by shifts in aggregate DEMAND, aggregate SUPPLY, or combinations of both. Changes in business INVESTMENT, CONSUMPTION spending, government purchases, fluctuations in EXPORTING, and IMPORTS, and changes in a country's MONEY SUPPLY all impact overall demand and supply in an economy. Discovery of new resources, wars, political upheavals, technological innovation, immigration, and population growth have all been suggested as factors contributing to business cycles. In the 19th century, sunspot cycles were suggested to have been similar to business cycles.

Economists try to predict business cycles. If businesses can anticipate changes in the economy, they can prepare for expansion and contractions in economic activity. If governments can anticipate changes in the economy, they can intervene with fiscal and MONETARY POLICY changes to reduce the severity of business cycle troughs and to sustain periods of economic expansion.

Economists use leading INDICATORS to predict changes in business cycles. Leading indicators, as the term suggests, shift in advance of changes in the economy. Changes in unemployment claims, stock prices, new plant and equipment expenditures, new building permits, and consumer expectations all tend to precede changes in economic output. Leading indicators are less than perfect predictors of business cycles, leaving business managers and policy makers uncertain about future changes in the economy.

Further reading

Boyes, William J., and Michael Melvin. *Macroeconomics*. 7th ed. Boston: Houghton Mifflin, 2007.

business ethics

PROFITS are the "bottom line" for businesses and CORPORATIONS, but should maximizing profits at any cost be the primary motivation of a business? Should responsibility to employees, customers, and the community be a concern as well? Can businesses act in ways that balance the duties they have to their SHAREHOLDERS with the duties they have to their STAKEHOLDERS?

Philosophers and other thinkers have contemplated ethics and ethical issues for thousands of years. However, it wasn't until the post-Watergate era that the development of ethical standards in business practices really began to evolve in response to highly publicized news about ethical issues in business. Some of these issues are: bribes and kickbacks, defective and harmful products, workplace discrimination and other unfair EMPLOYMENT practices, INSIDER TRADING, false ADVERTISING, deceptive accounting and AUDITING procedures, monopolies, whistle-blowing, hazardous work environments, and environmental pollution. These acts of misconduct have resulted in the creation and adoption of ethical standards into the structures of many businesses and corporations.

Just as individuals are guided by personal ethics when facing moral and other dilemmas, businesses (which are based on human activities, after all) also face challenges when they strive to earn profits and simultaneously try to maintain integrity in their practices in areas such as employee rights, workplace safety, and social responsibility. Therefore "business ethics" may be defined as the study and evaluation of both the moral implications of business behaviors and activities as well as the standards developed that promote moral policy-making at the individual, managerial, and organizational level.

Ethical business practices include acting within the law, providing a safe work environment for employees, treating employees fairly, giving back to the community through philanthropy, making safe products, and protecting the environment. To address these practices, businesses often codify ethical standards into the form of MISSION STATEMENTS, credos, or policies. Employees, managers, and executives may then refer to these policies for guidance when faced with situations that may have moral implications. Additionally, these policies may be applicable not only to existing and current problems but also to anticipated conflicts. These policies are then communicated to employees through handbooks and training, with notice that compliance with these policies is expected of employees, including the management and executives. Many companies also create ethics hotlines, committees, and training programs to further communicate their corporate values. Likewise, many professions and trade associations have their own codes of ethics developed in response to actual or anticipated ethical conflicts. These codes serve as guides for the professional behavior of members and set the standards of their profession.

An ideal world is one where businesses self-regulate according to ethical standards they have set and where corporations would always act ethically. However, external authority also exists to ensure adherence to legal standards addressing issues that are ethical in nature. Federal, state, and local laws, regulations, and codes are in effect to regulate business behavior and promote ethical practices. For example, OCCUPATIONAL SAFETY AND HEALTH ADMINISTRATION (OSHA) laws protect employees from hazardous work environments. The EQUAL EMPLOYMENT OPPORTUNITY COMMISSION (EEOC) oversees the legal protection of women, minorities, and the disabled against discrimination, harassment, and other injustices in the workplace. ENVIRONMENTAL PROTECTION AGENCY (EPA) legislation such as the CLEAN AIR ACTS and the CLEAN WATER ACT serves to protect the environment from industrial pollutants. The U.S. CONSUMER PRODUCT SAFETY COMMISSION is established to protect people from the risks of unsafe products. The SECURITIES AND EXCHANGE COMMISSION (SEC) has many rules and regulations that govern the financial disclosures of publicly traded companies.

With increasing GLOBALIZATION, business ethics must also extend internationally. Therefore the U.S. Department of Commerce has issued its "U.S. Model Business Principles" as a reference for businesses to use when framing their own ethical standards and policies—especially applicable in a global economy. Most recently, and in light of recent corporate scandals, the George W. Bush administration has initiated efforts to combat corporate FRAUD through its Corporate Fraud Task Force, to promote reforms to protect workers' pensions, and to protect stockholders through the "Ten-Point Plan to Improve Corporate Responsibility."

In recent years the media reported what seem like endless examples of unethical, illegal, and fraudulent corporate behavior by executives at Enron, WorldCom, Adelphia Communications, Tyco, Arthur Andersen, Qwest, and ImClone. These corporate scandals are probably the exceptions to the rule, since most businesses recognize that it benefits everyone to act ethically. An ethical business model will attract and keep high-quality employees, increase productivity, build a positive reputation for the business, inspire shareholder confidence, protect the environment, and make for good corporate citizenship in the form of philanthropy. All of these things have a tremendous impact on that bottom line: profits. It is therefore possible for businesses to adhere to high ethical standards and still please both their stockholders and stakeholders.

Further reading
Bender, David, pub. *Business Ethics.* Opposing Viewpoints Series. San Diego: Greenhaven Press, 2001; de George, Richard T. *Business Ethics.* Upper Saddle River, N.J.: Prentice Hall, 1999; Ethics Resource Center Web site. Available online. URL: www.ethics.org; Mauer, John G., et al., eds. *Encyclopedia of Business.* New York: Gale Research Group, 1995; Werhane, Patricia H., and R. Edward Freeman, eds. *The Blackwell Encyclopedic Dictionary of Business Ethics.* Cambridge, Mass.: Blackwell Business, 1997. For an excellent example of a corporate ethics credo, see the Johnson & Johnson Web site at www.jnj.com/connect/about-jnj/jnj-credo.

—Karen Brickman Emmons

business failure (bankruptcy)

Business failure or bankruptcy occurs when a firm cannot pay its debts on time or when liabilities exceed ASSETS. Bankruptcy is an ancient issue, critical to the development of an economic and social system. It is addressed both in the Old Testament of the Bible and the U.S. Constitution. The Bible states: "At the end of every seven years you shall grant a release and this is the manner of the release: every creditor shall release what he has lent to his neighbor . . ." The Constitution granted Congress the authority to establish "uniform laws on the subject of bankruptcies throughout the United States."

Business failure includes both legal and management issues. In the United States, The Bankruptcy Act, first passed in 1800 and amended numerous times since, serves several purposes:

- to ensure that the debtor's property is fairly distributed to creditors
- to ensure that some creditors do not obtain an unfair advantage
- to protect creditors from actions by the debtor to not relinquish assets to which the creditors are entitled
- to protect debtors from demands for payment by creditors

The Bankruptcy Code includes two levels or chapters of business failure status: straight liquidation (Chapter 7) and reorganization (Chapter 11).

There are also statutes for FAMILY FARM bankruptcy (Chapter 12) and CONSUMER BANKRUPTCY (Chapter 13). Under Chapter 7, known as "straight bankruptcy," a firm must disclose all property owned and surrender the assets to a bankruptcy trustee. The trustee sets aside certain assets that the debtor is allowed to retain and then sells the remaining assets in order to pay off creditors. Either a voluntary or involuntary petition (filed by the debtor or the creditor, respectively) can initiate Chapter 7 proceedings. Individuals, PARTNERSHIPS or CORPORATIONS can file voluntary petitions. Involuntary petitions are sought by creditors seeking to have a debtor declared bankrupt and have their assets distributed to creditors. There are numerous legal details and exceptions in bankruptcy proceedings as well as attorneys that specialize in bankruptcy law.

Under Chapter 11 of the Bankruptcy Act, a debtor is allowed to work out a plan to solve its financial problems under the supervision of a court-appointed representative. The debtor agrees to a reorganization plan, usually including some debt relief from creditors. The goal of Chapter 11 is to allow debtors, primarily businesses, to continue to exist and return to solvency. During the 1980s and 1990s many U.S. companies seeking to avoid major liability claims used Chapter 11 proceedings. Johns-Manville Corporation filed for bankruptcy because of asbestos claims. A. H. Robins filed for protection because of birth control device LIABILITY. When General Motors filed for Chapter 11 in 2009 it allowed the company to avoid debt repayment and cancel previous collective bargaining agreements.

As stated previously, business failure is also a management issue. As one official of the SMALL BUSINESS ADMINISTRATION (SBA) stated, "Poor management is the greatest single cause of business failure." Some common management mistakes include hiring the wrong people, inadequate employee training, trying to do too much, and misuse of management time. The SBA's Online Women's Business Center lists 11 common causes of business failure:

- choosing a business that is not very profitable
- inadequate cash reserves
- failure to clearly define and understand one's market, customers, and customers' buying habits
- failure to price one's PRODUCT or service correctly
- failure to adequately anticipate cash flow
- failure to anticipate or react to COMPETITION, technology, or other changes in the marketplace
- overgeneralization
- overdependence on a single customer
- uncontrolled growth
- believing one can do everything oneself
- putting up with inadequate MANAGEMENT

Further reading
Mallor, Jane P., A. James Barnes, Thomas Bowers, Michael J. Phillips, and Arlen W. Langvardt. *Business Law: The Ethical, Global, and E-Commerce Environment.* 14th ed. Boston: McGraw-Hill, 2009; U.S. Small Business Administration's Online Women's Business Center. Available online. URL: www.sba.gov/aboutsba/sbaprograms/onlinewbc/index.html.

business forecasting

Business forecasting is analysis of past and current situations in order to anticipate the future. The most widely used type of business forecasting is sales forecasting, predicting future sales, but businesses engage in a variety of other forecasting efforts. Major forecasting concerns for businesses include predicting future workforce requirements, CAPITAL investment needs, and materials. Forecasts are typically incorporated in BUSINESS PLANS.

Business forecasting can be either qualitative or quantitative and subjective or objective. Qualitative forecasts are generalized predictions about the future, while quantitative forecasts result in a specified number, percentage change in sales, additional workers needed, etc. Subjective forecasting is based on peoples' opinions. Subjective forecasting techniques include jury of executive opinion, DELPHI TECHNIQUE, sales force composite, and surveys of buyers' intentions. Objective forecasting methods include trend analysis, market tests, and regression analysis. (These techniques are discussed in greater detail in the SALES FORECASTING entry.)

Whether quantitative or qualitative, subjective or objective, businesses use forecasting to make decisions in the current time period affecting production, sales, and profits in the future. Anticipating and then meeting the future needs of customers is critical to MARKETING STRATEGY.

business intelligence   See MARKET INTELLIGENCE.

business language

Business language is the combination of slang, jargon, and acronyms used in the business world. Americans use a variety of terms and phrases that are not standard English. Businesspeople are often in a hurry. Slang and jargon are quick and easy ways to communicate. It saves time for people who know the terms, but for others it creates the potential for misunderstanding. A major problem in business communication is bypassing, where the speaker or writer knows what they want to communicate, knows what terms mean, and assumes the people they are communicating with also know the same terms. For example, a simple acronym AMA has at least three different meanings in American business: American Medical, Marketing, or Management Association. Similarly, "acid test" could mean the final decisive test or proof, or it could refer to a financial test for solvency. Users of business language need to consider their audience's level of understanding and the multiple meanings of terms and phrases.

Slang is a body of words intelligible to a large portion of the general public but not accepted as formal usage. *Jargon* is the technical vocabulary of a subgroup within the population. Slang and jargon are used more often in speech than in writing. "Baker's dozen," "bait and switch," and "bargain basement" are all examples of widely used slang phrases. "Keystone," "kicker," and "puff piece" are examples of jargon used in marketing but unfamiliar to most Americans.

Slang and jargon come from a variety of sources, usually industries or subgroups within society that are particularly important in a period of time. In the United States many colorful business language terms are historically rooted in the military (R&R, boot camp, deep six); sports (batting average, air ball, on the sideline, full-court press); immigrants (el jefe, fait accompli, schmuck, Chinese wall); and politics (kitchen cabinet, pork barrel, brain trust). In recent years financial markets (zombie BONDS, dead cat bounce, elves, zeros) and technology (DOT-COMS, chip jewelry, platforms, URLs, desktops) have been the major sources of new business language in the United States. U.S. business domination of electronic commerce has often led to worldwide acceptance of American business-language terms. Business language is constantly changing, challenging consumers and industry members alike.

Further reading

American business language Web site. Available online. URL: americanbusinesslanguage.googlepages.com; Chapman, Robert. *New Dictionary of American Slang.* New York: Harper & Row, 1987.

business logistics (physical distribution)

Originally the term *logistics* described the strategic movement of military personnel and equipment. During World War II, General George Patton's army was stalled by a lack of fuel. Patton called his problem "the iron grip of logistics." Transporting a large number of troops and a lot of equipment quickly and efficiently is often the key to military success. The business world now uses logistics (also referred to as physical distribution) to describe the process of distributing final goods efficiently to the consumer to ensure a PROFIT.

Seven elements comprise the logistics (physical distribution) system:

- customer service—to ensure that customers get what they ask for
- INVENTORY CONTROL—to determine where and how much inventory should be kept on hand
- transportation—how and from where goods should be shipped
- processing orders—how long it should take for orders to be processed
- packaging—how goods should be packaged. Goods need to be packaged according to their method of delivery and in a manner that is visually attractive and environmentally conservative

- handling of materials—determining whether materials be kept in a warehouse, where orders will be filled later, or shipped and transferred to other trucks on the loading dock (cross-docking) and then delivered to stores
- warehousing—determining whether it will be more cost effective to keep materials in warehouses in different locations or ship from one location?

Optimally, these seven elements work together to ensure the logistics system runs effectively from both the customers' and the firm's perspectives. If one element is not working efficiently, the other elements will not run as smoothly.

U.S. companies spend approximately $700 billion on logistics yearly. In some cases businesses are able to reduce distribution costs by hiring third-party logistics firms, companies that specialize in handling logistics for other firms. Hiring a third-party logistics firm will allow a company to focus more on the manufacturing of the product rather than its distribution. By contracting other companies to distribute goods, the producer may use less manpower, leading to greater profits.

In order to make a profit, companies need to find the most cost-efficient way to produce and deliver their products to customers. Logistics can make or break a company. Amazon.com, for example, started as an INTERNET bookstore that was distributed from the house of its creator, Jeff Bezos, is now one of the largest domains for on-line shopping.

Consumers are more likely to do business with a producer who is able to get products to them in a timely manner. Consumers will often pay more in order to get a product in a shorter amount of time.

See also LOGISTICS.

Further reading
Boone, Louis E., and David L. Kurtz. *Contemporary Marketing*. 14th ed. Fort Worth: South-Western, 2001; Czinkota, Michael R., et al. *Marketing Best Practices*. 2d ed. Fort Worth: Dryden Press, 2002.

—Jessica Lujick

business plan

A business plan is a document that describes a company's overall plans. The phrase is sometimes used to describe a plan for a segment of the company or for a specific initiative. It can also describe the document prepared in an effort to raise VENTURE CAPITAL.

A business plan describes the current business environment, the company's goals, and the progressive milestones for how those goals will be reached. The plan specifically reports the marketing, operational, staffing, and financial steps to be taken to attain each of the goals.

Here is an outline commonly used in business plans:

1. Executive Summary. This section summarizes the rest of the document. It should be interesting enough to entice the reader to read the rest of the document.
2. Company Profile. This section, which provides a description of the business, includes the company's MISSION STATEMENT.
3. Competitive Analysis. This section describes the business's competitive environment, specifies what competitors are currently in the business, and looks at their likely response to the actions described in the business plans.
4. Marketing Strategy. This section describes the marketing strategy to accomplish the company's goals and includes discussion of pricing and distribution issues.
5. Operational Strategy. This section tells about the operational milestones needed to accomplish the company's goals. It describes the development of new processes or technology and the progress being made in these areas.
6. Staff Qualifications. This section—one of the plan's most important—describes the team that has been marshaled to carry out the plans. Potential investors are often more interested in the "who" of the plan than the "what."
7. Financial Information. The business plan needs to include any financial information that helps describe (a) the company's current financial situation, (b) cost data relative to carrying out

the plan, and (c) the firm's financial condition if the plan is successful.

8. Appendices. This section contains any support documentation that makes the business plan more credible. For example, the financial information section may discuss the company's income growth over the past five years, and thus the appendix could contain the company's FINANCIAL STATEMENTS.

The sections described above serve only as an example of what often appears in a business plan. The more creative a person is in clearly presenting the plan, the more likely it is that the plan will get the attention of a potential investor.

Business Roundtable

The Business Roundtable is an association of CHIEF EXECUTIVE OFFICERS (CEOs) of major U.S.-based CORPORATIONS. The association's stated goal is "to promote policies that will lead to sustainable, non-inflationary, long-term growth in the U.S. economy." The Business Roundtable was formed in 1972 through the merger of three organizations: the March Group (a group of CEOs which had been meeting informally to discuss public issues), the Construction Users Anti-Inflation Round Table (a group focusing restraining construction costs), and the Labor Law Study Committee (a group of labor relations executives of major companies).

The Business Roundtable uses the power and visibility of major CEOs to influence government policies and regulations. At the annual meeting each June in Washington, D.C., Roundtable members discuss position papers developed by Task Forces on topics currently important to the group. In 2009, Roundtable Initiatives included Consumer Health and Retirement, Corporate Leadership, Education, Innovation and Workforce, International Engagement, and Sustainable Growth.

Roundtable position papers are often used by members in testimony before Congressional committees, lobbying efforts at Congress and the White House, and in media releases for the general public. The Business Roundtable is an important network for business executives, providing a forum for discussion of interests across industries and among competitors in the marketplace.

Further reading

Business Roundtable Web site. Available online. URL: www.businessroundtable.org.

business taxes

Business taxation is a constantly changing and controversial subject covering a wide array of taxes. Some are imposed by the federal government, others by state and local governments. Some are paid directly by businesses, while others are added into the price of products and, depending on the market, paid by consumers, producers, or combinations of both consumers and producers.

Taxes have existed as long as organized societies have existed, and the most powerful people in a society usually control taxation. For example, the Earl of Mercia in 11th-century Coventry, England, only agreed to reduce taxes after his wife, Lady Godiva, agreed to ride through the village naked on a horse. In U.S. elementary schools, students learn about the early American colonists' protests against taxation without representation, dramatized by the Boston Tea Party.

At its conception in 1781, the federal government was given no power to tax citizens. When Congress, in 1791, allowed an excise tax on spirits, it resulted in a revolt by farmers in western Pennsylvania, known as the Whiskey Rebellion. In 1798 Congress levied a tax of $2 million, apportioned among the states based on population, to pay off part of the debt accumulated during the Revolutionary War. The tax was levied based on the value of ASSETS including dwellings, land, and slaves.

Throughout the 1800s, TARIFFS were the major source of federal tax revenue. Tariffs were generally easier to impose, since most ports were open and visible, and they were less controversial than PROPERTY TAXES or excise taxes. Tariffs were imposed for two purposes: to raise money for government and to protect domestic industries against foreign COMPETITION.

During the Civil War, the federal government imposed both property and INCOME taxes. After the war, the income tax was discontinued, but the Bureau of Internal Revenue continued to collect "sin and vice" taxes on tobacco and liquor. Tariffs remained the major source of federal tax revenue until World War I. Income taxation, reimposed in 1913 as a popular response to the concentration of power and WEALTH among elite industrialists, was expanded and used to pay for U.S. involvement in the war.

Today, while most of the federal government's tax revenue comes from personal income tax and SOCIAL SECURITY payments, business taxation remains a significant and complex part of our tax system. Some of the major taxes imposed by the federal government on businesses include corporate income tax, excise taxes, Social Security, and Medicare. Corporate income tax is, as the name suggests, a tax on the net income of companies. It is a progressive tax, or the percentage of corporate income paid as taxes, increasing as income increases. Numerous deductions and allowances reduce the income subject to taxation. The federal tax laws contain thousands of special provisions for CORPORATIONS reducing or eliminating their tax liability. Businesses can also avoid corporate taxation by either electing sub-S classification (for small businesses) and distributing profits to SHAREHOLDERS, who then declare the profits as personal income; or by creating PARTNER-SHIPS, which also do not pay corporate taxes and, like sub-S corporations, distribute income to partners.

Excise taxes are taxes on the manufacture or sale of a PRODUCT. Businesses pay excise taxes to both the federal government and state governments. The major excise taxes in the United States are gasoline, tobacco, and alcohol taxes, taxed at a set amount per unit of output. For example, wine is taxed at $1.07 per gallon (for wine with less than 14-percent alcohol). Beer is taxed at $18 per barrel. As part of the TOBACCO SETTLEMENT, in 1998 the federal government significantly raised the excise tax on tobacco. There are also many obscure excise taxes, including taxes on coal, recreational vehicles, tires, and the production of machine guns and destructive devices.

To businesses, excise taxes are a cost of doing business, and as such they are included in the price of a product. How much of the tax is paid by consumers in the form of higher prices and how much is absorbed by businesses as a cost depends primarily on the ELASTICITY OF DEMAND for products. Elasticity of demand is consumers' sensitivity or responsiveness to price changes. For example, the government raised the excise tax on tobacco by 75 cents per pack in 1998 and settled the liability lawsuit costing the tobacco companies billions of dollars over the next 25 years. At the same time, the price of cigarettes went up an amount almost equal to the combined excise tax and settlement costs. Because demand for tobacco products is very inelastic (among addicted smokers), the tax was transferred to consumers. If, instead, consumers had significantly reduced their purchases of tobacco products in response to the higher price, much of the tax would have been incurred by the businesses.

The third major type of tax paid by businesses is Social Security. Employers and employees each contribute a set percentage of income, approximately 6 percent to Old Age, Survivors and Disability (OASDI), up to a limit of about $100,000 of wages and salaries annually. The limit increases with inflation. Both employers and employees contribute about 1.5 percent of wages, with no limit on income to pay for Medicare. Since these taxes are only paid on wage income, businesses, especially small businesses, can legally avoid paying some of these taxes by distributing income in the form of DIVIDENDS. On the other hand, self-employed people pay both the employer and employee's share of Social Security taxes.

Most states generate the majority of their tax revenue using sales, property, and personal income taxes. Business taxation varies considerably among states, with some states taxing business inventories and business income. Most cities impose property taxes on businesses but also offer tax breaks for companies bringing jobs to the community. Supporters of these practices call them incentives, while opponents call them CORPORATE WELFARE.

See also TAX SHELTERS.

Further reading

Tax Information for Businesses. Available online. URL: www.irs.gov/businesses.

—Jonathan S. Goldberg

business valuation

A business valuation is an estimate of the fair MARKET VALUE of a closely held business. There is no distinction between a valuation and an appraisal, but usually the term *valuation* is applied to estimating the value of a business and an *appraisal* is used to refer to estimating the value of a specific ASSET, such as real estate, jewelry, antiques, or art. *Fair market value,* an important term in business valuation, means what a willing buyer and seller would agree upon if neither had a particular compulsion to buy or sell and both had reasonable knowledge of all the facts.

Valuations are done for many reasons. The most obvious is the valuation done to assist in a genuine transaction, when, for example, a prospective buyer or seller hires a valuation expert to assist them in the process. But valuations are also done for other reasons. The estate tax levies a certain amount of tax on the value of property transferred to an heir, and so an estate must have a valuation of any family business that is inherited by the next generation. Sometimes the valuation of a family business is important in divorces. When the assets are being divided by the spouses, it is a relatively easy matter to establish a value for such things as cars and houses, but the value of the family plumbing business is a different matter. A valuation expert is important to guide the courts in the division of the assets.

In general there are three approaches used in estimating the value of a business: asset approach, INCOME approach, and the market approach. The asset approach is the easiest to understand: The company's individual are valued, then its debts are subtracted to find an overall fair market value.

The income approach estimates the company's future income and then uses DISCOUNTING techniques to estimate its current value. The difficulties with this approach include estimating the future income and determining an appropriate DISCOUNT RATE.

The market approach is theoretically very appealing. It compares certain characteristics of the company being valued to companies that have been sold recently; the person doing the valuation tries to find a comparable company in the same industry, with about the same assets and income size. The difficulty with this method is both in finding a comparable company and understanding the elements of the comparable transaction, which may include other considerations besides the company being sold. For example, the CONTRACT to sell a comparable company may include a certain amount of work to be done by the previous owner or some special financing provision. Such things have to be stripped from the comparable transaction before it is used as a basis for valuing the business. Finding a comparable company and understanding the transaction makes the market approach most difficult to apply.

The American Society of Appraisers and the AMERICAN INSTITUTE OF CERTIFIED PUBLIC ACCOUNTANTS have specialty designations or valuation credentials that they confer on members who accomplish certain prescribed training and testing and have pertinent experience.

Buy American Act and campaigns

The Buy American Act (1933) and traditions favor the purchase of goods and services from domestic suppliers. Almost every time the U.S. economy begins to decline, local and national politicians, supported by business leaders, develop campaigns promoting the purchase of American-made products. The Buy American Act requires the federal government to purchase American products unless (a) the purchase is for use outside the United States (such as U.S. military bases abroad), (b) there are insufficient quantities of acceptable quality products available domestically, or (c) it results in unreasonable costs.

As currently applied, the act requires federal agencies to purchase domestic goods unless the domestic bids are more than 6 percent higher than bids from foreign producers. Bids from U.S. companies must contain 50-percent or more American materials to be considered domestic. These rules apply to civil purchases made by the U.S. government but are suspended for purchasing subject to World Trade Organization rules.

The U.S. Department of Defense has its own Buy American rules giving preference to domestic suppliers. In addition, under the Small Business Act of 1953, federal agencies set aside 30 percent of their procurement for socially and economically disadvantaged businesses.

Many state and local purchasing requirements also support preferences for American producers. For example, California once had a regulation mandating purchase of American products, and cities in Massachusetts banned purchases from Myanmar (formerly Burma). These laws were declared unconstitutional on the grounds that they encroached on the federal power to conduct foreign affairs. State laws that copy the federal Buy American Act incorporating public interest and unreasonable cost exceptions have generally withstood legal challenges.

Many countries around the world have preferential buying laws similar to those of the United States. American laws can be used to deny procurement contracts to suppliers from countries that "maintain . . . a significant and persistent pattern of practice or discrimination against U.S. products or services which results in identifiable harm to U.S. businesses."

"Buy American" campaigns—business/political initiatives to encourage the purchase of American-made products—typically arise during downturns in the domestic economy. In the mid-1980s, Wal-Mart, the largest retail chain in the United States, initiated its "Keeping America Working and Strong" campaign. Led by founder Sam Walton, Walmart directed buyers to seek out U.S.-made products and encouraged vendors to do business with U.S. manufacturers.

"Buy American" campaigns generate favorable publicity and are good PUBLIC RELATIONS strategies. The federal government estimates that each additional $1 million spent on U.S. products results in 23 additional jobs in the country. "Buy American" campaigns are frequently associated with trade deficits and efforts to increase protectionism in the country. Economists have conducted numerous studies showing the huge cost to consumers for each job saved through TARIFFS and other competition-reducing trade legislation. In 2009, President Obama called for preferences for American companies in his economic stimulus legislation, resulting in cries of protectionism among trade partners.

Studies also show that, while Americans prefer U.S.-made products, they tend to purchase the best price/value products available regardless of where they are made. A frequent problem is determining what is American-made. For example, approximately half of the Japanese-brand cars sold in the United States are produced in this country. Similarly, many American-brand cars are produced elsewhere. Often consumers have to look on the inside passenger door to determine where their car was manufactured. In a controversial *Harvard Business Review* article entitled "Who Are US?," former Secretary of Commerce Robert Reich argued that if the goal is to create and maintain jobs in the United States, Americans should also support the many foreign companies producing products and employing workers in the country regardless of where the company is headquartered.

Further reading

"Buy American Campaign Gains Momentum," *Discount Store News* (9 December 1985): 24, 74; Folsom, Ralph H., and Michael Gordon. "International Business Transactions." 2d ed. Eagan, Minn.: West Group, 2002 (1999); Reich, Robert. "Who Are US?" *Harvard Business Review* (March–April 1991): 77.

buy-grid model

The buy-grid model is a business model depicting rational organizational decision making. Business marketers use the buy-grid model to portray the steps businesses go through in making purchase decisions. The model includes two components: buy phase and buy class.

Buy phase represents the logical eight steps businesses (or consumers involved in extensive problem solving) go through:

- need recognition
- definition of PRODUCT type needed
- development of detailed specifications
- search for qualified suppliers
- acquisition and analysis of proposals
- evaluation of proposals and selection of a supplier
- selection of an order procedure
- evaluation of product performance

Business-to-business marketers recognize that at each step in the buying process, business buyers have different needs, and different groups within the organization may be involved. Business marketers anticipate which step organizational buyers are in and attempt to provide the needed information and support for that stage of decision making. Marketers who can become involved early in the decision-making process have a greater chance of being considered in the final selection process. Many organizations, including government agencies, have formal purchasing procedures incorporating the buy-grid model. Set-aside programs targeting small and minority-owned businesses and bid solicitation requirements for government offices follow a similar defined procedure for PURCHASING.

Most business-buying situations do not involve all of the steps in the buy-grid model. The number of steps varies with the buy-class, the type of buying decision. There are three buy-class categories: new buys, straight rebuys, and modified rebuys. While the complete buying process is typically used for new buys (purchases of products or services never used before), a majority of business purchasing decisions are either straight rebuys or modified rebuys. In straight rebuy situations, only the need recognition (the company almost out of the product) and reordering steps are used. For business marketers it is critical for their products or services to be listed as approved vendors for straight rebuys. Marketers will use reminder ADVERTISING, relationship-building entertainment and hospitality, and PERSONAL SELLING to maintain their status as the preferred provider. In modified rebuy decisions (where a buyer is willing to "shop around"), the buyer may go through some or all of the purchasing steps. For marketers desiring to be considered during modified rebuy situations, comparison advertising and demonstrations are used to influence business buyers. Incumbent firms will use relationships, special offers, and anticipation of or quick response to customer needs to maintain their status when business buyers are considering alternatives.

Further reading
Dwyer, F. Robert, and John F. Tanner, Jr. *Business Marketing.* 4th ed. Boston: Irwin McGraw-Hill, 2008.

buying-center concept
The buying-center concept is the idea that in businesses and organizations, many people with different roles and priorities participate in PURCHASING decisions. Unlike consumer buying, where the consumer, alone or with assistance or influence from acknowledged opinion leaders, makes his or her own purchase decisions, in business buying a group often determines which PRODUCTS or SERVICES are purchased.

The typical business buying center will include a variety of participants:

- initiators: people who start the purchase process by defining a need
- decision makers: people who make the final decision
- gatekeepers: people who control the flow of information and access to individuals in an organization
- influencers: people who have input into the purchase decision
- purchasing agent: the person who actually makes the purchase order
- controller: the person who oversees the budget for the purchase
- users: people who use the product or service

In many situations, people play more than one role in business purchasing decisions. Sometimes, buying centers are formal committees created to make a purchase decision, but more often they are defined by organizational relationships. Depending on an organization's structure and the importance of the decision being made, there could be many or few layers of management involved in a buying center. Some members of a buying center will participate throughout the decision-making process, while others will only be involved briefly.

Marketers attempt to define who is involved in buying-center decisions. For example, in the 1990s it was often difficult to determine which people made purchase decisions for business computer systems. In many organizations there was no formal computer-systems department. Often important influencers were individuals within an organization who had taken the time to learn about and analyze computers, even though it was not part of their job requirements. Influencers were often also initiators of computer-systems purchases and upgrades but sometimes were thwarted by gatekeepers resisting changes in technology. For a marketer of computer systems, it was important to identify who played which roles in business buying centers.

Marketers have also recognized the importance of "champions"—advocates for a company's products or services within an organization. During the latter 1990s and early 21st century, many organizations expanded the use of OUTSOURCING—contracting for specific products or services from outside the organization. The jargon term *pilot fish* refers to individuals and businesses created by former employees now providing outsourcing services to the companies they previously worked for. These pilot fish know the company's structure and the buying-center process in the organization and depend on their champions to continue to influence and send business to them.

Further reading

Dwyer, F. Robert, and John F. Tanner, Jr. *Business Marketing*. 4th ed. Boston: Irwin McGraw-Hill, 2008.

bylaws

Bylaws define the organizational and operational structure of a CORPORATION. In addition to the articles of INCORPORATION (sometimes called a charter), which state the rights and responsibilities of the corporation, bylaws provide greater definition regarding the powers of managers, SHAREHOLDERS, and the BOARD OF DIRECTORS. Jane P. Mallor et al. note that a typical set of corporate bylaws cover:

- the authority of directors and officers, specifying what they may or may not do
- the place and time at which the annual shareholders' meeting will be held
- the procedure for calling special shareholders' meetings
- the procedures for directors' and shareholders' meetings, including whether a majority is required for approval of specific actions
- provisions for the creation of special committees of the board of directors, defining their scope and membership
- the procedures for the maintenance of records regarding shareholders
- the mechanisms for transfer of shares of stock
- the standards and procedures for the declaration and payment of DIVIDENDS

Bylaws are the rules guiding the behavior of shareholders, management, and the board of directors. Without them many disputes are likely to arise among owners and managers, and they provide greater transparency in corporate business decision making. Even with well-defined bylaws, corporate disputes and lawsuits frequently arise. In the 1900s, shareholders in many companies proposed changes in bylaws, including "shareholder-rights bylaws," which would require the company's board of directors to "pull the pill" when confronted with a hostile acquisition—that is, implementing anti-takeover actions to prevent another company from taking control of the company. Known as POISON-PILL STRATEGIES, shareholder-rights bylaws would direct specific action by the board of directors, but many legal scholars question their legality. In 2009, investors and government regulators pushed for bylaw changes increasing external membership to corporate boards.

Further reading

Goodchild, Seth, and Daniel J. Buzzetta. "Shareholder Bylaws: A Threat to the Board?" *Corporate Board* 19 (May–June 1998): 10; Mallor, Jane P., A. James Barnes, Thomas Bowers, Michael J. Philips, and Arlen W. Langvardt. *Business Law: The Ethical, Global, and E-Commerce Environment*. 11th ed. Boston: McGraw-Hill, 2009.

cafeteria plans

Cafeteria plans allow employers to compensate employees by offering a combination of cash and tax-favored "fringe" benefits (health/disability INSURANCE, dependent care, or group term life insurance). Generally, when cash is an option, it is taxable. However, under a cafeteria plan the employee can choose a nontaxable benefit and receive it free of both federal INCOME and payroll (SOCIAL SECURITY and Medicare) taxes. Cafeteria plans provide flexibility for the employee to elect benefits that meet individual needs. This ability to choose allows the employee to select cash in the early career years, dependent-care assistance when children are young, and life insurance when dependent care is no longer needed. The employer is relieved of offering the maximum benefits to all the employees, but can instead offer to fund a minimum level of benefits and include a contribution to the cafeteria plan, which would allow the employee to choose which benefits to maximize. Long-term care insurance is one tax-favored fringe benefit that is not includable in a cafeteria plan.

—Linda Bradley McKee

callable bond

A callable bond is a bond that the issuer can repurchase during certain time periods before its maturity date. To be callable, a bond must have a call feature, which enables the issuer to repurchase the bond before its maturity date. An issuer who chooses to call a bond generally pays the bond's holder a call premium upon repurchase, which is meant to compensate the holder for the disadvantage of having to find another way to invest his or her money.

Issuers like call features for several reasons. First, they can repurchase BONDS with call features and reissue them at a lower interest rate. If INTEREST RATES drop significantly, issuers sometimes need to repurchase and reissue their bonds to refinance their own debts. For example, if a 20-year callable corporate bond is issued at an 8-percent interest rate, and after five years interest rates drop to 4 percent, the CORPORATION could potentially waste a great deal of money if it did not recall the bond and reissue it at the lower rate. Issuers also sometimes like to recall bonds when they are rearranging their own capital structures or expanding. The flexibility afforded to issuers by the call feature enables them to do this.

A bond's call provision states whether the bond is noncallable, freely callable, or deferred callable. If a bond is noncallable, the issuer cannot repurchase it before the bond's date of maturity. Noncallable bonds are attractive to some investors because the issuer has to pay interest on them for the bond's full term, regardless of any prevailing level of interest rate. The drawback to these bonds for some investors, however, is that their interest rates are generally not as high as their callable counterparts. Noncallable bonds are sometimes referred to as bullets.

In comparison, an issuer can rescind a bond that is freely callable at any time. These types of bonds offer virtually no protection to investors and can be repurchased after as little as a few days.

A bond with a deferred call provision offers more protection to investors than a freely callable bond but less than a noncallable bond. Deferred callable bonds can be repurchased by the issuer, but only after the amount of time specified in the provision—for example, one, two, or 10 years after the date of purchase.

The only bonds that cannot be called are ones issued by the federal government. Other bonds, including state, municipal and corporate bonds, can be called when issuers are not able to meet interest rates, according to their own call provisions. Of the major types of bonds, corporate bonds are most likely to be called.

Further reading
Fabozzi, Frank J. *The Handbook of Fixed Income Securities.* 5th ed. New York: McGraw-Hill, 1997; Faerber, Esme. *All About Bonds and Bond Mutual Funds.* 2d ed. New York: McGraw-Hill, 2000; "What Is a Bond." Available online. URL: www.fool.com/bonds/bonds01/htm. Accessed on June 8, 2009; Woelfel, Charles J. *Encyclopedia of Banking and Finance.* 10th ed. Chicago: Probus Publishing Company, 1994; Wright, Sharon Saltzgiver. *Getting Started in Bonds.* New York: John Wiley & Sons, 2003.

—Carolyn McKelvey

capital
Along with labor, natural resources, and ENTREPRENEURSHIP (managerial ability), capital is one of the four factors of PRODUCTION. The sources of capital for a firm are represented by the items on the right-hand side of its BALANCE SHEET; debt, preferred stock, COMMON STOCK, and retained earnings. Capital is a major determinant of a firm's size. Since it is relatively more abundant for firms organized as CORPORATIONS than it is for PROPRIETORSHIPS and PARTNERSHIPS, the largest firms are corporations.

When various forms of debt, BONDS, and other liabilities are sources of capital, the cost of this borrowed capital is interest expense. When EQUITY (preferred and common stocks) and retained earnings are sources of capital, the cost of this capital is the return on equity to stockholders. On the other hand, the owners of capital earn interest income if they are creditors or bondholders; they earn DIVIDENDS and CAPITAL GAINS if they are stockholders.

Financial intermediation, the flow of capital from those who have to those who need, is necessary for ECONOMIC GROWTH. The more efficiently capital flows, the greater will be economic growth. A system of well-developed FINANCIAL INTERMEDIARIES is the cornerstone of all advanced economies, whose growth is attributable in large part to well-organized financial markets. Conversely, the lack of well-organized financial systems hinders economic growth. Lesser-developed countries are characterized by a paucity of financial intermediation. When financial intermediation is absent, capital is extremely scarce for those who need it.

See also VENTURE CAPITAL.

capital asset   See BETA COEFFICIENT, CAPITAL ASSET PRICING MODEL.

capital budgeting   See BUDGETING, CAPITAL BUDGETING.

capital expenditure, revenue expenditure
When a firm spends money, it is either for the purchase of an ASSET (a CAPITAL expenditure) or the payment of an expense (a revenue expenditure). Capital expenditures are recorded by debiting some asset account, and as a result, capital expenditures are reflected on the BALANCE SHEET. Revenue expenditures are recorded by debiting some expense account, and as a result, revenue expenditures are reflected on the INCOME STATEMENT.

Ordinary repairs to equipment or other assets are normal expenses—that is, they are revenue expenditures. However, extraordinary repairs, such as overhauls and rebuilds, are capital expenditures. Rather than debiting an expense account for the extraordinary expenditures, the asset account for the item being overhauled or rebuilt is debited. Thus ordinary repairs are revenue expenditures and show up on the income statement as normal expenses, and extraordinary repairs are capital expenditures and show up on the balance sheet.

In accounting, "extraordinary" means both unusual and infrequent. Changing the oil and buying tires for the delivery truck are normal, usual expenses—that is, revenue expenditures. However, overhauling the delivery truck's engine is both unusual and infrequent. This is a capital expenditure, and when this is added to the asset account for the delivery truck, this will increase the BOOK VALUE of the delivery truck.

capital gain, capital loss

CAPITAL gain (or loss) is the result of the purchase and subsequent sale of a capital ASSET. If a stock, bond, or piece of real estate is sold for more than was paid for it, a capital gain on the sale of that asset is realized. If that asset has been held for less than a year, it is a short-term capital gain. If the asset has been owned for more than one year, it is a long-term capital gain. If less is received from the sale of a capital asset than was paid for it, this incurs a capital loss.

For tax purposes, short-term capital gains are treated as ordinary INCOME and taxed along with an individual's other income. However, preferential tax treatment is given to long-term capital gains, on which there is a tax cap (limit), which may be lower than an individual's marginal income tax rate. Currently, the maximum tax rate applicable to long-term capital gains is 20 percent. Tax caps on long-term capital gains are especially beneficial to taxpayers with high marginal income tax rates. For example, an individual paying a 36 percent marginal income tax rate will have his or her income from long-term capital gains taxed at only 20 percent. There is no benefit to taxpayers with lower marginal income tax rates. A taxpayer in the 15 percent marginal income tax bracket will have his or her long-term capital gains taxed at 15 percent. The long-term capital-gains tax cap is a maximum limit and becomes relevant only when an individual's marginal income tax rate rises

above the 20 percent tax cap. Changes in capital-gains laws affect investor behavior.

capitalism

Capitalism is a social and economic system based on private property rights, private allocation of CAPITAL, and self-interest motivation. Capitalism is often referred to as a free enterprise or market system. Capitalism contrasts with SOCIALISM, in which most RESOURCES and industrial-PRODUCTION systems are state-owned or controlled; and with communism, in which most resources are state-owned and most decisions regarding output are made through central planning.

In the 18th century, capitalism replaced feudal control and MERCANTILISM as the primary basis for economic organization. Scottish philosopher Adam Smith described the benefits to society of rational self-interest, where producers would attempt to maximize their well-being by achieving the highest profit possible, and consumers would maximize their well-being by achieving the highest level of utility or satisfaction from the resources they controlled. Smith suggested that with private control and allocation of resources, ECONOMIC EFFICIENCY would result.

The distinguishing force of capitalism is self-interest motivation. Those individuals in control of capital will attempt to use it in a manner to maximize their profit, thereby increasing their WEALTH. Critics of capitalism, most notably 19th-century philosopher Karl Marx, suggested capitalism contained the seeds of its own destruction. Marx saw the English Industrial Revolution factory owners becoming increasingly rich, while workers, who were being replaced by machinery, were in excess SUPPLY and therefore were paid only minimal wages. Marx argued that capitalists, acquiring the "surplus value of labor," would add to the disparities between rich and poor, eventually leading to crises and social upheavals in which workers would overturn a minority's control of capital.

Ironically, the major characteristics of capitalism, private control and allocation of resources, depend heavily on the role of government. Many "free market" capitalists speak disparagingly about government, but without government laws and regulations defining who owns a resource, anarchy or dictatorial control would likely ensue. U.S. economic historians point to the excesses of the "robber baron" and AMERICAN INDUSTRIAL REVOLUTION eras as examples of the extremes of capitalism, and they credit the UNION movement and expansion of government control of resources as balancing forces in the evolution of U.S. capitalism.

Further reading

Ruffin, Roy J., and Paul R. Gregory. *Principles of Economics.* 7th ed. Boston: Addison Wesley, 2002.

carbon tax

A carbon tax is a tax based on how much carbon dioxide (CO_2) is emitted into the atmosphere. CO_2 is widely accepted among scientists as a major source of greenhouse gas emissions, which increase atmospheric temperatures and contribute to climate change.

The goal of a carbon tax is to increase the cost of producing goods and services that emit carbon, thereby reducing the quantity demanded and, in the process, reducing the amount of emissions in the atmosphere. In a press release on August 29, 2007, Representative John Larson (CT-1) announced that the bill he authored would "urge polluters to clean-up their act." In the release he also stated that "the goal of this legislation is to reduce the demand for fossil fuels and promote cleaner, more efficient energy sources. By shifting the burden of payroll taxes away from working Americans, this bill provides a transparent way to incentivize polluters to decrease their carbon emissions." Larson also argued: "Not only is this good environmental and energy policy, it is fair tax policy. The bill is an important move toward shifting taxes away from positive things, like labor, and onto negative things, like pollution."

Carbontax.org, an advocacy group, argues that "a carbon tax is the most economically efficient means to convey crucial price signals and spur carbon-reducing investment and low-carbon behavior."

A carbon tax is an indirect tax paid by consumers based on their usage or consumption. It is consistent with the economic concept of negative externalities, or costs not included in a market transaction, in this case climate change. Critics of carbon taxes note that low-income individuals and poorer countries use a higher percentage of their income for energy consumption and therefore a carbon tax would result in a greater burden on them than on richer individuals and countries.

A carbon tax is one of three options under consideration by policymakers to reduce carbon emissions. The second alternative is a cap-and-trade system under which a limit (cap) on emissions is set and firms buy or sell pollution rights depending on whether they have or have not reduced their emissions. The third alternative would be direct government regulation, mandating either emissions reductions or the use of specific technologies to reduce emissions.

In 1993 President Clinton advocated legislation to tax all fossil fuel energy sources based on their heat content (measured in British thermal units—BTUs). Nobel Peace Prize winner and former vice president Al Gore advocated for a carbon tax in his 1992 book *Earth in the Balance.* In the 1990s, most Scandinavian countries implemented carbon taxes. In 2009 Copenhagen hosted a United Nations Framework Convention on Climate Change (UNFCCC) forum on global warming with President Barack Obama and most of the world's major political leaders in attendance. The forum was expected to result in the implementation of either a cap-and-trade, or carbon tax system, to address global warming, but no agreement was reached.

Though most industrialized countries are now using less energy per billion dollars worth of economic output (gross domestic product) than they did several decades ago, the United States is often described as "five percent of the world's population using twenty-five percent of the world's energy resources." The use of carbon sources in developing countries, primarily the rapidly expanding use of coal in China and India, is expected to dramatically increase carbon emissions in coming decades unless incentives or disincentives alter prevailing patterns.

In theory, carbon taxes would go to a nation's government or a global authority. In turn that entity would use the funds to reduce carbon output, thereby slowing the process of climate change. Critics often refer to studies showing dairy cows as a major source of CO_2 and mockingly suggest dealing with this source of emissions first. *Super Freakonomics* authors Steven Levitt and Stephen Dubner challenged a carbon tax and other expensive efforts to reduce global warming, citing speculative research by former Microsoft engineers suggesting that helium balloons sending sulfur dioxide into the atmosphere could possibly reduce atmospheric temperatures at minimal expense.

In 2009, the U.S. House of Representatives passed legislation favoring a cap-and-trade policy as an alternative to a carbon tax. By late April 2010, the U.S. Senate had not taken up the House bill.

Further reading

Carbontax.org, Web site www.carbontax.org; "Larson Bill Would Urge Polluters to Clean Up Their Act," Press release, Office of John B. Larson, 29 August 2007. Available online. URL: www.larson.house.gov/index2.php?option=com_content&do_pdf=1&id=581. Accessed on July 11, 2009; Levitt, Steven D., and Stephen Dunbar. *Super Freakonomics.* New York: Harper-Collins, 2009.

—Alexia Scott

carry trade

Carry trade is an international financial market term referring to the practice of borrowing funds in countries with low INTEREST RATES and lending those funds in countries with higher interest rates, earning a profit on the difference. Most carry trade activity is conducted by major investment banking firms, with few individual investors engaging in this risky investment.

A typical carry trade example involves Japan and the United States. For decades, short-term interest rates in Japan have been held close to zero. Many Japanese and international investors borrowed in Japanese yen and then bought U.S. Treasury securities (in dollars) yielding 3 to 5 percent. Even with small spreads in interest rates, tremendous profits can be earned in the carry trade business. The obvious risk associated with the carry trade strategy is, if the exchange rate value of the yen increases and the dollar decreases, the investor will be paid back in lower valued dollars and have to pay back his loan in the higher valued yen.

A NATIONAL BUREAU OF ECONOMIC RESEARCH (NBER) paper found "carry traders are subject to crash risk: i.e. exchange rate movements between high-interest-rate and low-interest-rate currencies are negatively skewed . . . due to sudden unwinding of carry trades, which tend to occur in periods in which risk appetite and funding liquidity decrease. Funding liquidity measures predict exchange rate movements, and controlling for liquidity helps explain the uncovered interest-rate puzzle. Carry-trade losses reduce future crash risk, but increase the price of crash risk."

When, in 2008, the FEDERAL RESERVE, pursuing its monetary policy role, pushed U.S. short-term interest rates close to zero, the U.S./Japan carry trade activity disappeared and instead, speculators began using the dollar as their low-cost source of funds and lending those funds in markets with higher interest rates. One criticism of aggressive monetary policy measures is that it leads to this type of speculative movement of financial capital.

Carry trade can also refer to borrowing funds on a short-term basis and lending them on a long-term basis. This common strategy works when there is a "normal" YIELD CURVE, meaning short-term interest rates are lower than long-term rates. In December 2009, six-month U.S. Treasury bills yielded just 0.14 percent while 10-year Treasury notes yielded 3.02 percent, a spread of almost 3 percent. Many U.S. banks and investment firms were making huge profits by borrowing "short" and lending "long." The risk associated with this strategy is, when short-term interest rates eventually rise, lenders' costs go up while the value of their long-term loans—Treasury notes—goes down.

Further reading

Brunnerimeier, Markus K., Stefan Nagel, and Lasse H. Pedersen. "Carry Trades and Currency Crashes." National Bureau of Economic Research, NBER Working Paper No. 14473 (November 2008).

capital markets, money markets

CAPITAL markets are those in which stocks and long-term debt instruments are traded. Examples of these securities having maturities of greater than one year are COMMON STOCKS and preferred stocks, corporate and government BONDS, U.S. Treasury notes and bonds, and MORTGAGES. Thus capital markets are comprised of both EQUITY and debt instruments.

Money markets are those in which short-term debt securities with maturities of one year or less are traded. Examples of these securities are consumer loans, U.S. Treasury bills, COMMERCIAL PAPER, negotiable certificates of deposit, and MUTUAL FUNDS investing in short-term debt securities. Thus money markets are comprised entirely of debt securities.

From the investor's perspective, money-market instruments are attractive during periods of rising INTEREST RATES. Investing for the short term allows the investor to continually replace lower interest-bearing securities with those of higher interest rates as rates continue to rise.

Conversely, capital-market investments are more attractive when interest rates are falling. Being able to "lock in" a high interest with a long-term security protects the investor better than a series of short-term money-market instruments.

carrying value   See BOOK VALUE.

cartel

A cartel is an organization comprised of members of an industry who once competed against each other. Cartel members usually agree to set production quotas, reducing total output available to the market, based on the percentage market share each participant had when the cartel was formed. By collectively reducing output, the market price for the cartel's output will rise and cartel members'

profits will increase. Cartels, which can exist on local, regional, national, and international levels, are essentially formal agreements to restrict output, divide markets, or restrain price COMPETITION among firms in a market. As such they are illegal in the United States under the SHERMAN ANTITRUST ACT (1890).

Certain market conditions are necessary for creating and maintaining a cartel.

- few participants in the industry
- significant BARRIERS TO ENTRY
- similar PRODUCTS produced
- few opportunities to keep individual actions secret
- no legal barriers to production control agreements

Cartels are not easy to coordinate; if there are many members, it is difficult to gain consensus and cooperation. If new firms can enter the market once price has been driven up, the benefit of creating a cartel will quickly disappear. Likewise, if there are similar products that can be substituted for the cartel's product, the cartel will not be able to raise price because consumers will substitute other products. If members can cut special deals with customers, subverting the cartel agreement, the organization will quickly fall apart, and it will also disband or become an informal agreement if the agreement is deemed illegal in the markets where the cartel members participate.

Collusion, a secret agreement to restrict competition, has the same impact as a cartel and is also illegal in the United States. Most firms belong to industry associations and meet regularly to examine common issues. Frequently these meetings lead to discussion of prices. One industrial manufacturing lawyer cringed each time his company's executives went to annual industry gatherings, fearing they would return with secret agreements made with other executives in the industry.

The most famous cartel, ORGANIZATION OF PETROLEUM EXPORTING COUNTRIES (OPEC), is a group of countries (rather than firms) which coordinates oil production. When OPEC was formed in the 1960s, oil-producing countries were receiving $1–$2 per barrel of oil. In the 1970s OPEC members restricted SUPPLY while DEMAND was increasing, thereby raising oil prices to over $30 per barrel. (Oil prices vary slightly depending on the quality of the crude oil produced in different regions of the world.) Generally cartels contain the seeds of their own destruction, because members are reducing their output below their existing potential production. Once the market price increases, each member of the cartel has the capacity to raise output relatively easily. The tendency is for cartel members to "cheat" on their quota, increasing supply to the market and lowering the market price.

Most cartels are unstable agreements and quickly disband, returning the market to more competitive conditions. In the 1980s, OPEC began to fall apart, and the price of oil fell to $12 per barrel, when Saudi Arabia, the largest oil-producing country in OPEC, expanded output back to their agreed-upon OPEC quota. For most of the 1970s and 1980s, Saudi Arabia had cut its output below its quota to compensate for overproduction by other OPEC countries. This allowed OPEC to achieve the goal of higher prices but reduced Saudi Arabia's revenue. Frustrated with cheating by other members of the cartel, Saudi Arabia increased supply, and market prices plummeted. Reduced output due to the Iraq-Kuwait war in 1990, reduced cheating by OPEC members, and increased global demand brought oil prices back up over the $30-a-barrel level during most of the 1990s.

Over the years, many other cartels have been formed in tin, chrome, coffee, and diamonds. DeBeers controls the distribution of uncut diamonds, keeping prices high by restricting and coordinating supply to the market. Standard Oil—which in the 1890s gave John D. Rockefeller a near-monopoly in oil production and refining—created a cartel in petroleum distribution, shifting oil distribution among participants in the railroad cartel at agreed-upon levels. The railroads charged non-Standard Oil producers higher rates for oil distribution, facilitating Standard's acquisition of competitors and preventing new competitors from entering the oil-refining market. The Sherman Antitrust Act was a response to Standard Oil's monopolization activities.

While cartels are generally illegal in the United States, they are often legal in other countries and are sometimes sanctioned in the United States. The National Collegiate Athletic Association (NCAA) is a cartel of colleges and universities that sets athletic rules and behavior, determines distribution of television revenue from college sporting events, and penalizes institutions that violate NCAA rules. Many agricultural COOPERATIVES are legal cartels, raising prices for members' products or reducing costs through collective purchasing power. During bumper-crop years, one of the largest cooperatives in the United States, Sunkist, reduces market supply by mandating that members reduce production of citrus fruits. Cooperatives are legal in the United States.

Further reading
Boyes, William J., and Michael Melvin. *Microeconomics.* 7th ed. Boston: Houghton Mifflin, 2007.

case law   See COMMON LAW.

cash-flow analysis
Cash-flow analysis is a planning device that looks at the cash flows into and out of a new project, new venture, equipment purchase, new product, etc. The manager analyzes the cash-flow predictions to determine the relative desirability of doing the new activity.

One method of analyzing the cash flow is called the "payback period." This simple technique evaluates the wisdom of carrying out a project by looking at the relative time it takes to pay back the initial INVESTMENT in the project. With this method, projects that pay back their original investment the quickest are considered superior to those that take longer. The major disadvantage of this method, which is often used by business and criticized by academics, is that it ignores cash flows after the payback period. Thus one project that brings in large cash flows after its payback period may be discarded in favor of a project that pays back the original investment rapidly. On the other hand, many business managers rightly want to minimize the time they are "at risk" with the investment, so they prefer projects that give them back their original investment rapidly.

More sophisticated techniques involve discounted cash-flow analysis. These techniques look at the time value of money and the effect of interest compounding, using relatively simple mathematical calculations to convert future cash flows to their "present value," which is the present worth of future cash flows given a specified interest rate. Financial calculators do these calculations.

The project that produces the highest present value is considered superior to those that produce a lower present value. Another way to use the same concept is to calculate each project's internal rate of return—that is, the interest rate that the original investment earns in producing the project's resultant cash flows. Often a company has a target internal rate of return that it demands from its projects and approves those projects that surpass the target or those with the highest internal rate of return.

These cash DISCOUNTING techniques add a disarming degree of mathematical rigor to the cash-flow analysis, leading the unwary manager to ignore the underlying uncertainty of the cash flows themselves. To try to deal with this, some cash-flow analyses include analyzing the probabilities of the resulting cash flows prior to their being discounted. This produces an expected value of the cash flows.

cash-flow statement   See FLOW OF FUNDS.

cash management

Cash management is the cash collection, payment, and INVESTMENT activities involved in managing a business. This is done with the deliberate goal of minimizing the amount of cash the company has to borrow and maximizing its return from investments. Managers look for ways to hasten the collection of their ACCOUNTS RECEIVABLE, delay the payment of ACCOUNTS PAYABLE, and maximize the investment return of the resultant extra cash.

Hastening the collection of accounts receivable entails invoicing customers in a timely and accurate way, upon which the collected cash is hurried into investments. This happens in many different ways. The company must have an efficient way to process deposits. Banks offer a full array of services to speed cash into investments, such as bank lockboxes and sweep accounts. With a lockbox, a company lists the bank's address on its return envelopes used by its customers. The bank then directly receives all the payments on behalf of the company and immediately records these collections into the company's bank accounts, making copies of the collected checks and accompanying payment advices available to the company. This is now often done via an INTERNET site to which the company can, at its leisure, do its normal accounting for collections. Lockboxes are especially useful when the company's customers are widely dispersed. Strategically placed lockboxes minimize the amount of time the company's MONEY is tied up in the postal system instead of their bank account.

Another service offered by banks to maximize the amount of money in investments is a sweep account. The bank monitors needed cash levels in a cash account and then "sweeps" any excess into investments. Often this is done to sweep the account empty each night to get investment income on the otherwise idle cash.

To delay cash payments, the company maintains an accurate accounts payable system that carefully schedules payment dates and watches vendors' grace periods for taking cash discounts and avoiding late service charges. The payment is then made at the last possible moment.

At the heart of any cash management system is its cash accounting system and cash budget. Previously the cash account might be reconciled to the bank on a monthly basis, but today's accountants can download bank statements and reconcile them to the cash account almost daily. This close tracking of the cash account allows the company to keep a smaller cash safety cushion. As part of this focus on cash management, companies have dramatically reduced the number of bank accounts they maintain. This reduces the amount of cash that is tied up as safety balances for all of the accounts, and it allows the accounting staff to focus on the main accounts for the company.

Usually a cash budget is prepared as a part of a comprehensive BUDGETING process for the company. The cash budget predicts the inflow and outflow of cash and the resultant cash balances. This enables the company to minimize what it borrows and maximize the amount available for investments, but it involves more than just the simple scheduling of receivables and payables. Instead a good cash management system carefully studies each cash-flow item and determines the best strategy for its effective management.

International companies have developed an interesting cash management tool called *netting*. Instead of settling each transaction individually, where the receivable collected from the international client is collected, translated into the company's currency, and transmitted back to the company's main office, the company sets up a netting center where the company's collections for receivables in a certain currency are used to settle payables in the same currency. A version of this involves a joint-venture netting center where the receipts of one company are used to settle the payables of another. The resulting inter-company receivable/payable is settled between the two companies back in the home country. This solves some currency exchange and currency repatriation problems.

cause marketing, cause-related marketing (CRM)

Cause marketing, also known as cause-related marketing, is a MARKETING STRATEGY that combines efforts of a CORPORATION with a nonprofit entity for a shared benefit. The term is not to be confused with *social marketing* (a marketing message designed to influence social conduct, e.g., wear seat belts, don't drive drunk, or stop smoking) or *corporate philanthropy* (a tax deductible gift not expected to show a return). Cause marketing has been described as a blend of corporate philanthropy and sponsorship. By imple-

menting cause marketing, a corporation can reach marketing and business goals while satisfying a philanthropic component, ultimately "achieving self-interest through altruism."

The potential benefits for corporations include the ability to attract "new customers, reach niche markets, increase product sales, and build positive brand identity." The potential benefits for the nonprofit organizations include promoting their message to a more widespread audience, gaining access to a corporation's superior marketing resources, implementing a call to action to would-be supporters who may have not known how to participate, and obtaining the chance to generate additional direct donations outside the cause marketing campaign through increased visibility.

When a business decides to implement a cause-related marketing campaign, it is important that the firm chooses a "cause" that is relevant and closely related to the product or service the company sells. Customers need to fully understand why the company has chosen to promote the nonprofit's mission, and it needs to be a cause they can also support. Cause-related marketing can have a big impact on brand loyalty, and it can be targeted for specific groups and customized for individual customers. Therefore, it is imperative that the marketing campaign caters to the target market of the company and that it has a clear connection to the cause.

Cause marketing campaigns differ in scale and purpose, in the kind of nonprofits involved, and in the type of partnership between the nonprofit and the corporation. Contribution agreements vary from a specified dollar amount of each product sold to a promise of a portion of after-tax profits, or the offer may be valid for only one specific product or it may apply to an entire product line. Offers could be applicable for only a short promotional time period, or they may be open ended, leading to "Cause Branding," a long-term commitment that eventually becomes part of a corporation's identity.

While forms of cause marketing emerged earlier in the mid to late 1970s, the term "cause-related marketing" was coined and trademarked in 1983 by American Express with its Statue of Liberty

Restoration campaign. American Express donated one cent for every card transaction, one dollar for each new card issued, and also made donations based on purchases of their travelers' checks and travel packages, excluding airfares, sold through its vacation stores. In just three months, the Restoration Fund raised over $1.7 million, and use of American Express rose 27 percent, while new card applications increased by 45 percent compared to the previous year.

The success of the American Express campaign confirmed that mutually beneficial partnerships could be formed between corporations and nonprofits. It also proved that nonprofits had valuable assets and brands of their own and that, when joined with their corporate partner's brand and marketing, the result would appeal to the public and SHAREHOLDERS alike.

Cause marketing does have some controversy associated with it. Many grant seekers are uncomfortable when nonprofits enter into these relationships with publicly held companies and debate the ethics of lending their name and reputations to those corporations. Some think that cause-related marketing undermines traditional philanthropy, that nonprofits are changing their programs to attract cause-related marketing relationships, and that only well-established, noncontroversial causes can attract cause-related marketing relationships. For a business, it is important that it chooses a reputable nonprofit, with little or no controversy associated with it.

Sometimes, nonprofits have found their reputations hurt by the experience of pairing with a company that becomes synonymous with scandal. In 1992 United Way was embarrassed when its CHIEF EXECUTIVE OFFICER was accused of financial misconduct and replaced in an extremely public exposure of the organization's internal activities. The public was not quick to forget and it took some time for the nonprofit to restore its positive image as well as the reputation of the corporations that had aligned with the charity. In a separate incident, City Year, a successful youth outreach organization, had listed Enron as one of its major cause-marketing partners. In 2001,

when Enron became the subject of lawsuits and congressional hearings over mismanagements and possible crimes, City Year found unwanted publicity through a company that had misrepresented itself.

Even though American Express was able to raise money for the Statue of Liberty Restoration project, the company actually spent several more millions advertising its involvement in the campaign. This action has been a common obstacle for many corporations involved in cause marketing, with many making the argument that the money would be better spent going to the foundation directly.

The concept of cause marketing is replacing traditional anonymous corporate philanthropy with an "emphasis on bottom-line" and an opportunity to appear likable in the media. Supporting a specific cause and being public about it gives corporations identifiable personalities, demonstrates the values they represent, and helps connect them with customers, suppliers, investors, employees, and the community. In the 2006 Cone Millennial Cause Study, 89 percent of Americans aged 13 to 25 would switch from one brand to another brand of a comparable product (and price) if the latter brand was associated with a "good cause."

Examples of modern positive experiences in cause marketing include Nike and the Lance Armstrong Foundation. The company had been a longtime sponsor of Armstrong as an athlete, but in 2004 Nike decided to collaborate in cause marketing for Armstrong's cancer foundation. The idea was simple: a yellow rubber bracelet with the word "Livestrong" on it that showed support for the foundation when worn and resulted in a donation to the foundation when purchased. While Nike initially pledged to sell 5 million bracelets, a number that seemed impossible to many, over 50 million have been sold.

Yoplait Yogurt is another example, with its "Save Lids to Save Lives" campaign with the Susan G. Komen for the Cure foundation for breast cancer. Each October, Yoplait produces yogurt cups with specially designed pink lids encouraging buyers to mail the lids in, with a pledge of 10 cents for every lid, up to a $1.5 million donation, with a guaranteed donation of $500,000.

Further reading
The 2006 Cone Millennial Cause Study. Available online. URL: www.coneinc.com/news/request.php?id=1090. Accessed on April 26, 2010; Cause Marketing 101. Available online. URL: www.causemarketingforum.com/cause_marketing_101.asp. Accessed on April 26, 2010; Daw, J. *Cause-Marketing for Nonprofits: Partner for Purpose, Passion, and Profits.* Hoboken, N.J.: John Wiley & Sons, 2006; Kotter, P., and N. Lee. *Corporate Social Responsibility: Doing the Most Good for Your Company and Your Cause.* Hoboken, N.J.: John Wiley & Sons, 2005; Marconi, J. *Cause Marketing: Build Your Image and Bottom Line Through Socially Responsible Partnerships, Programs, and Events.* Chicago: Dearborn Publishing Group, 2002.

—Amanda Ramsden and Meg Park

caveat emptor

Caveat emptor is a Latin phrase meaning "Let the buyer beware." Associated most especially with the purchase of "as is" products, the doctrine of caveat emptor places the responsibility on the buyer to determine the quality and fitness of a product to meet his or her needs. In the early days of the U.S. economy, most commerce occurred between and among consumers and local businesses where buyers knew who was selling a product and could find the seller in the event of a problem. A seller's "word" and reputation were important to his success. As commerce expanded beyond local markets, consumers began to interact with traveling merchants and sellers representing goods produced elsewhere. Caveat emptor doctrine placed the responsibility on buyers to determine whether problems existed with the product being offered for sale.

For years, Wendy's restaurants used tables with depictions from late 19th-century newspaper ads. The ads frequently offered "cures" for whatever ailed people, often alcohol-based, morphine-laced cure-alls. The marketer would claim his product cured baldness, infertility, and even infidelity!

The caveat emptor doctrine, prevalent at the time, made it the responsibility of the buyer to accept or reject the claims being made.

More recently, caveat emptor was associated with the purchase of used cars and homes. After years of complaints from consumers, FEDERAL TRADE COMMISSION (FTC) rules and state laws were imposed requiring disclosure by sellers of any known flaws in the products being sold. Realtors now require home sellers to provide documentation of known existing conditions, and share that information with buyers. Mortgage lenders require home inspections to avoid costly repairs. Car dealerships offer warranties with their vehicles.

While caveat emptor doctrine places responsibility on the buyer, sellers can be held accountable if they conceal facts, engage in FRAUD, or make misleading representations. Over time, the premise of buyer beware has been weakened by laws and court decisions requiring sellers to provide merchantable products, products that do what they are intended to do, and an implied warranty of fitness, a promise that sellers make when their customers rely on the seller's advice that a product can be used for some specific purpose. Most retailers now provide limited or full warranties, detailing what they will be held responsible for, and requirements such as proof-of-purchase that customers must provide to be covered by the warranties.

The FTC is the primary federal agency responsible for protecting consumers. Truth in advertising, financial practices, marketing, and other business practices are monitored and enforced by the agency.

Further reading
Federal Trade Commission Consumer Protection Web site. Available online. URL: www.ftc.gov/bcp/index.shtml.

cease and desist (C&D)

Cease and desist is a legal term requesting or ordering a firm or individual to stop engaging in an activity. A cease-and-desist order is issued by a court directing a person or firm, under penalty of law, to stop the activity. The FEDERAL TRADE COMMISSION frequently issues "consent orders" that include cease-and-desist actions against firms engaged in unfair or deceitful trade practices. Sometimes a C&D order is the result of litigation, while often it is a temporary injunction imposed as an emergency measure to give complainants time to seek a permanent injunction against the objectionable activity. In construction and road building litigation, C&D orders are often requested when the potential exists for environmental damage.

Cease-and-desist letters are directives from a complainant to the firm or individual engaged in an objectionable activity. C&D letters are not issued by a court; rather, they threaten legal action if the activity does not end. C&D letters are common in homeowner association disputes, harassment claims, and trademark or copyright infringement. Critics of cease-and-desist letters point out that the letters may be used by wealthy individuals and organizations to silence or intimidate individuals or entrepreneurs who are unable or unwilling to engage in an expensive lawsuit, and therefore choose to comply with a cease-and-desist letter (even if it is unjustified).

Further reading
Federal Trade Commission Web site. Available online. URL: www.ftc.gov.

Center for Science in the Public Interest

The Center for Science in the Public Interest (CSPI) is an independent nonprofit organization focusing on food safety, nutrition, and alcohol abuse. Founded in 1971 by Michael Jacobson and headquartered in Washington, D.C., the CSPI has over 900,000 members and publishes *Nutrition Action Healthletter,* a widely read and respected source for information on health and nutrition.

In addition to disseminating information, the CSPI lobbies to pass health and nutrition legislation. The organization led efforts to pass the 1990 Nutrition Labeling and Education Act, which required all packaged and processed food sold in the United States to carry labels with nutritional

information. Many food-industry leaders opposed the CSPI's efforts, arguing that the requirements would be expensive to comply with and were not necessary. The Center also assisted with efforts to require warning labels on alcoholic beverages and to educate the public regarding the health dangers associated with fat, salt, and other substances in food.

In recent years the CSPI has gained widespread publicity for its efforts to educate consumers about high fat content in movie-theater popcorn and the questionable nutritional value of fast food and ethnic food restaurants. The CSPI is credited with gaining passage of the law requiring "Nutrition Facts" to be posted on packaged and processed foods sold in the United States. The center also has lobbied for increases in excise taxes on alcoholic beverages as a means to reduce alcohol consumption.

The CSPI has also influenced congressional legislation appropriating funds to reduce the risk of food-borne illnesses and to require safe-handling notices on meat and poultry products. The Center is advocating national menu labeling, food safety modernization, soft-drink taxes to reduce obesity, and improved school lunches.

The CSPI informs consumers regarding improvements and advances in nutrition and safety. With their newsletter and publicity, the CSPI significantly influences Americans' eating habits and government regulation of the food industry. Products criticized for deceptive labeling or given negative reviews in the *Nutrition Action Healthletter* can expect to see their demand decrease.

Further reading
Center for Science in the Public Interest Web site. Available online. URL: www.cspinet.org. Accessed on June 8, 2009; Johanna T. Dwyer. "Center for Science in the Public Interest," World Book Online Americas Edition. Available online. URL: www.aolsvc.worldbook.aol.com/wbol/wbpage/na/ar/co/102850; *Nutrition Action Newsletter.* Available online. URL: www.cspinetorg.nah/index.htm.

—Leah Kninde Frazier-Gaskins

centrally planned economy

A centrally planned economy is an economic system where the factors of PRODUCTION (RESOURCES) are controlled by the state. Resource allocation plans and decisions are made by the central government and then promulgated through government agencies. Regional managers allocate resources to production managers and collective farms, which are given output goals. Centrally planned economies require significant government bureaucracies to control resource allocation, coordinate information flows, and measure performance.

Centrally planned economies are considered synonymous with communism but are also associated with fascism and SOCIALISM. Centrally planned economies contrast with capitalism, where most resources are controlled privately. Many U.S. politicians equate capitalism with democracy. CAPITALISM is an economic system, while democracy is a political system. Dr. David Korten of Stanford University, a critic of GLOBALIZATION, argues that, "Contrary to its claims, capitalism's relationship to democracy and to the market economy is much the same as the relationship of a cancer to the body whose life energies it expropriates." Korten suggests the American democratic political system has been overrun by rogue capitalism, focusing on "money and materialism over life itself."

Like capitalism, centrally planned economies are associated with a political system—in this case a single-party system—yet most European countries have a social democrat political party, advocating democracy but greater collective control and allocation of resources. There are probably no purely capitalist or centrally planned economies. The differences among countries are a matter of the degree of control and allocation of resources made privately versus centrally.

As of 2009 the major centrally planned economies in the world are Cuba and North Korea. In both countries, powerful leaders direct and control a central government making most decisions regarding resource allocation. Because of its international isolation, much less is known about North Korea than Cuba. In many years there have been reports of severe food shortages in North Korea and fears of widespread starvation.

In 2002 Jimmy Carter became the first former American president to visit Cuba. In his farewell address, President Carter called for ending the American economic blockade of Cuba and increasing the freedom and rights of Cuban citizens. Cuba is a good example of the problems associated with centrally planned economies. When Cuban president Fidel Castro came to power in the early 1960s, he and his supporters overthrew the corrupt and dictatorial but pro-American Battista regime. Cuban resources, primarily land and tourism, were controlled by a wealthy elite, whereas communism advocates collective control of resources for the benefit of all of society. Castro had widespread support among Cuban citizens, because the vast majority of Cubans had few resources and a poor STANDARD OF LIVING.

After taking control of the government, Castro nationalized major industries in Cuba, mostly sugarcane plantations and rum factories. This infuriated the owners of these resources, in particular the Bacardi Rum family and the Boston-based United Fruit Company. Wealthy Cubans fled the country, and as the government seized control of the factors of production, many poor Cubans saw improved access to health care, education, and, initially, food supplies. But the major problem with centrally planned economies is efficiency. Private enterprise provides incentives for owners and managers to use resources efficiently and manage resources for long-term viability. If a business prospers, the owners profit, so efficient planning and allocating is desirable.

In a state-run enterprise, managers are given goals. If they achieve those goals, they may get some small bonus, a vacation at a government-run resort, or a larger apartment, but they do not get a share of any profit from achieving or exceeding the goal. Numerous stories report state farms being incredibly inefficient, but workers on the farms, given small plots of land for their own use, generate significant output crops, which they then sell for their personal benefit. State-run enterprises also create rigidity. The *Wall Street Journal* once reported about the instructions given to a greenhouse manager near Moscow for his winter crop. He told the reporter he could grow a lot of cabbage but instead was told to grow tomatoes—so he did, using huge amounts of energy to heat the greenhouses.

Similarly, it was not long before the Cuban economy declined due to inefficiency, government bureaucracies, and U.S. sanctions. (Until 1961 Cuba was a larger trading partner with the United States than Mexico.) To support the Cuban economy, Castro entered into a BARTER agreement with the Soviet Union, trading sugar cane for oil. Before long the Soviet Union was subsidizing the Cuban economy for as much as $5 billion annually. In return, Cuba allied itself politically with the Soviets and provided troops in cold war-era regional conflicts.

With the collapse of the Soviet Union in 1989, Soviet subsidies ended and the Cuban economy plummeted. Declining world sugar prices also hurt Cuban efforts, and before long the Castro government began allowing various private enterprises, but this meant attracting investors, one of the problems with centrally planned economies. Since Cuba had nationalized private enterprises in the 1960s and not compensated the owners, foreign investors were reticent about dealing with the Castro government. Eventually Spanish investors led hotel and tourism investments, and individual Cubans were allowed to create some private businesses, including transportation and other services. At first Cuban college graduates were not allowed to participate, based on the argument that they had benefited from an education provided by the state and therefore should contribute their services to the state. Desperate for foreign exchange earnings, the Cuban government allowed all citizens to create private enterprises.

Centrally planned economies replace market systems with government systems. Market systems are chaotic, often ruthless, and impersonal, but they send signals to produce more of this and less of that. Private control, rather than collective control, provides incentives for business owners to manage their resources effectively and efficiently. While Cuba and North Korea remain the major

examples of centrally planned economies, the Central European countries of the Warsaw Pact provide numerous examples of the problems involved in transitioning from a centrally planned economy to a market-based system.

The change from central planning to a market system requires addressing many issues including

- removal of price controls on necessities, usually food, housing, transportation, and utilities
- transfer of control of state-run enterprises to private enterprise
- changes in the legal system defining and enforcing property rights
- UNEMPLOYMENT and underemployment
- control of MONETARY POLICY
- privatization of finance and credit
- promises made by the state to retirees, military and others
- educating consumers and citizens about private enterprise

As the list suggests, the task is daunting. Some countries have adjusted better and more rapidly than others.

Further reading
Korten, David C. Web site. Available online. URL: www. davidkorten.com. Accessed on June 8, 2009.

certificates of deposit   See TIME DEPOSITS.

Certified Public Accountant

A Certified Public Accountant (CPA) is an individual who performs FINANCIAL ACCOUNTING services for the general public for a fee. While all CPAs are accountants, not all accountants are CPAs. Over 350,000 CPAs in the United States are members of the AMERICAN INSTITUTE OF CERTIFIED PUBLIC ACCOUNTANTS (AICPA). The AICPA was established in 1887 in New York City and originally had 31 members.

The AICPA Values and Vision Statement reads:

The AICPA is the premier national professional association in the United States. Our employees are a diverse, unified team who:

- Are committed to member service and the public interest, providing the highest quality products, services and support possible.
- Listen and respond to the needs and expectations of members, prospective members, the public and one another.
- Serve members with excellence.
- Act with the highest ethical behavior, performing with integrity and professionalism.
- Are committed to learning and using new or existing tools and technology to its maximum potential.
- Are responsive to others in a respectful and courteous manner.
- Embrace change and approach challenges with "can do" enthusiasm and creative thinking.
- Constantly seek opportunities to attract and retain members, offer additional products or services, reduce costs, and improve productivity.
- Are empowered to problem-solve and make decisions with the expectation of support by the AICPA.

The AICPA is committed to providing its employees with:

- Timely training to acquire the knowledge and skills needed for current and future jobs.
- Opportunity for professional and personal growth through job enlargement, rotation and education.
- A team environment that fosters participation, diversity, differences of opinion and a commitment to excellence.
- A system that recognizes and rewards outstanding performance, ongoing contributions and innovations of individuals and teams within the AICPA.
- EMPOWERMENT to problem-solve and make accountable and responsible decisions.
- A process that respects and utilizes contributions from staff throughout the Institute.
- Opportunities for promotion from within, when qualified and possible.
- Above all, a professional environment that values open and candid communications based on honesty, trust, respect, health COMPETITION and conflict resolution.

An accountant must earn the professional designation of CPA from the AICPA. As of 2002, the requirements to become a CPA included completing a program of study at a college or university with at least 150 hours of study; passing the Uniform CPA Examination; and completing required work experience in public accounting.

Further reading
American Institute of Certified Public Accountants Web site. Available online. URL: www.aicpa.org.

ceteris paribus
Ceteris paribus is a Latin phrase meaning "with other things the same." Commonly used by economists, ceteris paribus is often translated as assuming "all other things being equal," or "all other factors being unchanged." Economist William Elliott describes ceteris paribus as "both a blessing and the bane of an economist's existence. . . . It allows us to understand how changing only one factor in a complex world affects all other factors. . . . However, in its appeal, it has a major flaw. That flaw is also something economists know so well, endogeneity. In other words, everything in the world is connected and somehow affects everything else, therefore, ceteris paribus is not a realistic assumption."

Though it is often an unrealistic assumption, economists constantly use the assumption that all other factors remain unchanged to isolate and explain cause-and-effect relationships. A classic MICROECONOMICS example is the law of DEMAND, which states that there is an inverse relationship between price and quantity demanded (ceteris paribus). A higher price will result in less quantity demanded and a lower price will result in greater quantity demanded, assuming nothing else changes in the market being considered.

In a real-world example, one year a local university raised its tuition by 12 percent, yet enrollment increased. Ceteris paribus, the law of demand suggests that should not have happened but, during that time period, competing institutions also raised their tuition; students' (and their families') income declined, bringing more students back home to the local higher education market; new academic and athletic programs were initiated at the university, increasing interest among potential students; and the university expanded its promotion and recruitment efforts. All these changes made invalid the assumption that all factors other than price were held constant.

Market researchers also use the ceteris paribus assumption when conducting test market studies. To minimize the problem of having uncontrolled variables change during the course of the study, most test market studies are conducted over a short period of time and during "normal," as opposed to exceptional, market conditions.

In his seminal book *Principles of Economics,* 19th-century British economist Alfred Marshall described the effect of time on the ceteris paribus assumption:

> The element of time is a chief cause of those difficulties in economic investigations which make it necessary for man with his limited powers to go step by step; breaking up a complex question, studying one bit at a time, and at last combining his partial solutions into a more or less complete solution of the whole riddle. In breaking it up, he segregates those disturbing causes, whose wandering happened to be inconvenient, for the time in a pound called Ceteris Paribus.

A classic MACROECONOMIC example of ceteris paribus involves the quantity theory of money: $MV = P_1 Q_{real}$ where M represents the money supply, V is the velocity or turnover rate of the MONEY SUPPLY in an economy, P_1 represents the price level (inflation), and Q_{real} is real GROSS DOMESTIC PRODUCT (GDP). The quantity theory states that changes in the money supply will cause changes in the level of real GDP and/or INFLATION, ceteris paribus. Quantity theory assumes velocity does not change; historically, a reasonable assumption over relatively short periods of time but, during the U.S. financial crisis in 2008–09, access to credit "froze," reducing the flow of money in the economy and significantly reducing the velocity of money. Large injections of funds by the U.S. Treasury had little impact because financial institutions did not loan the money and therefore consumers and businesses did not have the money to spend.

The ceteris paribus assumption is also used in scientific studies in attempting to isolate and control variables, allowing researchers to assess cause-and-effect relationships.

Further reading
Marshall, Alfred. *Principles of Economics.* London: Macmillan and Co., 1890.

chain-of-command principle

The chain-of-command principle refers to the relationship of the reporting mechanism within an organization. A chain of command establishes the line of authority within the organization—i.e., who reports to whom and how all employees are linked within the company.

There are essentially two components that constitute a chain of command, namely unity of command and the scalar principle. "Unity of command" means that each individual reports to one (and only one) boss or supervisor. This is a vital issue in that all employees need to know from whom to accept commands and to whom they are directly accountable. Unity of command establishes the legitimate authority that a supervisor has over his/her workers. In reality, it legitimizes the right of the supervisor to make decisions, to allocate resources, and to direct an employee in his/her job. It gives authority to the supervisor to give an employee orders and then hold that person accountable in carrying out those orders. This legitimate authority is vested in the position and not the person.

Upholding unity of command in the organizational design provides structure and clarity for employees in the workplace. In MANAGEMENT, one organizational structure breaks the unity-of-command rule—specifically, the matrix design, which imposes a lateral reporting relationship on top of the traditional vertical reporting relationship that results from unity of command. Thus, a dual reporting relationship emerges, and the employee is accountable to two bosses or supervisors. A major disadvantage of the matrix is that it can result in inefficiency and discord if the two supervisors do not coordinate the employee's time. A major advantage is that the talents of one employee can be utilized more fully, resulting in greater efficiency in the use of a company's HUMAN RESOURCES. Ultimately, however, when an unresolved dispute arises between the two supervisors, the matrix design collapses to unity of command, with the one supervisor over the two disputing supervisors resolving the issue.

The second component in chain of command is called the scalar principle. This term means that an unbroken line can be traced from the lowest employee on the organizational chart to the CHIEF EXECUTIVE OFFICER (CEO). This unbroken line represents the line of authority and reporting relationship within the company.

Referring to the organizational chart, formal lines or channels of communication can be identified. Information within an organization is often passed through formal channels. This is especially the case with paperwork that needs approval to conform to company policies.

—Leanne McGrath

Chamber of Commerce

The U.S. Chamber of Commerce is a federation of businesses and business organizations coordinated at local, state, regional, and national levels. A voluntary organization, its goal is to promote business interests. At each level, chamber members typically include corporate, civic, and small-business owners.

The Chamber of Commerce grew out of a 1912 presidential commission review of the FEDERAL BUDGETING process. President William Howard Taft, in the first issue of *Nation's Business,* the official publication of the Chamber of Commerce, stated the need to "set forth periodically affirmative information and thought regarding our progress as a nation." Taft also cited the need for a single entity through which American businesses and government could deal with each other on a national level.

The most broadly represented business association in Washington, the Chamber of Commerce is an important voice in political, regulatory, and civil affairs affecting business. It has numerous committees that analyze and initiate policy positions in areas ranging from ANTITRUST LAW to taxation. The chamber influences legislation through congressional testimony, lobbying, and the grassroots efforts of local and state chambers. One of its more effective mechanisms is its "action call," a memorandum outlining its position on an issue and urging members to contact their representatives.

In 2009, the chamber's "Policy Priorities" constituted a wide variety of positions, including:

Activist Investor Agenda. Push back against the activist agenda that seeks to use the corporate governance process to gain benefit for minority shareholders with a political agenda. In particular, urge ISS Governance Services, a division of RiskMetrics Group, to move toward a more transparent and evidence-based policy-making process while eliminating core conflicts of interest.

Attorney-Client Privilege and Employee Access to Legal Representation. Continue to advocate for employee and business due process rights by supporting policies that protect the attorney-client privilege and right to counsel. Continue to oppose policies by the Securities and Exchange Commission (SEC) and other federal agencies that consider waiver of attorney-client privilege and payment of employee legal expenses as factors in determining whether a company is being cooperative in an investigation.

Auditing Profession. Strive to ensure a sustainable environment for the auditing profession by suggesting how to improve auditing and accounting practices and by encouraging a greater focus on long-term performance metrics.

Executive Compensation. Ensure careful and sensible rulemaking and implementation by the SEC and Congress on executive compensation and related party disclosure.

Innovation Economy. Promote ways to better value long-term investment, entrepreneurial risk taking, revolutionary research and development, and intangible assets.

International Financial Reporting Standards. Advocate for convergence of global accounting standards to reduce complexity and duplication.

Mutual Fund Regulatory Reform. Develop and advocate for bold and competitive new approaches to force change in investment company regulation and structures.

Local chambers of commerce provide members with information about business issues, resources, and opportunities to meet other businesspeople in their areas. The Chamber of Commerce is an important source of business information ranging from employee issues to taxes and money management. In many U.S. communities, the local chamber's "After Hours" receptions are an important chance for networking, exchanging ideas, and building relationships.

Further reading

"Affirmative Information and Thought Regarding Our Progress as a Nation," *Nation's Business* 80, no. 20 (September 1992): 83; Chamber of Commerce Web site. Available online. URL: www.uschamber.com.

Chicago Board of Trade

The Chicago Board of Trade (CBOT) is a market exchange where commodity and financial FUTURES and OPTIONS contracts are bought and sold. Created in 1848, the CBOT is used primarily by investors, managers, and broker/dealers to reduce risk in business transactions. Initially the CBOT focused on grain trade, allowing farmers and other agricultural-industry members to hedge or reduce their risk of price changes by using futures contracts.

Futures contracts—agreements to buy or sell a specific amount of a commodity at a particular price on or before a stipulated date—allow sellers to secure a price for their output and buyers to control the future cost of their inputs. If, in the time between their sale of the futures contract and when their products are ready for market, the commodity price goes down, farmers will be able to buy back their futures contract at a lower price. They profit by the difference and thus offset the lower market price for their product. If the price goes up, they will lose money on the futures contract but will profit from the higher price in the marketplace. Likewise, for a food-products company buying a futures contract, if prices rise in the interim, the value of their contract rises, offsetting the higher market price for their inputs. If prices decline, the food-products company's contract declines in value, but the cost of the inputs also declines in the marketplace.

Unlike stocks, which convey an ownership interest in a CORPORATION, futures contracts are standardized agreements defining the quantity, quality, delivery date, and location for a commodity or security. The CBOT estimates only 4 percent of all contracts result in delivery. The primary purpose of futures contracts is to provide protection against price changes for a specified period of time. As the maturity date of a futures contract approaches, traders who are "long" (having bought a futures contract) or "short" (having sold a futures contract) close their position by doing the opposite of their initial trade.

The CBOT is regulated by the COMMODITY FUTURES TRADING COMMISSION (CFTC), created to oversee the CBOT and other exchanges. In the last two decades, the CBOT, CHICAGO MERCANTILE EXCHANGE, Chicago Board of Exchange, NEW YORK MERCANTILE EXCHANGE, and other smaller regional markets have competed in providing new options and futures contracts to meet the needs of financial markets and managers. In addition to grains, the CBOT trades in U.S. Treasury bond futures, DOW JONES AVERAGES, silver, gold, and energy futures. Annually, the CME group handles over 1 billion contracts worth over $1,000 trillion.

Where futures contracts obligate the buyer and seller to a specified agreement, options contracts provide the buyer or seller the right to buy or sell at a specified price. If the option is not exercised by the maturity date, it expires with the buyer losing the amount of money they paid for the option.

Prices of futures and options can be quite volatile. In addition to being used by managers to reduce risk, speculators add liquidity to commodity and futures markets and profit when they correctly anticipate price changes in the market.

There are over 85 commodity exchanges around the world. Most, like the CBOT, are colorful places where traders in a "pit" shout and use hand signals to communicate their buy and sell orders. Pit activity can be quite physical. Professional football players have been known to find second careers working in the pits of the CBOT and Chicago Mercantile Exchange.

Further reading

Chicago Board of Trade Web site. Available online. URL: www.cbot.com.

Chicago Mercantile Exchange

The Chicago Mercantile Exchange (CME) is a market exchange where commodity and financial FUTURES and OPTIONS contracts are bought and sold. Created in 1898 as the Chicago Butter and Egg Board, the CME is used primarily by investors, managers, and broker/dealers to reduce risk in business transactions. Traditionally farmers and other agricultural-industry members used futures contracts—agreements to buy or sell a specific amount of a commodity at a particular price on or before stipulated date—to hedge their risk. Initially the CME specialized in butter-and-egg markets, while the Chicago Board of Trade focused on grain markets. Today both exchanges offer a wide array of futures contracts as part of the CME group, including the CBOT and NYMEX.

Farmers sell futures contracts for commodities they produce, thereby assuring themselves of a price for their products. If, in the time between their sale of the futures contract and when their products are ready for market, the commodity price goes down, farmers will be able to buy back their futures contract at a lower price. They profit by the difference, offsetting the lower market price for their product. If the price goes up, they will lose money on the futures contract but will profit from the higher price in the marketplace.

The CME is regulated by the COMMODITY FUTURES TRADING COMMISSION (CFTC), created to oversee the CME and other exchanges. Until they merged in 2001, the CME, CHICAGO BOARD OF TRADE, Chicago Board of Exchange, NEW YORK MERCANTILE EXCHANGE, and other smaller regional markets competed by providing new options and futures contracts to meet the needs of financial markets and managers.

Where futures contracts obligate the buyer and seller to a specified agreement, options contracts provide the buyer or seller the right to buy or sell at a specified price. If the option is not exercised by the maturity date, it expires with the buyer losing the amount of money they paid for the option. Prices of futures and options can be quite volatile. In addition to being used by managers to reduce RISK, speculators add liquidity to commodity and futures markets and profit when they correctly anticipate price changes in the market.

Today the Chicago Mercantile Exchange facilitates trading in a wide array of agricultural, currency, interest rate, and indexes including butter, cheese, frozen pork bellies, Australian dollars, Japanese Yen, Euros, 90-day U.S. Treasury Bills, 10-year Japanese Government BONDS, STANDARD & POOR's 500 Index, Russell 2000 Stock Price Index, and even heating and cooling degree indexes.

Further reading

Chicago Mercantile Exchange Web site. Available online. URL: www.cmegroup.com.

chief executive officer

The chief executive officer (CEO) is the primary leader in an organization. Though he or she may be known by many other names, such as president, executive director, and chief administrator, the CEO's role is more or less the same. The CEO's scope of authority varies, depending on whether the organization is a CORPORATION, PARTNERSHIP, sole PROPRIETORSHIP, or nonprofit organization. In corporations or nonprofit organizations with a BOARD OF DIRECTORS, the board has controlling power of the corporation. The CEO reports to the members of the BOARD OF DIRECTORS and sometimes the CEO also serves as the president or chairman of the board.

There are no standardized lists of the major functions and responsibilities of a CEO, though there are some things almost every CEO is expected to do. A CEO is expected to be a visionary, information bearer, and decision maker. As a leader, the CEO advises the board of directors, identifies and promotes changes, and is chief motivator of the people within the organization. While the CEO rarely oversees day-to-day operations, he or she is responsible for overall design, promotion, and delivery of products and services to achieve the organization's objectives. The CEO is also expected to be a visionary, looking forward and anticipating changes needed for long-term survival and growth. CEOs are sometimes the major community spokesperson for an organization.

As a decision maker, the CEO is expected to oversee operations of the organization, implement plans, and manage HUMAN RESOURCES as well as financial and physical resources. The CEO recommends yearly budgets to the board of directors and manages resources with the guidelines determined by the board. Most CEOs are energetic, articulate, and creative thinkers and leaders, with the ability to quickly comprehend information and solve problems. Depending on the nature of the organization, CEOs may also require a technical background in addition to a sound understanding of business practices.

Further reading

"Free Management Library," The Management Assistance Program. Available online. URL: www.managementhelp.org. Accessed on February 23, 2002; Carter McNamara. "Founder's Syndrome: How Corporations Suffer—and Can Recover." Available online. URL: www.mapnp.org/library/misc/founders.htm. Accessed on February 23, 2002; "Organization Management Theory," Academy of Management. Available online. URL: www.aom.pace.edu/omt. Accessed on February 27, 2002.

—Leah Kninde Frazier-Gaskins

chief financial officer

The chief financial officer (CFO), the highest-ranking financial executive of an organization, is responsible for all financial operations. The CFO oversees the preparation of budgets, treasury, internal AUDITING, forecasts, and qualitative information analysis for MANAGEMENT decisions; provides leadership to the financial services group; and contributes to the objectives of firm. The financial function includes internal and external reporting, treasury and tax matters, CAPITAL financing; contractual relations; the development of sound financial management systems and the management of investor/Wall Street relations.

Reporting to the CFO are the controller and treasurer, key leaders in the financial services group. The controller is the chief accounting executive who directs internal accounting programs, including cost accounting, systems and procedures, data processing, acquisitions analysis, and financial planning. The treasurer is concerned with the receipt, custody, INVESTMENT, disbursement, and protection of corporate funds and determines the ultimate cash position for the company. In smaller firms there may be an overlap of CFO and controller/treasurer responsibilities. While the CFO oversees the financial aspects of a business, the Chief Operating Officer (COO) oversees the company's production of goods and SERVICES. The CFO reports directly to the CHIEF EXECUTIVE OFFICER (CEO), the highest-ranking official of the company.

Typically the CFO position requires a bachelor's degree in accounting; an MBA, CPA, or equivalent postgraduate work; and a minimum 10 years of relevant, progressive experience. The experience may include numerous acquisitions, equity investments, divestitures, and JOINT VENTURES, both domestically and internationally.

Today's CFO requires a much broader knowledge base than just accountancy. The CFO job description is moving away from the super-accountant stereotype and towards someone more akin to a deputy chief executive officer. The changing global business environment has driven the trend towards diversification. In addition to being a financial manager, a CFO must be a strategic thinker, communicator, and team player, and must have an understanding of information technology (IT) systems.

The CFO must have the ability to clearly articulate the financial and operational results and strategic plans of the organization in a manner appropriate to a variety of audiences, including employee groups, the financial community, members of the BOARD OF DIRECTORS, and the corporate CEO. As a strategic planner, the CFO needs to understand the interrelationships between marketing, products, and production processes as well as understand the industry (market segment) in which the business operates.

The CFO's job has become more complex and demanding, and there are few general guidelines as to what one can expect when stepping into such a position. This will depend on the company—the nature of its business and its corporate structure, management style, strategic objectives, and executive resources.

—Asta Vaichys

Children's Online Privacy Protection Act
(COPPA)

The Children's Online Privacy Protection Act (COPPA) requires the FEDERAL TRADE COMMISSION (FTC) to issue and enforce a rule regarding children's online privacy. Effective since 2000, the rule is designed to give parents control over what information is collected from their children online and how such information may be used. COPPA does not protect children from what information is available to them, only what information is collected from them.

The online privacy rule requires Web site operators to:

- Post a privacy policy on the home page of the Web site and link to the privacy policy on every page where personal information is collected.
- Provide notice about the site's information collection practices to parents and obtain verifiable parental consent before collecting personal information from children.
- Give parents a choice as to whether their child's personal information will be disclosed to third parties.

- Provide parents access to their child's personal information and the opportunity to delete the child's personal information and opt out of future collection or use of the information.
- Not condition a child's participation in a game, contest, or other activity on the child's disclosing more personal information than is reasonably necessary to participate in that activity.
- Maintain the confidentiality, security, and integrity of personal information collected from children.

The COPPA rule applies to:

- Operators of commercial Web sites and online services directed to children under 13 years of age that collect personal information from them;
- Operators of general audience sites that knowingly collect personal information from children under 13; and
- Operators of general audience sites that have a separate children's area and that collect personal information from children under 13.

The COPPA rule sets out a number of factors for determining whether a Web site is direct to children, including whether its subject matter and language are child-oriented, whether it uses animated characters, and whether advertising on the site is directed to children. Web site owners who violate COPPA rules can be held liable for civil penalties of up to $11,000 per violation.

To encourage active industry self-regulation, COPPA also included a safe harbor provision allowing industry groups and others to request FTC approval of self-regulatory guidelines to govern participating Web sites' compliance with the rule. By 2009, four self-regulation programs had been approved, including:

- The Better Business Bureau's Children's Advertising Review Unit, Safe Harbor Program
- Division of the Entertainment Software Rating Board (ESRB) ESRB Privacy Online program
- TRUSTe's "Children's Seal Program Requirements"
- Privo's, PrivacyLock privacy assurance system

COPPA is sometimes confused with COPA, the Child Online Protection Act, enacted in 1998, which sought to prohibit online sites from knowingly making "harmful" material available to minors. COPA was challenged under First Amendment guarantees and was found unconstitutional in 2004.

Further reading
Federal Trade Commission Web site. Available online. URL: www.ftc.gov.

churning

Churning is excessive trading in an investor's portfolio to generate commissions for the stockbroker. Sometimes brokers or INVESTMENT advisors are given discretionary authority over an investor's account. Many investors do not want to or do not have the knowledge necessary to actively manage their investments. These investors will often entrust their investment CAPITAL to a broker, giving him or her general instructions about their investment objectives. With discretionary authority a broker can move a client's funds into different investments in order to take advantage of market opportunities. During the DOT-COM era of the 1990s, many brokerage houses allocated shares of INITIAL PUBLIC OFFERINGS (IPOs) to only their best customers. Some investors gave discretionary authority in order to get their broker to include them in these hot-issue stocks.

Churning is illegal; SECURITIES AND EXCHANGE COMMISSION Rule 10b-5 can be the basis for claims for state and federal securities FRAUD, COMMON LAW fraud, NEGLIGENCE, breach of CONTRACT, and breach of fiduciary duty. Churning usually involves a large number of trades, but *large* is a debatable term. Courts often use turnover ratios, the number of times the value of the account is traded in a given time period, as a basis for determining that churning has occurred. Because churning is defined as trading that is done to benefit the broker rather than the investor, even one trade can be considered churning if it has no legitimate purpose. For example, if a broker moves a client's money from one family of MUTUAL FUNDS to another, he or she must have a good reason for doing so. This is why most brokers use written confirmation that the customer wants to switch funds in spite of the fees that will be incurred.

Brokers who churn accounts often use frequent in-and-out trades of the same stock and "wash" transactions (simultaneous or roughly simultaneous buy-and-sell transactions that nullify each other). When adjudicating a churning claim, the courts evaluate whether the broker or advisor had control over the account in the form of either discretionary authority or practical ("de facto") control. The broker or advisor has de facto control when, as a practical matter, the investor lacks the knowledge and sophistication to make his or her own independent investment decisions and instead always follows the broker's recommendations. Bruce D. Fisher and Michael J. Phillips describe a case where the broker engaged in 147 separate purchases and sales for a customer's account, resulting in over $24,000 in commissions, fees, taxes, and margin interest against an account that started with only $25,000.

In addition to churning, the other major investor complaint against stockbrokers is inappropriate recommendations. Unethical brokers often convince unsophisticated investors to purchase high-risk (and high-commission) investments ranging from real estate scams to shares in obscure foreign companies.

See also STOCK MARKET, BOND MARKET.

Further reading
Fisher, Bruce D., and Michael J. Phillips. *The Legal, Ethical and Regulatory Environment of Business.* 8th ed. Cincinnati: Thomson/South-western, 2003; Investor Recovery Web site. Available online. URL: www.investorecovery.com.

circuit breakers

Circuit breakers are preannounced policies that halt STOCK or FUTURES market trading when prices drop rapidly. During periods of uncertainty, stock and futures markets trading can be quite volatile. Circuit breakers halt trading for a period of time, allowing market participants to evaluate new information and make informed buy and sell decisions. Effectively, circuit breakers are a method to allow investors to take a deep breath and ask, "Wait a minute. What is going on here?"

Interest in circuit breakers began after the October 1987 crash when the Dow Jones Industrial Average (DJIA) fell 508 points, or 22 percent, in one day, known as Black Monday. The Securities and Exchange Commission (SEC) created circuit breakers and other policies to reduce volatility and promote investor confidence.

The New York Stock Exchange (NYSE) circuit breakers are the most widely disseminated example. Initially, the NYSE circuit breakers halted market trading when the DJIA fell by 250 points in one trading session. When instituted in 1988, this represented a 12 percent fall in the market, but, as stock market prices rose by 1997, a 250 point fall represented only a 4 percent decline in the market. Called Rule 80B, effective April 15, 1998, the SEC's Trading Halts Due to Extraordinary Market Volatility changed "triggers" so as to halt trading based on a percentage of the DJIA calculated at the beginning of each calendar quarter of a year. Rule 80B halts trading for one hour if the DJIA declines by 10 percent, two hours if the DJIA falls by 20 percent, and halts trading for the rest of the day if the average falls by 30 percent. How long trading is halted depends on when in the trading day the market falls to the circuit-breaker trigger point. For example, in the first quarter of 2009, the NYSE trigger was an 850-point decline. If the decline occurred before 2 P.M. there would be a one-hour halt, between 2 and 2:30 P.M. a 30-minute halt, and after 2:30 P.M. no halt in trading.

Whether circuit breakers are good or bad for financial markets is debatable. Opponents argue that circuit breakers impede market efficiency, not allowing prices to change. Supporters argue that they "help prevent crashes by giving people time to respond with full information." Proponents argue that halts have prevented markets dropping as they did in October 1987.

Stock prices vary due to what economists call "fundamental volatility," that is, changes in information causing changes in the value of a firm's products and assets that, in turn, cause changes in the price of the firm's stock. When stock prices reflect all information known about a firm's prospects, resources are directed to firms with positive futures and away from firms with dismal prospects. Circuit breakers may increase volatility. If traders fear a halt is about to occur, they may submit orders earlier to avoid being locked out of trading.

Circuit breakers trigger a halt in all trading in the market. On average, trading is stopped about three times per day for individual stocks on the NYSE. The most common reasons for these halts are order imbalances, news pending, and news dissemination. For example, in September 2008, the NYSE halted trading in Fannie Mae and Freddie Mac, the two largest mortgage underwriters as rumors spread of their impending bankruptcy.

Further reading
Harris, Lawrence E. "Circuit Breakers and Program Trading Limits: What Have We Learned?" Brookings-Wharton Papers on Financial Services, December 1997.

circular flow model

A circular flow model is a diagram illustrating how the major sectors in a mixed-capitalism economy fit together. Circular flow models show how the value of output equals income in an economic system. The model also demonstrates the mutual interdependence of the various participants in an economy.

The five sectors in the model are households, firms, financial intermediaries, the government, and foreign countries. Households own and determine how to allocate resources—human, capital, and natural. For example, household members decide where and how to use their labor resources; control the use of any equipment like a computer or a machine; and control the use of land, minerals, or other natural resources they own. In a noncapitalist economic system, households control only a small percentage of resources, while the government controls most resources.

In capitalist economies, households receive payments for the use of their resources from firms or the government, depending on who purchases the resource. Gross household income is the sum of resource payments received. Households with greater resources receive more income than those with fewer resources. The quality of resources also influences the amount of income received. Education, an improvement in human capital, typically results in greater income. Likewise, land with minerals, beautiful views, or a lakeside site is more valuable than barren or polluted natural resources.

Households take the resource payments they receive and primarily use this income for CONSUMPTION spending—payments to firms for products and services. Some household income is saved, usually by depositing a sum with financial intermediaries, and of course some household income is taken by government in the form of taxes.

A circular flow model shows that firms complement the actions of households. Firms purchase or rent resources, paying wages, interest, DIVIDENDS and PROFITS to households, and use the resources to produce goods and services, which are then sold to households, the government, and foreign buyers. Firms that produce goods and SERVICES most desired by consumers will receive a greater portion of the flow of payments, allowing these firms to purchase more resources, produce more goods, and, in essence, grow. Those firms that produce PRODUCTS consumers do not want or only will purchase at lower prices see their revenue decline and eventually will be forced out of business.

In a mixed-capitalism circular flow model, the government plays many roles. The government purchases resources from households and provides goods and services to both households and firms. Employing teachers is an example of a government resource purchase to provide services to households. The government taxes portions of income from both households and firms. Changes in taxation redistribute the burden of paying for government goods and services among households and between households and firms.

Financial intermediaries primarily aggregate savings from many households and provide INVESTMENT capital to firms. In the process financial intermediaries reduce investor risk through knowledge of investment alternatives and portfolio diversification. Intermediaries also adjust for the diverse needs of savers. Households have many different levels of savings and periods of time they are willing to lend their savings. The savers' time frame and dollar amount preferences are unlikely to mesh with the needs of firms borrowing funds for investment. Financial intermediaries smooth the process of lending and borrowing in financial markets.

Foreign countries, through relationships with U.S. businesses, sell products and services to American consumers and purchase products and services from U.S. firms. TRADE BALANCES measure the net impact of EXPORTING and importing in the circular flow model.

Close inspection of a circular flow model shows that for each "real" flow of resources or goods and services, there is an opposite MONEY flow. One of the major roles of MONETARY POLICY is to provide the "right" MONEY SUPPLY to facilitate exchange of resources and goods in an economy. The "right" money supply is subject to debate and constant change as an economy grows or declines.

As stated earlier, one of the uses of circular flow models is to show how the value of output equals income in an economic system. Measuring either the flow of payments (income) or the value of goods and services (output) results in an estimate of the level of economic activity in an economy (GROSS DOMESTIC PRODUCT).

The circular flow model is analogous to the circulatory system in the human body. In the economy, the efficient flow of money between savers and borrowers is provided by financial intermediation, the process of bringing borrowers and savers together via financial intermediaries. Payments for goods and services (business revenues) flow in one direction, and payments for the factors of production (household incomes) flow in the opposite direction. One's spending becomes another's income. In the human body, blood flows from the heart via arteries and to the heart via veins. Just as leakages in the human circulatory system will cause declining performance, leakages in the circular flow model hamper the spending/income process, causing declining economic performance.

Civil Aeronautics Board

The Civil Aeronautics Board (CAB) regulated the U.S. airline industry until 1984. The CAB is most widely known as the first in a series of efforts toward government DEREGULATION, reducing government rules and regulations affecting American business.

The Civil Aeronautics Act (1938) mandated government regulation to promote "adequate, economical, and efficient service by air carriers at reasonable charges, without unjust discrimination, undue preferences or advantages, or unfair or destructive competitive practices." When passed, the U.S. airline business was similar to the pharmaceutical industry before creation of the FOOD AND DRUG ADMINISTRATION (1906); anyone with an airplane could and did establish an airline, flying wherever he/she wanted to, charging whatever the market would bear, and using equipment he/she deemed air-worthy. It was a classic "free market" industry.

Concerned over the airline industry's instability, safety record, and fierce price competition, Congress chose to regulate the industry. For almost 40 years the CAB regulated prices, routes, antitrust disputes, and CONSUMER PROTECTION. In the 1960s and 1970s, led by economic theorists, particularly Alfred Kahn, U.S. politicians began to question the role of government control of transportation industries. In response, in 1978 President Carter signed the Airline Deregulation Act, phasing out the CAB's role of controlling airline routes and prices by 1984. (Other roles of the CAB were transferred to the Justice and Transportation departments.)

Airline executives fought deregulation, arguing the United States had the strongest and safest airline industry in the world. Although they predicted chaos and disaster, the CAB was dismantled, and the U.S. airline market saw a surge in COMPETITION. Many new firms jumped into the market, and existing firms expanded into new

service areas. There were both winners and losers as airlines learned how to compete and customers saw choices expand and prices decline.

Some areas with small populations saw airline service eliminated. Travel agencies, who were supported under CAB commission-fixing agreements, saw their fees cut by the airline companies. Throughout the industry, a new emphasis on marketing arose. American Airlines created the first frequent-flyer program, a practice emulated by other airlines and service industry providers. Southwest airlines is the low-cost leader and a model for many new airlines.

Further reading

Daube, Scott. "From Precept to Practice (History of Deregulation)." *Travel Weekly* 47 (30 September 1988): 47.

Civilian Conservation Corps

The Civilian Conservation Corps (CCC) was one of the most popular "New Deal" programs initiated by the Franklin Roosevelt administration during the GREAT DEPRESSION. Begun in 1933, the program eventually involved over 3 million unemployed Americans in planting trees, controlling forest fires, and building state and national parks. At the time, almost 25 percent of American workers were unemployed. The CCC and the Works Project Administration (WPA) were one of the government's stimuli to a failing economy. The idea of government stimulating economic activity during a RECESSION challenged the prevailing doctrine of CLASSICAL ECONOMICS but was strongly supported by KEYNESIAN ECONOMICS in 1936.

The CCC was operated by existing federal agencies. The DEPARTMENT OF LABOR selected participants, mostly young men and women who were unemployed. (This broke traditional barriers of engaging women in the workforce.) The Departments of Interior and Agriculture planned the work projects. Participants were provided clothing, housing, and food and paid $30 per month but were required to send home $25 of their monthly earnings.

The CCC was the model for subsequent state conservation programs as well as the National and

Community Service Trust Act enacted by President Clinton in 1993. The CCC was disbanded in 1942 due to U.S. involvement in World War II and the need for labor associated with the war effort. The results of its programs can be seen today in many state and federal parks.

Further reading
Pagan, Kathleen Waltson. "Viewpoint (Civilian Conservation Corps)." *Planning* 59 (November 1993): 46.

civil procedure

Civil procedure refers to the rules by which civil (as opposed to criminal) legal proceedings are conducted. The Federal Rules of Civil Procedure apply throughout the FEDERAL COURTS. The rules of civil procedure in state courts can vary considerably. In general, rules of civil procedure concern pretrial "discovery" of evidence, including documents, answers to interrogatories (questions), and depositions (pretrial taking of testimony under oath) of witnesses and experts. The allowance of extensive pretrial discovery in civil proceedings is almost unique to the American legal system.

Civil-procedure rules also concern the pleading (filing) of complaints, answers to complaints, motions to dismiss complaints, requests for summary judgments (pretrial judgments on the merits of the case), and rules for the conduct of civil trials by judges or juries. Since the vast majority of business disputes are settled in advance of trial, pretrial discovery is the primary point of contact for businesspeople involved in civil proceedings. Common business-law civil proceedings include products liability, CONTRACTS disputes, and EMPLOYMENT matters.

Further reading
Kane, Mary K. *Civil Procedure in a Nutshell.* 4th ed. Eagan, Minn.: West Group, 1996.

Civil Rights Acts

As defined in *Black's Law Dictionary* (7th ed.), Civil Rights Acts are "several federal statutes enacted after the Civil War (1861–1865) and, much later, during and after the Civil Rights movement of the 1950s and 1960s, and intended to implement and give further force to the basic rights guaranteed by the Constitution, and especially prohibiting discrimination in EMPLOYMENT and education on the basis of race, sex, religion, color, or age."

The Civil Rights Acts, which are often called the most important U.S. laws on civil rights since Reconstruction, were a highly controversial issue in the United States when President John F. Kennedy proposed them. Although Kennedy was unable to secure passage of the bill in Congress, a stronger version was eventually passed by his successor, President Lyndon B. Johnson, who signed the first bill into law in July 1964.

The Civil Rights movement of the 1960s resulted in some of the most significant civil-rights ruling and legislation in U.S. history. There had already been many civil-rights court cases tried in state and federal courts by mid-century, but the Supreme Court decision in *Brown v. Board of Education of Topeka Kansas* (1954) set the tone for new legislation by directly challenging the "separate but equal" principle established by the 1896 *Plessy v. Ferguson* ruling. In *Plessy* the Supreme Court had authorized separate facilities for blacks and whites as long as the facilities were equal. In the *Brown* decision, the Court challenged the earlier ruling by declaring that segregation in public schools was unconstitutional.

Beyond crucial court decisions like *Brown,* the Civil Rights movement also resulted in and benefited from new legislation in the 1960s that expanded the social and political rights of minorities and women. The Civil Rights Act of 1964 prohibited discrimination in public facilities and schools on the basis of race, religion, or national origin and mandated equal opportunities for all workers irrespective of race, religion, national origin, or gender. The Voting Rights Act of 1965 guaranteed the right to vote for all citizens who were qualified by age, thus striking down literacy requirements that had been used effectively to disenfranchise many blacks. Three years later the Civil Rights Act of 1968 outlawed racial discrimination in housing and jury selection.

The Civil Rights Act of 1964 contained specific titles with specific applications. Title I of the act guaranteed equal voting rights by removing registration requirements and procedures biased against minorities and the underprivileged. Title II prohibited segregation or discrimination in places of public accommodation involved in interstate commerce. Title III banned discrimination by trade UNIONS, schools, or employers involved in interstate commerce or doing business with the federal government. This section also applied to discrimination on the basis of sex and established a government agency, the EQUAL EMPLOYMENT OPPORTUNITY COMMISSION (EEOC), to enforce the provisions. Title IV called for the desegregation of public schools. Title V broadened the duties of the Civil Rights Commission. Title VI assured nondiscrimination in the distribution of funds under federally assisted programs. Title VII prohibited employment decisions based on stereotypes and assumptions about abilities, traits, or the performance of individuals of certain racial groups. Title VII also prohibited both intentional discrimination and neutral job policies that disproportionately exclude minorities or are not job-related.

Title 28 of the U.S. Code Sec. 1343, Civil rights and elective franchise, states that "the district courts shall have original jurisdiction over any civil action authorized by law to be commenced by any person (1) to recover DAMAGES for injury to his person or property, or because of the deprivation of any right or privilege of a citizen of the United States, by any act done in furtherance of any conspiracy mentioned in section 1985 of Title 42; (2) to recover damages from any person who fails to prevent or to aid in preventing any wrongs mentioned in section 1985 of Title 42 which he had knowledge were about to occur and power to prevent; (3) to redress the deprivation, under color of any state, law, statute, ordinance, regulation, custom or usage, of any right, privilege or immunity secured by the Constitution of the United States or by any Act of Congress providing for equal rights of citizens or of all persons within the jurisdiction of the United States; (4) to recover damages or to secure equitable or other relief under any Act of Congress providing for the protection of civil rights, including the right to vote."

—Joi Patrice Jones

Further reading

Civil Rights and Elective Franchise States, U.S. Code, vol. 28, sec. 1343; *Encyclopaedia Britannica,* 2002, "Civil Rights Act"; Garner, Bryan. ed. *Black's Law Dictionary.* 7th ed. Eagan, Minn.: West Group, 1999; "Race Color Discrimination," Equal Employment Opportunity Commission. Available online. URL: www.eeoc.gov. Accessed on June 8, 2009.

class-action lawsuits

A class action is a device where large numbers of individuals whose interests are sufficiently related may bring suit. Thus it is more efficient to adjudicate their rights or liabilities as a group in a single action than to do so in a series of separate individual suits. Most class actions are called "plaintiff class actions," although in some cases the action may be brought against a defendant class as a defendant class action.

Most class-action lawsuits are filed for compensatory (money) DAMAGES. Class actions may also be filed to resolve disputes over a "limited fund," where the money available is inadequate to fully compensate all class members. A class action may seek injunctive relief, e.g., it may be filed to request that the court order the police or other authorities to discontinue an unconstitutional practice. Another type of class action is one that seeks a declaratory judgment, a court decision in a civil case telling the parties what their rights and responsibilities are without awarding damages or ordering any action be taken.

Generally, before a court certifies a class action (determines that the suit may proceed as a class-action suit), it must conclude that there are too many class members for them all to be named as parties in the lawsuit. The claims of the "class representatives" must arise from facts or law common to the class members. In most cases, class members do not technically join in the litigation but decide to participate by not "opting out." If the constitutional and procedural protections required for fairness are met in the underlying action, all absent class members are bound to the judgment or settlement of the case. However, if the action is primarily for compensatory damages, absent class members are entitled to notice and an opportunity to opt out (exclude themselves) from the proceedings. If a person opts out, he or she is not bound by any judgment or settlement of the class action.

The complex nature of many class actions and the danger of violating the DUE PROCESS rights of absent class members have led many rule-makers to provide the trial judge with authority to control and manage numerous aspects of the lawsuit. Further, in order to provide additional protection for absent class members, class-action provisions typically require court approval of any settlement or compromise of the class claims entered into between the class representatives and the defendant.

In recent years the subject of class actions has received more attention from the legal community and the media than any other area of CIVIL PROCEDURE, and it has even inspired film producers to make award-winning movies about them. Several high-profile cases involving tobacco litigation, asbestos claims, cases involving securities FRAUD, etc., have evoked public concern and stirred considerable debate. Some individuals claim that class actions should be used with greater frequency to spur major social change, to make CORPORATIONS pay up for their follies, and to provide recourse for those who otherwise would not find it economically feasible to litigate their grievances. Others argue that class actions are being brought not to defend the public interest but to enrich attorneys, force corporations into settlement with the threat of bigger jury awards, and waste the courts' valuable resources. They point to the fact that many of the suits have been extremely burdensome and expensive for litigants, and only a few have reached the stage of judgment.

Further reading
Friedenthal, Jack H., and Arthur R. Miller. *Civil Procedure: Sum & Substance.* 4th ed. Encino, Calif.: Herbert Legal Series, 1988; Klonoff, Robert H. *Class Actions and other Multi-Party Litigation in a Nutshell.* 3rd ed. Eagan, Minn.: West Group, 2007.

classical economics
Classical economics is the macroeconomic school of thought that suggests that real GROSS DOMESTIC PRODUCT (GDP) is determined by aggregate SUPPLY, while the EQUILIBRIUM price level is determined by aggregate DEMAND. Classical economics was the predominant theory from 1776 to the introduction of KEYNESIAN ECONOMICS in 1936. Classical economics is also defined as the study of an economy operating at full EMPLOYMENT, while Keynesian analysis portrays economies operating naturally at less than full employment.

According to classical theory, a major part of the self-correcting mechanism in an economy is flexible wages and prices. With this assumption, classical economists suggest real GDP is determined by the price of resources, technology, and expectations (the factors influencing aggregate supply). Prices would adjust depending on the overall level of demand. The assumption of flexible wages and prices distinguishes classical economics from Keynesian economics.

Classical economists believe economies tend to operate at or near full employment. Using Say's law (named after French economist Jean-Baptiste Say), supply creates its own demand; hence, desired expenditures will equal actual expenditures. According to classical economics, people produce goods and services because they desire to purchase other goods and services. The act of producing is based on their desire to trade their goods and services for other products, creating demand in the economy. From this reasoning, an economy would tend toward full employment of labor and other resources. Though temporary shocks may cause excessive UNEMPLOYMENT, this would be a temporary phenomenon.

Classical economists saw the GREAT DEPRESSION as a downturn in the BUSINESS CYCLE that would self-correct. Some politicians—U.S. president Herbert Hoover, for example—accepted classical theory. During the 1930 presidential election, Hoover said the current economic condition was just a mild recession, not a depression, suggesting this was a temporary situation that would self-correct. Political cartoonists compared Hoover to the Roman emperor Nero, famous for supposedly having fiddled while Rome burned. Hoover's opponent, Franklin Delano Roosevelt, advocated government intervention, a policy supported by Keynesian economics, leading to the New Deal.

See also MACROECONOMICS.

Further reading

Miller, Roger LeRoy. *Economics Today*. 15th ed. Boston: Addison Wesley, 2009.

Clayton Antitrust Act

The Clayton Antitrust Act (1914) specified and forbade activities that reduced COMPETITION. The act expanded on antitrust policy efforts initiated by the SHERMAN ANTITRUST ACT (1890), which was considered by many to be not specific enough and open to considerable judicial interpretation. Congress passed the Clayton Act to attack practices used by monopolists to acquire MONOPOLY power. Along with the FEDERAL TRADE COMMISSION Act passed in the same year, the Clayton Act prohibited four kinds of activities that would tend to lessen competition:

- PRICE DISCRIMINATION
- exclusive dealing and tying arrangements
- Certain types of MERGERS AND ACQUISITIONS
- Interlocking company BOARD OF DIRECTORS

Section 2 of the act prohibited local and territorial price discrimination by sellers. This was a practice often used by monopolists to bankrupt small competitors. A large company would sell its products at or below cost in markets where local competitors existed and at higher prices in markets where no local competitors existed. Small competitors were often driven out of business, allowing the monopolist to raise prices in markets where local competitors no longer existed. The ROBINSON-PATMAN ACT (1936) expanded and clarified anticompetitive PRICING STRATEGIES.

Tying agreements occur when a seller refuses to sell products to a buyer unless the buyer also agrees to purchase other products from the seller. If a firm has a monopoly on a critical product or component, it could use its monopoly power to pressure buyers into purchasing other products, for which the company does not have a monopoly, from them. Tying agreements reduce competition, and can be challenged under Section 3 of the Clayton Act, or under the Sherman Act. Exclusive dealing agreements require buyers of a particular service or product to purchase the product or service only from one seller. Like tying agreements, this reduces competition.

Section 7 of the Clayton Act bars mergers and acquisitions that may have an anticompetitive effect. To evaluate the impact of a merger or acquisition requires defining the market that would be affected. While this might seem simple, defining the relevant market or line of commerce is not always easy. Especially as technological advances allow markets to converge, defining who and how many competitors exist in a market is becoming increasingly difficult. For example, in the early 1990s the long-distance telecommunications market included three major firms—AT&T, Sprint, and MCI. A merger of any of these firms would have significantly increased MARKET CONCENTRATION. However, microwave, satellite, and fiber-optic cable company technologies are redefining telecommunications, thereby redefining competition in the industry.

Section 8 of the Clayton Act was designed to reduce the potential for price fixing or division of markets through coordination by INTERLOCKING DIRECTORATES. Section 8 prohibited any person from serving as a director of two or more corporations that were or had been competitors. The Antitrust Amendments Act of 1990 expanded the limitations on interlocking directorates by prohibiting individuals from serving as officers and/or directors of competing corporations.

See also ANTITRUST LAW.

Further reading

Mallor, Jane P., A. James Barnes, Thomas Bowers, Michael J. Philips, and Arlen W. Langvardt. *Business*

Law: The Ethical, Global, and E-Commerce Environment. 14th ed. Boston: McGraw-Hill, 2009.

Clean Air Acts

The Clean Air Acts (1970, 1977, and 1990) initiated and then revised a variety of programs to reduce air pollution in the country. The acts require the ENVIRONMENTAL PROTECTION AGENCY (EPA) to set national health-based air-quality standards to protect against ozone depletion, sulfur emissions, carbon monoxide, lead, and other air-borne pollutants. The 1990 revisions created the first attempt at market-based systems, POLLUTION RIGHTS, to address air pollution.

According to former U.S. senator Edmund Muskie, "the Clean Air Act of 1970 defined the air pollution control program we have today. . . . In the 1960s, air pollution was widely perceived as a Los Angeles smog problem. . . . Earth Day occurred during the [1970] hearings. That summer, Washington suffered the worst and longest air pollution episode in its history. . . . Three fundamental principles shaped the 1970 law . . . protection of public health . . . industry should be required to apply the best technology . . . American people deserved to know when they could expect their health to be protected." The 1970 act established regulations of the auto industry and allowed citizens to file lawsuits against violators.

The 1970 act and subsequent revisions have been controversial. Industry groups—including oil companies, coal producers, service station operators and land developers—have often opposed the acts. Various groups have intervened to delay and change Clean Air Act statutes.

The acts require states to carry out most of the monitoring and permitting of air pollutants. States are required to develop implementation plans to meet the various criteria defined in the act. Through the EPA, the federal government provides research engineering designs and financial support for state implementation plans.

Some of the specific measures in the Clean Air Act include

- *Ozone.* The 96 cities failing for ozone are ranked from *marginal* to *extreme,* with the more severe cases required to institute more rigorous controls but given more time to attain them. States may have to initiate or upgrade inspection/maintenance (I/M) programs, install vapor recovery at gas stations and otherwise reduce hydrocarbon emissions from small stationary sources, and adopt transportation controls that will offset growth in vehicle miles traveled. Major stationary sources of nitrogen oxides will have to reduce emissions.
- *Carbon monoxide.* The 41 cities failing for carbon monoxide are ranked *moderate* or *serious.* States may have to initiate or upgrade I/M and adopt transportation controls.
- *Particulate matter.* The 72 areas failing to attain for particulate matter (PM-10) are ranked *moderate.* States will have to implement reasonably available control technology (RACT), and use of wood stoves and fireplaces may have to be curtailed.

The Clean Air Amendments of 1977 primarily established federal standards for various pollutants and regulation of emissions through state implementation plans. The 1977 act also defined Class I, II, and III areas restricting particulate emissions in the most polluted (Class I) areas.

The 1990 act required all air-pollution-control obligations of an individual source to be contained in a single five-year operating permit. States have three years to develop permit programs and submit them to the EPA, which has one year to issue regulations describing the minimum requirements for such programs. Sources must pay permit fees to the states to cover the costs of operating the programs. The 1990 act also addresses

- *Vehicle emissions.* Tailpipe emissions of hydrocarbons, carbon monoxide, and nitrogen oxides were to be cut beginning with the 1994 model year, and standards would have to be maintained over a longer vehicle life. On-board charcoal canisters to absorb evaporative emissions may be required.
- *Fuels.* In 1995 reformulated gasolines having less aromatics were to have been introduced in the nine cities with the worst ozone problems; other

cities could "opt in." Beginning in 1992, oxyfuel gasolines blended with alcohol were to have been sold in winter in those cities having the worst carbon-monoxide problems.

- *Clean cars.* In 1996 a pilot program was introduce 150,000 cars to California that met tighter emission limits through a combination of vehicle technology and "clean" fuels (substitutes for gasoline or blends of substitutes with gasoline). Other states could "opt in."

According to the 1990 act, emissions of 189 toxic pollutants—typically carcinogens, mutagens, and reproductive toxins—had to be reduced within 10 years. The EPA was to publish a list of source categories within one year and issue Maximum Achievable Control Standards (MACT) for each category over a specified timetable. Companies that initiated partial controls before the deadlines set for MACT could receive extensions.

A two-phase, market-based system (pollution rights) was introduced to reduce sulfur-dioxide emissions from power plants. Electrical power plants account for approximately 70 percent of sulfur dioxide emissions. By the year 2000, total annual emissions were to be capped at 8.9 million tons, a reduction of 10 million tons from 1980 levels. Plants are issued allowances based on fixed emission rates set in the law and on their previous fossil-fuel use. Companies pay penalties if emissions exceed the allowances they hold. Allowances can be banked or traded. All sources are required install continuous emission monitors to assure compliance.

The 1990 act was rooted in the MONTREAL PROTOCOL, an international air-pollution agreement for restrictions on the use, emissions, and disposal of chemicals. It phased out production of chlorofluorocarbons (CFCs), carbon tetrachloride, and methyl chloride by 2000 and methyl chloroform by 2002; and it limited production of CFCs in 2015, phasing them out in 2030. Companies servicing air conditioning for cars were required to purchase certified recycling. The act mandated warning labels on all containers and products (e.g., refrigerators, foam insulation) that enclose CFCs and other ozone-depleting chemicals.

The Clean Air Acts have significantly impacted business in the United States and air quality in the country. According to the Clean Air Trust, a nonprofit organization established by former U.S. senators Edmund Muskie (Maine) and Robert Stafford (Vermont), the Clean Air Acts have been a "tremendous success." Lead emissions have been reduced by 98 percent primarily through removal of lead from gasoline in 1978. Emissions of sulfur dioxide (acid rain) and carbon monoxide emissions both decreased by 37 percent between 1987 and 1996.

Businesses have been required or motivated through pollution rights to change technology, production methods, disposal practices, and emissions levels. Changes in automobile technology, emissions from production processes, and smokestack emissions are examples of business responses to Clean Air act requirements. While not all goals have been achieved, as Senator Muskie stated, "[I]t was an 'experimental law.' It used innovative approaches to achieve the desired results on a more timely basis than provided under any previous law."

Further reading

"The Clean Air Act Amendments of 1990." Available online. URL: www.epa.gov/oar/cac/overview.text; Edmund S. Muskie. "NEPA to CERCLA The Clean Air Act: A Commitment to Public Health," Clean Air Trust Web site. Available online. URL: www.cleanairtrust. org./nepa2cercla.html.

Clean Water Act

Growing public awareness of water pollution and concern for controlling it led to enactment of the Federal Water Pollution Control Act Amendments of 1972. After being amended in 1977, this law became commonly known as the Clean Water Act, which established the basic structure for regulating discharges of pollutants into U.S. waters. It gave the ENVIRONMENTAL PROTECTION AGENCY (EPA) the authority to implement pollution-control programs such as setting wastewater standards for industry. The Clean Water Act continued requirements to set water-quality standards for all contaminants in surface waters, making it unlawful for any person to discharge any pollutant from a point source into navigable waters unless a permit was obtained under its provisions. It also provided billions of dollars for the construction of sewage treatment plants under a construction-grants program and recognized the need for planning to address the critical problems posed by non-point source pollution.

Subsequent laws modified some of the earlier Clean Water Act provisions. Revisions in 1981 streamlined the municipal construction-grants process, improving the capabilities of treatment plants built under the program. Changes in 1987 phased out the construction-grants program, replacing it with the State Water Pollution Control Revolving Fund, more commonly known as the Clean Water State Revolving Fund. This new funding strategy addressed water-quality needs by building on EPA-state partnerships. Other provisions in the 1987 revisions created programs to protect estuaries and focused attention on urban runoff issues.

For many communities, funding through the Clean Water Act facilitated needed construction of wastewater treatment centers both for community health and ECONOMIC DEVELOPMENT potential. When businesses look to create or relocate production facilities, wastewater treatment infrastructure is often a necessary component in those decisions.

Further reading
Environmental Protection Agency Web site. Available online. URL: www.epa.gov.

closed-end fund (CEF)
A closed-end fund, legally known as a closed-end company, is a mutual fund with a limited number of shares. Closed-end funds (CEFs) sell stock in the beginning to raise capital through an IPO, or initial public offering, and then, after that, no stock is sold directly from the company. These shares are held for a determined amount of time before they may be sold. The stockholder cannot sell the stock any time he wishes as he can through an open-end fund. The stock is later traded on the secondary markets and the price will fluctuate throughout the day according to market forces, meaning that at times the stock might sell for less than or more than the net asset value of the fund. Closed-end funds are regulated by the Investment Company Act of 1940, the Securities Act of 1933, and the Securities Exchange Act of 1934. The majority of closed-end funds are bond funds. The different types of closed-end funds include municipal bond funds, U.S. taxable funds, diversified U.S. equity funds, sector and specialty funds, global and international funds, and single country funds.

Closed funds are sometimes confused with closed-end funds because of the similar name. A closed fund generally refers to a mutual or open-end fund that is no longer selling new shares of stock for whatever reason. A closed-end fund, on the other hand, sells only a fixed number of shares of stock and will not create new shares to sell later on. Closed-end funds are generally a long-term investment, in some cases with stock being passed down from one generation to the next.

Further reading
Closed-End Fund Association. Available online. URL: www.closed-endfunds.com/Learn/Content/CEFBasics/ceftypes.fs Accessed on June 29, 2009. Closed-end Fund. Investopedia. Available online. URL: www.investopedia.com/terms/c/closed-endinvestment.asp Accessed on June 29, 2009. Closed-End Funds. In U.S. Securities and Exchange Commission Web site. Available online. URL: www.sec.gov/answers/mfclose.htm. Accessed on June 29, 2009.

—Robert Amerson

closely held corporation
A closely held or closed CORPORATION is a firm whose COMMON STOCK is owned by only a few individuals (often management) and is not publicly traded. PROPRIETORSHIPS and PARTNERSHIPS that eventually adopt the corporate form of organization often remain as closely held corporations with the original owners as the only stockholders. LEVERAGED BUYOUTS also result in firms being closely held.

In contrast are publicly owned corporations, large companies whose stocks are widely owned and are traded publicly. Usually closed corporations and publicly owned corporations are subject to the same state corporation laws. Many states, however, allow closed corporations greater autonomy in the operation of their business affairs than is granted to public corporations. For example, a closely held corporation may be allowed to operate without a BOARD OF DIRECTORS and be managed as if it were a partnership. The Close Corporation Supplement to the MODEL BUSINESS CORPORATION ACT (MBCA) allows SHAREHOLDERS in closely held corporations to have the same dissolution powers as partners in a partnership.

Closely held corporations may also institute supermajority voting requirements and restrictions on managerial discretion of the board of directors. Since most closely held corporations involve owner-managers, with some owners having more voting rights than others, sometimes closely held corporations establish rules such as requiring a three-fourths majority, unanimous approval to terminate owner-employees, or restricting management from reducing company DIVIDENDS.

See also STOCK MARKET.

Further reading
Mallor, Jane P., A. James Barnes, Thomas Bowers, Michael J. Philips, and Arlen W. Langvardt. *Business Law: The Ethical, Global, and E-Commerce Environment.* 14th ed. Boston: McGraw-Hill, 2009.

Coalition for Environmentally Responsible Economies
The Coalition for Environmentally Responsible Economies (CERES) is a group of environmental, investor, and advocacy groups coordinating efforts to promote sustainable development practices. (Ceres was the name of the Roman goddess of fertility and agriculture.) CERES is most known for its 10 principles, a 10-point code of environmental conduct. Companies that commit to these principles agree to "an ongoing process of continuous improvement, dialogue and comprehensive, systematic public reporting." Following are CERES' 10 principles.

Protection of the Biosphere We will reduce and make continual progress toward eliminating the release of any substance that may cause environmental damage to the air, water, or the earth or its inhabitants. We will safeguard all habitats affected by our operations and will protect open spaces and wilderness, while preserving biodiversity.

Sustainable Use of Natural Resources We will make sustainable use of renewable natural resources, such as water, soils and forests. We will conserve non-renewable natural resources through efficient use and careful planning.

Reduction and Disposal of Wastes We will reduce and where possible eliminate waste through source reduction and recycling. All waste will be handled and disposed of through safe and responsible methods.

Energy Conservation We will conserve energy and improve the energy efficiency of our internal operations and of the goods and services we sell. We will make every effort to use environmentally safe and sustainable energy sources.

Risk Reduction We will strive to minimize the environmental, health and safety risks to our employees and the communities in which we operate through safe technologies, facilities and operating procedures, and by being prepared for emergencies.

Safe Products and Services We will reduce and where possible eliminate the use, manufacture or sale of products and services that cause environmental damage or health or safety hazards. We will inform our customers of the environmental impacts of our products or services and try to correct unsafe use.

Environmental Restoration We will promptly and responsibly correct conditions we have caused that endanger health, safety or the environment. To the extent feasible, we will redress injuries we have caused to persons or damage we have caused to the environment and will restore the environment.

Informing the Public We will inform in a timely manner everyone who may be affected by conditions caused by our company that might endanger health, safety or the environment. We will regularly seek advice and counsel through dialogue with persons in communities near our facilities. We will not take any action against employees for reporting dangerous incidents or conditions to management or to appropriate authorities.

Management Commitment We will implement these Principles and sustain a process that ensures that the BOARD OF DIRECTORS and CHIEF EXECUTIVE OFFICER are fully informed about pertinent environmental issues and are fully responsible for environmental policy. In selecting our Board of Directors, we will consider demonstrated environmental commitment as a factor.

Audits and Reports We will conduct an annual self-evaluation of our progress in implementing these Principles. We will support the timely creation of generally accepted environmental audit procedures. We will annually complete the CERES Report, which will be made available to the public.

CERES was established in 1988 when the Board of the Social Investment Forum, an association of investment firms and pension funds supporting SOCIALLY RESPONSIBLE INVESTING, formed an alliance with environmental organizations. A year later the group created the 10 principles and began asking CORPORATIONS to endorse them.

Initially only environmentally friendly companies adopted the principles, but in 1993 Sonoco became the first Fortune 500 company to endorse them. By 2009 over 100 organizations and 80 companies have endorsed the principles, including 13 Fortune 500 companies, all of whom have benefited from endorsement of their companies. The coalition monitors the practices of participating companies to ensure compliance with the principles. As reported in a *Wall Street Journal* article, the relationship between CERES and major companies is not always harmonious.

The unlikely relationship between General Motors Corp. and the Coalition for Environmen-

tally Responsible Economies . . . resulted in GM decreasing pollution at some of its factories—a step that the company says is saving money by cutting energy bills and precluding expensive government-mandated cleanups. The tie also sheltered the auto giant from some criticism of its environmental record. Along the way, the collaboration became a high-profile example of a growing trend within the environmental movement: using quiet negotiation rather than noisy protest to change boardroom behavior.

Further reading

Ball, Jeffrey. "Rocky Road: After Long Détente, GM, Green Group Are at Odds Again," *Wall Street Journal,* 30 July 2002; CERES Web site. Available online. URL: www.ceres.org. Accessed on June 8, 2009.

Coase theorem

The Coase theorem suggests that when negotiation regarding an externality is possible, bargaining will lead to an economically efficient outcome regardless of which party initially controls the PROPERTY RIGHTS. Externalities are costs or benefits that affect people who are not part of that particular market. The standard economic textbook example is of people whose drinking water is polluted by an upstream manufacturer. ECONOMIC EFFICIENCY is a situation in which no one in society can be made better off without making someone else worse off. Named after Nobel Prize–winning economist Robert Coase, the theorem has been used to support market solutions for controlling pollution and other business activities that affect parties other than the buyer and seller of the product in question.

In 1959 Coase developed his theory in a dispute over the regulation of radio frequencies. At the time, competing radio stations would sometimes interfere with each other's broadcasts by using the same radio frequency. The problem was lack of clearly defined property rights. Each station owned a radio frequency in a market, but, with increasingly powerful broadcasting equipment, each could expand into new markets. Coase argued that it did not matter which station received the right to expand its broadcasting territory, through negotiation the station that could benefit the most from the right to broadcast would end up with that right, leading to economic efficiency. If the initial rights were given to the station that could make the best use of them, it would not be willing to sell those rights for an amount equal to the value to the other station. If the initial rights were given to the station that could not use them to their highest value, through negotiation it would sell those rights to the other station. This is referred to as the invariance thesis.

Implicit in the Coase theorem are the assumption that property rights can be defined and transferred and the assumption that transaction costs are negligible. Numerous tort law cases have been fought over who owns what rights, and often transaction costs can be significant. Economists William Boyes and Michael Melvin define the Coase theorem as: "the idea that if people can negotiate with one another at no cost over the right to perform activities that cause externalities, they will always arrive at an efficient solution."

Further reading

Boyes, William, and Michael Melvin. *Microeconomics.* 7th ed. Florence, Ky.: Cengage, 2009.

code of ethics

The written formalized statement of professional responsibilities is in aggregate called a "code of ethics." Any group organized or chartered to provide a product, service, or oversight of a service may define what are the proper means of production or uses of that service and, in so doing, define what an endorsement by that group or body means. This can be either voluntary or mandated by societal expectations or government. Ethics as here defined is not a code of laws or morals; rather, it is a compilation of acceptable behavior within that group's purview. In business, groups involved in activities such as design, acquisition, manufacture, transport, sale, marketing, government interaction of a trade group, final distribution, and use of a product or service may choose to define their own code of ethical behavior. Special statements

of responsibility and appropriate expectations are included in ethical codes of some professions charged with extraordinary service. Therefore, codes can govern such things as intellectual property, human resource management, use of natural resources, consumer safety, professional behavior, and government oversight.

At times, a code of ethics may be more easily structured by stating what is not acceptable behavior or practice. Possibly the most famous code of ethics of this type is Google's code of conduct "Don't be evil." A code is a group promulgation of what is a proper guide for the decision making and behaviors of members and what outside interested parties might expect as norms of activity. A code of ethics does not consider morality or a theoretical philosophy of ethics. Nor is it concerned with concepts of virtue and hierarchical approaches to the human condition. Rather, it defines what is acceptable and obligates members of the group, or those seeking inclusion or endorsement by the group, to a standard of behavior within the norms or "ethics" of the group code. It is definitional, therefore normative and practical.

Codes are constructed for the benefit of members and those parties who are anticipated to interact with loyalty to and respect for the credibility of a mission defined, in part, by the code of ethics. Without a sophisticated form of government, empowering some societal interpersonal expectations and decorum, ethical codes are unlikely to influence members' behavior. Conflicts may occur between ethical standards of competing groups. For example, a business may have goals of performance for its MANAGEMENT that are at odds with those of employees, the environment, or governmental interests. These potential conflicts can be regarded as "risks." Risk assessment personnel have the responsibility to identify conflicts before they become problematic and to work toward reconciliation of competing standards of performance by strategizing how things are approached or presented while maintaining the goals of the organization's mission statement and "code of ethics." In addition to "risk" or "compliance" review, organizations and governments have boards of review, or ethics commissions, to investigate conflicts and violations of the published, and, by extension, at times, intent of ethical codes of standards. Those on review boards of ethics usually are vetted for past compliance and any conflict of interest before appointment.

Noncompliance with the standards as they are publicly stated results in sanctions, which may include censure by the group, withdrawal of endorsement of that group, or referral to civil or criminal authorities. Examples of ethics codes violations include real estate brokers falsifying credit reports, physicians charging for services not performed, and manufacturers knowingly using inferior or hazardous material and false advertising.

Further reading

Google Code of Conduct. Available online. URL: investor.google.com/conduct.html. Accessed on December 31, 2009.

—Richard Fitzgerald

collection agencies

Collection agencies are private businesses that attempt to collect payments due to other firms from either consumers or businesses. Because collection agencies receive a significant percentage of amounts collected, typically creditors attempt to contact and collect debts directly rather than resort to use of a collection agency. Larger companies maintain debt collection departments or subsidiaries. Until recently, most debt collectors represented creditors, acting as "third-party agents," and in return received a fixed fee or percentage of the total amount recovered from the debtor. Today, many debt collection agencies purchase debts from creditors for a fraction of the amount owed and pursue the debtor for the full balance owed. Creditors typically are not specialists in debt collection and choose to sell debts to an agency to remove them from their accounts receivable, taking the difference between the amount received from the collection agency and the full value of the debt as a write-off.

In the United States, collection agencies have long had a reputation as "nefarious characters" that would trick, deceive, or intimidate consumers into making payments. Since 1977, collection agencies in the United States have been generally governed by the Fair Debt Collection Practices Act (FDCPA), administered by the FEDERAL TRADE COMMISSION. Many collection agencies belong to the ACA International, an industry trade group that promotes members' interests but also agrees to standards of behavior. In addition, many state and local governments have licensing and other regulations affecting collection agencies.

Before enactment of FDCPA, collection agencies were known to threaten, use obscene language, call in the middle of the night, and publicize the names of debtors to obtain payment. The act states: "a debt collector may not use any false, deceptive, or misleading representation or means in connection with the collection of any debt." Violations of the FDCPA can result in levying fines against the collection agency. In extreme cases, criminal proceedings have been pursued against debt collectors and damages awarded to debtors.

Rather than attempting to intimidate debtors, many collection agents use a "soft approach," attempting to first create a dialogue and offering to help people work out a solution to the debt owed. They may offer a payment plan or a discount on the principle amount that is owed. Knowing that collection agencies report debts owed to credit reporting agencies can influence consumers to make payments.

Executors of estates sometimes find the deceased person they represent had debts. Criminals have been known to scam relatives, presenting false debt claims. Relatives of deceased people are usually under no obligation to pay off the debts of the deceased with their own funds, but the deceased person's estate can be encumbered to pay off such debts.

Further reading

ACA International. Available online. URL: www.acainternational.org.; Fair Debt and Collections Act. Federal Trade Commission. Available online. URL: www.ftc.gov/bcp/edu/pubs/consumer/credit/cre27.pdf.

collective bargaining

Collective bargaining is the process through which representatives of UNIONS and management negotiate a labor agreement. The WAGNER ACT (National Labor Relations Act, 1935) defines collective bargaining as follows.

> For the purpose of (this act) to bargain collectively is the performance of the mutual obligation of the employer and the representative of the employees to meet at reasonable times and confer in good faith with respect to wages, hours, and terms and conditions of employment, or the negotiation of an agreement, or any question arising there under, and the execution of a written contract incorporating any agreement reached if requested by either party, but such obligation does not compel either party to agree to proposal or require the making of a concession.

This definition means that both labor and management are required by law to negotiate wages, hours, and conditions of EMPLOYMENT "in good faith"—that is, both sides are negotiating, putting forth proposals, and responding to proposals with counter proposals, though neither side is required to agree with what is proposed by the other side. Collective bargaining is seen by some economists as a countervailing force against the power of huge CORPORATIONS.

Through much of the early history of the United States, the few unions that existed had limited power to represent workers. Courts frequently treated unions as illegal criminal conspiracies and often sanctioned the use of police to counter union activity. In the early 20th century, with the expansion of industrialization in America, union membership grew and federal legislation began to recognize the rights of workers to organize and be represented by collective bargaining.

The Wagner Act was the third in a series of acts expanding the power of organized labor. In 1926 Congress passed the Railway Labor Act, regulating labor relations in the railroad industry. The NORRIS-LAGUARDIA ACT (1932) limited the circumstances in which FEDERAL COURTS could enjoin strikes and picketing in labor disputes and also prohibited federal-court enforcement of "yellow-dog" contracts (under which employees agreed not to join or remain a member of a union). The Wagner Act created the NATIONAL LABOR RELATIONS BOARD (NLRB), gave workers the right to organize and bargain collectively, and prohibited certain labor practices that were perceived to discourage collective bargaining, including

- interfering with employees' rights to form, join, and assist labor unions
- dominating or interfering with the formation or administration of a labor union
- discriminating against employees in hiring, tenure, or any term of employment due to their union membership
- discrimination against employees because they have filed charges or given testimony under the National Labor Relations Act (NLRA)
- refusing to bargain collectively with any duly designated employee representative

The NLRB and numerous court decisions have interpreted what is good-faith collective bargaining and what items are mandatory, permissible, and legal in collective-bargaining negotiations. ARBITRATION and mediation are often used to resolve collective bargaining disputes. The TAFT-HARTLEY ACT (Labor-Management Relations Act, 1947) rewrote NLRA powers, making secondary BOYCOTTS an illegal labor tactic, but also increased enforcement of collective-bargaining agreements.

In the 1980s, changes in the makeup of the NLRB reduced union power in collective-bargaining agreements. In the *NLRB v. Bildisco* (1984) case, the Supreme Court upheld a decision that employers may file a Chapter 11 bankruptcy petition and immediately break an existing collective-bargaining agreement without first communicating with the union. Congress then changed the bankruptcy code, requiring companies to consult with unions before using bankruptcy relief from collective-bargaining agreements. Bruce Fisher and Michael Phillips write "The Supreme Court has ruled that employers may shut down a plant permanently without committing an unfair labor practice, "provided the employer does not have the intent to discourage unionization elsewhere." Similarly, court decisions have addressed whether a successor company is liable for a collective bargaining agreement reached by the previous owners. Fisher and Phillips summarize the *NLRB v. Burns International Security Services* (1987) case, in which the NLRB ruled that "although the new employer is not bound by the substantive provisions of the predecessor's bargaining agreement, it has an obligation to bargain with the union so long as it is in fact a successor to the old employer and the majority of its employees were employed by the predecessor."

Employers can be charged with "Boulwareism," a violation of the duty to bargain in good faith. Named after a General Electric executive, Fisher and Phillips define Boulwareism as "an employer's careful study of all bargaining issues before meeting the union, and presenting its best offer to the union immediately on a take-it-or-leave-it basis." This process suggests a "closed-mind" attitude that violates good-faith collective bargaining.

Further reading
Dessler, Gary. *Human Resource Management.* 11th ed. Upper Saddle River, N.J.: Prentice Hall, 2007; Fisher, Bruce D., and Michael J. Phillips. *The Legal, Ethical and Regulatory Environment of Business.* 4th ed. Eagan, Minn.: West Publishing, 1992; Mallor, Jane P., A. James Barnes, Thomas Bowers, Michael J. Philips, and Arlen W. Langvardt. *Business Law: The Ethical, Global, and E-Commerce Environment.* 14th ed. Boston: McGraw-Hill, 2009.

collusion
Collusion is an agreement between two or more parties in an effort to fraud or deceive. Collusion is often practiced to coordinate efforts among firms, effectively lessening the degree of competition among them. As a result, collusion can be found in many areas of commerce.

An interlocking directorate, where a director sits on the boards of competing corporations, is an example of collusion. Because interlocking directorates facilitate the flow of information between competing firms, this exchange of knowledge reduces the competition between the two firms. The result is that the relationship between the two firms becomes more cooperative and coordinated and less competitive. Because interlocking directorates lead to more concentrated (more monopolistic or less competitive) market conditions, they have been made illegal (Clayton Act, 1914).

Collusion occurs most often in oligopolistic market structures, where markets or industries are made up of only a few firms. The output of these markets is concentrated in only a few firms, making the actions of each firm much more significant than if these markets were competitive, that is, comprised of many firms. Oligopoly, the presence of only a few firms in an industry, provides an optimal climate for collusion; it is much easier to monitor the actions of a few competitors than it is to keep an eye on many firms.

Overt and covert agreements are common in oligopolies. They take the form of social gatherings among the industry leaders, trade association conventions, and lists of representative prices. The goal of each of these practices is to facilitate the exchange of information among the competing firms in the industry. Price leadership is also common, either in the form of the dominant firm being the price leader or the more subtle form of collusive price leadership. As stated by economist F. M. Scherer, "industry members must recognize that their common interest in cooperative pricing behavior overrides any centrifugal aspirations toward independent behavior."

The most overt form of collusion is the cartel. A cartel is formed when a group of previously competing firms or countries organizes to set prices and control aggregate output from its members. Rather than competing against each other, the members now cooperate and their actions are coordinated. The United States' motto is "E pluribus unum," translated "from many, one." It portrays one nation formed from many states. The same idea applies to a cartel. Where there once were many competitors, now there is the cartel of once-competing members. OPEC, the Organization of Petroleum Exporting Countries, and De

Beers, the diamond cartel, are examples of successful cartels.

In general, because collusion leads to more market concentration rather than market competition, most forms of collusion have been made illegal in the U.S. The Sherman Antitrust Act (1890) and the Clayton Act (1914), and a few other acts outlaw various forms of cooperation and collusion. These acts attempt to discourage anti-competitive practices improve and, thus, market performance.

Further reading
Scherer, F. M. *Industrial Market Structure and Economic Performance.* Chicago: Rand McNally, 1970.

Commerce Business Daily

Commerce Business Daily (CBD) is a federal government publication that lists notices of proposed government procurement actions, contract awards, sales of government property, and other procurement information. A daily publication, CBD usually contains 500–1,000 notices, each of which appears only once.

The U.S. government is the single largest purchaser of goods and SERVICES in the nation, buying approximately $1 trillion of products and services each year. Selling to the government can be an important part of a firm's business operations, and the CBD is its major source of information. Many businesses pay service companies to monitor the CBD and alert them when procurement notices are listed in their areas of interest. Selling to the government can be daunting, since government procurement often involves considerable paperwork and understanding a distinct coding system.

The idea behind the CBD is that, by using this form of public notice, the government increases companies' access to its procurement, improving openness and increasing competition to supply to the government. Only procurement actions and CONTRACT awards over $25,000 are listed in the CBD. Certain procurement activities are not reported, including classified services and supplies and those needed for an emergency. The CBD can be found in federal depository libraries and online.

Further reading
Commerce Business Daily Web site. Available online. URL: cbdnet.gpo.gov.

commerce clause

Section 8 of the U.S. Constitution grants Congress the power to "regulate commerce with foreign nations and among the several states, and with the Indian tribes." This section is referred to as the "commerce clause." Originally Congress was given this power in order to block protectionist state restrictions. The original 13 states were, in many ways, like small, independent countries and, without the commerce clause, could have chosen to restrict IMPORTS from other states. For example, for over 100 years New Jersey financed its state government by levying a transport tax on wagons moving goods from Philadelphia to New York.

The U.S. Supreme Court has indicated in recent decades that Congress has broad authority to regulate commerce under the commerce clause, and that even internal state commerce affecting interstate commerce can be regulated. Many federal statutes, including some civil-rights laws, are constitutionally based on the commerce clause. As a practical matter, the commerce clause, in conjunction with the supremacy clause, supports the common economic market of the United States by minimizing state regulatory TRADE BARRIERS.

Congressional regulation of U.S. foreign commerce, which has been much more controversial, is discussed under EXTRATERRITORIAL JURISDICTION.

Further reading
Engdahl, David E. *Constitutional Federalism in a Nutshell.* Eagan, Minn.: West Group, 1987.

commercial law

Commercial law concerns the sale and distribution of goods, the financing of credit transactions on the security of goods sold, and legal documents related to such transactions (NEGOTIABLE INSTRUMENTS). In the United States, most state commercial law is governed by the widely adopted UNIFORM COMMERCIAL CODE (UCC). The UCC was heavily influenced by civil law commercial code principles, particularly from Germany via Professor Karl Llewellyn.

Article 2 of the UCC details the law of commercial sales contract formation (offer, counteroffer, acceptance), contract excusal (unforeseen circumstances, force majeure), interpretation of CONTRACTS, and contract-breach remedies (DAMAGES, performance orders). Article 2A concerns lease contracts, their formation, effects, performance, DEFAULT, and remedies. Article 3 of the UCC governs "negotiable instruments" (transferable documents representing title to goods). Article 4 deals with bank deposits and collections, Article 4A with the transfer of funds. Article 5 covers the LETTER OF CREDIT, a bank-issued financing device common to international sales transactions. Article 6 governs bulk sales, Article 7 warehouse receipts and bills of lading. Article 8 deals with investment securities and their issuance and transfer. Article 9 concerns "secured transactions," such as when the buyer provides collateral to the seller to guarantee payment. Typically in sales transactions, the collateral is the goods being sold.

Further reading

Stone, Bradford. *Uniform Commercial Code in a Nutshell*. Eagan, Minn.: West Group, 2001.

commercial paper

Commercial paper is a debt instrument—that is, a PROMISSORY NOTE issued by large CORPORATIONS that are also financially strong. To minimize the risk associated with commercial paper, it is traded among only the largest, most financially stable corporations, MUTUAL FUNDS, INSURANCE companies, banks, and other large intermediaries. Commercial paper is unsecured and short-term, with maturities ranging from 30 to 270 days.

For firms with large amounts of excess cash, commercial paper is a convenient, relatively risk-free way of earning interest on otherwise idle balances for short periods of time. For example, a corporation may be saving up for the payment of a cash DIVIDEND or seeking to retire a bond issue.

This pool of cash can be profitably and conveniently invested for a short term via commercial paper. In the financial crisis of October 2008, the commercial paper market froze when lenders, not being able to determine default risk, stopped making short-term loans.

For the borrower, commercial paper is a relatively inexpensive source of short-term CAPITAL. The interest rate on commercial paper is always below the prime rate and, in recent years, has closely paralleled T-bill rates.

See also INTEREST RATES.

Committee on Foreign Investment in the United States (CFIUS)

The Committee on Foreign Investment in the United States (CFIUS) is an interagency committee authorized to review transactions that could result in control of a U.S. business by a foreign person ("covered transactions"), in order to determine the effect of such transactions on the national security of the United States. In particular, the committee considers the national security implications of foreign takeovers of business assets in the United States. The CFIUS was created by the Defense Production Act of 1950, and amended by the Foreign Investment and National Security Act of 2007 (FINSA). Since 9/11, the CFIUS process has been the subject of greater political and national security scrutiny and the subject of several rounds of reforms.

The committee includes the heads of the following departments and offices:

DEPARTMENT OF TREASURY (chair)
Department of Justice
Department of Homeland Security
DEPARTMENT OF COMMERCE
Department of Defense
Department of State
Department of Energy
Office of the U.S. TRADE REPRESENTATIVE
Office of Science and Technology Policy

Reviews are conducted by the CFIUS in camera (in private) and no public record is available. With no statutory or regulatory definition of "national security" or "critical infrastructure," the committee has considerable latitude in determining whether foreign acquisitions pose a risk to the United States. If the CFIUS finds that a covered transaction presents national security risks and that other provisions of law do not provide adequate authority to address the risks, then CFIUS may enter into an agreement with, or impose conditions on, parties to mitigate such risks or may refer the case to the president for action.

Most Americans had never heard of the CFIUS until 2005, when Dubai Ports World (DPW) proposed acquisition of a British firm, P&O Ports, the lease operator of 22 ports in the United States. DPW already managed port facilities around the world but, in being owned by the government of Dubai in the United Arab Emirates, DPW engendered a political controversy when U.S. politicians fanned fears of Mideast control of potentially sensitive national security interests. President George W. Bush supported the acquisition, but the U.S. Congress voted against the deal. Eventually, DPW bought P&O Ports but sold its interest in U.S. operations to American International Group (AIG).

Further reading
The Committee on Foreign Investment in the United States Web site. Available online. URL: www.ustreas. gov/offices/international-affairs/cfius/.

Commodity Credit Corporation

The Commodity Credit Corporation (CCC), a federally owned and operated entity, was created to stabilize, support, and protect American farmers' INCOME and prices. The CCC aids agricultural producers through LOANS, purchases, payments, and other operations to support PRODUCTION and marketing of agricultural commodities. Initially a modest and popular government-support program, it has recently become part of a controversial agricultural subsidy issue.

When established in 1933, the CCC helped farmers attempt to attain and maintain PARITY. During the GREAT DEPRESSION, prices for farm PRODUCTS dropped to near zero. While farmers' costs declined, farm incomes were severely depressed. As portrayed in John Steinbeck's classic novel *The Grapes of Wrath,* many farmers left agriculture in search of opportunities elsewhere. Initially incorporated as part of President Franklin Roosevelt's New Deal program to combat the depression, in 1939 the CCC was transferred to the U.S. Department of Agriculture (USDA). In 1948 it was reincorporated as a federal corporation within the USDA.

The CCC's programs and policies have changed many times as U.S. policy toward agriculture and other economic support programs has changed. When it was established in 1933, a majority of U.S. congressional districts had large agricultural constituencies. As the United States has become more urbanized, agricultural political interests have declined as consumer and taxation political clout has expanded, and farm lobby power has also diminished.

Major CCC programs include

- *Support activities.* These include loan, purchase, and payment programs for wheat, corn, oilseeds, cotton, rice, tobacco, milk and milk products, barley, oats, grain sorghum, mohair, honey, peanuts, and sugar. Farmers may receive nonrecourse commodity loans on most of these commodities at a designated rate per unit (price) by pledging and storing a quantity of a commodity as collateral. When the commodities are harvested, farmers can choose to either pay back the loan and sell on the open market or deliver the commodity to the government at the support price. In years when market prices are higher than the support price, farmers naturally sell on the open market. When support prices are higher than market prices, the government winds up owning large quantities of agricultural commodities.

Two of the more controversial support programs are sugar and tobacco. Support prices for sugar are frequently significantly higher than world market prices, creating subsidies for sugar producers and higher costs for consumers. Tobacco support programs are both expensive and ethically questionable. Paying U.S. farmers to produce a harmful product is a dubious role for government.

- *Inventory, disposal, and domestic food assistance programs.* When the CCC acquires commodities through either collateral acquisition or nonrecourse loans, it stores and processes commodities through contracts with commercial warehouses. Sometimes the CCC will make loan-deficiency payments to farmers, based on the difference between the support price and the market price, rather than having farmers deliver products to the agency. The CCC sells commodities through its Farm Service Agency office in Kansas City, Missouri. To reduce inventories, it donates food commodities acquired through its price support programs to the Bureau of Indian Affairs and federal, state, and private agencies. The commodities are used in school-lunch programs, summer camps, and assistance of needy persons. Some commodities are provided to the U.S. military and federal and state prisons.
- *Export programs.* Through a variety of sales, payments, export credits, and other activities, the CCC, along with the Foreign Agricultural Services, promotes and sells U.S. agricultural commodities abroad. Through the Export Enhancement Program, the CCC pays cash to U.S. exporters as a bonus, allowing them to sell in targeted countries at prices matching those of subsidizing competitors.

In 1996 the Freedom to Farm Bill, amending the CCC, intended to reduce government subsidies of commodity producers. Instead, when commodity prices declined to near-record lows, the CCC was authorized to increase support for farmers to prevent further foreclosures and bankruptcies among farmers. By 2001 farm subsidies, distributed primarily through the CCC, amounted to over $27 billion, but almost two-thirds of those funds went to wealthy farm individuals and farm CORPORATIONS.

Supporting agricultural producers is a common practice in both industrialized and developing countries. Many international trade disputes center on "unfair" subsidies of domestic producers.

Support for agricultural producers traditionally has been a politically "sacred cow," but as the cost of subsidies and the balance of political power shifts, programs like the CCC have come under greater scrutiny.

Further reading
Farm Service Agency Web site. Available online. URL: www.fsa.usda.gov.; John Kelly, "Farm Fund Rules Mean Rich Get Richer," *Beaufort Gazette,* 10 September 2001, p. A1.

Commodity Futures Trading Commission
The Commodity Futures Trading Commission (CFTC) regulates FUTURES and OPTIONS markets in the United States, protecting market participants against market manipulation, abusive trading practices, and FRAUD. Created in 1974, the CFTC was a response to growing use and changes in futures and options markets. Traditionally, agricultural commodities dominated futures trading, but beginning in the 1970s, trading expanded to include FINANCIAL INSTRUMENTS, foreign currencies, U.S. government securities, and a variety of new commodity futures contracts. The CFTC's major activities include contract review, market surveillance, and regulation of futures market participants.

A futures contract is an agreement to buy or sell in the future a specific quantity of a commodity at a specified price. Most futures contracts consider that actual delivery of the commodity could take place; however, some futures contracts require cash settlement in lieu of delivery. For example, the NEW YORK MERCANTILE EXCHANGE offers an April contract in gold. Each contract is for 100 troy ounces, which at $300 per ounce represents $30,000 worth of gold. Most futures contracts are liquidated before the delivery date. An option on a commodity futures contract gives the buyer the right to convert the option into a futures contract. Futures and options must be executed through a commodity exchange and almost always through people and firms regulated by the CFTC.

The CFTC reviews all proposed futures and options contracts. Before an exchange is permitted to trade a future and option contract in a specific commodity, it must demonstrate that the contract reflects the normal market flow and commercial trading practices in the actual commodity. Normal trading practices are usually found in the "cash" market for a commodity, but if market norms are not well defined, the exchange must show why a contract should be structured as they propose.

The CFTC monitors trading in all commodity futures daily and can halt trading or take whatever action deemed necessary to restore order in any futures contract being traded. Trading in specific commodities is often conducted by relatively few individuals. Hedgers take a position in order to reduce the risk of financial loss due to a change in the price of their ASSETS, while speculators hope to profit by correctly anticipating changes in the price of an option or futures contract. In any market where there are relatively few participants, there exists the potential for market manipulation, raising or lowering prices by a few powerful individuals. For example, during the early 1980s, silver prices rose from $5 to over $50 per ounce, only to quickly fall back to the $5 range. Billions of dollars were made and lost in the silver market, and individuals were accused of market manipulation.

Companies and individuals who manage customer funds or give trading advice must apply to the National Futures Association, a self-regulating organization approved by the CFTC. The CFTC also requires registrants to disclose market risks and performance information to customers. One of the relatively new roles of the CFTC is to oversee trading in derivatives, contracts whose value is based on the value of the underlying financial asset or security. Derivatives LEVERAGE existing futures contracts, which in turn leverage the commodity they are based on. Leveraging allows buyers and sellers to benefit (or lose) from small changes in market prices while only having to pay a small percentage of the value of the contract being traded.

Further reading

Commodity Futures Trading Commission Web site. Available online. URL: www.cftc.gov.

commodity markets

Commodity markets are markets where basic goods and materials are exchanged. Commodity markets can be as small as a local farmers market or as large as the CHICAGO BOARD OF TRADE (CBOT), the first commodity exchange in the United States (established in 1848). Generally commodity markets are located near historic centers of PRODUCTION of major commodities or in major cities like Chicago and New York.

In the 19th century, the major commodity markets provided trading opportunities primarily in agricultural PRODUCTS. Initially the CBOT focused on grain trade, allowing farmers and other agricultural industry members to hedge or reduce their risk of price changes by using FUTURES contracts. Similarly, the CHICAGO MERCANTILE EXCHANGE (CME), created in 1898 as the Chicago Butter and Egg Board, allows investors, managers, and broker/dealers to reduce risk in business transactions. As ECONOMIC CONDITIONS changed, commodity markets like the CBOT and the CME expanded their trading to include currency futures, interest-rate futures, and stock-index futures.

Most commodity markets determine current market prices, called the cash price, by the interaction of buyers and sellers (DEMAND and SUPPLY). The CBOT and other commodity exchanges have colorful "pits" where traders, using hand signals, execute orders to buy and sell commodities and futures contracts. Within any major commodity market there is a variety of participants, including buyers, sellers, hedgers, floor traders, and speculators. Buyers are representatives of food companies purchasing commodities for use in production. Sellers are representatives of commodity producers.

Hedgers are firms and individuals who make purchases and sales in futures markets for the purpose of establishing a known price, weeks or months in advance, for commodities they intend to buy or sell in the cash market. HEDGING allows them to protect themselves against the risk of an unfavorable price change in the time before they are ready to buy or sell in the cash market. To a commodity producer, a decline in prices between the present and when the commodity will be available would be unfavorable. To a cereal company, where grains are input in production, a rise in commodity prices would be unfavorable. Both buyers and sellers of commodities can protect themselves against price changes.

For example, a farmer or farm corporation may plant 1,000 acres of winter wheat in the fall. Winter wheat is not harvested until the next year. The farmer knows that historically his/her land yields an average of 60 bushels per acre, so they expect to have 60,000 bushels at harvest time. The farmer can "lock in" the current price for wheat by selling 12 wheat futures contracts at the current price, say $2.90 per bushel. (The standard futures contract for wheat is 5,000 bushels.) If, in the interim, the price of wheat rises, the farmer will buy back the futures contracts at a higher price, losing money in the futures market, but then sell his or her wheat at the higher price in the cash market. If the price of wheat declines, the farmer will buy back the futures contracts at a lower price, profiting in the futures market, but then sell his or her wheat at a lower price in the cash market.

In addition to buyers, sellers, and hedgers, many commodity markets include floor traders and speculators. Floor traders are individuals who buy and sell for their own accounts. Like day traders in STOCK MARKETS, they buy and sell rapidly, hoping to earn PROFITS based on small changes in prices. Floor traders also provide liquidity to commodity markets. Speculators seek to profit based on anticipated changes in futures prices. Speculators will "go long," purchasing futures contracts, or "go short," selling futures contracts based on expectation that the price will decline, and profit by the difference. As one trading company states, "Commodity trading is risky and is not suitable for everyone."

Historically commodity-markets futures trading was designed to protect producers and manufacturers using commodities from price changes. Today commodity exchanges are used by a variety of nonagricultural buyers and sellers, such as power companies and airlines attempting to lock in their cost of fuel, multinational companies locking in their revenue or costs in other currencies, and investment companies locking in their cost or price of CAPITAL.

Further reading
Investor Learning Center at National Futures Association. Available online. URL: www.nfa.futures.org.

common law (case law)

Common law, also called case law or Anglo-American law, refers to the legal system developed in the common-law courts of England since the Middle Ages and transferred to much of the English-speaking world and Commonwealth nations, including the United States. It is distinguished from the civil-law system used in continental Europe and in the areas of other continents conquered and ruled by continental nations.

The common law evolved as a body of customary law based on judicial decisions and reports of decided cases of the common-law courts. Decisions by English grand juries, kings, magistrates and trial juries were written down and eventually catalogued according to the type of case. When the courts were called on to decide similar issues in subsequent cases, they reviewed the earlier decisions, and if they found one that was logically analogous to the contemporary case, they applied the principle of the earlier decision. This doctrine is called stare decisis—Latin for "to stand by decided matters." The common law thus consists of court opinions in specific disputes that state legal principles and must be followed in subsequent court cases about the same type of dispute.

The principle of stare decisis is the essence of common-law jurisprudence. Judges are usually reluctant to discard well-established rules. At the same time, the principles should reflect contemporary social values, and sometimes they have to be changed or modified to keep up with the times. For this reason, judges always attempt to write reasoned judgments, especially when their decisions mark a departure from the established precedent. However, different courts apply this general policy with varying degrees of strictness. The English courts, for instance, are inclined to be more rigorous than American courts in its application.

During America's colonial period, most of the English common-law tradition and many of the English statutes became firmly entrenched, though modified to some extent in accordance with the religious and cultural beliefs of the colonists. At the time of independence, the basic legal system did not change. The major difference was the creation of the U.S. Constitution, ratified in 1789. After that, the laws of Parliament and the edicts of King George III no longer had any power in the new United States. The Constitution became the foundation on which the American legal system was built. Both the law inherited from England and that enacted by Congress and state legislatures eventually had to stand the test of constitutionality in order to determine their validity.

In the centuries of American history following independence, the English common-law tradition has been modified to some extent. A number of common-law institutions have been rejected. For instance, in America, on death intestate (i.e., dying without leaving a will), all of the children inherited land and not just the eldest son, as was the case in England. Leaseholds owned by feudal landlords were replaced by freeholds in the American context, and there were no ecclesiastical (church) courts in America. Even in England, modern-day common law is considerably different from its feudal roots, and statutory law is widespread.

Especially during the past century, statutes and administrative regulations have become more important as instruments to make new law and to codify (put into a written, prescriptive form) broad principles developed by the case law. Even so, judge-made law remains an important component of American law. The courts in common-law jurisdictions have the right to interpret statutes, but they must do so in accordance with the rules of statutory interpretation. In the United States, the general policy of the courts has been to attempt to interpret the statute in the light of the legislature's intention. In England, on the other hand, the literal rule of interpretation is the predominant approach, i.e., the statute should be read literally, without reference to legislative intent.

Many laws affecting business evolve gradually through a series of court decisions. Major U.S. businesses closely watch product-liability, worker rights, environmental, and other court judgments. Companies and consumers (through their attorneys) often choose particular court venues where recent decisions have been advantageous to their interests.

One of the most widely reported issues involved tobacco companies' litigation. After decades of winning court decisions that smokers made the choice to smoke, in the mid-1990s, with new evidence that the companies knew their product was addictive, juries began finding in favor of smokers, creating an avalanche of lawsuits leading to the 1999 TOBACCO SETTLEMENT.

Further reading
Burnham, William. *Introduction to the Law and Legal System of the United States.* 3d ed. Eagan, Minn.: West Group, 2002; Meador, Daniel J., and Frederick G. Kempin, Jr. *Historical Introduction to Anglo-American Law in a Nutshell.* 3d ed. Eagan, Minn.: West Group, 1990.

common stock, preferred stock, treasury stock

Stock is an ownership interest in a corporation. If a CORPORATION issues only one type of equity security, it is called common stock, the kind normally issued by corporations. The common stockholders are the residual EQUITY in the corporation and are the only class of stockholders to have voting rights, one vote for each common share owned. Most common stock also carries a preemptive right, where existing stockholders have the privilege to purchase new issues before they are offered to the public for sale. This allows current stockholders to maintain the same percentage ownership in the corporation after a new issue is sold as they had prior to the new offering. The preemptive right is also crucial in preventing a dilution of value for existing stockholders when a new stock issue is sold at a lower market price than previous shares.

Par-value common stock and no-par-value common stock are issued by corporations. Originally conceived to establish a minimum legal CAPITAL to serve as protection for creditors, par value has little significance today. However, it still remains that if a common stock has a par value, that stock cannot be initially offered at less than its par value. When common stock is issued at a price above its par value, the excess of price over par value is recorded in the equity account: Contributed Capital in Excess of Par Value, Common Stock.

Preferred stock is also an equity security, but unlike common stock, it carries no voting rights. Preferred stocks have par values, a percentage of which is paid to the preferred stockholders when DIVIDENDS are declared. Preferred stock is named for the dividend preference that preferred stockholders enjoy over the common stockholders. The three types of dividend preference, listed here from the weakest to the strongest in terms of dividend-earning power, are current dividend preference, cumulative dividend preference, participating dividend preference.

Current dividend preference requires the preferred stockholders to receive dividends from a current dividend being paid and common stockholders to receive dividends only if there is any current dividend remaining after the preferred stockholders have been paid in full. In the case of a small dividend where there are insufficient funds to pay dividends to all stockholders, the preferred stockholders will receive dividends, and the residual, if any, will be shared by the common stockholders.

Cumulative dividend preference operates much in the same way as current dividend preference, but it is more powerful. In years when there is no dividend declared by the BOARD OF DIRECTORS or when the declared dividend has been so small as to be insufficient to pay in full the preferred dividends, the dividends which the preferred stockholders are entitled to but have not yet received are called "dividends in arrears." Cumulative dividend preference requires dividends in arrears to be paid before any other distributions of a current dividend. After the dividends in arrears are caught up and paid, then current dividend preference is applied to the remaining dividends to be distributed.

Participating dividend preference operates like cumulative dividend preference, except that when the cumulative dividend preference has been satisfied, the preferred stockholders then share the remaining dividends to be distributed with the common stockholders on a pro rata basis. By taking a larger share of the declared dividends, these dividend preferences benefit the preferred stockholders at the expense of the common stockholders.

Like common stock, when preferred stock is issued for more than its par value, the excess of price over par value is recorded in the equity account: Contributed Capital in Excess of Par Value, Preferred Stock. The issuance of common and preferred stocks is an important source of capital for corporations.

For a variety of reasons, occasionally a corporation will purchase (buy back) its own shares from the open market. Stock shares that have been previously issued but repurchased by the issuing corporation are called treasury stock. Treasury stock has the status of "issued, but not outstanding." The custom of "one vote per share" does not apply to treasury stock as long as it is held by the issuing corporation. Treasury stock is a contra equity account, has a normal debit balance, and reduces total stockholder equity as long as it remains not outstanding.

comparable worth (comparable pay, pay equity)

Comparable worth (also referred to as comparable pay or pay equity) is the idea that workers should receive equal pay for work of equal value. Comparable worth is most closely associated with differences in pay by gender. In the late 1960s, working women in the United States received only 59 percent of what working men were earning. During the 1980s, led by women in Oregon, pressure for pay based on comparable worth became a widely debated issue. Supporters argued women were shuttled into lower-paying professions, particularly education and nursing, and subjected to sex stereotyping, amounting to decades of under-valuing work done by women. In Oregon, women working for the state confronted the state legisla-ture and described their job responsibilities. When asked to guess their pay, the legislators overesti-mated women's pay by at least 15 percent.

The efforts of women in Oregon led to pay-equity projects where jobs were evaluated and compared according to the level of skill, effort, and responsibility required for the job. This resulted in numeric rankings of jobs and equalization of pay based on rankings. While comparable-worth legislation grew in Canada, with most provinces passing legislation calling for achieving equal pay for work of equal value, in the United States com-parable-worth laws have been limited to local and state public-sector workers. The EQUAL PAY ACT of 1963 has been interpreted in the courts as requir-ing equal pay only for workers in the same job and therefore has not affected efforts to equalize pay for jobs that are dissimilar but of equal skill and value.

By 2004 women workers in the United States were earning 76 percent of what men were earn-ing, reflecting their increasing shift away from traditional, low-paying occupations. The change also reflects a robust economy that has raised most workers' wages, due largely to efforts achieving pay based on comparable worth.

Further reading
Hallock, Margaret. "Pay Equity: The Promise and the Practice in North America," *Labour & Industry* 10 (December 1999): 53.

comparative advantage

The law of comparative advantage is the principle that firms, people, or countries should engage in those activities for which their advantage over others is the largest or their disadvantage is the smallest. First articulated by English economist David Ricardo (1772–1823), the law of comparative advantage demonstrated that both weak and strong nations benefit from trade by doing those things they do relatively more efficiently than others. At the time, Ricardo's ideas were revolutionary. The predominant economic doctrine, MERCANTILISM, espoused accumulation of WEALTH in the form of precious metals and maintaining a favorable TRADE BALANCE. The idea of comparative advan-tage was used to convince the English parliament to replace protective TARIFFS with a FREE TRADE policy. England's success with these changes influ-enced other countries to change their policies.

Comparative advantage is based on relative COSTS and exchange. Considering the alternative, self-sufficiency, raises the question whether qual-ity of life would improve or decline if one had to produce everything one consumed. There are few people who have the skills and other resources to come close to matching the quality of life they currently have in an economic system based on specialization and exchange.

Relative costs are also critical to the idea of comparative advantage. If one person (firm or country) can do something well, the OPPORTU-NITY COST (the value of the output foregone) of not using those resources in that capacity is quite high. Meanwhile the opportunity cost of using personal skills and resources in production of what one does well is relatively low. For example, Tiger Woods plays golf exceptionally well and earns sig-nificant INCOME doing so. Knowing golf courses, Mr. Woods could also probably do an excellent job cutting the grass on the courses he plays. If he chose to cut grass, his opportunity cost would be the income foregone from playing and winning on a lot of golf courses. By playing golf, Mr. Woods sacrifices the income he could earn cutting grass, but that is quite small compared to his income from playing golf.

The same principal, relative costs, applies to specialization and trade among firms and coun-tries. In the last decade, one of the trends in Ameri-can business has been OUTSOURCING. Firms are finding it less expensive to pay others for skills or products that would be expensive to produce inter-nally. Advances in communication technology are allowing firms to contract out a variety of service needs, including many human resource, account-ing, and development functions. Increasingly U.S.

countries are contracting for billing, engineering, and technology services with skilled English-speaking professionals around the world.

For the last two centuries, economists have studied the concept of comparative advantage, looking for the sources of relative-cost advantages. The Heckscher-Ohlim theorem suggests that relative factor endowments of countries are the principal determinant of comparative-cost differences. According to this theory, countries with highly skilled workers will have an advantage in the PRODUCTION of goods and SERVICES requiring skilled labor. Countries with significant mineral resources will have a comparative advantage in the production of those minerals. Empirical studies have both supported and challenged the Heckscher-Ohlim theorem. Other research suggests DEMAND considerations, ECONOMIES OF SCALE, and technology are important sources of comparative advantage. Governments sometimes attempt to create comparative advantage through subsidies to important domestic industries and tariffs placed on imported products.

Further reading
Folsom, Ralph H., and W. Davis Folsom. *Understanding NAFTA and Its International Business Implications.* New York: Matthew Bender/Irwin, 1996; Ruffin, Roy J., and Paul R. Gregory. *Principles of Economics.* 7th ed. Boston: Addison Wesley, 2001.

compensation and benefits
Compensation and benefits comprise the total rewards package that an employee receives for performing a job. Compensation is considered direct pay, since it is the amount of money the employee receives. Benefits are indirect pay, since they are monetary equivalents that can be converted later into cash or used to pay for selected expenses. For every dollar paid in compensation, the CHAMBER OF COMMERCE estimates that 39–40 percent is spent for indirect compensation, leaving 60–61 percent for direct compensation. These are composite averages; individual companies and specific situations may vary considerably.

Three factors influence the average pay for the organization and each employee's specific pay:

(1) competitive pressures from forces outside the organization, (2) the company's desire to compensate all of its employees fairly and equitably, and (3) what the individual employee brings to the organization.

The primary external pressure affecting pay rates comes from other companies within the marketplace (the geographical region in which companies recruit applicants). Each employer is in competition with other companies for applicants of similar qualifications. The competition may group employees within common industries or by level of knowledge, skills, and abilities. Through area surveys, companies identify what the collective marketplace pays and set their pay scales accordingly. Companies can pay less than others, more than others, or at the market average. The most common philosophy is to pay competitively (e.g., "at" the market scale), but a primary factor is the firm's ability to pay. Companies that can pay more than market scale are likely to be able to generate a larger pool of higher-qualified applicants, which translates to less required training time and higher operating efficiencies. Companies that pay less than market scale may be recent entrepreneurial start-up firms with limited CAPITAL. Sometimes these firms offer stock ownership incentives to attract highly qualified applicants. Compensation is directly linked the market's DEMAND for the products or services offered and the profits the company earns.

Every employee wants to be paid fairly in comparison with other employees. However, before pay rates are considered, each position needs to be studied and compared with other positions to assure an accurate hierarchy of jobs. This process assures internal equity, which is the second force that strongly shapes the company's compensation philosophy. Assuring internal equity requires that the company perform a thorough task analysis of each position. Task analyses look at the actual work performed by the job incumbent (job content) and the physical environment in which the work is performed (job context). In addition, the education, experience, knowledge, skills, and abilities of the desired job incumbent are identified. Common tasks are grouped and written into responsibility statements. Responsibility statements, budgetary responsibilities, reporting relationships, and a position summary statement are the bases for the job description. Care must be taken to ensure that essential job duties are accurately identified. (See EMPLOYMENT for additional information about this concern.) The job descriptions are then either compared to each other or to a predetermined measuring technique to determine their level of importance to the company. Job evaluations lead to the creation of a job hierarchy in which positions are listed in order of importance from most important to least important. Frequently positions are then grouped into labor (or salary) grades, and wage ranges are assigned using market survey data.

Individual considerations that are unique to each employee influence the actual salary or wage paid to the employee after the monetary range is defined. Individual salary determinants include the desire of the employer to hire the candidate, the level of performance as reflected by formal PERFORMANCE APPRAISALS, negotiating strength during the employment process and sometimes after employment, and SUPPLY and demand. Supply and demand recognizes the prevalence of applicants with unique knowledge and experiences in the recruiting area and the extent that the company needs someone with those unique capabilities.

A major portion of the employer's compensation expenses is allocated to pay for benefits that the company is either required to provide or offers voluntarily. Benefits that are voluntarily offered by employers are divided into three primary categories: (1) paid time off, (2) group INSURANCE, and (3) capital accumulation. Paid time off includes vacations and holidays but also may include work breaks, clean-up time at the end of the shift, sick pay, and personal time. Group insurance frequently includes medical, dental, life, and disability coverage. Capital accumulation includes the employers' portion of SOCIAL SECURITY payments and a wide variety of retirement benefit alternatives. Legally required benefits include Social Security, UNEMPLOYMENT insurance, WORKERS' COMPENSATION, and, in many cases, time off to attend to family medical needs. In a few states, employers are required to offer personal disability benefits, but this varies widely from state to state.

See also EMPLOYEE BENEFITS.

—John B. Abbott

competition

Competition has many meanings depending on the context in which the term is used. Almost all American businesspeople will say their market is highly competitive. Such business owners are concerned with both the actions of current competitors and the threats of potential competitors.

Companies often develop competitive strategies to differentiate themselves from other firms in their competitive environment. In this context, competition refers to the marketing strategies, product, pricing, distribution, or promotion strategies a firm uses to distinguish its offerings from competitors' offerings. A competitive environment is influenced by the actions of direct competitors, marketers of products that are substitutes for one another, and other marketers competing for the same consumers' purchasing power.

Sales managers use competition to motivate employees. In this context, competition is directed toward achieving a goal or measuring performance against other employees in the company. Sometimes sales managers will implement competitive PRICING STRATEGIES—that is, strategies designed to neutralize price as a competitive variable. A price-matching policy is one form of competitive pricing strategy.

The most common kind of competition is economic or market competition. This can range from a MONOPOLY, a market with only one seller, BARRIERS TO ENTRY, and no close substitutes; to PERFECT COMPETITION, a market with many sellers of similar products and ease of entry into the market. A market where there are many sellers of differentiated products is called MONOPOLISTIC COMPETITION. Perfectly competitive markets have the greatest degree of competition, while monopolistic markets have the least competition.

Business managers also use the term *nonprice competition*—that is, competing with other firms based on style, service, quality, availability, credit, or anything other than price. Nonprice competition is prevalent in markets where there are only a few firms (OLIGOPOLY).

See also MARKETING STRATEGY.

competitive advantage

Every day American businesses supply myriad products and services to consumers. The rational consumer is looking for the best value that can be found within his/her budget. Buyers evaluate products and services based on a variety of criteria. The primary purchasing criteria is the product's ability to satisfy the consumer's immediate need, but other decision criteria include price, appearance, quality, warranty, and service.

Producers understand consumers' buying habits and try to design into a product or service some unique characteristics that similar products from other producers do not have. Each producer hopes that the uniqueness of his or her product will induce the consumer to buy it instead of products made by other companies. This added uniqueness, intended to increase sales, is known as a *competitive advantage*.

Within the economic marketplace, producers also study products and services that compete with their own. If one company redesigns a product and includes new features, improves quality, or increases the product warranty, the changes are advertised with the goal of increasing the sales of their product and take potential sales away from the other producers. The uniqueness of competitive advantages like these, however, can be easily copied and duplicated by other producers. So most competitive advantages, such as quality, warranty, appearance, and product packaging, are short-lived.

Companies seek a competitive advantage that is not only unique but also is sustainable over extended periods of time. If the advantage cannot be easily duplicated, then it is sustainable over time. Probably the only sustainable competitive advantage that a company has is its employees—the human resources of the organization. It is only through a motivated, challenged, and rewarded workforce that the continuous stream of innova-

tive new and improved products, with controlled manufacturing and distribution costs, can be developed and maintained.

—John B. Abbott

competitive intelligence   See MARKET INTELLIGENCE; SOCIETY FOR COMPETITIVE INTELLIGENCE PROFESSIONALS.

compounding, future value

Compounding is the process of finding an unknown future value from a known present value. Using a time line, compounding is moving forward in time from the present to some point in the future. Given the time value of money (assuming that INTEREST RATES are always positive), future values are always larger than present values.

For deposits and other INVESTMENTS where interest can, in turn, earn interest, compounding can be quite powerful, especially at higher rates of interest. Because INFLATION builds upon itself—that is, it compounds—uncontrolled inflation is quite damaging to the value of money and its PURCHASING power.

For a lump sum, the future value of some present amount is determined by the compounding formula $FV_n = PV[1+ir]^n$, where FV_n is the future value at some future point in time n, PV is the present value (the current amount of the lump sum), ir is the interest rate (expressed in decimal form) applicable to the situation in question, and the exponent n is the same future point in time for which the future value is to be determined. For instance, find the future value in three years of a current deposit of $100 at 10 percent compounded annually: $FV_3 = 100 [1.10]^3$. Simplifying the formula reduces this to $FV3 = 100[1.331] = 133.10$. Notice that 10 percent of $100 is $10, yet the future value adds more than $10 interest per year for three years to the lump sum. Compounding (interest earning interest) added $3.10 to this lump sum over three years.

It is sometimes necessary to determine the future value of an ANNUITY. While there is a formula for this, it is much easier to use a commonly published table of interest factors. For compounding, there are tables of future-value interest factors for lump sums (FVIFs) and for annuities (FVIFAs). To find the future value of a lump sum: $FV_n = PV[FVIF_{i,n}]$, where $FVIF$ is the lump-sum future-value interest factor for some interest rate i and for some time period n. To find the future value of an annuity: $FVA_n = PMT[FVIFA_{i,n}]$, where PMT is the regular annuity payment and $FVIFA$ is the annuity future-value interest factor for some interest rate i and for some time period n.

While using the published tables of future-value interest factors is easier than manually doing the number-crunching, it is much more convenient to find future values for lump sums and annuities using a financial calculator. Remembering that the interest factor tables carry the interest factors to only four digits to the right of the decimal, the results obtained from the use of a financial calculator are more accurate than using the tables. The published interest factor tables list interest factors only for whole-number interest rates. A financial calculator can compound using any interest rate.

See also RULE OF 72.

Comptroller of the Currency

The Comptroller of the Currency directs the Office of the Comptroller of the Currency (OCC), which charters, regulates, and supervises all national banks. The office also supervises the federal branches and agencies of foreign banks. Headquartered in Washington, D.C., the OCC has six district offices and an office in London to supervise the international activities of national banks.

The four objectives of the Comptroller of the Currency are

- to ensure the safety and soundness of the national BANKING SYSTEM
- to foster COMPETITION by allowing banks to offer new products and services
- to improve the efficiency and effectiveness of OCC supervision, including reducing regulatory burden
- to ensure fair and equal access to financial services for all Americans

In 1861 Secretary of the Treasury Salmon P. Chase recommended the establishment of a system of federally chartered national banks, each of which would have the power to issue standardized national bank notes based on U.S. BONDS held by the bank. In the National Currency Act of 1863, the administration of the new national banking system was vested in the newly created OCC and its chief administrator, the Comptroller of the Currency.

The law was completely rewritten and reenacted as the National Bank Act (1864), which authorized the Comptroller of the Currency to hire a staff of national bank examiners to supervise and periodically examine national banks. The act also gave the comptroller authority to regulate lending and investment activities of national banks. Today the comptroller is appointed by the president, with the advice and consent of the Senate, for a five-year term. The comptroller also serves as a director of the FEDERAL DEPOSIT INSURANCE CORPORATION (FDIC) and of the Neighborhood Reinvestment Corporation.

OCC examiners conduct on-site reviews of national banks and supervise bank operations. The agency issues rules, legal interpretations, and corporate decisions concerning banking, bank investments, bank community development activities, and other aspects of bank operations. National bank examiners supervise domestic and international activities of national banks and perform corporate analyses. Examiners analyze a bank's loan and INVESTMENT portfolios, funds management, CAPITAL, earnings, liquidity, sensitivity to market RISK, and compliance with consumer-banking laws, including the Community Reinvestment Act. They review the bank's internal controls, internal and external AUDITING, and compliance with the law. They evaluate the bank management's ability to identify and control risk, particularly maturity matching (DURATION), and maintain collateral documentation.

In regulating national banks, the OCC has the power to

- examine the banks
- approve or deny applications for new charters, branches, capital, or other changes in corporate or banking structure

- take supervisory actions against banks that do not comply with laws and regulations or otherwise engage in unsound banking practices (i.e., remove officers and directors, negotiate agreements to change banking practices, and issue cease-and-desist orders as well as civil money penalties)
- issue rules and regulations governing bank investments, lending, and other practices

One of the reasons Congress passed the National Currency Act was to finance the Civil War. Although national banks no longer issue currency, they continue to play a prominent role in the nation's economic life. Today the OCC regulates and supervises more than 1,600 national banks and 50 federal branches and agencies of foreign banks in the United States, accounting for more than two-thirds of the total ASSETS of all U.S. commercial banks. Any bank with "national" in its name is chartered under the OCC. Banks can also choose to be chartered under state banking laws.

The OCC does not receive any appropriations from Congress. Instead, its operations are funded primarily by assessments on national banks. National banks pay for their examinations, and they pay for the OCC's processing of their corporate applications. The OCC also receives revenue from its investment INCOME, primarily from U.S. TREASURY SECURITIES.

Further reading
Office of the Comptroller of the Currency Web site. Available online. URL: www.occ.treas.gov.

computer-aided design, engineering, and manufacturing

Computer-aided design, engineering, and manufacturing (CAD, CAE, and CAM, respectively) are three stages in the industrial process that utilize computers to aid in the PRODUCTION of goods and SERVICES. CAD includes designing and drafting a product for manufacture. Many Americans have seen CAD systems in architects' offices, where architects take customers' ideas and requirements and create a computer model of the home or office.

In a manufacturing environment, a client company or marketing division within the company will develop ideas for products which are then designed using a CAD system.

CAE is the use of computer systems to define and refine the tooling needed to produce a product. As Gary S. Vasilach reports, "If you can design for manufacturability, you are well on your way to minimizing variability and achieving zero defects. . . . Run the part through more electronic versions. Do more testing. Get it right. Pack more upfront engineering into the same time frame."

CAM, also called computer-integrated manufacturing (CIM), includes manufacturing engineering tasks such as programming numerically controlled machine tools and generating process plans outlining the steps needed to produce a part. CAM includes links to factory automation equipment and production management as well. CAM systems often include quality-control systems, materials and components testing, and monitoring of final products to ensure that they are within tolerance specifications.

CAD, CAE, and CAM flourished in the 1980s and early 1990s as computers became more powerful and able to handle more complex quantitative relationships. As Vasilash states, manufacturers adopted computer-controlled machine tools to improve efficiency and precision. Their problem "was being able to feed those machines with data in a timely manner. At the same time, people were looking at the ways and means to automate designs, to create drawings faster. Thus, there were two different systems." Since then CAD/CAM systems including hardware, software, networks, and factory floor equipment have been integrated into complete systems. Many computer companies developed specialized systems for each industry. One company, Policy Management Systems, Inc., developed software systems just for INSURANCE companies, allowing parent companies and agents throughout their system to write policies, assess risks, and manage operations. In some industries, like architecture, standardized, off-the-shelf CAD/CAM systems are available, while in many industries customized systems are designed. CAD/

CAM systems are becoming increasing sophisticated and, with INTERNET communications, allow collaboration among design and manufacturing teams organized globally.

Further reading
Krouse, John, et al. "CAD/CAM basics," *Machine Design* 61, no. 15 (20 July 1989): C16–C22; ———. "CAE, CAD, and CAM at CMI." *Production,* 102, no. 5 (May 1990): 58–60; Vasilash, Gary S. "What Manufacturing Managers Should Know about CAD," *Production* 10, no. 1 (January 1989): 55–58.

Conference Board
The Conference Board is an international business organization headquartered in New York City. As stated on their Web site the Conference Board was created in 1916 during a period of intense criticism of "big business," and is a nonprofit group with a twofold purpose: "to improve the business enterprise system and enhance the contribution of business to society." Over 3,000 companies in 67 countries are members of the Conference Board.

While engaged in a variety of activities, the Conference Board is most widely known for its Consumer Confidence Index. Each month it sends a questionnaire to a sample of 5,000 households, with about 3,500 responses received. Households are asked to respond to five questions regarding

1. current business conditions in their area
2. expectations regarding business conditions in the next six months
3. current job availability in their area
4. expected job availability in the next six months
5. family income in the next six months

An index is constructed for each response covering the present situation and expectations, resulting in an overall Consumer Confidence Index, which is a leading indicator of future spending. Consumer confidence is closely correlated with UNEMPLOYMENT, INFLATION, and REAL INCOME changes.

Each month the index is compared to the previous month and a press release is issued and reported in the financial media. The base year is 1985, when the value was set at 100. In July 2000 the index was 141.7, a higher figure than the 139.2 rating for the previous month. But, in May 2009, the index stood at 54.9, up from 40.8 the month before. Along with the University of Michigan's Consumer Sentiment Index, the Conference Board's Consumer Confidence Index is a closely watched statistic among STOCK MARKET analysts and investors. The dismalscientist.com Web site posts the current Conference Board index along with many other economic indicators.

Further reading
Conference Board Web site. Available online. URL: www.conferenceboard.org; Dismal Scientist Web site. Available online. URL: www.dismal.com/dismal/ind_landing.asp.

conflict of interest
A conflict of interest can arise in almost any business situation where the well-being of individuals and businesses may differ. In business a conflict of interest exists when an employee's interests conflict with those of their employer, which may make the employee unable to represent the employer effectively. Employees are agents of the business they work for; implicitly or contractually, they are obligated to pursue the best interests of their employer. In a nonbusiness setting, the stereotypical example of a conflict of interest is the situation where a man or woman asks for advice about their loved one from a friend who is secretly in love with the same person.

Business law addresses numerous types of potential conflicts of interest. Agents are not allowed to deal with themselves as buyers. For example, a manager for a company that has a fleet of cars cannot sell a company car to himself. Similarly, employees in a grocery store will purchase something to eat from another cashier rather than themselves. In some situations conflict-of-interest rules extend to relatives of the agent, business associates, or other business organizations with which the agent is associated. If the employer consents to the sale, employees can sell company property to themselves. To avoid a potential conflict of interest, the employee must disclose all relevant information to the employer before dealing with the employer on his or her own behalf.

Another potential conflict of interest exists when an employee competes with the employer while acting as an agent for the employer. For example, employees generally cannot purchase property for themselves if their employer still desires to purchase the property, nor should they solicit customers for a planned competing business while still employed their current firm.

A third conflict-of-interest area exists when an employee acts on behalf of the other party to a transaction. Generally, an employee cannot act on behalf of the other party unless his or her employer knows about and consents to the action. As Mallor et al state, "Thus, one ordinarily cannot act as agent for both parties to a transaction without first disclosing the double role to, and obtaining the consent of, both principals."

The potential for conflict of interest exists in many business situations. The one most Americans encounter is in real-estate transactions. Only in the last decade have realtors been required to get signed acknowledgment from customers that they, the realtors, are agents of the seller. Also, in real-estate transactions it is common to have one closing attorney, acting on behalf of both the buyer and seller.

In recent years, conflicts of interest have become more important and visible in American business. In 2002, investment-banking firms were fined for pressuring company investment analysts to give favorable ratings to companies the investment-banking company was soliciting other business from. Investment-banking giant Merrill Lynch agreed to a $100 million fine and to change how it monitors and pays stock analysts, without admitting any wrongdoing. Similarly, accounting firms that audit companies and also provide business-consulting services to the same company are open to a potential conflict of interest. Since the Enron-Arthur Andersen case, many accounting firms have divested themselves of their business-consulting services, and many CORPORATIONS have discontinued the use of consulting services from their AUDITING company.

Part of the legal problems involving Enron Corporation concerned company dealings with PARTNERSHIPS created and owned by company executives. These partnerships purchased ASSETS from the company and then sold them for significant profits for the partnership, not the company.

Conflict of interest may also arise for members of a company's BOARD OF DIRECTORS. Most boards include outside representatives, people who do not work for the company but are knowledgeable about the business and industry in which the company operates. Members of the board are not agents of the company and thus are not subject to the same conflict-of-interest rules. Under the MODEL BUSINESS CORPORATION ACT, board members can avoid conflict of interests when

- the transaction has been approved by a majority of the informed, disinterested directors
- the transaction has been approved by a majority of the shares held by informed, disinterested shareholders
- the transaction is fair to the corporation.

Further reading

Mallor, Jane P., A. James Barnes, Thomas Bowers, Michael J. Philips, and Arlen W. Langvardt. *Business Law: The Ethical, Global, and E-Commerce Environment.* 14th ed. Boston: McGraw-Hill, 2009; Schroeder, Michael, "Merrill Deal Spurs More Inquiries," *Wall Street Journal,* 23 May 2002, p. A3.

conglomerate

A conglomerate is a business that operates in more than one market. Usually conglomerates produce and sell many dissimilar PRODUCTS for different markets. Unlike VERTICAL INTEGRATION, in which a firm expands by acquiring or establishing company-owned operations at different stages of the production process; or horizontal integration, a combination of firms at the same level of COMPETITION, conglomerates represent corporate expansion into diverse areas, levels, and markets. Conglomerates are typically created by multiple mergers of previously independent companies.

In the United States, the creation of conglomerates was quite popular in the 1960s and again in the 1990s. In the 1960s, the economic logic for creating conglomerates was that a well-established MANAGEMENT team could efficiently operate many different types of businesses. Management efficiency would increase PROFITS and SHAREHOLDER value. During the 1990s, the sudden creation of CAPITAL by DOT-COM companies via INITIAL PUBLIC OFFERINGS allowed these companies to purchase many other similar and dissimilar firms. Company executives often cite SYNERGY and mutual benefits when creating conglomerates. Many Japanese corporations, including Mitsubishi and NEC, are considered conglomerates. U.S. companies such as Raytheon, United Technologies, and Disney are examples of conglomerates.

Legal challenges to conglomerates focus on the potential for reduced competition. Reciprocal trade agreements among member units in a conglomerate can limit the access of outside competitors. Conglomerate control of newspaper, radio, and television companies has raised fears of corporate censorship of journalists fearful of reporting negative news about their parent organization.

consent decree

Consent decree refers to a judicial order agreed to by all parties in a litigation. Thus it typically embodies a litigation settlement, most commonly the settlement of a public (government) prosecution. The defendant consents voluntarily to a court order mandating certain conduct on his or her part in order to avoid a court trial on the merits. For example, businesses charged with violations of U.S. securities and ANTITRUST LAWS often settle with government prosecutors in advance of trial. The terms of these settlements are embodied in consent decrees, sometimes referred to as consent orders.

Most consent decrees do not involve an admission of guilt by defendants. They merely agree to alter their activities to avoid the risk of being found guilty at trial, the costs of litigation, and the possibility that an adverse judgment might be used as precedent against them. Consent decrees are used to settle both criminal and civil prosecutions. The court issuing the decree retains the power to monitor compliance and sanction any noncompliance.

Further reading

Kane, Mary K. *Civil Procedure in a Nutshell.* 4th ed. Eagan, Minn.: West Group, 1996; Cammack, Mark E., and Norman Garland. *Advanced Criminal Procedure in a Nutshell.* Eagan, Minn.: West Group, 2001.

consignment

Consignment is an arrangement in which the owner (consignor) delivers PRODUCTS to a seller (consignee), with the seller acting as agent for the owner in the sales process. The seller does not own the products; rather, the owner retains title to the products until they are sold. At that time the seller receives a commission for assisting with the sale of the item.

Consignment is typical in antique malls, art galleries, musical-instrument stores, and other businesses where an individual owner utilizes the skills and market contacts of an experienced businessperson to facilitate the sale of their possession. Consignment is one of three options within the category of sales transactions, called sales on trial. A sale on approval is an agreement in which goods are delivered to a buyer with the understanding that the buyer may use or test them to determine whether purchase is desirable. In a sale on approval, the title to the good and risk of ownership are not transferred until the buyer accepts the good. Because the title and risk of loss remain with the seller, goods held under a sale-on-approval agreement are not subject to claims from the buyer's creditors until the buyer accepts the good. Taking a car home from a dealership overnight would be an example of a sale on approval. If a buyer fails to notify the seller of his or her decision not to return the good, the buyer is considered to have purchased the good.

A second type of sales transaction is the sale or return in which goods are delivered to a buyer for resale to consumers with the understanding that the buyer has the right to return unsold items. Publishers and bookstores frequently use sale or return agreements allowing the bookstore to return for repayment unsold copies of a book.

Since the buyer (the bookstore) has accepted the goods, the buyer is at risk for loss or damage, and the goods will be considered part of the buyer's ASSETS in any bankruptcy litigation.

Sales on consignment need to be clearly documented to avoid problems associated with the seller's creditors. Under the UNIFORM COMMERCIAL CODE (UCC), a consignor must (1) make sure that a sign indicating the consignor's interest is prominently displayed at the place of business, or (2) make sure that the merchant's creditors know that the merchant is generally in the business of selling goods owned by others, or (3) comply with the UCC's filing provisions. Most individuals are unlikely to be familiar with the requirements to protect their rights in consignment agreements. Many American consumers have found their assets attached as part of business bankruptcy proceedings from failure to comply with consignment regulations.

In international trade, many EXPORTING agreements are sales on consignment. The owner ships the product to the buyer, retaining title to the goods, and the importer pays for the goods when they are sold. The importer's bank will often act as trustee for the goods in this transaction.

Consignment has been scrutinized when used as a means to control the resale price of a manufacturer's product. This is known as vertical PRICE FIXING or resale price maintenance. Manufacturers are allowed to state a suggested retail price for products they sell to retailers, but it is illegal for the manufacturer to obligate a reseller to a specific price. If a consignment selling systems restrains price competition, it may be deemed unlawful.

Further reading
Mallor, Jane P., A. James Barnes, Thomas Bowers, Michael J. Phillips, and Arlen W. Langvardt. *Business Law: The Ethical, Global, and E-Commerce Environment.* 14th ed. Boston: McGraw-Hill, 2009.

conspicuous consumption
Conspicuous consumption is the purchase and CONSUMPTION of goods and services with the intent of displaying INCOME or wealth. For most Americans, the purchase of very expensive cars, $1,000 bottles of wine, ostentatious jewelry, and huge mansions are examples of conspicuous consumption. In the housing crisis that began in 2007, many Americans found themselves stuck with "Mcmansions," huge homes, often on tiny lots, in subdivisions designed to provide an image and atmosphere of exclusiveness.

The term was first coined by sociologist and economist Thorstein Veblen in his 1899 book, *The Theory of the Leisure Class.* Veblen used the term to describe the buying patterns of Victorian-era nouveaux riches, as a large middle class evolved in the country during the American industrial revolution. While the wealthy class maintained control and limited access to the "better things in life," including business networks, clubs, estates, and elite colleges, entrepreneurs, immigrants, and merchant-class businesspeople used some of their newly acquired affluence to show others that they had "made it." The phrase "keeping up with the Joneses" comes from a comic strip created in the early 1900s, referring to neighbors who were talked about but never seen.

Conspicuous consumption is similar to invidious consumption, that is, the purchase of goods with the purpose of inspiring envy in others, and Veblen goods, products for which lower prices result in less quantity demanded. For Veblen goods, desirability decreases when many other consumers have the same product. As Veblen described, "Conspicuous consumption of valuable goods is a means of reputability to the gentleman of leisure." The consumption of status goods is more likely to be associated with socially visible goods than with goods consumed privately. Similarly, Veblen suggested that some consumers also practiced conspicuous leisure. He noted: "In one case it is a waste of time and effort, in the other case it is a waste of goods. Both are methods of demonstrating the possession of wealth."

In a period of economic "good times," conspicuous consumption typically results in envy and numerous "copy cat" products, but in a severe RECESSION, such as the one the United States experienced in 2008, conspicuous consumption goes out of style and is often criticized. During the early part of the 2008 recession, conspicuous consumption was epitomized by the automobile executives' use of corporate jets to fly to Washington, D.C., and then ask for bailout funds. Within months, the demand for corporate jets plummeted as executives experienced the wrath of shareholders and consumers. Corporate sponsorships of golf tournaments and other sports were questioned. Black-tie events and corporate retreats were canceled as conspicuous consumption became inappropriate during an economic recession.

Further reading
Veblen, Thorstein. *The Theory of the Leisure Class: An Economic Study in the Evolution of Institutions.* New York: Macmillan, 1899.

consumer advocacy (consumerism)
Efforts to protect the rights of consumers are the basis of consumer advocacy, also called consumerism. Consumer advocacy has a long history in the United States. Upton Sinclair's book *The Jungle* (1906), describing deplorable worker-safety and unsanitary conditions in the meat-packing industry led "muckrakers" to challenge business practices. During the 1960s, Ralph Nader's book *Unsafe at Any Speed* (1965) challenged design practices in the U.S. automobile industry, particularly the design of General Motors' Corvair. Consumer advocacy is often not welcomed by industry. General Motors unsuccessfully used detectives to find information that would undermine Ralph Nader's claims.

Major U.S. consumer advocacy groups and agencies include the CONSUMER PRODUCT SAFETY COMMISSION (CPSC), the Office of Consumer Affairs, the Consumer Federation of America, and CONSUMERS UNION. As stated on its Web site, the CPSC is a federal agency created in 1972 to "protect the public against unreasonable risks of injuries and deaths associated with consumer PRODUCTS." The CPSC's most visible consumer-advocacy effort is its quarterly publication highlighting unsafe toys for children. The Office of Consumer Affairs addresses consumer complaints

and provides consumer information services. Most states also have consumer-affairs offices.

The Consumer Federation of America, which includes approximately 280 organizations throughout the country, represents consumer interests in dialogues with policy makers and provides educational resources for consumers. Consumers Union, publisher of *Consumer Reports,* is a highly respected source of independent information for consumers. Unlike many industry magazines which derive their revenue from business advertisements, *Consumer Reports* is funded only by member contributions and grants. Consumers Union is well known for its independent testing of automobiles and other products. Positive and negative ratings by Consumers Union are closely watched by both consumers and businesses.

In addition to consumer education and publicity, consumer advocacy can include BOYCOTTS and CLASS-ACTION LAWSUITS. In the 1960s and 1970s, the UNITED FARM WORKERS, under the leadership of César Chávez, gained support for farmworkers' unionizing efforts through boycotts. More recently, boycotts of tobacco-company products have been used by consumer advocates to influence business practices. Class-action lawsuits are increasingly used to challenge business safety and responsibility issues.

The BETTER BUSINESS BUREAU (BBB) is a business-sponsored organization providing services to consumers. The BBB attempts to resolve consumers' complaints against businesses and maintains files documenting such complaints.

Further reading
Consumer Federation of America Web site. Available online. URL: www.consumerfed.org; Consumer Product Safety Commission Web site. Available online. URL: www.cpsc.gov; Consumers Union Web site. Available online. URL: www.consumersunion.org.

consumer bankruptcy (insolvency)
Consumer bankruptcy or insolvency occurs when individuals with regular INCOMES can no longer afford to meet their payment obligations. Consumer

bankruptcy is both a legal and business concern. Under Chapter 13 of the U.S. Bankruptcy Code, individuals can develop, under court supervision, plans to satisfy their creditors. Chapter 13 allows reductions in consumers' debts and/or extensions of time to pay debts. Consumers are also allowed to retain certain exempt ASSETS, usually their home, one motor vehicle, tools of their trade, and some other personal assets. Chapter 13 bankruptcy is available to individuals and sole proprietors of businesses, subject to limitations on unsecured debts and secured debts.

Chapter 7 of the U.S. Bankruptcy Code provides the option of liquidation or straight bankruptcy. Liquidation, selling all assets and dividing the proceeds among creditors, is available to individuals, partnerships or corporations operating in the United States.

Consumer bankruptcy is a major concern for U.S. businesses. CONSUMPTION spending represents two-thirds of U.S. GROSS DOMESTIC PRODUCT. Consumer spending is critical to the economy, but American consumers owe over $1 trillion to creditors. During the Bush administration business interests, particularly consumer-finance companies, complained U.S. personal-bankruptcy laws are too lenient, leading to passage of the Bankruptcy Abuse Prevention and Consumer Protection Act of 2005, which increased restrictions in consumer-bankruptcy laws.

CONSUMER ADVOCACY groups criticize lenders for inadequate disclosure of fees and rates to consumers and for irresponsible lending practices. Access to credit is critical to the sale of many consumer PRODUCTS. Businesses balance the need for sales against the credit-worthiness of customers. Lenders use the FIVE C'S OF CREDIT in evaluating lending requests and review credit-agency reports before extending credit. Nevertheless, consumer bankruptcy remains a major issue in the U.S. economy.

Further reading
Mallor, Jane P., A. James Barnes, Thomas Bowers, Michael J. Phillips, and Arlen W. Langvardt. *Business Law: The Ethical, Global, and E-Commerce Environment.* 14th ed. Boston: McGraw-Hill, 2009.

consumer behavior

Consumer behavior is comprised of the processes and factors consumers use to make purchase decisions. To most people, consumer behavior just "is." Many consumers only vaguely recognize the factors that influence their actions or the process they go through in making choices. But to marketers, understanding consumer behavior is critical to developing a successful MARKETING STRATEGY.

The first step in the CONSUMER BUYING PROCESS is problem or need recognition. Before consumers consider making purchases, a wide variety of social circumstances and psychological factors influence their problem or need recognition. This can be as simple as deciding one is thirsty or as complex as deciding to get married. In both situations, consumers are influenced by both personal and interpersonal forces in their decisions.

Personal or psychological factors—including needs, perceptions, attitudes, learning, and self-concept—can all influence people's actions. In MASLOW'S HIERARCHY OF NEEDS, there are basic physiological needs, such as thirst. People typically address their physiological needs before allocating time and money to meet higher-order needs. Perceptions are the process of receiving, organizing, and assigning meaning to stimuli detected by the five senses. Humans constantly receive stimuli from their environment. Some of the stimuli, like the sound of a bird, are natural, but others, like the roar of a jet, are man-made. Many man-made stimuli are marketing messages, and the typical American consumer is exposed to thousands of such messages daily—for example, commercials, signs, labels, and TRADEMARKS.

Marketers understand that one aspect of consumer behavior is reaction to stimuli. Consumers tend to pay selective attention to stimuli, screening out unpleasant or unfamiliar sensory information. As part of the perceptual process, people also distort meanings from stimuli, changing their interpretation to be consistent with their beliefs, in addition to selectively retaining sensory images. Relatively new studies indicate that significant events cause chemical changes in human brains, explaining why emotional situations can be recalled vividly many years later. Part of the task for marketers is to understand how people interpret stimuli. Understanding consumers' perceptions can help in designing products, packaging, and promotions, especially when considering new TARGET MARKETS.

Learning takes place through changes in behavior resulting from experience and observation. A thirsty person will observe signs of water keenly. Attitudes are consumers' learned predispositions. Dentists, for example, know most of their customers come into their offices with fear and trepidation developed from past painful learning experiences.

A last psychological factor influencing consumer behavior is people's self-concept, or personal "picture." This can include their "real" self, self-image, and ideal self. Numerous popular psychology books have been written about the differences in men's versus women's self-image, usually suggesting that men see themselves as better and women as worse than their real selves. Consumer behavior is often influenced by self-image and by ideal self-image—that is, how we would like to be seen. Even a simple need like thirst can be influenced by self-concept. In recent years, marketers have made millions of dollars selling bottled water. Chemical studies usually show bottled water to be of no better quality than tap water, but blue bottles and French names appeal to consumers' self-image.

As stated earlier, consumer behavior is influenced by both psychological and social forces. The power of others to influence behavior is well known to marketers. Social influences are typically categorized into four groups: culture, social class, reference groups, and families.

Culture refers to values, norms, tastes, and preferences passed from one generation to the next. Many people, for instance, buy the same goods and services that their parents purchased. Marketers also recognize many distinct subcultures in the United States, which are often the source of new ideas and trends adopted into the mainstream culture. The fastest-growing subculture in the United States is the Hispanic population. Both the Republican and Democratic parties recognize the importance of Hispanic voters and develop specific messages to appeal to them. (American marketers are also beginning to distinguish subcultures within the Hispanic population.)

Social class is a powerful influence on consumer behavior. Social class includes peoples' education, occupations, and habitats. The phrase "keeping up with the Joneses" refers to the common practice of people striving to display a lifestyle equal to that of their neighbors. Realtors often quietly relate stories of people selling empty houses, which had originally been purchased in order to live in the "right" neighborhood, even if it cost more than the family could afford.

Similar to the factor of social class is that of reference groups—that is, groups with which consumers identify. The behavior of a reference group often influences individual consumer behavior, as in the purchase of conspicuous items such as automobiles. Few Americans recognize that U.S. products and trends are closely watched and influence consumer trends in other countries. American music, movies, and dress are copied by teenagers around the world, and the use of celebrity spokespeople in marketing campaigns is often aimed at people who aspire to be like those celebrities.

Lastly, families influence individual consumer behavior. In the United States changing family DEMOGRAPHICS—including more single-parent households, children returning to the "nest" households, and two-adult but unrelated households—influence purchasing decisions. Home builders have constructed more two-bedroom, two-bath dwellings for the two unrelated adults market. Numerous time-saving products have been created for the single-parent market, and parents are still adjusting to children returning home after college. One source stated that 35 percent of college graduates move home.

Further reading

Boone, Louis E., and David Kurtz. *Contemporary Marketing*. 14th ed. Fort Worth: South-Western, 2009; Etzel, Michael J., Bruce J. Walker, and William J. Staunton. *Marketing*. 14th ed. Boston: McGraw-Hill, 2008.

consumer buying process

The consumer buying process is the series of steps consumers typically go through in making a purchase decision. Often the whole process will only take seconds or a few minutes, while other times it may take years. Regardless of how long it takes, consumers generally go through six steps when making a purchase decision:

- problem or need recognition
- search
- alternative evaluation
- purchase decision and action
- post-purchase evaluation

Problem or need recognition initiates the buying process. Dissatisfaction with current PRODUCTS, running out of supply of an item, or a changed financial status can stimulate consumer needs. Most consumers are creatures of habit and will repurchase the product they always use. This helps firms who are the established leaders in their markets but creates a barrier for new competitors. New competitors look for dissatisfied customers; those who are new to an area; and those who, through inheritance, divorce, or other situations have significantly changed their purchasing power.

In the search stage, consumers identify different products that will solve their problem. For everyday purchases like milk or bread, consumers usually quickly determine alternative sources of products to meet their needs. For high-involvement purchases like homes or automobiles, the search process will take longer and probably include searching for objective sources of information. Many consumers will only consider a few possible choices when searching for products to solve their problem. Marketers refer to the choices considered as the "evoked set." Firms that have severely disappointed consumers in the past or who are new to the market often have difficulty even being considered by consumers. For many years a significant portion of American consumers would not even consider American-made automobiles, having been disappointed with the performance of their last American-made cars.

In the alternative-evaluation stage, consumers consider and weigh the choices available. Again, with everyday-type purchases this stage can take seconds, while for a specialty item it may take months. Marketers respond to the alternative-evaluation stage by providing and promoting features they hope will influence consumers' evaluation of their products.

There can be considerable variation in the evaluation stage. One marketer found that it took him half the time it took his wife to do the family grocery shopping. Going to the supermarket together, he found out why. His wife read the ingredient labels, while he just purchased what was on the shopping list.

The purchase decision and action is, as the term suggests, the determination of which product will best satisfy one's need and the action of making the actual deal. Salespeople refer to this stage as the "closing." For everyday purchases, the goal is to make the purchase as quickly and effortlessly as possible. For complex decisions like a real estate closing, the purchase process can take weeks.

Post-purchase evaluation addresses the questions "Did I make the right decision?" and "Did I get a good deal?" Marketers refer to this anxiety as cognitive dissonance. Good marketers, recognizing that word-of-mouth is almost always the best form of promotion and that new customers are almost always more difficult and expensive to find than maintaining existing customers, try to reduce consumers' cognitive dissonance. Realtors will offer buyer's insurance, protecting the purchaser against unforeseen problems. Service providers like dentists and doctors will often call clients to see how they are doing after a procedure. Thank-you notes convey appreciation and also remind consumers about their purchase process.

Further reading

Boone, Louis E., and David L. Kurtz. *Contemporary Marketing.* 14th ed. Fort Worth: South-Western, 2009.

consumer credit counseling service

A consumer credit counseling service (CCCS) is a nonprofit organization that assists individuals and families in the United States with BUDGET-ING and credit resolution. CCCSs are members of the National Foundation for Credit Counseling (NFCC), which was established in 1951 by retail credit companies to provide financial counseling and education services. There are approximately 850 CCCSs in the country and over 3 million households who utilize their services annually.

CCCSs primarily provide debt-management services. In a debt-management plan, individuals document all of their financial liabilities as well as their INCOME and then voluntarily make payments to creditors through the CCCS. Payments are dispersed by the CCCS to creditors, who usually agree to eliminate interest and waive late or over-limit fees for consumers utilizing debt-management plans. Participants normally pay a $30 fee to set up a plan and are charged up to $24 per month to service the plan.

Debt-management plans are an alternative to filing for personal bankruptcy (Chapters 7 or 13), debt-consolidation loans, or home-equity loans. Personal bankruptcy filing is handled through the court system and stays on an individual's credit history for many years. Personal consolidation loans may reduce INTEREST RATES or monthly payments by extending the length of the loan, but they do not eliminate interest payments. Home-equity loans are tax-deductible and often at a lower interest rate than unsecured personal credit loans, but they use the borrower's home as security for the loan.

The major source of funding for CCCSs comes from the credit industry. Creditors who participate in CCCS programs contribute an amount equal to 15 percent of consumer payments to the local CCCS. The benefit to credit companies is they get their money back. The benefit to consumers is they restructure their loans into lower and usually interest-free payments that they usually can afford and thus get out of debt. The process also provides education to consumers about the use of credit. Excessive CREDIT CARD debt is a major problem in the United States, especially among young people with little knowledge of or experience in the use of credit.

See also PERSONAL FINANCE.

Further reading
National Foundation for Credit Counseling Web site. Available online. URL: www.nfcc.org.

Consumer Credit Protection Act

Passed in 1968, the Consumer Credit Protection Act (CCPA) protects employees from being discharged by their employers when their wages have been garnished and limits the amount of employees' earnings which may be garnished per week. Garnishment is the seizing of a person's property, wages, or money to satisfy a judgment. Generally creditors use garnishment as a last resort to gain payment from people they are owed money. Frequently there are few ASSETS available to garnish, aside from wages.

Employee earnings include salaries, commissions, bonuses, and INCOME from pension or retirement programs. The CCPA limits the amount a creditor can garnish to 25 percent of the debtor's weekly disposable income or the amount by which the person's weekly take-home income exceeds 30 times the current federal MINIMUM WAGE. The smaller of the two choices is the limit on the amount that can be garnished. In court orders for child support or alimony, the CCPA allows up to 50 percent of an employee's disposable earnings to be garnished. Disposable income is defined under the act as income after deductions for taxes, SOCIAL SECURITY payments, and state retirement-system contributions.

The CCPA is administered and enforced by the Employment Standards Administration's Wage and Hourly Division, a division of the U.S. DEPARTMENT OF LABOR. Violations of the CCPA may result in reinstatement of a discharged employee with back pay and the restoration of garnished amounts. Employers who willfully violate the discharge provisions of the law may be prosecuted and subject to up to a $1,000 fine and imprisonment of up to one year, or both.

The Consumer Credit Protection Act applies to all states, but states are allowed to pass laws that eliminate garnishment, and many have. Often employers have fired workers whose earnings have been garnished, citing the added bookkeeping expense associated with complying with a judgment. The law allows states to prohibit firing of employees whose wages have been garnished.

The FAIR DEBT COLLECTION PRACTICES ACT (1977), an amendment to the Consumer Credit Protection Act, defines forbidden debt-collection practices, including harassment, false or misleading representation, and other unfair practices.

Further reading
Fisher, Bruce D., and Michael J. Phillips. *The Legal, Ethical and Regulatory Environment of Business.* 8th ed. Cincinnati: Thomson/South-Western, 2003; U.S. Department of Labor Web site. Available online. URL: www.dol.gov/compliance/laws/comp-ccpa.htm.

consumer economics
Consumer economics is the study of how individuals and households allocate scarce RESOURCES. Consumer economics evolved out of 19th-century study of home economics and 20th-century emphasis on consumerism, the consumer's role in an economic system.

Today, in the United States, consumer spending accounts for approximately 70 percent of aggregate expenditures (the sum of consumer spending, INVESTMENT, government spending, and net trade). Economists and policymakers recognize the importance of consumer spending to a full-employment economy. In the 2008–09 recession, many pundits observed "consumers drive the economy." Efforts by the George W. Bush and Obama administrations to stimulate consumer spending included tax rebates and cuts, and monetary policy actions designed to lower INTEREST RATES.

Economists recognize consumer spending depends primarily on households' current disposable INCOME. For most Americans, current disposable income is their "take-home" pay. For more affluent Americans, disposable income also includes interest, dividend, and rental income as well as profits from investments and businesses. In addition to disposable income, changes in taxes, wealth, expectations, and demographics also influence consumers' decisions. Reduced tax rates increase consumers' disposable income. In the early 21st century, for most Americans increases in wealth came from higher property values and rising stock market prices. This led to what was called the "wealth effect," as consumers borrowed against the equity in their homes and spent more freely, comforted by the rising value of their portfolios. When the 2008 recession caused both housing and stock market prices to plummet, the wealth effect worked in reverse, curtailing consumer spending.

Consumers' expectations about the future also influence spending decisions. The University of Michigan's Consumer Sentiment Index and the Conference Board's Consumer Confidence Index are two national indicators assessing Americans' expectations. During economic expansions, consumers tend to feel positive about their future and spend and borrow more. During economic contractions, consumers tend to reduce spending and use added disposable income from tax cuts to pay off debt.

Demographics, consumers' age, race, gender, occupation, and income influence consumers' economic decisions through differences in marginal propensities to consume. Older consumers tend to spend less of their disposable income than younger consumers. Ethnicity and gender also influence consumer spending priorities. Marketers spend hundreds of millions of dollars annually trying to better understand their target market, the people who buy their products and services, and what influences their decisions.

CONSUMER BEHAVIOR, the processes and factors consumers use to make purchase decisions, is a fascinating and dynamic part of marketing, but it also provides insights for consumers as they assess what influences their consumer spending decisions. Psychologists divide factors that define consumers into personal and interpersonal determinants. Personal determinants include needs, perceptions, attitudes, learning, and self-concept. Interpersonal or social determinants include culture, social class, reference groups, and families. Consumer economics focuses on the choices people make, but many factors influence those decisions.

While economists, psychologists, and other social and behavioral scientists are constantly studying and developing theories about consumer behavior, consumer economics tends to focus on practical aspects of consumer decision making. Smart decision making requires knowledge. Consumer economics and consumer economics courses tend to focus on increasing consumers' ability to make sound judgments regarding quality, identify differences in features and value, differentiate advertising claims from factual information, weigh marginal benefits versus costs, and prioritize needs and wants.

To make sound economic decisions, consumers need good information. Consumer economics includes analysis of the role of government in providing objective information and preventing fraud, and study of the ability of consumers to detect false claims, counterfeit products, deceptive practices and attempts by criminals to steal from them. Though it is also used by criminals to deceive consumers, the Internet has become a powerful tool to help people make better choices.

One subject of debate in consumer economics is: where does it end and where does the study of personal finance begin? In addition to making spending decisions, individuals and households also make savings and investment decisions. The two areas of knowledge widely overlap. One textbook author titled his book "Personal Economics," recognizing the interrelationship of the two disciplines.

Further reading
Lee, Edgar Brown, and Fred F. Bartok: *Personal Economics.* Boston: Holbrook Press, 1977; Zelenak, Mel J. *Consumer Economics: The Consumer in Our Society.* Scottsdale, Ariz.: Holcomb Hathway, 2009.

Consumer Price Index

The Consumer Price Index (CPI) is a statistical measure of the average prices paid by consumers for a typical "market basket" of goods and SERVICES. Measuring the rate of change in prices is important to policy makers. Price changes are a critical concern in MONETARY POLICY, essential in

evaluating ECONOMIC CONDITIONS, and a major factor when indexing spending and taxes. The CPI is an important and controversial measure of price changes. The controversy centers on how the CPI is calculated and, thus, whether it is representative of INFLATION as experienced by American consumers. Most U.S. economists agree the CPI overstates the rate of inflation experienced by American consumers.

Calculated by the BUREAU OF LABOR STATISTICS (BLS) since 1917, the CPI is measured monthly by sampling prices around the country for a "typical market basket" of goods and services purchased. An average price for each good and service is derived from the sampling procedure, which is then multiplied by the assumed amount typical households purchase. This process "weights" the goods and services by the relative importance in consumers' budgets. The sum of the prices times quantities are then divided by the cost of the same goods and services in a base year to create a price index.

Price index = cost of market basket today × 100/
cost of market basket in base year

One of the problems with the CPI is what is "typical." Especially in the 1990s and early 21st century, rapid changes in technology have made many new products available to consumers. For example, cellular telephones, which have been available since the early 1990s, were not included in the CPI until 1998. Similarly, the CPI used the price of coal as a measure of the cost of heating long after it was replaced by heating oil and natural gas in most American homes.

Related to the problem of what constitutes typical purchases by consumers is the issue of quality changes. American consumers are paying more for health care but also have significantly improved products and services available to them. The CPI does not accurately distinguish between increased prices and higher prices for improvements in quality. The U.S. Congress created commissions to investigate the country's Consumer Price Index in 1961 (Stigler Commission) and again in 1997 (CPI

Commission). The CPI Commission estimated changes in quality and introduction of new PRODUCTS resulted in approximately a half percentage point upward bias in the index.

Another problem is that the CPI does not always capture changes in CONSUMER BEHAVIOR. Because the amount of each product is fixed in the index, the CPI does reflect consumer substitution. For example, if citrus fruit prices rise rapidly due to a freeze in the southern part of the country, consumers will likely substitute other fruit products in their purchases, but the CPI reflects the amount of citrus fruits typically purchased. Consumers' cost of fruit will therefore be lower than the amount estimated in the index. In 1997 the CPI Commission estimated this substitution bias overestimated inflation by 0.4 percentage points.

The CPI Commission also reported two other smaller sources of bias measuring the index. Most sampling takes place during the week, but retailers often reduce prices on weekends, and thus the index does not accurately reflect the prices paid by consumers. Similarly, the Bureau of Labor Statistics rotates the retail stores included in the sampling procedure each year, but the Commission found that the process does not fully reflect consumers' substitution of discount and superstore outlets for traditional retailers.

As stated earlier, the CPI is used to measure the change in prices paid, reflecting the cost of living. The CPI is used to address the question: "How much more INCOME will consumers need to be just as well off at the current price level as compared to old prices?" Private contracts for products, borrowing, and approximately one-third of the FEDERAL BUDGET are automatically escalated each year by the change in the CPI. Many union wage agreements (COST OF LIVING ADJUSTMENTS) and SOCIAL SECURITY payments are examples of contracts tied to changes in inflation as measured by the CPI. Even small changes in the CPI, when compounded over time, result in large changes in wages and payments.

The Bureau of Labor Statistics produces two other inflation indices, the PRODUCER PRICE INDEX (PPI) and the GDP deflator.

See also PRICE INDEXES.

Further reading
Boskin, Michael J. "The CPI Commission," *Business Economics* 32, no. 2 (April 1997): 60–63.

Consumer Product Safety Commission
The Consumer Product Safety Commission (CPSC) is a federal agency created in 1972. The CPSC's mission is to "protect the public against unreasonable risks of injuries and deaths associated with consumer PRODUCTS." The commission has jurisdiction over 15,000 types of consumer products and issues safety standards for everything from bicycle helmets to matchbooks.

Certain consumer products (automobiles and food products, for example) are under the jurisdiction of other federal agencies (DEPARTMENT OF TRANSPORTATION and FOOD AND DRUG ADMINISTRATION, respectively).

The CPSC uses a variety of methods to ensure product safety, including

- developing voluntary standards with industry
- issuing and enforcing mandatory standards; banning consumer products if no feasible standard adequately protect the public
- obtaining recall of unsafe products or arranging for their repair
- conducting research on potential product hazards
- informing and educating consumers

The CPSC administers five laws:

- Consumer Product Safety Act
- Flammable Fabrics Act
- Federal Hazardous Substances Act
- Poison Prevention Packaging Act of 1970
- Refrigerator Safety Act of 1956

The CPSC is composed of five members appointed by the president, by and with the consent of the Senate, for terms of seven years. The commission attempts to use voluntary standards and "product safety triangles"—government, industry, and consumers—to ensure product safety, and it will regulate industries when necessary.

Businesses do not want the negative publicity associated with the CPSC's determination that their product is unsafe. One of the most visible CPSC activities is the evaluation of toys that present choking hazards for children less than three years old. Some of the safety standards set by the CPSC include standards for lawn darts, swimming-pool slides, automated garage-door openers, insulation, and wood-burning appliances.

Further reading
Consumer Product Safety Commission Web site. Available online. URL: http://cpsc.gov.

consumer protection
Consumer protection refers to a wide variety of regulations, primarily issued and enforced at the federal level by the FEDERAL TRADE COMMISSION (FTC), affecting American consumers. Consumer protection includes regulation of consumer credit, product safety, warranties, and TELEMARKETING.

The major consumer-protection laws regulating consumer credit include the following:

- Fair Credit Reporting Act (1971): Requires credit-reporting SERVICES to maintain accurate, relevant, and recent information; provide access to credit information only to bona fide users; inform consumers who are turned down or have their interest costs raised and provide reasons for the change; allow consumers to review their files and correct any inaccurate information.
- Fair Credit Billing Act (1975): Requires creditors to mail bills at least 14 days prior to the payment-due date, customers to notify creditors in writing within 60 days regarding billing-error complaints; and allows merchants to give cash discounts.
- Equal Credit Opportunity Act (1975; expanded in 1977): Makes creditor discrimination based on sex, race, national origin, religion, age, receipt of public assistance, or marital status illegal.
- CONSUMER CREDIT PROTECTION ACT (1968): Requires prompt written acknowledgment of consumer billing complaints and investigation of billing errors by creditors.
- Consumer Product Safety Act (1972): Created the CONSUMER PRODUCT SAFETY COMMISSION as an independent regulatory agency issuing

safety standards and rules banning hazardous products; the commission also brings lawsuits against producers of hazardous consumer products.

- Magnusson-Moss Warranty Act (1975): Requires simple, clear, and conspicuous presentation of certain information in written warranties to consumers. The act does not require sellers to provide warranties, only requires clear presentation of information in warranties.
- Telemarketing and Consumer Fraud and Abuse Prevention Act (1994): Requires the FTC to develop regulations defining and prohibiting deceptive and abusive telemarketing practices. One regulation allows telemarketing only during the hours of 8 A.M. to 9 P.M., local time. Another regulation prohibits threats, intimidation, or use of profanity in telemarketing activities.

See also WARRANTY.

Further reading
Mallor, Jane P., A. James Barnes, Thomas Bowers, Michael J. Philips, and Arlen W. Langvardt. *Business Law: The Ethical, Global, and E-Commerce Environment.* 14th ed. Boston: McGraw-Hill, 2009.

Consumers Union
Consumers Union (CU) publishes *Consumer Reports* magazine, a premier independent source of information for American consumers. Founded in 1936 by a group of concerned professors, labor leaders, journalists, and engineers, CU is known for its testing and rating of consumer PRODUCTS. To maintain its independence, CU purchases every product tested and does not accept grants. Instead it relies on member subscriptions, which were only 4,000 in 1936 but today exceed 8 million.

A positive Consumers Union review can create significant impact in the marketplace. In the mid-1960s CU's recommendation of the Toyota Corolla helped the Japanese manufacturer break into the U.S. market. Ralph Nader, author of *Unsafe at Any Speed* (1965), a highly critical assessment of General Motors' Corvair, was a member of CU's BOARD OF DIRECTORS for eight years. CU also supported the publication of *Silent Spring* (1963), Rachel Carson's environmental classic, with a special CU edition of the book.

CU's National Testing and Research Center in Yonkers, N.Y., is the largest nonprofit education and consumer product-testing center in the world. CU's safety and repair reports for automobiles are among their most widely used consumer-information service. CU also maintains three advocacy offices in Washington, D.C., San Francisco, and Austin, testifying before federal and state legislatures, petitioning government agencies, and filing consumer interest lawsuits.

Further reading
Consumers Union Web site. Available online. URL: www.consumersunion.org.

consumption

In everyday living, consumption is the act of using or consuming things, but in business consumption refers to the level of current spending for new goods and services; in economics and business statistics, it is the amount of spending by households for currently produced goods and SERVICES. The purchase of a used car or home is not included in current consumption statistics, because it was included during the period of time when it was purchased.

Consumption spending is the largest component of total spending in NATIONAL INCOME ACCOUNTING. Because consumption represents two-thirds of total spending, it is the most closely watched component. Economists analyze the level and changes in the level of consumption spending in the economy. They have developed numerous theories regarding what factors influence consumption, the major one being current INCOME, since without income most people do little consumption spending. A variety of other factors influence peoples' consumption decisions, including expectations, WEALTH, and access to credit.

Expectations play an important role in current spending decisions. College seniors often purchase a car on the expectation of graduating and getting a good-paying job. Nobel Prize–winning economist Milton Friedman proposed the permanent-income hypothesis, suggesting consumption is determined by what people consider to be their permanent income rather than their actual income. Permanent income is what people expect to earn annually, not including transitory income or sudden windfalls such as prizes or one-time tax cuts, which temporarily increase their income.

Since the late 1990s, wealth has become an increasingly important consideration in consumption spending by Americans, many of whom first invested in the STOCK MARKET in the early 1990s. By 1999 most investors had accumulated significant increases in the value of their portfolios, especially if they had invested in technology companies. Sales of luxury cars and high-priced California real estate soared based on newly acquired wealth. When technology stocks began to fall in early 2000, many Americans' wealth declined, and with it their consumption spending diminished. Alan Greenspan, then chairman of the FEDERAL RESERVE SYSTEM, frequently analyzed the "wealth effect" on consumer spending. When U.S. housing prices collapsed in 2007, the wealth effect worked in reverse, reducing home-equity loans and consumption based on increasing wealth. Economists also recognize that expectations of wealth through inheritance influence current spending.

Credit and access to credit influence current consumer spending. Many college students have learned the hard way how easy it is to use credit for current consumption spending and become deep in debt as a result. Some consumer spending, for homes and automobiles particularly, is influenced by INTEREST RATES charged for financing, but much of this spending is limited by the maximum credit-level allowed.

Retail companies study changes in consumption spending to anticipate changes in DEMAND for their goods and services. Consumption of some products and services, such as health care, are relatively insensitive to changes in income or credit; while other products, leisure travel and appliances, are sensitive to changes in income. Manufacturers also study changes in consumption spending when making PRODUCTION-planning schedules and long-term CAPITAL investment decisions. Governments keep track of consumption spending in order to predict changes in sales tax revenue.

U.S. consumption statistics are available in the *Survey of Current Business Statistics,* published by the Department of Commerce.

Further reading
Department of Commerce Web site. Available online. URL: www.doc.gov.

consumption tax
Consumption taxes are the various taxes imposed on the purchase of goods and SERVICES. Sales, excise, and value-added tax (VAT) are the most common types of consumption taxes, with sales taxes being the most visible type. Many international visitors are shocked the first time a tax is added to the price of the PRODUCT they are purchasing. Americans, however, generally support the use of sales taxes over other forms of taxation, rationalizing that "everyone has to pay it" and "you only have to pay a little at a time." In the United States, sales taxes are commonly imposed by state and sometimes local governments, so sales-tax rates vary around the country. In addition, many states exempt certain categories of goods, usually food and clothing, from sales taxes.

A major controversy surrounds whether to require E-COMMERCE businesses to collect and remit sales taxes. Presidents since Bill Clinton have all delayed implementation of INTERNET commerce sales taxation. Supporters argue taxation would discourage growth of this new industry, while opponents, including many state treasurers and retail "brick-and-mortar" companies, complain it reduces tax revenue and gives an unfair advantage to Internet-based companies.

Generally excise taxes which usually comprise a fixed amount per unit of a good, are imposed by the federal government. The federal excise tax on gasoline is charged in the form of cents per gallon. Excise taxes on liquor and cigarettes are similarly based on cents per gallon and cents per pack, respectively. Government agencies rarely collect consumption taxes directly. Instead, sales and excise taxes are typically collected by retailers and remitted to the respective government treasuries. Excise taxes are sometimes used to implement the benefits principle in government policy: the idea that those citizens who benefit from the government program or service should pay for it, while those citizens who do not utilize the program or service should not have to pay for it. The excise tax on gasoline, which is directed into the national highway TRUST fund for building and maintaining roadways, is an example of an excise tax based on the benefits principle. Excise taxes are also sometimes called "sin and vice" taxes and are imposed to discourage CONSUMPTION of certain products. Higher excise taxes increase the price of products, and, given the law of DEMAND and ELASTICITY OF DEMAND, a higher price will have a major or minor impact on quantity demanded.

The United States, unlike Canada and most of Europe, does not have a value-added tax (VAT). Many economists argue a VAT would be preferable to the myriad of income taxes currently used in the country. In a VAT system, goods are taxed at each stage of the production process with the tax incorporated as part of the cost to producers. For example, farmers produce wheat, which is sold to flour companies. The difference between the revenue from the sale and cost of seed, fertilizer, and other inputs the farmer used is the farmer's value added; this would then be taxed. Next, the flour company would take the wheat, convert it into flour, and sell it to a bread company. The difference between the cost of the wheat plus other inputs and the INCOME received from the bread company would be the flour company's value added, and the VAT would be applied. The bread company would pay a VAT based on their value added, and it would be incorporated in the price consumers would pay.

Economists argue a VAT would discourage consumption and therefore encourage savings. Savings provide funds for investment, which in turn increases a country's CAPITAL resources, expanding its production capacity. Economists point to the current income-tax system as having almost infinite numbers of loopholes and discouraging productive activity through higher tax rates as peoples' incomes increase. Economists also recognize consumption taxes are regressive. Lower-income consumers typically spend a higher percentage of their income on sales-taxable items than upper-income consumers do, and therefore they pay a higher percentage of their income in the form of sales taxes.

Further reading
Ruffin, Roy J., and Paul R. Gregory. *Principles of Economics.* 7th ed. Boston: Addison Wesley, 2000.

contestable market theory
Contestable market theory suggests that in markets where the costs of entering and leaving are very low, existing firms are continually threatened by the entry of new competitors. Contestable market theory challenges one of the assumptions of PERFECT COMPETITION: that a large number of firms is needed to maintain COMPETITION and eliminate economic PROFITS.

A contestable market is one in which firms can enter and leave the market without incurring significant COSTS. Fixed costs—costs that are required to start a business and do not change as output expands—act as a barrier to entry to would-be competitors. If new competitors can enter and exit a market without large expenditures, they can take advantage of market conditions when prices and profits are high and leave a market when prices are low. Many types of direct consumer sales, such as cosmetics, health-care PRODUCTs, and consumer information SERVICES, can be entered and exited at relatively little cost. When a new product or service suddenly becomes popular, the few existing firms make economic profits. Seeing opportunities, new competitors enter the market, driving down prices and eliminating profits. Once the market price has dropped, some firms will exit the market.

Recognizing the threat of potential entrants into contestable markets, existing firms will often cut prices and expand output to reduce the incentives for new competitors to enter their market. Contestable market theory is used to explain why firms with local monopolies or few competitors

do not try to charge higher prices and maximize profits.

See also BARRIERS TO ENTRY; MONOPOLY.

Further reading
Miller, Roger Leroy. *Economics Today.* 15th ed. Boston: Addison Wesley, 2009.

contingency fee
A contingency fee is an arrangement between an attorney and his client in which the attorney is paid a percentage of the amount recovered in a legal action taken on behalf of the client. The payment to the lawyer depends, or is contingent, upon there being some monetary recovery or award in the case. The purpose of a contingent fee is to reward attorneys for proficiency and diligence in prosecuting disputed and litigated claims. Contingency fees are an alternative to retainer fees, paying an hourly rate for the attorney's services. The percentage of the award an attorney receives varies, typically 25 to 50 percent of the amount recovered, but can range as high as 100 percent. Many arrangements include different percentages depending on whether the case is settled out of court, goes to trial, or if the case is appealed. State laws require contingency fee arrangements to be written agreements and are subject to "reasonableness" restrictions determined by the courts.

Contingent fee agreements are not allowed in criminal cases but are common in civil cases, particularly personal injury cases. The derogatory term "ambulance chasers" refers to attorneys who seek out as clients people who have been injured in accidents, often targeting injured passengers in widely reported plane and train crashes. Court rules and statutes often regulate contingency fees in relation to the type of action and amount of recovery.

For individuals, contingent fee arrangements provide the benefit of allowing the party seeking recovery who cannot afford legal representation to retain an attorney and therefore possess an effective means of prosecuting a claim. A percentage fee arrangement provides an incentive for attorneys to work diligently and expeditiously, knowing they will only be paid if they succeed on behalf of their client. Contingent arrangements also benefit the legal system in reducing the number of lawsuits lacking merit.

Critics contend contingency fee arrangements induce attorneys to take on only the most promising and potentially remunerative cases, regardless of the merits associated with the claim. Citizens with costly or risky claims may not be able to find representation while highly publicized cases and class-action suits are adjudicated. Contingency arrangements are discouraged but not illegal in divorce proceedings. A fee arrangement could create a conflict of interest in which the attorney may discourage reconciliation between a husband and wife, if his fee depends upon the granting of a divorce.

Further reading

American Bar Association Web site. Available online. URL: www.abanet.org/publiced/practical/lawyerfees_contingent.html.

contingency theory

Contingency theory proposes that there is no one best approach to organizational problem solving. Contingencies include a variety of environmental forces internal and external to the organization such as market demands, technologies, management structure, and employee relations. Changes such as these require an organization and its leadership to respond to situations differently. Contingency theory suggests that organizations that adapt their structures to accommodate changing environments will thrive in an increasingly diversified global economy.

Contingency theory includes multiple behavioral, management, and leadership theories developed since World War II. Previously, discussions of leadership historically described leaders as hero-like individuals possessed of the ability to foresee the directions in which to lead society. Contingency theorists argued that organizational leadership is affected not merely by the influence of one leader, but also by many structural situations facing the organization.

In the late 1950s and early 1960s, Joan Woodward determined a correlation between an organization's technological mode of production and its management structure. Large companies with sophisticated systems of mechanized production had similar bureaucratic management structures. Organizations producing varying, individualized goods had smaller structures with less bureaucracy and more flexibility. Lawrence and Lorsch further documented the idea that external environmental fluctuations influence internal structural change within an organization in order for it to realign with the environment. This "survival-of-the-fittest" logic is a central tenet of contingency theory.

Fred Fiedler's contingency model classifies leaders as relationship-oriented or task-oriented. Leaders rank coworkers on a Least-Preferred Coworker (LPC) scale, using numerical values to indicate a range of preferences, such as Unfriendly/Friendly, where low LPC scores indicate task orientation and high LPC scores indicate relationship orientation. Fiedler's contingency model assumes that leaders do not change their LPC orientations and therefore it seeks to fit the best leader to the appropriate situation.

Examples of other contingency theories include Hersey and Blanchard's "situational theory" and Drotter's "leadership pipeline." Hersey and Blanchard assume that different styles of leadership are necessary in different situations, identifying three specific types of leadership: transactional (authoritative and status driven); transformal (charismatic and defined by each personality involved); and pluralistic (group defined). Drotter's "leadership pipeline" states that, to be successful, an organization should develop a core network of skilled, diversified leaders within the work environment. This eliminates the need to outsource leaders or frequently change leadership styles in response to contingencies.

Critics of contingency theory argue that it is opportunistic and that it is a tautology, a statement that is true by its own definition. By defining situations, contingencies, and their relationships as unique and in constant flux, opponents argue that contingency theory can never be challenged because it accurately reflects the nature of events in the real world.

Further reading
Articles Gratuits. *Contingency Theory.* Available online. URL: www.en.articlesgratuits.com/contingency-theory-id1620.php. Accessed on June 29, 2009; Babson College. *Contingency Theory.* Available online. URL: faculty.babson.edu/krollag/org_site/encyclop/contingency.html. Accessed on June 29, 2009; Contingency Theory. In 12 Manage: *The Executive Fast Track.* Available online. URL: www.12manage.com/methods_contingency_theory.html. Accessed on June 29, 2009; Kriger, M., and Y. Seng. "Leadership with Inner Meaning: A Contingency Theory of Leadership Based on the Worldviews of Five Religions." *Leadership Quarterly* 16 (October 2005): 771.
—Mark Lane and Kristin Rowan

contract

A contract is an agreement between two or more parties creating obligations (promises) that are recognized and enforceable by law. For example, the author of this book and its publisher have entered into a lengthy written contract detailing each others' obligations. Contracts may also be reached orally or electronically, but the Statute of Frauds incorporated as part of the Uniform Commercial Code and its successor statutes require certain contracts relating to realty, debts, marriage, sales, and those that take more than a year to perform to be in writing. Enforcement of contractual obligations is normally accomplished by means of court orders and remedies, although the parties to contracts may generally agree to submit their disputes to mediation or ARBITRATION or to pay a reasonable sum ("liquidated damages") in the event of a breach of contract.

There are many different types of contracts: sales, LICENSING, FRANCHISING, cost-plus, requirements, distribution, installment, procurement, etc. Some contracts, especially consumer contracts, are standardized on printed forms. Contracts and contract terms can be implied from the circumstances surrounding the parties' actions and have traditionally been governed by COMMON LAW doctrines regarding their formation, terms, and remedies.

Most U.S. commercial contracts are governed by the UNIFORM COMMERCIAL CODE (UCC), a widely adopted statutory body of law. International commercial contracts may be governed by the Convention on the International Sale of Goods (CISG), to which the United States is a party.

Further reading
Rohwer, Claude, D., and Anthony M. Skrocki. *Contracts in a Nutshell.* 5th ed. Eagan, Minn.: West Group, 2000.

contract theory

Contract theory, as defined in the field of economic research, is an applied (practical) tool for analyzing the process of contract formation within a framework of asymmetric (unequal) information. Contract theory is used to study how asymmetric (unequal) information affects the formation of contracts. A contract is formed when goods or services are offered in exchange for some value, and the specific terms offered by the seller are accepted by the buyer. If the contracting parties bargain from a position of equal power and equal knowledge, they reach an agreement in which each party to the transaction benefits equally. However, when parties to the contracting process hold private information, the bargaining process is altered by the strategies used to exploit that information.

When information is asymmetric, parties use private information to gain competitive advantage in the bargaining or contract formation process. Such private information is referred to as "information rent" because of the value or income that it produces as contracts are formed. For example, private knowledge that production of a new product will contribute to a shortage of raw material may prompt the party to bargain for a long-term, fixed-price supply contract. This is an example of the type of contract strategy that is studied through application of contract theory.

Economists study microeconomic theory by analyzing the effects of asymmetric information on the bargaining strategies and behaviors of contracting parties. Microeconomics is the branch of economics dealing with the behavior of individuals and firms within markets (whereas macroeconomics studies the economy from a broad, holistic perspective). Contract theory is applied to study microeconomic topics such as labor, corporate finance, executive compensation, corporate structure, credit markets, and insurance.

Asymmetric information, which results in an imbalance of bargaining power, is often represented in contract theory by the adverse selection and moral hazard models. In the adverse selection model, one or more contracting parties lacks information held by one or more of the parties during contract bargaining, as illustrated above. In the moral hazard model, knowledge of the actions of parties after contract signing is unequally shared.

The moral hazard model has two components: (1) one or more contracting parties lacks information about the ability of other parties to meet the terms of the agreement after it is signed, and (2) the uninformed party is unable to retaliate if the terms of the agreement are not met. For example, a moral hazard exists if, after signing an automobile insurance contract, a driver is less careful because collisions are insured. Even if it knew of the driver's carelessness, the insurance company has no means to void the contract based solely on the driver's attitude.

Two methods are used to overcome the effects of adverse selection and moral hazard: signaling and screening. Signaling uses a proxy, or substitute, to fill the information gap held by the contracting parties. For example, a good driving record "signals" that a driver is a good insurance risk. Screening is a method of uncovering missing information by asking questions designed to reveal the private information of the other party. For example, a health insurance applicant's answers to a questionnaire reveal the private information needed by the health insurance company to determine the risks associated with insuring the applicant.

Asymmetric information creates risks that the contracting process will not produce optimal, efficient economic transactions. Essentially, risks are the possibilities that one or more parties will not receive what they bargained for. While economic transactions depend on the enforcement mechanisms of legal institutions to mitigate at least some of that risk, contract theory studies the effects of risk tolerance on the contracting process and on relationships between contracting parties. For example, if all contracting parties are risk averse (not willing to accept risk) and they bargain from equal positions of strength and knowledge, the bargaining process is likely to result in an optimal economic transaction where the parties assume equal amounts of risk and/or purchase insurance to cover the risk.

A frequent application of contract theory is the analysis of labor markets, in which economists study the formation of labor contracts to predict the bargaining behavior of workers, who are usually risk averse, and employers, who are often risk neutral, under different economic conditions. In applications such as labor markets, contract theory is used to analyze the effects of asymmetric information on the bargaining process and the distribution of risks between the contracting parties.

Asymmetric information also creates distortions in the relationships of principals and agents, which affects contract formation. An agent possesses the legal authority to act in the place of the principal (the person or entity that designates the agent). An example of an agent is an employee of a company who carries out the actions of the company, such as a lawyer who negotiates contracts. Often, incentives (payments) are required to induce the agent to act for the principal. Constraints, or limits on incentives, produce measurable effects on the behavior of agents. Contract theory analyzes the behavior of agents and the effects of incentives during contract negotiations. For example, contract theory is used to study the effects of incentives on executive compensation and organizational structure.

Contract theory utilizes sophisticated mathematical models to describe and predict the outcome of the contracting process in specific situations. Gaming models, in which the success of individual choices depends on the choices of others, are often used to analyze and predict the behavior of contracting parties. Empirical (observational) studies of the contracting process and the associated behavior of contracting parties can be used to test contract theory models in real-world situations.

Specialized areas of contract theory include relational contracts, incomplete contracts, dynamic contracts, long-term contracts, and auctions. Relational contracts are informal (unwritten) agreements between firms, such as a verbal agreement to extend credit on a short-term basis. Relational contracts may also define relationships within firms. For example, unwritten agreements between managers and employees concerning promotions, retention, and assignments are representative of relational contracts. Incomplete contracts are common because it is not possible to specify the rights and obligations of the contracting parties in every situation. When situations arise that are not covered by the contract terms, additional terms are implied by the conduct of the parties or by courts. Models of incomplete contracts explore the actions of contracting parties in response to events not contemplated *ex ante* (before the event) in the original contract terms. For example, contract terms may be renegotiated in light of *ex post* (after the event) information, such as renegotiation of loan terms after a bankruptcy. Dynamic contract theory uses noncooperative gaming models to study contract formation as a framework for studying microeconomic theory. In dynamic contract models, competitive strength may vary over the term of the contractual relationship; information sharing may interact with other decisions; information may be perfect, imperfect but symmetric (shared by all parties), or asymmetric; disagreement may exist as to what decisions can be governed by contract terms; and agents may have different means of enforcing contract terms. Long-term contracts involve repeated interactions between the contracting parties, which creates complex information and incentive strategies over time. In addition to study of those strategies, contract theory is applied to study the renegotiation of long-term contract terms. Auctions are a subset of contract theory. In auctions, the principal (auctioneer) attempts to leverage the competition of the agents (bidders) to retain the maximum value (information rent) from private information. Each bidder has incomplete information about the information held by the other bidders, which increases the complexity of modeling auction behaviors.

Contract theory is applied to study microeconomic activity in many different segments of the economy. Among other areas, contract theory models are used to study labor markets, executive compensation, agricultural contracts, insurance, finance, credit markets, corporate structure, corporate governance, outsourcing, regulation, and organizational design. Researchers utilize contract theory to analyze and explain a variety of microeconomic activities.

Further reading

Baker, G., R. Gibbons, and K. Murphy. "Relational Contracts and the Theory of the Firm." *Quarterly Journal of Economics* 117, no. 1 (2002): 39–84; Bolton, P., and M. Dewatripont. *Contract Theory*. Cambridge, Mass.: MIT Press, 2005; Chiappori, P. A., and B. Salanié. *Testing Contract Theory: A Survey of Some Recent Work*. Invited Lecture, World Congress of the Econometric Society, Seattle, Washington, 2000. Available online. URL: home.uchicago.edu/~pchiappo/ wp/seattle4.PDF. Accessed on April 29, 2009; Crawford, V. P. "Dynamic Games and Dynamic Contract Theory." *Journal of Conflict Resolution* 29, no. 2 (1985): 195–224; DiMatteo, L. A. *Contract Theory: The Evolution of Contractual Intent*. East Lansing: Michigan State University Press, 1998; Freixas, X., and J. Rochet. *Microeconomics of Banking*. Cambridge, Mass.: MIT Press, 1997; Hart, O., and B. Holmström. "The Theory of Contracts." In N. Foss (ed.), *The Theory of the Firm: Critical Perspectives on Business and Management*, pp. 3–80. Vol. 2. London: Routledge, 2000; Laffont, J., and D. Martimort. *The Theory of Incentives: The Principal-agent Model*. Princeton, N.J.: Princeton University Press, 2002; MacLeod, W. B. "Three Solitudes in Contact: Law, Data, and Theory." *Scottish Journal of Political Economy* 54, no. 5 (2007): 601–616. Watson, J. "Contract and Game Theory: Basic Concepts for Settings with Finite Horizons." Available online. URL: repositories.cdlib.org/cgi/viewcontent.cgi?article=1057&context=ucsdecon. Accessed on April 20, 2009.

—Karen Miller

cookies

PC Magazine defines a "cookie" as a package of data sent from a web server that is stored by a receiving computer for various amounts of time, depending on the specifications of the cookie. Cookies, or http cookies, are embedded in the html code of a Web site to collect information about the user who visits the page. The cookie was created in 1994 by Lou Montulli who was employed by what would become part of Netscape Communications. He wanted to fix the problem of Web sites not remembering anything about users. He compared the problem to a store where the shopkeepers never remembered their customers. Montulli developed the cookie, which is a small file sent out by the Web site's computer to the user's computer to track information about the user. The cookie remembers buying habits or searching habits as well as passwords. An example of a cookie in action is when a user is shopping Amazon and she fills a virtual shopping cart. The cookies remember the information for the user. In the early days of computing, machines passed computer code back and forth known as magic cookies; hence, the name, cookie.

Many people are afraid of compromising their privacy but cookies really only collect a small amount of information that most people share willingly. It is easy for a user to delete cookies; however, the next time users visit their favorite page they have to reenter information. Blocking cookies by changing privacy setting on a web browser can cause a webpage to fail to load properly. A person using a frequent customer card at a local grocery store is probably sharing more information that way than they would with cookies.

Many people are afraid of cookies, but they are relatively harmless. Some common misconceptions about cookies are listed below.

- Cookies are like worms and viruses and cause harm to computers.
- Cookies are the same as spyware.
- Cookies are only there for advertisers.

None of the above are true. Cookies anonymously track the user's information, except when a user opts to store data such as passwords. Spyware can actually steal personal information and is more like viruses in that they can harm the computer. While advertisers use cookies to help select target groups, it is only one function of cookies. Some of the negative feelings toward cookies have been caused by what are known as third-party cookies that are embedded in information used by a Web site such as a photo borrowed from another place on the Web. The third-party cookies may cause the user to have to endure advertisements from third parties. Despite the negative feelings about cookies, many users find their web surfing experience to be more enjoyable because cookies remember the user and facilitate web browsing.

Cookies are not always accurate. One of the main problems occurs when several people use the same computer. Cookies have no way of differentiating among multiple users. Cookie information is not perfect and businesses should not rely on cookie information as their sole method of studying computer users.

Further reading

PCMag.com. Definition of Cookie. Available online. URL: www.pcmag.com/encyclopedia_term/0,2542,t=cookie &i=40334,00.asp. Accessed on April 27, 2010.
—Bill Boland and Sarah Shealy

cooperative

A cooperative is a business owned and controlled by the people who use its SERVICES and whose benefits are derived and distributed equitably on the basis of use. Cooperative user-owners are generally called members. Cooperatives are similar to private businesses, but members benefit based on their use of cooperative services, and earnings are allocated to members based on the amount of business they do with the cooperative. Usually incorporated under state laws, cooperatives elect a BOARD OF DIRECTORS and hire a manager to run day-to-day operations, but unlike private enterprises, they do not seek to make a profit.

Cooperatives are organized to

- improve bargaining power
- reduce costs

- obtain products or services
- create new and expand existing marketing opportunities
- improve the qualities of products or services
- increase INCOME

Because cooperatives are state-chartered, cooperative members, like SHAREHOLDERS of CORPORATIONS, have limited LIABILITY. Unlike corporations, where voting is based on the number of shares of stock held, in most cooperatives each member has one vote. In the United States, cooperatives, like S CORPORATIONS, are subject to single-tax treatment. Most PROFITS from a cooperative are distributed to members as patronage refunds, which are taxable income for members. CAPITAL for a cooperative comes from the members rather than from outside investors. Cooperatives, like any private enterprise, also borrow funds as needed from traditional lending institutions; the largest single category of cooperatives in the United States is CREDIT UNIONS. In addition, there are thousands of health-care, news-service, consumer, and agricultural cooperatives.

In the United States, the Philadelphia Contribution-ship for the Insurance of Houses from Loss by Fire, created in 1752, is said to have been the first cooperative in the country. Organized by Benjamin Franklin this cooperative is still in existence. Many cooperatives follow the principles adopted by the Rochdale Equitable Pioneers Society, established in England in 1844 by 28 craftsmen and entrepreneurs to purchase supplies and consumer goods cooperatively.

- open membership
- one member, one vote
- cash trading
- membership education
- political and religious neutrality
- no unusual risk assumption
- limitation on the number of shares owned
- limited interest on stock
- goods sold at regular retail prices
- net margins distributed according to patronage

The Grange, founded in Washington, D.C., in 1867, was a major agricultural cooperative, and by 1920 there were over 14,000 farmer cooperatives operating in the United States. By 1995 that number was reduced to 4,000, primarily farm-supply and grain and oilseed marketing coops. Farm Credit Service, established in 1916, is the country's oldest financial credit cooperative.

Further reading

U.S. Department of Agriculture. *Co-ops 101: An Introduction to Cooperatives.* Washington, D.C.: U.S. Department of Agriculture, Rural Development Cooperative Information Report 55, May 1999.

copy

Copy is a term for the words and illustrations used in an advertisement; *copy thrust* is what the words and illustrations should communicate to the target audience. A central part of any ADVERTISING campaign, copy is usually developed by advertising specialists for their clients.

Whether a part of billboard, brochure, television, radio, DIRECT MAIL, or other paid element of MARKETING COMMUNICATIONS, copy is generally designed to attract attention, hold interest, arouse desire, and result in action. This is known as the ATTENTION, INTEREST, DESIRE, ACTION CONCEPT (AIDA), and effective marketing attempts to accomplish one or more of these goals.

Author and copywriter Robert W. Bly states that his goal is to persuade buyers. He has collected numerous techniques he uses in writing copy, including the following:

- *The "so what" test.* If, after writing the copy for an advertisement, Bly thinks his target audience will respond, "So what," then he rewrites the copy until consumers will likely respond, "That is exactly what I am looking for."
- *Using key copy drivers.* The message should create one or more of the feelings that motivate people into action, including fear, greed, guilt, exclusivity, anger, salvation, or flattery.
- *The drop-in-the-bucket technique.* The copy should show that the price being asked is a "drop in the bucket" compared to the value it will provide.

- *Knowing the audience.* Use FOCUS GROUPS to probe into the feelings and motivations of target audiences.
- *Writing conversationally.* Use simple, easy-to-understand language that is appropriate for the target audience.
- *Leading with the strongest point.* Bly finds most writers end with their strongest point and suggests moving it to the beginning.
- *The tremendous whack theory.* If there is a strong point to make in the message, it is better not to be clever or subtle but to say it strongly, again and again.

Further reading

Bly, Robert W. "Persuasion Secrets of Marketing Pros." *DM News,* 21 October 2002; Perrault, William D., Jr., and E. Jerome McCarthy. *Basic Marketing.* 17th ed. Boston: Irwin McGraw-Hill, 2008.

copyright, fair use

The copyright law, Title 17 of the *United States Code,* includes all amendments enacted through the end of the second session of the 106th Congress in 2000. It includes the Copyright Act of 1976 and all subsequent amendments to copyright law; the Semiconductor Chip Protection Act of 1984, as amended; and the Vessel Hull Design Protection Act, as amended. The Copyright Office is responsible for registering claims under all three acts.

A copyright is a set of restricted, legal rights authors have over their works. Though copyright is most commonly applied to printed items like books and periodicals, it also includes music, videos, artwork, architectural works, software, databases, choreographic dances, pantomimes, images, graphics, and even sounds. Not only does copyright protect the use (copying) of these items, it also includes using parts of the work, distributing the work or performing the work as in a play. This protection is available to both published and unpublished works. The authors' rights begin when a work is created, and works published since March 1, 1989, do not have to bear a copyright notice to be protected under the federal law.

When an employee is creating a work as a job duty or on a commission, the employer, not the employee, is considered the author of the work. Examples of such situations could be a teacher creating a test, a graphic designer creating a company logo, a sound-effects recorder contributing to a motion picture, or a translator converting a text into English.

The copyright law does allow for a limited amount of an author's work to be copied or distributed without the author's permission; this is called fair use. The provisions outlined for fair use include the purpose of the use (mainly for educational purposes), i.e., students photocopying an article for a research paper or a teacher using a book, article, or artwork in the classroom; the nature of a work, i.e., a copy of a photo in a magazine or a clip of music from a CD selection; and using small "extracts" of a work that would not affect the value of a work. The idea of fair use is to copy or use a small portion of a work and not supplement or diminish its MARKET VALUE. Fair use does not allow for the user to distribute the work to the public, sale or lease the work, or profit from the work.

When using copyrighted material for personal or educational purposes, it is advised to make a reference to the authors of the materials, whether print, electronic, images, graphics, or sounds. If the material is used for a commercial venture, the author's permission should be obtained.

Some works that are not copyrighted include titles, names, slogans, familiar symbols, colloquialisms, colors, lettering, lists of ingredients, concepts, methods, and principles. Works that exclusively provide information, such as calendars, tape measures, rulers, height and weight charts and similar charts and tables, are not copyrighted.

Further reading

Copyright Office, Library of Congress. Available online. URL: www/copyright.gov; Title 17 Copyright Law. Available online. URL: www.copyright.gov/title17/.

—Susan Poorbaugh

corporate average fuel efficiency

Corporate average fuel efficiency (CAFE) is a series of rules established by Congress in 1975 to increase fuel efficiency of automobiles produced and sold in the United States. Initiated as a response to the oil crises of that time, CAFE standards apply to all manufacturers who sell cars and light trucks in the United States. The standards are administered by the National Highway Traffic Safety Administration (NHTSA).

Initially, CAFE standards required manufacturers to gradually increase fuel efficiency, thereby decreasing U.S. dependence on imported oil. Over the years, the auto industry blocked implementation of most changes in CAFE rules. In 2002, the standards required manufacturers' cars to average 27.5 miles per gallon and light trucks to average 20.7 miles per gallon. The distinction between light trucks and cars, when established in the 1970s, emphasized differences in the style and use of the two groups of vehicles. Since then, with changes in market DEMAND, manufacturers have classified minivans and sport utility vehicles (SUVs) as light trucks, which then requires them to meet only the lower fuel-efficiency requirement. In 2002 the expanded light-truck category represented approximately half of new vehicle sales in the country. Together, light trucks and cars consume over 40 percent of all oil used in the United States.

In recent years the "Big Three" U.S. automobile manufacturers (General Motors, Ford, and DaimlerChrysler) have produced larger vehicles that have barely met fuel-efficiency standards. If standards are raised as part of new national-security goals, these manufacturers could face significant investment requirements or face penalties under CAFE. BMW and Mercedes-Benz (part of DaimlerChrysler) regularly do not meet CAFE standards and pay federal fines, but most Japanese manufacturers easily meet the current standards. Imposition of higher standards would result in a competitive advantage for Japanese manufacturers, who would not have to invest in new technology.

In 2008, the Energy Independence and Security Act (EISA) mandated that the model year (MY) 2011 to 2020 CAFE standards be set sufficiently high to ensure that the industrywide average of all new passenger cars and light trucks, combined, is not less than 35 miles per gallon by MY 2020. President Obama issued a memorandum on January 26, 2009, requesting NHTSA to defer action on future model years to allow review of the approach taken by CAFE to standard setting.

Further reading
Ball, Jeffrey. "Detroit Again Tries to Dodge Pressures for a 'Greener' Fleet," *Wall Street Journal,* 28 January 2002, p. A1; National Highway Traffic Safety Administration Web site. Available online. URL: www.nhtsa.gov.

corporate culture
Culture can be described as the learned behavior patterns of any specific period, race, or people. Similarly, corporate culture refers to the beliefs, behaviors, values, and norms of an individual CORPORATION or of an organization. A corporation develops policies, procedures, and guidelines in order to establish and convey the concerns and priorities of the company. Corporate culture is what is "read between the lines" of those policies and procedures—that is, the "understood" or "unspoken" rules and regulations of a company. Informal, intangible, and ambiguous, corporate culture relates to the working environment or atmosphere of an organization and is very often based on the ideas and standards of the senior MANAGEMENT responsible for creating it.

For example, an organization's employee may understand that even though his or her boss is the nominal authoritarian figure, the boss's administrative assistant can often produce more results or has more "power" because he or she maintains more contacts throughout the company's INFRASTRUCTURE. Therefore she or he is the unofficial authority.

Corporate culture can be divided into four main categories: ritualized patterns, management styles and philosophies, management systems and procedures, and written and unwritten norms and procedures. Ritualized patterns refer to policies and procedures influenced by the political, economic, and social beliefs and behaviors of a society. An individual employee may affect a corporation's ritualized pattern when the employee brings his or her own ideas and beliefs to the organization. Collectively, the employee's work ethic, individuality, and relationships with fellow coworkers and customers create ideas and values that may shape a corporation.

LEADERSHIP, planning, motivation, and communication are all examples of areas influenced by management styles and philosophies. It is important that top managers constantly strive to improve and remain consistent in their management styles. Inconsistency can be seen by employees as unfair and frustrating. Motivating, training, and rewarding employees can provide a positive work experience, thereby causing them to be more productive and satisfied.

Management systems and procedures are those that are clearly stated as policy (in official documents) as well as assumptions made by staff for those instances that reach beyond the policy. Policies are developed in order to establish routines that employees should follow for certain situations. Training procedures followed during orientation and throughout the duration of EMPLOYMENT should be consistent with the established values of the organization. The organizational structure and company image are also important and can assist the firm when recruiting for new workers. The physical structure of the building can also send a message to employees and visitors. For example, if it is physically open and has many windows, this can create a pleasant atmosphere in which to work. Similarly, dress codes should be established in order to ensure that the staff maintains a neat representation of the company image. However, if codes and policies are too strict, it can lead to a negative work environment. It is always important to remember that a balance of structure and freedom should be maintained.

Assumptions made by employees during situations not officially covered by company policy relate to the fourth category: unwritten and written norms and procedures. Generating a certain working environment or atmosphere for employees will equip them to make judgments and assumptions according to the already established guidelines for situations that have not previously been anticipated.

For example, a customer may have a complaint about a product. The employee has guidelines to follow when dealing with the situation, but the actual resolution to the problem may be an individual judgment based on the employee's knowledge of the customer as well as the company's values and policies.

A good corporate culture allows a company the opportunity to be more successful. Typically, if an organization establishes a positive corporate culture, it can boost staff morale and foster creativity among employees, which can be used as an excellent public-relations tool. If a corporation fails to create a good corporate culture, productivity may suffer and employees may become unsatisfied. This can lead to high employee turnover and lack of creativity. It is important to remember that a corporation's culture can be considered one of the most important aspects of business, and having a contented staff can lead to greater profitability.

Corporate culture is continually changing. The days of smoke-filled meetings and company parties where the alcohol flowed freely died with changes in federal legislation and state laws governing tobacco, alcohol, and liability. Generations X (latchkey kids, divorced parents), Y (racially, ethnically diverse, materially well off), and Z (highly educated, technically savvy) have impacted corporate culture. They expect more and are unwilling to sacrifice personal quality of life. The current economic downturn is also affecting company culture. With more people scrambling for jobs, employees may again be more willing to tolerate tougher, less pleasant aspects of corporate culture.

Corporate culture also varies by industry or marketplace. The traditional eight-to-five workdays, formal suits, scheduled department meetings, and business on the golf course are still important in some industries but not in others. The culture of computer software and services companies of Silicon Valley is quite different from the banks and law firms of Wall Street and from small companies across the United States. Silicon Valley technology companies are known for their informal environments, including flex time, work from home, casual dress, free meals, and recreational diversions available to employees. Small companies across America tend to have a family culture of everyone knowing each other's personal business, as well as company business, and reflect the values of the families leading the firm.

Further reading

Goffee, Rob, and Gareth Jones. *The Character of a Corporation: How Your Company's Culture Can Make or Break Your Business.* New York: Harper Business, 1998; Sherriton, Jacalyn, and James L. Stern. *Corporate Culture/Team Culture: Removing the Hidden Barriers to Team Success.* Atlanta: American Management Association, 1997.

—Wanda Carter and Jennifer R. Land

corporate divestiture

Corporate divestiture is the disposing or relinquishing of a company's ASSETS or a portion of its business by way of sale, exchange, or liquidation. A CORPORATION may want to sell off a poorly performing division or spin off a subsidiary company through an exchange of stock with SHAREHOLDERS, or it may be forced to liquidate assets as a result of legal action.

A sell-off is one of the most common types of divestiture, where the divesting company sells a division or subsidiary to a third party for cash or some other asset such as stock. Companies usually sell off under-performing parts of the company and use the proceeds to strengthen other areas of the business. Likewise, if a company is experiencing financial trouble, it may decide to sell a segment of the business in order to generate INCOME.

Sometimes the business area is too small to sustain itself as an independent company and must be sold to another party. This leads to the second form of divestiture, a spin-off, which occurs when a parent company creates a new, independent company from a subsidiary company or division. Shareholders of the parent company are issued stock in the newly formed company to compensate for the asset loss of the parent company. This also serves the dual purpose of shifting some of the

investment responsibility and risk away from the parent company and places it on the shareholders' shoulders. Additionally, debt from the parent company can be transferred to the spin-off company during its creation. A spin-off can improve the overall operations of both companies by reducing red tape and overhead costs, allow each company to focus on their PRIMARY MARKETS, and give greater freedom to the management of the spun-off company.

There is also a modified version of a spin-off known as a split-off. The two are very similar; however, unlike a spin-off, where all the shareholders receive shares in the new company, in a split-off shareholders can choose if they want to exchange the shares they own in the parent company for shares in the new company, although sometimes exchange is mandatory. This exchange of shares is often done on an unequal basis. For instance, a shareholder may receive two shares in the new company for each exchange share of the parent company.

Finally, there is the case of liquidation, also known as a split-or break-up. A split-up occurs when a parent company exchanges all of its shares for a stake in two or more subsidiary companies. This is then followed by the liquidation of the parent company. This arrangement is typical in antitrust cases, when a split-up is used to break up a company into individual and independent companies.

During the late 1980s there was a growing trend among companies to diversify operations and expand into new markets. However, some companies found they had spread themselves too thin and were no longer competitive in all areas of their business. Thus, in the 1990s there was a growing amount of corporate divestiture as companies tried to refocus their businesses on core competencies. For example, in 1997 PepsiCo decided to spin off three fast-food restaurants in an effort to focus more on its "core" soft-drink and snack-food business lines. This action was in part prompted by PepsiCo investors who believed Pepsi had expanded in too many directions and wanted to see the company reorganize its business.

While not as common as a spin-off or sale, a break-up is often more widely publicized in the general press, usually because of its association with litigation and antitrust cases. For example, in 2000 one of the proposed solutions in the Microsoft antitrust case was to split the company into two new companies. One company would focus on operating systems, while the other would focus on software. After the new companies had formed, the "original" Microsoft would be liquidated, ceasing to exist as a company. Shareholders of the original Microsoft were to be issued stock in both of the newly formed companies. However, this plan never came to fruition, and Microsoft continued to operate as normal.

Divestiture works as a foil against excessive growth and expansion and as a counterbalance to MERGERS AND ACQUISITIONS. Companies will always try to improve their businesses, often through trial and error. When companies find they have overextended their operations, become too large, or have come to the attention of government watchdogs, they will often rely on these different divestment strategies to make their businesses more efficient, easier to manage, or complaint with legal regulations.

—Aaron S. Jones

corporate governance

Corporate governance—the consideration and evaluation of business and social goals by corporate leaders—addresses the ways in which CORPORATIONS balance the interests of SHAREHOLDERS, workers, and the community. In recent years, although corporate governance has attracted considerable public interest, its concept is poorly defined because it covers a large number of distinct issues. As a result, different people have come up with different definitions that basically reflect their special interests. Some definitions of corporate governance include

- "Corporate governance . . . can be defined narrowly as the relationship of a company to its shareholders or, more broadly, as its relationship to society . . ." (*Financial Times,* 1997)

- "Corporate governance is about promoting corporate governance fairness, transparency and accountability." (J. Wolfensohn, President of the World Bank, *Financial Times,* 21 June 1999)

- "Corporate governance can also be described as the system that controls and directs business corporations. The structure specifies the distribution of rights and responsibilities among different participants in the corporation. Some examples of the participants are the board, managers, shareholders, and other STAKEHOLDERS. Corporate governance spells out the rules and procedures for making decisions on corporate affairs. By doing this, it also provides the structure through which the company directives are set, and means of attaining those objectives and monitoring performance." (ORGANIZATION FOR ECONOMIC COOPERATION AND DEVELOPMENT, April 1999).

- As stated in the *OECD Principles of Corporate Governance,* "Some commentators take too narrow a view, and say it [corporate governance] is the fancy term for the way in which directors and auditors handle their responsibilities towards shareholders. Others use the expression as if it were synonymous with shareholder democracy. Corporate governance is a topic recently conceived, as yet ill-defined, and consequently blurred at the edges . . . corporate governance as a subject, as an objective, or as a regime to be followed for the good of shareholders, customers, bankers and indeed for the reputation and standing of our nation and its economy."

Further reading
OECD. *OECD Principles of Corporate Governance.* Paris, 1999; Organization for Economic Cooperation and Development Web site. Available online. URL: www.oecd.org.

corporate haven
A corporate haven is a state or country with laws that are particularly advantageous to businesses. Many companies choose to incorporate in these locations because of their favorable laws. Corporate havens typically permit greater secrecy, have

lower tax rates, and offer other advantages relative to the laws where the company is headquartered. In the United States, Delaware is known as a corporate haven while, internationally, Bermuda, the Cayman Islands, and Switzerland are among the most widely recognized havens.

In the United States, any corporation that operates in more than one state or country is considered a "domestic corporation" in the jurisdiction where it incorporates. In any other state the company must register to operate since it is considered a "foreign corporation." In the event of litigation, a corporation can choose to adjudicate under the law in the jurisdiction where it is incorporated. In practice this means that regardless of where a dispute occurs, if a corporation is formed in Delaware then the case will be tried in Delaware, where the corporation benefits from the state's advantageous secrecy/transparency laws.

To attract companies, Delaware enacted laws giving them more discretionary power in operating and controlling their corporations. This increased company control has resulted in diminished shareholder control, leading to the concept of a "haven" for corporations.

In the United States more than half of publicly traded companies are incorporated in Delaware. Note that a company may be incorporated in Delaware and be headquartered in a different state. While over 60 percent of Fortune 500 companies are incorporated in Delaware, only one of those companies is headquartered in Delaware.

Since Delaware has become home to a majority of corporations in the United States, it has more experienced courts and a better developed body of corporate case law than other states. Likewise the state is known for its governance lawyers and courts familiar with the intricacies of corporate governance. This gives Delaware-based corporations greater guidance and firmer precedents on matters of corporate governance and transaction liability issues.

Disputes regarding the internal affairs of Delaware corporations are filed in the Delaware Court of Chancery, a court with no jury, where cases are heard by a chancellor instead of a judge. (Since 2008, cases are heard by a chancellor and four vice chancellors.) After a case, a litigant may file an appeal to the state Supreme Court. In 2004 Borrus reported in *Business Week* that Delaware courts rarely second-guess a corporate board as long as the directors have acted reasonably and in good faith. In 2003, after Enron and other corporate scandals, the Delaware court became stricter on companies. In that year, a judge refused to toss out a lawsuit filed by a shareholder of the Disney Corporation challenging the company's multimillion-dollar CEO severance payment.

While many businesses incorporate in Delaware, it may not be the most advantageous idea for a small business. To incorporate in Delaware, a small business must appoint someone in the state to be an agent for the corporation. The company must also pay an annual franchise corporate tax to the state. This tax contributes as much as 20 percent to Delaware's revenue. Any company that is incorporated in the state of Delaware but does business in another state, including its home state, must file an application to conduct business as a foreign corporation. This requires a company to pay a franchise fee in addition to state income tax.

Further reading

Borrus, A. "Less Laissez-Faire in Delaware?" *BusinessWeek,* 22 March 2004; Business Law in Delaware. *Delaware Business Lawyers, Attorney.* Available online. URL: http://www.lawfirms.com/resources/business/business-law-delaware.htm Accessed on April 22, 2009; Jiraporn, P., and K. Gleason. "Delaware Incorporation and Earnings Management Analysis." *Journal of Applied Finance* 17, no. 1 (Spring/Summer 2007): 40–51.
—Rick Pelletier

corporate personhood

Corporate personhood is the concept and controversy over which rights that are provided to natural persons should also apply to a group of persons organized as a corporation or other entity. Until the AMERICAN INDUSTRIAL REVOLUTION (1870s) most businesses were small individual proprietorships. The corporate form of business, with shareholder-owners often separate from management, existed largely in educational charters and the banking industry. Also referred to as the "legal person" issue, as the corporate form of business expanded, questions arose regarding property ownership, lawsuits, and contracts engaged in by corporations and other groups of people. For example, under COMMON LAW tradition, only people could sue or be sued. Over time, court decisions established five corporate rights: the right to own property, sign CONTRACTS, enforce contracts, hire employees, and self-governance.

Industrialization brought with it the expansion of the use of the corporate form of business, leading to questions about what rights were provided for corporations in the U.S. Constitution.

Supporters of the corporate personhood concept argue that corporations, representing shareholders, were intended to have many of the same rights provided to natural persons, including the right to privacy, the right against self-incrimination, and the right to petition government to address their grievances. Opponents of corporate personhood focus mostly on this last issue, the right of corporations to engage in the political process, in arguing that corporations, by their size and financial power, unduly influence government.

Corporate personhood debate stems from interpretation of the First, Fifth, and Fourteenth Amendments to the U.S. Constitution. The First Amendment states: "Congress shall make no law respecting an establishment of religion, or prohibiting the free exercise thereof; or abridging the freedom of speech, or of the press; or the right of the people peaceably to assemble, and to petition the Government for a redress of grievances." The corporate personhood question is whether "people" also includes corporations and other groups such as cooperatives, unions, partnerships, churches, political action committees.

The Fifth Amendment states: "No person shall be held to answer for a capital, or otherwise infamous crime, unless on presentment or indictment of a Grand Jury, except in cases arising in the land or naval forces, or in the Militia, when in actual service in time of War or public danger; nor shall any person be subject for the same offense to be twice put in jeopardy of life or limb; nor shall be compelled in any criminal case to be a witness against himself, nor be deprived of life, liberty, or property, without due process of law; nor shall private property be taken for public use, without just compensation." Does the right of protection against self-incrimination also apply to corporations?

Section 1 of the Fourteenth Amendment states: "All persons born or naturalized in the United States, and subject to the jurisdiction thereof, are citizens of the United States and of the State wherein they reside. No State shall make or enforce any law which shall abridge the privileges or immunities of citizens of the United States; nor shall any State deprive any person of life, liberty, or property, without due process of law; nor deny to any person within its jurisdiction the equal protection of the laws." U.S. courts have often interpreted this clause as providing protections to corporations. The American Green Party has been a vocal opponent of protecting corporations' free speech rights, wanting to restrict political speech and donations of corporations, lobbyists, interest groups, and other non-natural persons. Former vice president Al Gore has also objected to the extension of political rights under corporate personhood. In a major decision (*Citizens United vs. Federal Election Commission*, 2010) the Supreme Court ruled against laws restricting corporations from "electioneering communications," that is, broadcast, satellite, or cable messages mentioning a candidate's name within 60 days of an election or 30 days before a primary. The Obama administration and others immediately called for new laws to restrict corporate influence in the election process.

Further reading

Mallor, Jane P., A. James Barnes, Thomas Bowers, Michael J. Philips, and Arlen W. Langvardt. *Business Law: The Ethical, Global and E-Commerce Environment.* 14th ed. Boston: McGraw-Hill, 2009; Reclaim Democracy for the People Web site. Available online. URL: www.freespeechforpeople.org. Accessed on May 4, 2010.

corporate security

Corporate security aims to protect the safety and viability of a business organization. Since September 11, 2001, corporate security has become an increasingly important issue. A survey of corporate executives a few months after the World Trade Center attack reported increased concern about mail processing, travel, protection of employees and INFRASTRUCTURE, and other security issues.

With the anthrax mailings shortly after 9/11, mail processing has become a major concern. The U.S. Postal Service provides guidelines, cautioning recipients about mail from unknown sources with multiple stamps and no return address. Companies have instituted a variety of mail-security practices, from the use of latex gloves and masks to the use of a separate room with no connection to the central ventilation system.

Building security is another area of concern for businesses. Simple changes such as increased surveillance cameras, ID badges, and visible security guards are being used in many companies, especially in headquarter buildings and among companies more likely to be threatened by terrorism. Concrete barriers, shatterproof glass, controlled access, and protection of a building's ventilation system are additional building-security measures that companies are instituting. Some firms are constructing safe rooms, providing safety kits, and redesigning floor plans with security in mind. One architect says the new question being asked is, "How do you get the last person in the corner office of the top floor out of the building safely?"

Business travel is another worry for corporations. Since 9/11 many companies have reduced and even banned employee travel abroad. While executives continue to pursue international expansion plans, companies are offering travel-security advice, hiring bodyguards and bullet-proof limousines for executives and purchasing security and intelligence bulletins for areas of the world where they do business. The general travel-security rules are: be more discrete, do not dress lavishly, replace business luggage tags, move through open areas of airports to secure areas as quickly as possible, and do not have pick-up drivers displaying signs with the company's name at arrival areas.

Even before 9/11, computer security was a major corporate concern, especially given constantly changing technology. The many stories of hackers accessing sensitive company data or destroying important data files had already increased corporate computer security efforts. Major companies often hire "ethical hackers" who attempt to find weaknesses in the firm's computer security system. The American Society for Industrial Security reported on-site contractors as the major threat to a company's INTELLECTUAL PROPERTY. Current employees and former employees were ranked the second and third sources of corporate-security problems. Most corporate losses due to contractor or employee sabotage are never reported or prosecuted. One story described a disgruntled employee who, sensing he was about to be terminated, set up a program to crash the company computer and, when dismissed, called his assistant, who mistakenly activated the program at his request.

The value of continual back-up data storage became apparent to many companies after the events of 9/11. Data storage, back-up facilities, disaster plans, and the federal "shadow" government facilities are all part of increased efforts and concerns about corporate security.

Further reading

American Society for Industrial Security Web site. Available online. URL: www.asisonline.org; Hymowitz, Carol. "Business's New Agenda," *Wall Street Journal,* 11 March 2002, p. R6; Warren, Susan. "Tools to Protect . . . Buildings," *Wall Street Journal,* 11 March 2002, p. R6.

corporate social responsibility

Corporate social responsibility (CSR) is business decision-making linked to ethical values, compliance with laws and regulations, and respect for people, communities, and the environment. A relatively new concept in western capitalism, CSR recognizes that CORPORATIONS are a legal entity chartered by society. To operate (legally) in the United States, all businesses are required to have a business license, whether from a city, county or state government.

Some corporations perceive social responsibility to be part of PUBLIC RELATIONS, any action or contribution that makes the company "look good" in the minds of the public. Advocates of CSR consider it to be policies, practices, and programs integrated into business decision making. Some of the most widely quoted examples of CSR include

- Ben & Jerry's company policy of donating 7.5 percent of PROFITS to charity
- Levi Strauss exiting business in China as a protest of human rights violations
- Body Shop's decision to use natural ingredients harvested using environmentally responsible methods
- Calvert Group's decision to exclude investment in companies producing guns, cigarettes, and vodka

Supporters of corporate social responsibility suggest these practices benefit companies in a variety of ways. Several studies have correlated socially responsible business practices with improved financial performance. CSR efforts to reduce wastes frequently result in reduced COSTS. Similarly, reduced wastes improve productivity and product quality. Corporate social responsibility improves BRAND images and company reputations, resulting in increased CUSTOMER LOYALTY. Companies practicing CSR find it is easier to attract and retain employees.

In the 1990s CSR supporters developed standards and awards. Some of these groups include the following:

- The Global Reporting Initiative, established in 1997, designed guidelines for preparing enterprise-level sustainability reports.
- Social Accountability 8000, developed by the Council on Economic Priorities Accreditation Agency, has set standards that include monitoring child labor, forced labor, nondiscrimination, wages and benefits, working hours, health and safety, freedom of association, and MANAGEMENT systems.

- The Caux Round Table, a group of senior business leaders from around the world, produced "Principles of Business," a document expressing their standards for ethical and responsible business practices.
- The Interfaith Center on Corporate Responsibility published "Principles for Global Corporate Responsibility," a "collective distillation of the issues of concern" to religious-oriented institutional investors.
- The Sunshine Standards for Corporate Reporting to Stakeholders developed a list of information that the creators believe should be included in ANNUAL REPORTS to STAKEHOLDERS, including customer, employee, community, and society information needs to evaluate corporate performance.
- The Keidanren Charter for Good Corporate Behavior, produced by the Japanese Federation of Economic Organizations, created a 10-point charter directing behavior by corporations.

The Business and Society Review has developed a remarkable Web site detailing examples of corporate social-responsibility efforts, implementation steps, links to other CSR organizations, and model policies for companies considering CSR initiatives.

See also PYRAMID OF CORPORATE RESPONSIBILITY.

Further reading
Business and Society Review Web site. Available online. URL: www.bsr.org; Green, Michael H. "Corporate Social Responsibility: Balancing Bottom Lines with Social Responsibility." Available online. URL: www.ziplink.net/~mikegree/career/social/htm. Accessed on June 10, 2009.

corporate welfare
Corporate welfare is a term used to describe special programs that benefit only specific CORPORATIONS or industries but not offered to others. In the United States, WELFARE—benefits to individuals or families for which no product or service is received in exchange—is a controversial area of social policy. Corporate welfare is less well-known and therefore less controversial, even though it

represents billions of dollars annually. What critics call corporate welfare, supporters refer to as economic incentives, enterprise zones, or development assistance.

It is difficult to determine what is corporate welfare and what is government spending but critics contend the federal government spends billions annually on corporate-welfare programs. In 2001 President George W. Bush's budget called for reductions in corporate welfare, including cuts in public-works projects, commercial-loan guarantees, shipbuilding programs, and export-import bank trade assistance programs. Supporters argue every country subsidizes exports and that export subsidies level the playing field in international trade. Similarly, in 2009, critics argued that much of the Troubled Asset Relief Program (TARP), begun under President George W. Bush and continued under President Obama, amounted to corporate welfare for the banking industry.

In an ongoing NAFTA (NORTH AMERICAN FREE TRADE AGREEMENT) dispute, the United States and Canada have been challenging each country's support of timber production. Both countries provide low-cost access to public land and subsidize road development and other transportation. The dispute centers on which country is providing greater subsidies, unfairly reducing the cost of timber harvesting and creating an artificial COMPARATIVE ADVANTAGE in lumber markets. Similarly, in 2001 the WORLD TRADE ORGANIZATION (WTO) ruled U.S. foreign-sales corporations (FSCs), offshore offices funneling paperwork for corporate exports to avoid federal income taxes on export PROFITS, unfairly subsidize U.S. corporations in world trade. The U.S. Congress responded by changing the language of laws allowing FSCs, hoping to continue to support the corporations without facing WTO sanctions.

In 1998 in a major exposé, *Time* magazine devoted almost an entire issue to the subject of corporate welfare. In addition to federal subsidies, *Time* presented numerous examples of state and local governments competing with each other to attract corporations. Typical corporate-welfare packages include cash, low-interest LOANS,

tax breaks, $1 real estate, and worker-training programs. States often compete to attract large corporations. In 2001 Boeing announced it was moving its corporate headquarters to Dallas, Denver, or Chicago. Chicago won the competition with a variety of "incentives." Among economic-development specialists, attracting Boeing or other large companies is known as an "elephant hunt." In the 1980s, to "bag" BMW, South Carolina leased land to the company for $1 a year, agreed to train workers, exempted the company from a variety of taxes, and even extended the runway on an area airport. Alabama subsequently offered hundreds of millions of dollars in incentives to bag Mercedes-Benz.

One of the problems with corporate welfare is the tendency for companies to "cut and run" once the incentive end. Throughout the southeastern United States, textile companies have long been known for this practice. *Time* describes the relocation of meat-packing operations around the Midwest. Rural communities lacking job opportunities build INFRASTRUCTURE (particularly waste-treatment facilities), spending millions to attract a company. When the company leaves for a better proposition, the community is left with huge indebtedness and little tax base to support the investment.

Critics say corporate welfare distorts allocation of RESOURCES and reduces ECONOMIC EFFICIENCY, but the question of how to stop it is difficult to answer. State officials from New Jersey and New York once agreed to stop "raiding" companies, but the truce was quickly ignored. Five possible measures have been suggested to reduce corporate welfare.

- Level a federal excise tax on incentives given to corporations from state and local governments. This would eliminate the value of the incentives and reduce the bidding war among communities.
- Challenge incentives as illegal under the COMMERCE CLAUSE of the U.S. Constitution.
- Create a special commission to propose ending corporate-welfare programs at the federal level.

- End funding for federal programs subsidizing loans to businesses.
- Challenge state and local incentive programs through lawsuits against companies receiving them.

See also EXPORT-IMPORT BANK OF THE UNITED STATES.

Further reading
Time, 30 November 1998, various pp.

corporation

A corporation is a legal entity owned by stockholders that is authorized by law to act as a single person. As such, the affairs of the corporation are separate from those of the owners, which gives them limited LIABILITY and thus a financial advantage. Under most circumstances, the owners' liability is limited to the CAPITAL they have invested in the company.

Corporations are created by acquiring a corporate charter from state offices, often the office of the secretary of state. In applying for a charter, a corporation submits its articles of INCORPORATION, listing the company name, address, number of shares of stock the company is authorized to issue, and usually the names and addresses of the individuals who will serve as the initial BOARD OF DIRECTORS. The board of directors represent the interests of stockholders and oversees the actions of managers. A corporation may have a few or many stockholders, based on who has purchased shares of COMMON STOCK in the company. For decades the most widely held stock in the United States was American Telephone & Telegraph (ATT), with over 80,000 shareholders. Only about 20 percent of businesses in the United States are incorporated, but they represent a majority of business activity in the country.

In addition to limited liability, the other major advantage of corporations is the ability to raise capital. Often a new business starts out as a sole PROPRIETORSHIP; expands by taking on partners; and, if promising or successful, funds further growth by incorporating. Selling shares of stock representing ownership interest in the company allows corporations to obtain funds needed to create or expand business operations without having to pay interest, but it reduces the ownership and control of initial owners of the business. Stockholders take an EQUITY interest in the company with the expectation of sharing in the company's future PROFITS, either through DIVIDEND payments or appreciation of the shares of stock in the marketplace as the company earns profits. Corporations also raise capital by selling BONDS and through bank LOANS issued in the corporation's name.

The selling of shares in a new corporation is called an INITIAL PUBLIC OFFERING (IPO). IPOs in technology stocks were highly sought after by investors during the rapid growth of the U.S. STOCK MARKET in the late 1990s. Since most new corporations often have only an idea, a BUSINESS PLAN, and little or no track record, shares of IPO companies are considered highly speculative investments.

Many times entrepreneurs create corporations to expand their PRODUCTS and SERVICES into larger markets. While they may have worked night and day for years developing their business and are reluctant to lose control of their enterprise, they need the capital and/or skill of managers to make their business grow. On the one hand, managers can provide new business expertise, but on the other they are unlikely to work as hard as the entrepreneur who created the business.

To overcome the problem of managers not being owners of companies, many U.S. companies offer employees STOCK OPTIONS—that is, the opportunity to purchase shares of stock at a specified price for a period of time. If the company does well and the stock price rises, employees can exercise their stock options, simultaneously buying stock from the company at the agreed-on price and selling the shares in the stock market at the current market price. This allows employees to share in a company's profits. Software developers at Microsoft Corporation were known to have cots put in their office cubicles so they could sleep in their offices after working 15- and 20-hour days.

Many of these employees have become Microsoft millionaires through stock options offered to dedicated employees. As demonstrated in the corporate corruption scandals stock options also provide incentives for executives to artificially increase share prices in order to cash in stock options for personal gain.

A disadvantage of corporations is double taxation. Because they are recognized as a separate legal entity, corporations pay taxes on their INCOMES. When they distribute income in the form of dividends, SHAREHOLDERS must report these distributions and pay personal income tax on them. Thus, profits are taxed first as corporate income and second as personal income. Similarly, when shareholders sell their stock for a profit, they must report the gain on their personal tax return.

Further reading

Mallor, Jane P., A. James Barnes, Thomas Bowers, Michael J. Phillips, Arlen W. Langvardt. *Business Law: The Ethical, Global, and E-Commerce Environment.* 14th ed. Boston: McGraw-Hill, 2009.

cost accounting   See MANAGERIAL ACCOUNTING.

cost-benefit analysis

Cost-benefit analysis looks at proposed transactions from an economic viewpoint, comparing the cost of the improvement to the benefits derived from the improvement. At the very least, business wants the economic benefits of the improvement to be greater than the cost of the improvement. In American businesses, supervisors and managers ask their superiors for money to purchase more supplies, new equipment, additional employees, and a variety of other reasons. Money, however, is a scarce resource, and, usually, the total amount of money requested is greater than the money available to be spent. Higher level managers must evaluate the spending requests and decide which ones to approve.

Cost-benefit analysis is a frequently used technique to evaluate spending requests. For instance, if production levels can be increased by 60 percent with the purchase and installation of new automated manufacturing equipment and the cost of the equipment is $100,000, the return to the company must be $100,000 before there is a break-even point. If the company cannot earn a good financial return on the expenditure, then it may decide to leave the money in the bank to earn interest or spend it on other projects with a higher rate of return.

Companies often set standards for the desired rate of return for an expenditure. If that standard is 2.0, then the improvement must generate economic returns that are twice its cost in the first year of operation. This introduces the term *payback*. If an improvement generates returns of twice its cost in a year, then the improvement has paid for itself in six months. The returns earned during the second six months of operation are incremental profits to the company. Companies are more willing to spend money for improvements with shorter payback times than longer.

Cost-efficiencies are related to be both cost-benefit analyses and payback period. When a manager compares different potential improvements that have the same potential benefit, he/she should select the improvement that has the lowest overall cost. This results in requesting the improvement with the greatest cost-efficiency and, similarly, the shortest payback period. Determining the lowest overall cost is important because it goes beyond the immediate purchase price and includes additional considerations, such as projected life of the machine, equipment reliability, and potential cost of repairs. When costs are incurred initially with benefits expected to be realized over a longer period of time, present value analysis is used to adjust costs and benefits into the current time period.

Cost-benefit analysis is an important consideration, but not all purchase decisions are primarily driven by economic factors. Improvements may be authorized to assure a safe work place, free of recognized hazards or to protect the environment from pollution.

See also DISCOUNTING, PRESENT VALUE.

—John B. Abbott

cost of goods sold

Cost of goods sold is an expense account with a normal debit balance found in the ledger of merchandising firms that buy and resell finished goods. Using the perpetual inventory system, when an item is sold from inventory, the merchandise inventory account is credited for the cost of the item, and cost of goods sold is debited for the same amount.

Because cost of goods sold is often the most important of all the expense accounts in a retail or merchandising firm, it is separated from the other expense accounts and subtracted first from sales revenues, with the remainder called gross margin. All the firm's other expenses are then subtracted from gross margin.

A well-known model for determining the cost of goods sold is:

beginning inventory
+ purchases of inventory
inventory available for sale
− ending inventory
cost of goods sold

Cost of goods sold provides important data for manufacturing firms, and their INCOME STATEMENTS give the same treatment to the cost-of-goods-sold account—that is, subtracting it first from sales revenues to obtain gross margin.

cost-of-living adjustment

A cost-of-living adjustment (COLA) is an increase in INCOME to compensate for INFLATION. As the general level of prices rises (inflation), the purchasing power of a fixed amount of income decreases. COLAs protect against inflation by raising incomes, or benefits.

Almost all COLAs in the United States are tied to the CONSUMER PRICE INDEX (CPI). The most widely cited use of COLAs is by the Social Security Administration (SSA). SOCIAL SECURITY (Old Age Survivors and Disability Income, OASDI) and SUPPLEMENTAL SECURITY INCOME (SSI) are adjusted annually based on changes in the Urban Wage Earners and Clerical Workers Consumer Price Index (CPI-W). Since 1975 the SSA has used the third-quarter-to-third-quarter change in the CPI-W to adjust benefits at the beginning of each year. In 1980 Social Security benefits were increased by 14.3 percent, while in 2010 benefits were not increased because the CPI had not risen the previous year.

In addition to being used to adjust government benefits programs, COLAs are often incorporated into UNION contracts and child-support orders. COLAs are also used to adjust for regional differences in the cost of living. Companies often adjust salaries of workers when transferring them to high-cost areas. Manhattan (New York City), Honolulu, and Alaska are relatively expensive places to live in the United States, while most midwestern cities and smaller towns are less expensive. The U.S. military also uses COLAs when transferring personnel to high-cost areas around the world.

People whose major sources of income are not protected by COLAs face declining purchasing power over time and rapid decreases in purchasing power during periods of severe inflation. Many pensioners in former Soviet countries saw their incomes vanish during the break-up of the Soviet Union.

Further reading

Social Security Administration Web site. Available online. URL: www.ssa.gov.

cost-push inflation (supply-shock inflation, sellers' inflation)

Cost-push inflation, also referred to as supply-shock or sellers' INFLATION, is an increase in the general level of prices caused by a leftward shift of an economy's aggregate SUPPLY curve. Aggregate supply/aggregate DEMAND (macroeconomic) analysis describes the interrelationship of real GROSS DOMESTIC PRODUCT (GDP) and the general level of prices (inflation). Assuming nothing else changes, a decrease in aggregate supply will result in both higher prices and reduced level of output (GDP).

The most widely quoted example of cost-push inflation in the United States is the period from

1973 to 1980, during which the price of oil went from $2 to $30 per barrel. When the ORGANIZATION OF PETROLEUM EXPORTING COMPANIES (OPEC) effectively reduced the supply of oil, driving up oil prices, western countries experienced supply shocks. During the 1990s the United States imported approximately 50 percent of its oil needs. Because there are few substitutes available, the demand for oil and products derived from it are inelastic; higher oil prices do not significantly reduce the quantity demanded. The result is a double negative: higher prices and higher UNEMPLOYMENT associated with reduced GDP.

Cost-push inflation is also a result of other pressures increasing prices while decreasing output. Wage increases greater than increases in productivity increase the cost of PRODUCTION, causing inflation. Increased market power by firms, allowing them to raise prices while reducing supply, results in cost-push inflation. When either wages or market power increases in many sectors of an economy, the economic system will experience cost-push inflation.

See also MACROECONOMICS.

Further reading

Ruffin, Roy J., and Paul R. Gregory. *Principles of Economics.* 7th ed. Boston: Addison Wesley, 2000.

costs

When business managers change the level of output, they do so by changing the quantity of resources, called inputs, used to produce the output. As the number of inputs change, the firm's costs change. There are many types of costs: total costs (TC), total fixed costs (TFC), total variable costs (TVC), average total cost (ATC sometimes shown as AC), average variable cost (AVC), average fixed cost (AFC), and marginal cost (MC).

To understand the various costs, it is necessary to distinguish between fixed and variable costs. Fixed costs are those that do not change during the period of time and range of output under consideration. When the planning period is relatively short, some inputs, such as the size of the factory and number of machines, are constant; while other

inputs—labor, materials, and energy—change with the level of output. Total costs can then be separated into fixed costs and variable costs. Using the table below, each of the cost concepts can be defined.

Units of Output (Q)	TC	TFC	TVC	ATC	AVC	AFC	MC
0	10	10	0	–	–	–	–
1	15	10	5	15	5	10	5
2	18	10	8	9	4	5	3
3	21	10	11	7	3.7	3.3	3

Total cost equals the sum of total fixed costs and total variable costs at each level of output: $TC = TFC + TVC$. Total fixed costs equal total costs minus total variable costs: $TFC = TC − TVC$. Note that in the table above, total fixed costs do not change as the units of output increase. By definition, fixed costs are fixed. Note also that when the firm has no output, total costs equals total fixed costs. When a firm has no output it has no variable costs, only fixed costs. For example, a new company, such as a bank, leases a building, gets a business license, obtains a charter with the banking authorities, hires office staff, rents computers and office equipment, and makes other expenditures before it ever opens its door for business. All of these costs are fixed costs.

Total variable costs equals total costs minus total fixed costs: $TVC = TC − TFC$. Variable costs are costs that change as the firm produces more output. For a bank, variable costs would include labor, communication costs, and costs of funds (interest paid).

Average total cost equals total cost divided by the number of units produced: $ATC = TC/Q$. Notice in the table above that there is no figure when the level of output is zero; division by zero is undefined. The same is true for average variable cost and average fixed cost.

Average variable cost equals total variable cost divided by the number of units produced: $AVC = TVC/Q$. Average fixed cost equals total fixed cost divided by the number of units produced: AFC

= *TFC/Q*. Notice that AFC decreases as output increases. This is known as "spreading your fixed costs." One of the reasons a small business, like a new bank, will want to grow as fast as possible is to spread the initial start-up costs (fixed costs) over a larger volume of output (loans and other ASSETS).

Marginal cost equals the change in total cost divided by the change in output: *MC = change in TC/change in Q*. In the table above, there is no figure for marginal cost when output is zero; there is no information to compare the change in total cost and change in marginal cost. But when output increases to one unit, total cost increases from 10 to 15, a difference of 5, and output changes from 0 to 1, a change of 1. Therefore marginal cost is 5/1 = 5.

Marginal cost is a very useful concept to business managers. Often managers are faced with new choices or situations. Open a new location. Add a new line of products. Stay open additional hours. Have the employees work overtime. In each of these situations, a manager would like to know how much more will it cost to do this. Marginal cost answers this important question.

There are other ways to calculate costs. *TC = TFC + TVC*. Total cost also equals average total cost times the number of units of output: *TC = ATC × Q*. Similarly, *TFC = AFC × Q*, and *TVC = AVC × Q*.

Average total cost can also be calculated by adding AFC + AVC at each level of output; therefore *AFC = ATC - AVC* and *AVC = ATC - AFC*.

Often, in a business situation, a manager will only have limited information about what costs are or will be. If a manager can estimate cost per unit (average total cost) in a range of output and then compare to the price they expect to be able to sell the product for, they can make the decision whether or not to pursue that activity.

Summary of cost relationships:

TC = TFC + TVC, or TC = ATC × Q
TFC = TC - TVC, or TFC = AFC × Q
TVC = TC - TFC, or TVC = AVC × Q
ATC = TC/Q, or ATC = AFC + AVC
AVC = TVC/Q, or AVC = ATC - AFC
AFC = TFC/Q, or AFC = ATC - AVC

See also MARGINAL ANALYSIS; PROFIT MAXIMIZATION; TRANSACTION COSTS.

counterfeit goods

Counterfeit goods are found in many markets, including the United States. Luxury brand-name articles are often counterfeited (Pierre Cardin, Louis Vuitton), but the phenomenon is by no means limited to them. Counterfeit auto and airplane parts, pharmaceuticals, and Levi jeans along with computer software, musical CDs and tapes, and even Apple and IBM computers exist. In China, a haven for counterfeiting, entirely counterfeit Jeeps have been produced.

Counterfeit goods are unlicensed and generally ride freely on the BRANDS identity and GOODWILL of TRADEMARK owners. Their quality, while often suspect, can be surprisingly good. Legal remedies against counterfeiting include customs seizures (the big problem being notice and identification of counterfeits), court orders, and DAMAGES. Members of the WORLD TRADE ORGANIZATION are required to provide such remedies, but their level of enforcement in developing countries varies substantially. Vested local interests (for example, the Chinese military) may block use of such remedies. The long-term solution is the emergence of local technology and brand-name supporters of INTELLECTUAL PROPERTY rights, as has occurred in Japan, Korea, and Singapore. When this occurs, counterfeiting as a cheap means of ECONOMIC DEVELOPMENT tends to move on to less-advanced nations.

Further reading

Folsom, Ralph H., Michael Gordon, and John Spanogle. *International Business Transactions in a Nutshell*. 6th ed. Eagan, Minn.: West Group, 2000.

countertrade

Countertrade is a reciprocal trading agreement between or among trading partners. In essence, countertrade is international BARTER. It is often used when there are problems with hard-currency generation and in TECHNOLOGY TRANSFER agreements. It is also often involved in the sale of aerospace and defense equipment.

Countertrade was the ancient basis for trade before MONEY was created and often became necessary during times of economic collapse. Between World War I and World War II, Germany was forced to barter for goods as its money became worthless. Countertrade became popular in the 1980s among companies wanting to trade with the Soviet Union and Eastern European countries. For example, PepsiCo traded billions of dollars worth of Pepsi PRODUCTS in exchange for Stolichnaya vodka and a few ships. Similarly, Coca Cola Company accepted Yugoslavian wine in exchange for their soft drinks.

In addition to straightforward barter agreements, there are many other types of countertrade transactions.

- *Counterpurchase.* This obligates the foreign supplier to purchase from the buyer goods and SERVICES unrelated to the goods and services sold, usually within a one- to five-year period.
- *Reverse countertrade.* This requires the importer to export goods equivalent in value to a specified percentage of the value of the imported goods—an obligation that can be sold to an exporter in a third country.
- *Buyback arrangements.* These obligate the foreign supplier of plant, machinery, or technology to buy from the importer a portion of the resultant production during a future time period.
- *Clearing agreements.* Two countries agree to purchase specific amounts of each other's products over a specified period of time, using a designated "clearing currency" in the transactions.
- *Switch arrangement.* Permission is granted to sell unpaid balances in a clearing account to a third party, usually at a discount; this may be used in producing goods in the country holding the balance.
- *Swap arrangements.* Products from different locations are traded to save transportation costs.

The Global Offset and Countertrade Association educates members concerning the use of countertrade by global firms. Countertrade specialists facilitate exchanges for companies wanting to sell products abroad but having no knowledge of products outside their industry.

Further reading

American Countertrade Association Web site. Available online. URL: www.countertrade.org; Boone, Louis E., and David L. Kurtz. *Contemporary Marketing,* 14th ed. Fort Worth: South-Western Press, 2009; "Nigeria: Market Will Not Be Easy to Do Business in This Year, As the Economy Continues to Face Difficulties," *Business America,* 14 April 1986.

countervailing duties (CVDs)

Countervailing duties (CVDs) are special TARIFFS imposed on imported goods to offset the benefits of subsidies provided to producers or exporters in the exporting countries. CVDs are designed to address unfair competition in global markets. Most countries subsidize domestic industries. U.S. law defines a subsidy as a financial contribution by a governmental entity that confers a benefit to the manufacturer of the subsidized product. The goal of subsidies is to expand output, creating jobs and income within the country. Subsidies can come in many forms, including grants, government-provided educational and training programs, tax credits, public infrastructure projects facilitating movement of goods and resources, financial subsidies, public sale of resources at below cost of production, and many other efforts to support domestic producers. For example, in the United States, the agricultural extension service provides free expertise and educational training to farmers. The U.S. EXIMBANK provides low-cost loans to international buyers of products produced in the United States. The U.S. Forest Service sells logging rights to public lands at prices below the cost of developing the timber resources. Local and state governments routinely offer tax holidays, low-cost land, free worker training, and infrastructure subsidies to attract new industries. Subsidies allow firms to produce at lower costs, making their products more price competitive in global markets. Subsidies have also been labeled "CORPORATE WELFARE," special programs designed to benefit specific firms or industries.

Theoretically, a countervailing duty would offset the unfair subsidy allowing firms to compete on a "level playing field." It is difficult to identify and quantify subsidies. Opponents of CVDs suggest if a foreign country wants to make its goods cheaper for consumers in other countries, let consumers benefit and let the taxpayers in the subsidizing country pay for the subsidy. If a country uses subsidies in a predatory manner designed to undercut and eliminate foreign competitors, most countries will attempt to use countervailing duties to prevent the elimination of domestic competition.

As part of the SMOOT-HAWLEY TARIFF ACT (1930) the United States can impose countervailing duties if a U.S. industry is "materially injured" or threatened by the foreign subsidy. More recently, the United States and the WORLD TRADE ORGANIZATION (WTO) classified actionable subsidies (ones for which countervailing duties may be imposed) as "red, yellow, amber, or green" light subsidies. "Red light," or prohibited, subsidies are financial support that requires firms to meet export performance requirements, or use local resources in production. "Yellow light" subsidies include financial contributions that benefit specific firms or industries but do not require minimum export targets. These subsidies can result in countervailing duties if they are found to materially injure domestic producers.

If a U.S. firm or industry thinks it is being harmed by unfair subsidies it can appeal to the International Trade Administration (ITA) of the U.S. COMMERCE DEPARTMENT to determine whether the imported products are being unfairly subsidized and to assess countervailing duties. WTO rules allow a country to impose CVDs under the "Agreement on Subsidies and Countervailing Measures" (SCM Agreement.) The WTO's substantive rule states: "A Member may not impose a countervailing measure unless it determines that there are subsidized imports, injury to a domestic industry, and a causal link between the subsidized imports and the injury." The causal link requirement places the burden of proof on the injured nation or industry.

In an attempt to reduce the imposition of countervailing duties during trade conflicts, the World Trade Organization has adopted an elaborate multinational dispute settlement procedure. The pro-cedure first provides a consultation between the countries. If a resolution is not reached, a panel of experts can be established to investigate and provide a report supporting or refuting the claims. If a prohibited subsidy is found to exist, the country providing the subsidy is obligated to remove it. If the subsidy is not removed within six months, the complaining country may take action in the form of retaliatory duties on exports from the subsidizing country. In 2009 the United States threatened to impose increased duties on a variety of gourmet foods from the European Union (EU) in response to the EU's ban on beef treated with hormones.

Further reading
Chung, Juliet. "Looming Tariffs Whet Appetite for EU Delicacies," *Wall Street Journal,* 31 March 2009, A3; World Trade Organization Web site. Available online. URL: www.wto.org.

countervailing power
Countervailing power is the economic concept that the power of a seller (buyer) in a market will eventually be offset by an equal, opposite power among buyers (sellers). As developed by John Kenneth Galbraith, countervailing power suggests that initial market dominance will evolve into complimentary power, reducing the control and pricing power of the firm or group that originally prevailed in the market.

The most frequently discussed case of countervailing power is a bilateral MONOPOLY. In this market situation, a monopsonist, or single buyer of labor, is offset by a UNION, or single source of labor. U.S. union history contains many examples of workers organizing to counter the power and abuse of a "company town," where the factory owner controlled EMPLOYMENT, housing, stores, banking, and even education. Factory owners, logically not wanting to give up market power and often believing that they acted in the best interests of the people they controlled, resisted union attempts to offset their power.

Today professional sports leagues—with owners acting collectively (having been granted exemptions from U.S. ANTITRUST LAWS) and unions representing players—create a bilateral monopoly. For example, in major-league baseball, the players' union's power evolved in the 1970s and 1980s. Early leaders in the players' union were sometimes blacklisted by team owners, but eventually the union became an effective countervailing force. When players' demands were not met, a 1990s strike hurt both players and team owners but established the players' union as an effective balance to the initial dominance of team owners. The union's power led to increased players' salaries, and negotiating terms in players' clauses allowing them to sell their services in the free-agent draft.

country-risk analysis

Country-risk analysis is the assessment of the level of political and economic RISK associated with doing business in another country. Risk analysis is used when extending credit to foreign buyers making foreign DIRECT INVESTMENT decisions. Country-risk analysis includes analysis of

- the level of political stability
- regulation of businesses
- protection for private property
- government WAGE AND PRICE CONTROLS
- government budgets and deficits
- INFLATION
- UNEMPLOYMENT
- INTEREST RATES
- EXCHANGE RATES

Business managers do not like surprises. Each aspect of country-risk analysis is a potential source of uncertainty, which can lead to unpleasant surprises for anyone doing business abroad. One of the reasons foreigners have invested huge sums of CAPITAL in the United States is the relatively low risk associated with American business ventures. By comparison, investors in Indonesia, Malaysia, Thailand, Argentina and many other industrializing countries have, at times, lost money due to changes in political and ECONOMIC CONDITIONS. For example, many U.S.-based companies invested in Indonesia during the 32-year reign of President Suharto. His government imposed strict controls, creating, through force, a stable political and

economic environment. The Indonesian economy grew rapidly, and its currency remained stable. In 1998 Suharto was forced out of office and replaced by President Wahid in national elections. With the Asian financial crisis that year, Indonesia's economy decreased by over 13 percent, its currency and STOCK MARKET plummeted, and political strife grew. In 2001, U.S. companies such as Newmont Mining and Exxon Mobil closed their Indonesian operations, citing risk of separatist revolt and conditions approaching anarchy. In 2008, when financial markets collapsed, many international investors bought U.S. government securities, some paying zero interest, fearing devaluation or default by other countries.

Typically, MULTINATIONAL CORPORATIONS (MNCs) conduct country-risk analyses before making major financial investments in new areas of the world. MNCs also pay consulting services to monitor changes in political and economic conditions around the world. One service provides a weekly update summarizing events in each country and providing analysis of the significance to businesses operating there.

To reduce country risk, companies will hedge against EXCHANGE-RATE RISK, seek assistance from U.S. government agencies, and insure INVESTMENTS through government-sponsored corporations including the OVERSEAS PRIVATE INSURANCE CORPORATION and EXPORT-IMPORT BANK OF THE UNITED STATES.

Further reading
Schuman, Michael. "How Big Mining Lost a Fortune in Indonesia: The Locals Moved In," *Wall Street Journal*, 16 May 2001, p. A1.

Court of International Trade
The U.S. Court of International Trade (CIT) was created under Article III of the U.S. Constitution to provide judicial review of civil actions from import transactions and certain federal statutes affecting international trade. The CIT replaced the Board of General Appraisers, a unit of the Treasury Department, and the U.S. Customs Court, which together reviewed U.S. CUSTOMS SERVICE

decisions concerning the amount of duties to be paid on IMPORTS. The president, with the approval of the U.S. Senate, appoints the nine CIT judges, with no more than five of the nine judges belonging to one political party.

The CIT has exclusive jurisdiction over civil actions taken against the United States, its agencies, or officers concerning any laws related to revenue from imports, duties, EMBARGOes, TARIFFS, or enforcement of customs regulations. Disputes regarding trade embargoes, quotas, customs classifications, and country of origin determinations are all heard by the Court of International Trade. Customs classifications and country of origin decisions affect the tariff rate importing businesses must pay. Information regarding country of origin can be obtained from (for example) reading stickers on automobiles sold in the country. Customs classifications are also important. For example, a small Michigan company, Heartland By-Products, imported molasses from Canada after U.S. Customs agreed molasses was not sugar. The company then reprocessed the molasses into sugar, selling it to candy and soft-drink manufacturers. The U.S. sugar lobby protested and brought legal action before the CIT, but the court affirmed products should be classified according to the way they are imported, not their ultimate use.

The CIT has authority to review agency decisions concerning antidumping and countervailing duty matters as well as TRADE-ADJUSTMENT ASSISTANCE. For example, the United States, under the NORTH AMERICAN FREE TRADE AGREEMENT (NAFTA) Worker Safety Act, provides assistance for U.S. workers who have lost their jobs due to import COMPETITION. Workers can seek assistance if a significant number of company employees have been or are threatened with losing their jobs due to NAFTA imports or shifting of jobs to Mexico or Canada. The CIT reviews disputes regarding whether workers in a company are eligible for benefits. In 2000 Save Domestic Oil, a U.S. political-action group went before the CIT with charges against oil-rich countries for DUMPING. In the same year, the CIT affirmed a dumping determination against heavy hand tools being imported

from China. CIT decisions can be appealed to the Court of Appeals for the Federal Circuit and ultimately to the U.S. Supreme Court.

Further reading
U.S. Court of International Trade Web site. Available online. URL: www.cit.uscourts.gov.

credit See DEBIT, CREDIT.

creative capitalism

Creative capitalism is "an attempt to stretch the reach of market forces so that more companies can benefit from doing work that makes more people better off." The term was first used by Microsoft CEO Bill Gates at the 2008 World Economic Forum where he described creative capitalism as "an approach where governments, businesses, and nonprofits work together to stretch the reach of market forces so that more people can make a profit, or gain recognition, doing work that eases the world's inequities."

Note the first definition includes only companies while the second definition also includes governments and nonprofits. Gates uses a number of examples to describe creative capitalism, including:

- The RED campaign in which major companies share profits from sales of RED branded products to the Global Fund to fight problems of AIDS, tuberculosis, and malaria around the world. (Red is the color symbolizing emergency.)
- To address the problem of meningitis in Africa, the World Health Organization (WHO) first went to the continent to assess what consumers could pay for the vaccine and then challenged manufacturers to make the product available at an affordable price.
- A Dutch company with rights to a cholera vaccine agreed to license its rights to manufacturers in developing countries for no royalty while retaining its rights in developed countries.
- A law passed in the United States allows any drug company that develops a treatment for a neglected disease, such as malaria or TB, to get a priority review for another drug from the FDA, expediting the drug approval process.

An economic argument for creative capitalism is that many of the sophisticated products created in recent years have low marginal costs, and thus the additional cost to a firm of providing those goods to low-income consumers around the world is quite small. For example, once a cellular phone system has been created (a huge initial CAPITAL EXPENDITURE), the extra cost of providing service to low-income customers is quite small. Similarly, the marginal cost of providing medicines, software, and information to make people with limited incomes better off is quite small.

CAPITALISM, as articulated by the famous 18th-century professor of moral philosophy, Adam Smith, is a system based on self-interest. Smith, considered the first modern economist, wrote,

> As every individual, therefore, endeavors as much he can both to employ his capital in the support of domestic industry, and so to direct that industry that its produce may be of the greatest value; every individual necessarily labors to render the annual revenue of the society as great as he can. He generally, indeed, neither intends to promote the public interest, nor knows how much he is promoting it. By preferring the support of domestic to that of foreign industry, he intends only his own security; and by directing that industry in such a manner as its produce may be of the greatest value, he intends only his own gain, and he is in this, as in many other cases, led by an invisible hand to promote an end which was no part of his intention. Nor is it always the worse for the society that it was not part of it. By pursuing his own interest he frequently promotes that of the society more effectually than when he really intends to promote it.

Gates argues: "The genius of capitalism lies in its ability to make self-interest serve the wider interest. The potential of a big financial return for innovation unleashes a broad set of talented people in pursuit of many different discoveries. This system, driven by self-interest, is responsible for the incredible innovations that have improved so many lives." He goes on to say, "Capitalism har-

nesses self-interest in a helpful and sustainable way, but only on behalf of those who can pay," referring to the fact that markets reflect the priorities of those households that have money but not the priorities of households without significant purchasing power.

Gates wants to refine the system, suggesting capitalism should have two missions: "making profits and also caring for others." Critics, including *Financial Times* commentator Clive Crook, argue that creative capitalism is just a new term for the idea of corporate social responsibility. Crook, citing Nobel Prize–winning economist Milton Friedman, suggests that efforts that benefit both business and society do not need a new champion like Bill Gates. "If it makes money, there should be no need for visionary exhortation about the social benefits." He goes on to state that in Europe and to some degree in the United States, corporate social responsibility has become the corporate equivalent of political correctness. "It seems to inspire a good deal of window dressing and bureaucratic overhead, to little or no economic purpose."

Bill Gates, considered one of the richest persons in the world, also heads (with his wife, Melinda) the world's largest nonprofit organization, the Gates Foundation.

Further reading

Gates, Bill. "Making Capitalism More Creative," *Time*, 31 July 2008. Available online. URL: www.time.com/time/business/article/0,8599,1828069,00.html. Accessed on February 25, 2009; ———. "Bill Gates: World Economic Forum 2008." Available online. URL: www.microsoft.com/Presspass/exec/billg/speeches/2008/01-24WEFDavos.mspx. Accessed on February 25, 2009; Crook, Clive. "A Creative Capitalism Compendium." Available online. URL: creativecapitalism.typepad.com/creative_capitalism/clive_crook/index.html. Accessed on February 25, 2009.

credit cards

Credit cards are a convenient method for consumers to secure short-term LOANS. In today's U.S. economy, credit cards and access to credit cards are ubiquitous; in many situations, such as hotels, it is difficult to purchase goods and services without use of a credit card. While most Americans probably cannot conceive of life without credit cards, they are a relatively recent phenomenon in U.S. business.

The AMERICAN BANKERS ASSOCIATION (ABA) credits Western Union with issuing the first consumer charge card in 1914. At the time there was no FEDERAL RESERVE SYSTEM, and the banking industry consisted of thousands of small-town banks and the large money-center institutions in New York. Credit was generally a locally based decision, and consumer credit was a new concept. Many hotels and department stores quickly followed Western Union's lead, issuing their own cards. Until the 1990s, locally based, high-interest-rate credit supported many main street businesses in small towns in the United States.

In 1950 Diners Club issued the first charge card accepted by a wide variety of merchants. Diners Club began the practice of charging merchants a small percentage "discount" for facilitating purchases by consumers. The next year Franklin National Bank (New York) issued its own card accepted by area merchants. Soon nearly 100 other banks issued similar cards for their market areas, but users were expected to pay their balances when presented with a statement.

In 1958 Bank of America issued its BankAmericard (later renamed Visa) for use throughout California. Bank of America was the first to offer credit rather than requiring consumers to pay their balances each month. By 1965 Bank of America had formed agreements with numerous banks, allowing them to issue BankAmericard outside of California. During the same period, a number of banks collectively created Master Charge (later renamed MasterCard).

The credit-card industry grew slowly until the advent of automated teller machines (ATMs). In the 1970s, American consumers did not readily accept ATMs; most preferred person-to-person bank transactions. Using both "carrots and sticks," incentives and disincentives, the industry gradually changed Americans' use of credit cards. Today Visa and MasterCard dominate the credit card industry in the United States, and in recent years they have been accused of anticompetitive behavior. The two associations have pushed the use of debit rather than credit cards, where consumers' accounts are directly debited and funds transferred to merchants as purchases are made. New technology now allows businesses to scan consumers' personal checks and directly debit their credit accounts.

Credit-card issuers are subject to a variety of legal requirements, most notably the TRUTH IN LENDING ACT (1968), which imposes a variety of disclosure requirements. They differ depending on how a credit-card application is solicited but basically require issuers to disclose the annual percentage rate (APR), annual fees, the grace period for paying without incurring a finance charge, and the method used for computing the balance on which a finance charge is based.

In the early part of the 21st century, credit-card usage boomed in the United States with Americans owing over $1 trillion, much of it borrowed using credit cards. Economists predicted that Americans saturated with credit would eventually have to slow CONSUMPTION spending to pay off past credit-card debt. Until 2007, card issuers aggressively pursued "subprime" borrowers, people with poor credit histories or previous personal bankruptcy. Credit-"repair" and CONSUMER CREDIT COUNSELING SERVICES expanded rapidly as Americans, in response to a recession, reduced their use of credit cards. In other countries, credit-card usage is much less prevalent, and consumer resistance to the use of credit cards has often surprised U.S. businesses expanding internationally.

See also DEBIT, CREDIT.

Further reading
"A History of Debit and Credit: How Plastic Cards Forever Changed our Lives," *Chain Store Age Executive with Shopping Center Age* 68, no. 9 (September 1992): 22.

Credit Card Accountability Responsibility and Disclosure Act of 2009 (CreditCARD Act of 2009)

The Credit Card Accountability Responsibility and Disclosure Act of 2009 was a major federal law passed in response to consumer and voter complaints about abusive practices in the CREDIT CARD industry. Technically, a series of amendments to the TRUTH IN LENDING ACT, and originally introduced as the Credit Cardholders' Bill of Rights in the previous session of Congress, the act changed laws regarding INTEREST RATES lenders can charge, late charges and fees, confusing and misleading terminology, allocation of payments toward debts, maximum fees that can be charged annually, and increased oversight of the credit card industry.

The Obama administration touted the act in stating:

- First, there have to be strong and reliable protections for consumers.
- Second, all the forms and statements that credit card companies send out have to have plain language that is in plain sight.
- Third, people must be assured that they can shop for a credit card that meets their needs without fear of being taken advantage of.
- Finally, more accountability is needed in the system, so that those who do engage in deceptive practices that hurt families and consumers can be held responsible.

Effective February 2010, the act:

- Bans retroactive interest rate increases except when a cardholder is more than 60 days late paying a credit card bill.
- Requires the credit card issuer must review the cardholder's account six months after increasing the interest rate, and return the APR to the previous lower level if the cardholder has been on time with payment.
- Prohibits interest rate increases within the first 12 months, and promotional rates must have a minimum of 6 months' duration.
- Requires advance notice of 45 days prior to significant changes in credit card terms, including the benefits and reward structure of a credit card.
- Bans the practice of universal default and double-cycle billing.
- Prohibits over-credit-limit fees unless consumers specifically agree to allow transaction to go through instead of being denied.

- Requires bills to be sent out no later than 21 days before the due date.
- Payments made by cardholders must be credited as on time if the payment is received by 5 P.M. on the due date.
- Requires clear disclosure on how long it would take to pay off a credit card balance if the cardholder makes only the minimum payment each month.
- Requires clear disclosure on the total cost in interest and principal payments if a cardholder makes only the minimum payment each month.
- Requires that a payment deadline and postmark date be clearly shown and disclosed to cardholders.
- Prohibits issuing credit cards to individuals under the age of 21 unless they have an adult cosigner or show proof that they have the means to repay the debt (proof of reasonable income).
- Requires college students to receive permission from parents or guardians to increase credit limit on joint accounts they hold with those adults.
- Requires gift cards to remain active for at least five years from the day of their activation.
- Dormancy or inactivity fees on gift cards can no longer be imposed unless there has been no activity in a 12-month period.
- Requires dormancy or inactivity fees to be clearly disclosed to gift card buyers.

The act followed directives from the FEDERAL RESERVE, which in December 2008 approved similar rules but delayed implementation until July 2010. The Fed had received over 60,000 comments on proposed regulatory changes affecting the credit card industry. One study showed major banks earning over half of their revenue from late fees and nonpayment charges. In 2007, Public Broadcasting System's *Frontline* series ran a powerful documentary, *The Secret History of the Credit Card Industry,* documenting practices that included

- "universal default," where nonpayment to any creditor was used to increase the interest rate on all credit charges
- Encouraging consumers to make even smaller minimum payments

- Changing billing cycles and payment due dates to increase late payment fees.

While consumer-interest groups applauded most of the measures in the act, critics argued it would decrease access to credit, cause lenders to eliminate popular rebate and credit card–based points programs, and subsidize "deadbeat" consumers.

Further reading

White House Office of the Press Secretary. "Fact Sheet: Reforms to protect American credit card holders." Available online. URL: www.whitehouse.gov/the_press_office/Fact-Sheet-Reforms-to-Protect-American-Credit-Card-Holders/. Accessed on June 26, 2009; "Breakdown: The Credit Card Act of 2009." Available online. URL: www.stopbuyingcrap.com/personal-finance/credit-card-act-2009/. Accessed on June 26, 2009.

credit counseling services

Credit counseling services provide credit information, advice, debt management plans, and sometimes bankruptcy assistance. Thousands of debt counseling services are available around the country, some more reputable than others. Reputable credit counseling organizations advise clients about managing their money and debts, help consumers develop a budget, and usually offer free educational materials and workshops. Their counselors are trained and certified in credit counseling. The FEDERAL TRADE COMMISSION (FTC) warns consumers that just because an organization says it is nonprofit does not guarantee that its services are free or affordable. Some counseling services are funded by credit card companies seeking to avoid personal bankruptcies. The FTC provides a series of "Tip-offs to Rip-offs" to avoid less than reputable groups, advising consumers to steer clear of debt consolidation companies that:

- Guarantee they can remove your unsecured debt
- Promise that unsecured debts can be paid off with pennies to the dollar
- Require substantial monthly service fees
- Demand payment of a percentage of the savings

- Tell you to stop making payments to, or communicating with, your creditors
- Require you to make monthly payments to them, rather than to your creditor
- Claim that creditors never sue consumers for nonpayment of unsecured debt
- Promise that using their system will have no negative impact on your credit report
- Claim that they can remove accurate negative information from your credit report.

State consumer advocacy offices, attorney general's offices, local consumer protection agencies, and the BETTER BUSINESS BUREAU are potential ways to check out the reliability of credit counseling organizations. Once creditable service organizations have been identified, the FTC provides a list of questions to ask, including:

- What services do you offer? Look for an organization that offers a range of services, including budget counseling, and savings and debt management classes. Avoid organizations that push a debt management plan (DMP) as your only option before they spend a significant amount of time analyzing your financial situation.
- Do you offer information? Are educational materials available for free? Avoid organizations that charge for information.
- In addition to helping me solve my immediate problem, will you help me develop a plan for avoiding problems in the future?
- What are your fees? Are there set-up and/or monthly fees? Get a specific price quote in writing.
- What if I can't afford to pay your fees or make contributions? If an organization will not help you because you cannot afford to pay, look elsewhere for help.
- Will I have a formal written agreement or contract with you? Do not sign anything without reading it first. Make sure all verbal promises are in writing.
- Are you licensed to offer your services in my state?
- What are the qualifications of your counselors? Are they accredited or certified by an outside

organization? If so, by whom? If not, how are they trained? Try to use an organization whose counselors are trained by a nonaffiliated party.

- What assurance do I have that information about me (including my address, phone number, and financial information) will be kept confidential and secure?
- How are your employees compensated? Are they paid more if I sign up for certain services, if I pay a fee, or if I make a contribution to your organization? If the answer is yes, consider it a red flag and go elsewhere for help.

If this series of questions seem daunting or aggressive, it is because so many Americans have been misled or taken advantage of by con artists posing as credit counselors. Criminals know they prey upon people who are vulnerable, including consumers who are in debt crises. Many consumers facing credit problems feel hopeless and are desperate for some form of relief. After a thorough credit review, a counselor may recommend a debt management plan (DMP) where the consumer deposits money each month with the credit counseling organization, which then disperses it based on a payment schedule the counselor has negotiated with the client's creditors. If the creditors agree to waive penalties and lower interest rates, the FTC states "get it in writing" before you begin the DMP and continue to make payments directly to creditors until the DMP has been approved.

Further reading
Federal Trade Commission. "Fiscal Fitness: Choosing a Credit Counselor." Available online. URL: www.ftc.gov/bcp/edu/pubs/consumer/credit/cre26.shtm Accessed on February 15, 2009.

credit default swaps

A credit default swap (CDS) is a financial contract that allows the transfer of credit risk from one market participant to another. Credit risk is the likelihood or potential that a borrower will default on a loan. In theory, credit default swap markets provide greater efficiency, diversification, and pricing of credit risk among financial market participants. In its simplest form, a credit default swap is an agreement between two parties in which the default protection buyer agrees to make periodic payments over a set period of years (usually the life of a loan) to the protection seller in exchange for payment should the third party, the borrower, referred to as a "reference entity," fail to make payment on his debt. If a default occurs, settlement can be made either in cash or physically, with the protection buyer having the right to sell the assets to the protection seller at the face value of the assets.

The major participants in credit default swap markets are large banks, followed by securities firms and insurance companies. A bank would typically use a credit default swap to reduce its risk associated with loans to one particular client without having to sell the loans they are holding. In some situations, the use of credit default swaps can reduce the amount of capital that banks are required to hold because the default risk has been transferred to another party. Securities firms and insurance companies both buy and sell default protection depending on their portfolio of assets and willingness to assume credit default risk.

Prices of credit default swaps depend on four factors: the credit risk of the reference entity, the expected recovery rates associated with the reference entity and the protection seller, the credit risk of the protection seller, and the default correlation between the reference entity and the protection seller. The fourth factor, the correlation between the reference entity and the protection seller, refers to the likelihood that both the credit default protection seller and the underlying borrower will default, leaving the buyer with both the loss of a loan and the insurance protecting him against default. As such, credit default swaps could be called insurance; but, as investors, politicians, and regulators learned during the 2008–09 financial crises, American International Group (AIG), a major writer of credit default swaps, argued that it constituted FINANCIAL INSTRUMENTS but not insurance, and therefore did not fall under the supervision of insurance industry regulators.

In a 2001 FEDERAL RESERVE report, the author ended by stating that "current market trends suggest increased participation of non-banks in the market and growing use of more complex credit derivatives in portfolio management." In the following years, the use of credit default swaps increased in exponential fashion. By the third quarter of 2008, when financial markets began to collapse, the Office of Comptroller of the Currency (OCC) reported that U.S. commercial banks had a credit exposure of $435 billion, up 73 percent from the previous year, and a notional value (face value of the securities against which default swaps had been written) of $175 trillion dollars. This compared with a reported face value of $33 trillion 10 years earlier.

The OCC reported that derivative activity was highly concentrated, with five large financial institutions accounting for 97 percent of activity, but, as would soon be proven foolish, it stated, "While market or product concentrations are a concern for bank supervisors, there are three important mitigating factors with respect to DERIVATIVES activities. First, there are a number of other providers of derivatives whose activity is not in the data in this report. Second, because the highly specialized business of structuring, trading, and managing derivatives transactions requires sophisticated tools and expertise, derivatives activity is concentrated in those institutions that have the resources needed to operate this business in a safe and sound manner. Third, the OCC has examiners on-site at the largest banks to continuously evaluate the credit, market, operation, reputation and compliance risks of derivatives activity."

When financial markets collapsed, in fall 2008, the U.S. government seized control of AIG, eventually injecting over $150 billion into the "insurance" company. In what became known as "too big to allow to fail" policy, Federal Reserve and Treasury Department regulators feared that default by the firm would create even larger problems in financial markets. AIG was a major writer of credit default swaps and other derivatives. AIG used government funds to then pay against defaults, with Goldman Sachs receiving billions of dollars, raising questions about relationships among financial market participants and government regulators.

One critic wrote, "Call it money laundering or cronyism, or just plain ugly, but for some AIG's bailout was money well spent."

Further reading

Bomfim, Antonio N. "Understanding Credit Derivatives and Their Potential to Synthesize Riskless Assets," Federal Reserve, 11 July 2001. Available online. URL: www.federalreserve.gov/pubs/feds/2001/200150/200150pap.pdf. Accessed on December 5, 2009; Colarusso, Dan. "The AIG Bailout Bargain," *The Business Insider,* 22 March 2009. Available online. URL: www.businessinsider.com/the-aig-bailout-bargain-2009-3. Accessed on December 5, 2009; "OCC's Quarterly Report on Bank Trading and Derivatives Activities Third Quarter 2008." Office of Comptroller of the Currency. Available online. URL: www.occ.treas.gov/ftp/release/2008-152a.pdf. Accessed December 5, 2009.

credit practices rule

Enacted in 1985, the Credit Practices Trade Regulation Rule prohibits many creditors from including certain provisions in consumer debt contracts. The rule was enacted in response to a variety of credit industry practices that were perceived as unfair, deceptive, or unethical. The rule covers all consumer credit transactions, except those involving the purchase of real estate. It covers loans made to consumers who purchase goods or services for personal, family, or household uses. The rule also applies to the sale of goods or services under lease-purchase plans.

The act contains three major provisions. First, it prohibits creditors from using contract provisions including confessions of judgment, waivers of exemption, wage assignments, and security interests in household goods. Second, the rule requires creditors to advise consumers who cosign obligations about their potential liability if the other person fails to pay. Third, the rule prohibits late charges in some situations.

Before passage of the Credit Practices Rule, creditors were allowed to include clauses that denied borrowers the right to receive notice of a lawsuit against them, to appear in court, and to raise any defenses that they might have. Usually called a "confession of judgment," this provision allowed a judgment to be entered for the creditor automatically when the creditor sued the debtor for breach of the contract. The rule prohibits creditors from including confession of judgment provisions in consumer credit contracts; however, it does not prohibit power-of-attorney provisions that allow creditors to repossess and sell collateral, as long as these provisions do not interfere with the consumer's right to be heard in court.

Before passage of the act, some consumer credit contracts contained "waiver of exemption" provisions that permitted creditors to seize (or threaten to seize) specific possessions or possessions of a specified value, even if state law treated them as exempt from seizure. Every state has a law that defines certain property (generally, property considered necessities) that a debtor is allowed to keep even if a creditor sues and obtains a judgment. By signing a waiver of exemption, a debtor made that property available to a creditor who obtained a judgment to satisfy a debt.

Previously, if consumers did not pay as agreed, some consumer credit contracts permitted creditors to go directly to the consumers' employers to have their wages, or some part of them, paid directly to the creditors. Under the rule's prohibition against "wage assignments," consumer contracts may not provide for the irrevocable advance assignment of any money due from consumers resulting from their personal services (usually through employment) if they do not pay as agreed. The rule's prohibition against "wage assignments" does not prohibit garnishment. If a creditor obtains a court judgment against a debtor, the creditor may continue to use wage garnishment to collect that judgment, subject to the consumer protections provided by federal (and sometimes state) law.

Until the Credit Practices Rule was passed, some consumer credit contracts contained nonpurchase money security agreements that allowed a creditor to repossess many household goods in the consumer's home if the consumer did not pay as agreed. Credit contracts cannot use language that provides for repossession of certain household goods, including necessities such as clothing, appliances, and linens, and some items of little economic value to creditors, but which may have personal value to consumers. These may include items such as family photographs, personal papers, the family Bible, and household pets. The act is quite specific, excluding from the definition of household goods such things as works of art, electronic entertainment equipment (except one television and one radio), items acquired as antiques (more than 100 years old), and jewelry (except wedding rings). The rule permits consumers to offer as security these valuable possessions to obtain credit as well as pianos or other musical instruments, boats, snowmobiles, bicycles, cameras, and similar items.

Under the rule, creditors may take "purchase money security interests" in any household goods when the consumer uses the loan proceeds or the credit advanced to purchase the household goods. If a creditor refinances or consolidates an agreement with a purchase money security interest in household goods, she may retain the purchase money security interest as a part of the refinanced or consolidated agreement to the extent permitted by state law. If the creditor takes possession of the secured property (as in pledge agreements that pawnbrokers commonly use), the rule permits a security interest even if the property pledged is household goods.

A second part of the Credit Practices Rule requires lenders to inform each cosigner of the potential liability involved before the cosigner becomes obligated for the debt. The rule specifies the following language that must be included in statements:

"You are being asked to guarantee this debt. Think carefully before you do. If the borrower doesn't pay the debt, you will have to. Be sure you can afford to pay if you have to, and that you want to accept this responsibility. You may have to pay up to the full amount of the debt if the borrower does not pay. You may also have to pay late fees or collection costs, which increase this amount. The creditor can collect this debt from you without first trying to collect from the borrower. The creditor can use the same collection methods against you that can be used against the borrower, such as suing you, garnishing your wages, etc. If this debt is ever in default, that fact may become a part of your credit record."

Finally, the rule imposed new restrictions on late fees charged by creditors. Previously, some creditors calculated late fees for delinquent payments using a practice called "pyramiding" of late charges. When one payment was made after its due date and a late fee was assessed but not paid promptly, all future payments were considered delinquent even though they were, in fact, paid in full within the required time period. As a result, late fees were assessed on all future payments. In other words, each successive payment was considered "short" by the amount of the previous late charge, with the result that another late charge was imposed.

The Credit Practices Rule applies to all creditors, all finance companies, retailers (such as auto dealers and furniture and department stores), and credit unions that offer consumer credit contracts. Similar rules passed by the FEDERAL RESERVE Board and the FEDERAL HOME LOAN BANK board apply to banks, SAVINGS AND LOAN ASSOCIATIONS, and other institutions under their jurisdiction. A state may petition the FEDERAL TRADE COMMISSION exemption from any of the rule's provisions. If the commission finds that the state law affords consumers a level of protection that is substantially equivalent to, or greater than, the protection afforded by the rule and the state has the ability to enforce and administer that law effectively, an exemption may be granted. The Federal Trade Commission can sue violators of the Credit Practices Rule in federal court. The court can impose civil penalties of up to $10,000 for each violation and can issue an order prohibiting further violations.

Further reading
Federal Trade Commission Web site. Available online. URL: www.ftc.gov.

credit-reporting services (credit bureaus)
Credit-reporting services, also called credit bureaus, are firms that maintain credit-history information on consumers and businesses. Credit-reporting services collect data about Americans' bill-paying practices and public-record information such as tax liens, court judgments, and bankruptcies. In the United States there are three major credit-reporting companies: Trans Union, Equifax, and Experian (previously named TRW). These firms own, or work with on a contractual basis, over 1,000 local and regional credit bureaus around the country, maintaining databases with credit information on more than 170 million individuals and businesses and producing over 500 million credit reports annually.

Credit-reporting services are an important resource used by lending institutions in making loan decisions. A typical credit report identifies the individual or firm; provides bill-paying history with retail stores, banks, finance and mortgage companies; and includes any public record credit-related documents. Credit-reporting services do not make decisions on LOANS, but their reports are the primary basis for many lending decisions.

Credit-reporting services produce credit scores based on consumers' payment history and other credit information. Scores range from 300 to 850, with the higher score representing a lower credit risk to lenders. CREDIT SCORING has, at times, been a controversial issue, with consumer groups complaining about the use of inaccurate data. Many dubious businesses have promoted their "credit repair" services to consumers turned down for loans.

The number and type of inquiries made about an individual's credit history is an important factor. Lending firms often make promotional inquiries into credit-reporting databases, gathering mailing lists of consumers who meet their inquiry criteria. Creditors also make periodic account-management inquiries, reviewing changes in the credit status of their customers. While these two types of inquiries do not affect consumers' credit scores, credit inquiries generated by consumers' requests for credit affect peoples' credit ratings. Too many inquiries suggest consumers are seeking a large amount of credit or have too much available credit.

The Fair Credit Reporting Act (1971) regulates credit information, requiring credit-reporting services to

- maintain accurate, relevant, and recent information
- provide access to credit information only to bona fide users
- inform consumers who are turned down or have their interest costs raised the reasons for these decisions
- allow consumers to review their files and correct any inaccurate information

Further reading

Mallor, Jane P., A. James Barnes, Thomas Bowers, Michael J. Philips, and Arlen W. Langvardt. *Business Law: The Ethical, Global, and E-Commerce Environment.* 14th ed. Boston: McGraw-Hill, 2009; Trans Union Web site. Available online. URL: www.tuc.com.

credit scoring

Credit scoring is mathematical modeling used by CREDIT-REPORTING SERVICES to generate a number rating a customer's credit risk. Fair Isaac and Company (FICO) is the leading provider of credit scores in the United States. Their system generates credit scores, ranging from 300 to 850 for each individual, which are used by lenders to make millions of lending decisions annually. The benefit to most consumers is that credit scores allow lenders to make quick, on-the-spot decisions based on past credit behavior, reducing the potential for bias. But credit scoring is only as good as the data used to create the number and can be a conundrum: How does one get a good credit rating without having access to credit? Critics argue the use of credit scores penalizes poor people, immigrants, and seniors, all groups who tend to pay their bills in cash and therefore do not have credit histories.

Based on past experience, FICO developed a predictive model that is used by the major credit-reporting services. This model uses

- payment history
- amount owed
- length of credit history

- new credit
- number of CREDIT CARDS
- total available credit
- finance company loans
- bank-issued versus department-store cards

In addition to evaluating consumer LOANS and issuing credit cards, credit scoring is used in making MORTGAGE decisions and determinations for auto- and homeowners-INSURANCE policies. Based on a correlation between credit quality and insurance claims, many insurance companies adjust their rates for potential customers.

Compared to the traditional FIVE Cs OF CREDIT, credit scoring introduces less potential for bias and less discretionary judgment.

Further reading

Quinn, Jane Bryant. "You Owe Yourself a Credit Check," *Washington Post,* 10 March 1996, p. H02; Simon, Ruth. "Looking to Improve Your Credit Score? Fair Isaac Can Help," *Wall Street Journal,* 10 March 2002, p. A1.

credit union

A credit union is a nonprofit cooperative financial institution that primarily provides consumer credit LOANS to its members, with funds deposited by its participants. Credit unions are mutually owned and run by their members, with a BOARD OF DIRECTORS, elected by the members, which sets policies and procedures. Most credit unions in the United States are members of the National Credit Union Association (NCUA), created to charter and supervise the industry; and participate in the National Credit Union Share Insurance Fund (NCUSIF), which insures credit union depositors.

The first credit unions were created in Germany during the 19th century. The first U.S. credit union was established by a group of Franco-American Catholics in Manchester, New Hampshire, in 1909. While banks provided business loans, and SAVINGS AND LOAN ASSOCIATIONS provided home MORTGAGE loans, credit unions grew to meet consumer-borrowing needs. In 1934 President Franklin D. Roosevelt signed the Federal Credit Union Act (FCUA), authorizing the establishment of federally chartered credit unions in all states.

After the FCUA was passed, Congress debated over which regulatory agency would preside over credit unions. Neither the COMPTROLLER OF THE CURRENCY (Treasury Department) nor the Federal Reserve Board wanted oversight of credit unions, so initially the Farm Credit Administration was responsible for managing them. Oversight then passed to bureaus within the FEDERAL DEPOSIT INSURANCE CORPORATION (FDIC); the Federal Security Agency; and the Department of Health, Education and Welfare. As the number of credit unions grew, responsibility for the system was shifted to the NCUA in 1970.

Because credit unions are nonprofit organizations, their INTEREST RATES on loans are typically lower than competing, for-profit, financial institutions. With DEREGULATION of the financial industry in the 1980s, credit unions expanded into mortgage and other lending activities. Like the savings and loan institutions, many credit unions failed during the 1980s, bankrupting the National Credit Union Share Insurance Fund (the credit union equivalent of Federal Deposit Insurance, FDIC). In 1985 the NCUSIF was recapitalized with deposits of member credit unions. The NCUSIF has three fail-safe features.

- Federal credit unions must maintain a one-percent deposit with the NCUSIF.
- Premiums are levied by the Board if necessary.
- When the equity ratio exceed 1.3 percent ($1.30 on deposit for every $100 insured), the Board sends a DIVIDEND to credit unions.

In 2009 there were over 10,000 credit unions with over $480 billion in ASSETS and 71 million members. Membership in credit unions is based on the principle of having a common bond. Workers in a particular factory, members of a local community or organization, or some other mutual relationship is usually required to join a credit union. During the 1990s credit unions greatly expanded membership, often redefining or relaxing the definition of the common-bond requirement. For-profit financial institutions challenged the actions of credit unions, and in 1998 the U.S. Supreme Court ruled against credit unions, stating government regulators too loosely defined the "field of membership" rule. In response, Congress passed the Credit Union Membership Access Act (1998), fostering local credit unions and expansion within "reasonable proximity" of existing credit-union service areas. Critics contend the NCUA continues to ignore and loosely interpret field of membership rules.

Further reading
American Banking Association Industry Issues Web site. Available online. URL: www.aba.com; National Credit Union Association Web site. Available online. URL: www.ncua.gov.

—Susan Poorbaugh

critical path method
Critical path method (CPM) was created in 1957 by J. E. Kelly of Remington Rand and M. R. Walker of DuPont to assist in the building and repairs of DuPont's chemical plants. In the following year, the Special Projects Office of the U.S. Navy created PROGRAM EVALUATION AND REVIEW TECHNIQUE (PERT) to help coordinate the duties of the thousands of contractors working on the Polaris missile program. Today CPM and PERT are essential planning tools used to help managers overcome the limitations of Gantt charts (horizontal bar charts used to track the progress of projects) and to determine which critical activities must be completed in order for a project to be finished in a timely and cost-effective manner. Although CPM and PERT do have some differences, which will be pointed out, they are often discussed synonymously because both are necessary quantitative techniques used for effective PROJECT MANAGEMENT.

In project management, determining CPM and PERT requires the creation of a network diagram, which gives the order of critical activities and the estimated time for completion of each activity. Loosely defined, a critical activity is any job in a project's schedule whose completion is necessary in order to have the entire project completed on time. Critical activities are found along a critical path, which therefore is "the longest path route through the network" because it is the path that will take the most time to complete. To reduce the time needed to complete a project, the number of activities found on the critical path would first have to be reduced.

Critical path method uses two time estimates for determining the time it will take to finish a project. The first is the "normal completion time" and the other is the "crash time." As the name implies, the normal completion time is the estimated time it will take to complete a project under "normal" conditions, or rather, a situation in which nothing unexpected happens to interrupt the course of the project. The crash time is the shortest time it would take to finish an activity if more money and other resources where added to complete the project.

Finding CPM and PERT requires project managers to perform a few simple calculations. CPM requires managers to find four quantities.

1. *Earliest Start Time (ES):* the earliest time an activity can start without violating any of the initial requirements for beginning the activity.
2. *Earliest Finish Time (EF):* the earliest time an activity is expected to end.
3. *Latest Start Time (LS):* the latest time the activity could begin without having the entire project lag.
4. *Latest Finish Time (LF):* the latest an activity could end without having the entire project lag (Render and Stair Jr., p. 635).

To calculate the earliest start and finish times for each activity in a project, project managers should begin by drawing a graph that looks something like this:

$$\text{(Earliest Start Time) } \underline{0} \qquad \underline{2} \text{ (Earliest Finish Time)}$$
$$0 \underline{\qquad} 2$$
$$t = 2$$

The Earliest Start Time is set at zero. Project managers should keep in mind that the earliest start time for each activity in the project will always be set at zero. Say, for instance, that activity "A" takes two weeks to complete; therefore, its ear-

liest finish time is represented as 2. The following calculation can be used to find the Earliest Finish Time: *Earliest Finish Time = Earliest Start Time + Expected Activity Time, or EF = ES + t.*

When computing the ES and EF for the activities in a project, there is one rule that must be followed. Before project managers begin one activity, all critical activities preceding that one must be completed first. For CPM, project managers are looking for the "longest path to an activity in determining ES" (Render and Stair Jr., p. 636). To calculate the ES and EF times for each activity in the entire project, project managers will make a "forward pass" through the network, where at each step EF = ES + t. Thus, say a project consists of projects A, B, C, D, E, and F; activity "F" cannot begin until the 11th week after starting the project, and it is expected to take two weeks to complete. The whole project will take exactly 13 weeks to be finished, since EF = ES + t; in this case, 13 = 11 + 2.

However, once the earliest finish time has been calculated, project managers still need to calculate the latest start and finish times for each activity in order to find the critical path. Now they will begin at the last activity, in this case activity "F," and work backward to activity "A." The formula used to find the latest start time is *Latest Start Time = Latest Finish Time - Expected Activity Time, or LS = LF - t.* For example, because LF equals 13 for activity "F," the latest start time for the activity is 11 weeks since LS = 13 - 2. The general rule here is that "the latest finish time for an activity equals the *smallest* latest starting time for all activities leaving that same event" (Render and Stair Jr., p. 637).

Another calculation that should be determined when finding the critical path of a project is the slack time, or the amount of time an activity can be put on hold without holding up the project as a whole. The calculation for slack is: *Slack = LS - ES or Slack = LF - EF.* However, it cannot be stressed enough that no critical activities can have any slack time because they are critical, and any delay in completing them will delay the completion of the entire project. Slack time can only be applied to those activities that are not considered critical to the outcome of the project.

Once the times for all activities on the critical path are computed, managers will apply PERT techniques to each activity to determine the variance of the entire project. Project variance is found by adding all the variances for each critical activity. Project variance equals sigma variances of each activity found on the critical path. The standard deviation for the project is the square root of the project variance. Once these calculations are made, project managers can determine whether the project will be completed on time.

While using CPM and PERT techniques is a necessary part of project management, it may not be necessary for a company to apply these tools to every job undertaken. Clearly there is a lot of analysis involved finding both CPM and PERT, and it takes a lot of experience on the part of the project managers to make the correct calculations. Managers who have little skills and knowledge working with the projects will surely make plenty of mistakes applying CPM or PERT because these techniques assume that managers already have plenty of understanding about the projects at hand and that each critical activity will be done in a known sequence, independent of one another. If the sequence is disrupted for any reason, the project could easily fail. Only when a job is expensive or important should this kind of detailed analysis be applied. Once these skills are crafted, however, project managers will have an extremely valuable tool that will enable them to remain in control of their projects from start to finish (Anderson, p. 338).

Further reading

Anderson, Carl R. *Management: Skills, Functions, and Organization Performance*. Boston: Allyn and Bacon, 1988; Cammarano, James. *Project Management: How to Make It Happen*. *IIE Solutions* 29, no. 12. Available from Dialog, Expanded Academic ASAP, article A20331320, 1997; Render, Barry, and Ralph M. Stair Jr. *Quantitative Analysis for Management*. Boston: Allyn and Bacon, 1988.
—Allison Kaiser Jones

cross-cultural communication

Cross-cultural communication is the ability to successfully form and maintain relationships with members of a culture different from one's own. Many factors contribute to success in communicating with a person of another culture; these include manners, social structure, and values.

Understanding cross-cultural communication is vital if one is pursuing a career in international business, and the best way to achieve this is by practice. Reading about other cultures is helpful, but understanding them cannot be done by reading alone. Practice, instruction, and experience are the three keys to success. Many U.S. CORPORATIONS send personnel who are being transferred abroad to cultural training seminars before they leave the country; often spouses also attend the seminars. Around the world, thousands of language-training centers offer immersion courses in local languages and culture.

Communication is the act of sharing information, often using both oral and written symbols as well as nonverbal symbols such as body language. For example, handshaking is a common form of nonverbal communication. In the United States, a solid, firm handshake is customary, whereas Orientals and Middle Easterners generally use a gentle grip. To many non-Westerners, using a firm grip may suggest that one is unnecessarily aggressive.

Another form of nonverbal communication is eye contact. Eye contact is used throughout the world, but the way it is interpreted varies. Americans are taught to look directly at people when speaking; not doing so suggests one is either not sure oneself or is trying to conceal something. In other cultures, making direct eye contact can convey disrespect or even convey sexual messages.

Culture also affects verbal communication. For example, the general tone in which one speaks varies among groups around the world. Many Americans consider raised voices to be rude and inappropriate, but other groups consider an increase in volume to be a sign of enthusiasm.

Even with accurate translation in business communications, many misunderstandings are caused by bypassing, where the sender and receiver "bypass," or miss, each other's meaning. Management professor Naoki Kameda writes that bypassing in cross-cultural communication is caused by the absence of general agreement, egocentric interpretation of received communications, and self-conceited conception of communications. People give their own meanings to words, and cultural differences result in misinterpretations. Even among English speakers there exists a strong potential for miscommunication. Language specialists often refer to "Englishes," recognizing that each country injects its own culture into the language.

Americans are often accused of being presumptuous in international business settings, assuming that others understand English and, in particular, American English. One area of frequent cultural miscommunication is in the use of acronyms. People situated within the "beltway" surrounding Washington, D.C. (Interstate 495), are masters of acronym-speak, a language that few people outside the beltway, never mind outside the United States, comprehend.

Marcelle DuPraw and Marya Axner describe six fundamental patterns of cultural differences that influence cross-cultural communication.

- *Communication styles.* Meanings of words, non-verbal communication, and BUSINESS LANGUAGE vary among cultures.
- *Attitudes toward conflict.* In the United States, conflict is generally avoided, but when necessary, it is dealt with directly. In many other cultures, conflict is considered embarrassing and addressed discreetly.
- *Approaches to completing tasks.* Americans are known for being task-oriented and developing relationships while working together. People from Asian and Hispanic cultures generally prefer developing relationships first and then approaching tasks together.
- *Decision-making styles.* In the United States, decision-making authority is often delegated, while in many other cultures it is highly centralized. Majority-rule decisions are common in the United States, while in Asian cultures consensus is preferred.
- *Attitudes toward disclosure.* In the United States, most businesspeople are up-front, willing to

discuss issues and problems. In many other cultures, candid expression or questioning can be considered shocking and inappropriate. Probing questions, often used to better understand a problem, may seem intrusive to non-Americans.
- *Epistemologies (approaches to knowing).* Americans emphasize cognitive knowledge gained through counting or measuring while other cultures incorporate transcendent knowledge gained through meditation, or spiritual understanding.

Further reading

DuPraw, Marcelle E., and Marya Axner. "Working on Common Cross-cultural Communication Challenges." Webster's World of Cultural Democracy Web site. Available online. URL: www.wwcd.org/action/ampu/crosscult.html; Folsom, Ralph H., and W. Davis Folsom. *Understanding NAFTA and Its International Implications.* New York: Matthew Irwin/Bender, 1996; East-West Business Strategies Web site. "What Is Cross-cultural Communication?" Available online. URL: www.ewbs.com/descr.html; Sabath, Ann Marie. *Business Etiquette, in Brief.* Avon, Mass.: Adams Media, 1996.

—Stan Yocco

cross-price elasticity of demand

Cross-price elasticity of demand is the responsiveness of DEMAND for one PRODUCT or service to changes in the price of another good or service. Cross-price elasticity is calculated by dividing the percentage change in demand for one product by the percentage change in the price of a related product.

$$E_{xy} = (\% \text{ change in demand good X}) / (\% \text{ change in price of good Y})$$

In most markets, managers can change price whenever they want. Managers of businesses selling related products will usually see a change in demand for their product in response to another firm's price change. One easy example is hot dogs and hot-dog rolls. If the price of hot dogs increases because hot dog manufacturers begin using higher-quality meat in their products, by the law of demand, fewer hot dogs will be sold, and sellers of hot-dog rolls (commercial bakeries) will see a decrease in demand for their products. Using the cross-price elasticity formula, a 20-percent increase in the price of hot dogs might cause a 15-percent decrease in demand for hot dog rolls. The cross-price elasticity is -.15/.20 = -.75. As would be expected, the two products are complimentary goods, and the cross-price elasticity is negative. If the two products were substitutes, an increase in the price of one good would result in an increase in demand for the other good, and the cross-price elasticity would be positive. If the cross-price elasticity is zero, the two products are not related.

Managers know changes in prices affect their business. Few small-business managers take the time to calculate the impact of price changes by other companies, but cross-price elasticity can be used to measure the degree of response to changes in prices of complements or substitutes for their products. This can be used in planning inventories, projecting sales, and developing PRICING STRATEGIES.

Examples of cross-price elasticity estimates include:

butter and margarine	0.67
natural gas and fuel oil	0.44
beef and pork	0.28
cheese and butter	-0.61

Further reading
Ruffin, Roy J., and Paul R. Gregory. *Principles of Economics*. 7th ed. Boston: Addison Wesley, 2000.

crowding-out effect
In its most narrow definition, the crowding-out effect refers to the impact of increased government spending financed through borrowing. The increased borrowing drives up INTEREST RATES through increased DEMAND for financial RESOURCES. Higher interest rates then reduce demand for, or "crowd out," private sector investment spending. A slightly broader definition of the crowding-out effect argues that expansionary FISCAL POLICY, whether financed through borrowing or not, will increase aggregate demand, which, in

turn, will increase the demand for money (to facilitate the increased aggregate demand) and drive up interest rates, thus decreasing planned private INVESTMENT.

Advocates of LAISSEZ-FAIRE, "free market," economic policies use evidence supporting the crowding-out effect to argue for less government fiscal policy intervention, claiming it takes away from private sector investment and future ECONOMIC GROWTH. Implicit in this argument is the assumption that there is significant planned private sector investment that would take advantage of lower borrowing costs, if government policies were not driving up interest rates. During periods of severe recessions, as the United States experienced in 2008–09 (which journalists have called the "Great Recession,") most businesses were laying off workers, putting on hold new plant and equipment expenditures, and canceling many major planned investments. When the Obama administration pushed through the huge, almost $800 billion stimulus package, interest rates remained largely unchanged due to the lack of private sector demand. The crowding-out effect is most likely to occur when an economy is expanding or near its potential output.

Crowding-out can also refer to changes in government policies or programs that decrease demand for private sector substitutes. In one report, researchers analyzed how increased access to Medicaid affected demand for private sector health care coverage.

Further reading
Dolan, Edwin G. *Introduction to Economics*. Redding, Calif.: Best Value Textbooks, 2007; "Medicaid Eligibility Policy and the Crowding-out Effect: Did Women and Children Drop Private Health Insurance to Enroll in Medicaid?" Center for Studying Health Care System Change, October 1969. Available online. URL: hschange.org/CONTENT/78/?topic=topic26. Accessed on December 5, 2009.

cultural industries
Cultural industries are those industries considered critical to maintaining the cultural heritage of a

region or country. Most often the term refers to the exclusion of certain industries from FREE TRADE agreements. (Citizens and politicians in many countries fear U.S. cultural dominance.) In addition to challenging existing cultural norms, cultural industries are a significant source of revenue. Many governments, including the United States, subsidize cultural industries in order to maintain them.

The U.S.-CANADA FREE TRADE AGREEMENT (1989) and NORTH AMERICAN FREE TRADE AGREEMENT (NAFTA) (1994) both contain provisions protecting primarily Canadian cultural industries. The acts restrict trade and control of publishing, distributing, or selling books, periodicals, newspapers, films, videos, audio or video music recordings, and printed or machine-readable music. The acts also define public-radio communications and all radio, television, and cable TV broadcasting as cultural industries; and allow unilateral retaliation against actions affecting cultural industries.

NAFTA also protects certain cultural products such as Mexican tequila and Kentucky bourbon.

Under the agreement, only producers in each country can use these terms to describe their products.

Further reading

Folsom, Ralph H., and W. Davis Folsom. *Understanding NAFTA and Its International Business Implications.* New York: Matthew Bender/Irwin, 1996.

CUSIP number

CUSIP stands for Committee on Uniform Securities Identification Procedures. A CUSIP number identifies most securities, including stocks of all registered U.S. and Canadian companies and U.S. government and municipal bonds. The CUSIP system is owned by the AMERICAN BANKERS ASSOCIATION and operated by STANDARD & POOR'S (S&P), a division of McGraw-Hill Company.

Historically, securities were created and identified by the issuing entity. Most securities were physical documents. In New York City, carriers would walk or bicycle around Wall Street carrying millions of dollars' worth of securities being transferred from one firm to another. The CUSIP

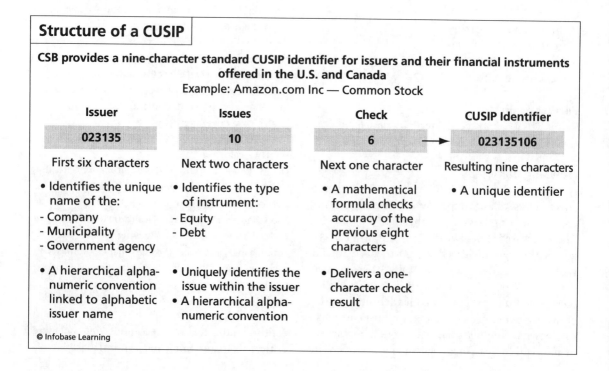

Structure of a CUSIP

CSB provides a nine-character standard CUSIP identifier for issuers and their financial instruments offered in the U.S. and Canada

Example: Amazon.com Inc — Common Stock

Issuer	Issues	Check	CUSIP Identifier
023135	10	6 →	023135106
First six characters	Next two characters	Next one character	Resulting nine characters
• Identifies the unique name of the: - Company - Municipality - Government agency	• Identifies the type of instrument: - Equity - Debt	• A mathematical formula checks accuracy of the previous eight characters	• A unique identifier
• A hierarchical alphanumeric convention linked to alphabetic issuer name	• Uniquely identifies the issue within the issuer • A hierarchical alphanumeric convention	• Delivers a one-character check result	

© Infobase Learning

system replaced the use of physical documents. In 1964 the New York Clearing House Association approached the American Bankers Association to develop a way to improve operating efficiencies across the industry by developing a standard method of identifying securities. The Committee on Uniform Security Identification Procedures (CUSIP) was organized, resulting in the establishment of the CUSIP system in 1968. The CUSIP Service Bureau (CSB) was formed to administer the CUSIP system.

The CUSIP number system was created to facilitate the clearing and settlement process of securities. CUSIP identifiers are available for more than 8.4 million unique FINANCIAL INSTRUMENTS issued by CORPORATIONS, municipalities, and government agencies throughout the world with thousands of new identifiers generated every day. The number consists of nine characters (including letters and numbers) that uniquely identify a company or issuer and the type of security. A similar system is used to identify foreign securities, namely, the CUSIP International Numbering System (CINS). Using Amazon.com Inc common stock, CSB's Web site illustrates the creation of a CUSIP number.

Further reading
CUSIP Service Bureau Web site. Available online. URL: www.cusip.com/static/html/webpage/welcome.html. Accessed on March 30, 2009.

customer loyalty (customer retention)
Customer loyalty (or customer retention) is the degree to which a company keeps its existing customers. Customer loyalty can be measured through repeat business and customer referrals. In most marketing environments, it is significantly more expensive to find and acquire a new customer than it is to retain an existing customer. Yet according to Paul R. Timm, author of *Seven Power Strategies for Building Customer Loyalty,* few companies measure customer retention rates or evaluate why customers do not return. Dr. Timm's research suggests three categories of "turnoffs" reducing customer loyalty: value, systems, and people.

Value turnoffs are situations in which customers think they are not getting what they paid for. Value turnoffs include inadequate guarantees, high prices relative to the perceived value, and a failure to meet quality expectations. A few years ago, a fast-food chain introduced a new "deluxe" hamburger, but in reality it added only lettuce and a tomato to its existing burger. The price was significantly higher, and consumers could easily see what they were paying extra for. Consequently, the product was a flop. Marketers of SERVICES often need to explain what they are providing in order to assure customers that they are getting good value for their purchase.

Systems turnoffs are situations where the purchase or distribution of PRODUCTS disappoints customers. Anyone who has gone through a telephone menu and, after spending five minutes on the phone, not found the desired choice has experienced systems failure. INTERNET marketers know they have about five seconds to catch viewer's attention. Simple features on Web sites, like "back" and "return to main menu" buttons are basic to facilitating consumers' needs. Slow service, lack of delivery choices, and unnecessary paperwork all reduce customer satisfaction and loyalty.

People turnoffs include lack of courtesy, failure to attend to the needs of customers, and unprofessional behavior. One retailer directed his employees to tell customers that any item the store did not have in stock was "on back order." People returned, expecting to find the product available and were usually disappointed; they soon went elsewhere. A television story described a telephone customer-service contractor in India using a scene with Jack Nicholson in the film *A Few Good Men* to train employees how to respond professionally and courteously to an angry customer. Occasionally a business will choose to lose a rude customer, but it is more expensive to replace a customer than retain one. Customers who have a poor experience with a firm are highly likely to tell others about their experience.

People turnoffs can also be subtle rather than blatant. Jeff Mowatt suggests customer loyalty is often affected by first impressions, including whether the business or business representative looks different from what a customer expected. Bankers know that clients like them to look professional and dress conservatively; flashy dress suggests that the banker might take excessive risks with their funds. Similarly, an electrician who shows up in a suit and driving a luxury car brings fear of fleecing to consumers. Mowatt also suggests consumer retention is affected by employees' communication skills and promises made to customers. If people do not understand what is being said, either through excessive use of technical jargon or inability to understand accents, they are likely to walk away and not return.

Many marketers also recommend understating promises to customers as a way of not building high expectations and setting an expectation that can be exceeded. When asked what advice he had for young people, new in marketing, one marketer said simply, "Be on time for your appointments and return your phone calls. You would be surprised how few people do this."

See also GAP ANALYSIS; RELATIONSHIP MARKETING.

Further reading
Keenan, William, Jr. "Customer Turnoffs," *Industry Week* 250 (11 June 2001): 25; Mowatt, Jeff. "The Shocking Truth about Your Image," *Canadian Manager* 26 (Fall 2001): 15.

customer-relationship management
Customer-relationship management (CRM) is an organization's efforts to build and maintain relationships with the people who buy their products and services. CRM became a popular buzzword among marketers in the last decade as new technology improved the ability of firms to gather information about and communicate with their customers using a variety of methods. But as Stephen Horne suggests, "In essence, CRM is your corner grocer knowing you by name, remembering what grade your child is in and suggesting that you pick up extra batteries for the big storm."

Customer-relationship management is based on the reality that, in most markets, it is much cheaper to maintain existing customers than to find new ones. Retailers know they spend hundreds or thousands of dollars for each new customer, but a thank-you note, sample, or discount coupon can stimulate additional purchases from existing customers.

A good customer-relationship management program involves applying the MARKETING CONCEPT, thinking of the customer in every aspect of the business, and involving everyone in the organization. Horne defines CRM as "process discipline," remembering and treating people well.

Customer-relationship management involves collecting and using information about existing customers to extend and strengthen relationships. In the 1990s, many marketers jumped on new CRM technology: DATABASE MANAGEMENT, INTERNET customization, and e-mails. But CRM is a process, not a technology. New technologies facilitate building relationships.

One of the major issues in American business today is PRIVACY. CRM is based on knowing one's customers, but some consumers are concerned about the use of technology to invade privacy and distrust institutions involved in collecting information. Direct marketers Michael Staten and Sheila Colclasure report one researcher has found that familiarity fosters trust. Those institutions with which consumers maintain positive relationships are trusted to act responsibly with information about them. "Thus, paradoxically, acquiring more information and showing greater interest in your customers can reduce privacy concerns."

See also CUSTOMER RELATIONS/SATISFACTION.

Further reading
Horne, Stephen C. "Cutting Through the CRM Hype," *DMNews*, 30 July 2001, p. 32; Staten, Michael, and Sheila Colclasure. "Using CRM to Enhance Privacy," *DMNews*, 30 July 2001, p. 38.

customer relations/satisfaction
Customer relations/satisfaction involves meeting or exceeding customer needs and expectations. CUSTOMER-RELATIONSHIP MANAGEMENT (CRM) is a philosophy and process of building and maintaining relationships with customers.

Customer relations and satisfaction begins with knowing what customers want, need, or expect. Most marketers develop a sense of understanding of their customers through experience. With good communications, marketers can often anticipate customers' needs and wants and, by fulfilling these needs, develop enduring business relationships. Understanding customers can be difficult, especially in new TARGET MARKETS. A common mistake is to assume new customers think and feel the same as past customers. Economic, demographic, and cultural differences, as well as lack of knowledge of a PRODUCT or service, can lead to different customer expectations.

Effective marketers constantly measure customer satisfaction through SURVEYS, complaints, and employee input. In almost every retail business, customers are offered customer-comment cards. These cards, if they have postage-paid mailing, are usually processed by marketing-research firms, which provide monthly summaries to the client. Some retailers have drop-in boxes at the checkout counter, while others ask customers to just leave their comment cards at their table. Like all MARKET RESEARCH, obtaining and interpreting information about customer satisfaction (or lack thereof) can be difficult. One restaurant had customers leave their comments at their table. Waiters and waitresses would read the comments and, if they were not complimentary, discard the cards. Some managers may overreact, using one complaint to change policy or procedures. Anyone who has worked in retailing knows it is impossible to please everybody. Market researchers recommend using complaints on customer-comment cards as a signal that there might be a problem.

In addition to customer-comment cards, some companies conduct surveys of their customers, assessing changes in perceptions and expectations. Whether conducted by mail, telephone, or personal interview, customer-satisfaction SURVEYS can provide valuable information to marketers. Armed with information about their customers, companies can develop better FAQ (Frequently Asked Questions) Web sites and information brochures, train call-center personnel, and adjust their MARKETING STRATEGY to better meet customer expectations.

The University of Michigan, along with the American Society of Quality Control, developed the AMERICAN CUSTOMER SATISFACTION INDEX, which tracks customer satisfaction across a broad range of companies, industries, and government agencies. Major companies watch the index and track their ranking relative to other competitors in their industry.

Improving customer satisfaction leads to better relationships. In almost every marketplace it is significantly more expensive to find new customers than retain existing customers. Effective customer-relationship management reduces marketing COSTS and improves word-of-mouth referrals. One study found that 95 percent of dissatisfied customers do not complain directly to the company but instead, on average, tell 11 friends or acquaintances about their negative experience. Marketers know word-of-mouth is almost always the most important source of promotion. Customer relations and relationship management can directly impact the success of marketing efforts.

With advanced DATABASE MANAGEMENT techniques in recent years, companies have adopted customer-relationship management strategies. CRM involves using information about customers to better meet and exceed their expectations. In the past, many times different divisions or individuals within a company had information about customers that was not centrally organized or accessible. CRM can tell managers simple things like which of the company's products and services the customer is already purchasing, leading to opportunities to cross-sell. It can tell marketers when customers have made most of their purchases, allowing predictions of when they will be ready to reorder. It can report which MARKETING COMMUNICATIONS and promotional methods customers respond to.

Some companies install CRM technology but do not institute a customer-relationship philosophy. A customer-relationship philosophy involves centering company efforts on the needs of their customers. Together, CRM and a customer focus can lead to enhanced customer satisfaction and retention and profitable business relationships.

Further reading
Boone, Louis E., and David L. Kurtz. *Contemporary Marketing.* 14th ed. Fort Worth, Tex.: South-Western, 2009.

customs union
A customs union is an agreement between or among countries to reduce or eliminate TRADE BARRIERS among its members and have a common set of external TARIFFS for trade outside the union. A customs union is one step beyond a FREE TRADE agreement but below a common market. A free-trade agreement only reduces or eliminates barriers to trade, while a common market also allows the free flow of CAPITAL and resources (including labor) among participating nations.

The most widely known customs union is Mercosur, an agreement among Argentina, Brazil, Paraguay and Uruguay, established in 1995. By this agreement, reductions in trade barriers among the four countries increased regional trade, and a common set of external trade barriers stimulated regional investment. Because a customs union is not an economic union (such as the EUROPEAN UNION), it does not include the creation of a common currency. In 2000 and 2001, currency crises in Brazil and Argentina altered EXCHANGE RATES, undermining the basis of trade within the customs union.

The only other major customs union is the Southern African Customs Union (SACU), which includes South Africa, Botswana, Lesotho, Swaziland, and Namibia.

cyberspace
Cyberspace is the electronic network of communications that includes the INTERNET and the WORLD WIDE WEB. Cyberspace is growing rapidly and creating a variety of new issues and concerns for global businesses.

In general, economists applaud the rapidly diminishing barriers to COMPETITION resulting from increased communication and access to market and other information through cyberspace. As with any revolution, rapidly changing market conditions are resulting in problems that did not exist just a few years before. Cyber-attacks (viruses diffused through cyberspace, crippling computer networks or gaining unauthorized access to proprietary computer systems) are a growing problem. Responding to fears of cyber-attacks on U.S. financial and electronic business systems, in 2009 President Obama ordered a review of cyber-security plans. The president's assistant for Counterterrorism and Homeland Security stated, "The national security and economic health of the United States depend on the security, stability and integrity of our nation's cyberspace."

Another major issue concerns domain names in cyberspace. Domain names are unique Internet addresses. In the United States, initially one company, Net Solutions, was the sole registry for domain names. Other companies now provide domain-name registration, but a variety of problems, including cybersquatting, cyberhustling, and typosquatting, have emerged. Cybersquatting is the registration of a domain name that has no meaningful relationship to the person or company registering it. Cybersquatters hope to either sell the domain name to someone who wants it or use it to draw traffic to their Web sites. One cybersquatter received $7.5 million for business.com, while Bank of America paid $3 million for loans.com.

Related to cybersquatting is the practice of cyberhustling. Cyberhustlers purchase the rights to domain names that are not renewed by the original owner. In an embarrassing situation, a technical college that switched its URL (universal resource locator) later found its old URL was purchased by a cyberhustler and then used to sell space to a variety of Web site promoters. People visiting the technical school's old URL found a variety of noneducational promotions, including pornography links.

Typosquatting is the registration of common misspellings. Cyberspace visitors typing in the wrong URL wind up at a typosquatter's site. Amazon.com challenged a typosquatter who had registered amazo.com. Businesses and individuals faced with typo- and cybersquatters can file complaints with the WORLD INTELLECTUAL PROPERTY ORGANIZATION (WIPO) and other arbitrators of names in cyberspace. The WIPO, an agency of the United Nations, uses three criteria in determining whether a complainant has been harmed.

- The domain name is identical or confusingly similar to a TRADEMARK or service mark in which the complainant has rights.
- The person who registered the domain name has no rights or legitimate interests in it.
- The domain name was registered or is being used in bad faith.

Cyberspace, like space itself, provides infinite possibilities for global businesses. Business use of cyberspace will continue to be a dynamic and important force requiring careful and continual scrutiny by managers.

Further reading
Harper, Timothy. "Cybersquatters." *Sky Magazine* (October 2001): 113; World Intellectual Property Organization Web site. Available online. URL: www.wipo. org.

cycle time

Cycle time—the minimum amount of time necessary for a task or series of tasks to be completed—is usually associated with manufacturing systems and depends on whether tasks are accomplished in a series or as parallel units. For example, in a textile factory production of a shirt requires cutting, sewing, and packaging. Assuming cutting requires 3 minutes per shirt, sewing 12 minutes per shirt and packaging 5 minutes per shirt, if the work is being done by one person (in a series of steps) then the minimum cycle time is 20 minutes. If three people are working in parallel, each performing one task, the minimum cycle time is 12 minutes, the time it takes to do the longest task.

PRODUCTION managers use the concept of cycle time to estimate the minimum amount of time needed to produce PRODUCTS, the maximum output in a fixed time period, and the coordination and allocation of resources to maximize efficiency. In the example above, the minimum time depends on whether the operations are conducted simultaneously or not. If it takes 12 minutes for a team of workers to make a shirt working in parallel, then in 8 hours the maximum number of shirts that could be produced is 8 hours ÷ 12 minutes = 480 minutes ÷ 12 = 40 shirts. But to maximize output, a manager would have to shift workers from one task to another. At 3 minutes per shirt, it will take only 120 minutes to cut the material for 40 shirts and only 200 minutes to package the 40 shirts.

In order to maximize output with a given level of workers and machines, production managers allocate machines and workers to fully utilize resources in production. In materials management, cycle time is defined as the time it takes from when materials enter the production process to when they leave the system. Similarly, one retail company sets as its goal to never have products in their distribution center for more than 24 hours. Recognizing that customers do not buy products from distribution centers, minimizing the time products are in storage increases the availability of products on the company's retail shelves. Reducing cycle time increases productivity. In complex production systems, statistical models are used to minimize variation in production and reduce cycle times.

Further reading
Stevenson, William J. *Production Operations Management.* 6th ed. Boston: McGraw-Hill, 1999.

D

damages

Damages, for legal purposes, are compensatory or punitive monetary awards. Persons suffering loss or injury (for example, in a car accident) sue in court to recover damages to which they are entitled by law. Damages can be awarded by court order for personal or property losses, for breach of CONTRACTS, and the loss of legal rights (such as COPYRIGHT infringement). Damages will only be awarded if the defendant acted unlawfully, negligently or in breach of contract and caused the damages alleged.

"Actual damages" refers to real damages suffered. In some cases, courts and juries may award "punitive" or "exemplary" damages when the defendant's conduct was outrageous and future deterrence is desired. Punitive damages are often a multiple of actual damages. At the other extreme, "nominal damages" may be awarded when little actual loss occurs. Some statutes, such as the federal ANTITRUST LAWS, mandate automatic trebling of actual damages, a kind of controlled version of punitive damages.

Further reading

O'Connell, John F. *Remedies in a Nutshell.* 2d ed. Eagan, Minn.: West Group, 1985.

database management

Database management is the process of organizing and manipulating a database. A database is a collection of organized data that is alterable (create, update, and delete), accessible, has a purpose, minimizes/eliminates redundancy, imports and exports data, has data independence, and has data integrity. It usually collects large amounts of data, which it organizes and stores in a computer system. The data are organized so the information can be searched or accessed quickly and efficiently.

The terms *database* and *database management* first appeared in the early 1960s with the introduction of computers into the business world. Computers allow businesses to store and retrieve large amounts of information in a database. Companies require a database-management system that is reliable and easy to maintain. This is a software package that assists in the organization and management of a database. Database-management systems were developed when existing systems no longer met the demands of businesses. The existing flat-file system was (and still is) ineffective, slow, inefficient, and unreliable, and the data were easily compromised. As databases increased in size, the flat-file system became even more redundant, unable to maintain the information in the database.

A flat-file system is unable to organize and manage data or to link them to other data. For example, a customer comes into a bank and asks for her checking account balance. She provides the bank teller with the checking-account number, and receives the account balance. Then the customer asks the bank teller for her savings-account balance, but she does not have the savings-account number. The bank teller is unable to give the customer the savings account balance without the account number. A flat-file system is unable to link the customer's checking account and savings account, whereas a database-management system allows the customer access to both the checking- and savings-account balances with only one of the account numbers. A database-management system allows for linking and flexibility in accessing information.

A database-management system also allows for multiple people to access, query, and update data simultaneously. A query or search retrieves specific information from the database. For example, several bank tellers can access the database simultaneously to assist numerous patrons. They can also query or search, all at one time, on specific account numbers to determine if patrons have accounts with that bank. If the information queried takes too long to retrieve, or if the information about a certain account is corrupted, patrons may determine the bank is unreliable and take their business elsewhere. The information in the database has to be accessed effectively and efficiently in order to better serve the customer.

A database-management system has to be organized properly or it may be just as inefficient and ineffective as a flat-file system. A downside to organizing a database-management system correctly is that it takes time, money, and resources. The database-management system has to be continually monitored and updated at regular intervals to maintain data integrity and efficiency.

Businesses now buy database-management software systems instead of creating a system from scratch, because it is more cost effective. There are two primary types of database-management systems: relational database-management systems (RDBM) and object-oriented database-management systems (ODBM).

The difference between ODBMs and RDBMs is how much the programmer can affect the data. Object-oriented databases can be fast and simple if the programmer is experienced in retrieving the information and understands the structure of the data storage, although a downside is that the programmer can also easily corrupt the data in the database. Relational-database programmers are restricted from interacting directly with the data, and the chance of corrupting the database is lower. Overall, relational databases tend to be faster and more efficient.

Not all database-management systems are created equal. Cost is an important factor in choosing the system that is right for an individual or business. For example, Oracle is an expensive database-management system to own and would rarely be purchased by an individual. Existing hardware and software are also factors in choosing a database-management system. Microsoft databases are not able to run on an Apple computer; Microsoft database systems are only able to run using a Microsoft operating system. Some database-management systems cater to individuals or small companies such as Microsoft Access, MySQL, and Progressql. Other systems cater to large CORPORATIONS such as Oracle, IBM's DB2, SYBASE, and Microsoft SQL server.

Further reading

Paul McJones SystemR Web site. URL: www.mcjones. org/System_R/; Date, C. J. *Introduction to Database Systems.* 7th ed. Addison-Wesley, 2000; Hoffer, Jeffrey A., Mary Prescott, and Fred R. McFadden. *Modern Database Management.* 6th ed. Englewood Cliffs, N.J.: Prentice Hall, 2002.

—Deborah Roth

Davis-Bacon Act

The Davis-Bacon Act, signed by President Herbert Hoover in 1931, requires contractors working for the federal government to pay the "prevailing" local wage. Expanded to include projects receiving federal funding or loan guarantees, the act effectively requires contractors to pay UNION scale wages. Rather than hire workers independently and pay union rates, most contractors rely on local unions to provide labor for federally supported construction projects. The act was later expanded to provide EMPLOYEE BENEFITS and require contractors or subcontractors to make necessary payments for these benefits. In right-to-work states, the act often accounts for the vast majority of union membership.

Originally the Davis-Bacon Act was intended to prevent itinerant labor from undercutting wages during the GREAT DEPRESSION. Supporters of the act argue it helps ensure stability in construction-market wages and provides skilled labor for federal projects. Opponents argue the act increases the cost of federal construction projects, costing taxpayers billions annually.

Further reading

"Should the Davis-Bacon Act Be Repealed," *Nation's Business* 71 (March 1983): 75.

day trading

The SECURITIES AND EXCHANGE COMMISSION (SEC) defines day trading as rapidly buying and selling stocks and other FINANCIAL INSTRUMENTS in the hope that the securities will continue climbing or falling in value for the seconds to minutes they are owned, allowing the trader to lock in quick profits. Day traders spend their time at computer screens, often using computerized systems or advisory services that claim to be able to predict the markets.

Day trading is complex and usually involves LEVERAGE, allowing traders to buy and sell large dollar amounts of securities while having a small percentage of their own capital invested in the trade. Under the rules of the NEW YORK STOCK EXCHANGE (NYSE Euronext) and the Financial Industry Regulatory Authority (FINRA), customers who are deemed "pattern day traders" must have at least $25,000 in their accounts and can trade only in margin accounts.

The SEC warns, "Day trading is extremely risky and can result in substantial financial losses in a very short period of time." The commission also created a publication *Day Trading: Your Dollars at Risk* in which it warns investors:

- Be prepared to suffer severe financial losses
- Day traders do not "invest"

- Day traders depend heavily on borrowing money or buying stocks on margin
- Don't believe claims of easy profits
- Watch out for "hot tips" and "expert advice" from newsletters and Web sites catering to day traders
- Remember that "educational" seminars, classes, and books about day trading may not be objective
- Check out day trading firms with your state securities regulator
- Day trading is an extremely stressful and expensive full-time job

The last SEC warning in the above list led the FEDERAL TRADE COMMISSION (FTC) to create a Web site posting "Day Trading Ads: Cutting Through the 'Bull'," in which it warns, "Advertisements for some day trading systems or advisory services make investing look like a virtual bonanza where everyone's a winner. But if one thing's certain about stocks, commodity futures, OPTIONS and similar investments, it's that they're uncertain. Any company that guarantees huge earnings is feeding you a load of 'bull'. . . . Every time investors make a trade, they pay a commission. That's true whether they buy or sell and whether they make money or lose their shirt."

The FTC continues, suggesting consumers interested in day trading should "Read Between the Lines. . . .

"If the ad promises . . . 'The potential to make a six or seven figure annual income from trading is at the ends of your fingertips.' Remember that . . . Many [profit claims] are based on hypothetical performance. . . . Actual results may not match the hypothetical performance—and even trading advisors with a long track record of success can lose a fortune suddenly.

"If the ad promises . . . 'The absolute best trading system with a profit-to-loss ratio of 12-to-1 and an average return better than 18 percent per trade . . .' Remember that . . . Even if the system really has had such successes, past performance is no guarantee of future results and nobody—not even financial experts—can guarantee what the market is going to do from day to day or even minute to minute. No matter how strong the market may seem and how solid a particular company may appear, prices can skyrocket or plummet faster than you can say 'Wall Street.'

"If the ad promises . . . 'Our software signals precisely when to buy and when to sell a particular security, allowing you the opportunity to make money regardless of the market going up or down . . .' Remember that . . . As tempting as it might be to leave your investment decisions in the hands of a software program, the ultimate responsibility for protecting your investment belongs to you.

"If the ad promises . . . 'Our recommendations returned an average annual return of 250 percent. If you can just follow our recommendations, you will make money.' Remember that . . . There's no fail-safe way to invest without any risk. High-yield investments tend to involve high risk. Be particularly suspicious of sales pitches that play down risk or portray written risk disclosures as routine formalities. Believe the risk disclosures that say you could lose your whole investment. Jumping on a 'hot' investment tip is a good way to get 'burned.'

"If the ad promises . . . 'Timothy Smith, who used our system wrote to us, ". . . at night I work with your trading system for a few hours and am averaging more than $500 a day."' Remember that . . . Everyone loves a good testimonial, but it's smart to be wary of them. The story may or may not be true. And it's highly unlikely that the testimonial reflects the actual experiences of other people using the system or advisory service—or the result you're hoping for."

The FTC concludes with the advice: "Invest Carefully, Whether or not you're a day trader, your best protection as an investor is to know what you're buying, what the ground rules are when you buy and sell, and what level of risk you're assuming." Most economists would disagree with the FTC's use of the term *investing* to describe day trading, arguing day trading is speculation at best and closer to gambling than investing. For economists, investing is a longer term commitment based on the hope and expectation of profit through the creation of goods and services valued in the marketplace.

The Connecticut Council on Problem Gambling (CCPG) includes "Investor Problem Gambling" as one of its concerns in stating,

Financial market gambling is the least studied major area of gambling by social scientists. In two separate studies by the CCPG, one with stockbrokers and the second with securities attorneys, the findings indicated that brokers and attorneys agreed that the financial markets provide a large number of vehicles in which investors gamble and that the level of risk in the more speculative areas of the markets is equal to or greater than the risk in a casino.

Clinical evidence indicates that problem gamblers who have gambled exclusively in the areas of business and the financial markets have met the same diagnostic criteria of pathological (compulsive) gambling as problem gamblers in recreational forms of gambling. Some problem gamblers move from the financial markets to recreational gambling and vice versa or may do both simultaneously.

Further reading

Connecticut Council on Problem Gambling, "Investor Problem Gambling." Available online. URL: www.ccpg.org/articles/investorgambling.html. Accessed on December 18, 2009; Federal Trade Commission, "Day Trading Ads: Cutting Through the 'Bull.'" Available online. URL: www.ftc.gov/bcp/edu/pubs/consumer/invest/inv01.sht. Accessed on December 18, 2009; Securities and Exchange Commission. "Day Trading." Available online. URL: www.sec.gov/answers/daytrading.htm. Accessed on December 18, 2009.

debenture

Debentures are debt securities issued by CORPORATIONS and governments. Debentures are similar to BONDS but they are not secured by collateral. Lenders who purchase debentures either trust the creditworthiness of the issuer or are paid higher-than-market INTEREST RATES for holding unsecured debt. Debentures are also issued by service companies that have few tangible assets that could be used as security. U.S. Treasury securities (T-bills, T-notes, and T-bonds) are government-issued debentures. General obligation bonds issued by state and local governments are also debentures since they are also unsecured debt. In practice, debentures are sometimes called bonds and vice versa.

Debentures come in several varieties, including convertible, senior, subordinated, convertible-subordinated, and sinking fund debentures. A convertible debenture allows the holder the option to convert the debt into shares of stock at a fixed ratio as stated in the debenture. A senior debenture has priority over other debt issued by the company. In the event of bankruptcy, holders of senior debt are paid off ahead of other creditors. Subordinated debentures follow senior debentures in the order of payment in the event of bankruptcy. Convertible-subordinated debentures combine the features of being convertible to shares of stock but also being lower in the debt repayment order. Sinking fund debentures are securities with commitments by the borrower to set aside periodic payments into a sinking fund usually held by a separate trustee that will be used to pay off the loan at the end of the loan agreement.

In the United Kingdom, debentures are frequently used for financing by clubs and by cultural and sporting organizations. The All England Lawn Tennis and Croquet Club issued debentures to finance refurbishing their facilities, known to Americans as the home of the Wimbledon tennis tournament. Holders of these debentures are entitled to a free seat at Center Court for five years. Similarly, the Green Bay Packers was initially financed by sale of stock to citizens in Green Bay, Wisconsin. These highly coveted shares are handed down from generation to generation, and they allow what is a relatively small town to continue to have a National Football League team.

The Trust Indenture Act (1939) administered by the SECURITIES AND EXCHANGE COMMISSION (SEC) regulates debt securities, including bonds, debentures, and notes that are offered for public sale. These securities may not be offered for sale to the public unless a formal agreement between the issuer of bonds and the bondholder, known as the trust indenture, conform to the standards of the act.

Further reading
Debentures. Available online. URL: www.answers.com/topic/debenture. Accessed on March 23, 2009; Securities and Exchange Commission Web site. Available online. URL: www.sec.gov.

debit, credit
The accounting terms *debit* and *credit* mean "left" and "right," respectively. Abbreviated *dr.* (from the Latin *debere*) and *cr.* (from the Latin *credere*), debits and credits are integral parts of financial or double-entry accounting.

When a transaction is recorded in the journal, the book of original entry, debit entries precede credit entries, and the dollar amount of the debit entry is placed in the debit (left) column of the journal. Credit entries follow the debit entries, and they are indented. Their dollar amount is placed in the credit (right) column of the journal.

In the ledger, the book of final entry, debit entries are recorded on the debit (left) side of the T-ACCOUNT; credit entries are recorded on the credit (right) side of the t-account.

Debit and credit by themselves do not signify an increase or a decrease in an account. It is only when debits and credits are associated with particular accounts that they take on the added meanings of increase or decrease. For example, to increase an ASSET account requires a debit to that account, because all asset accounts have normal debit balances. To decrease an asset account requires a credit to that account, because credit entries will offset the normal debit balances found in all asset accounts.

The converse holds true for the LIABILITY and owners' EQUITY accounts. Since they have normal credit balances, credit entries into these accounts will increase them. Debit entries will offset their normal credit balances, thereby reducing the balances in these accounts.

All of this is part of the double-entry accounting system developed in 1494 by Fra Luca Pacioli, a Venetian considered to be one of the most learned men of the Renaissance. Double-entry accounting has become the standard for FINANCIAL ACCOUNTING.

debt collection   See FAIR DEBT COLLECTIONS PRACTICES ACT.

debtor-in-possession financing/DIP financing

Debtor-in-possession financing is a special form of credit provided to companies in financial distress under Chapter 11 bankruptcy laws. Chapter 11 bankruptcy codes allow companies, sole proprietorships, or individuals to reorganize and hopefully return to profitability. Logically, lenders are reluctant to provide funds to companies that are in bankruptcy. Debtor-in-possession financing is a special type of financing that usually is more senior than existing debt, equity, or other securities issued by a company. This puts the lender at the "head of the line" should the company file for Chapter 7 (liquidation) bankruptcy. DIP financing gives a troubled company the potential for a new start while under strict conditions imposed by the bankruptcy court and monitored by court-appointed representatives.

DIP financing became a major concern during the financial crisis of 2008 when access to financing became difficult or impossible to find while the number of firms entering bankruptcy protection expanded dramatically. DIP financing is usually short term with restrictions or demands for quick actions by the firm's management. Some loans, known as defensive DIPs, DIPs of necessity, or exit financing, assist companies in staying afloat just long enough to find a buyer.

Given the risk of default, DIP financing is usually expensive, often tied to the LIBOR (London Interbank Offer Rate) rate plus five percentage points or more.

deceptive trade practices

Also known as deceptive acts, deceptive practices, and deceptive sales practices, deceptive trade practices are methods of doing business that are likely to mislead individual consumers or other businesses, usually through the use of deceitful, false, incomplete, or otherwise misleading statements. In other words, deceptive trade practices occur when someone in business acts in a misleading manner toward another party, often a buyer, in a commercial transaction. For example, sellers of a weight-loss product were recently found to have violated a federal law prohibiting deceptive acts and practices by falsely representing that their product could cause substantial weight loss in a short period of time without the need for diet or exercise. Another example would be an outlet store selling reconditioned blenders or stereos, without any indication that they were actually used and reconditioned rather than new.

Consumers and other businesses are protected from deceptive trade practices through laws prohibiting and punishing such practices. For example, today, many companies include explanatory statements in their ADVERTISING and product PACKAGING that are designed to prevent the misleading of consumers. Statements such as "some assembly required" in television advertisements for children's toys, "quantities limited" in sale circulars, and "serving suggestion" on boxes of breakfast cereal are the result, in part, of laws against deceptive trade practices.

Deceptive trade practices are prohibited by both federal and state laws. Enacted by Congress in 1914, the Federal Trade Commission Act (FTCA), which can be found at 15 United States Code § 45, prohibits "[u]nfair methods of COMPETITION in or affecting commerce and unfair or deceptive acts or practices in or affecting commerce." As the quoted text suggests, commercial acts or practices may be found to be unfair, deceptive, or both, but an act or practice need not be both deceptive and unfair to violate the FTCA. The FEDERAL TRADE COMMISSION is the federal agency primarily responsible for enforcing the FTCA.

While the FTCA governs unfair or deceptive trade practices occurring across state lines, all 50 states have also enacted laws prohibiting deceptive trade practices. Such laws may be known as consumer protection acts, unfair trade practices acts, or consumer fraud acts, among others.

While the specific provisions of each state's laws differ, they often have the following common features. First, both the state governmental authorities and private consumers or businesses can enforce the laws. The government can bring enforcement actions and individual consumers or businesses can bring lawsuits against those who engage in deceptive trade practices. For example, in Massachusetts both the Attorney General's Office of Consumer Protection and injured consumers or businesses can enforce the state's consumer protection act. Second, the government, consumers, or businesses may be able to get an INJUNCTION against deceptive trade practice through a court order requiring that the offending party stop engaging in the deceptive trade practice. Third, victims of deceptive trade practices may be entitled to sue for double or triple DAMAGES and attorney's fees for knowing violations of their state's deceptive trade practices laws.

Under some states' laws, the standards for what constitutes a deceptive trade practice may be different in the business-to-consumer context and the business-to-business context. Such standards are more protective of consumers than of other businesses. For example, courts in Massachusetts have decided that business conduct considered unfair or deceptive toward a consumer would not necessarily be unfair or deceptive toward another business. As one court put it, in the business-to-business context, "[t]he objectionable conduct must attain a level of rascality that would raise an eyebrow of someone inured to the rough and tumble world of commerce." (*Levings v. Forbes & Wallace*, 396 N.E.2d 149, 153, 1979)

Many states have adopted the Revised Uniform Deceptive Trade Practices Act (UDTPA), which was originally drafted and approved by the National Conference of Commissioners on Uniform State Laws, approved by the American Bar Association in 1964, and approved in its revised form in 1966. The original purpose of the UDTPA was to reconcile and update the states' conflicting laws in the area of deceptive trade practices. The UDTPA's drafters subdivided the types of business conduct that constitute deceptive trade practices

under the act into conduct involving either misleading trade identification or false or deceptive advertising. More specifically, the UDTPA enumerates 12 types of business conduct that constitute deceptive trade practices.

Under the UDTPA, a "person" (which includes individuals, CORPORATIONS, and many other entities) "engages in a deceptive trade practice when, in the course of his business, vocation, or occupation, he

1. passes off goods or SERVICES as those of another;
2. causes likelihood of confusion or misunderstanding as to the source, sponsorship, approval, or certification of goods or services;
3. causes likelihood of confusion or misunderstanding as to affiliation, connection, or association with, or certification by, another;
4. uses deceptive representations or designations of geographic origin in connection with goods or services;
5. represents that goods or services have sponsorship, approval, characteristics, ingredients, uses, benefits, or quantities that they do not have or that a person has a sponsorship, approval, status, affiliation, or connection that he does not have;
6. represents that goods are original or new if they are deteriorated, altered, reconditioned, reclaimed, used, or second-hand;
7. represents that goods or services are of a particular standard, quality, or grade, or that goods are of a particular style or model, if they are of another;
8. disparages the goods, services, or business of another by false or misleading representation of fact;
9. advertises goods or services with intent not to sell them as advertised;
10. advertises goods or services with intent not to supply reasonably expectable public DEMAND, unless the advertisement discloses a limitation of quantity;
11. makes false or misleading statements of fact concerning the reasons for, existence of, or amounts of price reductions; or

12. engages in any other conduct which similarly creates a likelihood of confusion or of misunderstanding."

Further reading
Sheldon, Jonathan, and Carolyn L. Carter. *Unfair and Deceptive Acts and Practices.* 5th ed. Boston: National Consumer Law Center, 2001.
—Laura M. Scott

decision tree
A decision tree is a map of the reasoning process businesspeople use to make choices. Decision trees are excellent tools for making financial or number-based decisions where a lot of detailed data needs to be considered. They provide guidelines in which alternative decisions and the implications of choosing those decisions can be organized and reviewed. Decision trees help people form an accurate and more realistic picture of the risks and rewards associated with a particular choice.

Creating a decision tree requires time. The first step is determining what decision needs to be made; a small square representing the decision is drawn on the left side of the paper. From this square lines are drawn toward the right for each possible solution, which are written on separate lines. The results of each solution are then considered. If the result is unknown, a circle is drawn; a different decision needs to be made, a square is drawn. When creating decision trees, squares represent decisions and circles represent unknown factors. The decision tree will thus expand until all possible outcomes and unknowns are included.

When the tree is completed, it is necessary to review the diagram and challenge each square and circle to see if there are solutions or outcomes that have not been considered. At this point, a decision tree will provide a range of possible outcomes. The next step is to evaluate the tree and calculate the decision that has the greatest worth. Once the values of expected outcomes have been established and the probability of the unknown outcomes have been assessed, it is possible to calculate the values needed to make the best decision. The benefit of each solution is its probability multiplied by its worth. When the benefit of each solution is calculated, the decision with the greatest benefit is selected.

Creating and using decision trees have many advantages when trying to make an important decision. Though it takes time to calculate the outcomes and probabilities, it is often time well spent. Decision trees allow managers to view all possible choices. They should be used in conjunction with common sense, identifying all considerations associated with a decision and recognizing that probabilities are usually professional judgments and subject to variation.

Further reading
"Decision Theory and Decision Trees," Mind Tools Ltd. Available online. URL: www.mindtools.com/dectree. html. Accessed on June 10, 2009; "Decision Tree," Mighetto & Associates. Available online. URL: www. eskimo.com/~mighetto/Isttree.htm. Accessed on June 10, 2009.
—Melissa Luma

decoupling
Decoupling refers to a variety of activities depending on the context in which it is used, but in business it refers to the theory that emerging countries are becoming less dependent on industrialized economies as a source of revenue and ECONOMIC GROWTH. An old saying goes something to the effect of "When the U.S. economy gets a cold, the world economies get the flu." Decoupling theory suggests that this is becoming less true as domestic economies in emerging nations, particularly Asian countries, expand and deepen to the point where they no longer depend on the United States and the European Union as outlets for their products.

With the publication in 2005 of *The World Is Flat* by Thomas Friedman, much of the international economics discussion has focused on GLOBALIZATION, namely, the expansion of world trade and therefore economic interdependence. Decoupling suggests the world's economies are less integrated and therefore a decline in the U.S. economy would not significantly impact many other countries. In 2007 decoupling theory was important for investors, suggesting that a recession in the United States would not significantly impact businesses in China, India, or other parts of Asia. The subsequent crash of global stock markets, many by a larger percentage than in the United States, challenges the theory.

Evidence presented in an article in *The Economist* suggests decoupling varies significantly among emerging economies. The articles states: "The four biggest economies, which accounted for two-fifths of global GDP growth last year [2007], are the least dependent on the United States: exports to America account for just 8% of China's GDP, 4% of India's, 3% of Brazil's and 1% of Russia's." For other countries, including Mexico and Malaysia, exports to the United States represent over 20 percent of GDP. If Asian economies continue to grow while the U.S. economy contracts, their exports as a percentage of GDP will decline, further reducing their economic ties to the U.S. economy.

Further reading

"The Decoupling Debate," *The Economist,* 6 March 2008.

default

Default is the failure of a debtor to meet the provisions agreed upon in a loan agreement. Typical consumer default involves the failure to make payments on a personal, automobile or home loan. Business default involves failure to make timely interest and principal payments on BONDS or corporate LOANS. When default occurs (which is usually defined in the lending agreement), the lender may make claims against the borrower's ASSETS in order to recapture the funds loaned to the individual or business.

In consumer credit markets, lenders often apply the FIVE Cs OF CREDIT: character, capacity, CAPITAL, conditions, and collateral. When a consumer defaults on a loan, lenders usually foreclose on the collateral provided by the borrower, entailing repossession of the asset. The repossession process varies from state to state depending on consumer-lending laws.

Lenders recognize that a certain percentage of loans will end in default. Most consumer defaults are caused by "trigger events" such as death, divorce, disease, or business downsizing. When making loans, the likelihood of failure to receive payments is referred to as default risk. Higher-risk loans are assessed higher INTEREST RATES. Consumer advocates are especially critical of lending practices in the subprime market, where borrowers are sometimes are sold products with payments they cannot feasibly make, resulting in excessively high default rates. Lenders in subprime or nonprime mortgage markets frequently repossess homes, sometimes literally towing manufactured housing off a borrower's property.

In securities markets, bonds are evaluated for the likelihood of default by MOODY'S RATINGS, STANDARD AND POOR'S, and other rating services. Junk bonds, considered riskier than investment-grade bonds, have a higher risk of default. In 2008 corporate bond defaults rose primarily in the housing industry due to over-investment and the economic recession.

Default is not limited to businesses and consumers. In the largest public-sector default action, Washington Public Power Supply System (WPPSS, known as Whoops) borrowed billions of dollars to construct nuclear power plants. In 1983 cost overruns, changing market conditions, and poor management led to the failure to complete construction and thus default on the WPPSS bonds. Many bondholders first learned about the difference between general obligation (backed by the taxation power of the government agency that issues them) and revenue bonds (backed by the anticipated revenue from the project they are used to fund) from experience with the default of the power-plant bonds.

Default rules are regulated by the UNIFORM COMMERCIAL CODE. Article 9 of the code is a set of rules that govern the taking of most types of collateral for loans, how to protect lenders' rights to collateral against claims by others, how to describe collateral in security agreements and FINANCIAL STATEMENTS, where to file financing statements, and what rights a lender has after default. Default rules are a complex but critical part of sound lending decisions.

Further reading

McElroy, John M. "Enforcing the Security Interest: The Lender's Rights & Duties After Default," *The RMA Journal* 83 (February 2001): 84.

deflation

Deflation is a sustained decrease in the general level of prices in an economy. It is the opposite of INFLATION, an increase in the general level of prices. Falling prices are a result from either increasing productivity, which allows producers to increase output and INCOME; or declining DEMAND. Increasing productivity benefits both the economy and producers, but decreasing demand results in lower prices and lower incomes. As illustrated in the CIRCULAR FLOW MODEL, when demand declines, output declines, and household income declines even further, causing further decreases in demand. The result can be a downward spiral in the economy.

Deflation has what economists call *distributive effects*. People with fixed incomes, including bondholders, benefit from deflation because it raises the value of the money income they are receiving, and thus their REAL INCOME or purchasing power increases. People with savings also see their purchasing power increase. Deflation hurts debtors because they are paying back money that has increased in purchasing power while their incomes have not increased commensurately.

Deflation can hurt creditors if declining prices put borrowers in a situation where the amount they owe exceeds the now-reduced value of the ASSETS they borrowed against. In the United States during the 1980s, when oil prices fluctuated dramatically, in some communities housing prices declined so much that owners "walked away" from their MORTGAGES. Banks and SAVINGS AND LOAN ASSOCIATIONS were forced to liquidate these mortgages and take losses, contributing to the savings and loan crisis and the creation of the RESOLUTION TRUST CORPORATION to bail out the industry. Similarly, declining prices in Japan have bankrupted many financial institutions, crippling the Japanese economy for over a decade. The most severe period of deflation in the U.S. economy occurred during the GREAT DEPRESSION, between 1929 and 1934, when prices decreased by 24 percent. Business bankruptcies skyrocketed, 9,000 banks failed, homeowners defaulted on mortgages, and UNEMPLOYMENT rose to 25 percent.

During a period of high debt levels, deflation is of particular concern to economic policy makers. With high debt levels, the potential for business and household DEFAULTS increases. In 2009 mortgage debt alone in the United States equaled GROSS DOMESTIC PRODUCT (GDP). According to the *Wall Street Journal,* "the last time debt rose to that level was in the late 1920s."

Policy makers fear deflation from decreased demand because it can make it hard for them to stimulate the economy. INTEREST RATES tend to change with inflation rates. When there is negative inflation (deflation), interest rates cannot go below zero. The Federal Reserve, the monetary authority in the United States, lowers interest rates to stimulate borrowing and spending, but the Fed cannot lower rates below zero. Without monetary policy options, the only ways to stimulate the economy are fiscal policy options, increasing government spending, and/or decreasing tax rates. These choices, though, increase budget deficits, increasing the national debt.

Generally businesspeople prefer stable prices. Increasing or decreasing prices create uncertainty, increasing the risk of business ventures.

Further reading

Ip, Greg. "Inside the Fed, Deflation Draws a Closer Look," *Wall Street Journal,* 6 November 2002, p. A1.

deleveraging

Deleveraging is the process by which individuals, businesses, and governments reduce their use of borrowed funds to finance current activities. Deleveraging became an important topic during the financial crises of 2007–09 as creditors, both for lack of funds and for fear of default RISK, reduced their lending activity and borrowers reduced their use of borrowed funds for current spending.

Deleveraging is the reverse of leveraging, using current income or assets as a basis for financing greater activity. For individuals, the major use of financial leverage involves the purchase of a home. Typically, the buyer puts down 5 to 10 percent of the price of the home and borrows the remaining amount. (Historically, lenders required 20 percent down, though in the peak of the housing market bubble in 2006–07, lenders often approved loans with no down payment.) Assuming a buyer put down 10 percent of the purchase price of the home, his leverage would be 9 to 1. Lenders provide the additional funds, based, in theory, on the borrower's ability to pay back the loan. As economist Donald Schunk states: "As we become more highly leveraged, we are able to do more with a given level of available INCOME."

During the housing market bubble (2004–07), home prices in many areas of the country increased 10 to 20 percent annually, creating what economists call the "wealth effect." Many homeowners, with encouragement from the lending industry, borrowed against the increased value of their property, increasing their use of leverage. When housing prices finally fell, many homeowners found themselves "upside down" or "under water" with mortgages greater than the market value of their homes. Combined with a RECESSION, homeowners both voluntarily and involuntarily faced foreclosure, adding more houses for sale in a depressed market. Similarly, rising stock market prices create a wealth effect, resulting in higher spending among households, particularly upper-income consumers holding financial assets. As Dr. Schunk states, "In addition to rising home and stock prices over the last decades, we have experienced a long period of historically low INTEREST RATES. Low interest rates combined with ongoing financial innovation provided easy access to credit affected households, businesses, and governments, and further allowed all groups to spend beyond our resource levels. All these factors allowed the global economy to become more highly leveraged."

For a business, deleveraging can affect a firm's level of inventory, expansion, or acquisition plans using borrowed funds. Typically firms start with equity capital provided by the entrepreneur or through shareholders and then borrow against

equity to expand business operations. During the financial market panic in October 2009, the commercial paper market, which provides short-term credit to businesses, froze when lenders could not determine who was and who was not a good credit risk. Businesses were forced to cut back on activities and use preestablished lines of credit to fund continuing operations. When markets stabilized, many firms issued new equity shares, reducing their use of leverage to finance business operations.

In 2009 the U.S. economy was in a process of deleveraging. In a matter of months, household savings rates jumped from near zero to over 5 percent. Businesses as well as state and local governments reined in spending. Dr. Schunk writes, "Just as increasing leverage boosts economic growth on the way up, deleveraging reduces economic growth on the way down because it involves lower spending along with higher savings and paying down debt. This deleveraging is likely to continue until a new balance is reached between household, business, and government resources and spending. Of course, there is now an important negative feedback loop at work. As market participants pull back in terms of spending, this has the effect of deepening and prolonging the recession. As the recession continues, job and income losses mount, and it becomes that much harder for a new balance to be found." The federal government with its macroeconomic tools, that is, its fiscal and monetary policies, attempted to counter the deleveraging activities in the private sector.

Further reading
Schunk, Donald. "Deleveraging the Economy," *Business & Economic Review* (April–May 2009).

Delphi technique

The Delphi technique—named after the Oracle of Delphi, to whom ancient Greeks would travel to seek advice about the future—is a marketing-management tool used by businesses for forecasting. Developed by the Rand Corporation, a major U.S. "think tank," the Delphi technique utilizes an anonymous group of knowledgeable individuals to estimate future trends or sales. Like the jury of executive opinion, in the Delphi technique managers solicit the opinions of people both inside and outside the organization. A series of QUESTIONNAIRES is used, and the results of each round of surveys are aggregated and returned to the participants until a consensus forecast is reached.

The Delphi technique is more time-consuming and expensive to administer than a simple jury of executive opinion. Because the individual responses in early rounds are anonymous, it prevents one individual, often a senior executive, from influencing the others in the group. As individuals compare their initial forecast, either for sales or predictions about some future trend, they can modify or justify their estimates in future rounds. As a consensus is being reached, often the final rounds are conducted by bringing the group together for discussion.

Further reading
Etzel, Michael J., Bruce J. Walker, and William J. Staunton. *Marketing*. 14th ed. Boston: McGraw-Hill, 2005.

demand
Demand, or the law of demand, is the relationship between price and quantity demanded for a good or service in a market. The law of demand states there is an inverse relationship between price and quantity demanded; that is, the higher the price the lower the quantity demanded, and the lower the price, the higher the quantity demanded.

A number of conditions are implicit in the analysis of demand. First, the market under consideration needs to be defined. For example does the term *automobile market* refer to the local, regional, national, or global market? Further, does it refer to the retail, wholesale, or manufacturing level? Demand relationships are usually studied with the assumption ceteris paribus (all other things being equal, or assuming nothing else has changed).

A demand schedule or graph shows the relationship between price and quantity demanded in a market in a period of time, ceteris paribus. In most markets, businesspeople have the power to change prices. Consumers respond to the changing prices by changing the quantity they are willing and able to purchase. Price is the independent variable, and quantity demanded is the dependent variable. A change in price causes a change in quantity demanded.

While a change in price causes a change in quantity demanded, other factors can cause a change in demand, which is a shift of the whole price/quantity relationship in a market. An increase in demand means that at every price, consumers are willing and able to purchase more of the good or service. Likewise, a decrease in demand means consumers are willing to purchase less of the good at each price.

Economists have identified six factors that can cause a change in demand:

- tastes and preferences
- INCOME
- price of compliments and substitutes
- expectations
- number of consumers
- EXCHANGE RATES

It is easy to envision how changing tastes and preferences affect demand in a market. Consider what were the most popular gift products in past holiday seasons. Some years it was a stuffed animal, other years a new electronic game. When PRODUCTs are "hot," they experience an increase in demand. Products that are no longer fashionable and those that receive unfavorable publicity experience a decrease in demand.

Income can affect market demand in two ways. Most often an increase in consumers' income increases demand for goods and services; if we have more money, we spend more. American business managers know that the demand for expensive products, automobiles, appliances, and electronic equipment is sensitive to changes in income. Automobile manufacturers consider changes in income when planning production levels. For some products, called economically inferior goods, as income increases, demand decreases. As an example, if someone wins the lottery, what would that person buy less of? College students often respond fast food, instant noodles, and used cars. A shrewd manager of an automobile repair business once observed that his business prospered during downturns in the economy. He recognized that when peoples' incomes decreased, they held on to their cars longer, creating an increase in demand for repair services.

The prices of complementary goods and substitute goods affect the demand for a product. For example, if the price of hot dogs increases, it would cause a decrease in the quantity of hot dogs demanded. This would cause a decrease in demand for hot-dog rolls. Business managers keep track of the prices of complementary products affecting the demand for their products. Similarly, managers monitor the prices of substitute products. Chicken producers know an increase in the price of beef products will increase demand for their products.

Economists have observed that consumer expectations affect demand for some goods and services. While most consumers will purchase basic goods and necessities without considering changing ECONOMIC CONDITIONS, the demand for home purchases, automobiles, and other significant purchases are affected by consumers' comfort and security about the future. The University of Michigan Survey of Consumer Expectations is a widely studied and quoted index of American consumers' attitudes.

Logically, the more consumers in a market, the greater the demand for most goods and services. Back in the 1950s, Aiken, South Carolina, then a town of 5,000 people, suddenly had an influx of 30,000 workers constructing the Savannah River Site Nuclear Weapons facility. The huge increase in number of consumers overwhelmed local markets. Landlords rented the same bed to two people, one working the day shift, the other working the night shift. Local grocery stores put canned goods out in boxes, never stacking the shelves. There were so many new customers, they opened and emptied the boxes themselves. Midwestern oil towns experienced the same boom, but it declined in the 1980s when low oil prices sent workers elsewhere.

Changes in exchange rates can increase or decrease demand for a product. DEPRECIATION of the Japanese yen makes products from Japan cheaper for American consumers, increasing this demand and decreasing demand for substitute products made by American businesses. Similarly, appreciation of the U.S. dollar increases demand for foreign products and decreases foreign demand for U.S. products.

While only a price change causes a change in quantity demanded, the above examples were changes in demand for a product.

Deming's 14 points

Deming's 14 points comprise a philosophy about business and efforts to achieve quality devised by Dr. W. Edward Deming (1900–93), a mathematical physicist. In 1950 Deming was invited to Japan to teach. His statistical quality-control methods were quickly adopted by Japanese manufacturers, and in 1951 a Deming Prize was established in his honor. Deming has had a significant impact on business managers, first in Japan and more recently in the United States.

Deming's 14 points, referred to as "A System of Profound Knowledge," are a basis for transformation for industry. Quality advocates suggest they apply anywhere, to small and large organizations, to the service industry, and to the manufacturing. As one of the first MANAGEMENT GURUS, Deming brought together ideas from many sources and emphasized the importance of human factors in achieving excellence. The 14 points are:

- Create constancy of purpose toward improvement of product and service.
- Adopt the new philosophy. We are in a new economic age.
- Cease dependence on mass inspection to achieve quality.
- Constantly and forever improve the system.
- Remove barriers.
- Drive out fear. Create trust and a climate for innovation.
- Break down barriers between departments.
- Eliminate numerical goals.

- Eliminate work standards (quotas).
- Institute modern methods of supervision.
- Institute modern methods of training.
- Institute a program of education and retraining.
- End the practice of awarding business based on lowest price alone.
- Put everybody in the company to work to accomplish the transformation.

Further reading

American Society for Quality Web site. Available online. URL: www.asq.org.

demographics

Demographics are population measures such as age, race, gender, occupation, and INCOME. Demographics are often used by businesspeople to define market segments on which to focus their efforts. No business has the resources to be "all things to all people"; marketers therefore use segmentation to identify which groups of consumers are or are likely to be most interested in their PRODUCTS and SERVICES.

Segmentation of markets based on demographics allows marketers to make more efficient use of RESOURCES. Consider the alternative, broadcast marketing—that is, promoting and distributing a company's products wherever and whenever possible. Also known as "spaghetti marketing" (throw it up on the wall and see if it sticks), broadcast marketing wastes resources and reduces the likelihood of success.

Often obtainable from U.S. CENSUS BUREAU data, demographics—in exacting detail for anywhere in the country—are a basic tool for marketing. Segmentation by gender is commonplace and logical. Some products, such as computerized action games, appeal more to males; while other products, such as cosmetics, appeal more to women. In the 1980s, racetracks, traditionally thought of as a male-dominated spectator sport, studied their demographics and found almost 50 percent of their patrons were female. This led to a huge increase in sponsorships by firms targeting women.

Age is also a basic demographic characteristic affecting CONSUMER BEHAVIOR. In the 1980s,

Chrysler recognized that "baby boomers," Americans born after World War II (1945–64), were finally starting to have children. Chrysler's vans appealed to this demographic group who needed room for a baby seat but did not want to drive station wagons like their parents. Demographers have come up with a variety of age-based labels, including "Generation X," people born between 1965 and 1976 perceived to be more egalitarian and environmentally oriented; and "Generation Y," young people in the 1990s, considered more conservative and materialistic than their predecessors.

Similar to age and gender segmentation, race, income, and occupational demographics are useful ways to look at consumer groups. Almost any television show or commercial radio station will have ADVERTISING that targets different demographic groups. Most advertising media maintain a listener, reader, and viewer demographic profile, allowing marketers to match their customer demographics with similar advertising media demographics.

Business markets are also divided based on demographic characteristics: size, geographic location, end-use applications, and customer type. Business marketers often use the NORTH AMERICAN INDUSTRY CLASSIFICATION SYSTEM to identify business customer groups. Business marketing organizational structures are typically based on business demographics. Sales organizations are usually divided based on customer types, geographic location, and business size, with representatives assigned to each group.

See also MARKET SEGMENTATION; TARGET MARKETS.

Further reading

Boone, Louis E., and David L. Kurtz. *Contemporary Marketing.* 14th ed. Fort Worth, Tex.: South-Western, 2009.

Department of Commerce, U.S.

The U.S. Department of Commerce (DOC) is the major department managing the federal government's domestic and international trade policies. Created in 1903 as the Department of Commerce and Labor, it has gone through numerous changes in activities as the U.S. economy has changed over the last 100 years. In 1913, a separate Department of Labor was created. In 1925 the Patent Office was transferred from the DEPARTMENT OF THE INTERIOR to the DOC. The Bureau of Mines has been moved in and out of the Commerce Department. The Radio Division was created in 1927 and then abolished in 1932. At various times the DOC has included bureaus of lighthouses, air commerce, weather, and marine inspection.

In 2009 the major bureaus within the Commerce Department include the following:

- Bureau of Industry and Security
- Economics and Statistics Administration
- Bureau of Economic Analysis
- Bureau of the Census
- Economic Development Administration
- International Trade Administration
- Minority Business Development Agency
- National Oceanic & Atmospheric Administration
- National Telecommunications & Information Administration
- Patent and Trademark Office
- National Institute of Standards and Technology
- National Technical Information Service.

The most widely known parts of the Commerce Department are probably the Bureau of the Census, the Patent and Trademark Office, and the National Oceanic and Atmospheric Administration (NOAA). The Census Bureau is charged with managing the U.S. population census, which is used to determine political representation and allocation of funds for many federal programs. The Patent and Trademark Office oversees patent and trademark applications in the United States. NOAA is widely known for its hurricane advisory service but also manages a variety of science, fisheries, and ocean management programs.

Most of the other bureaus and agencies within the Commerce Department manage federal functions explained by their titles. The International Trade Administration promotes exports of U.S. products, the Economic Development Administration stimulates economic growth in distressed communities, and the Minority Business Development Agency promotes growth and competitiveness of minority-owned businesses.

Further reading
U.S. Department of Commerce Web site. Available online. URL: www.commerce.gov.

Department of Labor, U.S.

The U.S. Department of Labor (DOL) is a cabinet-level agency in the federal government created in 1913 with a mission "to foster, promote, and develop the welfare of the wage earners of the United States, to improve their working conditions, and to advance their opportunities for profitable employment." The DOL was created by transferring four bureaus—Labor Statistics, Immigration, Naturalization, and Children's—from the old Department of Commerce and Labor.

Over the years, changing political and ECONOMIC CONDITIONS have expanded the DOL's role in addressing the needs of workers in the United States. During World War I, the department was placed in charge of the War Labor Administration, and during the Depression it operated EMPLOYMENT services and many New Deal–era programs. Some DOL responsibilities, including veterans' employment rights and immigration, have been shifted to other federal agencies. Today the DOL administers and enforces over 180 federal laws. Following are some of its major responsibilities.

- The FAIR LABOR STANDARDS ACT prescribes standards for wages and overtime pay. The act requires employers to pay covered employees at least the federal MINIMUM WAGE and overtime at a rate of at least 1½ times the regular wage. The act also restricts employment of children under age 16.
- The OCCUPATIONAL SAFETY AND HEALTH ACT (1970), administered by the OCCUPATIONAL SAFETY AND HEALTH ADMINISTRATION (OSHA), defines and regulates safety and health conditions for workplace environments in most industries in the United States. Additional acts protecting miners, longshore and harbor work-

ers, and child labor are also administered by OSHA.

- The EMPLOYEE RETIREMENT INCOME SECURITY ACT (ERISA) regulates employers who offer pension or WELFARE benefit plans for their employees. Before passage of ERISA, unscrupulous employers would "raid" employee pension funds for corporate and personal use, often bankrupting workers' funds. ERISA mandated fiduciary and disclosure requirements and created the PENSION BENEFIT GUARANTY CORPORATION requiring employers to insure retirement benefits with payments in to guaranty fund.
- The Labor-Management Reporting and Disclosure Act (also known as the LANDRUM-GRIFFIN ACT) created safeguards for the use and management of union funds. Protection of WHISTLE-BLOWERS—workers who report or complain about unsafe or illegal actions by their companies—is administered under OSHA.
- The WORKER ADJUSTMENT AND RETRAINING NOTIFICATION ACT (WARN) requires employers to provide employees with early warning of impending LAYOFFS or plant closings.
- The Employee Polygraph Protection Act (1988) prohibits most employers from using lie detectors on employees.
- The CONSUMER CREDIT PROTECTION ACT (1968) regulates the garnishment of wages by creditors.
- The FAMILY AND MEDICAL LEAVE ACT (1993) requires certain employers to provide up to 12 weeks of unpaid leave for eligible employees for the birth or adoption of a child or serious illness of the employee or a family member.
- The DAVIS-BACON ACT (1931) mandates payment of prevailing wages and benefits to employees of contractors engaged in U.S. government construction projects.
- The McNamara-O'Hara Service Contract Act (1965) sets wage rates and other labor standards for employees of contractors furnishing services to the U.S. government.
- The Walsh-Healey Public Contracts Act (1936) requires the DOL to settle disputes of awards to manufacturers supplying products to the U.S. government.

- The Migrant and Seasonal Agricultural Worker Protection Act (1983) regulates hiring and employment of agricultural workers.
- The Immigration and Nationality Act (1952) requires employers who want to hire foreign temporary workers to obtain certification that there are insufficient available and qualified Americans to do the work.
- The Federal Mine Safety and Health Act (1977) covers all people who work on mine property.
- The Copeland Act (1934) precludes "kickback" requirements, payments demanded from employees as a condition for employment with a federal contractor.
- The Longshoring and Harbor Workers' Compensation Act (1927) requires employers to assure that WORKERS' COMPENSATION is funded and available to eligible employees.

The DOL has many other regulatory and advisory responsibilities related to workers and working conditions in the United States. Critics of government involvement in the workplace often cite DOL regulations as bureaucratic interference that creates inefficiency.

See also BUREAU OF LABOR STATISTICS; LABOR FORCE.

Further reading
U.S. Department of Labor Web site. Available online. URL: www.dol.gov.

Department of the Interior, U.S.
The U.S. Department of the Interior (DOI) is the principal federal agency managing public land RESOURCES in the United States. Created in 1849, the DOI manages almost half a billion acres of federal property. The Department states as its mission:

1. to encourage and provide for the appropriate management, preservation, and operation of the Nation's public lands and natural resources for use and enjoyment both now and in the future;
2. to carry out related scientific research and investigations in support of these objectives;

3. to develop and use resources in an environmentally sound manner, and provide an equitable return on these resources to the American taxpayer;
4. to carry out trust responsibilities of the U.S. Government with respect to American Indians and Alaska Natives.

Since its inception, the DOI has managed a wide array of public projects including the water system and jail in the District of Columbia, the 1850s boundary with Mexico, U.S. trust territories, schools, hospitals, patents, and public parks. Today it is divided into 8 bureaus, each managing different aspects of federal natural resources. The roles of most DOI bureaus are obvious by their name: the National Park Service, Fish and Wildlife Service, Indian Affairs, Geological Survey, Land Management, Minerals Management, and Surface Mining. The Bureau of Reclamation manages federal dams, power plants, and canals, mostly in the western United States. The Bureau of Reclamation is the largest WHOLESALER of water and second-largest producer of hydroelectric power in the country.

Over the years, many DOI bureaus have been the center of controversy. The Bureau of Indian Affairs has been criticized for heavy-handed treatment of Native Americans and misuse of funds. The Bureau of Land Management has been criticized for mismanagement and subsidizing animal grazing on federal lands. Surface Mining has been challenged for not protecting natural resources during mining operations; and Reclamation has been denounced for water subsidies to western farmers, impairing salmon fisheries, and damming natural waterways. James Watt, DOI secretary during the Reagan administration, became the focus of environmental critics. Drilling in the Arctic National Refuge, proposed by the George W. Bush administration, is under the DOI's direction.

Further reading

Department of Interior Web site. Available online. URL: www.doi.gov.

Department of Transportation, U.S.

The U.S. Department of Transportation (DOT) is a federal agency responsible for national transportation policy. The DOT, established in 1966, oversees numerous federal regulatory programs ranging from intermodal transportation to the St. Lawrence Seaway. The DOT negotiates and implements international transportation agreements, ensures the safety of U.S. airlines, and regulates interstate surface-transportation systems. Changes in DOT regulations affect location and distribution decisions of U.S. and international business managers and safety standards for vehicles in the United States.

Following are some major DOT programs.

- The Bureau of Transportation Statistics compiles, analyzes, and publishes national transportation statistics. Commodity flow and American travel statistics are used to analyze changing patterns of U.S. business and consumer transportation.
- The U.S. Coast Guard, most widely known for rescuing stranded sailors, also manages waterway systems, intercepts illegal drug traffic, and promotes boater safety.
- The FEDERAL AVIATION ADMINISTRATION (FAA) oversees the safety of civil aviation. FAA regulations direct aircraft and airport management and maintenance procedures. FAA allocation of airport terminal space significantly affects airline market competition. The FAA has been criticized for lagging in upgrading airport traffic control systems.
- The Federal Highway Administration (FHWA) coordinates interstate highway programs. The Federal-Aid Highway Program, financed with gasoline taxes, is a major source of funding for highway development around the country. Critics of U.S. transportation policy often point to FHWA funding of highways, rather than mass transportation systems, as an example of misguided federal priorities.
- The Federal Motor Carrier Safety Administration, created in 2000, focuses on commercial motor vehicle safety.

- The Federal Railroad Administration promotes and inspects railroads, with a focus on safety and environmental concerns.
- The Federal Transit Administration assists in developing mass-transportation systems in urban areas.
- The Maritime Administration promotes the maintenance of U.S. merchant-marine (domestically owned marine transportation) resources through preferences for U.S.-flag vessels in transportation of goods involving federal funding or support; and provides subsidies for maintaining U.S.-flag vessels, repair, and shipbuilding facilities.
- The National Highway Traffic Safety Administration (NHTSA) directs highway safety programs, including defining and enforcing safety performance standards for motor vehicles, investigating safety defects, and setting and enforcing fuel economy standards. The NHTSA has frequently been criticized for capitulating to automobile manufacturers' demands, resulting in reduced fuel-economy standards.
- The Research and Special Programs Administration oversees rules governing safe transportation and packaging of hazardous materials.
- The St. Lawrence Seaway Development Corporation operates and maintains the Saint Lawrence Seaway.
- The Surface Transportation Board is responsible for economic regulation of interstate shipping, primarily rail transportation. The board adjudicates complaints regarding the pricing practices of railroads.
- The Transportation Administrative Service Center provides technical support for DOT administration of other government agencies.

Further reading

U.S. Department of Transportation Web site. Available online. URL: www.dot.gov.

Department of the Treasury, U.S.

The U.S. Department of the Treasury is the major financial management department for the federal government. As stated on its Web site, the major functions of the Treasury Department are:

- managing federal finances
- collecting taxes, duties and monies paid to and due to the U.S. and paying all bills of the U.S.
- producing all postage stamps, currency and coinage
- managing government accounts and the public debt
- supervising national banks and thrift institutions
- advising on domestic and international financial, monetary, economic, trade and tax policy
- enforcing federal finance and tax laws
- investigating and prosecuting tax evaders, counterfeiters, forgers, smugglers, illicit spirits distillers, and gun law violations
- protecting the president, vice president, their families, candidates for those offices, foreign missions resident in Washington and visiting foreign dignitaries

The most widely known bureaus of the U.S. Treasury are the Internal Revenue Service (IRS), the U.S. Mint, and the Bureau of Engraving and Printing, and the Alcohol and Tobacco Tax and Trade Bureau. The Internal Revenue Service (IRS) is probably the most controversial bureau, charged with administering income tax laws and collections. The U.S. Mint produces coins, while the Bureau of Engraving and Printing creates currency. The Alcohol and Tobacco Tax and Trade Bureau (ATF) was divided by The Homeland Security Act of 2002 Bureau of Alcohol, Tobacco and Firearms into two new agencies, the Bureau of Alcohol, Tobacco, Firearms, and Explosives, which moved to the Department of Justice, and the Alcohol and Tobacco Tax and Trade Bureau (TTB), which remains in the Department of the Treasury. The TTB, as ATF did before it, administers and enforces the existing Federal laws and tax code provisions related to the production and taxation of alcohol and tobacco products. These taxes amount to approximately $15 billion in excise taxes, including $100 million in occupational tax on the manufacture of firearms and ammunition.

Historically, the TTB was one of the most important parts of the U.S. Treasury. The department was created by an act of Congress in 1789.

During the early post–American Revolutionary era, Congress levied excise taxes on distilled spirits, tobacco, snuff, and other products to pay for the debts incurred during the Revolution. The TTB became the federal bureau responsible for collecting these taxes and enforcing tobacco and alcohol laws. During Prohibition, the TTB became known as the federal revenue agents, closing down and destroying thousands of illegal alcohol production operations. As tax laws changed, increasing the importance of income and employment taxes, the IRS became the major tax revenue bureau with the Treasury Department.

Today, as the major department managing federal finances, the U.S. Treasury oversees the government's budget, borrowing to finance the national debt (more than $12 trillion in 2010), and international financial and trade policy. In 2009, treasury Secretary Timothy Geithner led efforts to mitigate financial market crises.

Further reading

U.S. Department of the Treasury Web site. Available online. URL: www.ustreas.gov.

dependency ratios

Dependency ratios are statistics estimating the number of people in various dependent groups per 1,000 working-age adults. Dependency ratios are used by demographers to predict changing relationships and social patterns. The two most common are the youth-dependency and elderly-dependency ratios.

The youth-dependency ratio in the United States, or the number of children under age 18 per 1,000 adults between the ages of 18 and 64, is expected to decline by 11 percent between 1996 and 2020. This will lead to reductions in demand for public-school education as well as reduced SUPPLY of teenage labor, critical to many retail-business employers. In Indonesia a reduction in the youth-dependency ratio was found to alleviate household budget constraints and boost savings rates in the country. China's one-child-per-family policy significantly reduced the youth-dependency ratio but is contributing to a

crisis in the pension system, with fewer workers per pensioner.

The elderly-dependency ratio, the number of people over age 65 per 1,000 working-age adults, is expected to increase by 43 percent in the United States between 1996 and 2020. Political debates over SOCIAL SECURITY and Medicare begin with the reality of a declining ratio of contributors to recipients in the system. In the 1990s demographers found an increase in the mortality rate among working-age Russians resulted in an increase in the elderly-dependency ratio, further exacerbating problems with their social WELFARE system.

Further reading

"Fountains of Youth," *American Demographics* 18, no. 7 (July 1996): 60.

deposit expansion multiplier

The deposit expansion multiplier, also referred to as the deposit creation multiplier, is the ratio of the change in demand deposits to the change in bank reserves. Used by economists to estimate the impact of FEDERAL RESERVE actions to affect the MONEY SUPPLY, the simple deposit expansion multiplier (D) is expressed as:

$$D = 1/rr$$

where *rr* is the reserve requirement or percentage of deposits commercial banks are required to keep as cash in their vault or on deposit with the Federal Reserve. The actual reserve requirement is a complex formula based on the size of the bank and the types of assets the bank holds. (For a bank, consumers' deposits represent liabilities, while loans and investments are the bank's assets.) Banks operate under what is called a fractional reserve system, retaining only a small portion of the deposits under their control. Holding cash costs banks the amount of interest those funds could have earned, so banks attempt to minimize cash on hand.

Assuming for simplicity's sake that the reserve requirement is 5 percent of deposits, $D = 1/.05 =$

20, suggesting that an increase in bank reserves will result in a multiplier effect of 20, increasing the money supply by 20 times the initial injection. In the above explanation, two considerations are important. First, demand deposits, or checking account deposits, are money. Money is anything sellers will accept as a means of payment. Checks written against demand deposit accounts are widely accepted as payment. Second, injections into the money supply are called open-market operations, and they are the primary tool used by the Federal Reserve to influence the money supply. The Fed, through its New York Federal Reserve Bank, is constantly buying and selling U.S. Treasury securities (millions of dollars worth daily) to increase or decrease the amount of loanable funds in the banking system. Loanable funds are a bank's excess reserves once they have met the reserve requirement. When the Fed buys Treasury securities from banks, it pays by electronic deposit, increasing or injecting reserves into the system. This increase in reserves lowers interest rates, primarily the Federal Funds Rate, the rate at which banks loan reserves to each other to meet reserve requirements. Likewise, if the Fed sells securities, it receives electronic payment from banks, reducing their reserves and driving up interest rates.

If the reserve requirement is lowered it increases the deposit expansion multiplier and, if raised, it lowers the multiplier effect. (The Fed rarely changes the reserve requirement but, in 2010, China raised its reserve requirement to slow economic growth and the potential for inflation.) In addition, if banks or households hold excess reserves (as banks did during the financial crisis of 2008–09 and during the GREAT DEPRESSION) it lowers the multiplier effect.

Further reading

Federal Reserve. "Reserve Requirements." Available online. URL: www.federalreserve.gov/monetarypolicy/reservereq.htm. Accessed on November 16, 2009.

depreciation, depletion, amortization

Depreciation, depletion, and AMORTIZATION are accounting techniques associated with the long-term ASSETS of a firm. When a long-term asset that is used in the course of business helps to generate revenue, a portion of its purchase cost is systematically apportioned to expense to satisfy accounting's matching principle. The systematic apportionment from cost to expense for the firm's man-made, tangible assets is called depreciation. The systematic apportionment from cost to expense for the firm's natural resources in depletion, and for the firm's intangibles it is amortization.

When a long-term asset is purchased, this is a CAPITAL EXPENDITURE, and an asset account is debited for the purchase. When that asset is then used in the generation of revenue, a part of that purchase cost must be transferred to expense, a revenue expenditure. Thus the accounting for long-term assets requires an understanding of both capital and revenue expenditures.

Contra asset accounts are created when depreciation, depletion, or amortization expense is recorded as accumulated depreciation, accumulated depletion, and accumulated amortization. These contra asset accounts serve to systematically reduce the book (carrying) value of the long-term assets over their useful lives. When the BOOK VALUE of a long-term asset declines to the level of its residual (salvage) value, then the asset is considered to be fully depreciated, depleted, or amortized.

See also RESIDUAL VALUE.

deregulation

Deregulation is the reduction of government rules regulating business activities; it is a response to previous government decisions to regulate certain industries in the economy. Deregulation and PRIVATIZATION were popular political-economic policies in the United States during the latter half of the 20th century. In the United States, a variety of industries have undergone deregulation, including airline, railroad, banking, and trucking industries. Advocates of deregulation call for further action in such industries as helium, power PRODUCTION, and the U.S. Postal Service.

The debate over regulation and deregulation centers on the COSTS and benefits associated with government intervention into markets. Free-market economists argue that government intervention creates inefficiencies and that competitive markets will adjust and eliminate market problems. Most economists agree that one role of government is to correct for MARKET FAILURE—situations where there is a lack of COMPETITION, a misallocation of resources, and economic PROFITS. In the late 19th century, the social costs of living in an unregulated market environment were visible to all citizens. Large CORPORATIONS used their market power to extract higher prices from consumers, drive out competitors from markets, gain concessions from workers and suppliers, and procure support from the political establishment. Defective and dangerous products were sold to the public, and MONOPOLY profits concentrated in the hands of a few who became known as the "robber barons."

With a loss of trust in market solutions, public calls for business regulation became louder. The INTERSTATE COMMERCE COMMISSION (ICC), established in 1887, became the first in a series of government regulatory agencies. Earlier government subsidies had resulted in over-expansion of some rail routes and monopoly control in communities serviced by only one railroad. Some railroad owners colluded to fix prices in markets in which they were, in theory, competing, while in other markets competition drove prices to below operating costs. In response to the proposal to create a regulatory commission, railroad owners supported price stabilization at profitable levels, while grain shippers and small communities supported control over monopoly service. The ICC was seen as the solution to market failure at both extremes.

In Europe, rather than regulate private companies, many countries created government monopolies. Like regulation, the goal was to provide services on a least-cost basis. It clearly did not make sense to have two railroads connecting the same destinations or to have multiple sets of telephone lines in a community. In many industries where ECONOMIES OF SCALE exist, providing an ability to produce at a lower cost per unit as output expands, political leaders chose to either regulate existing firms or create government-run

monopolies. With greater numbers of government monopolies, in recent decades European governments have expanded privatization efforts rather than deregulation.

When railroads were first regulated in the United States, there were few alternative means of transportation. Automobiles and trucks did not exist, and waterways were limited by seasonal changes. With the advent of trucking, the monopoly power of railroads declined. Initially interstate trucking was included in ICC regulation. Similarly, AT&T was a regulated monopoly in the long-distance telephone market until the development of microwave technology created new sources of competition in long-distance communication.

In the 1960s and 1970s, critics of regulation cited the cost of huge regulatory bureaucracies, the slowness of regulators in approving changes, and the need to compete on a global basis, many times with firms that faced less regulation than U.S. firms, as reasons for government to deregulate. The ICC was disbanded, deregulating trucking and railroad transportation. The CIVIL AERONAUTICS BOARD (CAB) was dissolved, deregulating airline markets, and interstate banking restrictions were reduced and/or eliminated. Supporters of deregulation often point to the airline example citing lower fares that resulted from deregulation. Critics of deregulation point to increased airline overbooking practices, elimination of service to some communities, and increased safety problems.

In 2000 California experimented with deregulation of electrical power production. Prices power producers could charge were deregulated, while distribution fees and, more importantly, retail prices remained regulated. When, in 2000–2001, wholesale prices rose and retail prices were not allowed to also rise, a crisis occurred, severely challenging the financial survival of the power companies in California.

Further reading
Mallor, Jane P., A. James Barnes, Thomas Bowers, Michael J. Philips, and Arlen W. Langvardt. *Business Law: The Ethical, Global, and E-Commerce Environment.* 11th ed. Boston: McGraw-Hill, 2001; Moore,

Thomas G. "Deregulation, Privatization, and the Market," *National Forum: Phi Kappa Phi Journal* 70 (Spring 1990): 5.

derivative securities

In their basic form, derivative securities are agreements between two or more parties. The parties agree to pay each other based on some agreed benchmark. For example, two businesses agree to pay each other based on the behavior of INTEREST RATES. If interest rates rise above a previously agreed level, one company pays the other. On the other hand, if the interest rates fall below the agreed level, the other company pays the first. The amount that each company must pay is derived by the terms of the agreement, hence the name *derivatives*. Usually the higher the rate goes above the benchmark rate, the more one company must pay the other, and vice versa. This is similar to betting on a football game where the bet varies based on the difference in scores. To complicate things even more, the agreement can specify the way that payment is made—in currency; securities; or a physical commodity such as gold, silver, corn, or pork bellies (used to make bacon).

Although derivative securities are considered by some as nothing more than complicated gambling, they can serve a useful business purpose. To illustrate, suppose a resort hotel negotiates a CONTRACT with a Japanese tour operator, who wants to have the contract stipulate payment in yen. This protects the tour operator if the value of yen falls. The operator is charging his customers so many yen to come on the tour. If the value of yen falls and the hotel rooms were priced in dollars, the tour operator would lose. To avoid this risk, the tour operator forces the RISK onto the hotel. To get the tour operator's business, the hotel must accept payment in yen, but it does not want the risk of the yen falling in value, because when it exchanges the yen into dollars, it gets fewer dollars than it bargained for. On the other hand, the hotel could make an unexpected profit if the yen increased in value. To shift this risk, in essence it sells to someone else by using a derivative. The derivative contract specifies that the hotel will pay if the value of the yen increase, but if it falls

the other party pays the hotel. They are essentially betting on the change in the yen EXCHANGE RATE. The hotel puts the agreement together in such a way that the derivative contract will produce profits that make up for the amount it loses on the yen deal with the tour operator. If the hotel should make money on the agreement with the tour operator because the yen went up in value, it would lose a corresponding amount on the derivative arrangement. This effectively shifts the risk of the fluctuating yen to the other party to the agreement.

See also FUTURES; HEDGING.

developing countries   See EMERGING MARKETS.

direct investment

Direct INVESTMENT has two meanings in business: the creation of a business enterprise in another country or direct transfer savings from households to businesses without the use of FINANCIAL INTERMEDIARIES. In its first meaning, direct investment is one alternative for a business considering expansion abroad. Direct investment is an alternative to either EXPORTING or LICENSING. It usually involves a larger and longer-term commitment of CAPITAL and resources than either of those two alternatives.

Direct investment in foreign economies is typically done for any of three reasons. First, investment may be needed to extract or make use of raw materials. In the 1960s and 1970s, many U.S.-based oil and mining companies established facilities around the world to extract resources.

Second, many MULTINATIONAL CORPORATIONS (MNCs) establish manufacturing facilities in countries to take advantage of less-expensive, trained labor resources. For example, MAQUILADORAS, the production-sharing factories in northern Mexico employ over a million workers at significantly lower cost than in the United States or Canada. In recent years, many U.S. computer companies invested in software development facilities in India to take advantage of a highly skilled, English-speaking workforce.

Third, direct investment is often used as a means of overcoming TRADE BARRIERS protecting domestic industries. Production in a country, even by a foreign-owned company, is usually exempt from restrictions. In the 1980s, Japanese automobile manufacturers, fearing trade barriers, invested heavily in factories in the United States.

Globally direct investment is dominated by the United States, Europe, and Japan. For a developing country, direct investment brings new technology and production capacity. It also provides access to management and marketing methods used in international trade. But FOREIGN INVESTMENT is made based on earning profits, which are withdrawn from the country, and foreign companies are often criticized for lack of respect for cultural values and for creating and leaving behind environmental damage.

The second meaning of direct investment refers to direct interaction between lenders and borrowers. In the United States most savings are deposited with financial intermediaries, banks, CREDIT UNIONS, and SAVINGS AND LOAN ASSOCIATIONS, which then lend these funds to consumers and businesses. Financial intermediaries provide the benefits of aggregating funds, reducing risks through lending to multiple borrowers, and knowledge of sound lending practices. Like any business, financial intermediaries attempt to earn a profit for the services they provide. Since the 1980s, many U.S. financial intermediaries have experienced disintermediation: the withdrawal of funds by savers, who then directly purchase securities.

direct mail

Direct mail is the use of letters, brochures, samples, postcards, catalogs, and other printed material sent by mail to potential and current customers. Direct mail is a multibillion-dollar industry in the United States. If one person set aside all the direct mail received in a month, in one month he would probably have a huge pile of solicitations, depending on how many lists he is on.*

---

* To reduce the amount of direct mail received, write to Mail Preference Service, DMA, PO Box 9008, Farmingdale, NY 11735-9008. Consumers should specify whether they want their names to be removed from commercial lists, nonprofit lists, or both.

Marketers use direct mail because they can be highly selective in deciding which TARGET MARKETS to send MARKETING COMMUNICATIONS. The other advantages of direct mail as compared to other traditional media (television, radio, and magazine ADVERTISING) are as follows.

- The circulation can be controlled by the advertiser.
- Each mailing can be personalized.
- Consumers see only the company's message, not a competitor's as well.
- It is relatively easy to measure response rates.
- It can be used to stimulate a direct response.

Disadvantages of direct mail:

- It is considered "junk" by many recipients.
- It is expensive.
- It can be considered an invasion of privacy.
- It is only as effective as the list being used.

Mailing lists are the "lifeblood" of direct-mail marketing. Lists come from many sources: internal company lists of customers and requests, associations, and list-service agencies. Each issue of *DMNews,* a weekly newspaper for direct marketers, includes advertisements for thousands of direct-mail lists. List brokers represent businesses and organizations willing to rent out their mailing lists. Rental rates vary, but lists usually cost $100–$200 per thousand names. List renters usually agree to pay only for new names and addresses: the names remaining after they "merge and purge" the list received against their existing database. The selling of information about people is an important issue in business PRIVACY.

In the United States, direct mail traditionally has been used effectively by companies offering CREDIT CARDS, through magazine subscriptions, and via music clubs. With today's increasingly sophisticated database systems, many small businesses and nonprofit organizations are using direct mail to identify new customers and supporters and to sell their products. Contests are often a great way to generate names for future mailings.

Direct mail is expensive. The U.S. Postal Service offers discount rates for bulk mailings of 200 or more pieces of mail. But bulk-rate mail is easily identified by recipients and often is not even opened. Direct-mail marketers know the typical piece of direct mail is evaluated for only four seconds before people decide whether to throw it away or consider it further. The design of direct mail—including whether a label or hand-written address is used, a message on the outside of the envelope conveying the benefits of the product or service being offered, and the material included in the mailing—are critical to the effort's success. Direct-mail campaigns are often considered successful if the response rate is 2 percent.

Direct e-mail is becoming an increasingly effective form of direct mail. Companies ask consumers for their e-mail addresses and permission to send messages, then collect and rent lists of consumers who have agreed to receive direct e-mail solicitations. On-line newsletters and message-alert services allow companies to collect addresses and expand marketing communication using e-mails.

Further reading
DMNews Web site. Available online URL: www. dmnews.com; Etzel, Michael J., Bruce J. Walker, and William J. Staunton. *Marketing.* 14th ed. Boston: McGraw-Hill, 2005.

direct marketing
Direct marketing is MARKETING COMMUNICATIONS other than direct selling between consumers and companies. Although there is no consensus regarding what constitutes direct marketing and what is ADVERTISING, direct marketing includes catalog marketing, DIRECT MAIL, TELEMARKETING, direct-response television, and on-line retailing.

Catalog marketing, begun in the United States by Montgomery Ward in 1872, allows consumers to evaluate choices in a catalog and make purchases either by mail or telephone. There are over 7,000 catalog-marketing companies in the United States. American consumers spend over $100 billion annually on catalog sales. Many consumers in rural areas with few shopping alternatives, those in urban areas where travel is often congested,

and people working long hours and only able to shop for personal needs late in the evening prefer catalogs. Catalog marketers maintain extensive databases about their customers, customizing the catalogs consumers receive based on past purchases, mailing catalogs based on the timing of past purchases, and analyzing the effectiveness of each photograph used and number of items per page. Catalogs are expensive, so marketers attempt to maximize the effectiveness of their efforts.

Direct mail is the use of letters, brochures, samples postcards and other printed material sent by mail to potential and existing customers. Mailing lists are critical to the success of direct-mail marketing. Most companies maintain extensive databases about their customers, consumer requests for information, and other prospective customers. List brokers rent the names and addresses of magazine subscribers, association members, contributors to campaigns, credit-card applicants, and a variety of other groups. Direct marketers rent lists most likely to include people similar to their current customer groups. While expensive, direct mail allows marketers to personalize messages and focus on those consumers most likely to be interested in their goods and services.

Dedicated TV channels and INFOMERCIALS are forms of direct marketing. QVC and Home Shopping Network are the leading direct-response television marketers. Jewelry, housewares, clothing, and electronics products have been successfully marketed using direct-response television. Infomercials and dedicated television shopping networks are expensive but continue to be popular.

On-line retailing, often predicted to surpass all other forms of direct marketing, is the sale of products through computer connections. In the late 1990s, many companies created Web sites, promoted them through banner advertisements and other traditional advertising, and waited for consumers to come. To a large extent it did not happen. U.S. consumers initially used the World Wide Web to research companies and products but were reluctant to purchase products through computer connections. A few product categories—primarily books, music, and travel—dominate on-line retailing. The electronic retailing world is replete with DOT-COMS that were unable to gain consumer acceptance. Some on-line retailers added hyperlinked toll-free numbers at each stage of the on-line buying process, to reduce the "bail-out rate" (the high percentage of customers who begin to purchase online but do not complete the transaction). Many on-line retailers are using their Web sites to increase and improve communications with customers.

Further reading

Etzel, Michael J., Bruce J. Walker, and William J. Staunton. *Marketing*. 14th ed. Boston: McGraw-Hill, 2005.

disclosure duties

Disclosure duties in the context of the U.S. business environment ordinarily refer to information that companies and corporate officers must disclose on a timely basis to the public. Many disclosure duties originate in U.S. securities law and cover, for example, the PROSPECTUS that any stock, bond, or security buyer must receive. These disclosure duties relate to publicly traded companies, not privately held businesses. Other disclosure duties concern corporate accounts, ANNUAL REPORTS, materially significant events, and the securities transactions of company "insiders."

Some disclosure duties are specific to certain industries. For example, franchisers are obligated under federal and some state laws to disclose to prospective franchisees the nature of their franchise system and CONTRACT obligations. Other disclosure duties are consumer-oriented, such as the energy efficiency of household appliances and the fuel efficiency of automobiles. The economic premise behind disclosure duties is that information helps perfect markets by leveling the knowledge of buyers and sellers.

Further reading

Ratner, David L. *Securities Regulation in a Nutshell*. 7th ed. Eagan, Minn.: West Group, 2001.

discounting, present value

Discounting is the often-encountered process of finding an unknown present value from a known future value. Using a time line, discounting is moving backward in time from a given point of time in the future to the present time. Given the time value of money (that INTEREST RATES are always positive), present values are always smaller than future values.

Lottery and sweepstakes winners may be offered their winnings not as a lump sum paid presently but as a future stream of ANNUITY payments. For example, a sweepstakes participant may have won the grand prize of $1 million to be paid in yearly installments of $25,000 for the next 40 years. While the sum of the 40 payments is $1 million the present value of such a payoff is considerably less than $1 million. Finding the present value of this future stream of annuity payments will determine the true value for the grand-prize winner. Using a discount rate of 10 percent, the present value of receiving $25,000 each year for the next 40 years is only $244,476.27.

For a lump sum, the present value of some future amount is determined by the discounting formula $PV = FV_n \div [1+ir]^n$, where PV is the present value, FV_n is the future value at some future point in time n, ir is the interest rate (expressed in decimal form) applicable to the situation in question, and the exponent n is the same point in time for which the future value is known. For instance, find the present value $133.10 to be received three years from now, given a 10 percent interest rate, compounded annually: $PV = 133.10 \div [1.10]^3$. Simplification reduces the formula to $PV = 133.10 \div 1.331 = 100.00$.

It is sometimes necessary to determine the present value of an annuity. While there is a formula for this, it is much easier to use a commonly published table of interest factors. For discounting, there are tables of present value interest factors for lump sums (PVIFs) and for annuities (PVIFAs). To find the present value of a future lump sum: $PV = FV_n[PVIF_{i,n}]$, where $PVIF$ is the lump sum present interest factor for some interest rate i and for some time period n. To find the present value of an annuity: $PVA = PMT[PVIFA_{i,n}]$, where PMT is the regular annuity payment and $PVIFA$ is the annuity present value interest factor for some interest rate i and for some time period n.

While using the published tables of present value interest factors is easier than manually doing the number-crunching, it is much more convenient to find present values for lump sums and annuities using a financial calculator. Remembering that the interest-factor tables carry the interest factors to only four digits to the right of the decimal, the results obtained from the use of a financial calculator are more accurate than using the tables. The published interest-factor tables list interest factors only for whole-number interest rates. A financial calculator can compound using any interest rate.

discount rate

The discount rate is the interest rate charged by the FEDERAL RESERVE SYSTEM to member banks for short-term loans. Changing the discount rate is one of three "tools" used by the Federal Reserve (known as the Fed) to manage the MONEY SUPPLY. The discount rate is not a major tool; rather it is more of a "pencil tool." Like a builder changing the construction plans, changing the discount rate is a signal that the Fed is encouraging or discouraging banks to make more loans.

Banks are expected to exhaust alternative sources before the Fed provides discount-rate credit. Discount-rate borrowing is closely scrutinized. Excessive borrowing suggests a bank is not carefully managing its funds, and frequent borrowing might lead to closer evaluation of a bank's business activities by the Federal Reserve.

In the Fed's early days, banks would borrow funds for their short-term liquidity needs at the discount window of the New York Federal Reserve. In recent years, as banks have become better at managing their cash needs, fewer have utilized the Fed's borrowing at the discount window. A falling discount rate encourages banks to make more loans and signals that the Fed is practicing expansionary MONETARY POLICY. A rising discount rate signals contractionary monetary policy.

After September 11, 2001, the Federal Reserve publicly announced the discount window was available to provide liquidity to the BANKING SYSTEM. With the stock exchanges closed and major banks scrambling to reestablish operations, there was a liquidity problem in U.S. financial markets. The Fed stepped in to provide liquidity by providing loans through the discount window. As reported in the *Wall Street Journal*, that week the Fed loaned $45 billion, compared to a typical weekly amount in the range of $25–$300 million.

By opening up access to the discount window, the Fed was attempting to reduce volatility in the FEDERAL FUNDS MARKET, the short-term (usually overnight) lending among U.S. banks to meet the Fed's RESERVE REQUIREMENTS. Despite its name, the Federal Reserve does not operate or control the federal funds market. The Fed requires banks to keep a set percentage of their deposits as cash or other specified U.S. TREASURY SECURITIES. These required reserves, which are available when customers want their deposits returned, act as a source of liquidity for banks.

As banks receive more deposits, their reserve requirements increase. At the end of each business day, bank managers calculate their required reserves, determine whether they have excess or insufficient reserves, and lend or borrow reserves electronically in the federal funds market. Loans made in the federal funds market are returned the next business day.

Banks borrowing to meet their reserve requirement will compare rates in the market, attempting to minimize their costs. Federal funds rates tend to be uniform among participating banks and increase or decrease, depending on the demand for and supply of funds available.

In 2002 the Fed announced it would change its discount-rate policies. Federal Reserve governor Edward Gramlich was quoted as saying, "There is an alleged stigma to the discount window, and we intend to get rid of that." The Fed proposed setting the discount rate 1 percent above the targeted federal funds rate. Financially sound banks would be allowed to borrow at the new rate with "few questions asked and without requiring a bank to first exhaust alternatives." With the discount rate above the federal funds rate, banks will not likely borrow, but if a financial crisis arose, raising the federal funds rate temporarily, banks could borrow at the discount window, reducing pressure in the federal funds market. The new Fed program allows less financially sound banks to borrow at a rate one-half percentage point above the primary discount rate. The Fed goal is to reduce interest-rate volatility.

See also OPEN MARKET OPERATIONS.

Further reading
Ip, Gregg. "Fed Is Overhauling Procedure for Discount-window Loans," *Wall Street Journal*, 20 May 2002; Mishkin, Frederic S. *The Economics of Money, Banking, and Financial Markets*. 8th ed. Boston: Addison Wesley, 2006.

dispute settlement

There are many ways to settle business disputes. Litigation in courts is common in the United States, much less common elsewhere. Mediation and friendly consultations, which are not binding, are increasingly used and predominant in Asian countries like China. ARBITRATION is growing rapidly as a business dispute-settlement method in the United States and globally. Arbitration is typically binding and precludes going to court in most instances, although enforcement of arbitral awards in court may be required. One reason for the growth in the use of commercial arbitration to settle international business disputes is the so-called New York Convention. This international agreement, to which the United States and over 100 nations are parties, greatly facilitates the enforcement of arbitration awards across borders.

The U.S. Supreme Court has repeatedly demonstrated deference to arbitration as a method of settling business disputes, notably in the securities industry. Antitrust disputes can also be arbitrated. As a practical matter, many arbitrations result in compromises as opposed to the "winner-take-all" approach of litigation before courts.

Arbitrators are often chosen ad hoc by the disputing parties, say one for each side with a third arbitrator chosen by those two selected arbitrators. There are many arbitration centers, where the arbitrators and their procedural rules come pre-packaged. The American Arbitration Association hosts a wide range of business dispute-settlement options.

Further reading
Nolan-Haley, Jacqueline M. *Alternative Dispute Resolution in a Nutshell*. 2d ed. Eagan, Minn.: West Group, 2001.

distribution channels (marketing channels)

Distribution channels, also called marketing channels, are the systems used to move PRODUCTS and SERVICES from producers to consumers. At first glance, distribution seems like a simple and obvious process for a business: Find out where the customer is and get the product to him or her. But distribution channels can involve numerous structures depending on the needs of customers and producers.

Generally distribution channels involve two to five levels. In the simplest two-level system, manufacturers provide their good or service directly to consumers. With expanded use of the INTERNET, direct sales from producers to consumers are becoming more prevalent. Because of the direct contact needed, many service businesses have short, two-level distribution systems. Doctors, dentists, and lawyers rarely have market intermediaries between them and the customer.

Many manufacturers do not have the resources or skills needed to effectively market directly to consumers. These firms will sell to WHOLESALERS who then market the products to retailers, who in turn sell the product to customers. In recent years some U.S. retailers have used their market power to eliminate wholesalers, instead buying directly from manufacturers.

In addition to wholesale and retail levels in distribution channels, some markets have manufacturer's representatives who act as intermediaries between producers and wholesalers; in some markets jobbers or rack jobbers act as intermediaries between wholesalers and retailers. Manufacturers' representatives are often used for complex products where considerable explanation is needed. Rack jobbers provide physical distribution of products to small retail outlets that are not being serviced by wholesalers.

The number of levels in a distribution channel depends on who is performing which marketing channel functions. To be successful, all marketing functions must be accomplished. A manufacturer selling directly to consumers will need to advertise and promote the product, manage inventory and assortment, provide physical distribution, monitor customer satisfaction and feedback, and handle all financial aspects of the selling process. Many small E-COMMERCE entrepreneurs have learned there are reasons why intermediaries exist in distribution channels. The intermediaries provide benefits by managing distribution functions. Retailers assist with ADVERTISING and promotion, maintain an assortment of products available directly to consumers, manage returns, often offer credit, and complete the sales transaction. Wholesalers typically manage inventory and storage functions, have distribution systems, sometimes provide credit, and assist with advertising and promotion.

Sometimes a firm will want to control various aspects of its distribution channels. A manufacturer that creates or purchases retail outlets or creates its own wholesaling system is involved in VERTICAL INTEGRATION. For example, many U.S. cosmetic manufacturers lease space within retail department stores and hire their own sales staff to sell their products to customers in these stores, and oil companies now refine, distribute, and own the retail stores selling gasoline. Retailers sometimes contract to have products made by manufacturers to the retailer's specifications and with the retailer's brand name. Vertical marketing systems can also be created through contractual relationships. Many independent hardware stores are part of a voluntary wholesaling system, buying most of their merchandise from the group wholesaler and pooling funds for advertising.

Within distribution systems there exists channel power. One or more of the members of the distribution channel will determine which products are placed on retailers' shelves, which products are promoted, and which stores will be selected to sell exclusive products. Historically in the United States, manufacturers dominated distribution channels, determining how products were distributed and often dictating product and pricing decisions. In recent years, with an abundance of new products and limits to retail space, retailers have increased their power to influence manufacturers' and wholesalers' actions. Price concessions, shelving fees, and advertising allowances are a few examples of the increased channel power of retailers. Distribution channels are a dynamic part of a marketing system. Members of distribution channels are at the same time resistant to change, trying to maintain their part and power in the system but constantly changing in response to new threats and opportunities.

See also BRANDS, BRAND NAMES; ENTREPRENEURSHIP; RETAILING.

diversification

Diversification has two very different meanings depending on the business context. In personal finance, diversification is investing in a variety of assets. Diversification reduces risk. If one or a few companies go bankrupt, the investor does not lose all his or her assets. Investing in mutual funds that hold financial assets in many companies is one form of diversification. In 2002, Enron, WorldCom, and employees of other companies learned a painful lesson in the value of diversification. Many of these employees had, in addition to their livelihoods, all or most of their retirement funds in company stock. When the companies went bankrupt, they lost both their jobs and their pensions.

In a product/market growth matrix, diversification is expansion of a company into new markets with new products. This strategy for growth is more risky than expanding into new markets with existing products or expansion with new products into existing markets. While business diversification is more risky, if successful, it reduces a firm's business risk because, like personal financial investing, the company is less vulnerable if one product or one market fails. In the 1960s many U.S. conglomerates were formed, owning a diverse array of businesses. Conglomerate strategy was based on the idea that better management and financial backing would yield stronger growth than small, independent firms. In the 1980s and 1990s, many conglomerates, in an effort to become more efficient, sold off divisions, returning to their core business activities.

divestiture   See CORPORATE DIVESTITURE.

dividends, retained earnings

Dividends are a distribution of a corporation's earnings to its stockholders. A CORPORATION can do two things with its earnings: Pay them out in the form of dividends or retain them. Most corporations choose some combination—that is, they pay out a portion of earnings as dividends and retain the rest. A financial ratio called the *dividend payout ratio* measures dividends as a percentage of earnings.

The payment of dividends involves three dates. The first is the declaration date, the day on which the BOARD OF DIRECTORS announces the dividend and the time line for its processing and payment. A LIABILITY, dividends payable, is created by the announcement, and retained earnings are reduced on this date by the amount of the dividend.

Second is the holder-of-record date. The roster of stockholders as of this date determines who will receive the forthcoming dividend. Assume the holder-of-record date is June 24. Several days before June 24, the corporation's stock goes *ex dividend*. Sales of shares after this date will not include the upcoming dividend payment. If an investor buys shares of this stock on June 22, for example, the transaction is too close to the holder-of-record date for the new owner to be listed on the roster of stockholders to receive the dividend. As a result, the new owner will not receive the forthcoming dividend. The new owner is said to have purchased the stock *ex dividend*, that is, without the dividend. When a stock is purchased *ex dividend*, the price paid per share is normally the market price less the dividend not received.

The last date in the time line is the payment date. Checks are cut and mailed, effectively distributing a portion of the firm's earnings. The liability created on the declaration date is satisfied by the payment of cash dividends.

Retained earnings are the corporation's PROFITS not distributed as dividends. The cumulative amount of retained earnings accrues in an EQUITY account of the same name. Retained earnings belong to the stockholders and have the effect of increasing the value of the firm and the WEALTH of the common stockholders. Retained earnings do not usually exist in the form of cash. Rather, most firms use the retained earnings for CAPITAL EXPENDITURES—that is, to purchase ASSETS to foster growth and enhance the firm's profitability.

division of labor (specialization)

Division of labor is a form of specialization in which workers focus their efforts on producing one or a few of the products and services needed for survival and material well-being and then exchange the "fruits" of their labor for other goods and services. Division of labor often involves producing parts of a product or service by dividing workers' efforts into separate tasks. Whether determined collectively as in a family unit or administratively as in a business unit, workers' activities are based on their specialized skills, increasing total output with a given number of people. Managers or family leaders determine how to best allocate labor to maximize output. Division of labor is part of the basis of all modern economies and contrasts with earlier times when isolated individuals or small communities engaged in self-sufficiency in producing all of their requirements for survival.

The benefits of specialization and division of labor are easily demonstrated by the following hypothetical situation. Assume you and your classmates are the only people left on a luxurious island (Nantucket, Hilton Head, Sanibel, Padre, Oahu, Catalina, even Manhattan). Just you and your classmates have free access to all of the homes, businesses, and resources on the island. Will your quality of life be better or worse than it was the day before? Initially, you may "live well" basking in the riches left behind for you but at some point the infrastructure will need work (water, sewer, electricity) or you will need some specialized service (doctor, dentist) that none of you possess. Before long, your standard of living will decline because of the lack of specialized skills needed to provide a quality standard of living.

Drexel professor William King writes that the benefits of division of labor were an essential aspect of the ideas of 18th-century economist Adam Smith: "Like modern economists, Smith believed that the standard of living (the Wealth of a Nation) could rise only if the productivity of labor would rise. For Smith, the most important force leading to a rising standard of living was division of labor.

What most people associate with Adam Smith is the idea of the "invisible hand"; the idea, that is, that free markets restrain prices to some "natural" level and assure the supply of goods and services at the "natural" price. Indeed Smith's discussion of the invisible hand comes quite early in *The Wealth of Nations,* but it is not the first topic Smith takes up. In Smith's logic, it could not be. The very first topic Smith takes up is the division of labor.

Smith argues that increasing the division of labor increases productivity. In one of the most famous passages in the book, Smith illustrates this tendency by a description of work in a pin factory:

> But in the way in which this business is now carried on, not only the whole work is a particular trade, but is divided into a number of branches, of which the greater part are likewise peculiar trades. One man draws out the wire, another straights it, a fourth points it, a fifth grinds it at the top for receiving the head; to make the head requires two or three distinct operations; to put it on, is a particular business, to whiten the pins is another; it is even a trade by itself to put them in the paper; and the important business of making a pin is, in this manner, divided into about eighteen distinct operations, which, in some manufactories, are all performed by distinct hands, though in some others the same man

will sometimes perform two or three of them. I have seen a small manufactory of this kind where only ten men were employed, and where some of them consequently performed two or three distinct operations. But though they were very poor, and therefore but indifferently accommodated with the necessary machinery, they could, when they exerted themselves, make among them about twelve pounds of pins in a day. There are in a pound about four thousand pins of a middling size. Those ten persons, therefore, could make among them upwards of forty-eight thousand pins in a day. But if they had all wrought separately and independently, and without any of them having been educated to this particular business, they certainly could not each of them have made twenty, perhaps not one pin a day; that is, certainly, not the two hundred fortieth, perhaps not the four thousand eight hundredth part of what they are at present capable of performing, in consequence of a proper division and combination of their different operations. (pp. 4–5)

> . . . In the pin factory, each worker is taking a different part of the work, and in doing his part he is working along with—co-oper-ating with—the other workers in the pin factory. Each relies on the others for the part he or she does not do. They take different roles in production, and the roles are complementary. . . .

Smith's first great insight here is that cooperative production increases productivity. "The division of labor . . . occasions, in every art, a proportionable increase in the productive powers of labor. . . . It is the great multiplication of the productions of all the different arts, in consequence of the division of labor, which occasions, in a well-governed society, that universal opulence which extends itself to the lowest ranks of the people" (pp. 5, 11). In short, "In civilized society [one] stands at all times in need of the co-operation and assistance of great multitudes, . . ." (p. 14).

The division of labor into different trades is also an aspect (and perhaps the more important aspect) of the division of labor, according to Smith. "In the lone houses and very small villages which are scattered about in so desert a country as the Highlands of Scotland, every farmer must be butcher, baker and brewer for his own family. . . . A country carpenter deals in every sort of work that is made of wood . . . [he] is not only a carpenter, but a joiner, a cabinet maker, and even a carver in wood, as well as a wheelwright, a ploughwright, a cart and waggon maker" (p. 17). This is in contrast to a more developed region. "Observe the accommodation of the most common artificer or day-laborer in a civilized and thriving country, and you will perceive that the number of people of whose industry a part, though but a small part, has been employed in procuring him his accommodation, exceeds all computation" (p. 11). By accommodation, here, Smith means not only his residence, but also everything he consumes, and the example that Smith gives is his coat. "Conversely, the laborer's work usually will contribute, directly or indirectly, to meeting the needs of many others in society. This division of labor is so characteristic of modern society that we may fail to notice it, as a fish fails to notice the water in which he swims."

While Adam Smith reveled in the benefits of specialization and division of labor, modern economists also acknowledge real or potential costs, including dependence on others, repetitive motion injuries, and boredom from lack of creative input or a lack of a sense of satisfaction from completing a task. Major advances in technology facilitate greater global division of labor but also dependency on the actions of others without a shared sense of community and responsibility to others.

Further reading
Professor William King Web site "Adam Smith on the Division of Labor." Available online. URL: william-king.www.drexel.edu/top/prin/txt/Intro/Eco111g.html. Accessed on May 25, 2009; Smith, Adam. *The Wealth of Nations.* 1776. Reprint, New York: Barnes and Noble, 2004.

document-retention policy
A document-retention policy is a firm's written policies regarding which documents to retain and where and how to retain them. Document-reten-

tion policies serve a number of purposes, including maintaining whatever is needed to conduct business, what is needed for legal and regulatory purposes, and what is needed in case of litigation.

The first rule in creating a document-retention policy is to be constantly saving everything that is needed to conduct business. Following the September 11 tragedy, most companies operating in the World Trade Center were able to reestablish their operations due to continuous data backup systems located elsewhere. Many CORPORATIONS have since reviewed and revised their document-retention systems.

The second rule in document-retention policies is retaining what is required by law. For example, the SECURITIES AND EXCHANGE COMMISSION (SEC) and INTERNAL REVENUE SERVICE (IRS) regulate how long companies and individuals must retain financial documents. The IRS can audit tax-related records for up to seven years back.

The third rule in document-retention policies is to retain anything that may be subject to existing or pending litigation. In the United States, courts usually notify defendant parties when a lawsuit is initiated. Destroying documents once litigation has begun is called "spoilation." Attorney Brett Dorny defines spoilation as "the intentional destruction of evidence that is material to an ongoing or imminent litigation matter." Once litigation has commenced, both sides to a lawsuit engage in discovery, where each party is allowed to interrogate witnesses, take depositions, and request documents from the opposing party.

Discovery often is expensive. In most cases each party to a lawsuit bears its own expenses of discovery, including the costs of producing the documents requested. A well-organized document-retention system can mitigate these costs and allow a firm access to documents needed for its defense. One of the problems associated with document-retention policies is constantly changing technology. Often firms find they cannot easily access old documents saved under different software platforms.

Document-retention policies became widespread in the 1990s and drew public attention in 2002 during the Arthur Andersen LLP-Enron Corporation collapse. In the aftermath, former Arthur Andersen executive David Duncan pleaded guilty to obstruction-of-justice charges. He admitted participating in a meeting where Andersen partners decided to advise staff members assigned to Enron that they should begin implementing the firm's documentation-retention policy. The Andersen policy required personnel to destroy all files that were not supposed to be included in the firm's permanent records, including draft memos that often provide insight into the firm's decision-making process. Duncan testified that another Andersen executive suggested staff members be told to take care to not do "any more or any less" than the document-retention policy required.

The government's case against Andersen was based on the theory that when Andersen partners and employees directed staff members to implement the policy, they knew that an investigation of Andersen's audit of Enron was imminent. Ironically, Arthur Andersen, one of the country's "big five" accounting firms, created a nearly 500-page source book entitled "Document Retention . . . in the Face of Pending or Threatened Litigation," which has been licensed to many Fortune 500 corporations.

Further reading
Dorny, Brett. "Pitfalls for Pack Rats and Purgers." *CIO Magazine* 13, no. 19 (15 July 2000): 64–65; Jonathan Weil and Richard Schmitt, "Andersen Auditor Avoids Testifying," *Wall Street Journal,* 21 May 2002.

do not call registry

The National Do Not Call Registry allows U.S. consumers to opt out of receiving telemarketing calls from a variety of sources. Decried and challenged by marketers in the courts as un-American and infringing on their rights, the Do Not Call Implementation Act of 2003 was passed in response to volumes of complaints about intrusion and high-pressured sales techniques used by telemarketers. Within months, over 20 million Americans had signed up on the registry and, by 2007, over 70 percent of Americans had registered on the list. Telemarketers covered by the National Do Not Call Registry have up to 31 days from the date you register to stop calling you.

The National Do Not Call Registry is managed by the FEDERAL TRADE COMMISSION (FTC), and is enforced by the FTC, the FEDERAL COMMUNICATIONS COMMISSION (FCC), and state law enforcement officials. The registry was created to offer consumers a choice regarding telemarketing calls. The registry is only for personal phone numbers. Business-to-business calls and faxes are not covered by the National Do Not Call Registry. The FTC's decision to create the Do Not Call Registry marked the culmination of a three-year review of the Telemarketing Sales Rule (TSR). The FTC held numerous workshops, meetings, and briefings to solicit feedback from interested parties and considered over 64,000 public comments, most of which favored creating the registry.

Consumers can register online at www.donotcall.gov. Telemarketers are required to search the registry every 31 days and delete from their call lists phone numbers that are in the registry. Phone numbers in the registry also may be shared with law enforcement to assure compliance with federal and state laws. About every two years, e-mail messages circulate telling consumers that their cell phone is about to be assaulted by telemarketing calls. FCC regulations prohibit telemarketers from using automated dialers (speed dialers) to call cell phone numbers. Automated dialers are standard in the industry, so most telemarketers don't call consumers on their cell phones without their consent.

Registering your phone with the Do Not Call list does not stop all telemarketing solicitations. Calls from, or on behalf of, political organizations, charities, and telephone surveyors are still permitted, as are calls from companies with which you have an existing business relationship, or those to whom you've provided express agreement in writing to receive their calls. By purchasing something from the company, you established a business relationship with the company. As a result, even if you put your number on the National Do Not Call Registry, that company may call you for up to 18 months after your last purchase or delivery from it, or your last payment to it, unless you ask the company not to call again. In that case, the company must honor your request not to call. If they subsequently call you again, they may be subject to a fine of up to $11,000. An established business relationship with a company also will be created if you make an inquiry to the company, or submit an application to it. This kind of established business relationship exists for three months after the inquiry or application. During this time, the company can call you.

The Direct Marketing Association maintains a free Do Not Mail list for consumers who do not want to receive junk mail. A sign up for the list is available at www.directmail.com/directory/mail_preference/. The three major credit card companies maintain lists for consumers who do not wish to receive credit card offers. Some consumer advisers recommend signing up for this list as one way to reduce identity theft and fraudulent credit card activity. The link to the list is available below.

Further reading
Federal Trade Commission Web site. Available online. URL: www.ftc.gov. Credit card offer opt out link. URL: www.optoutprescreen.com/?rf=t.

dot-coms

Dot-coms are businesses that operate primarily or solely on the INTERNET. The term *dot-com* comes from the suffix for business domain names (.com). Dot-coms compete with traditional store-based businesses (called "bricks and mortar"), providing alternatives to consumer and business markets. Dot-coms have been more successful in fulfilling the needs of business customers who make repeat purchases of similar items and need relatively little customer assistance in making purchase decisions.

Because there are relatively low start-up costs associated with many dot-com businesses, the industry has attracted a wide array of entrepreneurs. In the late 1990s, the United States experienced a dot-com frenzy. Any business with even a whimsical Internet MARKETING STRATEGY was able to register a domain name and begin promoting itself as a global enterprise. Initially dot-coms used registration with Internet search engines and traditional media promotion to attract visitors and potential customers to their sites. Some dot-coms then used their click-rates (number of visitors to the site) to sell banner ADVERTISING to other dot-coms. Other early dot-coms also offered wireless modems, specialty hand-held gadgets, and Internet currencies for consumer purchases.

One dot-com offered up to 100-percent rebates for highly overpriced merchandise, betting few customers would collect the paperwork necessary for reimbursement. Another company's hand-held device offered entertainment and dining listings. When the company went bankrupt, the devices, which were not compatible with other hand-held technology, became worthless. The possibilities seemed endless, and almost any dot-com entrepreneur could find financial backing. INITIAL PUBLIC OFFERINGS (IPOs) of dot-coms created huge sums of money for businesses with meager sales and no PROFITS. Many companies with an Internet strategy changed their names, adding dot-com, hoping to attract investor interest and stock-price escalation.

The industry coined the term *burn rate* to quantify the rate the dot-com was using up investor CAPITAL in their quest for profitability. In March 2000 the dot-com "bubble" burst as investors finally recognized the lack of earnings and lack of prospects for future earnings among the vast majority of dot-coms. Media reports described the demise of dot-com millionaires whose paper WEALTH vanished as stock prices dwindled.

Many successful dot-coms use drop-shipping (taking orders from customers and then forwarding them to producers that ship directly to customers) along with traditional wholesaling channels to offer a wide array of products while maintaining minimal inventory. Amazon.com became the most successful dot-com using this business model.

See also ENTREPRENEURSHIP.

Further reading
Kaplan, Karen. "On Junk Heap of the Net," *Los Angeles Times*, 1 October 2001, p. 1.

double-entry accounting   See FINANCIAL ACCOUNTING.

Dow Jones averages

Dow Jones averages are the most widely quoted INDICATORS of the U.S. STOCK MARKET. There are three Dow Jones averages: industrials, transportation, and utilities. The Dow Jones Industrial Average (DJIA) is the oldest and best-known indicator.

In 1882 Charles Dow, Edward Jones, and Charles Bergstresser began producing a market newsletter delivered by messenger to subscribers in the WALL STREET area of New York. At the time the stock market was not highly regarded, being perceived as the province of speculators and market manipulators. Dow, Jones, and Bergstresser provided information to investors, and in 1884 they created their first index with 11 stocks, mostly railroad companies. Their business grew, and the newsletter quickly became a newspaper that would be called the *Wall Street Journal.*

In 1896 Dow Jones created their industrial average. At the time it included 12 stocks. The DJIA was calculated by adding up the closing price of these companies and dividing by 12. On May 26, 1896, the DJIA was 40.94. The average was increased to include 20 stocks in 1916 and 30 stocks in 1928. While the number of stocks in the DJIA has remained constant since then, the companies included in the index change infrequently. The editors of the *Wall Street Journal* select which stocks are included in the industrial average. The definition of "industrial" has changed as the U.S. economy has shifted away from primarily manufacturing to, increasingly, a service economy. Any stock (other than utility and transportation companies, which are included in the other Dow Jones averages) can be considered for inclusion in the index. In 1999 four companies—Union Carbide, Goodyear Tire & Rubber, Sears Roebuck, and Chevron—were removed from the DJIA, and Home Depot, Intel, Microsoft, and SBC Communications were added. In 2009 General Motors and Citibank were replaced with Travelers Insurance and Cisco Systems in the DJIA. A few companies have been added and deleted more than once, including General Electric, DuPont, U.S. Rubber, and IBM.

Changes to the index usually occur when a company is acquired by another company eliminating that stock from the market. While almost all other stock-market indexes are weighted by the market capitalization (price times the number of shares outstanding) of the stocks included in the index, the DJIA is an unweighted index. The DJIA is a relatively narrow indicator of the U.S. stock market, but because it is the oldest index, it is the most widely quoted. While it is well known, changes in the DJIA are neither a reliable indicator of future stock market changes nor a reliable predictor of changes in the economy. Generally changes in the stock market precede changes in the economy, but not always and not exactly by the same amount of lead time.

The Dow Jones Transportation Average (DJTA) and utilities average (DJUA) are, as their names indicate, industry-sector averages. Stock-market analysts use changes in the transportation and utilities averages as indicators of change in the larger market.

Dow Jones is a leading U.S. financial information service company. In addition to publishing the *Wall Street Journal,* they publish *Barrons, Far Eastern Economic Review,* Dow Jones newswires, and WSJ.com.

Further reading
Dow Jones Web site. Available online. URL: www. dowjones.com.

downsizing

Downsizing is the reduction of staffing levels necessitated by business reasons such as low sales or low profits. The number of employees required to build products is a variable expense directly related to the number of units being built. So if fewer people are on the company's payroll, labor expense is reduced, resulting in stabilized or increased profits.

People are a primary resource in virtually all businesses. People perform work necessary to the firm's success. Having either too few or too many employees may result in lower operating efficiencies and lower profits for the business. Determining the number of employees needed to operate the business is a primary management responsibility.

The following employee planning process is for a manufacturing firm; however, the process for a service company is virtually the same. With the best business forecast available, management estimates by product line the number of units that are projected to be sold over a time period of six months or more. Projected sales are totaled and existing finished goods inventory is subtracted to determine the number of units that need to be manufactured. Using existing manufacturing standards, by type of job and work station, management then estimates the number of positions needed and the requisite knowledge, skills, abilities (KSAs), and experience. After the positions, KSAs, and experience levels are identified, the employees are evaluated to determine which ones have the required background to perform the work. In the aggregate, if there are fewer employees than needed, new employees are hired; if there are more employees than needed, downsizing occurs.

The downsizing process can occur in several ways. If the sales forecasts, initially used by management to plan production levels, project a protracted slump in sales (that may last for a year or more), then those employees not needed are usually terminated. If the sales slump is expected to be relatively short and then sales are expected to rebound, then excess employees are usually laid-off. When an individual is laid-off, the assumption is that the person will be needed back within a reasonable period of time. The return to work process is known as a recall. A termination assumes that the employee will not return to work at that company.

Attrition is an attractive alternative to downsizing. Attrition occurs when an individual leaves a company's employment through either a voluntary resignation or being terminated for reasons other than low sales or low profits. The position is vacant, but the company does not fill the position with a newly hired employee. Total number of employees will decrease; however, this process is very slow and will not reduce the total number as quickly as downsizing.

—John B. Abbott

due diligence

Due diligence refers to any in-depth investigation, review, or effort to comply with requirements, expectations, or requests. The phrase originated in U.S. securities law. The laws require companies and the accountants, lawyers, and bankers who assist in the process issuing securities to provide accurate information about the securities. The company and its accountants, lawyers, and bankers must show that they were careful in complying with the disclosure requirements of these laws. The courts said that these groups must show due diligence in their efforts to comply with the law.

The phrase is now applied to any situation where in-depth information about a company is needed. For example, U.S. banking laws designed to reduce money laundering require banks to really know their customers fully, not just on a superficial level. To do this, banks employ due diligence to learn all they can about their clients, including such things as credit checks and background checks on a company's officers.

Due diligence also describes the procedure before one company buys another. It is common for the buyer and seller to agree on the selling price and other aspects of the deal based solely on the information the seller provides about the company. After both parties agree on a price, they have a due diligence period that allows the buyer and seller to check out the details of the transaction, ensuring that all the information is complete and accurate.

Due diligence can thus be interpreted as "to check something out to make sure it is true." Today it is often used just this way within a company. For example, a company adopts a tentative business plan to take a new initiative, such as starting a new product line. Before implementing the plan, a due diligence period will ensure its validity and check all its details.

due process

Under the Fifth and Fourteenth Amendments of the U.S. Constitution, everyone is guaranteed legal due process (fair treatment) under certain circumstances. There are two major subcomponents: procedural due process and substantive due process. Procedural due process refers to the constitutional provisions that prohibit federal and state governments from depriving persons of life, liberty, or property without a fair legal process. Substantive due process refers to the constitutional provisions that require all laws, federal and state, to be reasonable.

The Fifth Amendment to the U.S. Constitution, the part of the Bill of Rights that includes the due-process principle, applies only to the federal government—that is, it prohibits the federal government from violating the requirements of due process. In 1833, in the landmark case of *Barron v. Baltimore,* the U.S. Supreme Court determined that the Bill of Rights applied only to the federal government. However, due process, as provided in the Fifth Amendment, applies to state governments via the Fourteenth Amendment to the constitution, which is also known as the due-process clause.

The Fourteenth Amendment's due-process clause allows several provisions of the Bill of Rights to be applicable to state governmental conduct, including the Fifth Amendment's due-process provision. The Fourteenth Amendment's due-process clause "incorporates" several of the provisions of the Bill of Rights and makes them applicable to state governments. Thus, this function of the Fourteenth Amendment is known as incorporation.

The principles of due process under the Fifth and Fourteenth Amendments are very similar. However, a due-process case involving federal governmental conduct must be brought before the court by using the Fifth Amendment as the basis for the case, whereas a due-process case involving state governmental conduct must be brought before the court by using the Fourteenth Amendment. Failure to refer to the appropriate amendments in a due-process action may lead to the case being delayed or dismissed.

Procedural due process deals with the fairness of criminal and civil proceedings. Fair legal process generally includes providing notice of the proceeding to the relevant parties, bringing the case before an impartial tribunal or arbiter, and providing the parties with an opportunity to present evidence before the tribunal or arbiter hearing the case.

First, when a private, nongovernmental party deprives another of life, liberty or property, there is no due-process claim. However, there may be some other criminal or civil claim against that party, such as false imprisonment, theft, or WRONGFUL DISCHARGE. Corporate human resource managers often are involved with employee terminations in order to document that due process procedures were followed.

Second, if the deprivation involves something other than life, liberty, or property, there is no due-process claim. The U.S. Supreme Court is in charge of interpreting the meaning of "life, liberty, and property" for due-process purposes. The definitions of "liberty" and "property" have undergone periods of being both broadly and narrowly defined by the court, depending on the political climate or the sociopolitical beliefs of the majority of the court's justices.

When a federal or state government attempts to deprive a person of life, liberty, or property, some sort of fair legal process is required. However, whether the process is required before or after the deprivation occurs depends on the severity of the deprivation. The more severe the deprivation, the more likely predeprivation notice and a hearing will be required to satisfy procedural due process.

"Liberty" is defined as a significant freedom provided by the U.S. Constitution or state laws, including the right to CONTRACT, the right to engage in gainful EMPLOYMENT, the right to be free from unjustified intrusions of personal security, and the right to refuse medical treatment. One recent due process issue is employers' and employees' rights regarding use of a company's computer.

"Property" is defined as an entitlement right—that is, an interest that a person may reasonably expect to receive on a continuing basis. State laws may also create property interests, and where this is the case, those interests may not be terminated without procedural due process. The definition of property includes common-sense possessions such as PERSONAL PROPERTY, real property (land), and money, but it also encompasses less obvious interests such as

- the continued receipt of WELFARE benefits. If the government wishes to terminate a person's welfare benefits, there must be a pre-termination hearing that approves the termination.
- uninterrupted public education. When a public school attempts to suspend a student, that student must be given notice of the charges and an opportunity to explain his side.
- continued public employment. A public employee who has tenure, or who reasonably believes that his employment may be terminated only on sufficient grounds for termination, may not be terminated from employment without notice and a hearing.

Another component of due process, substantive due process, concerns the substance of laws. Substantive due process prohibits federal and state governments from creating laws that unreasonably infringe upon a person's fundamental rights and freedoms (generally involving matters related to sexual relations, marriage, bearing children, and child rearing). When a law restricts or regulates a person's fundamental rights, the court applies a standard called *strict scrutiny* in evaluating the validity of the law under substantive due process. Under strict-scrutiny evaluation, the government must prove to the court that the law is necessary to achieve a compelling state interest. As its name implies, strict scrutiny is very strict in its application and usually serves to invalidate state laws. Security changes since September 11, 2001, have redefined many areas of due process law.

Due process is still an evolving concept, and its boundaries will no doubt be continually tested in the U.S. Supreme Court in the future.

Further reading
Tribe, Laurence H. *American Constitutional Law.* 2d ed. Mineola, N.Y.: The Foundation Press, 2001.
—Gayatri Gupta

dumping

Dumping, in its most frequently used meaning, involves the sale of goods or SERVICES in a foreign market at prices that are below those in the seller's home country. Popular reports often refer to a specific country as the offending party, but in fact dumping is generally practiced by private businesses.

Dumping can also be viewed as PRICE DISCRIMINATION or predatory pricing. Price discrimination is the practice of charging different groups of consumers different prices for the same product or service. Price discrimination is based on market considerations, consumers' willingness and ability to pay for a product, and differences in price ELASTICITY OF DEMAND among consumer groups. Generally price discrimination is not against the law in the United States, but when done internationally, price discrimination and dumping appear to be very similar practices.

Predatory pricing is a pricing strategy where low prices are used to drive weaker competitors out of a market. Once the competitors have been eliminated (they are often sold to larger companies), the predatory-pricing firm can raise its prices and earn higher PROFITS. When practiced in international trade, predatory pricing can result in antidumping claims being filed by businesses and industries hurt by the actions of the exporting company. In the United States, the domestic steel industry has often filed charges of dumping against international competitors.

Dumping can also be the result of government subsidies to exporters, which artificially reduce the cost of production. Governments often subsidize export industries in order to create domestic jobs and INCOME. Consumers in importing countries benefit from lower-priced products, subsidized by foreign governments, but domestic producers are forced to compete on an unfair basis. Domestic businesses then ask their government to invoke antidumping statutes.

Antidumping laws have evolved since World War II through each "Round" of General Agreement on Tariffs and Trade (GATT) negotiations and through regional trade agreements such as the NORTH AMERICAN FREE TRADE AGREEMENT (NAFTA). Since the Uruguay Round in 1993, antidumping action can be brought against an importer if sales are at "less than fair value" and "material injury to a domestic industry" occurs. These phrases are open to interpretation, which has resulted in many dumping claims and counterclaims.

In the United States, dumping charges are forwarded to the U.S. INTERNATIONAL TRADE COMMISSION (ITC) for consideration. The ITC investigates PROFIT margins of the exporter in their home country versus in the United States and whether the exporter has injured or potentially could injure an existing U.S. industry. If the ITC concludes that dumping has occurred, representatives from the country are contacted to remedy the situation. If no agreement is reached, the U.S. president can order higher TARIFFS be placed on products from the offending country. While individual firms and industries are accused of dumping, government-to-government negotiations and dispute-resolution mechanisms are used to resolve dumping claims.

Another use of the term *dumping* refers to the selling of securities in financial markets. If a seller orders the sale of a large number of securities at whatever price he or she can get, the seller is said to have "dumped" the securities in the market.

Further reading
Folsom, Ralph H., and W. Davis Folsom. *Understanding NAFTA and Its International Business Implications.* New York: Matthew Bender/Irwin, 1996; Hill, Charles W. L. *Global Business Today.* New York: Irwin/McGraw-Hill, 1999.

—Gayatri Gupta

Dun & Bradstreet reports
Dun & Bradstreet (D&B) reports provide information about the creditworthiness of businesses around the world. D&B reports are the most widely used financial reports used by businesses in the United States in determining credit, marketing, purchasing, and receivables management decisions. D&B dominates the commercial credit-

data market. Many corporate financial officers rely solely on D&B reports to make credit decisions.

Created in 1841, Dun & Bradstreet is a long-established U.S. business that maintains files of information on more than 10 million firms worldwide. D&B analysts gather data by reviewing customer-supplied information, INTERVIEWING company executives, examining public documents about businesses, and reviewing credit references.

Over 100,000 companies use D&B reports to

- target market prospective companies
- assess risk of doing business with other companies
- set credit terms
- define collections methods for credit
- analyze COMPETITION
- evaluate potential vendors

Having a D&B report is often a prerequisite for doing business with major U.S. CORPORATIONS. Business managers tend to be RISK averse, not wanting to be surprised by either competitors or suppliers. Bankruptcy of an important supplier can create chaos and be costly to a company. Financial reports like those D&B supplies are used to reduce uncertainty.

D&B reports typically include a summary BALANCE SHEET, an INCOME STATEMENT, and a payments record indicating how timely the firm has been paying its bills. Background information about the company, its history, facilities, owners, litigation, bankruptcies, and settlements are also included.

D&B also published MOODY'S RATINGS, reports focusing on the status and details of corporate securities, but in 2000, Moody's was separated into its own publicly traded company.

Further reading
Dun & Bradstreet Web site. Available online. URL: www.dnb.com.

duration
Duration is a measure of interest-rate RISK (bond price volatility) that includes both the coupon rate and the time to maturity of the bond. Most BONDS,

both government and corporate debt instruments, are issued with a fixed interest rate (the coupon rate) for a set period of time (maturity). Duration incorporates both these features. A weighted average of each of the coupon payments plus final payment (return of principal) at the maturity date, duration is calculated by the formula

$$D = \frac{PB\,(t)}{PB}$$

where:

D = duration of the bond
PB = price of the bond = $\sum CF_t/(1 + i)^t$
CF = coupon or principal payment at time t
  i = interest rate
  t = time period in which the principal or coupon payment is made

In the formula, duration is the present value of all cash flows discounted according to the length of time until they are received and divided by the price of the bond, which is the present value of all cash flows.

Duration is directly related to maturity and inversely related to the coupon rate. The longer the time until maturity, the higher the duration, and the higher the coupon rate, the lower the duration. Since duration measures interest rate risk, financial managers can match the duration of their ASSETS and liabilities. Thus if INTEREST RATES rise (causing a decline in bond prices), decline values of financial assets will be offset by declining costs of liabilities. During the 1980s, many SAVINGS AND LOAN ASSOCIATION managers, faced with increased competition for deposits from nonbank financial institutions (particularly stock brokerage firms), used short-term deposits to finance long-term LOANS. When interest rates continued to rise, the value of their assets (loans) declined while their liabilities did not decrease, contributing to the S&L crisis.

Further reading

Kidwell, David S., David W. Blackwell, David A. Whidbee, and Richard L. Peterson. *Financial Institutions, Markets and Money.* 10th ed. Hoboken, N.J.: John Wiley & Sons, 2008.

earnings management

Earnings management is the controversial practice among publicly held corporations of adjusting the timing of reporting certain revenues and expenses by the company. In recent years, under pressure to meet WALL STREET analysts' earnings estimates, many U.S. corporations have deferred expense recognition or counted as revenue funds from sales that have not been fully completed. In 2000 the SECURITIES AND EXCHANGE COMMISSION (SEC), sensing an increase in abusive earnings-management practices, proposed new Supplemental Financial Information rules to address these abuses. The SEC recognized such problems were largely caused by a lack of transparency (openness and easily understood) in financial reporting, including problems associated with

- failure to comply with the disclosure requirements for changes in accrued liabilities for certain costs to exit an activity during periods subsequent to the initial charge
- grouping dissimilar items into an aggregated classification
- recurring "nonrecurring" charges
- inadequate disclosure of changes in estimates and in underlying assumptions during the period of change
- inconsistent application of SEC-required disclosures of valuation and loss accruals

- insufficient information about expected useful lives, changes in useful lives, and salvage values of long-lived ASSETS

A company's failure to comply with disclosure rules for changes in accrued liabilities can increase or decrease reported net INCOME. Information explaining changes provides investors with better estimates of present and future obligations. Grouping dissimilar items into an aggregated category has sometimes been used by companies to conceal something that is unfavorable and potentially a risk for investors. Reporting "recurring" charges as nonrecurring charges can be a misrepresentation of costs. Typical nonrecurring charges include restructured charges, merger expenses, and write-down of impaired assets. Investors assume nonrecurring charges are one-time costs, not costs that will have to be included in the future. Inadequate disclosure of changes in estimates is often associated with bad debt estimates or product returns. Increases in bad debt or product-return allowances reduce corporate income, but without adequate information, investors cannot easily assess the significance of the change being made. Inconsistent application of SEC-required disclosures of valuation and loss accruals is often associated with the value of future income-tax benefits. Lack of consistency in valuation can lead to over- and under-statements of net income. During the late 1990s, many of these problems were particularly evident among DOT-COMS attempting reach profitability or minimize losses and operating in markets where rapidly changing technology made standard depreciation allowances subject to considerable variation.

A related issue is the use of "pro forma" earnings. Companies issue pro forma (projected) earnings by adjusting net earnings reported using GENERALLY ACCEPTED ACCOUNTING PRINCIPLES (GAAP). Pro forma earnings exclude items such as restructuring charges, employee severance expenses, and write-offs of fixed assets that have declined in value (impairment charges). This increases a company's earnings and makes it look better to investors. The problem is there are no definitions of what pro forma earnings include or exclude. Thus investors looking at companies' pro forma earnings cannot easily compare them. In December 2001 the SEC warned companies they could face civil-FRAUD lawsuits for issuing misleading earnings numbers, and directed companies to fully explain how their pro forma results are calculated.

See also LEVERAGE; PROFITS.

Further reading

Cassell Bryan-Low, "Pro Forma Forecasts Are Hard to Decipher for Investors," *Wall Street Journal,* 28 May 2002, c1, Securities and Exchange Commission Web site. Available online. URL: www.sec.gov; Stanko, Brian B. "Improving Financial Reporting and Disclosure," *Business & Economic Review* 47, no. 4 (July–August, 2001).

e-business

The term *e-business* is often used synonymously with the term *e-commerce*. Technically e-business is a broader term that encompasses not only e-commerce but, importantly, all the internal processes of an organization—such as production, inventory, and HUMAN RESOURCES—that become digitally based functions. This often necessitates a rethinking of every aspect of the business. When the organization establishes its strategy and goals to include e-business concepts, the result is often a radical redesign of how the entire organization conducts business.

The entire business/economic environment has changed with the evolution of e-business and the introduction of digital-based design (DBD) models; many have described the new environment as dynamic, rapid, and reinventive. The speed at which information is exchanged globally has also increased the intensity and fierceness of business COMPETITION. Many companies have begun to think about competitors as partners in order to ensure their own survival. At the very least, many such businesses are building alliances and/or collaborating with competitors for survival.

E-business strategy involves system-wide integration from suppliers through customers. This entails many aspects within the organization and its interface with other organizations with whom it has a business relationship. Specifically, online sharing of information with customers, suppliers, manufacturers, and partners is an integral part of e-business. Terms such as enterprise-resource planning (ERP), CUSTOMER-RELATIONSHIP MANAGEMENT (CRM), supply-chain management (SCM), and KNOWLEDGE MANAGEMENT (KM) are common in e-business.

ERP integrates the entire organization's resource planning, payroll and accounting, inventory, PURCHASING, manufacturing, marketing, distribution, and so forth into one digitally based management system. ERP changes the way that almost everyone in every department in the organization does his/her job.

CRM involves all possible encounters with the customer. Designing a fully integrated system throughout the entire organization, regardless of the source of the interface, is often done with a call center. Interface originating online (e-mail and order form) or through telephone contacts resulting from catalogs or store visits can be handled from one location. This is sometimes achieved regionally or nationally to achieve economies.

Marketing is another area that has substantially changed with e-business. Use of the computer allows information tracking that has not been easily done with past processes. One-to-one marketing with individualized promotions targeted to the specific customer's needs has emerged because detailed information about the customer and his/her buying habits, interests, and so forth are readily available with data gathered online. Banners, affiliate programs, and links to promote the organization are new channels of marketing possible with e-business. Viral marketing, e-mail messages designed to encourage recipients to forward the message to their friends and colleagues, is an important aspect of an overall marketing strategy. Multichannel marketing, such as Web, catalog, and storefront, is linked and piggybacked. The newest marketing approach emerging as e-business matures is the use of social media, i.e. social networks, blogs, wikis, and so forth, to promote a company and its products.

Knowledge management changes the way information is gathered, shared, and disseminated throughout the entire organization and with customers, suppliers, manufacturers, and partners. The term *collaborative commerce* is being used to identify this information exchange on-line with business partners.

Supply-chain management (SCM) involves the information exchange about product flow and services, from suppliers, through the organization, and ultimately to customers and end users, i.e., the consumers. System compatibility becomes a major issue for this aspect of conducting e-business.

Overall, e-business requires structural changes in the way organizations conduct business. The sharing of information and resources across the organization changes the way people do their jobs. This also changes the relationship of the organization with other businesses for full integration to occur. Because it breaks down barriers and often necessitates a radical cultural shift for the organization, e-business changes the entire way that an organization conducts business. This new approach needs to be integrated into the strategy of the organization for successful implementation to occur.

See also INTERNET MARKETING.

—Leanne McGrath

e-commerce

Although the terms *e-business* and *e-commerce* are frequently used interchangeably, e-commerce is actually one component of e-business. Generally e-commerce covers the aspects of conducting business transactions via the INTERNET. This would include on-line marketing, sales, processing orders, customer issues, and supplier issues. From using the Internet, both business-to-business (B2B) and business-to-customer (B2C) relationships have evolved from traditional forms into a digital interface. To the extent that this interface involves sales and sales support and the exchange of goods and services for money or BARTER, it is defined as e-commerce.

An integral part of e-commerce is the Web site on the World Wide Web. There are various levels for which a company may use its Web site. The simplest level entails ADVERTISING an informational presence and display of products worldwide. Intermediate levels would be adding such features as e-mail and/or data-driven capabilities. The most complex level constitutes e-commerce, comprising a fully functional storefront that allows ordering and payment capability on-line. The latter requires addressing issues for payment security for the customer. Options for ordering on-line include CREDIT CARDS, electronic wallets, electronic cash, and smart cards.

A secure server protects information that is stored on it, and for some businesses like banks or investment brokers, this issue is a mandatory requirement for the customer. Use of encryption, for example a two-key public key system, protects the customer's information while it is being transmitted across the Internet.

The success of an e-commerce Web site includes development of effective INTERNET MARKETING for the Web site. Attracting traffic and building customers involve adding some new approaches to the traditional marketing approach. These include use of banners, links to other Web sites, affiliate programs, viral marketing, search-engine registration, and social media. The use of one-to-one marketing has become common because of the ease with which data can be accumulated, sorted, weighted, and evaluated through use of the computer. This one-to-one approach allows specific tailoring of SALES PROMOTIONS to the individual's need or area of interest. Of course, customer consent to gather and use personal information should be acquired before using this promotional technique. Including a policy statement on an e-commerce site concerning use of information gathered helps create a vital comfort level for the customer.

When a bricks-and-mortar company also establishes a presence on the Web, the term "bricks and clicks" is often applied to define the new multichannel e-commerce venture. Some businesses, however, exist only on the Web. For example, Amazon.com does not have any physical retail outlets. It conducts only e-commerce and exists as an e-business, utilizing its computer software for all aspects of its existence. In contrast, Talbots.com is a "bricks and clicks" example, with physical stores, a catalog, and an Internet presence.

See also DOT-COMS.

—Leanne McGrath

economic conditions

Economic conditions are the current state of the economy and are usually characterized by macroeconomic measures, including aggregate output, INFLATION, UNEMPLOYMENT, and INTEREST RATES.

Aggregate output is measured by GROSS DOMESTIC PRODUCT (GDP). Changes in aggregate output and changes in aggregate INCOME are closely related. Changes in GDP are the most widely watched measure of current economic conditions. The U.S. Department of Commerce issues monthly estimates of percentage change in GDP. Changes in GDP result in changes in DEMAND for natural resources, workers, and credit, causing prices to rise or fall.

Declining GDP reduces DEMAND for oil and in LABOR MARKETS, and it tends to reduce interest rates. Because the United States is the largest economy in the world, changes in U.S. economic conditions impact industries and economies globally. OPEC (Organization of Petroleum Exporting Countries) oil ministers know expanding or declining output in the United States directly affects demand for oil. Major trading partners of the United States are also affected by changing conditions in the United States. One exaggeration frequently used is: "If the United States sneezes, the world economy gets a cold."

As changes in aggregate output/income cause changes in demand, the overall level of prices, inflation, also changes, and as inflation changes, interest rates change. Inflation causes lenders to demand higher interest rates to compensate them for the reduced purchasing power associated with inflation.

Changes in output also cause changes in demand for workers. Cyclical unemployment is unemployment caused by changes in BUSINESS CYCLES, the ups and downs of economic activity. A 1-percent decrease in GDP results in over a million jobs lost in the U.S. economy.

Economic conditions are usually evaluated using leading and coincident INDICATORS. Coincident indicators change at the same time as changes in real output in the economy. Coincident indicators include

- payroll employment
- industrial production
- personal income
- manufacturing and trade sales

Leading indicators project future economic conditions. Leading indicators of the U.S. economy include

- average workweek
- UNEMPLOYMENT claims
- manufacturers' new orders
- stock prices
- new plant and equipment orders
- new building permits
- delivery times of goods
- interest-rate spread
- money supply
- consumer expectations

STOCK MARKET reporters frequently say, "The stock market anticipates changes in the economy." Historically, the U.S. stock market has gone up or down six to eight months in advance of changes in economic conditions. Similarly, consumer expectations are measured by the University of Michigan's Consumer Expectations Index and the CONFERENCE BOARD's Consumer Confidence Index.

See also MACROECONOMICS.

Further reading

Boyes, William, and Michael Melvin. *Macroeconomics.* 7th ed. Boston: Houghton Mifflin, 2007; Conference Board Web site. Available online. URL: www.conference-board.org.

economic development

Economic development is the process by which a country's economic system changes. This includes ECONOMIC GROWTH, an increase in a country's output, and changes in resource allocation and control, improvement in a country's INFRASTRUCTURE, and expansion of CAPITAL formation. Economic development occurs in all countries but is most closely associated with the process of change in poorer countries. Development economists study the process by which countries' economic systems grow or fail to grow, labeling them lesser-developed, underdeveloped, or developing economies.

To understand economic development, consider first the circle of poverty: low INCOME leads to low levels of savings, which leads to low levels of investment, which leads to low levels of income. In many developing countries, few households have sufficient income to save. If savings were available, households could choose to send their children to schools, expanding human capital and the productivity of future generations. With savings, farmers could purchase new equipment, seeds, simple tools, or storage bins to improve their productivity, but with only subsistence levels of income, most households in poorer countries cannot afford to save.

Development economists ask the question, "Why are some countries so much poorer than others?" Obviously some areas of the world are endowed with greater quantities of natural resources and more hospitable climates, but geographic differences only explain some of the differences in economic development among countries. Differences in political and social systems also contribute to explaining differences in economic development. One of the roles of a government in a capitalist economic system is to define and enforce property rights. Without control over their resources, households cannot effectively and efficiently allocate RESOURCES. Many resource-allocation decisions involve a long-term commitment of resources, which, if undermined by political instability, encourages people with portable resources, knowledge, and financial capital to seek alternatives elsewhere. With political instability, owners of land and other nonportable resources will attempt to extract as much income as possible in the short term, often at the expense of SUSTAINABLE GROWTH AND DEVELOPMENT of their resources.

Social customs and practices also influence economic development. Social systems that encourage maintaining existing social structures and customs such as limitations on work roles based on gender, restrictions to access to education, or nonacceptance of entrepreneurial efforts influence economic development. Corruption adds to the cost of doing business, limiting resource and business development.

Countries pursuing economic development typically adopt one or more of three strategies: primary production, import-substitution-industrialization, or export promotion. Many Mideast countries have developed their primary natural resources, oil and natural gas, as a means to economic growth and development. The kingdom of Saudi Arabia, until the 1930s a series of small tribal groups, grew rapidly with a joint agreement to extract oil from its land with ARAMCO (Arab American Oil Company), a consortium of U.S. oil companies. ARAMCO provided the capital and technology to develop Saudi Arabia's natural resources. MULTINATIONAL CORPORATIONS (MNCs) frequently participate in primary production development around the world. Supporters argue that without foreign capital and technology, developing countries would not be able to expand development of their primary products.

Supporters contend MNCs are an agent of change and modernization. Critics argue that MNCs align themselves with the political elite in developing countries, maintaining the status quo, and once the primary products are depleted, they leave the developing country, sometimes in worse economic and environmental condition than when it arrived.

A second development strategy is import-substitution-industrialization (ISI). This strategy focuses on replacing previously imported products with domestically produced substitutes. Many developing countries have assisted domestic industry development through combinations of low-cost capital and TARIFFS on competing imported products. ISI development can stimulate domestic production and income but has two inherent problems: market limits and lack of COMPETITION. The assisted producers can produce for the domestic market, but if the market is small, they may not be able to achieve ECONOMIES OF SCALE. Domestic producers protected from global competition often will produce goods of sufficient quality to sell domestically but not up to global standards, when or if the company tries to expand internationally. Mexican leaders, fearful of U.S. economic dominance, pursued ISI development in the 1960s and 1970s. Only in the 1980s, after a series of economic collapses, did Mexico move away from ISI and gradually toward export promotion.

Since the 1950s, many developing countries, particularly the so-called Asian Tigers (Japan, Korea, Hong Kong, Taiwan, and Singapore), have stimulated economic growth and development through export promotion. With government support and subsidies, domestic producers are encouraged to produce output for sale in global markets. Although export promotion requires producers to meet world-class standards, is vulnerable to changing prices and FOREIGN EXCHANGE problems, and requires access to major markets, it has been a successful development strategy for many countries. At some point government subsidies have to be withdrawn, which has created problems for many countries and companies.

Critical to economic development is access to capital. There are five general ways businesses and governments pursuing economic development acquire capital. Foreign direct investment (FDI), the development of factories or purchase of interests in existing businesses, is sometimes encouraged and sometimes discouraged. One of the major features of the NORTH AMERICAN FREE TRADE AGREEMENT (NAFTA) was the reduction in restrictions on FDI in Mexico. In the 1990s, portfolio INVESTMENT became an increasingly popular way to raise capital, particularly in countries like Mexico, where there was some existing level of industrialization. U.S. investors, often pursuing diversification, bought shares of stock or AMERICAN DEPOSITORY RECEIPTS in business around the world. Before the expansion of portfolio investment, commercial bank LOANS were a major source of capital for development. In the 1980s, U.S. banks were close to bankruptcy when loans to foreign businesses and governments failed. In 2008, international credit markets froze, creating panic in markets around the globe. Trade credit, the extension of short-term loans by exporters to importers, is often an important source of capital to businesses in developing countries. Foreign aid acts as a source of capital, mostly for governments in developing countries. The WORLD BANK and the U.S. AGENCY FOR INTERNATIONAL DEVELOPMENT are major sources of foreign aid for economic development.

In a World Bank study, "Where Is the Wealth of Nations?" economists found that "intangible" factors including trust among people in a society, an efficient judicial system, clear property rights, and effective government significantly affect the level of economic development. The study states: "Human capital and the value of institutions (as measured by the rule of law) constitute the largest share of wealth in virtually all countries."

Further reading
Bailey, Ronald. "The Secrets of Intangible Wealth," *Wall Street Journal,* 29 September 2007; Boyes, William, and Michael Melvin. *Microeconomics.* 7th ed. Boston: Houghton Mifflin, 2007; Folsom, Ralph H., and W. Davis Folsom. *Understanding NAFTA and Its International Implications.* New York: Matthew Irwin/Bender, 1996.

economic efficiency

Economic efficiency is defined in a variety of ways. Most simply stated, efficiency is the lack of waste. Economic efficiency in production is using the method that requires the least amount of resources to produce a given level of output. Efficiency is also associated with producing at the lowest point on a firm's average total-cost curve, producing at the least cost per unit possible.

Economic efficiency is also defined as a situation in which any reallocation of resources cannot make one person better off without harming someone else. This is known as Pareto Optimality, named after the Italian economist Vilfredo Pareto. Optimality is a bit misleading in that it usually infers the "best" outcome possible, whereas in reality many economic situations present multiple outcomes that are nearly equally efficient.

Economists also use a PRODUCTION POSSIBILITIES CURVE (PPC) to portray efficiency for an economic system. A country or business is said to have achieved economic efficiency when it has produced any combination of output that maximizes their production capability with existing RESOURCES and technology. Economic growth is portrayed by a rightward shift of the PPC through expansion of the quantity of resources, improvements in technology, or improvement in the quality of resources.

The 18th-century Scottish philosopher Adam Smith is credited with first describing economic efficiency of markets. In his famous "invisible hand" analogy, Smith suggested that self-interested individuals, both sellers and buyers, act as if driven by an invisible hand to produce economic efficiency. Buyers will attempt to maximize their benefits from the scarce resources they own. Sellers will attempt to maximize their return from the products they produce and sell. In the process, sellers and buyers will reduce and eliminate waste, producing what is most desired in the marketplace and purchasing those goods that maximize utility.

Advocates of LAISSEZ-FAIRE economic theory argue that economic efficiency is maximized when markets are allowed to act freely without government control or intervention. Critics counter that economic efficiency depends on having competition, and the assumed goal of businesses, maximizing PROFITS, is best achieved by reducing competition. Therefore government is needed to ensure markets operate as competitively as possible in order to achieve economic efficiency.

Further reading
Boyes, William, and Michael Melvin. *Macroeconomics.* 7th ed. Boston: Houghton Mifflin, 2007.

Economic Espionage Act

The Economic Espionage Act of 1996 was enacted to protect economic PROPRIETARY INFORMATION. With the end of the cold war in 1990, many governments and former espionage agents redirected efforts from political to business espionage. The act established penalties of up to $500,000 and 15 years in prison for agents of foreign powers and up to $10,000,000 in fines for organizations in cases where any "foreign government, foreign instrumentality, or foreign agent knowingly:

1. steals, or without authorization appropriates, takes, carries away, or communicates, or by FRAUD, artifice, or deception obtains TRADE SECRETS;
2. without authorization copies, duplicates, sketches, draws, photographs, downloads, uploads, alters, destroys, photocopies, replicates, transmits, delivers, sends, mails, communicates, or conveys a trade secret;
3. receives, buys, or possesses a trade secret, knowing the same to have been stolen or appropriated, obtained or converted without authorization;
4. attempts to commit any offense described in any of the paragraphs 1 through 3."

In cases of commercial espionage the same actions are illegal, but the penalties are: for persons, $500,000 and 10 years; for organizations, $5 million.

Like U.S. drug-smuggling laws, the act adds the potential of criminal forfeiture, meaning the seizure and disposition of property associated with the economic espionage activity. The act also directs prosecutors to "take such other action as may be necessary and appropriate to preserve the confidentiality of trade secrets," consistent with the requirements of federal laws. Civil court actions are also possible under the act. The act exempts law enforcement activity that might be in violation of the act.

See also MARKET INTELLIGENCE; SOCIETY FOR COMPETITIVE INTELLIGENCE PROFESSIONALS.

Further reading
Society for Competitive Intelligence Professionals Web site. Available online. URL: www.scip.org.

economic freedom

Economic freedom is the ability of individuals to exercise control over their property. Though there is no single, accepted definition Steve Hanke and Stephen Walters found that economic freedom includes

- secure rights to property
- freedom to engage in voluntary transactions both domestically and internationally
- freedom from governmental control of the terms on which individuals transact
- freedom from governmental expropriation of property

Economic liberty is perceived as distinct from political liberty, when people are free to participate in the political process on an equitable basis; and civil liberty, which involves protection against unreasonable searches and the right to fair trials, free assembly, free speech, and the practice of religion.

In the 1980s economists and political-interest groups became increasingly interested in measuring economic freedom and the relationship of economic freedom to ECONOMIC GROWTH. Part of the interest is ideologically based. Free-market advocates and critics of government scrutiny of business practices wanted to demonstrate a relationship between economic freedom and economic growth. Three organizations—Freedom House, Fraser Institute, and the Heritage Foundation—all developed measures of economic

freedom by country. Each organization identified crucial elements of economic freedom, quantified measures of these elements, and weighted the elements in order to create an index or score of economic freedom.

The first attempt to measure economic freedom was developed by Raymond Gastil and Lindsay Wright for Freedom House in 1983. Their efforts grew out of Freedom House's annual assessment of political and civil liberties. Since 1972 Freedom House has published an ANNUAL REPORT categorizing countries as "free," "partly free," or "not free" based on an average of the political- and civil-liberties ratings. Gastil and Wright supplemented this data with estimates of property rights, labor rights, business-operation rights, investment freedom, international trade openness, and anti-discrimination, and absence of corruption. Since 1995 Freedom House has published a separate *World Survey of Economic Freedom*. In the 2008 survey, only 89 nations were rated as free, representing 47 percent of the world's countries while 22 percent were rated as not free.

Fraser Institute publishes its Economic Freedom Index using five indices of economic liberty based on weighted averages of 21 components. Using a scale of 1–10, their average economic freedom index rose from 5.46 in 1980 to 6.65 in 2008. During that period, the score of 102 nations rose while the score of 13 nations declined. The three nations with scores that declined by over 1 point since 1980 included Zimbabwe, Venezuela, and Myanmar. Hong Kong had the highest score in the most recent survey (8.94) while the United States ranked eighth with 8.04. Their index uses measures of

- sound money
- size of government
- legal structure and security of property
- regulation of credit, labor, business
- freedom to exchange with foreigners.

Money supply growth, INFLATION rate, foreign currency accounts, and bank accounts abroad measure sound money. Size of government is measured by government spending as a share of total

CONSUMPTION, transfers, subsidies as a share of GROSS DOMESTIC PRODUCT (GDP), private versus state-run enterprises, and marginal tax rates. Judicial independence, impartial courts, protection of INTELLECTUAL PROPERTY, and military interference with the rule of law measure legal structure. Regulation of credit, labor, and business is measured by credit, labor, and business market regulations. Level of TARIFFS, regulatory TRADE BARRIERS, absence or presence of black-market EXCHANGE RATES, size of the trade sector, and absence of CAPITAL controls measure freedom to exchange with foreigners.

Beginning in 1994, the Heritage Foundation started publishing its annual *Index of Economic Freedom*. The Heritage Foundation's goal is to provide evidence on the impact of externally funded development assistance on facilitating economic growth. The foundation wants to discredit foreign-aid programs. The Heritage ranking of countries from mostly free to mostly unfree was then correlated with receipt of foreign aid and showing that many countries receiving foreign aid also lacked economic freedom and had not developed economically.

While some variation exists depending on the emphasis given to size of government and monetary stability, economic freedom index rankings are fairly consistent. Ironically, in 1996 Hong Kong (then independent of China) was ranked as one of the most economically free countries. New Zealand, Switzerland, the Netherlands, and the United Kingdom were also ranked high on each scale, followed closely by the United States. Not surprisingly, North Korea, Cuba, and Myanmar (Burma) ranked among the least free countries. In 2009, Hong Kong led their rankings followed by Singapore. The United States ranked 6th while Cuba, North Korea and Zimbabwe were at the bottom of the Heritage rankings.

Part of the interest in economic freedom comes from the question "How does economic liberty contribute to economic growth?" After each economic-freedom index was developed, economists correlated economic freedom ratings with measures of prosperity, usually GDP per capita. As expected, economic freedom (as defined by each organization) and economic growth are positively related. As Hanke and Walters observed, "They [economic researchers] have focused on the nature of institutions and on the structure of rules and norms that constrain economic behavior as a way of understanding the development process. And they have rediscovered [Adam] Smith's ancient insight that economic liberty is a crucial precondition for sustained, vigorous economic growth."

Further reading
Fraser Institute Web site. Available online. URL: www.fraserinstitute.ca; Freedom House Web site. Available online. URL: www.freedomhouse.org; Hanke, Steve H., and Stephen J. K. Walters. "Economic Freedom, Prosperity, and Equality: A Survey," *Cato Journal* 17, no. 2 (1998); Heritage Foundation Web site. Available online. URL: www.heritage.org.

economic growth

Economic growth, in its most limited definition, is an increase in real GROSS DOMESTIC PRODUCT (GDP), the primary measure of output in an economy. GDP comprises the total MARKET VALUE of final goods and services produced in an economy in a period of time, and increases in GDP are economic growth. Economies tend to go through periods of expansion and contraction of GDP.

Economic growth can be either extensive (resulting from greater quantity of labor, materials, and CAPITAL input) or intensive (resulting from technological advances and more efficient use of existing RESOURCES). Whether as a result of increasing quantities of resources or more efficient use of resources, output increases. Studies have documented growth in industrial economies as being largely attributable to intensive factors, while growth in developing economies tends to be derived from extensive sources. In an often-cited study, economist Edward Denison analyzed U.S. economic growth during the 20th century. He found that in the period from 1929 to 1948, over 50 percent of the growth in GDP was attributable to increases in the quantity of labor, with capital contributing to less than 5 percent of overall economic growth. From 1948 to 1973, the overall U.S. economic growth rate was 40 percent higher than the earlier period, but the contribution of labor to growth was almost unchanged. The quantity of capital accounted for over five times as much growth, and technological change accounted for three times as much growth in the later period. Denison attributed the added economic growth to the combination of increased capital, incorporating knowledge gains and technological advances in the period. Similarly, most economists attribute U.S. productivity gains in the 1990s to capital and human investment in computer technology.

Developing economies often face numerous obstacles in pursuit of economic growth. In many developing countries, resources for investment are concentrated among a small wealthy class and government. If these resources are spent on current CONSUMPTION, future economic growth will be limited. In what economists call the circle of poverty, low investment leads to low levels of output, which results in low levels of saving, which leads to low levels of investment.

In *The Stages of Economic Growth,* economist Walt Rostow posited that economies go through a series of five stages of economic growth: traditional society, preconditions for takeoff, takeoff, drive to maturity, and mass consumption. In the traditional-society stage, well-established economic and social systems and customs limit economic change and growth. In the preconditions stage, traditional constraints are removed and new methods and technology introduced. In the takeoff stage, an economic growth begins and investment expands rapidly. The takeoff stage is a period of intensive development. Rostow dated the takeoff stage in the U.S. economy as the period from 1843 to 1860, when major railroad investment opened new markets and expanded access to resources throughout the country. In the drive to maturity stage, an economy shifts from its original industrial base to expanding into new products and services. In the fifth stage, mass consumption, an affluent population leads to a well-developed consumer goods and SERVICES economy.

Austrian economist Joseph Schumpeter argued that economic growth depends on creative destruction. Schumpeter suggested that, in competitive markets, businesses attempt to find new ways to produce goods and better PRODUCTS in order to survive and prosper. In the process, existing methods and products are constantly being replaced. During periods of rapid economic growth, new technologies and new products are constantly being introduced. During periods of economic stagnation, innovation and INVESTMENT are low.

See also BUSINESS CYCLES; SUPPLY-SIDE ECONOMICS; TRICKLE-DOWN ECONOMICS.

Further reading
Folsom, Ralph H., and W. Davis Folsom. *Understanding NAFTA and Its International Business Implications.* New York: Matthew Bender/Irwin, 1996; Rostow, Walt W. *The Stages of Economic Growth.* 3d ed. Cambridge: Cambridge University Press, 1991; Ruffin, Roy J., and Paul R. Gregory. *Principles of Economics.* 7th ed. Boston: Addison Wesley, 2001.

economic institutions

Economic institutions are both specific organizations and government agencies and generally accepted economic behavior and arrangements. Economic institutions directly and indirectly affect commerce, policy, and customs within an economic system. A "top ten" list of specific U.S. economic institutions would likely include:

- FEDERAL RESERVE: responsible for monetary policy and oversight of the banking system
- U.S. TREASURY: responsible for management of the government's finances, national debt, coinage, and taxation
- SECURITIES AND EXCHANGE COMMISSION: responsible for oversight of public corporations and financial securities markets
- FEDERAL DEPOSIT INSURANCE CORPORATION: responsible for insuring deposits in commercial banks and oversight of state-chartered banks
- Department of Defense: responsible for national defense but also has the largest budget of any nonentitlement agency of the federal government (over $600 billion in 2010)

- FEDERAL TRADE COMMISSION: administers numerous acts and statutes affecting competition and consumer protection
- U.S. Supreme Court: the highest legal authority in the country, whose decisions often have a significant impact on consumers and business
- U.S. Congress: the legislative branch of government that, combined with the executive branch, initiates and implements the federal budget (over $4.5 trillion in 2009)
- SOCIAL SECURITY ADMINISTRATION: responsible for management of Old Age Survivors and Income (OASI), Supplemental Social Security (SSI), and Medicaid (over $350 billion in 2009)
- U.S. DEPARTMENT OF COMMERCE: responsible for a variety of federal government institutions, including the patent office, INTERNATIONAL TRADE COMMISSION, and the BUREAU OF ECONOMIC ANALYSIS

While all of the above are direct or government-sponsored institutions, many other government and nongovernment organizations influence economic decisions in the United States, including political action committees (PACs), labor unions, consumer interest groups, and religious organizations.

As stated earlier, economic institutions can also refer to written and unwritten rules of behavior. Visitors to the United States are often surprised by some of the "ways we do business." For example, in most of the industrialized countries workers receive and are expected to take at least five weeks vacation. Foreigners often perceive Americans as "workaholics." Also, most other industrialized countries have national healthcare systems and offer welfare assistance to all citizens, not requiring recipients to have dependent children.

Unwritten economic institutions include customary tipping, corporate attire, organizational expectations, and financial remuneration. For example, in major corporations around the world, the ratio of the highest to lowest paid employees is about 30 to 1, while in the United States it is over 400 to 1. In Europe most restaurant workers are paid a full-time salary with tips representing only a small part of workers' income. In many parts of the world, people live on property that they neither rent nor own. Economist Hernando de Soto has documented what is known as a parallel economy; people working outside the existing economic institutions because access to them is either impossible or costly.

Further reading
De Soto, Hernando. *The Other Path: The Invisible Revolution in the Third World.* New York: Harper and Row, 1989. Available online. URL: www.econlib.org/library/Topics/HighSchool/EconomicInstitutions.html. Accessed on May 25, 2009.

economic policy
Economic policy is a nation's use of its RESOURCES and power to achieve economic goals and objectives. Generally the central government has three types of economic policies—fiscal, monetary, and INCOME—that it can utilize.

FISCAL POLICY is the use of government taxation and/or spending to achieve economic objectives. For example, in early 2008 the Bush administration and Congress approved a $600 per taxpayer rebate to stimulate consumer spending but many households used the funds to pay off debt and pay for higher-priced gasoline.

MONETARY POLICY is controlling the MONEY SUPPLY to achieve economic growth with stable prices. In the United States, the primary goal of monetary policy is to attain and maintain price stability. Monetary policy is based on monetarism, a school of macroeconomic thought emphasizing the impact of changes in the supply of MONEY on the aggregate economy. Economic policies regarding the control of the money supply are often referred to as "tight money" or "easy money" plans. Generally the goal of monetary policy makers is to increase the money supply, but the question is at what rate to increase the supply. In the United States, the FEDERAL RESERVE SYSTEM determines monetary policy.

Income policies, also called WAGE AND PRICE CONTROLS, are government-imposed limits on increases in wages and prices. Income policies are typically imposed during wartime to limit INFLATION. during wars, government spending usually expands rapidly to provide the materials and weapons needed for defense. This increases DEMAND for labor and products and, in absence of wage and price controls, would likely result in inflation.

Economic policies can be directed to achieve a variety of objectives. As already stated, common economic objectives include price stability and ECONOMIC GROWTH. Other objectives include full EMPLOYMENT, economic choice and freedom, economic security for the elderly and ill, improvement in economic well-being, and equitable distribution of income among members of society. Some of these objectives are complimentary. Economic growth leads to increased employment and income, but some objectives present potential for conflict. Many economists, using Philips curve analysis, suggest there is a tradeoff between price stability and economic growth in the short run. A more significant conflict exists between ECONOMIC FREEDOM and social objectives. Economic freedom implies individual control and allocation of resources and receiving the rewards and returns from those resources. Economic security for the elderly and ill and equitable distribution of income in a society require economic policies that take resources or income from one group and provide resources and income to another group. Economic policies significantly affect what is produced, how it is produced, and who gets the output of an economic system.

economic rent

Economic rent is any payment to an owner of a productive resource in excess of the minimum amount necessary to keep the resource in its current use. In capitalist economic systems, individuals and households control most RESOURCES and choose how to allocate those resources. To keep a resource (land, labor, or CAPITAL) in its current use, the resource owner will demand, as minimum payment, a price equal to what they could receive for the best alternative use of that resource (OPPORTUNITY COST).

Economists distinguish between economic rent and quasi rents. Economic rent is the price paid to a productive resource that is perfectly inelastic in supply. Perfectly inelastic SUPPLY means there is a fixed quantity of the resource, and a higher price will not increase the quantity supplied in the market. The standard example of pure economic rent is agricultural land. There is a fixed quantity of useable land, and competing sources of DEMAND for the land determine the market price. A high percentage of agricultural land in the United States is rented out. Depending on the expected profitability of crops that can be grown, demand will increase of decrease and price will rise or fall, depending on demand. In many areas of the country, nonagricultural uses, generating higher use values for agricultural land, result in the conversion of agricultural property into commercial or residential areas. This activity, once approved by zoning officials, increases the economic rent to the resource holder.

Quasi rent is a payment in excess of the resource owner's short-run opportunity cost. The difference between economic rent and quasi rent is the response of suppliers to changing prices. Economic rent assumes quantity supplied does not change with price, while quasi rent assumes higher prices induce greater quantities supplied. Quasi rent is the difference between the current price and the price suppliers would have accepted. For example, if an employer offers a job-seeker $10 per hour more than he or she would have accepted, that is a quasi rent. In most markets, word will get out that higher-than-expected wages are being paid by an employer or industry, resulting in an increase in supply and a lowering of market wages. Thus the quasi rent is a short-run phenomenon, disappearing in the long run.

Further reading

Ruffin, Roy J., and Paul R. Gregory. *Principles of Economics*. 7th ed. Boston: Addison Wesley, 2001.

economic systems

Economic systems address a society's choices regarding control and allocation of RESOURCES, decisions regarding the products and services produced, and the distribution of that output. Economic systems can be classified into three general categories: CAPITALISM, SOCIALISM, and communism, with many variations within each category. Almost every economic system is a blend of the three basic categories, giving rise to the term *mixed economies.* Given economics is defined as how people allocate scarce resources, economic systems address the three fundamental questions: What to produce? How to produce it? And, who gets the output?

Capitalism is a social and economic system based on private property rights, private allocation of capital, and self-interest motivation. It is often linked with free enterprise and the use of markets to allocate resources and determine what is produced. Capitalism is associated with the ideas of 18th-century philosopher Adam Smith, who in his often quoted passage stated,

> It is not from the benevolence of the butcher, the brewer or the baker, that we expect our dinner, but from their regard to their own self interest. We address ourselves, not to their humanity but to their self-love, and never talk to them of our own necessities but of their advantages.

The distinguishing feature of capitalism is the assumption of self-interest as the primary guiding force in household and business decision making. Households are assumed to utilize their scarce resources so as to maximize their economic well-being, making informed decisions regarding alternative uses of the resources, and consumption decisions. Similarly, business owners and managers are assumed to make informed decisions regarding what resources to employ, products and services to produce, and markets to participate in. Advocates of capitalism argue government should have a minimal role in controlling and allocating resources, allowing markets to operate freely. Free-market capitalism is most associated with the ideas of the late Nobel Prize–winning economist, Milton Friedman. Called neoliberal economic theory, the ideas of Friedman and others argued for free trade,

deregulation, and small government. In the 1970s, Friedman's video series, *Free to Choose,* was widely distributed and used in economics education. Somewhat ironically, Friedman used Hong Kong as his example of an efficient capitalist economic system. Typically, the United States, Canada, and some European countries are most associated with capitalism.

In a socialist economic system, individuals control the use of their human capital but the government owns most other, nonhuman resources, including natural resources and economic capital. Land, factories, and major machinery are typically publicly owned in socialist economic systems. In 2009, opponents of the Obama administration's economic policies, including bailout of the banking and automobile industries and proposed changes in the healthcare system, accused the administration of taking the United States down the road of socialism. As stated earlier, no purely capitalist, socialist, or communist economic systems exist. In the banking industry bailout, the government acquired significant shareholder interests in private corporations but the bank leadership remained largely intact and in control. In the auto industry bankruptcy action, the government again gained a significant shareholder interest in General Motors (GM) and Chrysler and insisted on new management at GM and government representation on the board of directors, but both companies remained private corporations. In the 2009 healthcare proposal, the government would take a stronger role in negotiating price and cost controls, and it may wind up providing a government-sponsored insurance plan as an alternative to ones offered by the private sector. In each endeavor the government increased its influence on the private sector but did not own and decide the allocation of resources, as in a fully socialist economic decision.

In theory, incentives in socialist economic systems are based upon the individual's good will toward others, rather than serving as a function of individuals' self-interest as in a capitalist system. In socialist economies, individuals are urged to consider the well-being of others. As stated by socialist philosopher Karl Marx, "From each according to his ability, to each according to his need (or needs)." Most European countries have a major political party that advocates social democracy, with greater government control or influence over resource and output decisions than in the United States. For example, in 2009, the federal budget of the United States was about $4.5 trillion dollars while the country's gross domestic product was approximately $14 trillion. The federal government thus controlled approximately one-third (4.5/14) of the resource allocation decisions. In most European countries the government controls 40 to 45 percent of the resource allocation decisions, providing most of the same government services found in the United States, but also free healthcare and free or low-cost higher education. Part of the difference is citizens' perceptions of the role of government. In *Sixty Million Frenchmen Can't Be Wrong: Why Americans Love France but Hate the French,* the authors suggest Americans look at government as impeding the pursuit of their individual rights and as a source of problems, while the French look at government as a source for solutions to social problems.

Under a communist economic system, almost all resources, both human and nonhuman, are controlled or influenced by the state. Through central planning, the government directs both production and consumption in what is assumed to be a socially desirable manner. In theory guided by what they believe to be good for the country, central planners make most of the decisions regarding what, how, and for whom. Movement of resources, including the movement of labor, is strictly controlled. In the old Soviet Union and the eastern European countries then communist-controlled, workers were guaranteed a job but the state would determine which jobs and where. Government officials sometimes bragged that no unemployment existed in their country. Young women were often given a choice of becoming nurses or teachers but no other options. State factories controlled manufacturing, and trade barriers prevented global competition. One of the symbols of that era was the Trabant, a poorly made, less than 60

horsepower, two-cycle engine (which mixed the gas and oil) automobile built in an East German government-run factory. Less than 100 miles away, West Germans were manufacturing BMWs and Mercedes Benz automobiles. Central control is also evident in China with its one child per family rule and government mandate that factories close to clean up the air for the 2008 Olympics.

Economic and political control are both exercised by the government in a communist economic system. China has one "ruling party" that directs social, political, and economic policy, but, since the 1980s, it has encouraged economic growth through private enterprise. In 2010, the two major dictatorships, Cuba and North Korea, exert even greater control over both political and economic policies. However, in recent decades, Cuba has allowed foreign investment in resort complexes, generating revenue and creating local jobs. Cuba also has a unique tax on citizens wishing to emigrate, charging people based on the education they received from the government-sponsored system.

Further reading
Halsall, Paul. Adam Smith's *Wealth of Nations.* Summary available online. URL: www.fordham.edu/halsall/mod/adamsmith-summary.html. Accessed on July 3, 2009.

economies of scale, economies of scope
Economies of scale are production efficiencies realized when per-unit costs are reduced as the quantity produced increases. In business, scale is size, and in many business situations, as a company produces more output, the average cost of that output declines. Economies of scale are the result of efforts that improve efficiency.

Generally specialization and use of larger machines allow firms to become more efficient. Greater levels of output allow firms to spread the fixed COSTS associated with specialized equipment or personnel. For example, a manager is a fixed cost to a business; it does not change over a range of output (until the business is large enough to need a second manager). Every business needs a manager, and a manager's salary has to be included in the cost of doing business. If a company produces more output (in a manufacturing firm) or generates greater sales (in a retail firm), the cost of the manager per unit of output or sales decreases.

Economies of scale result in lower average costs of PRODUCTION up to the point where a firm reaches its minimum efficient scale (MES). MES is the level of output where the firm's average cost is lowest. Many times there is a range of output over which a firm achieves its MES. Production levels beyond MES result in diseconomies of scale, or rising costs per unit. Diseconomies of scale occur when the cost of additional RESOURCES rises, managers face so many demands that work slows, or new equipment is necessary to expand output.

Economies of scale are an important factor in market COMPETITION. Often cost advantages from large-scale production act as a BARRIER TO ENTRY in oligopolies and monopolies. Potential competitors are forced to start out with large levels of production in order to compete with existing firms.

Government often allows the creation of a regulated MONOPOLY in order to achieve economies of scale. Economists call these situations natural monopolies. Electric utilities, local cable and telephone service, and water companies are all examples of situations where one large firm can produce at a lower cost per unit than many competing firms. In many countries these services are directly provided by government, but in the United States private companies whose prices are regulated (public utilities) are more prevalent.

While economies of scale are the result of specialization, economies of scope are the result of production of similar products. A firm producing shirts can use the same equipment to also produce blouses or pants. A farmer growing one crop has the land and much of the equipment needed to grow other crops. These firms have an advantage, economies of scope, over other potential competitors based on their existing knowledge and resources.

See also OLIGOPOLY.

Further reading
Ruffin, Roy J., and Paul R. Gregory. *Principles of Economics.* 7th ed. Boston: Addison Wesley, 2001.

efficient market theory (efficient market hypothesis)

Otherwise known as the efficient market hypothesis, this theory concludes that investors cannot expect to outperform the STOCK MARKET over an extended period of time. This is not to say that some investors cannot outperform the stock-market indexes. The theory does suggest, however, that investors will not outperform the market on a RISK-adjusted basis over a longer time frame.

The efficient market theory is based on the assumptions that securities markets are highly competitive, information for research purposes is readily available at low cost, and transactions may be executed at low cost. Since securities prices adjust rapidly to new information and other market-driven effects, day-to-day price changes are unpredictable. The RANDOM-WALK THEORY suggests that the pricing pattern of securities is accidental, and techniques such as charting, moving averages, or purchases relative to sales will not lead to superior selection. The term *random walk* is occasionally misunderstood to mean that securities prices are randomly determined. To the contrary, securities prices are efficiently determined by the markets. It is the changes in securities prices that are random, as is new and unpredictable information. If new information were predictable, then securities price changes would also be predictable and investors could consistently outperform the market, assuming the same risks, and securities markets would not be efficient.

During the 2007–09 financial crises, efficient market theory came under considerable criticism from investors and economists who asked why markets did not adjust rapidly to changing conditions and negative information about securities. Market "bubbles" such as the 2001 dot-com bubble and 2006–07 housing market bubble challenge the assumption that markets process and incorporate risk in securities prices. Former FEDERAL RESERVE chairman Alan Greenspan's famous term *irrational exuberance* is often quoted by critics of efficient market theory. Finance professor Burton Malkiel, a supporter of efficient market theory, suggests that in markets in which information is not transparent or subject to government manipulation, securities prices cannot reflect market and economic conditions.

Further reading
Mayo, Herbert B. "The Valuation of Common Stock." In *Investments—An Introduction.* Greenwood Village, Colo.: College for Financial Planning, 2000.

e-government
E-government refers to government initiatives to provide information and SERVICES electronically and over the INTERNET; the means used include Web sites and e-mail. E-government has been linked to efforts to change or reform government to provide services to citizens, other governments, and the business community more efficiently and effectively.

The federal government, all of the state governments, and most larger cities and counties established a presence on the Internet by developing Web sites that provide information about their mission and how to obtain services. Many people have no idea how to reach various government agencies or even what services are available. Government Web sites provide much of this information to the public through on-line links to other government agencies and services. In many cases, government entities are able to streamline service provision for the general public and the business community as well.

In 2000 the federal government established a gateway, or portal Web site, to provide the public with one central location for accessing information about federal government agencies and services. For example, consumers can print up a passport application, find a zip code, or obtain information about many government benefits. Businesses can file taxes electronically, learn about subcontracting opportunities, report employee wages electronically, and access information about international trade. From a link to the federal legislative branch, one can reach the Web sites of members of the House and Senate to contact them with questions, provide feedback on issues, or request assistance. Links are also provided to the Web sites of Native American tribal governments and to state and local governments. The federal government's Web site can be accessed at http://www.usa.gov.

State and local governments provide a variety of information on their Web sites. The virtual visitor can learn a great deal about a state's history, culture, and laws, places to visit, the organizational structure of its government, and the services it provides. Typical services include information about business opportunities, taxes, EMPLOYMENT opportunities, and public health. Some state and local governments provide on-line forms and information to reduce waiting and travel time as well as time spent on telephone queries. For example, a government entity may provide information about how to obtain a copy of a birth or death certificate or a marriage license. The library system in one major city experimented with an on-line pay research service to fill requests for information from other governments and from businesses. A West Coast county allows contractors to apply for permits on-line and then schedule an appointment with a building inspector. In one East Coast city, traffic violators can track their case on-line through all the stages of the legal process. E-mail links contribute to government responsiveness by allowing consumers to contact government officials with specific questions and concerns that may save multiple trips to a bricks-and-mortar facility. City and county Web sites vary from those with an extensive presence to those with minimal Web sites or no presence on the World Wide Web at all. Most have at least a minimal presence. Scholars find that local governments tend to utilize their Web sites to supplement rather than to substitute for traditional services provided face to face. Due to cost considerations, governments have been slow to move toward a transactional approach, where more services are provided on-line.

Technology is changing the ways that citizens and the business community interact with government in other respects. Some communities provide on-line coverage of government meetings, either live or through archives, so citizens can "watch" a meeting from the comfort of their own homes or at their convenience. Some high schools and many colleges offer "virtual" classes where students never meet their teachers face to face. A traffic court goes paperless, and offenders can track each step of their cases on-line. Some communities are integrating a mapping and data-analysis technique known as geographic information system (GIS) with the Internet. In one community, citizens can use GIS to report the exact location of a pothole. In other communities, economic development offices are using GIS to provide information to businesses searching for new locations. Some local governments utilize GIS to garner other information of interest to citizens and business. For example, transportation officials can determine where to place roads and public safety agencies can map out the locations of murders.

E-government also provides new opportunities for businesses to establish partnerships with government entities by contracting for technology-related services. For example, the U.S. Postal Service contracted with several private companies to upgrade its hardware and software as it moved toward Web-based services.

New problems have developed along with the new technology. One key concern is how to balance the needs for national security and the free flow of information in a democratic society. In an effort to make government more "customer-friendly," federal and state government agencies provided public access to an enormous amount of information on topics as varied as nuclear power plants, chemical site security, pipeline mapping, and crop dusters. Following the terrorist attacks of September 11, 2001, government agencies began to reexamine what information was made available to the public through the Internet and other means, including via federal FREEDOM OF INFORMATION ACT requests. Subsequently, federal and state officials removed some information from the Internet that was deemed too sensitive and subject to abuse by terrorists. To what extent limits should be placed on public access to information about government is a subject for debate in the political arena.

A second concern is how to ensure the security of a Web site. Staying a step ahead of hackers who maliciously attack and damage Web sites for fun or for profit is a challenge for experts in computer security in both the public and the private sectors. Computer-savvy criminals may hack into Web sites to gather data that will allow them access to personal finances and to engage in identity theft. Hackers have breached thousands of computer systems around the world, including many government Web sites. For example, in 2009, officials at a major California public university campus revealed that overseas hackers had broken into databases at the university's health center, gaining access to the confidential records and Social Security numbers of thousands of students and alumni. In Virginia, hackers gained access to millions of electronic prescription records, including birth dates and other personal information. A terrorist attack on the nation's computer network would have serious ramifications for government operations and for the economy. Security experts use a variety of mechanisms to keep hackers from gaining access to data stored on computers, including firewalls, secure configuration of software, keeping security patches up to date, and designing "trust relationships" that prevent hackers who break into a system from accessing all the computers in a network (i.e., someone using a computer in the network must provide proof of identity in order to access other computers). Hackers also gain access to computer systems through social engineering or phishing—i.e., by tricking people into giving them their usernames and passwords. Experts agree that one of the best ways to prevent social engineering is by educating computer users to exercise care in giving out such information. Another security issue is related to transmission of data over the Internet, where it is readily accessible. Security experts recommend encryption of sensitive data so that it will be meaningless gibberish to those who are not authorized to use it, although hackers may develop new computer programs to gain access.

A related concern is maintaining the PRIVACY of personal data that may be available through the Internet and electronic records. A wide variety of information about clients, citizens, and government employees exists in both paper and electronic form. A widespread belief in the right to privacy exists in the society at large, buttressed by laws and court decisions. Many citizens object when government agencies gather personal data and fear that it will be misused by both government entities and by the private sector if they obtain this information. However, government agencies seeking to prevent terrorism may need to share data in order to better coordinate their activities. Maintaining confidentiality and ensuring appropriate safeguards of such data while at the same time allowing public officials access to the information needed for homeland security and national defense is difficult. Governments may also have a legitimate need for client data in order to determine what services a particular client is receiving from other agencies. For example, a county in an east-coast state purchased a program that allows it to track homeless people and lets social workers determine which benefits clients are receiving without contacting each separate service provider. They encrypted the data to maintain confidentiality.

A different kind of concern centers on the "digital divide." The "digital divide" is the gap between those who have Internet access and those who do not. Lower income persons especially are less likely to have home computers. But studies find that the "digital divide" is shrinking as the price of laptop computers drops and as more handheld devices become available at a low cost. By 2008, around three-quarters of all Americans were using the Internet, although access was still more limited for some, including many racial minorities. Rural residents were much less likely to have broadband, or faster Internet access, although more were adopting it as it became available. A 2008 Pew Center study found that those who do not use computers are most likely to be over the age of 70, non-English speakers, and have less than a high school education. Some state and local governments have addressed this problem by providing more computers in places like libraries and shopping malls. Most community colleges have developed programs to teach older people, some of whom need new skills to return to the job market, how to use

computers. Sometimes joining with partners in the private sector, government initiatives have made more computers available to schools. However, the cost of providing and maintaining technology is a problem when the economy slows and there are more demands on limited dollars. In a climate of strong opposition to tax increases, public officials may apply user fees, where the person who uses the service pays for it, as a viable alternative for maintaining Web-based services. But neither small business nor low income citizens may be able to afford to pay costs, thus creating new barriers to Internet access.

E-government has its limitations. In and of itself it will not solve all the problems inherent in service delivery. But ultimately it may change the way governments operate. New issues arise along with the new technology. For example, as governments become paperless, public officials must determine what records have to be retained under federal and state laws. Questions will be raised about what should be saved for the historical record as well. Another issue that may arise is that of increased citizen participation in government. Governments are already subject to many demands from a wide range of interest groups and from the general public. As government becomes more "user-friendly," the public may find it easier to understand how it operates and to access more specific information about how government spends the public's money. Government officials may find themselves responding to a new set of constituents who will closely question the day-to-day operations of government organizations. A challenge for governments at all levels will be how to best use new and changing technology to coordinate and maximize service provision.

Further reading

Chen, Yu-Che, and Kurt Thurmaier. "Advancing E-Government: Financing Challenges and Opportunities," *Public Administration Review* 68, no. 3 (May–June 2008): 537–548; Coursey, David, and Donald F. Morris. "Models of E-Government: Are They Correct? An Empirical Assessment," *Public Administration Review* 68, no. 3 (May/June 2008): 523–536; Daukantas, Patricia. "What on Web Merits Saving?" *GCN Government Computer News.* Available online. URL: www. gcn.com/ cgibin/udt/im.display.printable?client.id=gcn2&story. id=18754. Accessed on May 28, 2002; Davies, Thomas R. "Throw E-Gov a Lifeline," *Governing* (June 2002): 72; Fox, Susannah, and Jessica Vitak. "Degrees of Access (May 2008 Data)," Pew Internet and American Life Project (July 9, 2008); Gurwitt, Rob. "Behind the Portal," *Governing Online.* Available online. URL: www/ governing.com/8egweb.htm. Accessed on May 28, 2002; Harris, Shane. "Bridging the Divide," *Governing* (September 2000): 36; ———. "E-Commerce at the Library," *Governing* (April 2000): 56, 58; Horrigan, John B. "Home Broadband Adoption 2008," Pew Internet and American Life Project (July 2008); Kittower, Diane. "Welcome to Cyber High," *Governing* (April 2000): 52, 56; Marriott, Michelle. "Digital Divide Closing as Blacks Turn to Internet," *New York Times,* 31 March 2006; McDowell, Mindi. "Avoiding Social Engineering and Phishing Attacks," U.S.-Cert, a division of the U.S. Department of Homeland Security (2004). Last updated July 19, 2007; Miller, Jason. "USPS looks to travel light via Web," *GCN Government Computer News.* Available online. URL: www.gcn.com/ cgi-bin/udt/im.display.printable?client.id=gcn2&story. id=18709.; Mohn, Tanya. "That Digital Divide, Bridged in a Classroom," *New York Times,* 29 November 2008; Newcombe, Tod. "Conservative Growth," *Government Technology* (March 2002): 26, 28; Palumbo, John. "Social Engineering: What Is It, Why Is So Little Said About It and What Can Be Done?" SANS Institute, Information Security Reading Room. Available online. URL: rr.sans.org/social/social.php. Accessed on June 3, 2002; Perlman, Ellen. "Gavel to Gavel Online," *Governing* (April 2000): 52; ———. "Maps That Sell," *Governing* (December 2000): 68, 70, 7; Perlman, Ellen, and Melissa Maynard. "Working in Wiki," *Governing* (May 2008); Stanton, Sam, and Ted Bell. "Hacking Bares Key Data on All State Employees," *Sacramento Bee* (25 May 2002). Available online. URL: www.sacbee.com/content/ politics/story/2882520p-3704154c.html. Accessed on May 25, 2002; Swope, Christopher. "Total Disclosure," *Governing* (April 2000): 58; Tolbert, Caroline J., Karen Mossberger, and Ramona McNeal. "Institutions, Policy Innovation, and E-Government in the American States," *Public Administration Review* 68, no. 3 (May–

June 2008): 549–563; Walsh, Trudy. "Software Helps Lancaster, Pa., Aid Its Homeless," *GCN Government Computer News.* Available online. URL: gcn.com/21_11/ statelocal/18634-1.html. Accessed on May 28, 2002; Whitaker, Barbara. "Technology, Reveals Worlds to Map," *New York Times,* 12 August 2007; Zanko, Pete L. "Labor Department Launches New Web Site," *Washington Post On-line.* Available online. URL: www. washingtonpost.com/ac2/wp-dyn/A2566-2002Apr29? language=printer. Accessed on May 28, 2002.

See also the entire February 2002 issue of *Government Technology,* which focuses on network security.

—Carol Sears Botsch

80-20 principle

The 80-20 principle is the general observation that, in many markets, the vast majority (80 percent) of sales and/or PROFITS come from a small percentage (20 percent) of a firm's customers. Likewise, 20 percent of a firm's sales and/or profits come from 80 percent of its customers.

Italian economist Vilfredo Pareto first articulated the 80-20 principle in the 1890s. Pareto observed that 80 percent of the WEALTH in Italy was owned by 20 percent of the population. More recently marketers have utilized the 80-20 principle to evaluate and design marketing strategies. One example is the growth of affinity programs. First developed nationally by American Airlines, frequent-flyer programs reward the small percentage of customers who generate a large percentage of sales. Recognizing the benefits of catering to their most important customers, other airlines, hotels, and auto rental companies quickly adopted similar programs.

With today's CUSTOMER-RELATIONSHIP MANAGEMENT systems, marketers can better evaluate which customers are generating the lion's share of their profits. Personal sales efforts, customized products, specialized services, and alternative delivery systems are just a few of the many marketing strategies that can be used to retain and cultivate relationships with a firm's most important customers. Ultimately, the goal is to win and maintain the trust of valued customers.

Another example of the 80-20 principle can be used in MARKET RESEARCH surveys. Sometimes a marketer may not want a random sample of all of their customers. Instead, the opinions of their important customers (the 20 percent generating 80 percent of the company's profits) may be needed. Marketer Tony Cram makes an important insight about the 80-20 principle. Some customers may not generate significant sales or profits but may benefit a firm by sharing its planning process, collaborating on NEW PRODUCT DEVELOPMENT, or being a source of referrals and recommendations; they thus also prove valuable to a marketer. Like many aspects of business, the 80-20 principle should not be taken as an absolute guide for MARKETING STRATEGY decisions.

Of course, the 80 percent of customers who generate 20 percent of sales or profits should not be ignored. Manufacturers often use independent representatives to call on small customers. Catalog companies change the size, composition, and frequency of mailing depending on past customer purchases. College textbook publishers provide 800-number services for small campuses while sending sales reps to major institutions. The INTERNET allows companies to customize offerings for different customer groups.

Further reading
Cram, Tony. "How to Care for Customers Who Count the Most," *Marketing,* 12 July 2001, 21; Etzel, Michael J., Bruce J. Walker, and William J. Staunton. *Marketing.* 14th ed. Boston: McGraw-Hill, 2007.

elasticity of demand
In most market situations, business managers raise or lower price as they judge in their best interest. Elasticity of demand is a quantitative way to measure consumers' sensitivity or responsiveness to price changes.

Starting from the current price a firm charges, elasticity of demand is measured by the percentage change in quantity demanded in response to a percentage change in price. If, for example, price is raised by 10 percent and quantity demanded decreases by 10 percent (the law of

DEMAND states the higher the price the lower the quantity demanded and vice versa), the increase in revenue from the higher price is exactly offset by the decrease in quantity demanded. Total revenue for the firm will remain the same, though PROFITS may increase because the firm is now selling less quantity of their product and receiving the same amount of revenue. When a price change results in no change in total revenue, the elasticity-of-demand coefficient is one or unitary.

The elasticity-of-demand coefficient is the absolute value of the percentage change in quantity demanded divided by the percentage change in price.

$$E_D = (\% \text{ change in quantity demand}) / (\% \text{ change in price})$$

The elasticity-of-demand formula initially appears quite daunting, but looking closely it is just a percentage divided by a percentage. If the percentage change in quantity demanded is greater than the percentage change in price, demand is said to be elastic, or people responded significantly to the price change. However, demand is inelastic if consumers do not respond much when a business changes price.

For example, if a firm raises its price by 10 percent and quantity demanded goes down by 5 percent, the elasticity of demand is the absolute value of 5/10 or 0.50. This is less than 1.0 and considered inelastic. If, instead, when the firm raises price by 10 percent, the quantity demanded decreases by 50 percent, the elasticity coefficient is the absolute value of 50/10 or 5.0. This is considered very price-elastic; when the firm raises prices by 10 percent, people significantly reduce their quantity demanded.

The assumed primary goal of a business is to maximize profits, which are the excess of total revenues over total costs. Since elasticity of demand measures relative changes in quantity demanded in response to a change from an initial price, it can be used to estimate what happens to total revenue when price is changed. In the example of inelastic demand above, a 10-percent increase in price resulted in a 5-percent decrease in quantity demanded. The firm is now selling 5 percent less of their product but receiving a price that is 10-percent higher than what they were charging previously. The increase in price has more than offset the decrease in quantity sold. Their total revenue, therefore, is increased. In the example of elastic demand, the firm is charging 10-percent more for their product, but the number of products sold decreased by 50 percent. They are getting a higher price but losing a lot of sales. Their total revenue has decreased.

An easier way to remember the relationship of price elasticity is this axiom: For inelastic demand, price and total revenue move in the same direction, and for elastic demand, price and total revenue move in opposite directions.

Large companies often hire economists and MARKET RESEARCH professionals to estimate the price elasticity of demand for their products, but small-business owners can also use this concept. There are four rules of thumb used to make an educated judgment whether the demand for a product will be sensitive or insensitive to price changes.

- necessities versus luxuries
- short time frame versus long time frame
- few competitors versus many competitors
- inexpensive items versus expensive items

Generally people are more likely to purchase necessity goods even if the price of those goods rise, but they are less likely to buy luxury goods when those prices go up. For example, airlines keep some seats open on flights for last-minute business travelers who need to get to some destination to conduct business. Business travel is price-inelastic, while vacation travel is generally price-elastic; when the price of vacations increase, more people will decide not to travel for their vacation.

People are less likely to respond to a price change initially but more likely to change given time to adjust. When gas prices rose in early 2005, American consumers did not respond significantly to the price increase. But when they were ready to trade in their cars, they bought smaller, more fuel-

efficient cars, reducing their demand for gasoline. Thus, over time consumers were more responsive to oil-price increases than they were in the short run.

If monopolists raises prices, especially for necessity goods like electricity or water, people will reduce their quantity demanded very little, as they have few or no other choices. But if one fast-food company raised their price, consumers would fairly quickly substitute competitors' products. When there are few substitutes, demand tends to be price-inelastic, and when there are many substitutes demand tends to be price-elastic.

If the price of an ice cream cone goes up by 50 percent, most people will buy it anyway. But if the price of a new car goes up by 50 percent, many will keep driving their old clunkers. What one person considers expensive could be considered inexpensive to someone with significant INCOME, but generally consumers are more sensitive to price changes for expensive items than inexpensive items.

Using these four rules of thumb, business managers can estimate the degree of response to a price change. Small-business managers learn over time which customers are sensitive to price changes and also how much of a price decrease they need to make in order to sell end-of-the-year items. Though a theoretical concept associated with economics, price elasticity of demand has many practical uses for business managers.

Further reading

Boyes, William, and Michael Melvin. *Microeconomics*. 7th ed. Boston: Houghton Mifflin, 2007.

electronic data interchange

Electronic data interchange (EDI) is the electronic transfer of business documents such as purchase orders, invoices, and bills of lading between companies using a structured, machine-readable data format. A manufacturer using EDI can transmit purchase orders directly from its company computer to a supplier's company computer over a telecommunications network or the INTERNET, eliminating the time-consuming and expensive manual processing of paper documents. By streamlining data flow within an organization, companies can reduce inventory, lower labor costs, shorten CYCLE TIME, and enhance customer service.

The U.S. shipping industry first implemented electronic data interchange in the 1970s. EDI grew rapidly in the 1980s, especially in large manufacturing industries such as the automotive sector. For example, as a key step in streamlining their manufacturing processes to remain competitive, General Motors Corporation, Chrysler Corporation, and Ford Motor Company implemented EDI. They also expected their suppliers to use EDI to automate the procurement cycle, reducing inventory in support of a just-in-time (JIT) production philosophy.

However, EDI was often complex and expensive to implement, since large companies typically used many suppliers. It was common for each company to use different types of computer systems and software packages and to require different features from an EDI application, all of which complicated EDI implementation. Generally only large companies could afford to implement EDI, sometimes with only limited success. In the mid-1990s the growth of the Internet fueled the first attempts at E-COMMERCE, introducing a simpler, less-expensive way for smaller companies to conduct business transactions electronically. Today implementing Web-based EDI is a viable alternative for small and medium-sized companies pressured by their larger customers who prefer to complete their business transactions electronically using EDI. In the future it is likely that businesses not using EDI will be at a competitive disadvantage, as CORPORATIONS continue to embrace flatter, decentralized organizational structures in an effort to remain competitive in the global marketplace.

The EDI process itself is quite simple: companies, or trading partners, first agree on the specific format of each EDI transaction, including the format, content, and structure of the business document. Standardized formatting ensures that each trading partner's computer can correctly interpret the data it sends or receives. Document content standards such as ANSI X.12 or EDIFACT typically provide the standard format for EDI transmissions. Most American companies adhere to the American National Standards Institute (ANSI) X.12 standard, while global business partners use the international EDI for Administration, Commerce, and Trade (EDIFACT) standard supported by the United Nations. Computer software applications translate each trading partner's documents into the proper standardized format.

After translating the business document into machine-readable form, one business partner can electronically transmit it to the other. A direct telecommunication line between trading partners, telecommunication lines via an intermediary value-added network (VAN), and the Internet are all methods used to transmit electronic data. Using a third-party value-added network, companies can transmit all of their EDI transactions for all of their trading partners at the same time. The VAN separates the EDI transactions by company and places them in each trading partner's electronic mailbox. At regular intervals, each trading partner's company computer dials the VAN's computer and extracts any pending EDI transactions. Translation software then transforms the EDI transaction into the specific format used internally by the trading partner.

Increasingly, smaller companies are turning to the Internet for EDI transmissions. Web-based EDI uses the Hypertext Markup Language (HTML) as a document format standard and maintains security during transaction transmission over the Web through the Secure Hypertext Transfer Protocol (SHTTP) or Secure Sockets Layer (SSL) protocol. As more vendors embrace the concept of e-commerce and offer inexpensive Web-based EDI software and VAN services, Web-based EDI has become a less costly and more attractive alternative to traditional EDI for even the smallest companies.

Further reading

Busby, Michael. *Demystifying EDI*. Plano, Tex.: Wordware Publishing, 2000; Jilovec, Nahid. *The A to Z of*

EDI & Its Role in E-Commerce. 2d ed. Loveland, Colo.: Twenty Ninth Street Press, 1998.

—Karen S. Groves

Electronic Fund Transfer Act

The Electronic Fund Transfer Act (EFTA, 1978) defined the LIABILITY rules governing electronic fund transfers. As defined in the act, electronic fund transfers are "any transfer of funds, other than a transaction originated by check, draft, or similar paper instrument, which is initiated through an electronic terminal, telephone instrument, or computer or magnetic tape so as to order, instruct, or authorize a financial institution to DEBIT or credit an account. Such term includes, but is not limited to, point-of-sale transfers, automated teller machine transactions, direct deposits or withdrawals of funds, and transfers initiated by telephone."

At the time it was passed, the EFTA was far-reaching legislation, affecting the E-COMMERCE that is commonplace today. The act provides CONSUMER PROTECTIONS requiring financial institutions providing EFT services to inform the customer regarding

- the customer's liability for unauthorized transfers caused by loss, or the loss of the card, code, or other access device
- whom to call and the phone number if there is a theft or loss
- the charges for using the EFT system
- what systems are available, including limits on frequency and dollar amounts
- the consumer's right to see transactions in writing
- ways to correct errors
- the consumer's right to stop payments
- rules concerning disclosure of account information to third parties

Probably the EFTA's most important aspect to consumers is the $50 limit on their liability when their access device is lost, stolen, or misplaced. This limit applies if the consumer notifies the financial institution within two business days of learning of the loss or theft. A consumer's liability rises to $500 if notification is made after two business days, and unlimited liability occurs if notification does not take place within 60 days after receiving a periodic statement reflecting the unauthorized transfer.

The act also provides sanctions and DAMAGES against financial institutions that violate the EFTA. Actual, punitive, and criminal sanctions can result from failure to comply with the act.

Further reading

Fisher, Bruce D., and Michael J. Phillips. *The Legal, Ethical and Regulatory Environment of Business.* 8th ed. Cincinnati: Cengage, 2003.

electronic funds transfer

Electronic funds transfer (EFT) is the movement of funds using an encrypted electronic format. Moving money electronically is generally more efficient, more secure, and less costly than handling cash or paper checks. Although payments by cash and checks still dominate in the United States, nonpaper, or "e-payments," are growing rapidly through integration of existing and new electronic technology.

The predominant means of electronic funds transfer are CREDIT CARDS, debit cards, and automatic clearing house (ACH) transactions. In a credit-card transaction, cardholders, merchants, card-issuing banks, merchants' banks, and credit-card companies are all linked electronically. Scanning credit cards simply activates accounts of participants in their banking and credit-card companies, recording the transaction that is taking place.

Debit cards are similar to credit cards, but the electronic funds-transfer system is more direct. Debit cards create point-of-sale (POS) transactions, eliminating the issuance of credit between the buyer and seller and instead directly debiting the buyer's account and crediting the seller's account. Like automated teller machine (ATM) transactions, debit cards are linked to a customer's bank account.

In the 1990s the federal government began using electronic funds transfer systems to provide electronic benefits transfer (EBT) programs, in part to reduce costs and also to reduce FRAUD. Most states have joined the federal program and provide cash entitlement assistance (AID TO FAMILIES WITH DEPENDENT CHILDREN) and food assistance (Food Stamps), using cards that allow recipients to make cash withdrawals from designated ATM machines or to pay for food purchases at grocery stores using the equivalent of a debit card.

Another category of electronic funds transfer involves wire and ACH systems. Wire transfers are payments made among banks and other financial institutions through either of two electronic payments systems, CHIPS and Fedwire. CHIPS (Clearing House Interbank Payment System) is operated by the NEW YORK CLEARING HOUSE ASSOCIATION and is primarily used to settle FOREIGN EXCHANGE transactions among major banks. Fedwire is operated by the FEDERAL RESERVE SYSTEM and is used to settle interbank transactions.

ACH is a nationwide electronic funds-transfer system facilitating payments among individuals, businesses, and governments. Created in the 1970s, ACH is a network used for payroll direct deposit, automatic bill payments, and corporate tax payments. It is also used as the settlement mechanism for ATM, credit card, and debit card transactions. Settlement means balancing of debits and credits. During the course of any business day, there are likely to be thousands of electronic payments on the behalf of customers and businesses between any two large banks. Settlement determines which bank transfers funds electronically to compensate for the balance in exchanges between the two institutions. Each bank settles with all other banks with which it had funds transfers, also done electronically through the clearinghouse.

There are four ACH operators in the United States. The largest is the Federal Reserve, which clears almost 80 percent of all ACH transfers. The major ACH transfer is direct deposit of employee salaries. Approximately 50 percent of employees in the U.S. utilize payroll-deposit programs, and 75 percent of Social Security recipients utilize electronic transfer. The second major use of ACH transfer is cash concentration. Companies with

many branches or sales outlets lose ACH to aggregate funds into a central cash account. The third major use of ACH operators is bill payment by the federal government, businesses, households. The Debt Collection Improvement Act (DCIA, 1996) directed the federal government to expand its use of electronic funds-transfer systems. As per the DCIA:

1. The government should be able to maximize on collection of delinquent accounts.
2. Debt-collection costs can be minimized by consolidating functions and activities.
3. The reduction of losses from debt-management activities is achieved by conducting proper screening for potential borrowers, monitoring accounts, and sharing information between federal agencies.
4. The federal government will ensure the public is fully aware of their debt-collection policies so debtors are cognizant of the obligation to repay amounts owed.
5. Debtors are afforded all DUE PROCESS rights, including the ability to challenge, verify, and compromise claims and have access to administrative appeals procedures.
6. When appropriate, agencies are encouraged to sell any delinquent debt, especially debts with underlying collateral.
7. The experience and expertise of private-sector professionals should be employed to help provide debt-collection services for federal agencies.

Electronic funds transfer also includes electronic bill presentment and payment and e-money. In the increasingly popular method of electronic bill presentation and payment, bills are received over the computer, and payment is initiated or authorized electronically. Bills received in the mail may also be paid via the computer or telephone.

E-money has been attempted by a number of electronic service providers, with minimal success to date. One type of e-money system is prepaid stored-value cards, by which consumers pay in advance for set dollar amounts, which are then scanned to execute purchases. Most stored-value cards are designated for specific purchases, such as telephone, photocopying, and mass-transit cards. Multipurpose stored-value cards are gaining acceptance in Europe but more slowly in the United States. E-cash systems, dominated by Pay-Pal, have created an on-line currency exchanged among customers and merchants, thus avoiding the use of credit cards and the potential for credit-card FRAUD. These forms of electronic funds transfer have not yet been widely accepted.

See also DEBIT, CREDIT; E-COMMERCE.

Further reading
Electronic Funds Corporation Web site. Available online. URL: www.achnetwork.com; Financial Management Service Web site. Available online. URL: www.fms.treas.gov/eft; Weiner, Stuart E. "Electronic Payments in the U.S. Economy: An Overview," *Economic Review* 16, no. 2 (1999): 44.

embargo
An embargo is a government-sponsored INJUNCTION against the sale of goods to a foreign country and/or the importation of goods from another country. Though embargoes are designed to adversely affect the economy of another country, they are usually motivated by political reasons—i.e., to punish an offending country. Embargoes are less costly than military intervention, both in money and lives, and they are less likely to be opposed by other countries in the region or world.

The United States' use of embargoes against specific goods is justified on the grounds of national security. Under Section 232 of the Trade Expansion Act of 1962, the president is authorized to take actions to "adjust the IMPORTS" of any good that may impair the national security. In addition to national defense, economic welfare is considered part of national security under the act. In the United States, complete embargoes of goods from some nations are undertaken through the International Emergency Economic Powers Act, or the Trading with the Enemy Act. U.S. embargoes against goods from North Korea, Libya, Vietnam (until 1994), and Cuba all originated under the Trading with the Enemy Act.

The longest-lasting and most famous U.S. embargo has been the ban against trade with Cuba. Enacted in the early 1960s, the Cuban embargo was a reaction to the expropriation of private businesses, many of them owned by Americans, and the communist rhetoric of Fidel Castro's government. For over 40 years, the United States has prohibited trade with Cuba. In 2009, the United States increased sanctions against North Korea in response to expansion of that country's nuclear weapon program.

An embargo is not a blockade; it is an economic sanction. For any embargo to be effective, other countries must agree to cooperate with the sanction. Before the rise of Fidel Castro, Cuba was a major trading partner with the United States. In 1959 Cuban exports to the United States exceeded those from Mexico. After the embargo, Cuba expanded trade relations with the then Soviet Union and Eastern Bloc countries under Soviet control, trading sugar for oil and other goods previously imported from the United States. With the collapse of the Soviet Union, trade and Soviet subsidies of the Cuban economy ended. The Cuban government then turned to other trade partners, primarily Spain and Mexico, developing new business arrangements and investments.

In 1992 the U.S. government attempted to expand its embargo against Cuba, passing the Cuban Democracy Act. Designed to force developing countries to adhere to the U.S. embargo, the act prohibits trade by subsidiaries of U.S. firms with Cuba and bars ships using Cuban ports from entering U.S. ports for six months after leaving Cuba. A provision of the act also terminates eligibility for U.S. economic aid, debt reduction, and debt forgiveness for any country providing assistance to Cuba. Most U.S. trading partners objected strongly to the Cuban Democracy Act, passing legislation prohibiting U.S. subsidiaries operating in their countries from complying with the act.

Sometimes the United States has banned specific products from entering the country, including oil imports from Iran (1979) and Libya (1982) and wheat from the Soviet Union (1978). The wheat embargo, in response to the Soviet invasion of Afghanistan, had little impact as Soviet buyers found ready suppliers of grains from South American producers.

Further reading

Folsom, Ralph H., and Michael Gordon. *International Business Transactions.* 5th ed. Eagan, Minn.: West Group, 2002.

embezzlement

Embezzlement occurs when employees steal from a company. Whereas theft and larceny involve an outsider's taking funds or property, embezzlement is the misappropriation of funds or ASSETS by someone within an organization. Most business owners actively work to reduce shoplifting (called *shrink,* short for inventory shrinkage, by retailers), but fewer businesses develop policies and strategies to reduce embezzlement.

Almost any business is vulnerable to embezzlement. Experts report that it most often occurs in financial institutions and small businesses. A typical case of embezzlement involves a bookkeeper who, using multiple accounts, electronic transfers of funds, and phony paperwork, removes funds from the company into his or her own accounts. Once established, an embezzler can repeatedly extract funds, covering his acts with receipts and accounting transfers. This type of WHITE-COLLAR crime is rarely prosecuted and often repeated at subsequent places of EMPLOYMENT. Logically, a thorough review of references would prevent embezzlers from repeating their crimes, but given the potential LIABILITY associated with a negative reference and without a criminal conviction, former employers usually will volunteer little information beyond dates of employment.

To reduce embezzlement, experts recommend establishing

- policies and procedures regarding cash-handling and internal accounting controls, and rotating responsibilities in sensitive areas where embezzlement is most likely to occur, segregating office shipping, sales, and bookkeeping functions

- a code of conduct for personnel, including notice the company will conduct periodic credit checks on employees and all applicants
- a documentation system that restricts access to FINANCIAL INSTRUMENTS allowing transfer of funds and an AUDITING system to ensure accuracy of information
- control of access to facilities, including having a least two people open and close the facility, and documentation of who has keys, security, and alarm-system information
- review of a fidelity bonding company's reputation and performance

One of the largest cases of embezzlement in the United States involved a group of executives in Phar-mor, a chain of retail drug stores. In 1992 the company lost $350 million in a FRAUD and embezzlement scheme. The company was forced into Chapter 11 bankruptcy protection, fired 16,000 employees, and closed 200 stores to recover from the crime.

emerging markets

Emerging markets are economies that present high RISK but also potentially high rates of growth; they have low per capita GROSS DOMESTIC PRODUCT (GDP). Economists and investors use a variety of terms to differentiate among economies. In the 1960s, economies were divided among first-, second-, and third-world countries. Considered elitist by many, these terms were replaced with industrialized, newly industrialized (NICs), and developing countries. With increased GLOBALIZATION and the end of cold-war economic barriers, many developing countries are now referred to as emerging markets.

In recent years many U.S. mutual fund companies have created emerging-market funds. Emerging markets are predominantly capitalist political/economic systems, with the potential for growth. In addition to relatively low per capita GDP, emerging markets tend to have lower literacy rates, lower life expectancies, and higher infant mortality rates. Most emerging markets also lack INFRASTRUCTURE, roads, ports, and utilities needed for ECONOMIC GROWTH.

Emerging markets differ from agrarian econo-mies in that there is the potential for growth. In very low-INCOME countries, the circle of poverty limits the potential for economic growth. Low incomes prevent households from saving. Lack of savings limits INVESTMENT. Lack of investment limits the potential for economic growth.

One problem for many emerging markets is the dependence on commodities, with prices that vary greatly from year to year. In many emerging markets, people have become the major export, called guest workers in the Middle East and tem-porary workers in Europe. Throughout the later part of the 20th century, remittances sent home to developing countries from these young men and women working abroad have been a major source of hard-currency income. The worldwide recession beginning in 2008 has reduced these remittances and resulted in a reverse migration of labor.

In his *The Stages of Economic Growth,* Walt Rostow describes how economies go through a series of five stages of economic growth: tradi-tional society, preconditions for takeoff, takeoff, drive to maturity, and mass CONSUMPTION. In the traditional society stage, well-established eco-nomic and social systems and customs limit eco-nomic change and growth. In the preconditions stage, traditional constraints are removed and new methods and technology introduced. In the take-off stage, an economic growth begins, and invest-ment expands rapidly; this is a period of intensive development. Rostow dated the takeoff stage in the U.S. economy as the period from 1843 to 1860, when major railroad investment opened new mar-kets and expanded access to resources throughout the country.

Today many emerging markets are in what Rostow would label the preconditions for take-off. Removal of centrally planned economic systems, creation of STOCK MARKETS, and economic aid to stimulate infrastructure development are all occurring in emerging markets around the world.

One source of CAPITAL for emerging markets is MULTINATIONAL CORPORATIONS (MNCs). These are firms that operate in more than one country. The common image of an MNC is a giant CORPO-RATION engaging in business around the world. The *Fortune* 2006 list of "The World's Largest Cor-porations" is led by ExxonMobil, followed by Wal-Mart (later, Walmart), Royal Dutch Shell and BP.

The contribution of multinational corporations and their subsidiaries to the emerging markets they operate in is debatable. Two contrasting theo-ries center on issues of dependency versus mod-ernization. The dependency theory suggests that market CAPITALISM in the form of large MNCs entering small, less-developed countries leads to exploitation and dependency on the MNCs and inhibits indigenous ENTREPRENEURSHIP. Depen-dency theorists argue that MNCs monopolize local industrial, capital, and LABOR MARKETS. Economic growth occurs, but it is largely to the benefit of the "triple alliance": MNCs, government-owned enter-prises, and the local capital elite.

Modernization theorists, on the other hand, suggest multinational corporations are agents of change, promoting economic growth and devel-opment. When a multinational corporation enters an emerging market, it brings with it new technol-ogy, managerial training, infrastructure develop-ment, and access to modern business practices. Management scholar Peter Drucker contends MNCs are "the only real hope" for less-developed countries (LDCs). They alter traditional value sys-tems, social attitudes, and behavior patterns and encourage responsibility among political lead-ers of LDCs. Some economists, however, ques-tion whether replacing traditional systems with "modern" values is always beneficial to the local population.

In today's economy, global sourcing is a com-mon practice. MNCs purchase materials and components around the world, assembling and producing wherever costs are lowest. With INTER-NET communications, corporations now hold ven-dor auctions, inviting selected suppliers to bid on production of parts and products. Managers argue this results in increased COMPETITION and lower prices. Critics counter that it leads emerging economies to cut their prices by ignoring social costs, including pollution, in the race to keep any EMPLOYMENT and income in their economy.

In addition to lack of capital and potential exploitation by multinational corporations, emerging markets face a variety of other hurdles to economic growth and development. Political instability, corruption, protection of property rights, and other risks impair investment and growth in emerging markets.

Further reading
Folsom, Ralph H., and W. Davis Folsom. *Understanding NAFTA and Its International Implications.* New York: Matthew Bender/Irwin, 1996; Lamb, Charles, Joseph Hair, and Carl McDaniel. *Marketing.* 10th ed. Cincinnati, Ohio: Cengage, 2007.

eminent domain
A legal term for one of the "sovereign" powers inherent in all governments, eminent domain allows for the taking (with "just compensation") of private property for public use without the consent of the owner. The government exercises this right, by either judicial or administrative proceedings, through condemnation.

The need for eminent domain is predominately based on growth. As population increases, the demand for land use also grows, along with increasing needs for all kinds of public goods and SERVICES such as sewage-treatment systems, hospitals, bridges, highways, cemeteries, and other forms of INFRASTRUCTURE.

The idea of eminent-domain compensation comes from 17th-century judges and legal scholars, such as Hugo Grotius and Samuel Pufendorf. In the early 1600s, the English Parliament would authorize the taking of property and the amount to be paid as compensation, or it would provide a judicial review to determine the amount. In the American colonies, legal proceedings evolved allowing for landowners to make statements concerning the question of compensation.

Unlike Anglo-American law, the French and German systems require that compensation be paid in advance of the takings. There are fewer general statutes allowing for blanket authorization of condemnation for specific public projects (such as highways) than there are in the United States,

and often each case of condemnation has to be authorized by that country's government.

The U.S. Constitution deals specifically with eminent domain in the last clause of the Fifth Amendment, stating: ". . . nor shall private property be taken for public use, without just compensation." The issue of property takings is not limited to those at the federal level. Section 1 of the Fourteenth Amendment extends the limits to state and local levels by declaring: ". . . nor shall any State deprive any person of life, liberty, or property, without the DUE PROCESS of law."

Additionally, several state constitutions limit eminent-domain powers. As the Industrial Revolution developed in the United States, quasi-public CORPORATIONS such as railroads were able to acquire private property for their own use. Some STATE COURTS reacted to this by interpreting the "public use" clause in its strictest sense, that public access must be allowed to the property taken, while other states required only that the public benefit in some manner from the taking. This situation created a legal debate that lasted for decades, although current U.S. courts' interpretation of the amendment tends towards the "public benefit" theory. Until the 1930s, "public use" was defined to include schools, roads, dams, government buildings, and other public entities. Lately the concept has been expanded to include the resale of private property to private owners for urban renewal, housing developments, and similar programs that generally benefit the public. Critics claim that governments often tread a fine line between what benefits the public and what is essentially ECONOMIC DEVELOPMENT in the guise of public interest.

In a basic condemnation situation, a single person owns the property; however, a great deal of property in the United States is not held in such a simple manner. Often ownership involves holders of easements, MORTGAGES, OPTIONS, and leases. Leaseholders are particularly significant in number, since land is often leased for residential, agricultural, industrial and commercial reasons. This situation creates a two-step legal situation: the government is only required to settle with the landowner, but often another hearing determines how those LEASING the property are compensated. Many states and the federal government have "quick taking" statutes that allow the government to take title and possession before the price is decided by the courts, provided an adequate security deposit is offered.

Generally the amount of compensation due is the fair MARKET VALUE of the property taken. Fair market value is interpreted as the price for which the property would have sold in the absence of condemnation, including not only the existing use value but also the best use for which the property may be utilized. Problems often arise from the definition of a fair market: when there is no market or DEMAND for the condemned property; when adjacent properties rise or fall in value because of the government projects (some of which end up being condemned at a later date); or when the taking involves less than full ownership of the property. Some states, such as California, allow for the compensation for business GOODWILL losses (based on the reputation and location of the business), but these are not recoverable in federal-takings cases.

Probably the biggest eminent-domain issue in recent years has been the case of regulatory takings. In this situation, a new law, regulation, or government action under an existing statute (such as the ENDANGERED SPECIES ACT) results in a decrease in the value of the property, generally because of restrictions placed on its utility and development. This instance, where land has not actually been formally seized under eminent domain, is known as inverse condemnation, and critics maintain that the owner is still entitled to compensation for the loss of property value. As of this writing, almost every state in the union has introduced legislation regarding regulatory-takings compensation.

Eminent Domain in Action

In recent years, possibly the most famous case involving the use of eminent domain was *Kelo v. City of New London* pitting the city of New London, Connecticut, against Susette Kelo. In 1997 Ms. Kelo bought a Victorian fixer-upper house overlooking Long Island Sound. A few months after moving in, Pfizer Pharmaceutical Company announced plans to build a large research facility in the area and the city development agency, using a grant from the state, began buying up adjoining properties in an attempt to upgrade the neighborhood. The city wanted to remove the modest houses and allow private developers to build a corporate park, hotels, and condominiums, which would significantly increase the city's tax base.

When Ms. Kelo and a few neighbors objected, litigation ensued, finally reaching the U.S. Supreme Court, which in 2005, ruled in favor of the city. By a vote of 5 to 4, the justices ruled the city had acted within its rights in using eminent domain for public use and did not violate the Fifth Amendment's takings clause, which states ". . . nor shall private property be taken for public use, without just compensation."

Ms. Kelo received a settlement that allowed her to purchase a new house on a hill overlooking the water and her home was disassembled and moved to a another part of New London, "where a plaque in the front yard explains its significance." In response to the Supreme Court's decision, 43 states amended their eminent domain laws expanding private property rights protections.

Further reading

Benedict, Jeff. *Little Pink House: A True Story of Defiance and Courage.* New York: Grand Central Publishing, 2008; Fellows, James A. "The Legal Doctrine of Regulatory Takings: An Evolving Issue," *Appraisal Journal* 64 (October 1996): 363 (12); Guidry, K., and A. Quang Do. "Eminent Domain and Just Compensation for Single-Family Homes." *Appraisal Journal* 66 (July 1998): 231(5); Melton, B. "Eminent Domain, 'Public Use' and the Conundrum of Original Intent." *Natural Resources Journal* 36 (1996): 59–85.

—Patricia Giddens

employee assistance program

An employee-assistance program (EAP) is a series of company-sponsored services designed to address employees' work and personal problems affecting their performance. In the 1980s many U.S. companies, recognizing the benefits of healthy, focused employees, implemented EAPs as part of EMPLOYEE BENEFITS packages. Most often employee assistance programs are associated with counseling services, which help to address stress, family difficulties, drug abuse, and other problems. The North Dakota Public Employees Retirement System works to give employees assistance "in guidance and counseling and to determine appropriate diagnosis and/or course of treatment to employees and their eligible dependents in cases of alcoholism, drug abuse and personal problems." The North Dakota program, like most EAPs, allows employees a set number of visits per year. EAPs can also include wellness programs, financial counseling, and legal advice.

The economic logic behind providing employee assistance programs is productivity. Focused workers not distracted by personal crises will be more productive, and burnout and work frustration is lessened, improving worker loyalty and reducing turnover costs. EAPs provide a confidential resource for employees, rather than employees having to discuss personal issues with their managers. After the events of September 11, 2001, employees at many U.S. companies, most of them far removed from the direct impact of terrorism, utilized employee assistance programs to deal with emotional stress.

Most companies contract with independent providers of employee assistance programs. Typically employers pay a set dollar amount per month per employee to the EAP provider, regardless of how often employees use the service. Kevin Host, director of Family Services Employee Assistance Program, suggests employers use five criteria in choosing an EAP provider.

- *Location.* Is the EAP provider local or national? Which is best suited for the particular business?
- *Contract terms.* Is it subcontracted? Will employees interact directly with the EAP or a variety of subcontractors?
- *Pricing and value.* Different levels of service result in varying prices and benefits.
- *Accessibility.* How easily accessible is the EAP? How long will employees have to wait to gain assistance?

- *Relationships.* How does the EAP provider's philosophy and practice fit with the mission and philosophy of the company?

One of the difficult parts of employee assistance programs is evaluating their effectiveness. Simple measures like reduced absenteeism and turnover are a starting point; reductions in conflicts and accidents can also be measured. In *Human Resource Management,* Cynthia Fisher, Lyle Schoenfeldt, and James Shaw describe the approach taken by Phoenix, Arizona. A company determined its average annual wage costs and then multiplied this by 0.17, which is the national average percentage of troubled employees. They then multiplied this figure by 0.25 on the assumption that personal problems reduce performance by 25 percent. Assuming EAP intervention could reduce losses due to troubled employees by 50 percent, the savings from their EAP would be 50 percent of the calculated improvement in performance. Net benefits would then be the savings minus the cost of the program, which the city estimated to be $2.5 million annually.

Further reading

Fisher, Cynthia D., Lyle F. Schoenfeldt, and James B. Shaw, *Human Resource Management.* 6th ed. Boston: Houghton Mifflin, 2006; Host, Kevin. "How to Choose an Employee Assistance Plan," *Puget Sound Business Journal,* 17 August 1998.

employee benefits

Benefits are one part of the COMPENSATION AND BENEFITS package that an employee receives as a member of the workforce of a particular company. Total compensation costs to an employee include salary or wages, incentives, and benefits. During the time around World War II, the description was "fringe benefits," because the benefits constituted a minor part of an employee's compensation, but this has changed over time. In this new millennium, employee benefits can add an average 40 percent or more of salary (payroll) costs to the employer's costs. In current economic times, shrinking of benefit packages through cost cutting, cost sharing, deductibles, and fewer benefits offered is occurring. Some major categories of benefits are discussed below, although the list of possibilities is broad, and employers have the flexibility to customize for their specific company needs.

Benefit packages called CAFETERIA PLANS or flexible-benefit packages are common today. With these the company pays a certain dollar amount per pay period for the purchase of various benefits. Any coverage chosen above the company limit can be purchased by the employee at the company's group rates. Thus the employee has a benefits package that is tailored to his or her needs.

INSURANCE is a broad category that includes such items as hospital, medical, dental, vision, life, disability, and long-term care coverage. Each of these can include several choices as to level of coverage. For the medically related insurances, usually several options are offered involving a range of costs for employees. In general a higher deductible and co-pay are associated with a lower premium for the employee. Preferred Provider Organizations (PPOs) and HEALTH MAINTENANCE ORGANIZATIONS (HMOs) are common options offered by most employers today.

RETIREMENT PLANS, if offered, are guaranteed when an employee becomes vested with a company. Vesting traditionally comes after a designated number of years of service, although it can be part of a phased-in system. For example, an employee can earn 20 percent per year with full vesting at five years or another time schedule designed by the company. Pension plans can be fully funded by the employer or be proportionately funded by both employer and employee. Some companies are using the option of a 401K program as their total pension benefit for employees. In this arrangement the employer contributes some dollar amount such as 30 or 50 cents per dollar contributed by the employee up to a certain limit—for instance, 6 percent of earnings. This is further capped by law as to the maximum amount that can be contributed to a 401K plan per year. It is possible and preferable for a company to offer both the traditional pension plan and a 401K plan.

In many companies, "leave banks" have replaced the traditional separate programs for vacation, sick leave, and holidays. Commonly these forms of paid absence from work have been combined into a maximum number of days per year for the employee in his/her leave bank. Whether an employee uses these days for vacation, sickness, or other purposes is immaterial to the employer. The FAMILY AND MEDICAL LEAVE ACT is a separate issue. This is unpaid leave that, by law, an employee may take under certain circumstances and within certain specified guidelines.

Finally, additional leave areas that are traditionally paid by the employer include jury duty, leave due to death of an immediate family member, and military service.

A partial listing of other areas for benefits would include memberships in various clubs like Sam's Club or country clubs; paid educational expenses; paid travel expenses; programs or assistance for child care and elder care; employee discounts; food services; use of a company car; membership in CREDIT UNIONS; and EMPLOYEE-ASSISTANCE PROGRAMS for such items as counseling, financial planning, or legal advice.

Legally required benefits include SOCIAL SECURITY insurance, UNEMPLOYMENT compensation (most employees are eligible), and WORKERS' COMPENSATION (compulsory in most states).

—Leanne McGrath

employee motivation

Employee motivation involves the willingness of people to work towards and obtain their goals at work. Multiple factors affect employee motivation, including the nature of the organization's formal reward structure, perceived pay equity, employee benefits, interesting work, leadership style and quality, and individual needs.

The formal structure of the company's reward system, or the means through which employees earn promotions, salary increases, or other rewards, can either increase or decrease employee motivation. As discussed in MOTIVATION THEORY, incentives or external rewards often motivate people, provided that the incentives are used in an informative manner rather than a controlling manner. Reward structures that promote professional development and provide recognition for employees' contributions to company success are associated with higher levels of JOB SATISFACTION and likely increase employee motivation. On the other hand, inadequate or unfair reward structures may decrease motivation and tempt employees to reduce their efforts at work.

Perceived equity in rewards, such as pay, is a key factor in determining employee motivation. Good wages, which are distributed fairly, serve as an important external motivator. People tend to make social comparisons with other individuals or groups, comparing the level of their own contributions and subsequent rewards with those of their peers. When employees feel either over- or underpaid for their work, it affects motivation. People who feel overpaid may increase their outputs in order to match the high level of pay, benefiting the organization. On the other hand, employees who feel underpaid may respond in a variety of ways. They may decrease their efforts to match the low pay, ask for a raise, try to change the contributions or rewards garnered by other individuals, or search for another job.

Part of the perception of pay equity depends on whether employees believe that their supervisors are qualified to assess their work and that they make fair use of objective standards in evaluating employee performance. Although many employees agree that merit-based pay, or pay related to actual performance, is appropriate and desirable, few believe that such systems are successful when applied to them. In addition, perceptions of pay equity sometimes depend on the appropriateness of the comparison group. Because many companies keep salary information confidential, it may be difficult for employees to select an appropriate comparison group when assessing pay equity. For example, women tend to compare their salaries with those of other women performing the same job, especially if this information is more readily available to them, rather than compare their pay with men performing the same job. In cases where pay inequity does exist between men and women

for the same job and level of experience, women may be relatively unaware of the difference.

Although many organizations may have a difficult time raising employees' salaries due to budget constraints, there are other actions they can take to motivate their workers. Supervisors can strive to maximize the intrinsic value of a job by making it more intellectually stimulating, challenging, or interesting for employees. In addition, providing clearly defined goals for the employees and stating how their performance will relate to potential rewards helps reduce ambiguity about job responsibilities. Providing interesting and stimulating work is as essential to employee motivation as providing fair and equitable pay.

Leadership style and quality also affect employee motivation. Directive leaders, or those who are task-oriented, tend to do the best when the organizational needs include defining a problem or goal and keeping employees focused while working on it. Of course the success of this type of leader depends in part on the leader's ability to provide clear direction to employees. However, leaders who adopt a more democratic style, for instance including employees in the decision-making process, may be more effective at promoting motivation and morale. These leaders are concerned both with the employees' needs and relations and with the organizational goals. Research indicates that leaders who are flexible enough to use either style when the situation dictates, or who at least can recognize when a situation is not well matched for their style, tend to be the most effective.

Finally, employees vary in their individual needs for different kinds of motivating rewards. For example, some employees are high in ACHIEVEMENT MOTIVATION and thrive on accomplishment. Providing these employees with challenging or complex tasks may increase their motivation. Other employees derive motivation primarily from recognition for a job well done. Although organizations should strive to provide full recognition for the work of each employee, extra praise and attention may work especially well in motivating these employees. For others, the need for belonging and affiliation is important. These employees may be highly motivated when working in democratic groups where they can play a role in making decisions and in shaping the group outcome. Still other employees are competition-oriented and may be motivated most when they are provided with opportunities to compete and succeed. Tailoring rewards to employees' personal needs can be an effective means of motivation. However, employing this one-on-one strategy requires a perceptive, creative, and highly effective supervisor.

The importance of facilitating employee motivation should be underscored. Organizations that treat their employees well by providing fair and equitable wages, a stimulating atmosphere, high-quality LEADERSHIP, and full and suitable appreciation for a job well done will be the most successful at retaining talented and motivated employees.

Further reading
Myers, David G. *Exploring Psychology in Modules.* 7th ed. New York: Worth Publishers, 2007; Schultz, Duane, and Sydney Ellen Schultz. *Psychology and Work Today.* 9th ed. Upper Saddle River, N.J.: Prentice Hall, 2006.
—Elizabeth L. Cralley

employee recruiting
People are the one resource that every organization needs to accomplish its mission successfully. How, when, and where to find these people; determination of appropriate COMPENSATION AND BENEFITS; and then securing their EMPLOYMENT constitute the essence of employee recruitment. Effective recruiting begins with HUMAN RESOURCES planning. This includes (but is not limited to) determining job tasks and duties; the education, skills, and experience required of the hired individuals; the level of responsibility for process, people, and product; and the market prices for specific talent. In implementing the organizational strategy, the need for certain employee talent becomes evident for success.

In order for hiring to be effective, it must be tied to organizational goals and result in the desired performance (accomplishing the mission). The human resources that a company hires can provide the sustainable competitive advantage needed to win in the marketplace. No two individuals will bring to the organization identical abilities, experience, or skills, and what they bring will be unique for each and every company. For this reason alone, the recruiting process should be a top priority for all companies. Any and all parts of the process must adhere to all employment laws, including but not limited to the 1964 CIVIL RIGHTS ACT, Age Discrimination Act, Pregnancy Act, and EQUAL PAY ACT.

Many times the initial screening for employees involves reading or scanning résumés, which is done to get a preliminary idea of the person's suitability for a position, Résumés, however, contain only the information that a candidate wants to reveal, and this is always presented in a most positive light. In contrast, a carefully designed application form tells an employer what he/she wants to know about the candidate. This consistency of information gathering allows better comparison of candidates and helps in the event of legal challenge to the final hire.

Tests are used frequently by employers to measure candidates' intangible dynamics as well as job-performance skills. These tests need to be both reliable and valid to be useful and to pass possible legal challenge. The available battery of tests is quite extensive, including paper-and-pencil integrity or honesty tests, personality tests, physical-ability tests, mental-ability tests, and job-knowledge tests. All tests that an employer uses in screening applicants need to be able to demonstrate direct relatedness to job performance. This helps provide a rationale for the candidate hired and helps to defend the employer against a possible discrimination in hiring charge.

INTERVIEWING is a common screening step used in the hiring process. Because of cost considerations, a two-step process is often used. The first pass can be a phone call to screen candidates; this often includes asking behavioral-type questions to gain insight into the candidate's work performance. The second step often consists of a series of face-to-face interviews that occur at the company with managers and those with whom the new hire would be working. A consistent set of questions should be employed and used for all candidates for the position, and the scores of raters should be checked for interrater reliability.

Reference and background checks are another integral part of the recruiting process. Failure to do such checks can result in charges against an employer for negligent hiring if the new hire proves unfit or harms a third party. Both personal and work references are sources for candidate information. Again, specific and consistent questions need to be asked about all candidates to allow accurate comparison. A check of employment facts for verification of information given should also be done. Other types of background checks include credit, educational credentials, and criminal background.

Drug tests are common today as a preliminary screen done early in the recruiting process. A complete medical examination, if required of all new hires, is usually completed after the offer of hire is extended. The offer then is made contingent upon passing the medical exam successfully.

The list of possible sources for qualified candidates for a job opening is very extensive and includes the following: private employment agencies; public employment agencies; ADVERTISING venues such as newspaper, radio, and television; bulletin boards; professional publications; INTERNET employment sites; employee referral; recruitment from competitors; unsolicited applicants; current (in-house) employees; and universities, colleges, and other educational institutions. Using as many of these sources as possible helps the organization find qualified candidates.

Overall the employee recruitment process needs to be designed well and to be understood by all managers. Then its implementation can result in effective hiring.

—Leanne McGrath

Employee Retirement Income Security Act

The Employee Retirement Income Security Act (ERISA, 1974) imposed requirements, on covered employers, to manage employee pension funds for the benefit of their workers. For years many U.S. employers engaged in a variety of practices such as arbitrary termination in pension-plan participation, arbitrary benefit reductions, and mismanagement of pension-fund ASSETS. ERISA was passed to address many of these abuses. The act does not require an employer to establish or fund a pension plan but does impose FIDUCIARY DUTIES for fund managers.

Three important rules within ERISA include the "prudent man" rule, which stipulates that employee pension funds cannot be invested in FINANCIAL INSTRUMENTS that prudent trustees of other pension funds would not purchase. This was intended to reduce the risks taken by pension-fund managers with employees' retirement funds. Under the prudent man rule, most fund managers diversify investments as way to reduce risk.

The second rule requires ERISA fund managers to be registered brokers with the SECURITIES AND EXCHANGE COMMISSION (SEC). This often prevents fund managers from investing in FUTURES markets, because futures-market managers are regulated by the COMMODITY FUTURES TRADING COMMISSION, not by the SEC.

Third, ERISA only applies to pension funds for private-sector employees, not public pension funds. While many states have adopted ERISA guidelines, state employees' pension funds have often been "tapped" to purchase risky investment decisions. In one of the more famous cases, New York City employee pension funds were loaned to the city to prevent the city from filing for bankruptcy. If the prudent man rule had applied to the New York City pension fund managers, it is unlikely that they would have made that investment decision.

The DEPARTMENT OF LABOR (DOL) is charged with enforcing ERISA. Most companies hire professional fund managers to oversee investment of pension funds, but the DOL has ruled that corporate directors and officers are still liable for prudent management of their employees' retirement funds. ERISA requires record-keeping, reporting, and disclosure requirements on companies, as well as requirements guaranteeing employee participation and vesting in pension plans.

Further reading
Gold, Jackey. "The Rape of Public Pensioners: or Why Public Pension Funds Aren't under ERISA, and What Happens as a Result." *Financial World* 160 (23 July 1991): 22; Mallor, Jane P., A. James Barnes, Thomas Bowers, Michael J. Philips, and Arlen W. Langvardt. *Business Law: The Ethical, Global, and E-Commerce Environment.* 14th ed. Boston: McGraw-Hill, 2009.

employee stock-ownership plan
Employee stock-ownership plans (ESOPs) are programs where a CORPORATION contributes shares of the company's stock into a TRUST, which then allocates the stock to employee accounts within the trust.

Shares are typically allocated in proportion to compensation and employees usually begin receiving allocations after one year of service, the shares must vest, meaning the employees become entitled to the shares, before the employee can choose to diversify his or her account. By law, vesting must occur within seven years of service, but many companies vest employees within shorter waiting periods. Employees waiting receive the vested portion of their accounts at termination, disability, death, or retirement. In publicly traded companies employees may sell their distributed shares on the market. In privately held firms, the company must give employees an option to sell the stock to the company. In the United States, ESOPs, created by the EMPLOYEE RETIREMENT INCOME SECURITY ACT of 1974, allow both publicly owned and closely held corporations to transfer ownership interest in the company to its employees.

ESOPs are typically used to buy the stock of a retiring owner in a privately held company and as an employee benefit or incentive plan.

Employees can also benefit from the creation of ESOPs, which are often used to establish a pension plan and add incentives for workers. ESOP distributions and DIVIDENDS are tax-deferred, and laws require financial disclosure to employees. Researchers have found that employee ownership heightens worker involvement and productivity. Drawbacks to ESOPs include the cost of starting a plan, administrative expenses, and compliance with government regulations.

Further reading
Dessler, Gary. *Human Resource Management.* 11th ed. Upper Saddle River, N.J.: Prentice Hall, 2007. Employee Stock Ownership Association Web site. Available online. URL: www.esopassociation.org.

employment
Every organization needs to be staffed with knowledgeable personnel. When evaluating applicants, there are two major concerns: hiring the right person for the available position and being sure that the applicant is right for the company. The person-job fit evaluates whether the applicant has the appropriate knowledge, skills, abilities, and other requirements to perform the job. Factors such as education, experience, and the applicant's desire to perform the job duties are also included in the evaluation. The person-company fit looks beyond the applicant's immediate capacity to perform the current open position and evaluates such factors as the long-term potential of the applicant with the company. Important questions to be answered include: Is the applicant capable of assuming greater responsibilities that are inherent with promotions? Will the applicant fit in with the CORPORATE CULTURE and appreciate the organization's guiding beliefs and values?

The employment process typically consists of three phases: EMPLOYEE RECRUITING, selection, and socializing. Recruiting assures a supply of qualified applicants from which the appropriate selection(s) of new hire(s) can be made. While recruiting and selection are the two steps in employment that receive the most attention, the process of socializing—acclimating the new employee into the organization—should also be an integral part of the employment process. Socialization reduces the potential of psychological shock that the new employee may experience during the first few weeks or months of employment.

Applicants can be recruited from either within or outside the organization. Many companies emphasize developing and promoting their own employees, so these firms conduct an internal search before looking elsewhere. There are several techniques for notifying employees that a position is open and will be filled. Job-posting and job-bidding systems allow the individual employee to tell the company that he/she is interested in the position. Other internal recruiting techniques include data and skills banks that the company may maintain. This information may have been encapsulated from career discussions the employee had with his/her supervisor. The company typically has many applicants for only one opening, so another valuable technique is to maintain information from earlier applicants for previous jobs.

Regardless of whether the position is to be filled with an internal or external candidate, knowledge of the position's availability is crucial. Many applicants are drawn to apply because other individuals already employed by the company have told their friends and family members about the position. Current employees are an effective source of applicants because the referring employee often believes if his/her recommendation results in an unsatisfactory hire, it could negatively reflect on him- or herself. More common external-recruiting methods include ADVERTISING available positions in newspapers and technical journals, on radio stations, and on the INTERNET. Public and private employment agencies are frequent sources of candidates. State employment security commissions are the primary public employment agencies; their services are provided without fees since they are publicly funded. Private employment agencies are paid for their services either by the applicant or the potential employer. Finally, many candidates simply walk into the office and ask if the company is hiring individuals with their qualifications.

Evaluating the applicant's qualifications and determining to whom the employment offer will be made is the purpose of the selection phase. Selection usually involves multiple steps including (1) a series of interviews with the HUMAN RESOURCES representative, the supervisor and/or manager with the opening, and other knowledgeable individuals; (2) verbal and written comprehension and ability tests; and (3) a physical examination that

may include a screen for illegal drug use. A unique type of interview is the realistic job preview (RJP). This interview technique involves the employee in performing actual job duties on the job site. The applicant sees where the work is done and is encouraged to ask questions of current employees whom he/she will be working alongside. RJPs give the applicant more information about the job than would be otherwise obtained. Companies vary widely, however, in their use of these specific techniques.

"Job relatedness" is a critical concern in determining which selection techniques will be used. The ultimate purpose of interviews, tests, and other screening techniques is to predict the potential on-the-job success of the applicant. If a specific question or technique does not predict success, then it should not be used. Employment techniques must be both reliable and valid. Reliability is concerned with the consistency of results if the test or technique is used multiple times. Validity asks the question, "Did the test measure what it was supposed to measure?"

Employment specialists must be careful that the employment process conforms to the requirements of the AMERICANS WITH DISABILITIES ACT. This federal law was passed to help applicants with physical or emotional limitations find meaningful employment. The applicant, after reviewing an up-to-date job description based on a thorough job analysis, is asked whether he/she can perform the essential job duties. At this time the candidate can ask the company to make reasonable accommodations in the job to enable him/her to perform the duties. The company must then evaluate the applicant's request(s) and decide whether it can implement the requested accommodation. Duties that are not essential to the position may be reassigned to other positions.

—John Abbott

employment-at-will

Employment-at-will is the concept that EMPLOYMENT is a CONTRACT between an employer and an employee and therefore subject only to the terms of the agreement between the two. As such, workers are hired for an indefinite duration, and either the employee or the employer may end the relationship for any reason and at any time. Implicit in employment-at-will is the idea that government does not determine employment relationships.

The concept of employment-at-will evolved out of the AMERICAN INDUSTRIAL REVOLUTION as workers and employers shifted from small-scale, local craft guilds to an industrial system employing hundreds and thousands of workers. Employment-at-will became part of American COMMON LAW based on rulings in the 1870s and 1880s.

Most discussion of employment-at-will focuses on an employer's right to terminate a worker without having to justify the action. Contracts, union agreements, and federal discrimination laws limit the right of employers to terminate employees. Until the WAGNER ACT of 1935, UNIONS had relatively little power. Union strikers were often prosecuted under criminal conspiracy laws. The Wagner Act gave union members the right to COLLECTIVE BARGAINING and through these contracts, workers often gained protection from being fired, except for JUST CAUSE.

Law Professor Jane Mallor and her coauthors note that public employees are also often protected from termination without just cause. In what is called the public-policy exception, recognized by about 80 percent of the states, terminated public employees can claim WRONGFUL DISCHARGE based on "(1) refusal to commit an unlawful act, (2) performance of an important public obligation (jury duty or whistle-blowing), (3) exercise of a legal right or privilege (e.g., making a WORKERS' COMPENSATION claim or refusing top take an illegal polygraph test)."

Other limitations on employment-at-will relationships are based on federal antidiscrimination laws. Generally workers are protected against termination based on personal traits, age, and disabilities. In some states, promises by employers and implied good faith and fair-dealing covenants also limit employment-at-will. But as Cynthia Fisher, Lyle Schoefeldt, and James Shaw summarize, ". . . between 70 and 75 percent of employees in the United States have no such explicit protection."

Further reading

Fisher, Cynthia D., Lyle F. Schoenfeldt, and James B. Shaw. *Human Resource Management.* 6th ed. Boston: Cengage, 2006; Mallor, Jane, A. James Barnes, Thomas Bowers, Michael Philips, and Arlen Langvardt. *Business Law: The Ethical, Global, and E-Commerce Environment.* 14th ed. Boston: McGraw-Hill, 2009.

employment taxes   See PAYROLL TAXES.

empowerment

Empowerment in business is participatory decision making and teamwork within organizations. Empowerment includes greater worker control, accountability, and, often, flexibility in scheduling, work hours, and prioritizing of tasks.

Empowerment became a popular management concept in the United States during the 1990s. One story reported that in an empowered work environment, managers were called vision supporters. Empowerment is an alternative to hierarchical work environments, which many portray as places where bosses think they know more than they do and subordinates say what they think boss wants to hear, rather than saying what they believe is true. Hierarchical work environments discourage creativity and risk taking, essential to long-term growth and viability of the organization. MANAGEMENT consultants often advocate greater empowerment of workers. Managers frequently may say they encourage worker participation but instead fear and react against workers who suggest changes with which they are uncomfortable.

Empowerment can also refer to improving the choices available to minority groups struggling for equal opportunity, both in the work environment and in society. In this context, empowerment refers to taking greater control of personal decision making.

empowerment zones, enterprise zones

Empowerment and enterprise zones are areas identified by the Secretary of Housing and Urban Development or the Secretary of Agriculture that have a condition of persuasive poverty, UNEMPLOYMENT, and general distress. To help rebuild these distressed urban or rural areas, tax incentives encourage businesses to locate in these areas and to hire the people who live there. Eligible regions meet certain criteria concerning population, size (urban, less than 20 square miles; rural, less than 1,000 square miles), and poverty rate (minimum 20 percent).

Businesses operating within the designated areas are entitled to an empowerment-zone employment credit (EZEC) of a percent of wages paid to employees who are residents of the empowerment zone, with a maximum credit per employee per year. The employer's deduction for wages must be reduced by the amount of credits allowed. To further encourage development, businesses within an enterprise zone are also entitled to increase the amount they can expense under the Internal Revenue code for the purchase of tangible business property that is not real estate.

—Linda Bradley McKee

Endangered Species Act

The Endangered Species Act, passed by Congress in 1973, provides for the protection and conservation of endangered species and their habitats. The act refers to all species of plants and animals with the exception of pest insects.

The Fish and Wildlife Service (FWS) in the DEPARTMENT OF THE INTERIOR and the National Marine Fisheries Service (NMFS) in the Department of Commerce administer the act and are responsible for identifying and listing "endangered" and "threatened" species. The act defines "endangered species" as "any species which is in significant danger of extinction throughout all or a significant portion of its range." A "threatened species" is "any species which is likely to become an endangered species within the foreseeable future throughout all or a significant portion of its range."

Before a species is listed, its status is evaluated by biologists, scientists, and government agency officials using set criteria. Factors considered when determining species status are: habitat instability, disease or predation, overutilization, inadequacy of existing regulatory mechanisms, and "other natural or manmade factors affecting its continued existence." The Endangered Species Act requires all proposed and officially listed species to be published in the *Federal Register*. Once listed officially, conservation programs are designed for the species' ultimate recovery.

The Endangered Species Act of 1973 builds upon two previous species-protection acts: the Endangered Species Preservation Act of 1966 and the Endangered Species Conservation Act of 1969. Although these acts were important because they established endangered-species listings, they did little to protect the listed species. The Endangered Species Act of 1973 provides enforceable rules for endangered-species protection. All federal agencies are required to participate in the conservation of listed species and are prohibited from taking any action that could harm listed species or their habitats. Additionally, under the 1973 act, the importing or EXPORTING of endangered species is illegal.

One widely publicized controversy involving the Act erupted in 1990 between conservationists and the timber industry when the northern spotted owl of the Pacific Northwest forests was listed as a "threatened" subspecies. (The northern spotted owl is a subspecies of the spotted owl.) Because the owl's "critical habitat," the old-growth federal forestland in the Pacific Northwest, is protected under the provisions of the act, the U.S. government proposed limits on the harvesting of timber in the area. The timber industry protested the limits, fearing the loss of jobs. Conservationists proposed that not enough of the forestland was being protected from logging. In 2009, the northern spotted owl remained on the "threatened" species list and the controversy between forest workers and conservationists continues.

Further reading

"The Spotted Owl's New Nemesis." Available online. URL: www.Smithsonian.com. Accessed on June 15, 2009.

—Paula Maloney

enterprise zones   See EMPOWERMENT ZONES, ENTERPRISE ZONES.

entrepreneurship

Entrepreneurship is the ability and urge to find new, creative solutions to problems. Entrepreneurs forsake the security of regular EMPLOYMENT in pursuit of their dreams. Their compensation is measured by their initiative, skill, and performance. An academic definition states that entrepreneurs are individuals willing to risk investing time and money in a business activity that has the potential to make a PROFIT or incur a loss. Entrepreneurs are innovators who make things happen. The potential for success often blinds an entrepreneur to obstacles, creating a single-mindedness hard to ignore and nearly impossible to stop.

CAPITALISM provides endless opportunity to achieve business success and accumulate WEALTH. People who are excited about profitable opportunities and vigorously pursue them are a business force of unquenchable desire and inexhaustible energy. Economic textbooks typically categorize resources as human, natural, and capital. Some texts use the land, labor, CAPITAL, and entrepreneurship categories. Entrepreneurship is a resource. In the 1990s, as they discarded socialist economic systems, many Central European countries recognized the need to develop entrepreneurial resources. Often the first entrepreneurs were the people who previously had been operating in the black market.

In the United States, people like Bill Gates, Mary Kay, Jeff Bezos, and Steve Jobs fit the definition of *entrepreneur*. Their dreams involved risking time and money on an idea with no guarantees. Destiny, freedom, and money motivated them. Today Microsoft, Mary Kay Cosmetics, Amazon.com, and Apple are household names.

Entrepreneurs are not held to the restrictions of corporate rules and regulations; they decide how to manage their personal lives and businesses. Many people crave the freedom from direct supervision, and this is very important to entrepreneurs. Entrepreneurs answer to consumers and the requirements of their individual business; their supervisor is the person who stares back at them from the mirror. Even though money is important, it is hardly ever at the top of the list of entrepreneurial motivation. Entrepreneurs simply want to be rewarded in direct proportion to their own efforts. Most realize that profitability is usually not immediate but can be the end result of hard work, a good idea, and perseverance.

What exactly is an entrepreneur? Marketing professor Dr. Jerry Moorman has a unique definition: "An entrepreneur is simply a capitalist in heat!" Ignoring the crudeness of this analogy, it is probably an accurate description.

Further reading

Moorman, Jerry, and James W. Halloran. *Contemporary Entrepreneurship.* Cincinnati, Ohio: Southwestern, 1995.

environmental impact statement

An environmental impact statement (EIS) is a public report of a government-funded project, usually industrial, and its potential impact on the environment. An EIS summarizes the project's long-term and short-term effect on noise, water, and air pollution as well as the impact on EMPLOYMENT and living, social, and local service standards. An EIS explains the proposed project and describes any alternatives to it.

An EIS is written by any federal agency either on its own behalf or on the behalf of a state agency and, given the complexity of the report, is usually authored by numerous professionals including scientists, social scientists, and engineers. The drafting of an EIS is required by the National Environmental Policy Act of 1969 (NEPA). The NEPA created a Council on Environmental Quality (CEQ), a three-member board that advises the President with respect to environmental matters. The CEQ directed the creation of guidelines used in writing environmental impact statements. An EIS is required if a project involves federal licensing or federal funding or is undertaken by the federal government.

An EIS is required to address all the possible questions a "reasonable person" might ask. Most environmental impact statements are lengthy documents containing a wealth of information from experts, community groups, and individuals affected by the proposed action. As a brief example, there is the St. Augustine (Florida) Bridge of Lions (details available at www.fdotbridgeoflions.com). The EIS begins by outlining the bridge's importance, the history of the city, and the importance of the bridge for tourism, together with a description of the action that must be taken to rehabilitate, replace, or continue to maintain the existing bridge. The EIS explains three alternatives and their effect on the environment, the public, and businesses and individuals who would have to be relocated. The report states the cost of land acquisition, the method of appraising land values, and additional costs to be paid to individuals affected by the project. The potential economic impact of the bridge project is also evaluated.

Initially the requirement for federal projects and agencies to conduct environmental impact studies was seen as a way to minimize community and activist opposition to federal activities. Businesses benefitting from federal contracts are often closely involved in EIS development. A whole industry has now developed to provide consulting services to federal agencies required to produce environmental impact statements. Opponents of particular federal projects have learned to use the EIS requirement to stall projects they oppose and bring public attention to questionable practices.

Further reading
U.S. Dept. of Agriculture, Water and Environmental EIS. Available online. URL: www.usda.gov/rus/water/ees/eis.htm. Accessed on June 15, 2009.
—Karen M. Cimino

Environmental Protection Agency (EPA)
The Environmental Protection Agency (EPA) is the major federal agency responsible for protection of the natural environment. The EPA's mission is "to protect human health and to safeguard the natural environment—air, water, and land—upon which life depends. For 30 years, EPA has been working for a cleaner, healthier environment for the American people."

The EPA employs over 17,000 people in 10 regional offices and 17 laboratories around the country. As stated on their Web site, "The EPA is responsible for researching and setting national standards for a variety of environmental programs and delegates to states and tribes responsibility of issuing permits, and monitoring and enforcing compliance. Where national standards are not met, EPA can issue sanction and take other steps to assist the states and tribes in reaching the desired levels of environmental quality. The agency also works with industries and all levels of government in a wide variety of voluntary pollution prevention programs and energy conservation efforts."

The EPA was established in 1970 in response to public outcries for better management of air, water, and land. A major contributing factor to this pressure was the publication of *Silent Spring,* Rachel Carson's 1962 classic about the indiscriminate use of pesticides and their impact on bird reproduction. Though skeptics accused Carson of "shallow science," her passionate concern and "literary genius" lead to calls for environmental protection. At the time, environmental management was spread among a wide array of federal agencies. In response to the public pressure, in 1969 Congress passed the National Environmental Policy Act (NEPA), calling for the creation of a Council on Environmental Quality (CEQ) and

- "To declare a national policy which will encourage productive and enjoyable harmony between man and his environment."
- "To promote efforts which will prevent or eliminate damage to the environment and biosphere and stimulate the health and welfare of man."
- "To enrich our understanding of the ecological systems and natural resources important to the Nation."

President Richard Nixon, not known for environmental leadership, signed the NEPA on January 1, 1970, beginning what became known as the "environmental decade." The first Earth Day, April 22, 1970, brought out 20 million citizens demonstrating for environmental reforms, and by the end of the year the Environmental Protection Agency was formed.

The EPA was initially cobbled together from personnel and programs at other federal departments. Responsibility for air and water pollution came from Department of Health, Education, and Welfare (HEW) and the DEPARTMENT OF THE INTERIOR. Pesticide management came from the FOOD AND DRUG ADMINISTRATION (FDA) and the Department of Agriculture. EPA Web site history notes the National Air Pollution Control Administration (NAPCA) and the Federal Water Quality Administration (FWCA) "represented the core of the federal government's pollution-control apparatus prior to the birth of EPA." Both the NAPCA and the FWCA "gained enforcement and standard-setting powers in the 1960s, but the actual exercise of these powers fell far short of expectations."

On December 1, 1970, William Ruckelshaus was confirmed as the first EPA administrator, and by the end of that month the first major piece of environmental legislation, the CLEAN AIR ACT of 1970 was signed. This act required the EPA to establish national air-quality standards as well as standards for significant new sources and for all facilities emitting hazardous substances. The act focused on automobile emissions.

The 1970s are sometimes considered the hey-day of environmentalism, yet Ruckelshaus blames the idealism of the time for subsequent problems. In an interview he said,

> "We thought we had technologies that could control pollutants, keeping them below threshold levels at a reasonable cost, and that the only things missing in the equation were national standards and a strong enforcement effort. All of the nation's early environmental laws reflected these assumptions, and every one of these assumptions is wrong . . . the errors in our assumptions were not readily apparent in EPA's early days because the agency was tackling pollution in its most blatant form."

Since then the Clean Air Act has been amended twice, in 1977 and 1990. In addition, other major environmental acts enforced by the EPA include the

- Federal Insecticide, Fungicide and Rodenticide Act (1996)
- Food Quality Protection Act (1996)
- Toxic Substances Control Act (1976)
- National Environmental Policy Act (1969)
- Pollution Prevention Act (1990)
- Environmental Research, Development and Demonstration Authorization Act (1976)
- RESOURCE CONSERVATION AND RECOVERY ACT (1970)
- CLEAN WATER ACT
- Marine Protection, Research and Sanctuaries Act
- Rivers and Harbors Act (1899)
- Safe Drinking Water Act

The EPA is involved in all major international environmental negotiations, including global warming and ozone-depletion efforts. It has also been involved in cleanup after major environmental disasters, including Love Canal, *Exxon Valdez,* Times Beach, and Three Mile Island. Love Canal was a small ditch dug in the early 1900s to create electrical power using water from Niagara Falls. When the project failed, it became a municipal and industrial chemical dump. In 1953 Hooker Chemical Company filled in the canal and sold it to the city for $1, and in the late 1950s houses were built on the land. In the late 1970s Lois Gibbs and other area home owners began documenting and questioning the exceptionally high rate of birth defects among Love Canal residents. Eventually, using SUPERFUND monies, the EPA relocated 1,000 residents. The Superfund was created by its federal government in 1980 to clean up abandoned and accidentally spilled hazardous waste.

The *Exxon Valdez* was the infamous oil tanker that had a disastrous spill in Prince William Sound, Alaska, in 1989. The EPA oversaw bioremediation efforts, while Exxon paid over $1 billion in fines. Less well known than the *Exxon Valdez* was Times Beach, a small community south of St. Louis, Missouri. Dioxin-contaminated oil had been sprayed on area roads in the 1970s in efforts to control dust. The EPA managed permanent relocation of Times Beach residents and brought a portable thermal incinerator to the area to burn dioxin-laced soil.

The EPA was actively involved in the aftermath of the 1979 Three Mile Island nuclear accident. Mechanical failure at the nuclear power plant near Harrisburg, Pennsylvania, created the potential for nuclear meltdown, which fortunately did not occur. No nuclear power plant has been built since then. The EPA is responsible for long-term monitoring of the impact of radioactive releases from Three Mile Island.

Environmental critics of the EPA often complain the agency does not conduct "good science" research, leading to lax environmental regulations. Social critics complain about the lack of enforcement of environmental laws. Business and industry groups complain about the cost of reporting and compliance with EPA regulations.

See also GREEN MARKETING.

Further reading
Environmental Protection Agency Web site. Available online. URL: www.epa.gov.

environmental scanning

Environmental scanning is the process of monitoring and collecting information about business conditions affecting a market. As marketers develop and then implement their marketing strategies—combinations of pricing, PRODUCT, distribution, and SALES PROMOTION decisions for each target market—businesses must keep track of changes in the marketplace. Yet most business managers have more than enough to do directing day-to-day operations; one analogy of a typical businessperson's day is that it is spent swatting mosquitoes. In addition a manager must also hire new workers, meet government requirements, decide which products to produce or terminate, and cultivate relationships with customers and distributors, resulting in workweeks that are often 70–80 hours long. Often managers can become so consumed with these necessary activities that they fail to notice the "lion"—some change in the marketplace that can create a major new opportunity or a dire threat to their enterprise. Thus, environmental scanning is needed to look beyond all the mosquitoes and see if there are any lions coming.

The main purpose of environmental scanning is to track changes in ECONOMIC CONDITIONS, GROSS DOMESTIC PRODUCT, INFLATION, UNEMPLOYMENT, technology, COMPETITION, international trade agreements, and other cultural, political, and legal factors that affect business decisions. Businesses consider changes in economic conditions, which usually do not change very quickly, when making long-term planning decisions. On the other hand, changes in technology can rapidly redefine markets and sources of competition or of COMPARATIVE ADVANTAGE. For example, while the U.S. Postal Service has a MONOPOLY in mail service, the fax machine and cellular and INTERNET technologies are changing the ways people communicate, often bypassing standard mail service.

When conducting competitive environmental scanning, marketers consider three types of competition: direct competitors producing similar products, competitors producing substitute products, and firms competing for the same consumers' spending. Most marketers can name their direct competitors instantly, and they are usually aware of producers of substitute products. Many companies maintain MARKET INTELLIGENCE efforts to monitor the activities of these sources of competition.

Changing social and cultural conditions require marketers to be aware of and sensitive to changing values and to changes in market DEMOGRAPHICS. For example, since 2001 California no longer had a majority white population as Hispanic and Asian Californians together represented a majority of the state's residents. Cultural groups have different values, consumer preferences, and buying activities. Some groups, such as Japanese consumers, are reluctant to use CREDIT CARDS, and many cultural groups in the United States tend to be very brand-loyal consumers. During environmental scanning, marketers attempt to identify changing social and cultural trends and adjust their marketing strategies to meet changing market opportunities.

Political and legal changes can harm or help a business. Often firms or business organizations will attempt to influence regulatory processes affecting their markets. Industry associations use environmental scanning to monitor proposed changes in laws, testify at public forums for and against legislation, and lobby on behalf of their interests.

See also MARKETING STRATEGY.

Further reading
Boone, Louis E., and David L. Kurtz. *Contemporary Marketing.* 14th ed. Fort Worth: South-Western, 2009.

Equal Credit Opportunity Act (ECOA)

The Equal Credit Opportunity Act (ECOA) was enacted to give all consumers an equal chance to obtain credit. Passed in 1974, the ECOA protects consumers when dealing with any creditor who regularly extends credit, including banks, small loan and finance companies, retail and department stores, credit card companies, and credit unions. Anyone involved in granting credit, such as real estate brokers who arrange financing, is covered by the law. Factors such as INCOME, expenses, debt, and credit history can be used in determining creditworthiness. The ECOA was written in response to past practices in which factors including sex, race, national origin, or religion influenced lending decisions. Businesses applying for credit also are protected by the law.

Under the ECOA, when you apply for credit, a creditor may not:

- Discourage you from applying because of your sex, marital status, age, race, national origin, or because you receive public assistance income
- Ask you to reveal your sex, race, national origin, or religion. A creditor may ask you to voluntarily disclose this information (except for religion) if you are applying for a real estate loan. This information helps federal agencies enforce anti-discrimination laws. You may be asked about your residence or immigration status.
- Ask if you're widowed or divorced. When permitted to ask marital status, a creditor may use only the terms married, unmarried, or separated.
- Ask about your marital status if you are applying for a separate, unsecured account. A creditor may ask you to provide this information if you live in a "community property" state: Arizona, California, Idaho, Louisiana, Nevada, New Mexico, Texas, and Washington. A creditor in any state may ask for this information if you apply for a joint account or one secured by property.
- Request information about your spouse, except when your spouse is applying with you; your spouse will be allowed to use the account; you are relying on your spouse's income or on alimony or child support income from a former spouse; or if you reside in a community property state.
- Inquire about your plans for having or raising children
- Ask if you receive alimony, child support, or separate maintenance payments, unless you're first told that you don't have to provide this information if you won't rely on these payments to get credit. A creditor may ask if you have to pay alimony, child support, or separate maintenance payments.

When deciding whether or not to offer you credit, a creditor may not:

- Consider your sex, marital status, race, national origin, or religion
- Consider whether you have a telephone listing in your name. A creditor may consider whether you have a phone.
- Consider the race of people in the neighborhood where you want to buy, refinance, or improve a house with borrowed money
- Consider your age, unless:
  you are too young to sign contracts, generally younger than 18 years of age;
  you are 62 or older, and the creditor will favor you because of your age;
  it is used to determine the meaning of other factors important to creditworthiness. For example, a creditor could use your age to determine if your income might drop because you're about to retire.
  it is used in a valid scoring system that favors applicants age 62 and older. A credit-scoring

system assigns points to answers you provide to credit application questions. For example, your length of employment might be scored differently depending on your age.

When evaluating a consumer's income, a creditor may not:

- Refuse to consider public assistance income the same way as other income.
- Discount income because of your sex or marital status. For example, a creditor cannot count a man's salary at 100 percent and a woman's at 75 percent. A creditor may not assume a woman of childbearing age will stop working to raise children.
- Discount or refuse to consider income because it comes from part-time employment or pension, annuity, or retirement benefits programs.
- Refuse to consider regular alimony, child support, or separate maintenance payments. A creditor may ask you to prove you have received this income consistently.

When applying for credit, consumers have the right to:

- Have credit in your birth name (Mary Smith), your first and your spouse's last name (Mary Jones), or your first name and a combined last name (Mary Smith-Jones)
- Get credit without a cosigner, if you meet the creditor's standards
- Have a cosigner other than your husband or wife, if one is necessary
- Keep your own accounts after you change your name, marital status, reach a certain age, or retire, unless the creditor has evidence that you're not willing or able to pay
- Know whether your application was accepted or rejected within 30 days of filing a complete application
- Know why your application was rejected. The creditor must give you a notice that tells you either the specific reasons for your rejection or your right to learn the reasons if you ask within 60 days. Acceptable reasons include: "Your income was low" or "You haven't been employed long enough." Unacceptable reasons are: "You

didn't meet our minimum standards" or "You didn't receive enough points on our credit-scoring system." Indefinite and vague reasons are illegal, so ask the creditor to be specific.

- Find out why you were offered less favorable terms than you applied for—unless you accept the terms. Ask for details. Examples of less favorable terms include higher finance charges or less money than you requested.
- Find out why your account was closed or why the terms of the account were made less favorable unless the account was inactive or delinquent

The FEDERAL TRADE COMMISSION's ECOA guidelines recommend consumers who suspect discrimination in credit decisions can take action, including:

- Complain to the creditor. Make it known you're aware of the law. The creditor may find an error or reverse the decision.
- Check with their state Attorney General to see if the creditor violated state equal credit opportunity laws.
- Bring a case in federal district court. If you win, you can recover damages, including punitive damages.
- Join with others and file a class action suit. You may recover punitive damages for the group up to $500,000 or 1 percent of the creditor's net worth, whichever is less.

Along with the many other problems and irregularities associated with the subprime mortgage lending crisis, investigators found that many "prime rate," meaning qualified borrowers, were pushed into subprime loans by mortgage lenders. Under ECOA, borrowers had the right to ask what terms were used to determine their loan status, but many consumers were unaware of their rights.

Further reading
Federal Trade Commission Web site. Available online. URL: www.ftc.gov.

equal employment opportunity and affirmative action
Two terms commonly used in American business but often misunderstood are *equal employment*

opportunity and *affirmative action.* In general, "equal employment opportunity" means that individuals will be considered for jobs or employment actions without any regard to their race, color, religion, sex, or national origin. These five demographic criteria are specifically named in Section 703 of the Civil Rights Act (CRA) of 1964, (see CIVIL RIGHTS ACTS) as amended. Considering one or more of the criteria in personnel activity is to engage in discrimination, which is prohibited by the act. The definition of covered employers, governments, labor unions, employment agencies, and training and apprenticeship sponsoring groups is so extensive that equal employment opportunity is considered a fundamental principal in employment law.

Since equal employment opportunity prohibits the use of artificial criteria (race, color, religion, sex, or national origin) in personnel activities, the concept is considered to be facially neutral. Affirmative action, however, is not facially neutral. Affirmative action encourages giving special consideration because of an individual's membership in a protected category, such as racial or sexual. Affirmative action is a voluntary program. It is above and beyond equal employment opportunity and intended to help correct injustices that occurred in the past. Through this concept when qualified applicants have similar qualifications for the same job opportunity, additional consideration is given to the minority and/or female applicant.

The practice of affirmative action was promulgated with the issuance of Executive Order 11246 in 1965. Issued by President Lyndon Johnson, this Executive Order established regulations for companies doing business with the federal government. Covered federal contractors and primary subcontractors are prohibited from discriminating based on race, color, religion, sex, or national origin. Covered companies which employ 50 or more people and have more than $50,000 in government contracts must have a written affirmative action program for minorities and females, with identified goals and timetables. The plans include a comparison of the internal utilization of minorities and females, by job group, compared with their external availability. When the external availability is greater than the internal utilization, underutilization exists and a goal to eliminate the utilization must be developed. Companies with government contracts of $10,000 or less are exempted from this executive order.

The elimination of discrimination in America was the goal of the 1964 Civil Rights Act. It is a very broad and far-reaching act. Section 7 specifically addresses employment. Other laws such as the 1968 Federal Fair Housing Act, as amended, assures equal housing opportunities regardless of race, color, religion, national origin, gender, as well as handicap and familial status. This act prohibits the red-lining of geographic areas (an area where loans are not made) or failure to finance housing to people living in inner cities or low-income census tracts.

—John B. Abbott

Equal Employment Opportunity Commission

The Equal Employment Opportunity Commission (EEOC) is a federal agency created by the passage of the CIVIL RIGHTS ACT of 1964. The EEOC's mission is "to promote equal opportunity in EMPLOYMENT through administrative and judicial enforcement of the federal civil rights laws and through education and technical assistance." In addition to enforcing Title VII of the Civil Rights Act of 1964, which prohibits discrimination in employment based on race, color, religion, sex, or national origin, the EEOC enforces the following statutes.

- The Age Discrimination in Employment Act of 1967 makes it illegal for employers to discriminate against individuals 40 years of age and older.
- The EQUAL PAY ACT of 1963 prohibits discrimination based on gender in compensation for similar work performed under similar conditions.
- Title I of the AMERICANS WITH DISABILITIES ACT of 1990 makes it illegal for employers in the public and private sector, excluding the federal government, to discriminate on the basis of disability.
- The Civil Rights Act of 1991 provides for monetary DAMAGES in cases where intentional

discrimination can be proved and clarifies legislation regarding disparate impact actions. (Disparate impact actions are those which, although not intentionally discriminatory, can be shown to have a disproportionately negative effect on a group defined by race, color, religion, sex, or national origin.)

- Section 501 of the Rehabilitation Act of 1973 prohibits discrimination in employment against federal employees with disabilities.

In order to fulfill its mission, the EEOC

- investigates charges brought by individuals who believe they have experienced discrimination in employment, as well as charges initiated by Commissioners themselves
- attempts to "conciliate" substantiated charges by negotiating voluntary resolution between the party bringing the charge and the employer
- brings suit in federal court in cases where conciliation is not successful
- interprets the laws it enforces by means of regulations and other forms of guidance
- provides funding and support to state and local agencies, as well as training and assistance programs to employers

Individuals may file charges of employment discrimination at the EEOC headquarters in Washington, D.C., or at any one of the commission's 50 field offices. Once charges have been filed, the commission assigns them to one of three categories. Category A charges receive highest priority, in terms of investigation, resource allocation, and settlement effort. Category B charges are identified as those needing more investigation before action is taken. Category C charges are those over which the commission does not have jurisdiction or where the charges are unsupported. Category C charges are not pursued by the EEOC, although complainants are free to file civil suits in such cases.

The EEOC encourages all parties to negotiate settlements without resorting to litigation, and it has instituted a program to help individuals and employers reach mutually acceptable solutions with the help of trained mediators. When mediation fails, the commission represents victims of employment discrimination in federal court, obtaining monetary judgments against employers of all types and sizes who violate the statutes under the EEOC's jurisdiction.

In addition to investigating and resolving employment discrimination cases at the federal level, the EEOC contracts with state and local fair-employment practices agencies (FEPA's) to handle charges and claims that arise under state and local statutes. The commission's Federal Sector Program provides for the enforcement of antidiscrimination laws on behalf of employees of the federal government and serves as the point of appeal for complainants against federal agencies. Additionally, the commission coordinates individual federal departments' and agencies' equal-opportunity programs, policies, and regulations.

The EEOC offers education and training to employers, employees, groups representing companies and workers, community organizations, and the general public. Its outreach and education programs include speakers, seminars, booths and displays, a Web site, and interactive workshops, which are provided free of charge to small businesses, employee groups, job fairs, cultural festivals, and other interested parties. Technical assistance and training programs are fee-based (with fees limited to the cost of providing training and producing training materials) and cover a wide variety of seminars and training courses on general and customer-specific topics aimed at the private sector as well as local, state, and federal government agencies. The goal of the commission's outreach and education programs is to provide information that will clarify the requirements of the laws and encourage voluntary compliance.

The EEOC is also responsible for gathering, tabulating, and publishing data on the employment status of women and minorities in a wide variety of private- and public-sector occupations. An important component of this effort is the annual Employer Information Survey, which requires certain employers and government contractors to complete and file an EEO-1 report with the EEOC every year. In addition to processing the information generated by these reports, the commission provides guidance and training for employers in completing the EEO-1.

The EEOC is made up of five commissioners who are appointed by the U.S. president, subject to the consent of the U.S. Senate. Commissioners serve for five years; terms are staggered, and a chairman and vice chairman are chosen by the president. Other key positions include an executive officer, general counsel, inspector general, and legal counsel, as well as directors of communications and legislative affairs; equal opportunity; federal operations; field programs; financial and resource management; HUMAN RESOURCES; information resources management; and research, information, and planning. The EEOC budget for FISCAL YEAR 2009 was $341 million. Approximately 90 percent of the commission's budget is spent on personnel costs (salaries, benefits) and rent. At the end of fiscal year 2008, the commission had the equivalent of 2,174 full-time employees, down from a high of 3,390 in 1980.

EEOC statistics for fiscal year 2009 indicate that

- 35.6 percent of the 95,042 individual charge filings in that year alleged race-based discrimination
- 29.7 percent of cases were for gender-based discrimination
- 11.1 percent alleged discrimination on the basis of national origin
- gender-based discrimination charges included pregnancy-related discrimination as well as allegations of SEXUAL HARASSMENT; of the sexual harassment charges filed in FY2008, 15.9 percent were filed by males

Further reading

EEOC Web site. Available online. URL: www.eeoc.gov/; Office of the Federal Register, National Archives and Records Administration. *The United States Government Manual, 2000/2001.* Washington, D.C.: United States Government Printing Office, 2000; Quain, Anthony J. *The Political Reference Almanac, 2001/02.* Arlington,

Va.: PoliSci Books, 1999; Rothstein, Mark, et al. *Employment Law.* 2d ed. St. Paul, Minn.: West Group Publishing, 1999.

—Janet Hadwin Brackett

Equal Pay Act

The Equal Pay Act (1963), which makes pay discrimination based on gender illegal, was designed to correct the wage gap for women. At the time female workers were being paid 60 percent of what male workers were making. By 1999 women were earning 75 percent of men's wages. Until 1999 the Equal Pay Act had rarely been a major concern for businesses. In that year the Clinton administration pushed for expanded use of equal-pay auditors, raising the importance of addressing pay discrimination.

In 1999, after the DEPARTMENT OF LABOR conducted a "glass ceiling" audit, Texaco paid female employees over $3 million. Other companies and government agencies scrambled to assess and address pay discrimination. The general provisions of the Equal Pay Act (referred to as the EPA in HUMAN RESOURCES literature) requires equal pay for equal work and prohibits paying an employee of the opposite gender less if the work both employees in an establishment do is the same or substantially the same.

Close examination of the act requires legal assistance, but according to the law, "same or substantially the same work" refers to job content, not job titles or descriptions. "Opposite gender" means the EPA protects both men and women from pay discrimination. Under the EPA, pay refers to all payments and benefits including PROFIT SHARING, bonuses, and expense accounts. An establishment is defined as a distinct physical place of business. Thus employers can pay different wages to people doing the same work at different locations. the act exempts certain categories of employees, but in 1999, when faced with the potential of a pay audit, many companies were forced to look closely at their pay practices.

While the EPA challenges gender-based pay discrimination, generally pay differences are legal when based on

- differences in level of skill
- unequal effort
- differences in responsibility
- differences in working conditions
- differences based on a SENIORITY system
- differences based on a merit system

Many pay-discrimination lawsuits have defined and redefined the legal parameters associated with the Equal Pay Act. The EPA is enforced by the EQUAL EMPLOYMENT OPPORTUNITY COMMISSION.

Further reading

Bland, Timothy S. "Equal Pay Enforcement Heats Up," *HRMagazine* 44, no. 7 (July 1999): 138; Mallor, Jane P., A. James Barnes, Thomas Bowers, Michael Philips, and Arlen Langvardt. *Business Law: The Ethical, Global, and E-Commerce Environment.* 14th ed. Boston: McGraw-Hill, 2009.

equation of exchange

The equation of exchange is a mathematical statement showing that the MARKET VALUE of all goods and services sold equals the amount of money paid for the goods and services. The equation is $MV = PQ$, where M is the MONEY SUPPLY, V is the velocity of circulation of money (the number of times that money changes hands during a year), P is the level of prices (in most circumstances, retail prices), and Q is quantity of goods and services sold to final consumers. In the equation of exchange, P times Q is the monetary value of final goods and services—that is, national INCOME. The equation of exchange is used to relate monetary aspects of an economy and ECONOMIC POLICY to output and INFLATION in the economy.

The quantity theory of money, developed by Yale economist Irving Fisher (1867–1947), stated that under most circumstances V and Q are constant, and therefore an increase in the money supply will cause an increase in the price level (inflation). Historical data do not support Fisher's theory. Velocity, while often assumed to be constant, varies over time with changes in technology and CONSUMER BEHAVIOR. The quantity of goods and services sold (Q) also cannot be assumed to be constant.

Monetarists, using the ideas of the late Milton Friedman, use the equation of exchange to demonstrate the importance of the money supply in affecting inflation. They assume velocity is constant, at least over short periods of time, suggesting that changes in the money supply result in changes in the price level and/or changes in real output of an economy. Most monetarists believe economies tend toward EQUILIBRIUM at the level of potential real GROSS DOMESTIC PRODUCT; thus, changes in MONETARY POLICY primarily affect inflation. Because of the time lag between a change in the money supply and its impact in the economy, monetarists argue government intervention heightens peaks and troughs of BUSINESS CYCLES, rather than smoothing out variations in the level of economic output. Milton Friedman and many other monetarists suggest establishing a fixed rate of growth in the money supply, thereby eliminating money-supply changes as an uncertainty in the business environment.

Further reading

Boyes, William, and Michael Melvin. *Macroeconomics.* 7th ed. Boston: Houghton Mifflin, 2007.

equilibrium

In economics, equilibrium refers to situations in which individuals, firms, markets, and systems are operating at optimal level and there is no current need or motive to change. One analogy to equilibrium is dropping a marble into a bowl. The marble will roll back and forth but will eventually come to rest. Unless something disturbs the bowl, the tendency will be for the marble to stay in the same place. Similarly, when circumstances change for individuals, firms, or societies, economic systems adjust to attempt to attain a new equilibrium.

At the individual level, equilibrium is attained when consumers allocated their INCOME among available choices to obtain the maximum level of satisfaction. Also at the individual level, a firm achieves equilibrium when it chooses levels of inputs and outputs that maximize PROFITS, given current market conditions.

Market equilibrium is portrayed by the Marshallian cross, named after British economist

Alfred Marshall. Market equilibrium is achieved where there is a market-clearing price, meaning a price at which those consumers who want to purchase the PRODUCT can do so, and those producers who want to sell their product at that price can find buyers. It is the price at which quantity demanded equals quantity supplied, ceteris paribus (other things being equal).

Macroeconomic equilibrium occurs when all the markets within the economic system are in balance. Like market equilibrium, macroeconomic equilibrium is a price level at which aggregate demand equals aggregate supply. Changes in monetary and FISCAL POLICY, consumer and business decisions, and global social, political, and climatic conditions are major causes of changes in equilibrium of economic systems.

Realistically, economic forces are in constant change. In the time it takes to read this entry, markets, economic policies, and individual and household priorities are changing. Nevertheless, equilibrium is an important concept portraying the direction of efforts within economic systems. A story in the *Wall Street Journal* once described pricing activity by airline companies, noting that managers changed 1 million airline-ticket prices each day. These firms were adjusting their price, attempting to maximize profits depending on market forces: the number of people who bought tickets that day, the time until the flight departed, the actions of competing firms, the capacity of the plane, and past experience with last-minute DEMAND. While most markets do not change as rapidly as that for airline tickets, markets are nonetheless constantly changing, and therefore equilibrium, the state of balance, is also changing.

Further reading
Ruffin, Roy J., and Paul R. Gregory. *Principles of Economics*. 7th ed. Boston: Addison Wesley, 2002.

equity

Equity has different meanings, depending on the business context. In general, equity is the ownership interest of SHAREHOLDERS; in accounting it is the portion of a company's ASSETS owned by share-

holders, as opposed to the amount the company has borrowed. In this context, equity equals assets minus liabilities, or net worth. This is also referred to as stockholders' equity. Similarly, in banking equity is the MARKET VALUE of a property minus the loans against the property. Equity LOANS are based on this type of equity.

Equity, equity interest, and equity markets are all a critical part of any capitalistic economic system. By definition, CAPITALISM is a social and economic system based on private property rights, private allocation of CAPITAL, and self-interest motivation. Capitalism is often referred to as a free-enterprise or market system. Capitalism contrasts with SOCIALISM, in which most RESOURCES and industrial PRODUCTION systems are state-owned or controlled; and with communism, in which most resources are state-owned and most decisions regarding output are made through central planning. Equity and the ability to transfer equity interests are essential to the flow of capital. In the CIRCULAR FLOW MODEL of an economic system, households provide savings, either directly or indirectly, through FINANCIAL INTERMEDIARIES to businesses. Businesses use savings to purchase capital to produce goods and services, which in turn are purchased by consumers. In exchange for their savings, households receive either interest INCOME for loans or an ownership interest in the business—equity.

Equity interests are often exchanged among investors in stock exchanges. While these venues create new equity interests through INITIAL PUBLIC OFFERINGS (IPOs), most stock trading is a transfer of ownership interests. In the United States the oldest and most prominent stock exchange is the NEW YORK STOCK EXCHANGE (NYSE Euronext). Established in 1792, along a wall that had been used to keep wild pigs out of settlers' gardens in lower Manhattan, the NYSE is the largest stock exchange in the world based on dollar value of shares traded. In January 2009 the exchange traded 62 billion shares, valued at $1,521 trillion dollars.

While NYSE dominates the stock exchanges in dollar volume traded, the over-the-counter (OTC) market is the largest stock exchange in terms of the number of different CORPORATIONS whose stocks are traded there. The backbone of the OTC market is NASDAQ, the NATIONAL ASSOCIATION OF SECURITY DEALERS AUTOMATED QUOTATIONS. Geographically dispersed securities dealers connected by computers are the intermediaries for the OTC stock traders. The enormous size of the OTC market is illustrated by the fact that NASDAQ surpasses NYSE in annual share volume.

As important as equity markets are to the U.S. economy, they are sometimes even more important to countries that are transitioning from socialism to capitalism. In the 1990s Mongolia, with the advice of former Secretary of State James Baker, privatized its few industries, issuing each adult shares of stock in what had been government-controlled industries, including the electrical company, railroad, and a few factories. The old opera house in Ulan Batur, Mongolia's capital, was converted into the national stock exchange. Government representatives held numerous education forums, explaining what shares of stock were and what value they might have.

Romania was one of the last post-communist countries to move toward capitalism. After the assassination of dictator Nicolae Ceaușescu, Romania was pressured by the INTERNATIONAL MONETARY FUND (IMF) and WORLD BANK to "establish the INFRASTRUCTURE for a market economy." In response, Romania created two small stock exchanges modeled after the U.S. system. One, the Bucharest Stock Exchange (BSE), trades "listed securities." Starting with six listings and 24 brokerage companies, by 2009 the BSE had shares of over 140 companies being traded daily. Romanian managers were initially shocked that the exchanges required financial transparency; disclosure of the BALANCE SHEETS, and other financial information. They quickly learned that attracting equity investment in EMERGING MARKETS like Romania required transparency. Similarly, the Iraq stock exchange, established in 2004, had trading in only 24 companies on June 11, 2009.

The U.S. Securities and Exchange Act of 1934 defines an equity security as "any stock or similar security, certificate of interest or participation in any profit sharing agreement, pre-organization certificate or subscription, transferable share, voting trust certificate or certificate of deposit for an equity security, limited partnership interest, interest in a JOINT VENTURE, or certificate of interest in a business TRUST or any security convertible, with or without consideration into such a security, any such warrant or right; or any put, call, straddle, or other option or privilege of buying such a security from or selling such a security to another without being bound to do so."

See also OWNER'S EQUITY.

Further reading
"Romania Builds Infrastructure for Economic Reform," *Securities Industry News,* 11 March 2002; The Iraq stock exchange. Available online. URL: www.isx-1Q.net/page/index.htm. Accessed on June 15, 2009.

equity income theory
Equity income theory suggests that employees determine whether they are being fairly treated by management by comparing their own input/outcome ratio to the input/outcome ratio of others. Inputs are the experience, education, effort, time worked, and special skills workers bring to a job. Outcomes are pay, benefits, recognition, and other rewards given to workers.

Equity income theory attempts to address almost every worker's question, "Am I being treated fairly?" People develop a sense of inequity when a comparison of inputs and outcomes leads to a perceived imbalance relative to others. For example, teachers frequently complain that relative to their education and responsibilities, they are not paid equitably. In situations where employees perceive they are not being paid equitably, they often resort to any of three alternatives:

1. Reduce effort.
2. Work with colleagues to lobby for higher pay for each member of the affected group.
3. Seek EMPLOYMENT where pay is better.

Successful employee COMPENSATION AND BENEFITS systems incorporate the concept of equity income theory. Equitable compensation plans address internal, external, and individual equity concerns. Internal equity is the pay relationship among jobs within the organization. Employees expect senior executives to earn more than production workers, but when the differences become huge, the system is not perceived as internally equitable. Ben & Jerry's Ice Cream company was legendary in the 1980s for mandating that the president receive no more than seven times the INCOME of the lowest paid worker. Enron executives apparently did not adhere to that sense of social, internal equity.

External equity refers to workers' comparisons of similar jobs in different organizations. In many rural areas of the United States, federal government jobs pay more than similar local, private-sector jobs. Local businesses often hire, train, and then lose employees to government and government-funded jobs in the area. In the 1990s, U.S. postal workers threatened to strike. When the postal workers' pay scale became known, public ire over perceived pay inequity relative to the skills and effort required created resentment against postal workers, leading to such comments as "I will do their job for that pay."

Individual equity refers to comparisons among individuals doing the same or very similar job within an organization. Those in HUMAN RESOURCES management suggest this is the most important comparison. In the United States, most workers accept the concept of paying senior employees more than newer employees and paying more-productive employees more than less-productive employees. Problems arise in defining and differentiating productivity. In service environments, measuring differences in productivity are difficult. Subjective evaluations often become popularity contests and create resentment among the workforce. Equity income theory suggests managers need to address all three types of equity concerns. Unionized work environments address pay differences in COLLECTIVE BARGAINING. New workers understand the pay system before they choose to join the workforce. In nonunion environments, pay inequities are a frequent source of conflict and sometimes litigation.

The EQUAL PAY ACT (EPA, 1963) made illegal any pay discrimination based on gender. The act was designed to correct the wage gap for women at a time when women workers were being paid 60 percent of what men workers were making. By 1999 women were earning 75 percent of men's wages, and many companies were closely evaluating their pay practices.

See also FORCED RANKING SYSTEMS; UNION.

Further reading
Fisher, Cynthia D., Lyle F. Schoenfeldt, and James B. Shaw. *Human Resource Management.* 6th ed. Boston: Cengage, 2006; Mallor, Jane P., A. James Barnes, Thomas Bowers, Michael Philips, and Arlen W. Langvardt. *Business Law: The Ethical, Global, and E-Commerce Environment.* 14th ed. Boston: McGraw-Hill, 2009.

ergonomics

Ergonomics is an engineering science concerned with the psychological and physical relationship between workers and their work environment. Ergonomics evolved after World War II as production managers recognized the physiological impact of workers' repetitive actions. The term *ergonomics* comes from the Greek words *ergon,* meaning work, and *nomos,* meaning laws. Initially ergonomics focused on improving productivity through developing a more worker-friendly environment, but in recent years with increased concern about repetitive stress syndrome, it has grown increasingly important in workplace health and safety.

Ergonomics is most closely associated with repetitive-stress syndrome, encompassing such injuries as carpal-tunnel syndrome; lower back pain; and problems with tendons, nerves, ligaments, and joints from performing the same manual task over and over. In 2000 the OCCUPATIONAL SAFETY AND HEALTH ADMINISTRATION (OSHA) issued over 300 pages of new ergonomics regulations. The new rules detail which job categories, what activities are covered, and the minimum number of hours per day a worker can do a repetitive task before they are covered by the OSHA rules. For example, workers using a keyboard are covered if they work at that task for four or more hours per day. Workers who lift 55-pound objects over 10 times per day are also covered by the new regulations. In 2003 OSHA created a four-pronged approach to ergonomics including guidelines, enforcement, outreach and assistance, and a National Advisory Committee.

OSHA justified the new ergonomics rules using benefit-cost analysis, claiming it would cost U.S. businesses $4.5 billion to comply but result in over $9 billion saved annually from reductions in lost employee time due to injuries and lost productivity from long-term disabilities. Business managers differed with the OSHA analysis, claiming the cost of compliance would be significantly greater. Business managers complained they would have to frequently shift workers to different job activities, losing work time and the benefits of specialization.

Further reading
Calderwood, James A. "Ergonomic Rules Become Final," *Ceramic Industry* 151, no. 3 (March 2001): 24; OSHA ergonomic Web site. Available online. URL: www.osha.gov/SLTC/ergonomics/index.html. Accessed on June 15, 2009.

escalator clause
An escalator clause is a stipulation in CONTRACTS that adjusts the agreed-on price when costs change. Generally business transactions include an agreed price, but often market conditions are volatile, and the seller can potentially lose money if his or her costs increase between the time the price is agreed on and when the transaction is completed. Escalator clauses protect sellers against this risk.

Escalator clauses are common in business-supply contracts, labor agreements, utility pricing, and lease arrangements. Usually an escalator clause is tied to changes in a cost index such as the CONSUMER PRICE INDEX (CPI), the price reported in a market exchange such as the CHICAGO MERCANTILE EXCHANGE or some other industrial cost index to which both parties agree.

Escalator clauses are more common during periods of uncertainty and INFLATION. In recent years, with dramatically changing oil and natural gas prices, utility companies, airlines, and chemi-

cal manufacturers have all resorted to escalator clauses. In the 1980s, most union contracts added escalator clauses to protect workers' wages against inflation. Many long-term rental agreements contain clauses raising the rent a set percentage annually.

Critics contend escalator clauses reduce producers' incentives to operate efficiently, instead just passing along cost increases to customers. When escalator clauses are used, it is important to clearly define what index or price is to be used and how often prices are to be adjusted. In multimillion-dollar transactions, small details such as using the national CPI or regional index, end-of-the-day or average for the day price on a commodity exchange can significantly affect costs and PROFITS.

ethics   See BUSINESS ETHICS; OFFICE OF GOVERNMENT ETHICS.

ethnocentrism
Ethnocentrism is a form of bias in which people believe their own ethnic group to be generally superior to others. An ethnic group typically shares common values, beliefs, customs, and history, along with a common language. Thus, the feelings and reactions a person has toward members of other ethnic groups tend to be relative to their own ethnic group experiences.

Ethnocentrism likely stems from multiple sources. To begin, people have a cognitive tendency to categorize others into groups, allowing perceivers to process copious amounts of social information efficiently. Basic categorizations include in-group versus out-group classifications, such as whether a target person is a member of the person's own group (an in-group member) or a member of some other group (an out-group member). Given our propensity to think in terms of groups, it is not surprising that, in addition to classifications based on physical characteristics such as sex and age, classifications tend to occur along lines of ethnicity.

Additionally, specific values, customs, beliefs, and languages are passed from generation to generation by members of ethnic groups. Role models, such as parents, teachers, the media, and respected members of the community, pass on information through direct instruction and reinforcement. They also pass on information about ethnicity through indirect means, such as the modeling of desired ethnic behaviors. Given that individuals are born within various ethnic communities throughout the world, it is likely that everyone experiences at least some level of ethnocentrism at some point in life.

The very tendency to categorize people into in- and out-groups can result in an "us" versus "them" mentality. Moreover, role models tend to teach and reinforce that their own culture's beliefs and customs are the "correct" ones. Together, these tendencies can affect out-group members in many ways. For example, people tend to favor their in-group members when distributing resources and rewards. Thus, they tend to be inclined to share valued resources with their own ethnic group members before considering the needs of out-group members. Some research suggests that, at times, in-group members would rather short-change their own group in terms of resources to be sure that their in-group appears to have a distinct advantage over an out-group. Additionally, ethnocentric people tend to prefer that new group members assimilate into the ethnic group by completely replacing their old ethnic values and customs with those adopted from the new in-group. This leaves little room for new group members to retain their own ethnic heritage while assimilating into a new culture.

Decreasing ethnocentrism may be possible by using strategies that are effective in decreasing other types of biased thinking. For example, people can be encouraged to try to understand others as individuals first, rather than categorizing them as members of any particular group. Alternatively, they may be encouraged to find their common ground, resulting in a new and more inclusive in-group identity. Last, individuals can be taught through direct and indirect means that although other ethnic groups may have different customs, languages, and histories, they still have important value.

Organizations would be wise to bear in mind that ethnocentrism may affect them at multiple levels. For example, left unchecked, ethnocentrism may affect hiring choices, leading managers to favor workers who fit into their ethnic in-group while overlooking qualified out-group candidates. Additionally, business practices that are rooted in one culture may not apply or work as effectively in other cultures, leaving organizations at risk for failure when they do not consider the implications of their ethnic perspective. Ethnic out-group members may ignore or be alienated by marketing strategies and campaigns that are heavily based on one cultural perspective. Finally, techniques for motivating and retaining employees that are based on an ethnocentric understanding of employee motivation may undermine an organization's success with a multicultural workforce or in a global marketplace.

—Elizabeth L. Cralley

European Recovery Program   See MARSHALL PLAN.

European Union

The European Union (EU) comprises 27 European countries joined in economic and political cooperation. The member countries are Austria, Belgium, Bulgaria, Cyprus, Czech Republic, Denmark, Estonia, Finland, France, Germany, Greece, Hungary, Ireland, Italy, Latvia, Lithuania, Luxembourg, Malta, the Netherlands, Poland, Portugal, Romania, Slovakia, Slovenia, Spain, Sweden, and the United Kingdom. While each country retains its independence and own political system, member states of the EU join together to establish policies they abide by for mutual benefit. Today, while the driving force of the European Union continues to be economic, its goals include issues of law, citizenship, and social justice.

The European Union has five main objectives: (1) to promote economic and social progress; (2) to assert the identity of the European Union on the international scene; (3) to introduce European citizenship; (4) to develop a geographic area of freedom, security, and justice; and (5) to maintain and build an established EU law (europa.eu.int/abc-en.htm).

Annual meetings take place between members of the EU's governing bodies and U.S. government representatives. The United States and the European Union are interdependent on one another regarding trade and because of this have established a number of areas of cooperation and conflict.

Combined, the gross domestic product (GDP) of EU countries exceeds that of the North American countries (United States, Canada, and Mexico). The evolution and expansion of the EU created a fear of "fortress Europe," with increased power and economic integration within the union and barriers to businesses outside of the union. The North American Free Trade Agreement (NAFTA) was, in part, a response to fears about the growing economic power of the EU. Though all countries in the EU and NAFTA are members of the World Trade Organization (WTO) there are continuing trade conflicts. Two of the more publicized disputes were the banana wars, preferential access to European markets for bananas from former European colonies, and the bovine growth hormone (bgh) restriction on U.S. meat exports to the EU. While trade disputes gain headlines in the news, historically the EU countries and the United States have been closely linked.

After World War II, there was a desire to integrate the economies of European countries in order to avoid another war in Europe. Leaders believed that by fostering cohesion among European nations through unified trade and economic policies, countries would be less likely to fight against one another. In the early 1950s, proposals for how to establish a united Europe were developed. In 1951 Belgium, France, Germany, Italy, Luxembourg, and the Netherlands signed the European Coal and Steel Community Treaty (ECSC), which came into effect on January 1, 1952. This treaty created an official body known as the High Authority that regulated coal and steel production, creating a single economic market for these products for all of the member countries. This group was extremely successful, and coal

and steel trade increased dramatically, benefiting all six countries. Based on this success, the countries started working towards creating a common market for additional goods for mutual economic benefit.

In 1957 two treaties were signed by the six members of the ECSC, establishing the European Economic Community (EEC) and the European Atomic Energy Community (EAEC or EURATOM). The EEC established common markets for goods in addition to those already established for coal and steel. EURATOM established agreements regarding atomic and nuclear energy with regards to research. These treaties came into effect on January 1, 1958. In 1967 the members of these three treaties (the ECSC, the EEC, and the EAEC) established one governing authority known as the European Communities (EC) that had four divisions: the European Commission, the Council of the European Union, the European Parliament, and the European Court of Justice. The EC existed until 1993, when it was incorporated into what is now the European Union.

In 1973 Denmark, Ireland, and the United Kingdom officially joined the EC. In 1981 Greece joined, followed by Spain and Portugal in 1986.

Due to the success of the trade policies created by the EC and growing interest in establishing even more integration, the countries continued to work together to create a more unified governing structure. The Treaty on the European Union, more commonly known as the Maastricht Treaty, came into effect on November 1, 1993. The Maastricht Treaty essentially revised the original treaties that were effective under the EC and created the European Union, as it is known today. The treaty established what are termed the three pillars of the European Union. The first pillar incorporates the original three treaties, the second pillar created the Common Foreign and Security Policy, and the third pillar created the Justice and Home Affairs Policy. One of the most important outcomes of the Maastricht Treaty was the establishment of the European Monetary Institute (EMI), which, created a FREE TRADE zone known as the European Economic Area (EEA), effective January

1, 1994. In addition, the treaty included the plan to create a single currency and citizenship for all member countries. The United Kingdom and Denmark only agreed to the treaty once they had been exempted from some of its provisions.

Austria, Finland, and Sweden joined the EU in 1995. In 2004 10 countries joined the EU. Any European country can join the EU provided it has a stable democratic government, a decent human-rights record, a functioning economy, and the ability to follow the membership requirements. Croatia, Macedonia, and, the most controversial, Turkey were candidate countries to join the EU in 2009.

The EU's structure is based on a democratic system to ensure that member states and citizens are represented fairly while at the same time the institutions work for the good of the whole union. There are five main governing bodies.

- The European Commission consists of 20 commissioners including the president of the union. The commission proposes legislation; implements directives, regulations, and the budget; and acts as the EU's official representative.
- The European Council, also referred to as the Council of Ministers, is made up of representatives of each of the 27 member countries and is considered the EU's main decision-making body. Council meetings cover various topics such as the environment, finance, and foreign affairs. The council enacts legislation for the union as a whole in conjunction with the European Parliament. In addition, the council makes decisions on foreign policy and deals with cooperation among member countries in criminal matters.
- The European Parliament is a political body whose members are elected by the citizens of the EU countries every five years. Representation in the Parliament is based on the population size of each member country. The Parliament deals with the legislative process, plays a role in the budget process, approves the nominations to the European Commission, and supervises the other governing bodies.
- The Court of Justice operates as the EU's supreme court. The court makes decisions

regarding treaty interpretations and is made up of one justice from each member country.
- The Court of Auditors oversees the management of the EU budget and controls expenditures.

There are additional governing bodies to support the five main branches of the EU.

- The Committee of Regions addresses issues of local identities and plays a role in decisions involving regional policies, the environment, and education.
- The Economic and Social Committee has 222 members and represents the views of organizations and groups that deal with topics such as labor and consumer rights.
- The European Central Bank handles the EU's monetary policies.
- The European Investment Bank is the EU's financial institution.
- The European Ombudsman handles complaints from EU citizens regarding the EU's administration.

Common policies adopted by member countries have allowed for freer movement of both goods and people throughout member countries. For example, citizens of member countries now have EU passports rather than passports from their individual countries, allowing for freer travel. Common policies deal with topics such as agriculture, the environment, education, and transportation. The EU has established uniform foreign policies and plays an active role in distributing humanitarian aid. It collects revenue from the value-added tax (VAT), import duties, and contributions from each of the member countries.

The EU's common currency, the euro, was introduced on January 1, 1999, and has been adopted by 11 countries: Austria, Belgium, Finland, France, Germany, Italy, Ireland, Luxembourg, the Netherlands, Portugal, and Spain. Denmark, Sweden, and the United Kingdom have not yet agreed to adopt the euro. On January 1, 2002, the euro became the official legal tender of participating states, and each country's individual currency was permanently replaced by the common currency.

Further reading

European Union Web site: Europa. Available online. URL: europa.eu.

—Stephanie Godley

exchange-rate risk

Exchange-rate risk is the effect on profitability and ASSETS that can occur as a result of changes in EXCHANGE RATES. Exchange rates are the value of one country's currency in terms of another country's currency. As the value of one currency increases, the value of the other currency decreases. For most of the 1990s, the U.S. dollar appreciated against most of the other world currencies. As the dollar increased in value, U.S. companies doing business in other parts of the world saw their PROFITS, earned in other currencies, decrease when converted to dollars. For example, in 2000 Coca-Cola Company warned investors of declining profits from foreign operations due to appreciation of the dollar. By contrast, foreign companies earning profits in dollars saw their earnings increase when converted to their home country's currency.

After increasing in value in the 1990s, the U.S. dollar decreased in value in the early 21st century reaching a low against the euro in 2008. With the uncertainty associated with the financial crises later that year, the value of the dollar increased as investors looked for relatively safe places to store their wealth.

Many factors influence exchange rates, including changing DEMAND for U.S. products and foreign products, changes in investment opportunities both in the United States and elsewhere, and changes in expectations of speculators in FOREIGN EXCHANGE markets. Most business manager try to make profits not by successfully predicting the direction of exchange rates but by selling their products and services. To reduce exchange-rate risk, managers

- hedge in foreign exchange markets
- diversify operations
- borrow in the currency used for investing

HEDGING involves buying or selling FUTURES currency contracts. Many exchanges (in the United States, particularly the CHICAGO MERCANTILE EXCHANGE) offer currency futures contracts. A company, expecting payment in another currency six months from now, when the job is completed, could sell a futures contract for that amount of the currency. If, in the interim six months, the value of that currency declined, they will be able to buy back the futures contract at a lower price, offsetting the decline in value of the payment they receive.

By diversifying operations, MULTINATIONAL CORPORATIONS (MNCs) can also reduce their exchange-rate risk. Many global automobile manufacturers have set up factories in the markets they sell in. By producing in markets where they sell, companies incur their costs and generate their revenue primarily in the host country's currency. This reduces the impact of changing exchange-rate values.

Similarly, MNCs reduce exchange-rate exposure by borrowing in the currency they are investing in. By borrowing in U.S. dollars, Japanese automobile manufacturers building plants in the United States incur their financial costs in the same currency as their received revenue.

While most of this discussion has focused on MNCs involved in or exposed to exchange-rate risk, almost every business is vulnerable to changing exchange rates. In the early 1990s, when the U.S. dollar was declining, a *Wall Street Journal* article described the impact of the dollar decline against the Japanese yen in Troy, Ohio.

- Japanese automobiles were $2,000 more than comparable domestic models.
- The price of pearls and cameras also rose.
- Japanese robots used in the production of U.S. cars became more expensive.
- Farmers hoped the declining dollar would increase demand for local corn and soybeans.
- A local economic development officer speculated Japanese companies would be more interested in building factories in the area.

Further reading

Hill, Charles W. L. *Global Business Today.* Boston: McGraw-Hill, 1999; Reitman, Valerie. "Global Money Trends Rattle Shop Windows in Heartland America," *Wall Street Journal,* 26 November 1993, p. A1.

exchange rates

Exchange rates are the domestic price of a unit of foreign currency. Exchange rates impact international trade, part of a country's CIRCULAR FLOW MODEL of economic output and INCOME. When the value of a country's currency rises relative to another country's currency, the currency is said to have appreciated. Likewise, when a currency decreases in value relative to another currency, it has depreciated. For most of the 1990s and early 21st century, the U.S. dollar appreciated against most of the other world currencies. For example, on January 9, 1998, the Canadian dollar was worth 0.6992 U.S. dollars; on June 15, 2009, it was worth 0.8827 U.S. dollars, 26 percent more than it was worth 11 years earlier. The same relationship can be expressed in terms of how many Canadian dollars are required to be exchanged for one U.S. dollar. In 1998, 1.4303 Canadian dollars equaled one U.S. dollar, while in 2009 it took 1.133 Canadian dollars to equal one U.S. dollar.

Two important questions when studying exchange rates are: What is the impact of appreciating and depreciating currencies, and what exchange-rate policies can and do governments pursue?

When a country's currency appreciates, its exports become more expensive to foreign buyers and IMPORTS become less expensive. This increases DEMAND for imports and decreases demand for exports. In recent years the U.S. TRADE BALANCE, both the merchandise trade balance and the current account, have been negative, reflecting the relative value of the U.S. dollar against world currencies. In 2003 the United States' current account deficit was approximately $400 billion, meaning foreigners held more ($400 billion worth) claims against the U.S. output than U.S. sellers had against foreign output. Ceteris paribus (other things being equal), the U.S. dollar should fall in value as foreigners increase the supply of U.S. dollars in exchange markets and increase demand for their currencies. Instead foreigners have been buying U.S. securities, both government BONDS and corporate stocks and bonds, and purchasing U.S. ASSETS, mostly U.S. companies. Because foreigners are not exchanging the U.S. dollars, the value of the dollar has not declined.

Economists are quite concerned about the potential impact of a change in international investment in the United States. A sudden shift in international sentiment would decrease the supply of investment CAPITAL and thus the value of the dollar in world markets, increasing the price of imports and adding to INFLATION. This can happen in a system of floating exchange rates. Since 1973, when the gold standard created at BRETTON WOODS at the end of World War II was abandoned, a variety of exchange-rate policies have evolved in world trade, including floating, fixed, pegged, and managed floating exchange-rate systems.

Floating exchange-rate systems, as stated earlier, allow SUPPLY and DEMAND for a country's currency to determine the exchange rate. Floating exchange rates create uncertainty for businesses engaged in foreign trade, allow countries to pursue independent economic policies, and tend to ease balance-of-payments adjustments. Fixed exchange-rate systems reduce business uncertainty but require government intervention to maintain the fixed exchange rate (buying or selling currencies to adjust for the imbalance of supply and demand for the currency). If two countries have similar rates of inflation, they will be able to maintain a fixed exchange-rate policy. If one country's inflation rate is consistently greater than the other country's inflation rate, the first country's currency will be overvalued in a fixed exchange-rate system. The PESO CRISIS was largely a result of higher inflation in Mexico than in the United States, without sufficient devaluation of the Mexican peso.

At the time of the peso crisis (1994), Mexico had a crawling-peg exchange-rate system: a predetermined monthly rate of DEPRECIATION of the peso against the U.S. dollar. Some countries that have experienced rapid inflation have "pegged" their currency to another country's currency, creating a fixed exchange rate. Argentina and Ecuador pegged their currencies to the U.S. dollar. Many former French colonies peg their currencies to the French franc.

The European Union, through the European Monetary System, negotiated a fixed exchange rate among the participating members and a floating exchange rate with respect to the rest of the world. Not all members of the EU agreed to the terms of the historic Maastricht Treaty, but those that did agreed to coordinate domestic macroeconomic policies including budget deficits and inflation rates as part of agreement to create a unified currency.

See also EXCHANGE-RATE RISK; FOREIGN EXCHANGE; MACROECONOMICS.

exchange traded funds (ETFs)

Exchange traded funds (ETFs) are INVESTMENT funds that hold assets designed to achieve a financial objective. ETFs are traded on the major stock exchanges and in many ways are similar to traditional mutual funds. Like a mutual fund, ETFs usually hold a basket of securities, and most ETFs track an index like the Dow Jones Industrial Average (DJIA) or S&P 500. Unlike traditional MUTUAL FUNDS, ETFs do not sell or redeem their shares at net asset value (NAV). Instead, major FINANCIAL INSTITUTIONS purchase and redeem shares of an ETF, but only in large blocks called "creation units." These baskets typically represent 10,000 to 200,000 shares of the ETF in question. The financial institution deposits a "purchase basket" of certain securities and other assets identified by the ETF and receives a creation unit. The purchase basket is held by the Depository Trust Clearing Corporation, the federal agency that oversees stock market transactions. The basket generally reflects the assets of the ETF's portfolio and is equal to the aggregate NAV of the ETF shares in the creation unit. After purchasing the creation unit the financial institution may hold the shares or resell them on the secondary market. ETFs have become popular because, like mutual funds, they offer diversification but also because of their relatively low trading costs, tax efficiency, and liquidity.

By holding a portfolio of securities, ETFs offer diversification. ETF trading costs are typically lower than management fees charged by mutual funds and do not include "load" or sales charges like many actively managed mutual funds. They are generally more tax efficient than mutual funds because they typically have lower portfolio turnover, creating fewer reportable short-term capital gains. Like a stock, ETFs provide liquidity. They can be bought and sold on the market exchanges and allow limit orders, short selling, and options.

The first exchange traded funds were SPDRs, created in 1993 with a portfolio reflecting the S&P 500 index. Initially, ETFs were perceived as a threat to the mutual fund industry, but, with their advantages and popularity, they have grown rapidly. As ETF products have evolved, the regulation of exchange traded funds also has evolved. Because SPDRs were different from traditional mutual funds, they were approved by the SECURITIES AND EXCHANGE COMMISSION (SEC) under a series of exemptions from provisions of the Investment Company Act. Exchange traded funds are registered as investment companies under the act, which regulates open-end funds, closed-end funds, and unit investment trusts, or UITs. Exchange traded funds are hybrid products. Like an open-end mutual fund, exchange traded funds issue redeemable shares; however, those shares can be issued or redeemed only in large creation units. Like a closed-end fund or a stock, the individual shares of exchange traded funds trade in the secondary market at negotiated prices. Investors can also sell those shares short or purchase them on margin. Because exchange traded funds are not typical mutual funds, they did not fit perfectly into the Investment Company Act's regulatory regime. Today, only four ETFs are organized as UITs. Most exchange traded funds launched today are organized as open-end funds, the form of organization of a traditional mutual fund. The SEC first allowed exchange traded funds to organize as open-end funds in 1996 and began allowing actively managed ETFs in 2008.

By 2008, there were over 680 ETFs with assets totaling $610 billion. Assets in ETFs still equal only 7 percent of the total held in traditional mutual funds.

The most popular ETFs include:

Standard & Poor's 500 index Depository Receipts (SPY: AMEX)
NASDAQ-100 Tracking Stock (QQQ: AMEX)
DIAMONDS Trust (DIA: AMEX) which tracks the DJIA.

More recently, ETFs have been created tracking commodity prices, currencies, and market shorting positions, moving up as the underlying index (DJIA, S&P 500 etc) moves downward.

ETFs have been criticized as facilitating short-term speculation and offering insufficient diversification. Some have been criticized for being "black boxes," using untested or unknown techniques to obtain their investment objective. In 2008 some ETF managers shocked the marketplace by issuing large, end-of-the-year dividends, creating significant tax consequences for holders of those securities.

Further reading
Securities and Exchange Commission Web site. Available online. URL: www.sec.gov; New York Stock Exchange Web site. Available online. URL: www.nyse.com.

excise tax   See BUSINESS TAXES; CONSUMPTION TAX.

exit strategies
Exit strategies are methods used by companies to discontinue PRODUCTS, businesses, or relationships with customers or suppliers. They are generally not considered as part of a company's BUSINESS PLAN; rather, they are decisions made when a business plan does not work as anticipated.

One of the trends in the United States is RELATIONSHIP MARKETING—development and maintenance of long-term, cost-effective exchange relationships with customers, suppliers, employees, and partners. Most businesspeople are optimists, rarely accepting the end of a project, product, or enterprise. An often-neglected part of relationship marketing is establishing when, how, or on what terms the relationship will end. Exit strategies

devised in advance are like prenuptial agreements, easing the pain of breaking up.

Exit strategies are important because they influence consumers' and business partners' image of a company. In the 1970s, when Texas Instruments announced it was abandoning its line of early computer equipment, many consumers expressed distrust for the company. It took decades for the company to recover its reputation. Conversely, when IBM sold its personal computer division to a Chinese company, Lenovo, in 2005 by maintaining its U.S. employees, warranty, and service support, the companies did not harm their reputations.

Marketers recognize most products and product categories go through what is known as the PRODUCT LIFE CYCLE (PLC)—market stages that include introduction, growth, maturity, and decline. Exit strategies are part of the decline stage. Generally as sales and PROFITS decline, firms can sell the product line to another company, create a separate company (called spinning-off), or abandon the product line. Which exit strategy is chosen depends on market conditions, the current status of the product line, and company resources. Sometimes products in the decline stage gain new life as "retro" products sought out by a small number of loyal consumers. These consumers are often willing to pay more for the product, creating a profitable niche market. For example, the Coca-Cola Company still sells Tab, their early diet drink, even though sales represent less than 1 percent of Diet Coke sales. A small, vocal group of consumers continues to prefer Tab, and rather than chance losing those customers to their rival Pepsi, Coca-Cola continues to produce the soda.

expectancy theory
Expectancy theory states that motivation depends on an individual's expectations of his or her ability to perform a job and the relationship between performance and attaining rewards valued by that individual. First proposed by management specialist Victor Vroom, expectancy theory can be used in sales management to stimulate sales-force productivity. Sales managers apply a five-step process.

1. Provide each salesperson with detailed information regarding what management expects in terms of selling goals, service standards, and other areas of performance. For example, one study found that sales performance was enhanced by setting goals more frequently. In many companies, sales representatives are given annual goals. Quarterly or monthly goals can increase sales-force motivation.
2. Assign salespeople to appropriate tasks by assessing the needs, values, and abilities of each salesperson. For example, some salespeople like to travel while others do not. Some people are great at getting to know clients but poor at closing a deal.
3. Make goals achievable. Sales managers should provide the LEADERSHIP, training, and support salespeople need to be successful.
4. Provide specific and frequent feedback to salespeople.
5. Offer appropriate rewards that reinforce the values of each salesperson. Most salespeople are motivated by making money, but recognition, prizes, vacation time, and other incentives motivate some people.

Further reading

Boone, Louis E., and David L. Kurtz. *Contemporary Marketing*. 14th ed. Fort Worth: South-Western, 2009.

experience and learning curves

Experience and learning curves are behavioral models demonstrating that individuals and organizations learn and become more efficient through work. Experience and learning curves are a source of COMPARATIVE ADVANTAGE in competitive markets.

The concept of improved efficiency and productivity through learning is relatively easy and can be understand by considering some new activity that has been initiated (learning a new software, language, sport, etc.). The more often one practices or studies, the more proficient one becomes at the activity. Generally everybody learns by doing, and while the results can be dramatic initially, eventually doing more of an activity results in smaller marginal improvement.

The early 20th-century management consultant Frederick W. Taylor studied productivity under different working conditions, focusing on the size of shovel used at a coal company. He believed the company would be much more efficient if each worker learned to do a smaller portion of the entire job, which would increase overall workers' productivity. Using observation and experimentation, he answered a few key questions:

1. Will a first-class worker do more work per day with a shovelful of 5, 10, 15, 20, 30, or 40 pounds?
2. What kinds of shovels work best with which materials?
3. How quickly can a shovel be pushed into a pile of coal and pulled out properly loaded?
4. How long does it take to swing a shovel backward and throw the load a specified horizontal distance at a specified height?

Experience and learning curves can be used to measure the productivity improvement of individual workers and organizations. Critical to the success of any organization is being able to respond quickly to opportunities and challenges. The collective knowledge within a business provides information about what has been done before, who knows where resources exist to meet an opportunity or challenge, or why something failed in the past. This collective experience allows a firm to act faster than competitors with no experience and to be more efficient by avoiding mistakes from the past.

Experience and learning curves as a source of comparative advantage depend on retaining that knowledge and experience within an organization. With greater use of OUTSOURCING, contract workers, and turnover, particularly in knowledge-based businesses, it is often difficult to control the transfer of knowledge and experience among industry competitors.

Further reading

Hellriegel, Don, Susan E. Jackson, and John W. Slocum Jr. *Management*. 8th ed. Cincinnati: South-Western College Publishing, 1999.

export controls

The United States has a detailed system of export controls intended to protect scarce RESOURCES, further U.S. foreign policy, and enhance national security. The controls are contained in the Export Administration Act (2001) as implemented by a host of regulations. Broadly speaking, all exports from the United States are controlled under two categories, those permitted with or without a license. These categories reflect country of destination and product-type analyses.

The first step in ascertaining whether a license is needed is to examine the "Country Control List." This list specifies which destination countries are license-free and which are not. For example, Libya, Iraq, Iran, Cuba, and North Korea are countries for which an export license is often required. Canada, Mexico, France, South Africa, and Japan are not ordinarily on the Country Control List.

The second step is to examine the "Commerce Control List" to ascertain which products require a license for EXPORTING. Supercomputers and military goods will almost always require licenses. Personal computers and most consumer goods will not. If a U.S. export is not on the Commerce Control List and the country of destination is not subject to licensing, the goods may be freely shipped subject to completion of a Shipper's Export Declaration form.

If the country or the PRODUCT (or both) is on a control list, then a license from the U.S. Bureau of Export Administration is required. Obtaining such a license takes considerable time and expense. Violations of the Export Administration Act can incur very large company fines and penalties. Individual violators can be sentenced criminally. In extreme cases, the right of U.S. businesses to export can even be revoked. These sanctions are severe.

Further reading

Folsom, Ralph H., Michael Gordon, and John Spanogle. *International Business Transactions in a Nutshell.* 6th ed. Eagan, Minn.: West Group, 2002.

Export-Import Bank of the United States

The Export-Import Bank of the United States (Ex-Im Bank) is a government-held CORPORA-TION created in 1934 to finance and facilitate U.S. exports. To stimulate exports to the former Soviet Union at the end of World War II, the Ex-Im Bank supported reconstruction of Europe and Asia. More recently, the Ex-Im Bank shifted its focus to supporting exports to developing countries. The Ex-Im Bank is managed by a BOARD OF DIRECTORS chosen by the U.S. president and confirmed by the Senate.

The primary goal of the Ex-Im Bank is to support exports and in the process stimulate ECONOMIC GROWTH in the United States. The bank has three primary programs: working-CAPITAL loans, LOANS to foreign purchasers, and credit guarantees. Working-capital loans provide funds for companies to bid on projects, facilities, build production, or complete foreign CONTRACT awards. Loans to foreign purchasers provide financing subject to U.S. content rules, generally 50 percent, and other restrictions. Credit guarantees protect U.S. exporters against debtor DEFAULT for political or commercial reasons.

Critics contend the Ex-Im Bank is a form of CORPORATE WELFARE, subsidizing U.S. MULTINATIONAL CORPORATIONS. Private-sector banking and business INSURANCE companies contend the Bank unfairly competes with their lending business. In 2001 President George W. Bush surprised many critics and supporters by recommending significant cuts in federal support for the Ex-Im Bank.

Further reading

Export-Import Bank of the United States Web site. Available online. URL: www.exim.gov.

exporting

Exporting—the production and sale of goods from one country to another—is both a business decision and part of a country's economic and political policies. Businesses export PRODUCTS and SERVICES to markets where they expect to earn PROFITS. From a business perspective, exporting is part of a firm's MARKETING STRATEGY. Countries exchange goods and services based on COMPARATIVE ADVANTAGE.

Because the U.S. market is the largest in the world, for many years American companies did not feel the need to participate in global markets; domestic DEMAND created sufficient opportunities. For some U.S. companies, export expansion resulted from needs generated by World War II; for others creation of the General Agreement on Tariffs and Trade (1947), now part of the WORLD TRADE ORGANIZATION, led to export expansion.

Most trade is conducted among industrialized countries and among large MULTINATIONAL CORPORATIONS (MNCs). MNCs often produce raw materials, components, and partially assembled products in many different countries, shipping these products to other factories and markets around the world. Intrafirm trade is a major part of total exports. One of the issues associated with this type of trade is transfer pricing, the price assessed for goods "sold" from one division of a company to another in a different country.

Exporting contributes to a country's GROSS DOMESTIC PRODUCT, adding output and INCOME to an economy. Many countries create TRADE BARRIERS, blocking IMPORTS while supporting domestic exporting activity. In the 1980s Japanese automobile manufacturers, fearing the creation of new BARRIERS TO ENTRY into the U.S. market, agreed to voluntary export constraints, limiting the number of cars shipped annually. With decreased SUPPLY and increasing demand, retailers of Japanese cars raised prices in the United States. One study found this voluntary export constraint program cost American consumers $250,000 for every domestic job saved.

Exporting depends heavily on price competitiveness in world markets, and this, in turn, depends on EXCHANGE RATES. The relatively high-valued dollar in the 1990s reduced U.S. exports while stimulating demand for imports, contributing to a continuing U.S. trade deficit.

As the dollar decreased in value in the early 2000s, exports rose but imports also rose when oil prices skyrocketed. The United States (as well as the governments of most other industrialized countries) provides support for business exporting. The OVERSEAS PRIVATE INVESTMENT COR-PORATION and the EXPORT-IMPORT BANK OF THE UNITED STATES provide INSURANCE and investment CAPITAL for U.S. companies. The Department of Commerce and many state commerce departments provide a variety of trade seminars, trade-show services, and other assistance to businesses attempting to expand their export-marketing efforts. The U.S. State Department provides assistance through commercial attaches to U.S. businesses seeking opportunities abroad.

See also EXPORT CONTROLS.

externalities (spillover effects)

Externalities, also called spillover effects, are COSTS (negative externalities) or benefits (positive externalities) associated with a market but not included in the price of a good or service. An external cost occurs when the PRODUCTION or CONSUMPTION of a good inflicts a cost on someone other than the producer or consumer. A standard example of an external cost is pollution. Many producers are allowed to dump wastes into streams or send emissions up their smokestacks. By releasing their wastes into the environment, these firms are avoiding costs of pollution control or mitigation. Because they do not have to bear them, market prices do not reflect these costs, and this encourages greater consumption of their products. Instead, the cost of pollution is transferred to others, either people trying to use the water downstream from the polluter or people breathing the polluted air.

Business groups sometimes argue that forcing them to reduce their emissions will make them unable to compete in global markets. Referring to demands for reduction in emissions associated with the use of oil products, President George H. W. Bush once said, "I am an environmentalist too, but we cannot afford these new regulations." From a business perspective, unless everyone, including international competitors, has to incur the same costs, they will become higher cost producers and less competitive. Developing countries, eager to have new jobs and sources of INCOME, are often willing to ignore negative externalities (spillovers of costs and negative effects onto society) in the name of ECONOMIC GROWTH.

The air and water pollution examples illustrate MARKET FAILURE, with an overallocation of resources into production of the polluting firm's products. These two examples can also be used to illustrate how society can correct the problem. In a market environment, a downstream user of water could simply pay the upstream user not to pollute the water. Naturally the downstream user does not want to pay, but faced with no other choice and needing clean water, paying is one option. More likely the downstream user will complain to a government agency, which in turn will force the polluter to stop.

Regulation is one option to correct the problem, but that requires the government agency to develop an appropriate set of regulations and enforce them. Often it is difficult to come up with a standard set of rules that can be applied among many firms and across various industries. In the United States, business managers frequently complain about the time, cost, and lack of logic in many government environmental regulations. Another option is for government to tax the polluting firm based on the amount of pollution it creates. This will encourage the firm to reduce its pollution, alleviating the problem for the downstream user of the water.

In the case of water pollution, the third party, the downstream user of the water, can easily be identified and will pressure the upstream polluter to pay to clean up its pollution or internalize the externality. In the case of air pollution from the same factory, it probably will be more difficult to identify the people hurt by the air pollution. If these people do not recognize the impact of the pollution on them, or if only a few citizens complain, the company may not be forced to stop polluting the air. This is the problem of lack of clearly defined property rights. The downstream water user demanded the right to clean water, but no one person or group owns the air.

Beginning in the 1970s, the U.S. ENVIRONMENTAL PROTECTION AGENCY (EPA) experimented with an alternative to regulation or taxation of pollution. Recognizing that the environment can accept some level of pollution without being significantly harmed (called environmental carrying capacity) and that some firms can reduce their pollution more cheaply than others, the EPA helped create a market for pollution credits. After defining an acceptable level of overall pollution, firms were given an allocation of pollution credits. Firms that could reduce their emissions most cheaply did so and sold their pollution credits, while firms that would have to incur significant costs to reduce their pollution bought credits. A market for pollution credits was established, allowing firms to choose which was a more efficient method of achieving the government-imposed standard. Some environmental groups also bought pollution credits, reducing the overall supply of credits, thereby increasing the price of polluting, making it more efficient for firms to clean up the air than to continue to pollute.

Like an external cost, external benefits are not reflected in the price of a product. An external benefit is derived when some of the benefits of consumption of a good or service are enjoyed by a third party. If, for example, just as Mr. Smith is ready to put his home up for sale, his neighbor cleans up her house and yard, Mr. Smith receives a benefit from her action—that is, his house will probably sell for a higher price due to his neighbor's efforts. Similarly, everybody benefits from other people being more educated. Education enhances peoples' productivity, increasing their incomes, reducing overall taxes, and providing the public with better products and services. Recognizing that society benefits from having educated people, U.S. education DEMAND and SUPPLY are both subsidized. This results in a greater quantity of education being produced than would be if consumers had to pay the full cost of education. This is called internalizing a positive externality.

Further reading

O'Sullivan, Arthur, and Steven M. Sheffrin. *Economics: Principles, Applications, and Tools.* 6th ed. Upper Saddle River, N.J.: Prentice Hall, 2009.

extraterritorial jurisdiction

Extraterritorial jurisdiction most often refers to laws that are applied to activities, businesses, and persons located outside the United States. These activities, businesses, and persons may or may not involved Americans, but they are subject to U.S. laws reaching beyond U.S. territorial boundaries. Laws regarding antitrust, securities, export control, EMPLOYMENT, and TRADEMARKS provide good examples of U.S. extraterritorial jurisdiction. The SHERMAN ANTITRUST ACT does so by being specifically applicable to U.S. "foreign commerce."

Extraterritorial jurisdiction has been extremely controversial among U.S. trading partners. Many, including Britain, France, Canada, and Australia, have enacted "blocking statutes" intended to make it difficult to apply U.S. laws extraterritorially. These statutes typically deny access to documents, people, and information; deny enforcement of U.S. extraterritorial judgments; and sometimes retaliate by authorizing in local courts actions for DAMAGES against successful U.S. extraterritorial plaintiffs.

In an increasingly integrated global economy, the effects of business are often felt beyond territorial boundaries. The EUROPEAN UNION applies its competition (antitrust) laws extraterritorially, doing so specifically to block the U.S.-based General Electric/Honeywell merger in 2001, although U.S. antitrust authorities had already approved that same merger. Resolving extraterritorial conflicts like this one is a major problem. The United States has "antitrust cooperation" agreements with Canada, Australia, Germany, and the European Union, which attempt to reduce the potential for conflicts over extraterritorial jurisdiction in that field.

See also ANTITRUST LAW.

Further reading
Folsom, Ralph H., Michael Gordon, John Spanogle. *International Business Transaction in a Nutshell.* 6th ed. Eagan, Minn.: West Group, 2000.

factoring

Factoring is selling ACCOUNTS RECEIVABLE to another business in order to obtain cash payment before the due date on the account receivable. In many businesses, cash flow—the stream of revenues and expenses—is a major problem. Creditors want payment on delivery or shortly afterwards, and customers tend to delay payment, often for 30–90 days after receiving the good or service. Factoring allows businesses to get their money (at a discount) by selling the right to receive the future payment from a customer.

Once factored, the account receivable becomes the property of the company (factor) purchasing the CONTRACT. The factor, assuming the risk that a customer may delay or DEFAULT on payment, pays the seller a discounted amount below the amount owed. To effectively assess RISK, factors have to be familiar with the firms and practices in the markets they operate in. Factoring is most associated with the garment industry and is conducted primarily by large factoring finance companies.

Further reading

Kidwell, David S., David W. Blackwell, David A. Whidbee, and Richard L. Peterson. *Financial Institutions, Markets, and Money.* 10th ed. Hoboken, N.J.: John Wiley & Son, 2008.

factory tours

Factory or industrial tours show consumers how a company's PRODUCTS are manufactured. Sometimes used as part of a firm's MARKETING STRATEGY, factory tours are a relatively new promotional tool as many companies are just beginning to realize the benefits of demonstrating to consumers how their products are made. One company, Celestial Seasonings Tea, opened their manufacturing facilities to customers in the mid-1990s. Within five years more than 500,000 people were visiting the factory annually. The company sells teas, mugs, t-shirts, and other company-logo products in the factory tour store and also includes visitors in taste tests of new products it is considering.

Three business concerns when considering creating a factory tour include INSURANCE, plant organization, and MARKET INTELLIGENCE. Having nonworkers walking around a factory creates a potential insurance liability. Plant design can incorporate factory tours by including showcase windows and walkways to facilitate visitors. One company discontinued factory tours when competitors used the tours to gain access to the facility and view proprietary production technology.

The book *Watch It Made in the USA* (1998) lists hundreds of factories around the country open to the public. York County, Pennsylvania, promotes itself as the United States' factory-tour capital, with 14 free factory tours. HowStuffWorks.com has developed virtual tours of U.S. factories. Many factory managers offer tours when asked but consider factory tours a distraction from their primary activity; production.

See also SALES PROMOTION.

Further reading
Axelrod, Karen, and Bruce Brumberg. *Watch It Made in the USA.* 2d ed. Santa Fe, N. Mex.: John Muir Publishing, 1998.

FAFSA

Free Application for Federal Student Aid (FAFSA) is provided by the Federal Student Aid Office, a division of the U.S. Department of Education (DOE). The office functions to provide eligible individuals with federal financial assistance or federal funding for educational purposes. The office cooperates with educational and financial institutions in the Title IV student financial assistance programs to help provide aid to families and individuals looking to further their education. The Federal Student Aid Office is the first government Performance-Based Organization (PBO) and operates under congressional authority. Its duties include processing 14 million student financial aid applications per year, resulting in the distribution of more than $80 billion in financial aid; enforcing rules and regulations; servicing student loan accounts; securing loan repayment from borrowers; educating students and their families about the process; partnering with institutions; and operating information technology systems.

Financial aid is awarded on a first-come first-served basis. There is no penalty for estimating income on the form; however, this should be corrected once taxes are completed. Students must fill out a FAFSA form each school year to continue to be considered for financial aid programs.

Nearly every student regardless of income, financial status, and other barriers is eligible for some type of financial assistance. Students eligible for assistance must meet requirements, including U.S. citizenship or eligible noncitizen; a valid Social Security Number (there are a few exceptions); registry with Selective Service (if they are male 18 to 25 years old), having a high school diploma, GED, or passing an exam approved by the DOE; having no drug conviction for an offense occurring during a period in which the student was receiving student aid; and be enrolled or accepted as a regular student working toward a degree/certificate in a school participating in the federal student aid programs.

FAFSA is used by most states, universities, and colleges to determine eligibility for other types of aid, including grants, loans, and work-study programs. Some institutions may require additional forms for aid. All students will be expected to contribute toward their educational cost. The amount, or Expected Family Contribution (EFC), is determined by the student's financial situation. This is determined by the FAFSA through a "needs analysis" in taking under consideration income, assets, and other contributing factors.

Congress recently took steps to help improve access for higher education, including passage of the College Cost Reduction, Affordability and Access Act, which resulted in a reduction of interest rates on student loans, cutting them in half over a period of five years. The act also increased the amount of funding students could receive through programs, and it increased funding for the Pell Grant. Other initiatives include the Ensuring Access to Student Loan Act of 2008, which increased the borrowing limits in the Unsubsidized Stafford Loan program, and the Higher Education Opportunity Act, which reauthorized the Higher Education Act.

Further reading
FAFSA Web site. Available online. URL: www.fafsa.com; Federal Student Aid Web site. Available online. URL: federalstudentaid.ed.gov.

—Jenna Lasseter

Fair and Accurate Credit Transactions Act (FACT or FACTA)

The Fair and Accurate Credit Transactions Act (FACT) of 2003 allows consumers to obtain a free copy of their credit report from each of the three major credit reporting agencies. A credit report typically includes information on where consumers live, how they pay their bills, and whether they have been sued or arrested, or have filed for bankruptcy. Nationwide consumer reporting companies sell the information in consumers' reports to creditors, insurers, employers, and other businesses that use it to evaluate applications for credit, insurance, employment, or renting a home.

FACT was an amendment to the 1970 Federal Fair Credit Reporting Act (FCRA) passed to promote the accuracy and privacy of information in the files of the nation's consumer reporting companies. FACT was enacted because of continued consumer complaints about inaccurate information in credit reports and because of the increasing need to protect consumers against identity theft. As reported on the FEDERAL TRADE COMMISSION's Web site, under the Fair and Accurate Credit Transactions Act,

- Consumers have the right to receive a copy of their credit report. The report must contain all the information in an individual's file at the time of the request.
- Each of the nationwide consumer reporting companies—Equifax, Experian, and TransUnion—is required to provide consumers with a free copy of their credit report, at their request, once every 12 months. (The companies implemented this across the country during a nine-month period in 2005.)

To order a copy of their report, consumers can go to www.annualcreditreport.com, call 1-877-322-8228, or complete the Annual Credit Report Request Form available at the Federal Trade Commission's Web site, www.ftc.gov/credit and mail it to: Annual Credit Report Request Service, P.O. Box 105281, Atlanta, GA 30348-5281.

Consumers may order their reports from each of the three nationwide consumer reporting companies at the same time, or they can order their report from each company one at a time. Most consumer advisers recommend staggering requests, ordering one from each company on a rotating basis every four months. If problems are encountered, consumers are advised to order reports from all three companies. Under the original FCRA, consumers were entitled to a free report if a company takes adverse action against them, such as denying an application for credit, insurance, or employment. Consumers are also entitled to one free report a year if they are unemployed and plan to look for a job within 60 days; if they are on welfare; or if their report is inaccurate because of fraud, including identity theft. Otherwise, a consumer reporting company may charge consumers up to $9.50 for another copy of their report within a 12-month period.

The FTC also provides a warning about "imposter" Web sites, stating:

> Only one Web site is authorized to fill orders for the free annual credit report you are entitled to under law—annualcreditreport.com. Other Web sites that claim to offer "free credit reports," "free credit scores" or "free credit monitoring" are not part of the legally mandated free annual credit report program. In some cases, the "free" product comes with strings attached. For example, some sites sign you up for a supposedly "free" service that converts to one you have to pay for after a trial period. If you don't cancel during the trial period, you may be unwittingly agreeing to let the company start charging fees to your credit card. Some "imposter" sites use terms such as "free report" in their names; others have URLs that purposely misspell annualcreditreport.com in the hope that you will mistype the name of the official site. Some of these "imposter" sites direct you to other sites that try to sell you something or collect your personal information. Annual-creditreport.com and the nationwide consumer reporting companies will not send you an email asking for your personal information. If you get an email, see a pop-up ad, or get a phone call from someone claiming to be from annualcreditreport.com or any of the three nationwide consumer reporting companies, do not reply or click on any link in the message. It's probably a scam. Forward any such email to the FTC at spam@uce.gov.

Further reading
Federal Trade Commission Web site. Available online. URL: www.ftc.gov.

Fair Credit Reporting Act (FCRA)

The Fair Credit Reporting Act (FCRA) provides consumers the right to know what information credit reporting agencies are collecting and conveying about them to creditors, insurance companies, and employers. Historically, American consumers rarely borrowed money or had access to personal credit. The first widely circulated credit card was introduced by Diners Club in 1950. Within one year, 20,000 Diners Club cards were issued. With the huge growth in this industry during the 1960s, consumers complained that the information in their credit reports was inaccurate. Prior to 1970, consumers' credit files were accessible only to creditors. The FCRA of 1970 required that consumers:

- be told the name and address of the consumer reporting agency responsible for preparing a report that was used to deny them credit, insurance, or employment, or to increase the cost of credit or insurance
- be told the nature, substance, and sources (except medical data) that a consumer reporting agency collects about them
- be able to take anyone with them to the credit bureau to review their file
- obtain their credit information free of charge when the consumer has been denied credit, insurance, or employment, within 30 days of the denial
- be told who has received a consumer report within the preceding six months (or within the preceding two years if the report was furnished for employment purposes
- have incomplete or incorrect information reinvestigated and, if the information is found to be inaccurate or cannot be verified, to have the information removed from their file
- have the consumer's version of the dispute placed in the file and included in subsequent consumer reports when a dispute between the consumer and the reporting agency cannot be resolved

- request the agency to send the consumer's version of the dispute to businesses that received the report previously
- have their consumer report withheld from anyone who, under the law, does not have a legitimate business need for the information
- sue a company for damages if it willfully or negligently violates the law and, if successful, to collect attorney's fees and court costs
- have most adverse information not reported after seven years; ten years for bankruptcy information
- be notified that a company is seeking information that would constitute an "investigative consumer report"
- request from a company that orders an investigative report further information as to the nature and scope of the investigation
- discover the nature and substance (but not the sources) of information that was collected for an investigative report.

The 1997 amendments to the FCRA required credit reporting agencies to:

- investigate disputed items quickly and thoroughly (within 30 days)
- disclose corrections to the consumer within 5 days of the investigation
- retain deletions of adverse information unless the creditor has certified the accuracy of the information and the consumer has been notified of the reinsertion
- expand the circumstances under which consumers can request free reports
- require employers to obtain written permission before obtaining credit reports
- increase the penalties against creditors who violate the law.

The FCRA constituted a major consumer protection law and continues to be expanded, most recently by the 2003 FAIR AND ACCURATE CREDIT TRANSACTIONS ACT.

Further reading
Federal Trade Commission Web site. Available online. URL: www.ftc.gov.

Fair Debt Collections Practices Act

The Fair Debt Collections Practices Act (FDCPA, 1977, and amended since then) is a federal law designed to prohibit abusive practices by debt collectors. Congress stated, "It is the purpose of this title to eliminate abusive debt collection practices by debt collectors, to ensure that those debt collectors who refrain from using abusive debt collection practices are not competitively disadvantageous, and to promote consistent State action to protect consumers against debt collection abuses." The act applies to debts incurred by consumers involving money, property, INSURANCE, or services. At the time, Congress found that

> (A) There is abundant evidence of the use of abusive, deceptive, and unfair debt collection practices by many debt collectors. Abusive debt collection practices contribute to the number of personal bankruptcies, to marital instability, to the loss of jobs, and to invasions of individual PRIVACY. (B) Existing laws and procedures for redressing these injuries are inadequate to protect consumers. (C) Means other than misrepresentation or other abusive debt collection practices are available for the effective collection of debts. (D) Abusive debt collection practices are carried on to a substantial extent in interstate commerce. Even where abusive debt collection practices are purely intrastate in character, they nevertheless directly affect interstate commerce.

The act generally prevents debt collectors from contacting anyone other than the person who incurred the debt. Previously debt collectors often contacted relatives, employers, and friends, attempting to intimidate or embarrass people into paying the debt. The act states that any debtor communicating with any person other than the consumer for the purpose of acquiring location information about the consumer shall "only ask location information; not state that the consumer owes any debt; not use postcards or any symbols or language in mailings referring to debt collection; and not communicate with any person other than the attorney, after the debt collector knows the consumer is represented by an attorney."

Without the prior consent of the consumer given directly to the debt collector, a debt collector may not communicate with a consumer at the consumer's place of EMPLOYMENT or at any unusual time. (Generally debt collectors can only contact consumers between 8 A.M. and 9 P.M. local time.) The act also requires the collector to provide details regarding the debt within five days of initial contact. If a consumer notifies a debt collector in writing that they refuse to pay a debt or that they wish the debt collector to cease further communication with the consumer, the debt collector must not communicate further with the consumer regarding the debt.

The act states that the debt collector may not engage in any conduct to harass, oppress, or abuse any person in connection with the collection of a debt. The following list provides an idea of the types of practices utilized before the FDCPA.

- The use or threat of use of violence or other criminal means to harm the physical person, reputation, or property of any person.
- The use of obscene or profane language or language the natural consequence of which is to abuse the hearer or reader.
- The publication of a list of consumers who allegedly refuse to pay debts, except to a consumer reporting agency.
- The advertisement for sale of any debt to coerce payment of the debt.
- Causing a telephone to ring or engaging any person in telephone conversation repeatedly or continuously with intent to annoy, abuse, or harass any person at the called number.

The act states further: a debt collector may not use any false, deceptive, or misleading representation or means in connection with the collection of any debt, including

- the character, amount, or legal status of any debt
- any services rendered or compensation which may be lawfully received by any debt collector for the collection of a debt

- the false representation or implication that any individual is an attorney or that any communication is from an attorney
- the representation or implication that nonpayment of any debt will result in the arrest or imprisonment of any person or the seizure, garnishment, attachment, or sale of any property or wages of any person unless such action is lawful and the debt collector or creditor intends to take such action
- the threat to take any action that cannot legally be taken
- the false representation or implication that a sale, referral, or other transfer of any interest in a debt shall cause the consumer to lose any claim or defense to payment of the debt, or become subject to any practice prohibited by this title
- the false representation or implication that the consumer committed any crime or other conduct in order to disgrace the consumer
- communicating or threatening to communicate to any person credit information which is known or which should be known to be false, including the failure to communicate that a disputed debt is disputed
- the use of distribution of any written communication which simulates or is falsely represented to be a document authorized, issued, or approved by any court, official, or agency of the United States, or which creates a false impression as to its source, authorization, or approval
- the use of any false representation of deceptive means to collect or attempt to collect any debt or to obtain information concerning a consumer
- the false representation or implication that accounts have been turned over to innocent purchasers for value
- the false representation or implication that documents are legal process
- the use of any business, company, or organization name other than the true name of the debt collector's business, company, or organization
- the false representation or implication that documents are not legal process forms or do not require action by the consumer

- the false representation or implication that a debt collector operates or is employed by a consumer reporting agency

The FEDERAL TRADE COMMISSION is the primary federal agency responsible for enforcement of the FDCPA, which also allows individual civil actions and class actions by consumers or consumer groups.

See also CONSUMER CREDIT PROTECTION ACT.

Further reading
Mallor, Jane P., A. James Barnes, Thomas Bowers, Michael J. Philips, and Arlen W. Langvardt. *Business Law: The Ethical, Global, and E-Commerce Environment.* 14th ed. Boston: McGraw-Hill, 2009.

fair disclosure (SEC Regulation FD)

Fair disclosure is providing information to all parties at one time. The SECURITY AND EXCHANGE COMMISSION's (SEC) Regulation FD, effective October 2000, is designed to eliminate "selective disclosure" of financial information by officials of publicly traded CORPORATIONS in the United States. Historically, STOCK MARKET analysts "cover" stocks in particular industries, analyzing trends, making predictions about future profitability, and offering recommendations to investors. These WALL STREET insiders get to know managers and officials of the companies they cover and are often provided reports from and interviews with company executives, thus obtaining information in advance of individual traders in the marketplace. For decades this was standard practice on Wall Street, but with the advantage of online trading and the huge increase in individual traders, non-Wall Street investors complained about the unfair advantage given to industry analysts and the firms they represented.

In addition to eliminating selective disclosure, the fair disclosure regulation, as SEC Regulation FD is known, also addresses "analyst independence," recognizing that the firms analysts work for often have other business relationships with the companies they evaluate. The SEC and the

SECURITIES INDUSTRY ASSOCIATION direct stock market firms to separate analysts' pay from other relationships with the companies they cover.

The fair disclosure guidelines provide flexibility for companies to comply with disclosure requirements. The guidelines allow companies to issue press releases through conventional media and encourage firms to announce in advance Web site disclosures and teleconferencing announcements. Companies continue to have investor conferences, but with the new fair disclosure rules, all information provided at these conferences must also be made available to the general investing public.

Further reading
Securities and Exchange Commission Web site. Available online. URL: www.sec.gov.

fair housing laws
Fair housing laws refers to a series of statutes and amendments enacted in the last 40 years to provide equal access and opportunity for renters and homebuyers. Title VIII of the Civil Rights Act of 1968 prohibited discrimination in the sale, rental, and financing of houses based on race, color, religion, sex, or national origin. The Federal Department of Housing and Urban Development (HUD) administers national fair housing laws. Some states and communities have additional housing discrimination laws.

Specifically, in the sale and rental of housing, federal fair housing laws prohibit actions based on race, color, national origin, religion, sex, familial status, or handicap, including:

- Refusal to rent or sell housing
- Refusal to negotiate for housing
- Making housing unavailable
- Denying a dwelling
- Setting different terms, conditions, or privileges for sale or rental of a dwelling
- Providing different housing services or facilities
- Falsely denying that housing is available for inspection, sale, or rental
- For profit, persuading owners to sell or rent (blockbusting) or

- Denying anyone access to or membership in a facility or service (such as a MULTIPLE LISTING SERVICE) related to the sale or rental of housing.

In MORTGAGE lending, the laws prohibit any of the following actions based on race, color, national origin, religion, sex, familial status, or handicap (disability):

- Refusing to make a mortgage loan
- Refusing to provide information regarding loans
- Imposing different terms or conditions on a loan, such as different interest rates, points, or fees
- Discriminating in appraising property
- Refusing to purchase a loan or
- Setting different terms or conditions for purchasing a loan.

It is also illegal for anyone to:

- Threaten, coerce, intimidate, or interfere with anyone exercising a fair housing right or assisting others who exercise that right
- Advertise or make any statement that indicates a limitation or preference based on race, color, national origin, religion, sex, familial status, or handicap.

In 1988 amendments to the 1968 act greatly increased HUD's fair housing role, expanding protection against discrimination to include people with disabilities and family status (presence of children under the age of 18) and pregnant women. The amendments expanded Justice Department jurisdiction, allowing that agency to sue on behalf of victims in federal district courts, and also established administrative enforcement mechanisms allowing HUD attorneys to bring actions on behalf of victims of housing discrimination. Housing discrimination complaints filed with HUD are investigated by the Office of Fair Housing and Equal Opportunity (FHEO). If the complaint is not successfully conciliated, FHEO determines whether reasonable cause exists to believe that a discriminatory housing practice has occurred. Where reasonable cause is found, the parties to the complaint are notified, and a hearing is scheduled before a HUD administrative law judge. Either party—complainant or respondent—may cause the HUD-scheduled administrative proceeding to be terminated by electing instead to have the matter litigated in federal court.

Passage of the Americans with Disabilities Act in 1990 led to changes in housing laws, requiring new buildings that have an elevator and four or more units to have public and common areas that are accessible to persons with disabilities as well as doors and hallways wide enough for wheelchairs.

In 1995 federal fair housing laws addressed the problem of senior-only housing with passage of the Housing for Older Persons Act (HOPA), which eliminated the requirement that age 55 and older housing have "significant facilities and services" designed for the elderly, but required that operators of senior housing publish and follow policies and procedures that demonstrate the intent of the premises to be used for housing for persons 55 and older.

Further reading
Department of Housing and Urban Development Web site. Available online. URL: www.hud.gov.

Fair Labor Standards Act
The Fair Labor Standards Act (FLSA), passed in 1938 and amended many times since then, is a major labor-management law regulating wages and hours, child labor, equal pay, and overtime pay. The act entitles covered employees to a specified MINIMUM WAGE and a time-and-a-half rate for work exceeding 40 hours per week.

One of the critical and complicated aspects of FLSA is the question of who is covered by the act. Generally, hourly employees for business engaged in interstate commerce or producing goods and services for interstate commerce are covered by the act. Federal employees were added to coverage in 1974. Most executive, administrative, and professional personnel are exempted from coverage. Whether or not an employee is covered is important in determining which workers can be expected to work beyond 40 hours per week without compensation and which employees must be compensated.

FLSA also contains provisions regarding child labor. "Oppressive" child labor is considered to include most EMPLOYMENT of children below the age of 14. Employment in certain occupations is allowed for children aged 14–15, and the act contains restrictions for employment of children aged 16–17 in certain hazardous occupations. Changes in minimum-wage laws are amendments to the original FLSA.

Interpreting the FLSA is a complex process with numerous legal precedents. Whole books have been written and are continually updated regarding labor-law requirements under the act. International businesses opening operations in the United States need to become familiar with labor practices acceptable and unacceptable under FLSA.

Further reading
Mallor, Jane P., A. James Barnes, Thomas Bowers, Michael J. Philips, and Arlen W. Langvardt. *Business Law: The Ethical, Global, and E-Commerce Environment.* 14th ed. Boston: McGraw-Hill, 2009.

fair use   See COPYRIGHT, FAIR USE.

Fair Packaging and Labeling Act
The Fair Packaging and Labeling Act (FLPA), enacted in 1967, directed the FEDERAL TRADE COMMISSION (FTC) and the FOOD AND DRUG ADMINISTRATION (FDA) to issue regulations requiring that all "consumer commodities" be labeled to disclose identity of the commodity, net contents, and place of business of the product's manufacturer, packer, or distributor. The act was enacted in response to numerous consumer complaints regarding deceptive labeling and packaging practices. FLPA is consistent with competitive market theory, which requires knowledgeable buyers and sellers.

The FLPA authorized additional regulations where necessary to prevent consumer deception or to facilitate value comparisons with respect to descriptions of ingredients, slack fill of packages, use of "cents off" or lower price labeling, or characterization of package sizes. The

FDA administers the act with respect to foods, drugs, cosmetics, and medical devices. The FTC also administers the act with respect to other consumer goods, though numerous products are exempt from regulation.

Recent food labeling controversies include tracking sources of meat production during the mad cow crisis, whether herbal dietary supplements are properly labeled, the use of "all natural" in package and ingredient labeling, and the U.S./EU disagreement on labeling of genetically modified organisms (GMO).

Further reading
Federal Trade Commission. "Fair Packaging and Labeling Act." Available online. URL: www.ftc.gov/os/statutes/fpla/outline.shtm. Accessed on December 8, 2009; Miller, Henry I., and Peter VanDoren. "Food Risks and Labeling Controversies," Cato Institute. Available online. URL: www.cato.org/pubs/regulation/regv23n1/miller.pdf. Accessed on December 8, 2009.

Family and Medical Leave Act
One of the first legislative acts signed by President Bill Clinton in 1993, the Family and Medical Leave Act (FMLA), entitles eligible employees to take up to 12 weeks of unpaid leave in a 12-month period for specific family and medical needs such as the birth of a child, adopting or fostering a child, serious health care for immediate family (spouse, parent, or child), and medical leave when an employee has a serious health condition. The employer has a choice of using either a calendar year or the company's FISCAL YEAR. The law protects the employee who takes the leave by guaranteeing job continuation after the leave, health benefits during the leave, and the right to take the leave.

This law applies to all employees who work for public agencies; local, state, and federal government employers; and educational institutions such as local public schools, colleges, and universities. For employees in the private sector, their company must have 50 or more employees and have 20 or more workweeks in the current or preceding calendar year and be engaged in commerce or any industry or activity that affects commerce.

For employees to take leave under the FMLA, they must have worked in the job for 12 months, have worked at least 1,250 hours for those 12 months, and worked in the United States or any territory or possession of the United States. For spouses employed by the same employer, they are jointly entitled to a combined total of 12 workweeks.

Under some conditions, the family leave may be taken in blocks of time (intermittently) or by reducing their normal workday. Intermittent leave must be approved the employer. Employees may also combine earned leave (vacation or sick time) with the FMLA upon approval of the employer.

It is unlawful for any eligible employer to interfere or deny their employees' rights to the FMLA. It is also illegal to fire or discriminate against the employee for participating in the FMLA. The DEPARTMENT OF LABOR will bring action against any eligible employer for denying an employee participation in the FMLA.

The FMLA does not take the place of state or local laws, which offer better leave provisions, nor does it prevent an employer from offering better benefits to their employees.

Further reading
Flynn, Gillian. "The Latest Focus on the Fuzzy FMLA," *Workforce* (February 2001): 94–95; U.S. Department of Labor Web site. Available online. URL: www.dol.gov.
—Susan Poorbaugh

family farm
A family farm is officially defined by the 1998 Agricultural Resource Management Study as any farm organized as a sole PROPRIETORSHIP, PARTNERSHIP, or family CORPORATION. Family farms exclude those organized as nonfamily corporations or COOPERATIVES or firms with a hired manager. Family farms are those legally controlled by one operator, or the person who makes daily decisions, and are run by their family or household. The U.S. Department of Agriculture (USDA) defines small family farms as those with sales of less than $250,000, large family farms as those with sales of $250,000–$499,999, and very large family farms

as those with sales of $500,000 or more. Farms were first defined for census purposes in 1850, and their definition has changed nine times. The current definition of a farm is any place from which $1,000 or more of agricultural PRODUCTS are sold or would normally have been sold in a given year.

The 2001 Family Farm Report by Economic Research Services of the USDA illustrates that there is a wide variety of small family farms. These include are limited-resource farms with sales less than $100,000 and an operator household of less than $20,000; retirement farms, whose owners are retired; and residential/ lifestyle farms, which are small farms where the majority of household INCOME comes from an occupation other than farming.

Family farms declined dramatically in number during the 20th century. The census of agriculture has shown that the number of farms decreased by two-thirds between 1935 and 1974, from 6.8 million to 2.3 million. The average farm was 155 acres in 1934; it was 487 acres in 1998. Agricultural PRODUCTION is heavily concentrated on large and very large family farms. While these two groups accounted for only 8 percent of all farms in 1998, they made up 53 percent of the total production of agricultural products. Although the limited-resource, retirement, and residential/lifestyle types make up 62 percent of farms in the United States, they produce only 9 percent of farm output. Family farms in the United States also tend to specialize in production, and half of all farms produce just one commodity.

In addition, family farmers are an aging and mostly rural population. The average age of a family farmer is typically around 50 years old. Many younger people have moved off family farms as more nonfarm EMPLOYMENT became available. Almost two-thirds of U.S. farms are in nonmetropolitan counties. One of the biggest problems that these farms face is a heavy debt burden. A USDA-recommend strategy for these farmers by the USDA is to lease land and farm equipment rather than purchase it in order to eliminate the need for CAPITAL financing. A large number of family farms are simply too small for their owners to do anything other than supplement other types of employment.

Farm policy has always been a difficult issue for the United States, especially in the 19th century when the populist movement was a major force in U.S. politics. This movement lasted until the early 20th century and was widely supported by farmers who hoped to have some control over crop prices and determining credit policies toward farmers. During the New Deal of the 1930s, legislation was passed that was designed to protect farmers from wide price changes during the GREAT DEPRESSION, and a farm policy called the Parity Program was developed. This resulted in the COMMODITY CREDIT CORPORATION (CCC), which made LOANS to farmers whenever prices fell below the cost of production. Farmers could consequently hold crops back from the market to force prices back up and repay their loans with interest. This program also regulated farm production in order to balance crop supply with DEMAND and created a national grain reserve.

Controversial legislation passed in 1996 sought to alleviate the problems of family farmers. The Federal Agriculture Improvement and Reform Act (FAIR), also known as the Freedom to Farm Act, is a seven-year farm program that put an end to New Deal production controls and eliminated federal price supports. FAIR gave farmers a guarantee of fixed but declining payments that were to end in 2002 as well as the flexibility to plant whatever crops they want. By eliminating PRICE FLOORS and production controls, FAIR was supposed to give farmers some control over the price of their crops so that they could increase EXPORTING by offering more competitive prices on the world market. Critics of this legislation have argued that in the last four years, exports of key crops such as corn, wheat, and soybeans have dropped 10 percent. They also suggest that this law has not allowed farmers a means of controlling the SUPPLY of crops on the market, even if there is already a surplus that has greatly depressed prices. Finally, critics argue that legislators have failed to consider the reality of increased production by other exporting countries, and that lower commodity prices do not increase overall demand.

The decline in the profitability and number of family farms has also led to great debate over their future role in the American economy. Some economists have argued that in a global economy, small family farms have simply become too inefficient and that those who support them cling to a romantic notion rather than economic reality. In the last 20 years the agriculture industry has seen a great deal of concentration. In 2000 the top packing companies in the beef business accounted for 81 percent of cattle slaughtering, up from 30 percent in 1980. In hog processing, four farms control 56 percent of the market. Several recent mergers have also created huge new CONGLOMERATES, often referred to as agribusiness companies. In 1999 Cargill Inc., the country's largest grain processor, acquired Continental Grain Company, the third largest. In order to prevent this new conglomerate from becoming a complete MONOPOLY, the Justice Department required that they make some significant CORPORATE DIVESTITURES of ASSETS.

As corporate farms have become steadily larger, some critics have warned about potential environmental and health dangers associated with them. Factory farms such as hog farms often create pools of waste that can leak into ground water and rivers. While agribusiness companies insist that that mergers will lead to a growing efficiency in production and lower consumer prices, many small farmers argue that such mergers are driving them out of business.

Supporters of agribusiness suggest that family farms are simply unproductive and outdated in face of the large-scale efficiency offered by large corporations. They suggest that family-farm supporters exaggerate the environmental threat, that America is no longer a rural culture, and that agriculture policies should be developed to favor international trade, rather than small rural farmers. FAIR was passed in great measure to support the U.S. commitment to the WORLD TRADE ORGANIZATION and the General Agreement on Tariffs and Trade (GATT). Nonetheless, some staunch family-farm supporters, such as Senator Bryan Dorgan

of North Dakota, argue that family farms do not struggle because they are inefficient but because of inappropriate federal legislation and trade agreements that favor agribusiness. He suggests that the most important element family farms provide to the country is a sense of community and family values. The place of family farms in American life was important throughout the 18th and 19th century, but their decline in the 20th century has been significant, and their future economic viability remains in question.

Further reading

Dorgan, Byron. "Don't Be Down on the Farm." *The Washington Monthly,* January/February 2000; Ghent, Bill. "Agriculture: Mergers Squeeze Family Farms," *National Journal* (15 July 2000): 32; "Structural and Financial Characteristics of U.S. Farms: 2001 Family Farm Report," U.S. Department of Agriculture Economic Research Service. Available online. URL: www.ers.usda. gov/publications/aib768/. Accessed on May 31, 2001.

—Alison Jones

family-friendly business practices

Family-friendly business practices are policies and benefits provided to employees to assist them with their family needs and obligations. The idea of family-friendly business practices was part of the 1992 presidential debates regarding "family values" and the FAMILY AND MEDICAL LEAVE ACT (FMLA), vetoed by President George H. W. Bush and later passed under the Clinton administration. Under FMLA, a covered employer must grant an eligible employee up to 12 workweeks of unpaid leave during any 12-month period for one or more of the following reasons.

- for the birth and care of the employee's newborn child
- for placement of a son or daughter with the employee for adoption or foster care
- to care for an immediate family member (spouse, child, or parent) with a serious health condition
- to take medical leave when the employee is unable to work because of a serious health condition

Beyond the Family and Medical Leave Act, there is no one definition of what constitutes a family-friendly business, but two surveys provide guidelines. A group in Horry County, South Carolina, created the *Employee Certified Family-Friendly Business Initiative.* To be certified at their minimum (bronze) level, a firm needs to offer

- health INSURANCE with the organization paying at least 50 percent of the premium and offering some dependent coverage
- paid time off for critical family needs
- dependent care assistance
- some type of savings program
- school/educational support
- community/neighborhood support
- paid vacation or leave
- opportunity for skill development and progression
- some type of dissemination of family, work/life information
- sponsored seminars or workshops on family/work/life topics
- employee recognition for work service, community work, and personal events
- life insurance for employees
- selected benefits for part-time/seasonal employees
- a written MISSION STATEMENT emphasizing employees and family

By 2001, 21 area organizations had been certified as family-friendly.

In a second study, 28 benefits or policies were identified as family-friendly business practices, including

- timing of employee training
- equal pay for equal work
- vacation time
- time for family emergencies
- MINIMUM WAGE
- health insurance
- COMPARABLE WORTH
- flexible working hours
- college tuition reimbursement
- overtime guidelines for salaried employees

- family counseling services
- moving expenses reimbursement
- preretirement planning services
- freedom to refuse transfers
- family leave
- pretax account for dependent care
- consideration of spouse in transfers
- voluntary reduced time
- CAFETERIA PLAN for benefits
- benefits for part-time workers
- job-sharing opportunities
- satellite offices/branches
- work-at-home capability
- release time or flexible hours for sick-dependent care
- release time or flexible hours for elderly care
- paid time off for volunteer work
- dependent care provision or referral
- career break plan

Relatively few firms offer all or most of these benefits or policies. Traditionally in the United States, employees were expected to "leave their personal problems at the door." During the labor shortage that occurred in many industries in the 1990s, many U.S. companies became more flexible in accommodating and supporting their employees' personal needs. Surveys show that companies offering family-friendly work environments have greater worker loyalty, initiative, and teamwork.

Further reading

Department of Labor Family and Medical Leave Act Fact Sheet. Available online. URL: www.dol.gov/esa/regs/compliance/ whd/whdfs28.htm; Folsom, Davis, and Robert Botsch. "Is Your Company Family Friendly?" *B&E Review,* April–June 1993; Rogers, Jim R. "Is Your Business Family-Friendly?" *B&E Review,* July–September 2001.

family life cycle

The family life cycle is a series of typical stages that families go through, from family formation to dissolution. At each stage individual and family needs and wants differ, creating opportunities for marketers to change and provide what will best suit their customers.

The family life cycle can comprise up to eight stages, including bachelor, young married, full nest, single parent, divorced and alone, middle-aged and married, full nest again, and empty nest. The usefulness of family life-cycle analysis is looking at customer groups based on their life stage rather than age or other demographic measure. For example, in the United States the average age at which people get married for the first time has been increasing, which means consumers remain in the bachelor stage for a longer period of time. Bachelors are more likely to need apartment furnishings, purchase economy or sports cars, and pursue adventure travel. Another phenomenon within the bachelor stage is that young people are staying longer in their parents' home. Especially in areas where housing costs are high, many young singles live at home and will have different needs than those moving into their own dwellings.

Young married couples are an attractive group to many marketers. Anyone who has recently become engaged has probably been overwhelmed with a vast array of promotions from wedding services, jewelers, travel agents, and INSURANCE companies. Many new choices and decisions are made in a short period of time among young married couples, creating needs and opportunities for marketers.

Even before the arrival of first children, full-nest families (and filling-the-nest families) change their CONSUMER BEHAVIOR. Sports cars often cannot hold safety seats and are traded in for vans and SUVs. Larger apartments and first-home purchases create changing needs for products. Insurance, health care, and other service needs also change.

Single parent and divorced and alone are two similar and typical family life-cycle stages. The splitting up of households creates changing needs for products and services and undoes many existing CONTRACTS, including home ownership and insurance coverage.

Those families that make it through the full-nest stage or remarry after the single-parent stage become the middle-aged and married segment. These households tend to have higher INCOMES, established relationships with firms, and greater interest in quality and timesaving products. Often, within a few years, these families are surprised to find themselves in the full-nest-again stage, as college-graduate children return home. This can create needs for remodeling, changing insurance needs, and a variety of products to accommodate different needs under one roof.

Eventually the family life cycle leads to the empty-nest stage. At this point families often shift from homes to condominiums or purchase a second home in a warmer climate, leaving offspring behind to take care of the homestead. Travel demand increases, and at some point health-care needs grow.

Of course, many adult groups do not go through the family life cycle. Marketers refer to DINKS (Double Income, No Kids) as one segment of affluent consumers who choose to not have children.

Further reading

Boone, Louis, and David Kurtz. *Contemporary Marketing*. 14th ed. Fort Worth, Tex.: South-Western, 2009; Etzel, Michael J., Bruce J. Walker, and William J. Staunton. *Marketing*. 14th ed. Boston: McGraw-Hill, 2005.

Fannie Mae   See FEDERAL NATIONAL MORTGAGE ASSOCIATION.

Farm Credit System

The Farm Credit System (FCS) is a national financial cooperative providing LOANS to farmers, COOPERATIVES, rural homeowners, agribusinesses, and rural utility systems. In 2007 the FCS made over $115 billion in loans to borrowers and provided approximately one-fourth of the credit extended to U.S. agricultural producers.

The Farm Credit System, the earliest government-sponsored enterprise (GSE), sells FCS BONDS and notes and then lends funds through a network of 200 Farm Credit lending institutions. The Farm Credit Administration (FCA) based in McLean, Virginia, is an independent federal regulator responsible for examining and ensuring the FCS's financial soundness. The FCA's three-member BOARD OF DIRECTORS are nominated by the U.S. president and confirmed by the Senate.

To people not involved in agriculture, the FCS is a maze of acronyms. To anyone involved in agriculture, the FCS is a major source of government support and funding. The FCS includes a variety of financial institutions including Farm Credit Banks, CoBank, Federal Land Bank Associations (FLBAs), Federal Land Credit Associations (FLCAs), Production Credit Associations (PCAs), Agricultural Credit Associations (ACAs), and Farm Credit Council (FCC).

There are six Farm Credit Banks (FCBs), including AgAmerica and Western FCBs (western and northwestern U.S.), Agribank, FCB (midwestern states), AgFirst, FCB (primarily southeastern U.S.), FCB of Wichita (south-central states), and FCB of Texas (Louisiana to parts of New Mexico). The FCBs provide financial services and finds to local associations, which in turn lend those funds to agricultural and rural borrowers.

The CoBank, created in 1989 through the merger of 10 of the 12 district cooperative banks, is one of three Banks for Cooperatives. A Bank for Cooperatives in turn provides lending and other financial services to farmer-owned cooperatives and rural utility systems.

The Federal Land Bank Associations (FLBAs) are affiliates of the Farm Credit Bank and provide long-term MORTGAGE loans to farmers, ranchers, and rural homebuyers. The Federal Land Credits Associations (FLCAs) provide lending for long-term loans. The Production Credit Associations (PCAs) provide short- and intermediate-term loans to farmers and ranchers. The Agricultural Credit Associations (ACAs), formed through mergers, are the successors to the FLBAs and PCAs, providing long- and short-term agricultural and rural loans. The Farm Credit Council (FCC) is the national trade association of the FCS, representing the interests of the FCS with respect to federal agricultural policies and providing INSURANCE and business services to the FCS.

The history of the Farm Credit System began with the Country Life Commission created by President Theodore Roosevelt in 1908. At that time, lending for agricultural real estate was extremely limited. In 1913 federal law prohibited national banks from making loans with maturities greater than five years. (The government was attempting to reduce interest-rate RISK in banking and reduce bank failures after the crash of 1907.) The commission's report eventually led to the passage of the Federal Farm Loan Act of 1916, which created the 12 Federal Land Banks, using $125 million in government funds and private CAPITAL to create credit institutions for agricultural producers. The land banks prospered with World War I and increased DEMAND for food products but collapsed in the postwar economic decline. In response Congress created 12 Federal Intermediate Credit Banks, but they faltered with the GREAT DEPRESSION. The Agricultural Marketing Act of 1929 provided support prices for agricultural products and financial support for agricultural cooperatives. By 1933 the government consolidated federal farm programs into the Farm Credit Administration, creating the basis for today's Farm Credit System.

Historically, support for U.S. agriculture has been strong, based on widespread political representation. In recent decades, as agricultural interests have been supplanted by manufacturing, technology, service industries, and greater consumer interests, support for farm programs have been sometimes challenged in the political arena. In response the Farm Credit System has come under greater scrutiny to become financially sound and self-sustaining.

See also GOVERNMENT-SPONSORED ENTERPRISES.

Further reading
Farm Credit Council Web site. Available online URL: www.fccouncil.com.

fast track (trade promotion authority)

Fast track is the media term for the authority, granted by Congress to the U.S. president, to negotiate trade agreements. Fast track allows the president to negotiate a trade agreement with the understanding that Congress will ratify or reject the treaty but will not amend the agreement. By granting the president fast-track authority, Congress limits its right and duty under the U.S. Constitution to ratify any agreement the president enters into.

Every U.S. president since 1974 has been granted fast-track authority. Ronald Reagan used fast-track authority to negotiate the U.S.-CANADA FREE TRADE AGREEMENT (1989), and Bill Clinton used his fast-track authority to complete the NORTH AMERICAN FREE TRADE AGREEMENT (NAFTA), initiated by George H. W. Bush in the early 1990s. At the 1994 Conference of the Americas in Miami, President Clinton assured Chile that they would be the next country allowed to join NAFTA. Congress then refused to renew Clinton's fast-track authority, ending the expansion of NAFTA for the rest of his presidency.

In 2001 President George W. Bush met with the leaders of 33 Western Hemisphere countries in Quebec, Canada, to initiate plans for the Free Trade Area of the Americas (FTAA). At the conference, the president renamed fast-track authority "trade promotion authority." Even though the leaders agreed to create a FREE-TRADE AREA by 2005, the agreement was never completed. Fast track authorization expired in 2007.

Further reading
Public Citizen Web site. Available online. URL: www.citizen.org/trade/fasttrack/. Accessed on June 16, 2009.

featherbedding
The term *featherbedding* describes UNION efforts to require employers to hire more workers than needed for the task. Featherbedding agreements require companies to pay union members wages whether their work is needed or not. As LABOR MARKETS change, often certain skills and tasks are no longer needed. However, if the union/MANAGEMENT agreement calls for workers to be employed, then the company is required by the CONTRACT to pay the workers. A classic example was firemen on trains. In the days of wood and coal engines, having a fireman on board a train was a reasonable requirement. But as diesel and electric engines came into use, railroad companies were often required by the union contract to continue to employ firemen.

The TAFT-HARTLEY ACT (1947) attempted to outlaw featherbedding by making it an unfair labor practice to demand payment of wages for services that are not performed or will not be performed. Nevertheless, featherbedding exists. In one case the Supreme Court ruled that only payments for workers not to work are prohibited. A union may require that the employer pay workers for useless or totally unnecessary work, as long as the work is actually performed. For example, a newspaper accepted ads from customers that had been prepared by the customer. However, the union agreement required the employer to recopy the prepared work using union workers. In another case, companies have been forced to pay union workers who do nothing as long as they remain willing to work. For example, a theater that brought in out-of-town orchestras still had to pay union musicians, even though no work was performed.

Featherbedding is a basis for major criticism of labor unions in the United States. In recent years many unions have become more flexible in union/management negotiations about minimum crew sizes and "make-work" agreements.

Further reading
Regulation of Economic Pressure. Available online. URL: /web./missouri/edu/~labored/1997-30.html.

Federal Aviation Administration
The Federal Aviation Administration (FAA) is an agency in the U.S. DEPARTMENT OF TRANSPORTATION responsible for the safety of civil air transportation. Its other roles include RESEARCH AND DEVELOPMENT, implementing programs to control noise pollution resulting from air traffic, and regulating launches of commercial space payloads.

Originally called the Federal Aviation Agency, the FAA was created when Congress passed the Federal Aviation Act of 1958. Its responsibilities included overseeing licensing and certification of pilots and aircraft, development of air navigation and air traffic-control systems, and adopting the safety rules and policy-making functions of the

CIVIL AERONAUTICS BOARD. In 1967 it became part of the Department of Transportation and took its present name.

The FAA is comprised mainly of seven organizations whose leaders report to the administrator and deputy administrator. Other significant programs are managed by assistant administrators. The FAA's primary role is to enforce safety and security policy within the industry. The National Transportation Safety Board frequently makes recommendations for safety inspections and aircraft repair as a result of accident investigations. It is at the FAA's discretion to enforce such recommendations.

The FAA oversees all activities with regard to aviation operations, and its activities are a pivotal part of the business aspects of the aviation industry. Airlines and the aviation industry in general are strongly affected by FAA mandates. Inspection orders, requirements for hiring policies for employees and contractors, upgrades to equipment, and updated procedures are some of the common directives issued by the FAA. These directives can be determining factors in how safe or successful the industry will be. Ordered inspections, for example, are time-consuming and costly for airlines. Grounding aircraft for inspection and repair often requires cancellation of flights and incurred costs ultimately reach the consumer.

Past air disasters, particularly the TWA Flight 800 explosion over Long Island, New York, in July 1996, raised questions about the FAA's performance in maintaining air safety and security. Many critics claim that mandates for inspection, upgrades, and policies regarding aging aircraft have come only in response to tragedy. However, in 1998 the FAA responded immediately by ordering the inspection of older Boeing 737s when frayed wiring was found during routine maintenance.

Following the TWA disaster, when initial evidence suggested terrorism, President Bill Clinton directed the FAA to put into operation specific recommendations dealing with airport and airline security. Few have been fully implemented, others

not at all. Scrutiny regarding security increased after the terrorist attacks on September 11, 2001.

Other FAA functions include promoting aviation safety abroad, constructing and maintaining navigational facilities, developing new aviation technology, providing air-travel advisories, awarding grants and scholarships, and participating in outreach programs.

Further reading
Federal Aviation Administration Web site. Available online. URL: http://www.faa.gov.

—Jennifer McGeorge

federal budget

The federal budget is the spending activity of the U.S. government. At almost $3.1 trillion in 2009, the federal budget is larger than the GROSS DOMESTIC PRODUCT (GDP) of every country in the world except Japan, China, and Germany. Yet federal government spending represents only about 22 percent of U.S. GDP, a smaller percentage than almost every other industrialized country in the world.

The federal budget is a source of constant debate. While politicians often complain the federal government is too big, few political leaders are willing to cut spending programs for fear of offending important constituents. Until 1998 there were often cries to cut the federal budget as a means of achieving a balanced budget. Beginning that year, budget surpluses (a result of modest growth in the federal budget), tax increases, use of the presidential line-item veto, and increased government revenue and reduced spending from a growing economy allowed political leaders the option of reducing the GOVERNMENT DEBT. Tax cuts under the George W. Bush administration and increased spending for defense and wars in Iraq and Afghanistan quickly erased the budget surpluses at the end of the Clinton administration.

The major components of the U.S. federal budget include defense spending, SOCIAL SECURITY, Medicare and Medicaid, other INCOME security, and interest on the government debt. The federal government groups budget spending into mandatory and discretionary spending. The year 2009 budget is summarized below.

Outlays:	Billions of Dollars
Discretionary:	
Department of Defense (DoD)	515
Global War on Terror	145
Non-DoD discretionary	550
Mandatory:	
Social Security	644
Medicare and Medicaid	632
Means-tested entitlements	360
Other	123
Net interest	260
Total	3,106
Receipts (taxation)	2,700
Unified budget surplus	406

The budget process begins in the government's executive branch. Every January the president sends to Congress a budget containing spending proposals for all departments and agencies for the coming FISCAL YEAR, which begins October 1. The OFFICE OF MANAGEMENT AND BUDGET represents the president in budgetary matters, and proposed allocations in the federal budget are examined by committees in Congress. Hearings are held with representatives of the government departments and other interested parties testifying for or against the budget proposal. Congress must approve funding for each budget allocation. Some years, when political control is divided between Democrats and Republicans, the approval process has been contentious and often delayed past the beginning of the fiscal year. Congress then passes continuing resolutions, allowing government agencies to operate under the last budget allocation.

Because of the federal budget's size, nearly every industry or business group in the United States watches it closely and attempts to influence spending. The U.S. CHAMBER OF COMMERCE represents the interests of U.S. business groups in general, while industry associations focus on specific parts of federal legislation and spending. Industry

association newsletters, Web sites, and magazines generally summarize pending federal legislation affecting their industry.

Further reading
U.S. Office of Management and Budget Web site. Available online. URL: www.whitehouse.gov/omb.

Federal Communications Commission

The Federal Communications Commission (FCC) is a government agency regulating interstate and international communications by radio, television, wire, satellite, and cable. The FCC was established by the Communications Act of 1934 as part of government regulation of evolving technologies. Like the FEDERAL AVIATION ADMINISTRATION and the Nuclear Regulatory Commission, the FCC was created to regulate the growth and use of communications systems, such as television and radio, that require the use of an electrical frequency spectrum transmitted through the air.

Like other federal agencies, the FCC is directed by a five-member commission, with no more than three members from one political party and one member rotating off annually. Commissioners are nominated by the U.S. president and confirmed by the Senate. The FCC has seven bureaus organized by function, including Cable Services, Common Carrier (telephone), Consumer Information, Enforcement, International, Mass Media (AM-FM radio and television broadcast stations), and Wireless Telecommunications (cellular and PCS phones, pagers, and two-way radios). Each bureau develops and implements regulatory programs, analyzes complaints, conducts investigations, and processes licenses.

One of the most important functions of the FCC is LICENSING. Mass-media companies are required to file license renewal requests every eight years, demonstrating that they are serving local communities. Licenses are limited in most mass-media markets. In recent years the FCC also expanded the sale of broadcast frequency licenses. These licenses sold for billions of dollars to telecommunications companies anticipating expanded wireless communications systems. The Telecommunications Act of 1996 attempted to increase COMPETITION in the communications industry. The act directed incumbent local exchange carriers (telephone companies) to lease part of their network "at cost" to competitors. Numerous legal challenges have blocked many of the act's goals.

Further reading

Federal Communications Commission Web site. Available online. URL: www.fcc.gov.

federal courts

The U.S. judicial system, which is based on England's system of COMMON LAW, was established by the authority found in Article I and Article III of the U.S. Constitution. In England between A.D. 476–1450, judges developed common law through their procedures and rulings. Eventually laws passed by legislatures replaced common law. Article I of the Constitution, provides the legislature (Congress) authority to establish courts inferior to the supreme Court [sic]—legislative courts. Constitutional courts are established by Article III, which states that the "judicial power of the United States, shall be vested in one supreme Court," but allows Congress the authority to "ordain and establish" inferior courts when necessary.

Common-law principals are still important to the American federal court system in that they emphasize protecting the individual from state abuse in two ways. First, the individual is presumed innocent until proven guilty; the burden of proof rests upon the state, and therefore the individual need not prove innocence. Second, common law provides individual protection from state abuse through a jury system (grand and petit juries).

Grand and petit juries consist of panels of ordinary citizens. Federal courts cannot prosecute defendants unless they are first indicted (charged with a crime) by the grand jury. The grand jury determines whether enough evidence exists to prosecute the individual for the charged crime in a trial court (petit jury). Petit juries consist of jurors who hear evidence from the prosecution and defense attorneys and then render a verdict of guilty or not guilty. Once a defendant is convicted, the judge imposes the sentence, or punishment. As previously noted defendants are protected from state abuse during these two stages of the judicial process.

Federal courts are distinguished by two major criteria: (a) the authority that establishes the court—constitutional and legislative courts, and (b) the jurisdiction the court has when hearing cases—original and appellate jurisdiction. Article III established constitutional courts, specifically the Supreme Court, but also gave Congress the power to establish lesser federal courts deemed necessary to exercise the "judicial power of the United States" (Article III Section 1). Constitutional courts include the Supreme Court, the U.S. Court of Appeals, and the U.S. District Courts. Legislative courts are lesser federal courts established by Congress with their vested authority in Article I. These special courts have limited jurisdictions to areas as defined by Congress. Examples of legislative courts include Military Courts, U.S. Tax Courts, U.S. Courts of Appeals, and the U.S. Claims Court. When cases are heard in court for the first time, they are heard under original jurisdiction. If an individual appeals the decision from the lower federal court, the case is then heard under appellate jurisdiction. Attorneys for major corporations monitor court decisions, particularly Tax and Claims court rulings, for their potential impact on business actions and strategies. Tax court rulings often influence accounting and business location decisions.

The United States has 89 Federal District Courts, each state having at least 1 and larger states having as many as 5. These courts are the country's major federal trial courts in which a single judge presides and a jury decides a verdict.

There are 12 circuit Courts of Appeal throughout the country. Precedence is determined by three judges (no jurors, witnesses, or attorneys present) and interpretation of the law, rather than case facts, is used to establish (hand down) an opinion. In most cases, decisions of the federal appellate courts are final—only a small number of cases are accepted (heard) by the Supreme Court proceeding appellate court rulings.

Further reading

Baradat, Leon P. "The Judiciary." In *Understanding American Democracy*. New York: HarperCollins, 1992; Janda, Kenneth, Jeffrey M. Berry, and Jerry Goldman. "The Constitution." In *The Challenge of Democracy*. 7th ed. Boston: Houghton Mifflin, 2002.

—Frank Ubhaus Jr. and Jerry Merwin

Federal Deposit Insurance Corporation

The Federal Deposit Insurance Corporation (FDIC) is a government agency administering federal deposit INSURANCE funds and regulating state-chartered "nonmember" banks. The FDIC is directed by a five-member BOARD OF DIRECTORS, appointed by the U.S. president and approved by the Senate. The FDIC was created in 1934 in response to the collapse of more than 9,000 U.S. banks between 1929 and 1933. Less than two days after Franklin Roosevelt was elected president, he declared a "banking holiday," closing all banks in the country while Congress enacted legislation to strengthen the BANKING SYSTEM. The FDIC, part of the 1933 Glass-Steagall Act, created insurance for bank depositors.

Banks play important roles in any economic system, including acting as FINANCIAL INTERMEDIARIES, aggregating funds from depositors, and making LOANS to businesses for INVESTMENT. In the CIRCULAR FLOW MODEL of an economy, most households save a small portion of their INCOME for varying periods of time, but they do not have the time or expertise needed to evaluate business investment proposals. Without a sound banking system, it is difficult for businesses to find the needed CAPITAL to make investments. Fearful of bank failure, individuals store their savings under the mattress, bury it in jars, or hold precious metals, none of which provides the capital most needed for investment and thus ECONOMIC GROWTH.

The bank failures of the GREAT DEPRESSION were not the first experience with problems in the U.S. financial system. Bank panics had occurred almost every 20 years beginning in 1819. Between 1929 and 1933, almost 40 percent of U.S. banks closed their doors, with depositors losing their savings. In 1934 the FDIC began by insuring deposits up to $2,500 per depositor, the goal being to restore bank customers' confidence. Over time FDIC insurance was raised to a limit of $100,000 per depositor. During the 2008 financial crisis, the FDIC raised the amount to $250,000. Insurance premiums are paid by member banking institutions into an FDIC-managed fund that contains only a small portion of the outstanding guarantees but is backed by the federal government.

The $250,000 insurance amount is available per depositor per institution. This means if one customer has savings, checking, and certificate of deposit accounts in an FDIC-insured institution, the sum of that depositor's accounts is insured for $250,000. (INDIVIDUAL RETIREMENT ACCOUNTS and KEOGH PLANS are insured separately.) During the 1980s, when almost 3,000 banks and SAVINGS AND LOAN ASSOCIATIONS failed, invariably individuals and groups lost parts of their deposits. In one case, a church group saving for a new building had over $200,000 in one account but received only the $100,000 maximum coverage. Since FDIC insurance is applied on a per-depositor per-institution basis, consumers with deposits exceeding $250,000 frequently spread their savings among financial institutions in order to be covered by FDIC insurance.

In addition to insuring bank customer deposits, the FDIC monitors about 6,000 state-chartered "nonmember" banks. These are commercial and savings banks that are not members of the FEDERAL RESERVE SYSTEM. The FDIC audits these financial institutions for sound banking practices and, when necessary, manages the liquidation of failed institutions. Typically the FDIC comes in and reorganizes a failed institution by merging it with a financially sound institution. The FDIC will often provide subsidized loans and buy questionable ASSETS of the failed institution from the merger partner. In the purchase-and-assumption method, customers of the failed bank become customers of the new bank, with their deposits continuing to be insured by the FDIC. When the FDIC cannot find another institution to assume the role of the failed institution, it will take over the failed bank, pay depositors, and liquidate the institution's assets.

Further reading
Federal Deposit Insurance Corporation Web site. Available online. URL: www.fdic.gov; Mishkin, Frederic S. *The Economics of Money, Banking, and Financial Markets.* 8th ed. Boston: Addison Wesley, 2006.

Federal Financial Institutions Examinations Council

As stated on their Web site, the Federal Financial Institutions Examinations Council (FFIEC) is a "formal interagency body empowered to prescribe uniform principles, standards, and report forms for the federal examination of financial institutions by" the major regulatory agencies responsible for supervision of the financial industry in the United States. The five member agencies of the Council are the Board of Governors of the FEDERAL RESERVE SYSTEM (FRS), the FEDERAL DEPOSIT INSURANCE CORPORATION (FDIC), the National Credit Union Administration (NCUA), the Office of the COMPTROLLER OF THE CURRENCY (OCC), and the Office of Thrift Supervision (OTS).

While the FFIEC has existed since 1979, it has rarely attracted public attention or industry concern. In July 2002, however, the council released draft guidelines on account management and loss-allowance guidance for credit-card lending. The council "found disparities in the quality of account management practices and inconsistencies in the application of existing guidance. The practices can increase institutions' credit RISK profile to imprudent levels. Further, the inconsistent application of accounting and regulatory guidance can affect the transparency and comparability of financial reporting for all institutions engaged in credit card lending."

As the *Wall Street Journal* reported, the FFIEC "issued new guidelines in an attempt to clean up inconsistent accounting methods, slow down the providing of credit to consumers who can't pay it back and to insure credit-card companies are adequately reserved for bad loans and fees tied to the loans." The council's actions followed the numerous financial accounting scandals that arose during 2002.

The FFIEC also has the responsibility to facilitate public access to depository institution data required under the Home Mortgage Disclosure Act of 1975. As required in the statute creating the group, the council has established an advisory State Liaison Committee composed of five representatives of state financial supervisory agencies.

See also CREDIT CARDS; CREDIT UNION.

Further reading
Federal Financial Institutions Examinations Council Web site. Available online. URL: www.ffiec.gov; Mollenkamp, Carrick. "New Scrutiny on Credit Cards Already Squeezes Some Lenders," *Wall Street Journal,* 19 August 2002.

federal funds market

The federal funds market is the short-term (usually overnight) lending and borrowing among banks in the United States to meet the FEDERAL RESERVE SYSTEM's reserve-requirement ratio. Though it is called the federal funds market, the Federal Reserve does not operate or control the market. Banks are required by the Federal Reserve to keep a set percentage of their deposits as cash or other specified U.S. TREASURY SECURITIES. These required reserves are available when customers want their deposits returned and act as a source of liquidity for banks.

As banks receive more deposits, their RESERVE REQUIREMENTS increase. At the end of each business day, bank managers calculate their required reserves, determine whether they have excess or insufficient reserves, and lend or borrow reserves electronically in the federal funds market. LOANS made in the federal funds market are returned the next business day.

Banks borrowing to meet their reserve requirement will compare rates in the market, attempting to minimize their COSTS. Federal-funds rates tend to be uniform among participating banks, but they increase or decrease depending on the DEMAND for and SUPPLY of funds available. Depending on the Federal Reserve's MONETARY POLICY, the Federal Reserve will increase or decrease the supply of funds in the federal funds market through OPEN-MARKET OPERATIONS. By purchasing securities from banks, the Federal Reserve increases the supply of funds in the market, which tends to decrease the federal-funds rate. Sale of securities by the Federal Reserve would have the opposite effect. Increasing federal-funds rates increases the costs to banks, which in turn increases rates charged to borrowers, decreasing borrowing from banks.

Further reading

Mishkin, Frederic S. *The Economics of Money, Banking, and Financial Markets.* 8th ed. Boston: Addison Wesley, 2006.

Federal Home Loan Bank System

The Federal Home Loan Bank System (FHLBS) was created by Congress in 1932 to stimulate housing financing in the United States. Through its 12 regional Federal Home Loan Banks, the FHLBS provides support to member financial institutions for residential MORTGAGE lending by providing access to CAPITAL MARKETS. In 2009, over 8,000 commercial banks, thrift institutions, CREDIT UNIONS, and INSURANCE companies were members of the FHLBS.

The Federal Housing Finance Board regulates the 12 Federal Home Loan Banks and has regulatory oversight for the Office of Finance, which supervises its members' financial practices. The 12 Federal Home Loan Banks are privately capitalized, government-sponsored enterprises. Each member of the regional banks is a shareholder in the institution, which receives no direct funding from the federal government. The FHLBS sells debt securities in capital markets, generating funds that are used by the regional FHL banks to provide mortgage credit to home buyers.

The FHLBS, like the FEDERAL RESERVE SYSTEM, serves as lender of last resort for its members, but it also provides long-term mortgage funds and provides advances to member institutions at competitive INTEREST RATES. In 1989 the mission of the FHLBS was expanded to include lending for affordable housing and community development.

Most SAVINGS AND LOAN ASSOCIATIONS (S&Ls) are members of the FHLBS. Unlike the Federal Reserve System, where loans are made for short periods of time at the discount rate, the FHLBS provides long-term loans at rates lower than the S&L would have paid in the open market. In this way the FHLBS subsidize mortgage lending.

This system of government-sponsored, privately owned financial institutions supported growth in residential housing for almost 50 years. In the early 1980s, new financial PRODUCTS, negotiable order of withdrawal (NOW) accounts, money-market funds, junk BONDS, and SECURITIZATION threatened traditional business lending practices by commercial banks and S&Ls. The Depository Institutions Deregulation and Monetary Control Act (1980) and the Depository Institutions (Garn-St. Germain) Act of 1982 allowed banks and S&Ls to move into risky lending areas while still protecting depositors through the FEDERAL DEPOSIT INSURANCE CORPORATION (FDIC) and the Federal Savings and Loan Insurance Corporation (FSLIC) insurance.

S&L managers increased investment in new areas of real estate lending beyond their traditional market, residential housing. RISKS were either ignored or not understood by S&L managers and regulators. A RECESSION in 1981–82 combined with a collapse in oil prices resulted in huge DEFAULTS on S&L LOANS, bankrupting many S&Ls. The Federal Home Loan Bank Board and its deposit insurance subsidiary, FSLIC, failed to close insolvent institutions. Finally, in 1989 the George H. W. Bush administration proposed new legislation (the Financial Institutions Reform, Recovery, and Enforcement Act [FIRREA]) eliminating the FHLB Board and the FSLIC. The act created a new fund, the Savings Association Insurance Fund; and a new agency, the RESOLUTION TRUST CORPORATION, to manage and liquidate insolvent thrifts.

Bailout of S&Ls cost an estimated $150 billion, with funding coming partly from FHLBS member institutions but mostly from the sale of government debt securities. FIRREA imposed new restrictions on S&L lending practices and new supervision of the thrift industry.

In 2009 at least one of the 12 home loan banks (Seattle) ran into financial difficulty, falling short of capital requirements due to a continued drop in the value of mortgage-backed securities held by the bank. Though the home loan banks are cooperatively owned by the financial institutions they serve, the federal government was expected to step in and provide resources to the ailing bank system.

Further reading

Federal Home Loan Bank Web site. Available online. URL: www.fhlb.gov; Mishkin, Frederic. *The Economics of Money, Banking, and Financial Markets.* 8th ed. Boston: Addison Wesley, 2006.

Federal Home Loan Mortgage Corporation
(Freddie Mac)

The Federal Home Loan Mortgage Corporation (FHLMC), better known as Freddie Mac, is a government-sponsored enterprise that purchases MORTGAGES from lending institutions and packages them into securities sold to investors (SECURITIZATION). Freddie Mac and Fannie Mae (FEDERAL NATIONAL MORTGAGE ASSOCIATION), the two major competitors in the mortgage securitization market, grew out of government desire to support mortgage lending and help stimulate economic activity. Freddie Mac was established in 1970 to buy conventional (not federally insured) mortgage LOANS. In 1989 it became a private stockholder-owned CORPORATION, but with a mixture of oversight. Freddie Mac's BOARD OF DIRECTORS includes 13 members elected by stockholders and five members appointed by the president of the United States. In 2001 Freddie Mac was the 27th largest corporation in the country, with over $500 billion in ASSETS, but Freddie lost billions in the sub prime housing crisis (2007) and went into conservatorship (bankruptcy) in September 2008.

In addition to purchasing mortgages for its own portfolio, Freddie Mac creates pass-through securities (called participation certificates) and guaranteed mortgage certificates. The participation certificates are similar to GOVERNMENT NATIONAL MORTGAGE ASSOCIATION (Ginnie Mae) pass-through certificates, except that they contain conventional mortgages. The mortgage pools are assembled directly by Fannie Mae (not mortgage lenders). The mortgages are usually much larger than government-insured mortgages, and participation certificates are sold in minimum amounts of $100,000.

Freddie Mac's government mortgage certificates (GMCs) are also pass-through securities, guaranteed by the FHLMC. As such, GMCs are similar to conventional BONDS where the borrower guarantees payment of principal and interest over the life of the security.

Like Fannie Mae, Freddie Mac is subject to market and government scrutiny. In 1992 Congress passed the Federal Housing Enterprises Financial Safety Act to provide regulatory oversight over Freddie Mac and Fannie Mae. The act did not go into effect until 1995, and the initial report was published in 2002. Critics of Freddie and Fannie, most notably the lobbying group FM Watch, argue that GOVERNMENT-SPONSORED ENTERPRISES compete unfairly in the secondary mortgage market due to their implied government sponsorship. This allows Freddie Mac and Fannie Mae to borrow at lower rates in the market. Critics also contend the FHLMC has undermined the private lending industry through creation of Loan Prospector, an automated underwriting system created by Freddie Mac.

Further reading

Freddie Mac Web site. Available online. URL: www. freddiemac.com; Kidwell, David S., David W. Blackwell, David A. Whidbee, and Richard L. Peterson. *Financial Institutions, Markets, and Money.* 10th ed. Hoboken, N.J.: John Wiley and Sons, 2008.

Federal Housing Administration

The Federal Housing Administration (FHA) provides mortgage insurance on loans made by FHA-approved lenders throughout the United States and its territories. FHA insures MORTGAGES on single family and multifamily homes, including manufactured homes and hospitals. Congress created the Federal Housing Administration (FHA) in 1934. FHA became a part of the Department of Housing and Urban Development's (HUD) Office of Housing in 1965. It is the largest insurer of mortgages in the world, insuring over 34 million properties since its inception during the depths of the GREAT DEPRESSION.

When the FHA was created, the housing industry was experiencing tremendous declines:

- Two million construction workers had lost their jobs.
- Terms were difficult to meet for homebuyers seeking mortgages.
- Mortgage loan terms were limited to 50 percent of the property's market value, with a repayment schedule spread over three to five years and ending with a balloon payment.
- America was primarily a nation of renters. Only four in 10 households owned homes.

As stated on its Web site, "FHA provides a huge economic stimulation to the country in the form of home and community development, which trickles down to local communities in the form of jobs, building suppliers, tax bases, schools, and other forms of revenue." During the 1940s, the FHA along with Veterans Administration (VA) programs helped finance military housing and homes for returning veterans and their families after World War II. In the 1950s, 1960s, and 1970s, FHA guarantees helped to expand production of privately owned apartments for the elderly, handicapped, and lower income Americans. By 2007, the nation's homeownership rate had soared to an all-time high of over 70 percent, largely due to FHA, FEDERAL NATIONAL MORTGAGE ASSOCIATION (Fannie Mae), and FEDERAL HOME LOAN MORTGAGE CORPORATION (Freddie Mac) programs.

FHA mortgage insurance provides lenders with protection against losses as the result of homeowners defaulting (known as credit risk) on their mortgage loans. Because loans must meet certain requirements established by the FHA to qualify for insurance, FHA guidelines heavily influence private-sector lending decisions. Banks and mortgage lenders structure loans to "conform" to FHA guidelines. Unlike conventional loans that adhere to strict underwriting guidelines, FHA-insured loans require less cash investment to close a loan. There is more flexibility in calculating household income and payment ratios. The cost of the mortgage insurance is passed along to the homeowner and typically is included in the monthly payment. In most cases, the insurance cost to the homeowner will drop off after five years or when the remaining balance on the loan is 78 percent of the value of the property, whichever is longer. FHA mortgage insurance does not vary based on the credit history of the borrower, in effect subsidizing low credit-quality borrowers by higher credit-quality borrowers.

Historically, the FHA operated entirely from its self-generated income. The proceeds from the mortgage insurance paid by the homeowners are captured in an account that is used to operate the program. During the recession of 2008–09, FHA's two competitors, Fannie Mae and Freddie Mac, which were stockholder owned but implicitly federal government-sponsored programs, quickly failed, becoming "wards of the state." The FHA along with a U.S. Department of Agriculture program became the leading lenders to low-income and first-time home buyers. In November 2009, the FHA reported, "The volume of FHA insurance guarantees has increased since 2008, as private sources of mortgage finance have retreated from the market. Nearly 80 percent of FHA's purchase-loan borrowers in 2009 were first-time homebuyers. In the second quarter of 2009, nearly 50 percent of all first-time buyers in the entire housing market used FHA-insured loans." A 2008 General Accounting Office (GAO) report projected a multimillion-dollar shortfall in the department's budget as a result of surging foreclosures.

Further reading
Federal Housing Administration Web site. Available online. URL: portal.hud.gov/portal/page/portal/HUD. Accessed on December 8, 2009; General Accounting

Office, "A Single Regulator Will Better Ensure Safety and Soundness and Mission Achievement," 6 March 2008. Available online. URL: www.gao.gov/new.items/d08563t.pdf. Accessed on December 8, 2009; Department of Housing and Urban Development. "HUD Secretary, FHA Commissioner Report on FHA's Finances, FHA." Available online. URL: portal.hud.gov/portal/page/portal/HUD/press/press_releases_media_advisories/2009/HUDNo.09-214. Accessed on December 8, 2009.

Federal Mediation and Conciliation Service

The Federal Mediation and Conciliation Service (FMCS) is a federal agency created by the TAFT-HARTLEY ACT (1947) to assist labor and MANAGEMENT relationships. The FMCS offers six categories of services, as follows.

- mediation of disputes and CONTRACT negotiations for private, public, and federal sectors
- preventive mediation, providing services and training in cooperative labor and management relationships
- alternative dispute resolution, providing services and training in a variety of problem-solving approaches that can be used in lieu of litigation, agency adjudication, or traditional rule-making by federal, state, and local governments
- ARBITRATION services, maintaining a computerized roster of qualified arbitrators
- labor-management grants, administering a grants program to fund cooperative, innovative joint labor-management committees
- international services, providing international dispute resolution and international labor education

The goal of the FMCS is to minimize labor-management conflict and, in the process, support ECONOMIC GROWTH. The FMCS is a very small agency, with less than 300 workers and a budget of less than $40 million annually. Its director is appointed by the U.S. president with the advice and consent of the Senate.

Further reading
Federal Mediation and Conciliation Service Web site. Available online. URL: www.fmcs.gov.

Federal National Mortgage Association
(Fannie Mae)

The Federal National Mortgage Association, better known as Fannie Mae, is the nation's largest secondary MORTGAGE financial institution. Fannie Mae was initially chartered during the GREAT DEPRESSION as a government-owned enterprise to buy federally insured mortgage LOANS. In 1968 Fannie Mae became a private, shareholder-owned company trading under the symbol FNM. In 2002, Fannie Mae was the United States's third-largest company in terms of ASSETS ($859 billion).

Fannie Mae's principal activity is SECURITIZATION of mortgage loans. Securitization is the purchase of loans from lenders in the United States and then issuing securities, backed by the loan agreements, to investors. Fannie Mae buys mortgage loans from SAVINGS AND LOAN ASSOCIATIONS, commercial banks, mortgage bankers, CREDIT UNIONS, and state and local housing-finance agencies. Fannie Mae then sells mortgage-backed securities to investors and mortgage lenders. Mortgage-backed securities, which provide low-risk, diversified portfolio returns to investors, are liquid investments that can be bought and sold through securities dealers. Mortgage lenders sell loans to Fannie Mae but receive a fee for handling mortgage payments and use the proceeds from the sale of the loan (the principal) to make new loans.

The 1934 National Housing Act established the Federal Housing Administration (FHA), to be headed by a federal housing administrator. As one of the principal functions of the FHA, Title II of the act provided for the INSURANCE of home mortgage loans made by private lenders. Title III of the act provided for the chartering of national mortgage associations by the administrator. These associations were to be private corporations regulated by the administrator, and their chief purpose was to buy and sell the mortgages to be insured by FHA under Title II. Only one association was ever formed under this authority: the National Mortgage Association of Washington, formed on February 10, 1938, as a subsidiary of the Reconstruction Finance Corporation, a government CORPORA-

TION. Later that same year its name was changed to the Federal National Mortgage Association.

By amendments made in 1948, the charter authority of Fannie Mae's administrator was repealed, and Title III became a statutory charter for the Federal National Mortgage Association. By revision of Title III in 1954, Fannie Mae was converted into a mixed-ownership corporation, its preferred stock to be held by the government and its COMMON STOCK to be privately held. It was at this time that Section 312 was first enacted, giving Title III the short title of Federal National Mortgage Association Charter Act.

By amendments made in 1968, the Federal National Mortgage Association was partitioned into two separate entities: GOVERNMENT NATIONAL MORTGAGE ASSOCIATION (Ginnie Mae) and Federal National Mortgage Association. Ginnie Mae remained in the government, and Fannie Mae became privately owned by retiring the government-held stock.

Fannie Mae and its competitor, Freddie Mac (FEDERAL HOME LOAN MORTGAGE CORPORATION) are often at the center of financial-industry controversy. Because they were created as GOVERNMENT-SPONSORED ENTERPRISES and continue to have the implied backing of the federal government, Fannie Mae and Freddie Mac are able to raise funds in CAPITAL MARKETS at lower costs than competitors. They also maintain significant lobbying and campaign finance operations in Washington, D.C., designed to protect other benefits. (Fannie Mae and Freddie Mac donate millions of dollars annually to the major political parties.) Though Fannie Mae is not connected to the federal government, it is exempt from PROPERTY TAXES and from SECURITIES AND EXCHANGE COMMISSION (SEC) securities registration fees. (Fannie Mae and Freddie Mac are the second- and third-largest issuers of securities behind the U.S. Treasury.) Fannie Mae is also exempt from SEC quarterly and annual disclosure requirements.

When it was created in the 1930s, Fannie Mae was needed to restore confidence to failing financial markets. Since it became a private corporation in 1968, other FINANCIAL INTERMEDIARIES have questioned the fairness of retaining special benefits for one private enterprise. Competitors have pressured Congress to restrict Fannie Mae's advantages, including efforts to eliminate its emergency line of credit with the U.S. Treasury, ending its property-tax exemption, and requiring SEC disclosure.

General Electric Capital, Wells Fargo, Household Finance, JP Morgan, Chase, and other financial institutions funded FM Watch, an industry-lobbying group to challenge Fannie Mae and Freddie Mac. Fannie Mae refers to FM Watch as a "group of mortgage insurers, high-cost lenders and their allies who want to roll back Fannie Mae policies that cut costs to consumers." Though it is a for-PROFIT business, Fannie Mae claims it "is in business to lower consumer costs and expand home ownership." In 1992 Congress created the Office of Federal Housing Enterprise Oversight (OFHEO) to ensure the CAPITAL adequacy and financial safety of Fannie Mae and Freddie Mac.

Another controversy surrounding Fannie Mae was its use of derivatives and purchase of lower-quality debt. Derivatives are CONTRACTS based on the changes in value of some underlying financial asset. Stock-options values are derived from the value of the stock they are tied to. Financial derivatives are complex, highly leveraged investments. In 1999 the Federal Reserve led the bailout of Long Term Capital Management, which became insolvent when its derivatives on the spread between short- and long-term INTEREST RATES proved wrong. Because Fannie Mae is exempt from some SEC disclosure requirements but also has a line of credit with the U.S. Treasury, congressional critics have asked whether Fannie Mae was creating RISK exposure for the federal government.

In 2008, the government took over a bankrupt FNMA, and agreed to inject up to $200 billion to restabilize the company.

Further reading

Federal National Mortgage Association Web site. Available online. URL: www.fanniemae.com; O'Leary, Christopher. "Bush Budget Raps Fannie Mae: Political Grousing Causes Stir in Mortgage, Agency Bond Markets," *Investment Dealers Digest,* 18 February 2002.

Federal Reserve System

The Federal Reserve is the central bank of the United States, issuing currency, directing MONETARY POLICY, and supervising commercial banks in the country. The Fed, as it is often called, is a uniquely American institution that was created in 1913 after a series of financial panics and bank failures. Given the long history of distrust in centralized control of political and ECONOMIC POLICY in the United States, Congress created the Federal Reserve System, an independent agency, to oversee commercial banks and coordinate monetary matters in the country.

The key word in the Federal Reserve System is *system*. Unlike most industrialized countries where control of banking and monetary policy is a cabinet-level function within the central government, the United States has a decentralized, semiautonomous system to direct these critical economic functions. The three important parts of the Fed are the Board of Governors, Federal Reserve Banks, and Federal Open Market Committee.

The Board of Governors includes seven members, nominated by the president of the United States and confirmed by the U.S. Senate. The Board members serve 14-year terms, staggered so that a new appointment is made every two years. A two-term president nominates four member of the Board of Governors, and the chairperson of Board of Governors is appointed by the president for a four-year term. In recent times the president has frequently renewed that appointment. The chairman of the Federal Reserve has considerable influence and is often referred to as "the second most important person in Washington."

There are 12 Federal Reserve District Banks in the system. Located in Boston, New York, Philadelphia, Cleveland, Richmond, Atlanta, Chicago, St. Louis, Minneapolis, Kansas City, Dallas, and San Francisco, these banks are technically separate CORPORATIONS owned by their members, commercial banks in each district. All national banks—banks given a charter to operate by the COMPTROLLER OF THE CURRENCY in the U.S. Treasury—and some state-chartered banks in each district purchase shares in their District Federal Reserve Bank. The members of each district bank elect a BOARD OF DIRECTORS who then appoint a district bank president.

Together, the Fed's Board of Governors and five of the 12 Federal Reserve District Bank presidents form the Federal Open Market Committee (FOMC). The FOMC, whose goals are to maintain price stability and support ECONOMIC GROWTH, meets on a regular basis in Washington and directs monetary policy. Its primary activity, OPEN-MARKET OPERATIONS, involves buying and selling government securities in order to increase or decrease the MONEY SUPPLY in the economy.

The Fed's monetary-policy decisions, which affect all Americans and many other people around the world, are made in secrecy by seven people, appointed by the President for long terms, and five Federal Reserve District Bank presidents. Some people argue that monetary policy is too important to be left in the hands of this group of bankers and economists largely removed from the democratic process. Others have argued that monetary policy is too important to be left in the hands of politicians. However, critics and supporters of the Federal Reserve System have generally complimented the Fed's decisions and leadership in recent years.

See also DISCOUNT RATE; MONEY.

Further reading

Boyes, William, and Michael Melvin. *Fundamentals of Economics.* 4th ed. Boston: Cengage, 2009.

Federal Trade Commission

The Federal Trade Commission (FTC), created in 1914, provides administrative enforcement of ANTITRUST LAWS. Section 5 of the Federal Trade Commission Act prohibits "unfair methods of COMPETITION." While the CLAYTON ANTITRUST ACT, enacted in the same year, created judicial remedies for some anticompetitive activities, the FTC Act created a commission to review and regulate unfair competition.

The FTC is composed of five people nominated by the U.S. president and confirmed by the Senate; no more than three members can be from the same political party. While structured as an independent agency, the FTC is subject to political influence, most often through budgetary constraints imposed by Congress. The commission's primary antitrust remedy is issuance of "cease and desist orders" against parties found to violate Section 5 of the FTC Act. The commission can also impose civil penalties and restitution requirements. In recent years its primary activity has been evaluating mergers under the premerger-notification rules of the Clayton Act. When major companies announce a merger, the announcement almost always includes the statement "subject to government approval." This approval includes review by the Antitrust Division of the U.S. Justice Department and review by the FTC.

While review of mergers is the FTC's primary activity, the commission is charged to enforce 46 laws in three categories: statutes relating to both competition and CONSUMER PROTECTION, statutes principally related to competition, and statutes principally related to consumer protection. Statutes relating to both competition and consumer protection include

- the Federal Trade Commission Act
- the Energy Policy and Conservation Act, which directs the commission along with the Justice Department to develop, implement, and monitor plans established by oil companies to deal with emergency international oil shortages. The act also addresses "energy efficiency ratings" on appliances, and, with the DEPARTMENT OF TRANSPORTATION, assesses penalties against automobile manufacturers for violating fuel-economy standards
- portions of the Lanham Trade-Mark Act (1946), authorizing the FTC under specified conditions to apply to the PATENT and TRADEMARK Office for the cancellation of registered trademarks
- the Packers and Stockyards Act, extending FTC jurisdiction to some activities of meat packers

The FTC enforces 10 acts related to competition.

- the Clayton Antitrust Act, preventing and eliminating unlawful TYING CONTRACTS, corporate

mergers and acquisitions, and INTERLOCKING DIRECTORATES

- the Hart-Scott-Rodino Antitrust Improvements Act of 1976, establishing waiting periods for certain acquisitions and requiring premerger notification to the FTC and the Antitrust Division of the Justice Department
- the Webb-Pomerene Act, providing for supervision of export-trade associations allowed under the act and allowing collaborative trade activities among companies that compete in the U.S. market
- the Deepwater Port Act of 1974 along with the Attorney General, mandates the FTC to assess the expected competitive effects of proposed licenses for deepwater ports
- the Defense Production Act of 1950, by which the FTC participates in establishing and monitoring voluntary agreements by oil companies to deal with domestic oil shortages, along with the Department of Justice
- the Conservation Service Reform Act of 1986, allowing the FTC to adjudicate complaints concerning the supply and installation of energy conservation measures by public utilities
- the Deep Seabed Hard Minerals Act (1980), providing the FTC with the opportunity to review and make recommendations regarding the antitrust implications of proposed licenses for extraction of minerals from deep seabed sites
- the National Cooperative Research and Production Act of 1993, providing regulatory protection for joint research and development ventures
- the International Antitrust Enforcement Assistance Act of 1994, authorizing the FTC and the Justice Department to enter mutual assistance agreements with foreign antitrust authorities
- the Interstate Commerce Commission Termination Act of 1995 along with other agencies the FTC files reports regarding possible anticompetitive features of rate agreements among common carriers.

The Federal Trade Commission administers 31 statutes related to consumer protection.

- The Wool Products Labeling Act (1939) concerns the manufacture, introduction, sale, transportation, distribution, or importation of misbranded wool. The statute requires that wool-product labels indicate the country in which the product was processed or manufactured and that mail-order promotional materials clearly and conspicuously state whether a wool product was processed or manufactured in the United States or was imported.

- The Fur Products Labeling Act (1998) requires that articles of apparel made of fur be labeled and that invoices and ADVERTISING for furs and fur products specify, among other things, the true English name of the animal from which the fur was taken and whether the fur is dyed or used.

- The Textile Fiber Products Identification Act (1960) requires disclosure in the labeling, invoicing, and advertising of textile fiber products.

- The Federal Cigarette Labeling and Advertising Act of 1966 requires the FTC to submit ANNUAL REPORTS to Congress concerning (a) the effectiveness of cigarette labeling, (b) current practices and methods of cigarette advertising and promotion, and (c) recommendations for legislation. The act also establishes the text of four health-related warning labels and requires that cigarette packages and advertisements carry these warnings on a rotating basis.

- The Fair Packaging and Labeling Act (1966) directs the FTC to issue regulations requiring that all consumer commodities other than food, drugs, therapeutic devices, and cosmetics be labeled to disclose net contents, the commodity's identity, and the name and place of business of the product's manufacturer, packer, or distributor. The act authorizes additional regulations where necessary to prevent consumer deception (or to facilitate value comparisons) with respect to descriptions of ingredients, slack fill of packages, use of "cents-off" or lower-price labeling, or characterization of package sizes.

- The TRUTH IN LENDING ACT (1968) gives the FTC responsibility for assuring compliance by nondepository entities with a variety of statutory provisions, including certain written disclosures concerning all finance charges and related aspects of credit transactions (i.e., disclosing finance charges expressed as an annual percentage rate). The act also establishes a three-day right of rescission in certain transactions involving the establishment of a security interest in the consumer's residence and establishes certain requirements for advertisers of credit terms.

- The Fair Credit Billing Act (1975), amending the Truth in Lending Act (1968), requires prompt written acknowledgment of consumer billing complaints and investigation of billing errors by creditors. The amendment prohibits creditors from taking actions that adversely affect the consumer's credit standing until an investigation is completed, and it affords other protection during disputes. The amendment also requires that creditors promptly post payments to the consumer's account and either refund overpayments or credit them to the consumer's account.

- The Fair Credit Reporting Act (1971) protects information collected by consumer reporting agencies such as credit bureaus, medical information companies, and tenant-screening services.

- The Fair Credit and Charge Card Disclosure Act (1988), amending the Truth in Lending Act (1968), requires credit- and charge-card issuers to provide certain disclosures in DIRECT MAIL, telephone, and other solicitations to open-end credit and charge accounts and under other lending circumstances.

- The Equal Credit Opportunity Act (1976) prohibits discrimination on the basis of race, color, religion, national origin, sex, marital status, age, receipt of public assistance, or good-faith exercise of any rights under the CONSUMER CREDIT PROTECTION ACT.

- The FAIR DEBT COLLECTION PRACTICES ACT (1977) prohibits third-party debt collectors from employing deceptive or abusive conduct in the collection of consumer debts incurred for personal, family, or household purposes.

- The ELECTRONIC FUNDS TRANSFER ACT (1978) establishes the rights, liabilities, and responsibilities of participants in electronic fund-transfer systems.

- The Consumer Leasing Act (1976) regulates personal property leases that exceed four months in duration and that are made to consumers for personal, family, or household purposes.
- Magnuson Moss Warranty-FTC Act (1975) authorizes the Federal Trade Commission to develop regulations for written and implied warranties.
- The Hobby Protection Act (1973) outlaws manufacturing or importing imitation numismatic and collectible political items unless they are marked in accordance with regulations prescribed by the Federal Trade Commission.
- The Petroleum Marketing Practices Act authorizes the FTC to prescribe requirements for the calculation and posting of gasoline octane ratings by gasoline distributors and retailers.
- The Postal Reorganization Act of 1970 authorizes the FTC to prosecute any use of the mails to send unordered merchandise as an unfair or deceptive practice in violation of the FTC Act.
- The Comprehensive Smokeless Tobacco Health Education Act of 1986 requires manufacturers, packagers, and importers of smokeless-tobacco products to place one of three statutorily prescribed health-warning labels on product packages and in advertisements. It also prohibits advertising of smokeless tobacco products on radio and television.
- The FEDERAL DEPOSIT INSURANCE CORPORATION Improvement Act of 1991 amends the Federal Deposit Insurance Act to impose certain disclosure requirements on non-federally insured depository institutions and to require that the FTC prescribe the manner and content of those disclosures.
- The Dolphin Protection Consumer Information Act (1990) makes it unlawful under section 5 of the Federal Trade Commission Act for any producer, importer, exporter, distributor, or seller of any tuna product that is exported from or offered for sale in the United States to deceptively claim that its tuna is "dolphin safe."
- The Energy Policy Act of 1992 requires the FTC to issue disclosure rules regarding the energy efficiency of lightbulbs, plumbing fixtures, and other energy-related products.
- The Telephone Disclosure and Dispute Resolution Act of 1992 regulates advertising, operation, and billing for "900 number" services.
- The Telemarketing and Consumer Fraud and Abuse Prevention Act (2001) regulates deceptive TELEMARKETING practices.
- The Violent Crime Control and Enforcement Act of 1994 establishes domestic content requirements for products labeled "Made in America" or "Made in USA."
- The Telecommunications Act of 1996 expands the definition of "pay-per-call service."
- The Home Equity Loan Consumer Protection Act requires creditors to provide certain disclosures for credit plans secured by consumers' dwellings and imposes limitations on such plans.
- The Home Ownership and Equity Protection Act (1994) establishes disclosure requirements and protection from abusive practices in connection with high-cost MORTGAGES.
- The Credit Repair Organizations Act (1996) prohibits untrue or misleading representations regarding "credit repair" services.
- The Children's Online Privacy Protection Act (1998) provides protection of information from children collected online.
- The Identity Theft Assumption and Deterrence Act of 1998 directs the FTC to create a central clearinghouse for identity-theft complaints.
- The Gramm-Leach-Billey Act requires the FTC and other agencies to issue regulations ensuring that financial institutions protect the PRIVACY of consumers' personal financial information.

Further reading
Federal Trade Commission Web site. Available online. URL: www.ftc.gov; Folsom, Ralph H., and Michael Gordon. *International Business Transactions*. 5th ed. Eagan, Minn.: West Law, 2002.

fiduciary duties
Fiduciaries are people and businesses that by law owe others a high duty of care when acting on

their behalf. Corporate officers are fiduciaries for SHAREHOLDERS; trustees are fiduciaries for TRUST beneficiaries; executors are fiduciaries for estates and heirs; conservators and guardians are fiduciaries for wards. Fiduciaries can be individuals or CORPORATIONS, and sometimes cofiduciaries are both. They owe duties of loyalty, prudent INVESTMENT, disclosure, accounting, and integrity to those whom they benefit. Unless specifically authorized, for example, fiduciaries should not undertake speculative investments with other people's money.

The powers of fiduciaries are controlled by the legal documents creating the fiduciary relationship and by statutory law. Other commonly existing fiduciary relationships include attorneys and their clients, stockbrokers and their customers, and persons acting for others under powers of attorney.

Further reading

Mennell, Robert L. *Wills and Trusts in a Nutshell.* Eagan, Minn.: West Group, 1994.

financial accounting (double-entry accounting)

Financial accounting, also called double-entry accounting, is the system of collecting, processing, and periodically reporting a firm's transactions. First described in 1494 by a Franciscan monk, Fra Luca Pacioli, double-entry accounting was largely an oral tradition which, for centuries, was passed down through the generations. In the 20th century, two organizations, the FINANCIAL ACCOUNTING STANDARDS BOARD (FASB) and the AMERICAN INSTITUTE OF CERTIFIED PUBLIC ACCOUNTANTS (AICPA), were instrumental in codifying the accounting principles that had become widely accepted and generally agreed upon over time. No longer an oral tradition, this comprehensive set of published rules and methods is now referred to as GENERALLY ACCEPTED ACCOUNTING PRINCIPLES (GAAP). The establishment of GAAP has served to standardize the practice of accounting among all firms and organizations, and the federal government, most notably the INTERNAL REVENUE SERVICE (IRS) and the SECURITIES AND EXCHANGE COMMIS-

SION (SEC), requires that all published accounting information be collected, processed, and reported in accordance with GAAP.

Accounting is often called double-entry accounting because of the nature of the data (a firm's transactions) that are collected and processed in an accounting system. Since a transaction is an exchange of equal-valued RESOURCES between two parties, a double entry is required to record a transaction: one entry recording what is received in the transaction and one entry recording what is given up. The first entry is the debit (abbreviated *dr.* from the Latin *debere,* meaning "left") and the second entry, which is indented to the right, is the credit (abbreviated *cr.* from the Latin *credere* meaning "right"). Because equal-valued resources are exchanged in a transaction, the dollar amount of the debit entries must equal the dollar amount of the credit entries.

While account names have evolved over time and new accounting principles have been added to comply with governmental and tax regulations, the practice of accounting today is in many ways much the same as what was developed over 500 years ago.

See also DEBIT, CREDIT; INCOME STATEMENT, GROSS MARGIN.

Financial Accounting Standards Board

The Financial Accounting Standards Board's mission is "to establish and improve standards of FINANCIAL ACCOUNTING and reporting for the guidance and education of the public, including issuers, auditors, and users of financial information." It serves the "investing public through transparent information resulting from high-quality financial reporting standards, developed in an independent, private sector, open due process."

Since 1973 the Financial Accounting Standards Board (FASB) has been the designated organization in the private sector for establishing standards of financial accounting and reporting that govern the preparation of financial reports. The FASB is officially recognized as authoritative by the SECURITIES AND EXCHANGE COMMISSION and the AMERICAN INSTITUTE OF CERTIFIED PUBLIC ACCOUNTANTS.

In further explaining its mission, the FASB states that "accounting standards are essential to the efficient functioning of the economy because decisions about the allocation of resources rely heavily on credible, concise, and understandable financial information. Financial information about the operations and financial position of individual entities also is used by the public in making various other kinds of decisions."

Further reading
Financial Accounting Standards Board Web site. Available online. URL: www.fasb.org.

financial instrument
Financial instrument is a broadly used term to refer to almost any obligation of one party to give financial ASSETS to another. There are three types of financial instruments, the first of which is cash. The second type is any agreement that is settled only with the payment of a financial instrument (usually cash); this would make LOANS, BONDS, notes, derivatives, and receivables all financial instruments. The third type of financial instrument is EQUITY securities, which represent ownership in a company; this makes COMMON STOCK and preferred stock in a company financial instruments. Equity securities give owners residual rights (remaining assets after all liabilities have been satisfied) in the company and the right to share the company's PROFITS.

CONTRACTS between two parties that are not settled with financial instruments (including cash) are not themselves financial instruments. For example, contracts to buy a piece of real estate, equipment, or inventory or to deliver services are not financial instruments.

Many financial instruments are negotiable. There are dozens of types of negotiable financial instruments, and more are created every day as others pass off the scene. Some of the more common type of NEGOTIABLE INSTRUMENTS would be COMMERCIAL PAPER, bonds, corporate debt securities, banker acceptances, treasury bills, repurchase agreements, and some PROMISSORY NOTES.

These financial instruments are created in a primary market and traded in a secondary market. The primary market consists of INVESTMENT banks that enter into the agreements with the issuing companies and then sell a portion of the negotiable instruments to other investors who are free to trade the instruments with others; this is the secondary market. Thus an investment bank may buy all the new stock issued by a company and then sell it to investors. When these investors then sell, these are secondary-market transactions.

See also U.S. TREASURY SECURITIES.

financial intermediaries
Financial intermediaries are institutions that take funds saved by households and in turn make LOANS to others. The process of taking savings and providing funds to borrowers is called intermediation, or indirect finance. While most people think of banks as financial intermediaries, in the United States, SAVINGS AND LOAN ASSOCIATIONS, mutual INSURANCE companies, CREDIT UNIONS, pension funds, finance companies, MUTUAL FUNDS, and money market funds all function as financial intermediaries.

Generally financial intermediaries specialize in particular types of lending practices and provide services for certain segments of the overall market. For example, savings and loan associations came into existence to provide lending to consumers for the purpose of building or purchasing homes. Early savings and loan organizations (many were mutual organizations rather than for-PROFIT businesses) were established by groups of immigrant workers who brought together their savings, which were then loaned to other members of their group. Until the 1980s savings and loan crisis (see RESOLUTION TRUST CORPORATION), one group of German Americans in Cincinnati, Ohio, ran their savings and loan out of a bar where they and their ancestors had socialized for almost 100 years.

Financial intermediaries perform the following basic services.

- denomination divisibility: providing lending and savings options for different dollar amounts
- maturity flexibility: providing lending and savings options for different time periods

- credit RISK diversification: reducing risk through lending to multiple borrowers
- liquidity: providing access to funds when needed by depositors

Financial intermediaries pool the funds of many small savers and make loans in varying amounts to borrowers. This is preferable to the alternative, where a borrower would have to find and negotiate with tens or hundreds of savers in order to get sufficient funds. Financial intermediaries create securities with a wide range of maturities, from overnight to 50 years and also reduce RISK through diversification. Lending money to one person results in concentrated risk—that is, it depends on the repayment of one borrower. Financial intermediaries make loans to many borrowers, spreading the risk of DEFAULT among many loans and thereby reducing risk through diversification. Intermediaries also provide liquidity, facilitating the conversion of financial ASSETS into money.

In the 1990s many Americans and American businesses decreased their use of financial intermediaries. With greater information obtained through INTERNET technology, more lenders and borrowers interacted directly with each other, with individuals buying shares of stock, businesses purchasing COMMERCIAL PAPER issued by CORPORATIONS, or direct placement of tax-exempt BONDS by state agencies. Nevertheless, financial intermediaries provide three basic benefits over direct borrowing and INVESTMENT: ECONOMIES OF SCALE, reduced transaction costs, and information.

Because they handle a large volume of transactions, financial intermediaries can spread the fixed costs and start-up COSTS associated with lending. With their experience in lending, financial intermediaries lower the cost of searching and evaluating information associated with saving and lending actions. Most importantly, financial intermediaries generally have better knowledge of credit criteria and risk associated with particular financial instruments and borrowers.

See also FIVE Cs OF CREDIT.

Further reading
Kidwell, David S., David W. Blackwell, David A. Whidbee, and Richard L. Peterson. *Financial Institutions, Markets, and Money*. 10th ed. Hoboken, N.J.: John Wiley & Sons, 2008.

financial markets

The primary function of financial markets is to facilitate the transfer of funds from savers to borrowers. Theoretically, financial markets are part of the CIRCULAR FLOW MODEL with households supplying excess INCOME (beyond CONSUMPTION spending) to FINANCIAL INTERMEDIARIES, which aggregate funds from multiple sources, evaluate alternatives, make and manage loans or investments, and pay back interest, dividends, and/or profits to the lending household. Realistically, financial markets constitute a wide variety of physical and electronic markets operating on local, national, and international levels.

The most widely quoted financial market in the United States is the stock market, historically the NEW YORK STOCK EXCHANGE (NYSE, now part of Euronext). The NYSE began as an open-air market on WALL STREET in New York City, where investors, brokers, and entrepreneurs bought and sold securities. The first securities traded in 1790 were bonds issued by the new U.S. government to finance the American Revolution war debt. Two years later, 24 brokers and merchants under what is referred to as the Buttonwood Agreement committed to selling securities on a commission basis. Eventually, they moved indoors, created their own exchange rules and membership requirements and, over time, became the dominant financial market for issuing new equity securities trading existing equity securities (secondary market operations). EQUITY securities, commonly called shares of stock, represent an ownership interest in the business. From the 1860s until 2005, most purchases and sales of stock on the NYSE were handled by specialists, brokers who "made a market" in one or a few stocks on the floor of the exchange. Prices rose or fell based on the supply versus demand for a company's shares. Specialists made a profit based on the spread between offer and bid prices.

Today in the United States, the NATIONAL ASSOCIATION OF SECURITIES DEALERS AUTOMATED QUOTE SYSTEM (NASDAQ) is equally as important as a secondary equity financial market. Created in 1971 by the National Association of Securities Dealers (NASD), NASDAQ is a system of linked computer terminals that match buy and sell orders. (The NYSE now uses a similar linked computer system.)

While the NYSE and the NASDAQ handle the vast majority of equity market exchanges, investment banks, in 2009, dominated by Goldman Sachs and JP Morgan, create markets for debt, initial public offerings of stock, collateralized financial securities, and other types of financial instruments. Unlike the stock exchange and NASDAQ system, no formal market for most of these financial products exists. In 2005, after years of complaints about the lack of transparency, the Securities Industry and Financial Markets Association (SIFMA) was created to provide information and education for investors, including recent prices for debt securities.

Investment banks also "make markets" for a wide variety of thinly traded securities, including the shares of small companies, public-sector debt, including municipal bonds or "muni's," and other types of debt issued by public or public-sponsored entities. Municipal bonds can be either general obligation bonds (GO bonds), backed by the taxing authority of the city or state issuing them, or revenue bonds, backed by the projected revenue stream from the project being financed.

In addition to state and local governments, the federal government is a major force in U.S. financial markets through both regulatory activities and government financing. After the collapse of the stock market during the GREAT DEPRESSION, the SECURITIES AND EXCHANGE COMMISSION (1934) was created to oversee financial markets. The FEDERAL RESERVE buys and sells Treasury securities as part of its role as managers of MONETARY POLICY and, over time, has been given expanded power to oversee banking and other financial institutions. The federal government is a major borrower in financial markets, financing the national debt

through sale of Treasury securities through the major financial institutions.

While New York is the headquarters of most major financial institutions in the United States, London dominates European financial markets, and Hong Kong dominates Asian markets. Foreign investors and governments are a major source of savings loaned through the financial markets in the United States. The financial market "meltdown" in 2008–09 illustrated the interconnectedness of today's global financial system.

Further reading
New York Stock Exchange Web site. Available online. URL: www.nyse.com; Securities Industry and Financial Markets Association (SIFMA) Web site. Available online. URL: www.investinginbonds.com.

Financial Planning Association

The Financial Planning Association (FPA) is an organization that trains and certifies financial planners. Financial planning is the process of establishing personal financial goals and allocating resources to obtain those goals. The FPA was created in 2000 through a merger of the Institute of Certified Financial Planners and the International Association for Financial Planning.

The FPA and its earlier organizations grew rapidly in the 1980s and 1990s due to changes in business pensions and changes in STOCK MARKET trading. Until the 1980s, most corporations in the United States provided defined-benefit pensions for their employees (see RETIREMENT PLAN). The employer put aside funds in a TRUST account to meet future obligations to retirees based on a percentage of what salary employees were receiving when they retired. Depending on how much the trust fund earned, a company could have either an over-funded pension plan or unfunded pension liabilities.

With the advent of 401(K) PLANS, employers shifted the RISK associated with pension LIABILITY to employees. The 401(k)s, along with similar 403b and 457 plans, allow employees to contribute a portion of their salary into a tax-deferred retirement fund. The money can be invested by the employee in MUTUAL FUNDS, individual stocks, and other INVESTMENT options. The employee's pension benefits are determined by how well their investments do and are not the responsibility of the employer.

The new retirement plans led to tremendous growth in the DEMAND for and SUPPLY of financial planners. Virtually every personal finance-related salesperson, from INSURANCE representative to stockbroker, began to call himself a financial planner. Since a planner's INCOME depended on how many policies or stock trades he or she made, it often led to a CONFLICT OF INTEREST when the best objective advice did not generate sales commissions.

The Financial Planning Association's major role is to certify financial planners. Members must pass the FPA examination and acquire three to five years of financial planning–related experience to become a Certified Financial Planner (CFP). In addition, members ascribe to the FPA code of ethics and obtain a minimum of 30 hours of continuing education every two years.

The second factor contributing to the rapid expansion in the financial-planning industry was the advent of discount stock-brokerage firms. Pioneered by Charles Schwab Company, discount-brokerage firms allow individuals to trade stocks without paying huge commissions to full-service brokerages. Today individuals can buy or sell stock for $10 per trade or less, but in the 1980s trades often cost $100 to $200 each and had to be conducted through a full-service broker. Brokers acted as financial planners for people with investment funds, recommending strategies and appraising risks for investors. Discount brokers offer fewer financial planning services creating a need for, and opportunity for professional financial planners.

The Financial Planning Association states the following as their "core values."

- competence
- integrity
- relationships
- stewardship

The objectives of the FPA are

- Unify the voice, focus and resources of the financial planning community.
- Grow the organization by bringing together those who champion the financial planning process.
- Cultivate the body of knowledge of financial planning.
- Advance brand awareness for professional financial planners, building the CFP credential as the hallmark brand.
- Define and effectively communicate a common understanding of the discipline of personal financial planning and the benefits of its use.
- Facilitate the success of our members.

Further reading

Financial Planning Association Web site. Available online. URL: www.fpanet.org.

financial ratios

FINANCIAL STATEMENTS are analyzed by MANAGEMENT and investors to predict and plan for the future. Financial ratios, fractions that show relationships between accounts found on the financial statements, are the tools used in financial-statement analysis. Some ratios are useful in the analysis of a single firm, while other ratios have meaning only when compared to those of other firms or to industry averages. A few of the more common financial ratios follow.

A firm's creditworthiness—that is, its ability to service its debt on a timely basis—can be determined by the current ratio and the acid-test ratio. A rough measure of a firm's ability to pay its debt on time is the current ratio: current ASSETS divided by current liabilities (CA/CL). The numerator is the firm's current assets and the denominator is the firm's current liabilities (current debt). The current assets are the firm's resources it will use to pay its current debts. If the current assets exceed the current liabilities, the current ratio will have a value greater than 1, an indicator that there are sufficient current assets to pay the current liabilities. Thus current ratios greater than 1 indicate that a firm can take on more debt. If the current assets are equal to the current liabilities, the current ratio will have a value of 1. All of the firm's current assets are used to cover (pay) the current liabilities, and the firm has no excess assets with which to assume additional debt. If the current assets are less than the current liabilities, the current ratio will have a value less than 1, and the firm is having problems paying its current debt. In fact, a current ratio less than 1 is indicative of a firm that is slow in paying its bills.

Working CAPITAL is the current assets of a firm: cash, short-term investments, ACCOUNTS RECEIVABLE, and inventories. Net working capital (CA–CL) is a measure of a firm's liquidity, the amount of current assets remaining after the current debt of the firm is paid. The current ratio (CA/CL) can be used to compare net working capital among firms.

Included in a firm's current assets are merchandise inventories, but in reality inventories aren't very liquid. If a buyer is found, the sale may be a sale on credit, in which case no monies are currently received. Many creditors understand the lack of liquidity associated with inventories, and as a result they prefer using the acid-test (quick) ratio, in which inventories are not included with the current assets of the firm: (CA–inventories)/CL. Because inventories are subtracted from the current assets, the acid-test numerator is smaller than the one used in the current ratio. This causes the acid-test ratio to be a stricter measure of the debt worthiness of a firm; the acid-test ratio is more commonly than the current ratio for this purpose.

The debt ratio (total liabilities/total assets) is an indicator of a firm's capital structure. For example, a debt ratio of 60 percent indicates that debt (liabilities) comprises 60 percent of a firm's capital and EQUITY (stocks) comprises 40 percent.

The days' sales outstanding (DSO) ratio (accounts receivable/average sales per day) analyzes a firm's accounts receivable by determining its average collection period, the average number of days a firm waits after making a credit sale before receiving cash. The number of days' sales tied up in accounts receivable is compared with that of other firms or with industry averages to determine how well a firm manages its investment in accounts receivable.

The asset-turnover ratio (sales/total assets) measures a firm's sales volume relative to its INVESTMENT in total assets. For example, a firm with an asset-turnover ratio of 1.4 times operating in an industry with an industry average of 1.7 times is not generating sufficient sales volume, given its investment in total assets.

The price/earnings (P/E) ratio (price per share/earnings per share) indicates how much investors are willing to pay per dollar of current earnings. When compared to industry averages, a low P/E ratio generally indicates that investors view the firm as being riskier than other firms in its industry. A high P/E ratio relative to the industry average generally indicates that investors view this firm as having a greater potential for growth and, therefore, less riskier.

PROFIT margin is the relationship between a firm's net INCOME and its sales volume, indicated by the profit-margin ratio (net income/sales). This ratio measures a firm's income per dollar of sales. A firm's relative profitability can be determined by comparing its profit margin ratio with that for the industry.

Return on equity (ROE), the ratio of net income to common equity, measures the rate of return earned by the common stockholders' investment in a firm. The ROE ratio is net income/total common equity. In order for a firm to attract the interest of investors and thus retain their investment in the firm, its ROE must be greater than or equal to its industry average. A firm with a low ROE as compared to its industry average will be viewed by investors as an unattractive investment, and investors will be attracted to those firms with greater earnings potential.

Financial Stability Institute   See BANK OF INTERNATIONAL SETTLEMENTS.

financial statements

FINANCIAL ACCOUNTING is the system of collecting, processing, and periodically reporting a firm's financial information; thus, its ultimate purpose is the dissemination of a firm's financial data. This is accomplished by the publication of financial statements, all of which must be constructed in accordance with GENERALLY ACCEPTED ACCOUNTING PRINCIPLES (GAAP). The more common financial statements are the INCOME STATEMENT, the statement of OWNER'S EQUITY, the BALANCE SHEET, and the statement of cash flows.

The income statement measures the performance and success (or lack thereof) of a firm for a specific period of time, usually a year. When the accounting period coincides with the calendar year (January 1–December 31), the firm is said to be reporting on a calendar-year basis. If the accounting period is any other 12-month period (say, July 1–June 30), the firm is reporting on a FISCAL YEAR basis. The equation upon which the income statement is based is *revenues - expenses = net income*. Revenues are resources flowing into the firm from the sale of goods and/or services. Expenses, necessarily incurred in the process of earning revenue, are resources flowing out of the firm. The difference between revenues and expenses is "the bottom line"—i.e., net INCOME. Whether the firm has made a PROFIT or a loss for the period being reported, the bottom line is always labeled "net income."

The statement of owner's (or owners') equity illustrates the changes that occurred in owner's equity during the accounting period being reported. Positive net income and additional investment by the owner are the primary factors that increase owner's equity. Negative net income and withdrawals will decrease owner's equity.

The balance sheet measures the assets, liabilities, and owner's equity of the firm at a point in time that is the last day of the accounting period. The equation on which the balance sheet is based is *assets = liabilities + owner's equity*. Assets are resources owned by the firm; they are necessary for the generation of revenue. Liabilities are the firm's debts; they are one major source of CAPITAL for the firm. Equity is the firm's ownership and forms the other major source of capital for the firm. The right side of the balance-sheet equation represents the sources of capital; the left side, the uses of that capital. Thus, the equation must always be in balance. The format for the balance sheet is identical to the balance sheet equation: assets on the left side of the balance sheet, liabilities and equity on the right side. Just as the equation is always in balance, the two sides of the balance sheet are also always in balance.

Important for effective liquidity management, the statement of cash flows details the cash flowing into and out of the firm for the accounting period being reported. This is not the same as an income statement. The income statement, constructed on the ACCRUAL BASIS as required by GAAP, includes more than just cash flows; it also contains accruals (such as revenues earned but not yet received and expenses incurred but not yet paid). The income statement also contains many non-cash expenses such as DEPRECIATION, DEPLETION, AMORTIZATION. The statement of cash flows makes adjustments for accruals and noncash expenses to give a true picture of a firm's actual flows of cash.

The SECURITIES AND EXCHANGE COMMISSION requires CORPORATIONS whose stocks are publicly traded to publish their financial statements at least annually. To meet this requirement, a corporation will group these financial statements and others with reports from management and the BOARD OF DIRECTORS to form the ANNUAL REPORT.

first in, first out; last in, first out

First in, first out (FIFO) and last in, first out (LIFO) are inventory-costing methods. Inventory costing methods are used to assign values to a firm's ending inventory and to COST OF GOODS SOLD. For tax purposes, a firm will use the inventory-costing method that maximizes its cost of goods sold and minimizes the value of its ending inventory. When unit costs are rising, as is normally experienced with INFLATION, LIFO is the inventory costing method of choice.

To illustrate the effects of FIFO and LIFO, assume the following inventory data where unit costs are rising:

Jan. 1	Beginning inventory	
	100 units @ $10 each	$1000
Jan. 12	Inventory purchase	
	100 units @ $12 each	$1200
Jan. 23	Sale 150 units	

For the month of January, what is the firm's cost of goods sold? What is the value of the ending inventory at the end of the month? To answer these questions, the firm must first select an inventory-costing method.

Using FIFO, cost of goods sold and the value of ending inventory are determined as follows:

Beginning inventory	
100 units @ $10 each	$1000
+ Purchases	
100 units @ $12 each	1200
Goods available for sale	
200 units	$2200
Units sold	
100 units @ $10	$1000
50 units @ $12	600
Cost of Goods Sold	
150 units	**$1600**
Ending inventory	
50 units @ $12 each	$600

Using LIFO, cost of goods sold and the value of ending inventory are determined as follows:

Beginning inventory	
100 units @ $10 each	$1000
+ Purchases	
100 units @ $12 each	1200
Goods available for sale	
200 units	$2200
Units sold	
100 units @ 12	$1200
50 units @ $10	500
Cost of Goods Sold	
150 units	**$1700**
Ending inventory	
50 units @ $10 each	$500

Using FIFO, cost of goods sold is $1,600; using LIFO, $1,700. In order to maximize cost of goods sold and, in turn, reduce gross margin and taxable INCOME, a PROFIT-maximizing firm uses LIFO when unit costs are rising.

When unit costs are falling over time, FIFO is the inventory-costing method that maximizes the cost of goods sold.

first-mover advantage (first-to-market)

First-mover advantage, also called first-to-market, is the benefit a company gains by being first to market with a new PRODUCT or service. First-mover advantage is part of MARKETING STRATEGY—the coordination of product, pricing, promotion, and distribution decisions for each target market.

In the late 1990s many of the frenetic marketing efforts of DOT-COMS were based on the idea of first-mover advantage. The first company offering a new INTERNET product or service gained significant publicity, attracted additional financial support, and created a BARRIER TO ENTRY for other potential competitors. As Latin American Internet expert Lucas Graves states, "It's absolutely true that nothing can make up for first-mover-advantage, and the proof is that Yahoo! remains where it is today and eBay remains where it is, despite the entry of many other companies into those vertical categories."

First-mover advantage is based on attracting consumer innovators—customers who purchase a product as soon as it reaches the market. Often people are consumer innovators in specific categories of products. Serious photographers try out the latest equipment, committed golfers are always looking for something new, and fashion-conscious consumers keep abreast of the latest styles. With today's Internet communications technology, consumer innovators quickly evaluate and recommend or reject products. Marketers recognize that word-of-mouth referrals from consumer innovators can ensure the success of their new product.

First-mover advantage is offset by the potential for mistakes from rushing a product or concept to the marketplace. An old saying in marketing is,

"You only have one chance to make a first impression." Many dot-coms and other companies died quickly when the promised benefits of their new products did not meet consumer expectations.

Further reading
Hemlock, Dorren. "Mass Production Hits the Web," *Sun-Sentinel*, 3 December 1999.

fiscal policy
Fiscal policy is the use of the federal tax and spending process to influence the level of economic activity. In its simplest form, fiscal policy involves changing taxes and/or government spending in order to expand or contract aggregate DEMAND toward a targeted level of equilibrium national INCOME. Contractionary fiscal policy dictates a decrease in spending and/or an increase in taxes in order to reduce economic activity. Expansionary fiscal policy is the opposite, an increase in spending and/or a decrease in taxes in order to stimulate economic activity.

In the United States, fiscal policy became an accepted, important part of macroeconomic policy during the GREAT DEPRESSION. In the absence of private CONSUMPTION spending and business INVESTMENT, government spending was used as an alternative source of demand. As advocated by the British economist John Maynard Keynes, President Franklin Roosevelt's "New Deal" administration greatly expanded government spending through programs such as the CIVILIAN CONSERVATION CORPS and the WORKS PROGRESS ADMINISTRATION. Many of today's state parks and older government buildings were created during the Depression. Similarly, President Obama's 2009 Stimulus bill amounting to over $700 billion was designed to offset declining consumption and investment spending during the deepest recession since the 1930s.

When estimating the impact of fiscal policy, economists consider how the policy is financed and the indirect impacts of the fiscal-policy measure. For example, if an increase in government spending is financed by an increase in taxes, the increase in government spending will be largely offset by a decrease in consumption spending. An increase in government spending financed through borrowing will have a larger immediate impact on the economy but will also likely increase INTEREST RATES due to the government's increased demand for funds. This, in turn, will likely increase interest rates, reducing consumption spending and private investment. Economists call this the crowding-out effect.

Many economists support the use of discretionary fiscal policy along with a consistent MONETARY POLICY to stabilize the overall economy. Other economists argue the time lag between the implementation of fiscal-policy measures and their impact causes these efforts to exacerbate rather than mitigate peaks and troughs in BUSINESS CYCLES.

In addition to discretionary fiscal policy, the U.S. political economic system also includes AUTOMATIC STABILIZERS. During periods of economic expansion, progressive tax rates—tax rates that increase as income increases—automatically reduce consumers' incomes, reducing their spending and slowing the rate of growth in aggregate demand. During periods of economic contraction, UNEMPLOYMENT and WELFARE benefits offset some of the loss of income and spending when workers lose their jobs. These are referred to by economists as automatic stabilizers.

In the U.S. political system, the use of fiscal policy during periods of economic decline to stimulate the economy is widely accepted. The logical corollary is to advocate a decrease in government spending and/or an increase in taxes during periods of an inflationary, full-employment economy. Few politicians want to run for reelection after having increased taxes or to cut voters' favorite government programs, which is why monetary policy is often needed to counterbalance excessively expansionary fiscal policy.

fiscal year
In the United States most CORPORATIONS are legally required to report the results of their business activities at least once a year. In their initial INCORPORATION documents, companies define

when their business year starts and ends; this is their fiscal year. Some retail businesses end their business year at the end of January, corresponding to the end of the holiday sales season. Companies usually also conduct inventories at the end of each fiscal year.

The U.S. government begins their fiscal year on October 1. Many U.S. agencies engage in a flurry of PURCHASING just before the end of the government's fiscal year, and frequently Congress and the executive branch will fail to pass spending legislation in time for the beginning of the next fiscal year. In those years government agencies will be allocated funds based on the previous fiscal year's budget. State governments also have varying fiscal years, with many states starting new budget years in July.

In recent years STOCK MARKET watchers have closely scrutinized the quarterly earnings reports of leading companies. The release of quarterly earnings statements are tied to corporations' fiscal years, which is why the statements do not all appear at the same time. When a leading company in any industry reports unexpectedly high or low earnings, the stocks of other companies in the same industry are usually affected by the one company's report.

five Cs of credit

The five Cs of credit are character, capacity, CAPITAL, collateral, and conditions. To analyze the risk of DEFAULT by a borrower, lenders typically evaluate a customer's five Cs. *Character* refers to a borrower's integrity, credit history, and past relationships with the lender. Credit history is an important determinant in predicting whether a borrower will default or not. In the United States, three major CREDIT-REPORTING SERVICES provide lenders with information about customers' past credit experiences. *Capacity* is the borrower's ability to pay off the loan requested. Lenders often use ratios of loan payment to monthly INCOME and total monthly payments to income in evaluating a borrower's ability to pay.

Capital is a borrower's net worth or WEALTH, some of which may be offered as collateral against a loan. *Collateral* is comprised of ASSETS that

the lender could seize and sell if the borrower defaulted on the loan. *Conditions* refer to ECONOMIC CONDITIONS. Lenders know from experience that borrowers' ability and likelihood of paying off LOANS are influenced by changes in the economy. U.S. banking institutions are regulated by state banking commissions or the FEDERAL RESERVE SYSTEM. During declining economic conditions, regulatory authorities often examine more closely how lenders apply the five Cs of credit in making loan decisions.

By the nature of their business, banks and other lending institutions consider borrowers their most important customers. Generally lenders can attract deposits or capital by offering competitive INTEREST RATES. Finding good borrowers is more difficult. Lenders make a PROFIT by the spread, the difference between the cost of funds and the rate being received for LOANS or INVESTMENTS. Because lenders are RISK-averse, borrowers whose five Cs indicate a higher potential for default are charged higher interest rates, compensating lenders for the higher percentage of defaults.

During the 1990s many U.S. lending institutions made money through credit-card lending to low-quality customers at very high interest rates. When a recession started in late 2007, lenders who ignored the 5Cs quickly found themselves facing escalating default and foreclosure rates.

Further reading

Kidwell, David S., David W. Blackwell, David A. Whidbee, and Richard L. Peterson. *Financial Institutions, Markets, and Money.* 10th ed. Hoboken, N.J.: John Wiley & Sons, 2008.

flowchart

A flowchart is a graphic illustration of the steps to follow in the process of production. Flowcharts are important in understanding a project and the different sequences to follow. They are also important for decision making, helping people better understand a project, the possible outcomes, and possible solutions to consider.

A flowchart consists of various standard-shaped boxes, circles, or other shapes that are interconnected by flow lines. The flow lines have arrows indicating the direction of flow between the boxes, and if flow continues elsewhere, connector lines show this. Flowcharts are drawn on white, unlined paper on one side only.

Some of the standard flowchart symbols include

- circles representing the on-page connector (used to connect remote parts of the flowchart to one another)
- rectangles representing processing or activities (each activity is represented by a separate rectangle)
- diamond shapes used to represent decisions or questions
- rounded-edge rectangles representing the beginning and terminal activities (start or end)

Constructing a flowchart involves a series of steps, the first of which is determining the process and the purpose of the diagram. The next step is determining who will work in constructing the flowchart and how accurate and reliable the information available is, an important consideration. Defining the relationship between each of the diagrams and how they are connected is a third step.

Flowcharts are convenient because they are easy to read and understand. Flowcharting in business is useful because it helps a business consider all its possibilities and all the outcomes of the decision they might or might not make. Flowcharts are often created by teams within an organization to coordinate new projects.

Further reading
Chaneski, Wayne S. "Process Flow Chart: A Tool for Streamlining Operation," *Modern Machine Shop* 72 (March 2000): 52.

flow of funds
The term *flow of funds* has both business and economic meanings. In business, flow of funds refers to a statement of the sources and application of funds in the organization. In this context it is often referred to as a funds-flow statement or cash-flow statement. More often flow of funds refers to data showing the movement of savings and the sources and uses of funds through the economy.

Since 1955 the FEDERAL RESERVE SYSTEM has published quarterly and annual data on flow-of-funds accounts. These data measure the financial flows across sectors of the economy, tracking funds as they move from those sectors that serve as sources of CAPITAL through FINANCIAL INTERMEDIARIES (such as banks, MUTUAL FUNDS, and pension funds) to sectors that use the capital to acquire productive and financial ASSETS.

The flow-of-funds accounts are useful in identifying economic trends. They show, for example, how the growth of debt for each sector changes in the sources of household credit as well as the development of new FINANCIAL INSTRUMENTS for providing credit. In recent years flow-of-funds data have been used to document the widely discussed "WEALTH effect"—the effect of change in households' net worth on savings and CONSUMPTION decisions. The data are also used to estimate the impact of changing credit conditions on output and spending in the economy.

The Federal Reserve's flow-of-funds accounting system tracks over 40 types of financial instruments, including savings accounts, MORTGAGES, corporate BONDS, STOCK MARKET shares, mutual fund shares, and bank LOANS. Financial transactions are recorded for 30 economic sectors, including nonfinancial sectors (households, nonprofit organizations, businesses, and government) and financial sectors (banks, INSURANCE companies, pension funds, and other financial intermediaries). In flow-of-funds accounting, total sources of funds must equal total uses of funds. Analysis of the data allows macroeconomic forecasters to estimate the impact of policy measures and project the impact of changing market conditions on output and INCOME in the economy.

Further reading
Teplin, Albert M. "The U.S. Flow of Funds Accounts and Their Uses." *Federal Reserve Bulletin,* July 2001, p. 431.

FOB   See FREE ON BOARD.

focus groups

Focus groups are small groups of individuals brought together by market researchers to discuss a particular topic. Most focus groups include 8–12 people and a moderator. Individuals are chosen based on interest or involvement with the subject to be discussed and are often paid $50–$100 to participate in the session. A typical focus group will last 1–2 hours, be taped for later detailed review, and observed by market researchers and the client through a one-way mirror.

Focus groups are often used during the exploratory stage of the MARKET RESEARCH process to provide quick, in-depth information about people's attitudes and motivations. They are often used to screen ADVERTISING designs, learn about the interests and values of hard-to-research market segments, provide feedback during NEW PRODUCT DEVELOPMENT, and help structure market-research SURVEYS. Marketers recognize they are often "too close" to a particular project or PRODUCT to be objective about it. Focus groups can be used to get consumers' opinions before a product is launched, helping to avoid costly marketing failures.

Focus groups are vulnerable to a variety of problems. First, they only include a small number of participants and therefore may not be representative of the ideas and opinions of the larger target market. Second, the moderator must be chosen carefully, since his or her role is critical in successfully probing participants' feelings and controlling group dynamics. Third, critics contend focus groups tend to result in people saying what they think the sponsor wants to hear rather than honest opinions. Finally, there are "professional" focus groupers, people who participate in numerous studies and tend to dominate group discussion.

Further reading

Boone, Louis E., and David Kurtz. *Contemporary Marketing.* 14th ed. Fort Worth, Tex.: South-Western, 2009.

Food and Drug Administration (FDA)

The U.S. Food and Drug Administration (FDA) is a federal agency charged to protect public health.

The agency, created by the 1906 Food and Drugs Act, defines its mission as

1. To promote the public health by promptly and efficiently reviewing clinical research and taking appropriate action on the marketing of regulated products in a timely manner;
2. With respect to such products, protect the public health by ensuring that foods are safe, wholesome, sanitary, and properly labeled;
3. Participate through appropriate processes with the representatives of other countries to reduce the burden of regulation, harmonize requirements, and achieve appropriate reciprocal arrangements.

The original act prohibited interstate commerce in misbranded and adulterated foods, drinks, and drugs; the Meat Inspection Act was passed the same day as the Food and Drugs Act. The historian James Harvey Young describes the evolution of pure-food regulations as a combination of seven Cs: change, complexity, COMPETITION, crusading, coalescence, compromise, and catastrophe.

Change refers to the rapid industrialization in the United States during the late 1800s, including discoveries in chemistry leading to synthetic medicines and changes in markets as consumers moved away from the village merchants they knew and trusted for pure food. *Complexity* refers to the problem of how the federal government should address the problems of deceptions and hazards in food and drugs. Some products were regulated under individual laws, but how could the government address the many products that existed and the continuing flow of new products coming into the market?

Competition refers to the reality at the time that adulterated food could be produced and sold more cheaply than healthier and safer foods. With lower prices, questionable and unsafe foods were competing with reputable food makers, and an uninformed public had little basis for judging the difference in quality. Throughout the 1890s, business groups pressured Congress for protection. Many state laws were enacted, but they were often contradictory, creating inefficiency for national producers.

The fourth C, *crusading,* evolved when animal-rights groups, the National Consumer League, and the General Federation of Women's Clubs began pushing for tougher food-and-drug safety laws and the U.S. Department of Agriculture (USDA) began to oversee food-adulteration practices. Initially food adulteration was perceived as a harmless FRAUD, but with USDA research, the threat to consumers' health was explored and articulated. Harvey Wiley, a chemist and physician who became the chief chemist for the USDA, joined forces with other agricultural groups, medical professionals, and sympathetic journalists, creating the fifth C, a *coalescence* of forces for reform. *Compromise* recognized the many different groups and interests among government, business, and consumer interests. Wiley organized three National Pure Food and Drug Congresses between 1898 and 1900 to work out agreements.

As James Harvey Young states, "In the end it took the seventh 'C,' *catastrophe,* to fuel the final compromise and get the law enacted." Investigations showing that "embalmed beef" had been shipped to troops in the Spanish-American war and the publication of Upton Sinclair's *The Jungle,* describing filthy conditions in meat-packing plants, pressured politicians into passing the Food and Drug Act.

Since the act's passage, numerous responsibilities have been assigned to the Food and Drug Administration, including medical labeling, narcotic-substance control, cosmetic and therapeutic device supervision, ADVERTISING of FDA-regulated products, hazardous-substance labeling, sanitation programs, and many others. In 1997 Congress pressured the FDA to speed up its drug-review process. Consumers and pharmaceutical industry representatives pointed to European drug-review processes, which often took one or two years less than the FDA's system, allowing new therapies to be available sooner.

Further reading
Food and Drug Administration Web site. Available online. URL: www.fda.gov.

forced-ranking systems (forced distributions, "rank and yank")

Forced-ranking systems are employee performance review systems where workers within groups or departments are rated best to worst with the lowest ranked workers either terminated or considered for termination. Also called forced distributions or "rank and yank," forced-ranking systems were popular in the 1990s among many major companies including General Electric, Cisco Systems, Ford, Microsoft and Intel. Even the infamous Enron Corporation had a forced-ranking system. At Enron workers rated "needs improvement" meant "you have one leg hanging out the window," while "there are issues associated with an employee" meant "you're gone."

Ford's system probably received the most negative publicity and was dropped after numerous employee complaints and lawsuits. The most common criticism has been that forced-ranking systems are biased, often using subjective criteria and favoring younger and majority employees over minorities. These systems can also be demoralizing, especially when their criteria are not well understood. Another criticism is that forced ranking might make a mediocre employee in a poorly performing unit look good and penalize a strong performing employee in an exceptional unit.

Many senior managers like forced-ranking systems. Legendary General Electric CEO Jack Welch Jr. touted the system as the best way to eliminate the least productive employees. Welch is quoted as saying, "A company that bets its future on its people must remove that lower 10 percent, and keep removing it every year—always raising the bar of performance and increasing the quality of its LEADERSHIP."

An Intel spokesperson says of forced ranking systems, "It rewards good performance, not seniority, not cronyism, not teacher's pets. We think it is a pretty accurate reflection of people's performance."

However, as Bonnie Kabin, a workforce-training consultant, notes, "What happens with forced distribution is that there is no place to hide. If your performance is poor, a manager is forced to make a decision." Often managers, especially first-line supervisors, are reticent to make critical evaluations and decisions. Called the "halo effect," or "Lake Wobegon" evaluations, everyone is rated above average.

See also 360-DEGREE FEEDBACK.

Further reading
Bruman, John. "Performance Reviews: Perilous Curves Ahead." Available online. URL: deming/eng.clemson. edu/pub/den/archive/2001.05/msg00114.html; Johnston, Mark, Neil M. Ford, Greg W. Marshall, Orville C. Walker, and Gilbert A. Churchill. *Sales Force Management.* 6th ed. Boston: McGraw-Hill/Irwin, 2002.

Foreign Corrupt Practices Act
The Foreign Corrupt Practices Act (FCPA, 1977) makes it illegal for any U.S. firm to offer, promise, or make payments or gifts of anything of value to foreign officials. The FCPA was a response to a 1970s investigation documenting that over 400 American companies had given bribes or made otherwise questionable payments in excess of $300 million to foreign officials for the purpose of obtaining or keeping business. The act is one of the toughest anti-BRIBERY laws among trading countries in the world.

The FCPA, technically an amendment to the Securities and Exchange Act of 1934, applies to issuers of registered securities in the United States and "domestic concerns" (any individual who is a citizen, national, or resident of the United States). Payments are prohibited if the person making the payment knows or should know that some or all of the funds will be used to influence government decisions. The FCPA prohibits payments to foreign political parties and candidates as well as officials. Payments to foreign companies and executives are not prohibited unless it is known or should be known that the payments will be distributed to government officials.

As amended in 1988, the FCPA allows "facilitating payments" for "routine governmental action." This may include payments for obtaining permits, licenses, or other official documents; processing of governmental papers; providing public services; and scheduling inspections.

As documented in the investigation, many U.S. companies hid bribes for foreign government officials, accounting for these payments as commissions or payments rendered for professional services. As part of the FCPA, U.S. firms engaged in international trade are subject to periodic disclosure requirements. The act requires the making and keeping of records and accounts "which, in reasonable detail, accurately and fairly reflect the transactions, and disposition of the ASSETS."

Criminal penalties for violation of the FCPA are significant. Firms are subject to fines up to $2 million; officers, directors, employees, and agents are subject to fines up to $100,000 and imprisonment up to five years. Civil penalties are also possible as well, and other federal criminal laws apply for bribery of international officials. While bribery remains a global business issue, the FCPA has significantly influenced American international business practices.

Further reading
Business Information Service for the New Independent States (BISNIS) Web site. Available online. URL: www.bisnis.doc.gov; Mallor, Jane P., A. James Barnes, Thomas Bowers, Michael J. Philips, and Arlen W. Langvardt. *Business Law: The Ethical, Global, and E-Commerce Environment.* 14th ed. Boston: McGraw-Hill, 2009.

foreign exchange
Foreign exchange is the trading of one country's currency for another's. There are many reasons why this must be done in the normal course of business. For example, a company may need a foreign currency to purchase items priced and sold in another currency. Also some people (often poorer people) see holding the currency of another country as a hedge against the INFLATION in their own currency. Most U.S. currency is held outside the United States, probably for this reason.

Many countries try to manage the rate at which their currency exchanges with other countries. A too-weak currency makes the purchase of foreign goods more expensive and indicates a weak economy. A too-strong currency makes the purchase of foreign goods cheaper, leading the country's citizens to buy IMPORTS instead of domestically made goods. (The 1994 PESO CRISIS in Mexico is an example of what happens when a currency becomes overvalued.)

Some countries try to control currency value fluctuations by establishing fixed or legal EXCHANGE RATES that currency exchanges must use. This usually produces devastating results in the local economy. In most cases there emerges an illegal black market where the common people and small businesses exchange the country's currency. The degree of seriousness of this situation depends on how vigorous the government enforces the official exchange rate. China has been repeatedly accused of keeping its currency (yuan) undervalued in order to stimulate exports and reduce imports. U.S. critics have attempted to get the U.S. Trade Representative to investigate as an unfair trade practice but Clinton, Bush, and Obama administrations have declined to pursue these allegations.

In some cases an "official" exchange rate is set, but everyone, including the government, uses the unofficial market rate. This has little impact on the economy, allowing the country's officials to delude themselves that the economy is behaving well. On the other hand, if the government strictly enforces the dictated exchange rate, large business may not be able to function in the country, and no foreign investor would dare invest money there.

A less disruptive way to manage the exchange rate is for the government's central bank to manage it by open-market activities. The central bank will purchase its own currency in an attempt to raise its value in the market and then sell its currency in an attempt to lower its value. This behavior is less troublesome but is usually only effective to manage minor currency fluctuations on an ongoing basis. It is largely ineffective in managing large shocks to an economy. For this reason, small countries are becoming more wary of draining their foreign-currency reserves by buying large amounts of their own currency to support its value.

The reasons for the foreign-currency exchanges discussed above are the results of normal economic activity within a country. However, for years foreign-exchange markets (some very informal) have existed for solely speculative reasons. People in France are buying Indian rupees from people in Australia solely in anticipation of gains in the value of Indian rupees. These speculative exchanges combined with the routine ones discussed earlier have produced a financial market of gigantic proportions. The worldwide foreign-exchange market has a typical volume of $1.5 trillion per day, more than three times the amount of stocks and BONDS traded in the United States per day. Unlike STOCK MARKETS, which have central exchanges, the foreign-exchange market has no physical location. It operates 24 hours a day, solely through an electronic network of banks, CORPORATIONS, and individuals. Even though there are some regulations on the participating banks and corporations, the foreign-exchange market is virtually unregulated.

foreign investment

Foreign investment includes both portfolio INVESTMENT and DIRECT INVESTMENT; these two investment types vary in the degree of RISK and control.

Foreign-portfolio investment is investment in foreign stocks, BONDS, and other FINANCIAL INSTRUMENTS. Usually there is no intention on the part of the investor to be involved in the MANAGEMENT of the company in which he or she is investing. Investing in the stock of, say, an Indian company can be lucrative, but it involves risks that do not exist in investing in a domestic company. Here is a short list of such risks.

Currency risk. Changes in the currency EXCHANGE RATES will affect the profitability of the investment. The Indian company may pay its normal 10,000-rupee DIVIDEND. If the rupee strengthens in value relative to the dollar, the value of the dividend increases to the U.S. investor, and vice versa.

Political risk. Favorable political actions, government changes, and events or increased stability will increase the value of the stock, and vice versa.

Diplomatic risk. Diplomatic relations between the two countries will affect the value of the investment. Improved relations and an openness of currency exchange between the United States and India will improve the value of the stock, and vice versa.

Information risk. Changes in the regulatory environment in either the United States or the foreign country can affect the value of the foreign investment. The foreign investment carries what could be characterized as an information premium. This could be stated in terms of the increased returns the foreign company must pay because of the low quality or quantity of information it provides compared to a U.S. company. So if information is improving just in the United States, this premium widens and the price will fall in order to provide the needed return to compensate the investors for the poorer quality information from the foreign investment, and vice versa.

Foreign-direct investment occurs when an investor company in, say, the United States invests in a subsidiary company or project with intentions of being involved in the management of that company. Typically the investing company invests in the ASSETS directly by providing EQUITY funding to a subsidiary in the foreign country. Foreign-direct investment also includes the parent company leaving INCOME in the subsidiary company or loaning money to the subsidiary.

Most developing countries consider foreign-direct investment an important part of their development strategy. Consequently they spend a great deal of energy in providing incentives and reforming their legal systems, all in an effort to attract foreign-direct investment.

See also EMERGING MARKET.

Foreign Sovereign Immunities Act

Immunity can be defined as being exempt from or not responsible for things such as illness, problems, or governance. Specifically, the Foreign Sovereign Immunities Act states that foreign countries are immune to the U.S. judicial system, with the exception of certain limitations.

The Foreign Sovereign Immunities Act (FSIA) refers to Title 28, Section 1330, and Sections 1602-1611 of the U.S. Code. This law, passed by Congress in 1976, is complex and states the exceptions with which the United States and its citizens have the right to file suit against a foreign country. Some of these general exceptions include a waiver of immunity by a foreign state, commercial activity of a foreign country which involves the United States, and the personal injury or death of a U.S. citizen caused by any foreign entity.

The need for a law such as the Foreign Sovereign Immunities Act has grown throughout the last century. With increased international commercial activity and GLOBALIZATION, obtaining the ability to hold a foreign country responsible in case of illegal actions is necessary.

Earlier in the history of the United States, foreign countries were given almost absolute immunity. In 1812 Chief Justice John Marshall, ruling in *The Schooner Exchange v. McFaddon*, developed the theory of foreign-sovereign immunity. Eventually the United States adopted the "restrictive theory" or "absolute theory," which gave foreign countries immunity for public acts of government offices but not for commercial or private activity. The U.S. courts found this difficult to apply because of a lack of standards and the frequent deference of cases to the State Department. Political considerations often influenced decisions, and during the 1950s many countries were competing unfairly by treating commercial activities as government actions to remain immune. In 1976 Congress passed the Foreign Sovereign Immunities Act to provide clear standards, making it more difficult to hide commercial activities and avoiding the use of political branches, such as the State Department, when making decisions.

The purpose of the FSIA is not only to establish standards but also to define "foreign state." According to the U.S. Code, a "foreign state" is considered any political subdivision, agency, or instrumentality of a foreign country. This act also sets forth standards for the extent of LIABILITY and counterclaims.

Through the years the FSIA has been amended several times. In 1999, it was amended to include terrorist actions by foreign countries. It is under this amendment that victims' families from September 11, 2001, are provided the ability to file suit against the country or countries sponsoring such terrorist actions, but the FSIA was invoked in 2008 to prevent lawsuits by families of the September 11th attacks who alleged the Saudi Arabian government indirectly financed al Qaeda.

Further reading

Fisher, Bruce D., and Michael J. Phillips. *The Legal, Ethical and Regulatory Environment of Business.* 8th ed. Cincinnati: Cengage, 2003; *Foreign Services Immunities Act U.S. Code.* Vol. 28, sec. 1330 (1976): 1,602–11; Lowenstein, Andrew. "The Foreign Sovereign Immunities Act and Corporate Subsidies of Agencies or Instrumentalities of Foreign States," *Berkeley Journal of International Law* 19 (Spring 2001): 350; Tessitore, Michael A. "Immunity and the Foreign Sovereign: An Introduction to the Foreign Sovereign Immunities Act," *Florida Bar Journal* 73, i10 (November 1999): 48.

—Jennifer R. Land

foreign-trade zones

Foreign-trade zones (FTZs), also known as free-trade zones, are facilities, usually established in enclosed areas near U.S. ports of entry that receive special treatment with regard to taxation of imported of goods. Technically FTZs are treated as being outside the customs territory of the United States and are subject to local and state labor, public health, and other laws. However, state regulations regarding food, drugs, or cosmetics do not apply to imported goods transshipped through foreign-trade zones.

Although FTZs have existed in Europe since the 1800s, they were first established in the United States after passage of the Foreign Trade Zone Act in 1934 as an attempt to mitigate the impact of protective TARIFFS imposed during the GREAT DEPRESSION. FTZs were not widely used until the 1980s and 1990s. In 1970 there were only eight FTZ projects; by 2001 there were over 230 FTZs.

Goods imported into FTZs are treated for tariffs primarily as either "privileged foreign merchandise" or "nonprivileged foreign merchandise." Privileged foreign merchandise is assessed tariffs based on condition upon the entry into the zone,

but the actual duties are deferred until the merchandise is removed from the FTZ and enters the United States. In addition to having the tariffs deferred, privileged foreign merchandise status continues even if the goods are manufactured or processed before leaving the zone. This avoids additional tariffs if the good is changed from one classification to another and would otherwise be subject to a higher tariff.

Nonprivileged foreign merchandise is not categorized for tariff purposes until it leaves the FTZ. Thus its value, classification, condition, and applicable tariff rate are determined by the PRODUCT leaving the zone. Because of the ability to take advantage of differences in the U.S. tariff structure, there has been substantial growth in the use of foreign-trade zones in the United States. In one case, Japanese steel plates were brought into an FTZ on a nonprivileged basis and left the zone as barges. The steel plates would have been subject to a U.S. tariff, but barges are not subject to tariffs.

Another advantage of foreign-trade zones is that U.S. quotas do not apply. If an import quota has been filled, FTZs can be used to store products until the next quota period. Goods from countries not subject to most-favored-nation status can be brought into foreign-trade zones and, if they are transformed into products subject to lower most favored nation (MFN) tariffs, receive the lower tariff rate. Even though foreign-trade zones are intended to benefit U.S. exporters, allowing them to bring products into the U.S. for processing and then reexport without having to pay tariffs, many foreign companies use FTZs to bring products into the United States subject to lower tariffs.

The National Association of Foreign Trade Zones list of FTZ benefits include

1. duty deferral
2. exports
3. reduced or eliminated duties related to defects, damage, obsolescence, waste, and scrap
4. nondutiability of labor, overhead, and PROFIT
5. inverted customs duty savings
6. international returns
7. spare parts

8. U.S. quotas
9. simplification of import/export procedures
10. QUALITY CONTROL
11. cargo insurance
12. security
13. INVENTORY CONTROL
14. consumed merchandise (generally not subject to duties)
15. inventory taxes
16. exhibition of market goods before payment of duty
17. reduced INSURANCE costs
18. country of origin marking and labeling
19. zone-to-zone transfer
20. transfer of title.

See also RULES OF ORIGIN.

Further reading
National Association of Foreign Trade Zones Web site. Available online. URL: www.naftz.org; U.S. Customs Web site. Available online. URL: www.customs.ustreas. gov.

401(k) plan
The term *401(k)* comes from a section of the Internal Revenue Code allowing special tax consideration to help people save for retirement. Americans, particularly "baby boomers," have relatively low savings rates. The 401(k) plan was created to induce Americans to increase their savings. This plan, along with similar 403b and 457 plans, allows employees to contribute a portion of their salary into a tax-deferred retirement fund. The funds can be invested by the employee in MUTUAL FUNDS, individual stocks, and other INVESTMENT options.

A 401(k) plan has a maximum pretax amount that an employee can contribute each year. For 2009 the limit was $16,500, with increases indexed for inflation. 401(k) rules also allow a "catch-up" provision of an extra $5,500 for people 50 or older in 2009.

401(k) plans offer a variety of benefits. Tax deferment means contributors do not have to pay taxes on their contributions until the funds are withdrawn, usually during retirement. Tax deferment also reduces workers' current taxable income. In addition, 401(k)s facilitate savings, since the funds are taken out of a worker's pay. Many companies also match workers' contributions to 401(k)s, increasing the amount set aside for retirement.

In the 1990s, 401(k)s and other defined-contribution RETIREMENT PLANS replaced traditional defined-benefit plans. In a traditional retirement plan, a worker's retirement pension was a set percentage of their salary, often 50–60 percent of their highest three-year average salary. In defined-contribution plans, employers match employees' contribution. If an employee elects to contribute 3 percent of their salary, the employer would match that amount. The employee's retirement pension would be the future value of those funds and would depend on the growth in value of the investments chosen.

Employers often put contingencies on their contributions to employees' 401(k)s—for instance, not allowing employees access to the employers' contributions until they had been with the company a set amount of time, often 3–5 years (vesting) and making employer contributions in the form of company stock. (Beginning in 2002, the longest a company can require is three years.) These contingencies contributed to the hardship of Enron employees who, in 2001, seeing their 401(k)s "vaporizing," were unable to sell their Enron stock.

Most 401(k) plans allow employees access to funds in an emergency through LOANS or withdrawals. Loans, which are paid back, are not subject to taxes or penalties, but they have their own danger; if an employee leaves or is laid off, he or she will probably have to repay the loan immediately. Withdrawals are restricted by INTERNAL REVENUE SERVICE (IRS) rules and are subject to taxes. The IRS allows withdrawals for

- certain nonreimbursable medical expenses
- purchase of primary residence
- payments for post-secondary education
- to prevent eviction or foreclosure on a home

401(k)s are also portable, meaning they can be carried with an employee when they change employers. When changing jobs employees can

- directly roll an old 401(k) plan into the new employer's plan
- keep the old 401(k) account and start a new one
- directly roll the old 401(k) into an INDIVIDUAL RETIREMENT ACCOUNT (IRA), and start a new plan with the new employer.

Further reading

PAI-Pension Services Web site. Available online. URL: www.paipension.com; Fidelity Investments' 401K Web site. Available online. URL: www.401k.com; CNN money Mutual Funds Web site. Available online. URL: www.mutual-funds.com.

—Rachel Archangel

franchising

Franchising is a contractual agreement between a manufacturer or business-idea owner—the franchiser—and a WHOLESALER or retailer—the franchisee. The franchiser sells to the franchisee the right to market its products or ideas and to use its TRADEMARKS and brand names. The franchisee agrees to meet the franchiser's operating requirements, usually pays an initial fee for the franchise, and agrees to pay a percentage of sales to the franchiser.

Franchising is big business in the United States. While it has existed for centuries, it boomed in the country after World War II. Growth of the interstate highway system in the 1950s and 1960s stimulated travel in the United States, and franchises offered travelers the expectation of standardized PRODUCTS or levels of service. Ray Kroc's McDonald's fast-food restaurants and the many hotel chains symbolized the growth of this type of business. Today over one-third of all retail sales in the United States are transacted through franchises. Critics argue the growth of franchising is creating "sameness" in America, reducing local and regional differences and creating cultural homogenization.

Franchising is a business strategy that allows rapid and flexible penetration of markets, growth, and CAPITAL development. In the United States, franchises are typically distinguished as either product franchises or business-format franchises.

Product franchises involve manufacturers who produce goods that are distributed through franchise agreements. Many ice-cream stores, soft-drink bottling outlets, and gasoline retailers are product franchises. Business-format franchises involve the LICENSING of INTELLECTUAL PROPERTY rights in conjunction with a unique "formula for success" of a business. Many service businesses, including hotels, fast food restaurants, and employment services, are examples of business-format franchising.

Franchising provides both advantages and disadvantages to the franchiser and franchisee. Based on the growth of franchising in the United States, generally both sides benefit from this type of business relationship. For the franchisee the benefits include use of trademarks and brands that are recognized and preferred by customers, support and training from the franchiser organization, national ADVERTISING, a protected territory, reduced costs through bulk buying, and reduced risk from a proven business concept. The disadvantages for the franchisee include payments for use of the franchise trademark or brands, restrictions on business practices, and the potential to be hurt by actions taken by the franchiser or other franchisees.

From the franchiser's perspective, franchising allows faster growth into new markets before competitors copy its ideas, expansion without additional CAPITAL EXPENDITURES, royalty payments from franchisees, and ECONOMIES OF SCALE through larger operations. Franchising also allows firms to expand internationally in conjunction with franchisees who understand and adapt to cultural differences.

Franchises are subject to significant government regulation both from state and federal agencies. Many states and the FEDERAL TRADE COMMISSION enacted disclosure statutes for franchise agreements. The typical franchise-disclosure statute created criminal penalties for material misrepresentation or omission in franchise promotions. It usually permits withdrawal from any franchise agreement if the franchisee did not receive a copy of the PROSPECTUS. In the 1950s and 1960s, franchising was known for having many unscrupulous operators promising instant success and making unsubstantiated claims to potential franchisees. Franchising was and is often promoted as a way for people who do not have business experience to start their own enterprise, and it does reduce the RISK for new businesspeople through the knowledge gained by the franchiser.

Most state franchise-disclosure laws require the franchiser to register with an agency by filing a franchise-offering circular. The state agency reviews the circular to ensure it meets the necessary disclosure requirements. Once registered, the franchiser is licensed to sell franchises in that state. Many states also review franchisers' capitalization before permitting the sale of franchises. This is done to protect potential investors from franchisers who have made little initial investment in the proposed franchise system. States have also enacted laws dealing with the termination of franchise agreements. These laws typically prohibit franchisers from initiating termination of the franchise CONTRACT without "good cause," which is usually defined as a material breach of the franchise agreement.

Franchising is designed to provide standardized products and services even though the parent company (franchiser) does not own all the business outlets. Franchise agreements protect the image and reputation of the franchiser and the other franchisees from inappropriate actions by individual franchisees.

See also BRANDS, BRAND NAMES.

Further reading

Boone, Louis E., and David L. Kurtz. *Contemporary Marketing*. 14th ed. Fort Worth: Dryden Press, 2009; Folsom, Ralph H., and Michael Gordon. *International Business Transactions*. 5th ed. Eagan, Minn.: West Group, 2002.

fraud

Fraud is intentional misrepresentation and has long been a major problem both for businesses and consumers. In 17th-century England, a law on oral contracts prohibited parties to a lawsuit from testifying on their own behalf. This frequently led to third parties offering false testimony about the existence of an oral CONTRACT. To reduce this problem, in 1677 Parliament enacted the Statute of Frauds, requiring written evidence before certain types of contracts would be enforced.

American legislatures adopted similar rules, and today statutes of frauds vary from state to state. Most contracts covered by statutes of fraud require written evidence. Contracts for sale of real estate are the most common written agreement Americans encounter. Fraud statutes also cover executor or administrator contracts, contracts associated with marriage, and collateral contracts (in which a person promises to perform another person's obligation).

Today fraud against businesses includes a variety of misrepresentations with the intent to deceive. Employee EMBEZZLEMENT is a constant problem for businesses. Sham transactions, by which a company executive sells a PRODUCT, division, or other ASSET in order to record a PROFIT while agreeing to purchase the asset back in some future time period, is another type of fraud. The Enron fiasco of 2001 included significant use of sham transactions to boost reported earnings in order to bolster the firm's stock price while executives were selling their shares.

Bogus invoices are another serious type of fraud against businesses. Large companies are often fooled into paying what appear to be legitimate business expenses. Bogus checks, counterfeit currency, and devious contract agreements all challenge business managers. Misrepresentation in EMPLOYMENT is another problem. One sales representative courted a young woman, offering her a fantastic job with his company. Fortunately the woman was shrewd enough to contact the company's HUMAN RESOURCES department in the company and find out that the sales rep had no authority to hire anyone.

While businesses contend with a variety of frauds, criminals posing as businesses confront American consumers with numerous fraudulent representations. The FEDERAL TRADE COMMISSION has identified what they call their "Dirty

Dozen" of fraudulent solicitations likely to be received by consumers by bulk mail or e-mail, including

- business-opportunity scams offering financial success with little or no effort. Often these are pyramid schemes, requiring the individual to find and sell the business opportunity to others in order to create a "downline" and profit from sales to others.
- making money by sending bulk e-mail—that is, offers to sell the consumer bulk e-mail distribution lists and products, services, or software to promote through e-mail.
- chain letters, a classic fraud received through the mail or e-mail, asking people to send money to the person on the top of the list. The recipient adds his or her name to the bottom of the list, and supposedly, when that name rises to the top, he or she will receive huge sums of money. Sometimes these solicitations include some type of information package designed to suggest that something of value is being exchanged and therefore it is not fraud.
- work-at-home schemes, which usually involve stuffing envelopes with promises of earning hundreds and even thousands of dollars per month. These are often advertised in classified ads and on signs tacked onto telephone poles. Like the old saying, "If it sounds too good to be true, it probably is too good to be true," these solicitations prey upon the least sophisticated and usually poorest people in society.
- health and diet scams—miracle cures for every ailment that have been around for centuries. In the 19th century, tonics often included codeine and a high percentage of alcohol to numb anyone who might doubt their efficacy.
- effortless income—offers that promise ways to earn huge profits, usually from currency exchange. Charles Ponzi, after whom the PONZI SCHEME was named, promised investors a 40-percent profit on their investment in 90 days. At the time, prevailing INTEREST RATES were around 5 percent, making the Ponzi proposition very attractive to investors. Ponzi's proposi-

tion was based on International Postal Reply Coupons, which were redeemable at fixed rates of exchange negotiated by the participating governments. However, EXCHANGE RATES for currency fluctuate. Ponzi convinced investors he would take their funds, invest in International Postal Reply Coupons in countries where the currency had depreciated significantly, and then redeem the coupons in strong-currency countries, making a significant profit. After being caught and sent to jail, Ponzi moved to Florida to sell real estate.

- free-goods offers that promise expensive products such as computers for free if one pays to join the club and get so many other people to join.
- offers for investment opportunities, which, like Ponzi schemes, promise huge returns using "scientifically proven" trading methods or inside information of some upcoming breakthrough. Like health and diet claims, these are "snake oil" schemes for an INVESTMENT portfolio.
- cable descrambler, INTERNET services, pay-per-call scams, and other communications service offers that either do not work or contain hidden clauses costing unsuspecting consumers much more than they thought.
- guaranteed LOANS or credit scams offering, for instance, home-equity loans and CREDIT CARDS to anyone regardless of credit history. One of the worst types is the PREDATORY LENDING scheme in which homeowners are conned into refinancing their MORTGAGES with low interest rates but huge fees, leaving the homeowner (often an elderly person) with payments that cannot be sustained.
- credit repair schemes involving companies that claim they will repair someone's credit rating with the credit-rating services. Under U.S. law, consumers are allowed to request a copy of their credit-rating reports once a year for free and submit documentation refuting claims made to the reporting agency by any creditor.
- vacation prize promotions, a classic fraud that involves claims of deluxe accommodations on luxury cruise ships and other sorts of misrepresentations.

To reduce the chances of being defrauded, experts recommend the following.

- Use common sense. If it sounds too good to be true, it is probably a scam.
- Watch out for "processing fees," whether to borrow money, register for prizes, or to receive "free" things.
- Do business with companies one knows and trusts.
- Protect financial information. One of the latest frauds is a bogus form saying it is from the INTERNAL REVENUE SERVICE, looking to update personal information.
- Scrutinize charitable solicitations. Two common frauds are sound-alike charitable organizations—i.e., the soliciting group sounds like a well-known national charity—and the use of a paid, professional solicitor, with the charity receiving only a small percentage of the donations received. After September 11, 2001, many fraudulent solicitations duped millions from well-meaning Americans.
- Avoid the classic Nigerian money order fraud, in which callers or e-mailers requests help getting money that is "theirs" but need help transferring the funds to a U.S. bank account—the consumer's. With that account information, they liquidate the account.

Internet fraud is expanding rapidly. See the FBI's INTERNET FRAUD COMPLAINT CENTER entry for current examples of Internet fraud.

Further reading

Mallor, Jane P., A. James Barnes, Thomas Bowers, Michael J. Philips, and Arlen W. Langvardt. *Business Law: The Ethical, Global, and E-Commerce Environment.* 14th ed. Boston: McGraw-Hill, 2009; National Consumers League Web site. Available online. URL: www.nclnet.org; FBI's Internet Fraud Web site. Available online. URL: www.fbi.gov/majcases/fraud/internetschemes.htm. Accessed on June 16, 2009.

Freddie Mac   See FEDERAL HOME LOAN MORTGAGE CORPORATION.

Freedom of Information Act

The Freedom of Information Act (FOIA), which can be found in Title 5 of the U.S. Code, Section 552, was enacted in 1966 and provides that any person has the right to request access to federal agency records or information. FOIA requires government agencies to respond to public requests for documents within 20 days after the request is received. All states have their own statutes governing public access to state and local records. Federal agencies unwilling or unable to respond within the 20-day period must justify their denial of a FOIA request. The FOIA exempts from public disclosure documents that:

1. are of national security interest
2. concern internal agency personnel practices
3. are specifically exempted from disclosure by federal statute
4. contain TRADE SECRETS or other confidential information
5. reflect internal agency deliberations on matters of proceedings or policies
6. are part of personnel or medical files
7. jeopardize law enforcement investigation's or individual's rights to a fair trial
8. relate to regulation or supervision of financial institutions
9. contain geological or geophysical data

All agencies are required by statute to make certain types of records created by the agency on or after November 1, 1996, available electronically. FOIA requests are not needed to obtain access to (1) final opinions and orders made in adjudicating cases, (2) final statements of policy and interpretations which have not been published in the *Federal Register,* (3) administrative staff manuals and instructions to staff that affect a member of the public, (4) copies of records that have been the subject of a FOIA request and that are of sufficient public interest or curiosity that the agency believes other persons are likely to request them, and (5) the agency's annual FOIA report.

There is no initial fee to file a FOIA request, and in the majority of requests made to the Justice Department, no fees are ever charged. By law, however, an agency is entitled to charge certain fees, which depend on the requestor's category.

FOIA is important to businesses in that media, public-interest groups, companies, and industry trade associations use FOIA requests to learn about their competitors. Competitive intelligence professionals "mine" government documents, whether EPA documentation or SECURITIES AND EXCHANGE COMMISSION reports, to gather public information about competitor's products and activities.

Further reading

Mallor, Jane P., A. James Barnes, Thomas Bowers, Michael J. Philips, and Arlen W. Langvardt. *Business Law: The Ethical, Global, and E-Commerce Environment.* 14th ed. Boston: McGraw-Hill, 2009; U.S. Department of Justice Web site. Available online. URL: www.doj.gov.

free on board (FOB)

Free on board, most commonly called FOB, is a shipping term that has much significance in the accounting for a firm's ASSETS. There are two FOB situations: FOB shipping point and FOB destination. When a seller needs to ship goods to a buyer, the two parties will negotiate the manner in which the goods are transported, either FOB shipping point or FOB destination. The shipping point is usually the seller's shipping docks, and the destination is usually the buyer's receiving docks.

When goods are transported FOB shipping point, the title (ownership) to the goods being shipped is passed to the buyer at the shipping point—that is, when the goods leave the seller. Though the buyer may not receive the goods for several days or weeks, it is the buyer who now owns the goods and must include them in his inventory, despite the fact that he doesn't have physical possession of them. It is also the buyer who is liable for the goods while in transit, as it is he who owns them. Because the goods were shipped "free on board," the shipping agent (transportation company) will send the freight bill to the buyer, the owner of the goods while in transit.

When goods are transported FOB destination, the title (ownership) to the goods being shipped is not passed to the buyer until the goods reach their destination. Thus the seller owns the goods while they are in transit, and it is she who is liable for the goods while they are being transported. The seller will continue to include the shipped items in her inventory until such time as they reach their destination. The freight bill will be sent to the seller, the owner of the goods while in transit.

free trade

Free trade is international trade without restraints imposed by governments. For a variety of reasons, governments often impose limitations on trade, and thus totally free trade does not exist in the world. Limitations on trade include TARIFFS, quotas, and other NONTARIFF BARRIERS. Tariffs can be used to generate revenue or increase the price of imported PRODUCTS, making domestically produced products cheaper and more competitive in the marketplace. Quotas are quantitative limits on the amount of a specific import that can be brought into a country during a period of time. To protect domestic textile jobs for decades the United States imposed quotas on textiles coming into the country.

Today nontariff barriers are often the biggest restraint on free trade. Nontariff barriers include labeling requirements, "voluntary export quotas," technical standards, and health and safety constraints. For example, the United States, ignoring rulings by the NORTH AMERICAN FREE TRADE AGREEMENT (NAFTA) and the WORLD TRADE ORGANIZATION (WTO), used safety concerns to prohibit Mexican trucks from having full access to U.S. highways. In the 1980s Japan, fearing the imposition of quotas, voluntarily restricted automobile shipments to the United States for several years.

The argument for free trade is based on the ideas of Adam Smith, author of the *An Inquiry into the Nature and Cause of the Wealth of Nations* (1776), and 19th-century economist David Ricardo. Smith argued against MERCANTILISM, the idea that a country's WEALTH and power could be increased through the accumulation of precious metals and by maintaining a favorable balance of trade. Mercantilism was the dominant economic doctrine of his time, but Smith proposed free trade, or unrestricted access to markets, instead. (Ironically, he ended his career as port tax collector in his native Scotland.)

David Ricardo, building on Smith's ideas, was the originator of the concept of COMPARATIVE ADVANTAGE. The law of comparative advantage is the principle that firms, people, or countries should engage in those activities for which their advantage over others is the largest or their disadvantage is the smallest. Trade is then based on doing those things that can be done relatively more efficiently than others can do. Logically, free trade encourages individuals, firms, and countries to specialize in doing those things they can do well and trading for those that they cannot do as efficiently. Also, logically, comparative advantage depends on access to markets to make exchanges—free trade.

The other arguments for free trade are that exports pay for IMPORTS and the cost of protection of domestic industries. Countries that attempt to limit imports usually find that their exports face similar restrictions, offsetting any economic gain from reducing imports. Restricting free trade also creates a strange dichotomy. Using the example of Japan's voluntary export limits in the 1980s, economists found for each American automobile industry job retained because Japanese producers were limiting exports, American consumers paid approximately $250,000 more for cars. The benefits of trade restrictions usually are concentrated, in this case in the U.S. automobile industry, while the costs are dispersed among consumers in general. Because of this dichotomy, there is often a strong, vocal group of supporters for restricting free trade and no strong group opposing it on an economic basis.

Trade among countries has existed for thousands of years, well before the ideas of Smith and Ricardo, but there are many economic and social-justice reasons countries and individuals do not always support free trade (as evidenced in the WTO meetings in Seattle in 1999). One argument against free trade is to prevent unfair foreign COMPETITION. Free trade and fair trade do not mean the same thing. Free trade, as stated earlier, is trade without restraints, whereas in fair trade everyone "plays by the same rules." Sometimes referred to as a market with a "level playing field," fair trade precludes DUMPING, export subsidies, and, more recently, abuse of workers and the environment. As the largest economy in the world, the U.S. market is important to any multinational firm. U.S. businesses often ask government to restrict access to the U.S. market, claiming unfair trade practices on the part of firms from other countries. Under section 301 of U.S. trade rules, the U.S. trade representative must investigate and report findings regarding claims of unfair trade practices.

NAFTA, the NORTH AMERICAN FREE TRADE AGREEMENT, is often cited as an example of the benefits of free trade. Since 1995 NAFTA has significantly increased trade among the United States, Canada, and Mexico, but close inspection of the agreement (more than 1,100 pages long) shows a myriad of exceptions and limitations. Free trade would be trade without limitations; NAFTA significantly reduces the barriers to trade but does not eliminate restrictions. The World Trade Organization's goal is to increase world free trade. More than 135 countries are members of the WTO, but free trade is still a vision for the future among those who support that vision.

Further reading
Ruffin, Roy J., and Paul R. Gregory. *Principles of Economics.* 7th ed. Boston: Addison Wesley, 2000.

free-trade areas
Free-trade areas are regional agreements to reduce TARIFFS, quotas, and other barriers to trade among the participating nations while retaining national TRADE BARRIERS with respect to other countries. The goal in creating areas for FREE TRADE is to stimulate ECONOMIC DEVELOPMENT and increase economic bargaining power.

Since World War II, numerous free-trade areas have been established. The most widely known are the 130+-member WORLD TRADE ORGANIZATION (WTO), the 27-member EUROPEAN UNION (with plans to expand membership in the near future), and the 3-member NORTH AMERICAN FREE TRADE AGREEMENT (NAFTA).

Each region of the world has attempted to create regional agreements. In 1966, five Central African countries created the Customs Union of Central Africa (Union Douanière et Economique de l'Afrique Centrale, UDEAC). The following year Kenya, Tanzania, and Uganda created the East African Community (EAC). In 1974, six French-speaking West African countries formed the West African Economic Community (known by its French initials CEAO). The following year the CEAO became part of the Economic Community of West African States. In 1991, 51 African nations established the Organization of African Unity (OAU).

In Latin America and the Caribbean, the first free-trade area was the Central American Common Market (CACM), established in 1958. Many Latin American countries participated in the Latin American Free Trade Association (LAFTA, 1961). Eight island nations plus Belize created the Caribbean Community (CARICOM, 1973). In 1994, 37 nations became members of the Association of Caribbean States, agreeing to long-term economic integration.

The Persian Gulf states formed the Gulf Cooperation Council (GCC) in 1984 implementing trade and investment rules among participating states. In South America, two free trade areas have been established: MERCOSUR (Southern Cone including Brazil, Paraguay, Argentina, and Uruguay in 1991 and later joined by Chile and Bolivia); and ANCOM, the Andean Common Market established in 1969 by Bolivia, Chile, Columbia, Ecuador, and Peru. In South Asia the most prominent free trade area is ASEAN, the Association of Southeast Asian Nations, formed in 1967.

Most regional free-trade areas have had limited success in stimulating economic development. Often they are created as a counter-balance to the political and economic power of the United States, Japan, and European nations. Many countries retain special trade agreements based on historic and colonial relationships and political-military alignment. For example, the United States has a special trade agreement with Israel, established in 1985. The United States and the European Union (EU) got into what was known as the "banana wars" over preferential access to the EU for banana producers in former European colonies and Commonwealth countries.

Further reading
Folsom, Ralph H., Michael Gordon, and John Sproagle. *International Business Transactions in a Nutshell.* 7th ed. Eagan, Minn.: West Law, 2004.

futures, futures contracts

Futures or futures contracts are sales of commodities for delivery at some later time. In the United States, futures generally refer to CONTRACTS specifying a fixed quantity and quality of a commodity to be delivered to a location at a certain date. Futures contracts are traded under the rules of the COMMODITY FUTURES TRADING COMMISSION (CFTC).

Futures contracts eliminate or reduce the RISK associated with future price changes. Initially they were used by farmers and food-industry processors to hedge against the risk of price changes. Farmers would sell a futures contract at a specified price, "locking in" that price for the PRODUCT between planting and harvesting time; this is referred to as HEDGING. Food processors would buy futures contracts locked in the cost of raw materials. Over time a wide variety of futures contracts have been developed, including those concerned with FINANCIAL INSTRUMENTS, STOCK MARKET indices, INTEREST RATES, energy products, foreign currency, and precious metals.

In a futures market like the CHICAGO BOARD OF TRADE, someone who buys a futures contract is said to have "gone long." If, after going long, the price of the underlying commodity or ASSET rises, the price of the futures contract will rise, and the buyer profits. In the example of the food-processing company, the PROFIT from buying a futures contract would offset the increase in price of the commodity in the cash market. If, instead, the price of the commodity declined, the value of the futures contract would decline, causing a loss for the food processor, but the cash-market price would also have decreased, offsetting the loss associated with purchasing the futures contract.

Someone who sells a futures contract is said to have "gone short." If the price of the underlying commodity or security rises, the short seller loses, but if the price declines, the short seller can buy back the futures contract at a lower price and profit by the difference.

In most situations, buyers and sellers of futures contracts "close out" their trades before the expiration date of the contract. They could also take or make delivery of the commodity or security, as per the stipulations in the contract.

In addition to hedging, futures contracts are widely used as speculative investments. Holders of futures are required to pay an initial margin, usually equal to 10 percent of the value of contract. Thus, futures contracts provide significant LEVERAGE. For example, if a contract is worth $100,000, a buyer is only required to put up $10,000. Should the value of the underlying ASSET increase by 5 percent, the investor earns $5,000 (5 percent of $100,000), a 50-percent return on their INVESTMENT. The buyer could also lose money in the same leveraged manner if the value of the contract decreased by 5 percent. If the value decreased, the investor would receive a margin call, requiring him to put up additional funds or have the contract closed. The most famous recent example of the potential for profit from futures market speculation was the report that Hilary Clinton earned approximately $100,000 from an initial investment of only a few thousand dollars.

Futures markets are known for their widely varying prices. Changes in weather, political turmoil, and rumors cause rapid changes in futures markets, resulting in huge profits and losses. Futures markets are also known for their "pits," intense bidding rooms where brokers shout and use hand signals to exercise trades for their customers. Prior experience as a football player is considered a valuable training for work in futures market pits.

Further reading
U.S. Dept. Agriculture, Risk Management Agency Web site. Available online. URL: www.rma.usda.gov/pubs/rme/fsh_7.html. Accessed on June 16, 2009.

—Todd Devries

future value
Future value is the amount an investment is worth after a set period of time at a specific interest rate. Future values can be determined for assets with simple interest and for assets with compound interest. Future value is closely related to present value. Present value is the amount that a future sum of money is worth today at a specific INTEREST RATE. The value of a sum of money changes over time if it is put into an INVESTMENT that earns interest, such as a savings account or certificate of deposit (CD). Assuming a consistently positive interest rate, the future value of a sum of money will always be greater than the present value. Future value is a calculated numerical amount not to be confused with terms such as "futures" or "futures market." These terms refer to the purchase or sale of financial contracts that are then set to be delivered at a future date.

A number of formulas are used to determine an amount's future value. For the following formulas, FV is future value, PV is present value, ir is interest rate, and n is time period (such as number of years). This is the formula used to calculate the future value of an investment earning simple interest:

$$FV = PV \times (1+(ir \times n))$$

For example, the future value of $1,000 in five years at 6.5 percent interest would be: $1000 \times (1 + (0.065 \times 5))$ or $1,325. However, since interest earned is generally rolled back into the principal amount and interest is then earned upon that total, future value is usually computed using compound interest. This is the formula used to calculate the future value of an investment earning compound interest:

$$FV = PV \times (1 + ir)^n$$

In this case, the future value of $1,000 in five years with a 6.5 percent compound interest rate would be: $1000 \times (1 + 0.065)^5$ or approximately $1,370. Because the interest is compounded, an investment earns more over the same period than if the sum were earning only simple interest (in this case, about $45 more). Numerous online tools can help in calculating future value. Users can input their different variables into an online calculator and are able to determine future and present values for simple interest and for compound interest.

An ANNUITY is income from an investment that is paid out in fixed, regular payments in the future. Calculating the future value of an annuity can be a bit more difficult. The formula used for calculating this is:

$$FV = PMT \times (((1 + ir)^n - 1)/ir)$$

In this formula, *PMT* equals the periodic payment. There are many types of annuities, so determining their future value can be complicated. A number of tables are available on the Internet and in print that show the future value of an annuity due for $1.00 at various interest rates. To figure for a particular amount, users multiply their dollar amount by the figure given for a particular interest rate and period on the table. For example, the future value of an annuity yielding 4 percent for 10 years is 12.48635 times the periodic payment.

Further reading

Frick, D. R. *Time Value of Money Concepts.* Available online. URL: www.frickcpa.com/tvom/TVOM_formulas. asp. Accessed on April 21, 2009; Investopedia. *Investopedia Dictionary.* Available online. URL: www.investopedia. com/dictionary/default.asp. Accessed on April 21, 2009.

—Jennifer Bell

gain sharing   See PROFIT SHARING, GAIN SHARING.

game theory

Game theory is a mathematical representation of situations in which two or more players strategize and make choices that affect the choices and outcomes for other players. There are many forms of game theory, and in a business environment it is defined by boundaries, players, and a set of rules within which outcomes are determined.

Game theory is often used in marketing to describe the results of strategies depending on strategies other participants in the market employ. Understanding the rules and theory of game theory, which occur in every business, are essential for success. Consumers, entrepreneurs and managers, regulators, courts, and other participants contribute to a market's design, directly or indirectly. Any change, either within the company or outside the company, will be reflected throughout the business system.

In game theory, nothing is fixed. The marketplace is constantly evolving, and players are constantly creating new markets. Buyers and sellers do not take products or prices as given. Game theory differs from conventional economic assumptions by which consumers are thought to behave in simple stimulus-response, i.e., sellers determine prices and consumers respond accordingly.

Mathematicians John Von Neumann and Oskar Morgenstern first developed game theory. Their theories were restricted to games in which no players could gain except at the expense of others. In the process of the game, each player strategized in order to gain what he or she wanted out of the interaction. For example, when purchasing a car, buyers go to the car dealership looking for the lowest price they can possibly obtain, while the salesperson will ask for a higher price than the minimum they will accept up to the point when he fears they will walk away. Buyers will continue to negotiate as long as they believe the seller still might come down on their price.

Nobel Prize–winning economist John F. Nash (portrayed in the Academy Award-winning film *A Beautiful Mind*) clarified the distinction between cooperative and uncooperative games. In an uncooperative game (unlike cooperative games), there are strategies that are used by players in such a way that neither player can benefit by changing the strategy if the strategies of the other players remain unchanged. Nash introduced the concept of "bargaining negotiation," or agreement between two players to produce an outcome, with both participants believing they will benefit from the ultimate outcome.

See also ZERO-SUM GAME.

Further reading

Roth, Alvin E. "Game Theory as a Tool for Market Design." Available online. URL: kuznets.fas.harvard. edu/~aroth/design.pdf.

—Karen M. Cimino

gap analysis

Gap analysis is a managerial tool used to compare a company's performance or customer expectations with current outcomes. It is used both in product MANAGEMENT and SERVICES marketing to evaluate and improve business performance.

In product management, gap analysis can be used to measure current PRODUCT quality against desired standards. Any difference between product quality and desired standards reveals a gap. Managers sometimes create product specifications based on PRODUCTION technology or regulatory standards, but they do not create product specifications consistent with their understanding of consumer's expectations. Changing product quality can take time and be costly, but it can also make the difference between success and failure.

Marketers use service gap analysis to measure the difference between expectations and perceived outcomes. One potential gap is the difference between management perceptions of consumer expectations and actual consumer expectations. Many marketers are surprised when consumers occasionally express their expectations (usually an expression of their disappointment with the service received).

A second potential gap can be the difference between managers' perceptions of consumer expectations and the service quality specifications that managers create. Service quality includes timeliness, accuracy, friendliness, and attentiveness. Managers who emphasize fast service may miss consumers' need for friendliness or attentiveness. United Parcel Service (UPS), known for its hustling employees, learned customers would like to talk longer with UPS delivery people. The company adjusted expected deliveries per hour to allow delivery people to take time to communicate with customers.

A third potential gap can exist between service quality standards set by management and the actual service quality delivered. Just because managers set a standard does not mean it will be attained or maintained. Another service quality gap can exist between what is provided and what is promised. Many marketing people have learned from customers about assurances made by senior managers. Communications gaps are a common problem between all levels of organizations.

An additional service quality gap can exist between received service and expected service. Consumers develop expectations regarding service quality through experience and observation. Miscommunication and misinterpretation can lead to a gap between expectations and perceived service received.

Gap analysis can help define problems. It often involves creating rating scales used to survey both internal staff members and external constituents. Differences in the average ratings between customers and companies signal a potential gap for further evaluation. Reducing and eliminating gaps improves CUSTOMER RELATIONS/SATISFACTION, leading to repeat purchases and stronger marketing relationships.

See also RELATIONSHIP MARKETING.

Further reading

Boone, Louis E., and David L. Kurtz. *Contemporary Marketing*. 14th ed. Fort Worth: South-Western, 2009.

garnishment

Garnishment is a legal process used by creditors to receive payment for a debt. Generally, the garnishment process begins when an individual stops paying a creditor, and, in response, the creditor goes to court and wins a case against the debtor. In court, the creditor then gets a judgment against the debtor, which is a court order detailing how much is owed, and the interest rate that can be charged on the unpaid amount. Garnishment can be an effective tool for the creditor, but it can have a devastating impact on debtors.

Garnishment laws and restrictions vary from state to state and are based on what is being garnished, namely, wages or real property. Sometimes, creditors get an additional court order to make debtors appear at supplemental proceedings, where they are required to answer detailed questions about their assets, wages, bank accounts, and other property. With this information, the creditor can get an order from the court to garnish the debtor's property. As reported by bankruptcy.lawyers.com, before a creditor can actually take anything—either property or wages—the creditor must give notice of the garnishment. The notice must include:

- A clear statement that garnishment has occurred
- A description of the primary "exemptions" from garnishment, that is, what the creditor can't take
- A description of the procedures that the debtor can follow to contest the garnishment.

After providing notice, the creditor can take the judgment and garnishment order to the local sheriff and ask that the judgment be "levied" or "applied." Generally, a creditor won't be interested in garnishment if the debtor does not have anything that can be taken to pay the judgment.

Vehicle garnishment can lead to repossession in some circumstances. But in many states, creditors aren't allowed to repossess and sell vehicles if the equity in the vehicle (the amount it is worth minus what is owed on it) is under a certain amount (around $2,000 or a little more in most states). News stories often describe automobile "bounty hunters" surreptitiously towing away cars in the middle of the night. In many cases, a vehicle dealer takes a lien on the vehicle to secure payment. In these cases, the lien laws, rather than garnishment laws, control the creditor-dealer's rights against you and the vehicle.

Wage garnishment is an order to an employer, usually served by a police officer, directing the employer to take out and remit to the creditor a certain amount from each paycheck, until the debt is paid off. Usually, a creditor will opt for wage garnishment if the debtor has steady work at more than the federal minimum wage. Under federal law, the creditor can take only a specified amount based upon a percentage of the debtor's "disposable earnings," for most working people, their

net paycheck. SOCIAL SECURITY benefits, retirement plan benefits, and public assistance benefits cannot be garnished, but creditors can garnish accounts where these funds are mixed with other sources of income.

Unless the judgment is for child or spousal support, a debtor's income cannot be garnished if it comes from workers' compensation awards or from unemployment or disability benefits.

Under the CONSUMER CREDIT PROTECTION ACT (CCPA), employers cannot fire a worker because of the inconvenience of having to cooperate with a garnishment for one debt. An employer who violates the law can be punished with fines of up to $1,000 and imprisonment for up to one year. But an employee can be fired for having more than one wage garnishment.

Many sources of funds otherwise exempt from garnishment can be garnished to pay child or spousal support, including veterans' benefits, military retirement, most workers' compensation benefits, and Social Security old age, survivors' and disability benefits. Also, the percentage of disposable income that can be garnished is higher for support than it is for other types of debt.

Through the automatic stay process, filing for bankruptcy can stop a garnishment. A stay is a court order directing creditors not to proceed with any further actions against the debtor. Actions taken in violation of the stay are void or invalid. As stated earlier, garnishment laws vary from state to state. During the 2008–09 recession, an Associated Press article reported "drastically lower rates" of personal bankruptcy filings in the five states (North Carolina, Pennsylvania, South Carolina, Florida, and Texas) that prohibit or limit wage garnishments.

Further reading

Bennett, Sherrie. "Garnishment," Bankruptcy.lawyers.com. Available online. URL: bankruptcy.lawyers.com/consumer-bankruptcy/Garnishment.html. Accessed on July 6, 2009; "Wage Garnishment," U.S. Department of Labor Web site. Available online. URL: www.dol.gov/compliance/guide/garnish.htm. Accessed on July 6, 2009; Baker, Mike. "Bankruptcies Low in States That Don't Seize Wages," Yahoo News, 6 July 2009.

Available online. URL: news.yahoo.com/s/ap/20090706/ ap_on_bi_ge/us_stress_map_bankruptcy. Accessed on July 6, 2009.

gender gap index

The gender gap index is an index of the gap or disparity between men and women within countries based on differences in economic and educational opportunity, political participation, and health-related measures. Sponsored since 2005, by the World Economic Forum, a major economic discussion group that meets annually in Davos, Switzerland, the index provides an overall ranking of the gap in gender equality. If women had equal access and opportunity, a country's ranking would be 100. In 2009, Iceland had the highest index, 82.8, while three other Nordic countries, Finland, Norway, and Sweden, followed closely behind.

As stated on the World Economic Forum Web site:

> The Global Gender Gap Index scores can be interpreted as the percentage of the gap between women and men that has been closed. The report's Index assesses countries on how well they are dividing their resources and opportunities among their male and female populations, regardless of the overall levels of these resources and opportunities. . . . Out of the 128 countries covered in both 2007 and 2008, more than two-thirds have posted gains in overall index scores, indicating that the world in general has made progress towards equality between men and women. Additionally, taking averages across the sub-indexes for these 128 countries reveals that, globally, progress has been made on narrowing the gaps in educational attainment, political empowerment and economic participation, while the gap in health has widened.

Between 2008 and 2009, South Africa and Lesotho had the largest gains in closing their gender gaps to enter the top 10, at sixth and 10th position, respectively. "The data reveals that South Africa in particular made significant improvements in female labor force participation. Gains

for women in parliament and women ministers in the new government also helped close the gender gap in the country."

The "Global Gender Gap Report" is based on methodology introduced in 2006 and includes detailed profiles that provide insight into the economic, legal, and social aspects of the gender gap in each country using four parameters:

- Economic participation and opportunity—outcomes on salaries, participation levels, and access to high-skilled employment
- Educational attainment—outcomes on access to basic and higher level education
- Political empowerment—outcomes on representation in decision-making structures
- Health and survival—outcomes on life expectancy and sex ratio

Coauthor Ricardo Hausman stated: "The Index assesses countries on how well they are dividing their resources and opportunities among their male and female populations, regardless of the overall levels of these resources and opportunities. Thus, the Index does not penalize those countries that have low levels of education overall, for example, but rather those where the distribution of education is uneven between women and men."

American coauthor Laura Tyson stated: "The Report also provides some evidence on the link between the gender gap and the economic performance of countries. Our work shows a strong correlation between competitiveness and the gender gap scores. While this does not imply causality, the possible theoretical underpinnings of this link are clear: countries that do not fully capitalize effectively on one-half of their human resources run the risk of undermining their competitive potential. We hope to highlight the economic incentive behind empowering women, in addition to promoting equality as a basic human right."

Further reading

Global Gender Gap Report 2009. Available online. URL: www.weforum.org/en/Communities/Women%20 Leaders%20and%20Gender%20Parity/GenderGap Network/index.htm. Accessed on May 5, 2010.

General Accounting Office

The General Accounting Office (GAO) investigates problems and issues for members of Congress. The GAO examines the use of public funds, evaluates federal programs and activities, and provides analyses, options, recommendations, and other assistance to Congress. Where the Office of Management Budget (OMB) provides analytical support to the executive branch of government, the GAO works for the legislative branch of government. The GAO is sometimes called the "congressional watchdog," investigating how the federal government spends taxpayer dollars. GAO reports are often used by members of Congress as a basis for drafting legislation, supporting or opposing legislation, and evaluating the economic impact of proposed policies.

Companies doing business with the federal government monitor and attempt to influence GAO reports. Critical GAO reports can hinder business-favorable legislation or result in termination of current government contracts with a business.

Since the U.S. Senate and House of Representatives contain members from both major political parties, the GAO faces challenges providing unbiased analyses. The GAO

- reports how well government policies and programs are meeting their objectives
- audits agency operations to determine whether federal funds are being spent efficiently, effectively and appropriately
- investigates allegations of illegal and improper activities
- issues legal decisions and opinions
- performs analyses and outlines options for congressional consideration

The GAO releases over 1,000 documents annually, often in the form of "blue book" reports, in response to requests for analysis of current issues being debated by Congress.

The GAO was created in 1921 in response to financial management problems after World War I. The Budget and Accounting Act transferred AUDITING responsibilities, accounting, and claims from the Treasury Department to the new agency. The agency grew rapidly during the New Deal era of President Franklin Roosevelt and the expanded government spending associated with World War II.

The GAO is directed by the Comptroller General, appointed for a 15-year term to insure the independence of the GAO from political pressures.

Further reading

General Accounting Office Web site. Available online. URL: www.gao.gov.

General Agreement on Tariffs and Trade   See WORLD TRADE ORGANIZATION.

generally accepted accounting principles

A double-entry system of accounting (now called FINANCIAL ACCOUNTING) was first described in 1494 by a Franciscan monk, Fra Luca Pacioli, living in the Tuscany region of Italy. As a result of his extensive treatment of the double-entry system, then known also as the Venetian system, Pacioli is regarded as the father of accounting. Born in 1445, he was one of the greatest minds of the Renaissance, distinguishing himself as a mathematician, college professor, and author. The accounting process Pacioli described is called a double-entry system because it takes two entries to record a transaction.

Drawing upon the nature of a transaction, an exchange where equal-valued RESOURCES are simultaneously received and given up, the accounting system uses one entry to record the resource received in a transaction and another entry to record the resource given in exchange. The first entry of the double entry is known as the debit, and the dollar figure of the first entry is placed in the left column of the journal. (Debit comes from the Latin word *debere* meaning "left" and is abbreviated *dr.*) The following entry is the credit, and the dollar figure of this entry is placed in the right column of the journal. (Credit comes from the Latin word *credere* meaning "right" and is abbreviated *cr.*) Because the double entry represents a transaction, an exchange of equal-valued resources, the amount of the debit entry is equal to the amount of the credit entry, and at any given time in the accounting cycle, the sum of all the debit entries must equal the sum of all the credit entries.

For centuries, accounting existed as an oral tradition passed from one generation to the next. The rules, methods, and formats for accounting became widely known and generally accepted over time by accounting practitioners. It was not until the 20th century that accounting rules were made more formal, rather than accepted as an oral tradition. Largely due to the efforts of the FINANCIAL ACCOUNTING STANDARDS BOARD (FASB) and the AMERICAN INSTITUTE OF CERTIFIED PUBLIC ACCOUNTANTS (AICPA), perhaps the two most important organizations governing the practice of financial accounting today, the rules for the practice of accounting are now codified and are regarded as "generally accepted accounting principles" (GAAP).

The SECURITIES AND EXCHANGE COMMISSION (SEC) requires that all published FINANCIAL STATEMENTS be constructed in accordance with GAAP. The INTERNAL REVENUE SERVICE (IRS) requires that the accounting for businesses follow GAAP. Because of the long oral tradition, the codification of GAAP, the various organizations concerned with the practice of financial accounting, and its backing from the SEC and IRS, financial (double-entry) accounting has become the standard among today's businesses and organizations.

See also DEBIT, CREDIT.

General Services Administration

The General Services Administration (GSA) is a major purchasing agent for the federal government. The GSA was created in 1949 through the consolidation of four small agencies involved in PURCHASING services, space, and PRODUCTS to support the activities of federal employees. After World War II the GSA directed disposal of war-surplus materials and managed emergency preparedness and stockpiling of strategic materials. Emergency-preparedness functions were later transferred to the Federal Emergency Management Agency (FEMA), and stockpiling functions were transferred to the Department of Defense.

Rather than have each of thousands of federal offices procure rental space, office equipment and supplies, and business services, the GSA oversees and coordinates these actions with the goal of obtaining the best value for federal expenditures.

The GSA also provides travel and transportation services, manages the federal motor vehicle fleet, oversees telecommunication centers and federal child-care centers, preserves historic buildings, manages a fine-arts program, and develops, advocates, and evaluates government-wide SERVICES. The GSA employs 12,000 people, has an annual budget of $26 billion, and directs $500 billion in federal spending. Businesses wishing to sell to the U.S. government must learn GSA's methods of purchasing, including paperwork and bidding procedures.

Further reading

General Services Administration Web site. Available online. URL: www.gsa.gov.

Giffen goods

A Giffen good is a product or service for which DEMAND increases as price increases. These goods defy the law of demand, which states that an inverse relationship exists between price and quantity demanded, that is, as price rises quantity demanded decreases and as price decreases, quantity demanded increases, CETERIS PARIBUS, assuming nothing other than the price of the good has changed.

The Giffen good is named after 19th-century British economist Sir Robert Giffen (1837–1910). Alfred Marshall in his *Principles of Economics* (1895) wrote:

> As Mr. Giffen has pointed out, a rise in the price of bread makes so large a drain on the resources of the poorer labouring families and raises so much the marginal utility of money to them, that they are forced to curtail their consumption of meat and the more expensive farinaceous foods: and bread being still the cheapest food which they can get and will take, they consume more, and not less of it.

The distinguishing qualities of Giffen goods include:

- There are few close substitutes
- They are economically inferior goods (demand increases as incomes decrease)
- Their purchase represents a significant part of consumers' incomes.

Using Alfred Marshall's example, logically, if substitutes existed, then as the price of bread increased consumers would purchase less of it and buy other sources of carbohydrates and starch. Bread, like potatoes, is a classic example of economically inferior goods; demand increases as income decreases and vice versa. With few alternatives, lower income consumers will buy more bread as the price of other food products and bread increases. As economists state, the income effect is stronger than the substitution effect. All Giffen goods are economically inferior goods but not all economically inferior goods are Giffen goods. The Giffen effect, or paradox, requires that other conditions to be present.

Status and prestige products are sometimes labeled Giffen goods because demand for them may decrease as price declines, the result of declining image and greater affordability to lower income consumers. These goods are called VEBLEN GOODS, named after economist Thorstein Veblen. The result is similar to the Giffen paradox but the cause is different, changes in consumers' tastes and preferences. Marketers of prestige products like Tiffany jewelry, Maserati sports cars, and first growth Bordeaux wines will often limit the supply of their products in order to maintain higher prices and the image of exclusivity.

Further reading

Marshall, Alfred. *Principles of Economics.* London: MacMillan, 1895.

Gini ratio

A Gini ratio is a measure of the distribution of INCOME in an economy. A Gini ratio (also called Gini coefficient) can range between 0 and 1. Zero means all families have the same income; 1 means one family has all of the income. Gini ratios are used in conjunction with LORENZ CURVES. Lorenz curves plot the cumulative income by quintiles (one-fifths) of the population in an economy. If each fifth of the population had 20 percent of the income, the Lorenz curve would be a 45-degree line and the Gini ratio would be 0.

Since no economy has an equal distribution of income, the Lorenz curve, with quintiles on the horizontal axis and cumulative percent of income on the vertical axis, is a bow-shaped line beneath the 45-degree line. The Gini ratio measures the gap between the Lorenz curve and the 45-degree line. The higher the Gini ratio, the greater the disparity of income in an economy. Since the area between the 45-degree line and the Lorenz curve is an irregular-shaped half ellipse, calculating the area requires a complex mathematical formula. See "Gini says: measuring income inequality" in the *Left Business Observer* (October 18, 1993) for details.

The Census Bureau calculates the Gini ratio for the U.S. economy. As the table below shows, income inequality decreased for approximately two decades after World War II, but beginning in the 1960s it has steadily increased. Economists suggest stagnant and declining minimum wages (in real terms) and increased executive compensation explain much of the changing distribution of income. Government Gini ratios are calculated using cash income and therefore do not take into account changes in tax laws and noncash benefits such as food stamps, AID TO FAMILIES WITH DEPENDENT CHILDREN, and employer-provided noncash benefits. Opponents of government WELFARE programs suggest that when noncash benefits are included in income-distribution statistics, lower income groups are receiving an increased share of national income.

U.S. GINI RATIOS FOR 1967 TO 2007

Year	Ratio	Year	Ratio	Year	Ratio
2007	0.463	1993	0.454	1979	0.404
2006	0.470	1992	0.434	1978	0.402
2005	0.469	1991	0.428	1977	0.402
2004	0.466	1990	0.428	1976	0.398
2003	0.464	1989	0.431	1975	0.397
2002	0.462	1988	0.427	1974	0.395
2001	0.466	1987	0.426	1973	0.397
2000	0.460	1986	0.425	1972	0.401
1999	0.457	1985	0.419	1971	0.396
1998	0.456	1984	0.415	1970	0.394
1997	0.459	1983	0.414	1969	0.391
1996	0.455	1982	0.412	1968	0.388
1995	0.450	1981	0.406	1967	0.399
1994	0.456	1980	0.403		

Further reading

U.S. Census Bureau Web site. Available online. URL: www.census.gov; "Gini Says: Measuring Income Inequality." *Left Business Observer,* 18 October 1993.

Ginnie Mae   See GOVERNMENT NATIONAL MORTGAGE ASSOCIATION.

glass ceiling

While there are many definitions of the term *glass ceiling,* the DEPARTMENT OF LABOR has concluded that it is most clearly defined as those artificial barriers based on attitudinal or organizational bias that prevent qualified individuals from advancing upward in their organization into MANAGEMENT-level positions. The phrase was first used in a 1986 *Wall Street Journal* article describing the invisible barriers women confront as they attempt to be promoted up to the top corporate hierarchy.

As part of the 1991 CIVIL RIGHTS ACT, the Department of Labor was directed to establish the Federal Glass Ceiling Commission, which issued its report in 1995. The commission found that the glass ceiling was real, and in many instances it existed lower in business organizations than expected. Evan Kemp, the chairman of the EQUAL EMPLOYMENT OPPORTUNITY COMMISSION (EEOC) stated, "I believe the glass ceiling is real, that it destroys morale, and that though we have made some progress, we are a long way from shattering it." In the report John W. Snow, President and CEO of CSX Corporation is quoted as saying, "It's clear that progress is possible when top management addresses the importance of women and minorities in a straightforward manner with real commitment to finding answers . . ."

The basic finding of the commission was: "Qualified minorities and women are all too often on the outside looking into the executive suite." Lynn Martin, secretary of labor in the George H. W. Bush administration, summarized the glass ceiling's impact: "The glass ceiling, where it exists, hinders not only individuals but society as a whole. It effectively cuts our pool of potential corporate leaders by eliminating over one-half of our population. It deprives our economy of new leaders, new sources of creativity the 'would be' pioneers of the business world."

The Glass Ceiling Commission pilot project randomly selected nine Fortune 500 establishments for review reviews that were conducted by senior officials from the national and regional offices of the Department of labor. They found that their conclusions generally applied to all nine companies, despite the vast differences that existed among them in terms of organizational structure, CORPORATE CULTURE, and business sector and personnel policies.

- If there was not a glass ceiling, there certainly was point beyond which minorities and women had not advanced in some companies.
- Minorities had plateaued at lower-levels of the workforce than women had.
- Monitoring for equal access and opportunity, especially as managers move up the corporate ladder to senior management levels where important decisions were made, was almost never considered a corporate responsibility or part of the planning for developmental programs and policies.
- Appraisal and total compensation systems that determined salary, bonuses, incentives, and perquisites for employees were not monitored.
- Placement patterns were consistent with research data.
- There was a general lack of adequate records.

Among the attitudinal and organizational barriers identified were

- recruitment practices involving reliance on word-of-mouth and employee-referral networking as well as the use of executive search-and-referral firms in which affirmative action/EEO requirements were not made known
- a failure to make available to minorities and women such traditional precursors to advancement as developmental practices and credential-building experiences, including advanced education, as well as career-enhancing assignments such as to corporate committees and task forces and special projects

- the failure of senior-level executives and corporate decision-makers to be accountable for Equal Employment Opportunity responsibilities

To help support the removal of glass ceilings, the Department of Labor annually honors outstanding federal contractors and contractor associations that have demonstrated innovative efforts to increase EMPLOYMENT opportunities for minorities, women, individuals with disabilities, and veterans. The OFCCP Exemplary Voluntary Efforts (EVE) Awards are presented for highly successful good-faith efforts and action programs.

The United States is not the only country facing the problem of glass ceilings. The Australian Human Rights & Equal Opportunity Commission studied "Glass Ceilings and Sticky Floors" in the finance sector. They found that "women were concentrated in part-time, lower-grade work with limited opportunities for training and advancement." The commission recommended the introduction of career and gender-awareness programs, development plans for managerial and nonmanagerial women employees, appropriate training, and examination of lateral and vertical career paths.

Further reading
Australian Human Rights & Equal Opportunity Commission Web site. Available online. URL: www.human rights.gov.au; Lynn Martin. "A Report on the Glass Ceiling Initiative." Available online. URL: www.mith2. umd.edu/WomensStudies/GenderIssues/GlassCeiling/LaborDeptInfo/glass-ceiling-initiative.

globalization
Globalization is an economic and cultural process in which countries are increasingly integrated through economic and political connections. Globalization began to grow after World War II, when falling TARIFFS and more efficient means of air travel promoted both an expansion and a reliance on world trade. In the immediate postwar era, TRADE BARRIERS were eased through international agreements, such as the General Agreement on Tariffs and Trade (GATT, 1947), as part of an effort by industrialized nations to reinvigorate the world economy. More recently, technological advances have linked financial markets, and today financial transactions can occur in an instant from across the world. As global markets have been established and become profitable, new open markets continue to emerge in countries that have formerly been closed and highly regulated.

Globalization has had many effects on the world economy. There has been an increase in the number of regional trade agreements, such as the EUROPEAN UNION (EU), the NORTH AMERICAN FREE TRADE AGREEMENT (NAFTA), and the Asia-Pacific Economic Cooperation (APEC). These agreements serve to enhance international economic opportunities for their member nations by easing economic barriers to international trade and business operations. In 1994 the WORLD TRADE ORGANIZATION (WTO) was created out of GATT negotiations. With over 130 participating countries, the WTO is currently the most prominent international organization responsible for setting and enforcing global-trade rules intended to lower trade barriers, institute international product standards, and provide a forum to settle international trade disputes.

With globalization there has been an increase in foreign direct investment by MULTINATIONAL CORPORATIONS, large companies with operations in more than one country. These CORPORATIONS take advantage of economic opportunities by utilizing variations in local conditions, such as lower wages, to promote a competitive advantage in the PRODUCTION, distribution, and marketing of their PRODUCTS. Some labor organizations have feared that globalization will allow corporations to exploit unequal standards of workers' rights in less developed countries and EMERGING MARKETS. For example, if workers were to strike in the United Kingdom or France, employers could move their operations to countries where workers have lower expectations. This has caused some labor organizations to be resistant to globalization forces.

Concerns over the negative impact of globalization have increased in the last decade. A 1999 WTO Conference in Seattle, Washington, was met with thousands of protesters who claimed that the WTO should leverage trade sanctions against nations with poor labor or environmental practices. In 2001 similar protests were made at the meeting of the Group of Eight industrialized nations in Genoa, Italy, where over 100,000 anti-globalization demonstrators congregated and one was killed in clashes with police. On the other hand, many developing countries have resisted the demonstrators' efforts, claiming that eased trade restrictions bring much-needed FOREIGN INVESTMENT to poorer countries, and that strict environmental and labor regulations would be prohibitively expensive for less-developed countries.

CONSUMER BEHAVIOR has also been influenced by globalization. The growth of the mass media and an increase in international travel has heightened cultural exchanges, which in many cases has made it easier for companies to operate and train personnel abroad. Many multinational corporations have developed brand awareness with consumers worldwide; for example, McDonald's, Coca-Cola, Fosters Lager, and Marks and Spencer have products that are sold in numerous countries. The INTERNET has also permitted consumers to purchase products from other countries online.

As the world becomes smaller through international coalitions, electronic exchanges from across the globe in a matter of seconds, the development of E-COMMERCE and E-BUSINESS, the proliferation of mass media, and the development of worldwide consumer tastes, globalization will continue to shape the world economy and culture in the years to come.

—Margaret C. Dunlap

global brand

A global brand is a symbolic representation of a company or subsidiary recognized on an international scale. Global branding creates an immediate image for the organization that universally conveys the values, services, and products offered. Global branding is increasingly important as international commercial trade networks expand and interrelate. Because global branding crosses many cultural channels, how to convey a steady and accurate image can be problematic.

In general, branding consists of creating a set of symbols, images, sayings, and logos that link up to the services and products offered. Simple image branding tools create a strong foundation for cross-cultural market communication. The Nike "Swoosh" symbol on athletic apparel strives to create a psychological link in the customer between athleticism and its products; when their logo is displayed on a backpack, for instance, it would be assumed to be athletic-related and perhaps therefore desirable. The logo of the Apple Corporation symbolizes user-friendly computers and consumer electronics; the Apple logo, independent of any words or additional images, would still advertise the firm's products. Sayings or "jingles" can also become branding tools, although their application on an international scale is more difficult. Corporate sayings such as "have it your way" from Burger King or "maybe she's born with it" from Maybelline have stronger effects within a set cultural/linguistic framework than outside of that framework. Because of this limitation, often global branding requires a more visual-figurative product-image replacement.

Global branding must take into account cultural differences in perception and value. Symbols provide the advantage of not having to translate the message from one language to another. Language-based brands create the potential for mistranslation. When Novartis Corporation was created through the merger of Ciba-Geigy and Sandoz, the company had its new name evaluated in over 100 languages to make sure it did not have a negative interpretation or connotation. A classic language-based brand is Coca-Cola. To convey value to Chinese consumers, the company linked its name to the Chinese words for "makes mouth happy." The nonprofit Red Cross organization's brand seeks to establish a standard of medical attention across borders in conflict yet its symbol is patently offensive to some Muslims and an alternative symbol, the Red Crescent, replaces it in these regions. Similarly, a swastika has extremely negative meaning in Western societies but symbolizes the four elements in Hindu cultures.

While global branding provides the opportunity for unified MARKETING COMMUNICATIONS and reduced costs, many firms find brand adaption, local brands, and multiple brands are more effective for international marketing and reduce the potential problems associated with cultural and language differences.

Further reading

Chandha, R., and P. Husband. *The Cult of the Luxury Brand.* London: Nicholas Brealey International, 2006; Gregory, J. R. *Branding Across Borders.* Chicago: McGraw-Hill, 2002; Lee, K., and S. Carter. *Global Marketing Management.* Oxford: Oxford University Press, 2005; Milberg, S., and F. Sinn. "Vulnerability of Global Brands to Negative Feedback Effects." *Journal of Business Research* 61, no. 6 (2007): 684–690; Yang, J. *Eastern Standard Time: A Guide to Asian Influence on American Culture from Astro Boy to Zen Buddhism.* Boston: Mariner, 1997.

—Andrew Blatchford

global shares

Global shares are COMMON STOCK shares that trade in multiple currencies around the world. Introduced in 1998 with the merger of DaimlerChrysler, global shares are an alternative to AMERICAN DEPOSITORY RECEIPTS (ADRs), which are indirect holdings of stock in a foreign company. With ADRs, a U.S. custodial bank holds the shares of stock of the foreign company and issues receipts to stock purchasers. Because ADRs are indirect holdings, they must be converted back to local shares if sold outside the United States. Also, holders of ADRs do not always have the same rights, including shareholder resolutions and sometimes voting privileges.

The market for creating ADRs is dominated by J. P. Morgan, Citibank, Deutsche Bank, and Bank of New York. In 1998 Bank of New York, along with Deutsche Bank, created global shares as an alternative to ADRs. Global shares were seen as part of the process linking STOCK MARKETS around the world and a way for the two banks to gain a greater share of the lucrative foreign stock-trading market.

Both ADRs and global shares offer the benefits of allowing companies to issue dollar-denominated stock to its U.S. employees, opportunities to broaden their investor base, and the use of proceeds to acquire companies in the United States. Most companies considering both alternatives have found global shares more expensive to initiate and requiring more coordination with back-office systems and regulatory agencies.

Further reading

Karmin, Craig. "What in the World? Global Shares May Leave Obscurity," *Wall Street Journal,* 20 August 2001, p. C1.

goal setting

In business, goal setting—the establishment of personal or professional objectives—can be an individual or organizational activity. Managers often use goal setting as a means of motivating employees. Many MANAGEMENT writers provide guidelines for people or groups attempting to set goals.

Selling magazine recommends not setting goals that are easily attained, suggesting that these types of goals do not inspire people. Instead they suggest:

- "Create a big-picture goal"—some long-term important objective.
- "Break it down into basics"—divide the overall goal into smaller more manageable tasks.
- "Be unreasonable"—goals should be appropriate but should also take effort to achieve.

Tom Ritchey, author of *I'm Stuck, You're Stuck: Break Through to Better Work Relationships and Results by Discovering Your DiSC Behavioral Style,* suggests that managers need to understand first what drives their own behavior and then what motivates their employees. Ritchey states there are four behavioral styles: dominance, influence, supportiveness, and conscientiousness.

For dominance-style employees, people who see problems and attempt to solve them, Ritchey suggests goal setting should include such questions as "What do you think needs to be done?" and "What can you do to help the company?" Dominance-style employees prefer autonomy and need only clearly stated rules and expectations to work effectively.

Influence-style employees take more time, as they want to discuss everything that is going on in the company and are more emotional than dominance-style workers. Influence-style employees are likely to be better at goals associated with working with others and generating enthusiasm for the objectives.

Supportiveness-style workers prefer to make lists and check off accomplishments; these workers need more guidance in goal-setting. Finally, conscientiousness-style employees tend to be careful and more reserved, needing specific information related to goals and time in order to achieve them.

Most people think of goal setting as having a New Year's resolution. Whether setting personal or business goals, *Investor's Business Daily* writer Linda Stockman-Vines suggests reviewing past goal-setting using statements like "I learned (fill in the blank) this past year." She then suggests asking oneself, "What risks am I running by going along just as I have been?" Experts in HUMAN RESOURCES state that working Americans will have, on average, seven major career changes in their professional life. Without setting goals and striving for them, businesspeople can leave themselves unprepared for change. Stockman-Vines also suggests going through lists of goals and eliminating any "shoulds," which are obligations, not goals.

Like almost every other aspect of business, there are a variety of Web sites that attempt to provide assistance with goal setting. *Business Week* writer Francesca Di Meglio reviewed several sites and came away unimpressed, noting, "All these sites have spiritual jive in common, instructing visitors to do things like overcome their fears and move metaphorical mountains. Of course, no Web site can move the mountains for you. This may not be a shock. But it's still worth saying."

See also PROBLEM SOLVING.

Further reading
Di Meglio, Francesca. "This Self-Help Site Needs Help." *Business Week Online.* Available online. URL: www.businessweek.com. Accessed on January 2, 2002; "Set 'Unreasonable' Goals." *Selling* (January 2002); p. 2; Stockman-Vines, Linda. "Decide on Your Dreams: Help

Workers Set Goals." *Investor's Business Daily,* 22 January 2002, p. 6. Ritchey, Tom. *I'm Stuck, You're Stuck: Break Through to Better Work Relationships and Results by Discovering Your DiSC Behavioral Style.* San Francisco: Berrett-Koehler, 2002.

gold standard
A gold standard is a monetary system under which a country defines its currency as convertible either to a fixed quantity of gold or to a fixed amount of the country's currency. For example, for decades the United States used a fixed exchange rate of $20.67 per ounce of gold; one U.S. dollar was exchangeable for 1.354 grams of gold. Guaranteeing the convertibility of a country's paper currency into gold was a way for a government to maintain consumers' confidence in the currency's value. Countries that maintained a constant EXCHANGE RATE were said to be on a gold standard.

Historically, gold has been the most common form of MONEY. To be used as money, a commodity needs to be scarce, divisible, and nonperishable. Because gold meets these requirements, for centuries it has been widely accepted as money. In the prerevolutionary period of U.S. history, gold and silver coins from many European countries circulated as money in the colonies. Sometime in the Middle Ages, goldsmiths effectively became bankers, creating an undefined exchange rate for gold versus paper currency. Because they had vaults, goldsmiths were paid by merchants to hold their gold for safekeeping. When traveling on business, merchants faced the risk of robbery and found it easier and safer to carry certificates issued by the goldsmith that were exchangeable for gold. Goldsmiths quickly figured out they could issue more certificates than they had gold in their vault and charge interest on the loan. Merchants used the added money to buy more products and increase their profits. Goldsmiths, under no regulatory authority, issued as many certificates as they wanted, fearing only the possibility of too many merchants showing up at the same time demanding gold in exchange for the certificates.

The process, known today as fractional reserve banking, continued on a local and regional basis (wherever the goldsmith's certificates were accepted as money) until the 16th and 17th centuries when governments took over control of defining and printing paper money. Often governments issued more paper money whenever they had a pressing need such a war, an ostentatious display of wealth, or to pay off creditors and citizenry. This led to frequent rounds of hyperinflation and debasing of the currency. In one infamous example, a Scotsman, John Law, proposed the creation of a new paper currency to increase the availability of credit, thereby expanding trade and prosperity. His idea was rejected in his homeland, as well as in Belgium, Austria, and Italy, but, in 1716, it was accepted in Paris, where he was allowed to create the Banque Générale largely capitalized with *billets d'état,* government-approved currency, that was then required to be used in making tax payments. With paper currency issued at a rate of 10 to 1 compared to the gold held by the bank, credit and trade expanded. Law then proposed an even grander idea, financing French expansion in Louisiana using state-sponsored debt and stock in his company, the Compagnie des Indes. All went well except few Frenchmen chose to move to the New World and therefore little commerce came from the colony. In 1720, when some members of the aristocracy demanded payment for their share in the company, Law resorted to printing billions of livres (the paper currency) to meet redemptions, debasing the currency, and wrecking havoc on the economy. In one instance, 16 people died of suffocation attempting to exchange their paper currency for gold.

Aware of the problems in Europe, in the Coinage Act of 1792, the United States prescribed the death penalty for any official who fraudulently debased the people's currency. While the use of paper currencies continued in Europe and elsewhere throughout the 18th and 19th centuries, the gold standard, a fixed exchange rate for gold versus a currency, was not introduced until 1821 by Great Britain, and it did not come into common use until around 1880.

Eighteenth-century Scottish historian and philosopher David Hume described the benefits of a gold standard, suggesting, when a country has a favorable balance of trade, that gold flows in to pay for the excess of exports over imports and the gold inflow expands the domestic money supply, which drives up prices and incomes. The price increases make exports more costly to foreigners, causing exports to decline, while the increased income stimulates increased imports. In addition, the increased amount of money (gold) drives down interest rates in the exporting country, causing an outflow of capital. As this process continues, the country with the initial favorable trade balance will see exports decline and imports increase, causing an outflow of gold, and thus a correction of the trade imbalance. While the trade imbalance will correct itself, countries will experience in the process fluctuations in prices, income, and interest rates.

In 2009, financial market analyst and critic James Grant described the operation of a gold standard as the following:

> A proper gold standard was a well-oiled machine. The metal actually moved and, so moving, checked what are politely known today as "imbalances." Say a certain baseball-loving North American country was running a persistent trade deficit. Under the monetary system we don't have and which only a few are yet even talking about instituting, the deficit country would remit to its creditors not pieces of easily duplicable paper but scarce gold bars. Gold was money—is, in fact, still money—and the loss would set in train a series of painful but necessary adjustments in the country that had been watching baseball instead of making things to sell. Interest rates would rise in that deficit country. Its prices would fall, its credit would be curtailed, its exports would increase and its imports decrease. At length, the deficit country would be restored to something like competitive trim. The gold would come sailing back to where it started. As it is today, dollars are piled higher and higher in the vaults of America's Asian creditors. There's no adjustment mechanism, only recriminations and the first suggestion that, from the creditors' point of view, enough is enough.

From 1880 until the beginning of World War I (1914) the United States and most European countries operated on a gold standard. Then, when warring countries financed their efforts through increases in the supply of their currency, the fixed exchange rate broke down. Between 1914 and the end of World War II (1945) no organized system for setting exchange rates existed, but the gold standard existed, at least on paper. Many countries raced to devalue their currency ahead of competitors. A global depression was helped in part by huge increases in tariffs (SMOOT-HAWLEY). Some economists argue that the gold standard contributed to the severity of the depression.

During the GREAT DEPRESSION, the Franklin D. Roosevelt administration devalued the dollar by changing the gold standard from $20.67 per ounce to $35.00 per ounce and limited convertibility to foreign governments and central banks. Previously, the FEDERAL RESERVE issued gold certificates, which entitled anyone to exchange paper currency for gold. Near the end of World War II, representatives of 44 countries met in BRETTON WOODS, New Hampshire, to create new standards for international trade. In what became known as the Bretton Woods System, the conferees agreed to a gold exchange system, in which each country fixed its currency in terms of gold. The United States continued to use a standard of $35 per ounce but, unlike the gold standard, where gold flowed in and out of a country's accounts, under the new system, a country bought and sold dollars in order to maintain a fixed exchange rate. In effect, the dollar became the world's "reserve currency," used to settle international debts and held by governments to use in foreign exchange markets.

The gold exchange system made sense at the time since the U.S. economy was strong and intact at the end of the war, and the United States, through the MARSHALL PLAN, was financing much of the postwar redevelopment throughout the world. The system worked well until the 1960s when expanding economies around the world held an excess of dollars. In 1971, President Nixon terminated the convertibility of dollars, ending the gold standard. In its place, floating currency exchange rates and relative interest rates signaled faith (or the lack thereof) in a country's currency.

Since the mid-1970s, the United States has run a "chronic" trade deficit, averaging over $700 billion annually in the last few years. Under a gold standard, this would have self-corrected without government intervention. As it is, China and Japan enable trade deficits to persist by returning some of their excess dollars into the U.S. economy through purchases of U.S. Treasury securities (called sterilization by economists), and in the process maintaining exchange rates that undervalue their currencies but are favorable to their export industries, discouraging imports from the United States and lowering interest rates in the United States. But, in recent years, finance ministers from China, Korea, and other creditor countries have also floated the idea of no longer using the dollar as the world's reserve currency. This would cause the dollar to lose value against other currencies but also decrease the value of central governments' dollar holdings.

Changes are in store to reduce global trade imbalances but what, when, and how the imbalance will be corrected is open to considerable debate. James Grant concludes:

A monetary economist from Mars could only scratch his pointy head at our 21st century monetary arrangements. What is a dollar? He might ask. No response. The Martian can't find out because the earthlings don't know. The value of a dollar is undefined. Its relationship to other currencies is similarly contingent. Some exchange rates float, others sink, still others are lashed to the dollar (whatever it is). Discouraged, the visitor zooms home.

Further reading

Grant, James. "Requiem for the Dollar," *Wall Street Journal,* 5 December 2009, p. C1; Train, John. *Famous Financial Fiascos.* New York: Random House, 1985; U.S. Treasury, History of the Treasury. Available online. URL: www.ustreas.gov/education/history/events/ Accessed on December 7, 2009.

goodwill, going concern

A going concern is an established business with a developed clientele and/or reputation. Because the business is "up and running" and has a following, such a business, if sold, will command a price higher than the BOOK VALUE of its ASSETS as listed on its BALANCE SHEET. The excess of price over the book value of the firm's assets is called goodwill, which can be recorded only when it is purchased; that is, a buyer may claim goodwill only when he or she pays for it. Goodwill is a long-term, intangible asset and is listed with the other long-term assets of the newly purchased firm.

Until 2002, goodwill was amortized over a period of time not to exceed 40 years. Under new rules, companies can leave goodwill on their balance sheets indefinitely, as long as it does not become impaired. After the Enron fiasco, many companies took a closer look at their accounting practices and incurring "impairment" charges under the new rules. Companies are now required to test the value of goodwill they carry on their FINANCIAL STATEMENTS every year and write it down if it is excessive. Discounted cash flow is often used to test the value of assets acquired.

It is not the seller of a going concern who determines the amount of goodwill associated with the firm; rather, goodwill is market-determined. If the market (selling) price is above the book value of the assets of the firm being sold, then the market views the established nature of the firm and its clientele as desirable and more profitable than a new, start-up firm. If the firm's selling price is in line with the book value of its assets, then the market does not view that any goodwill has developed over the life of that firm.

Further reading

Sender, Henry. "Flood of Firms to Take Goodwill Write-downs," *Wall Street Journal,* 24 April 2002, p. A1.

government debt

The government debt, also referred to as the federal, public, or national debt, is the cumulated sum of outstanding IOUs that a government owes its creditors. In the United States, the government debt refers to indebtedness of the federal government. (State governments have balanced-budget laws limiting or prohibiting the state government from running persistent budget deficits and creating a state-owed debt.) The federal debt, approximately $11 trillion in 2009 is the result of past budget deficits. Historically the U.S. government ran budget deficits during periods of war and RECESSIONS. Government spending and deficits rose during the GREAT DEPRESSION and World War II but declined after each period. However, beginning in the mid-1970s, the federal government began running persistent and expanding deficits, averaging $50 billion during the Jimmy Carter administration, almost $200 billion per year during the second Ronald Reagan administration, $290 billion during the last year of the George H. W. Bush administration (1992), and approaching $450 billion per year in the George W. Bush administrations (2008). Each year the U.S. Treasury Department borrows additional funds to pay for the difference between government revenue and government spending (the deficit). These additional amounts are added to the federal debt. Unlike households and individuals, the federal government rarely pays off its debt but does have to pay interest on it; otherwise creditors, primarily U.S. citizens, would no longer lend money to the government. Interest payments on the debt are included in the FEDERAL BUDGET and are generally the third- or fourth-largest category of federal government spending.

In 1998, for the first time in almost 30 years, the federal government began accumulating a budget surplus. Economic logic suggests it is normal for governments to run budget surpluses during periods of economic expansion, when government spending on programs for the poor tends to decline and revenues from progressive taxation tend to increase. If budget surpluses are used to pay off portions of the government debt, it can create what economists call a "virtuous circle." Decreased government borrowing reduces market INTEREST RATES, which in turn reduces government spending on interest payments. This increases budget surpluses, which then can be used to pay off more of the debt.

In recent years budget surpluses have been replaced by deficits. When the government increases its borrowing to fund deficit spending it can lead to higher interest rates, reducing business borrowing and investment. This is called the crowding-out effect and is a hotly debated topic among business economists.

There are several ways to consider and measure government debt. While the gross public debt was approximately $11 trillion in 2009, approximately 40 percent of it was interagency borrowing—for example, the FEDERAL RESERVE SYSTEM lending surplus funds to the U.S. Treasury and accumulating Treasury securities in return for the funds loaned to the government. Another way to look at the government debt is as a percentage of GROSS DOMESTIC PRODUCT (GDP). Like a growing business, it is normal and logical for government borrowing to increase as the economy grows. When compared to the size of the economy, the national debt peaked at the end of World War II at approximately 115 percent of GDP, declined to about 30 percent of GDP during the 1970s, and rose to about 60 percent in 1994, declined in the rest of that decade but has risen since then and was approximately 75 percent of GDP in 2009.

A third way to look at the debt is consider to whom is it owed. One common myth is that foreign governments control much of the U.S. debt, which could lead to political "blackmail" and international lenders dictating policies to the U.S. government. The overwhelming majority of the national debt (80 percent) is owed to Americans. Of the remaining 20 percent, most of it is held by foreign individuals, investors who decided the U.S. government was a good credit risk.

Another common question is: Why would people lend money to a government that already owed over $12 trillion? The U.S. economy is the largest and, by many measures, the most productive in the world. When private individuals borrow money, they are often required to provide collateral, ASSETS the lender could take title to and sell if the borrower defaulted on the loan. The federal government has the authority to tax its citizens, so in effect the collateral of the U.S. government is the assets and productive capacity of its citizens.

This leads to the question of whether the government debt is a transfer of indebtedness from present citizens to future generations. The Congressional Budget Office has developed "generational accounts" estimating the net-payment burden on future generations if the government debt is eventually paid off. This analysis showed that current retirees are, in fact, receiving benefits in excess of tax payments they have made, while younger workers' lifetime tax payments will likely exceed the present value of the benefits they will receive.

Further reading

Ruffin, Roy J., and Paul R. Gregory. *Principles of Economics*. 7th ed. Boston: Addison Wesley, 2001.

government, economic roles of

Consider for a moment, what if there was no government? Who would establish and enforce laws? How would decisions be made to allocate resources? What goods and services normally provided by government would be produced and which ones would not be produced? What would serve as MONEY? These are just some of the questions that lead to economic roles for governments.

The questions of how big should government be and how much control government officials should have in a capitalist economic system are ongoing. These questions prove contentious, but it is generally accepted that governments fulfill six basic economic roles:

- Provide public goods
- Provide objective information
- Correct for externalities
- Create and control monopolies
- Act as guardians of efficiency
- Intervene in BUSINESS CYCLES

Public goods are goods and services provided to all citizens regardless of their ability to pay for them, and whose consumption by one person does not diminish the availability of the good to others. Typical public goods include national defense, public parks, education and police and fire protection. Fire protection is an interesting example because today, and historically, it has not always been a public service. In many parts of the United States, citizens inside city limits are provided fire protection free as part of the services they receive associated with property taxes but homeowners outside the city limits are required to pay a fee for the same service. Also, historically, local fire companies sold insurance to homeowners, with numerous private firms providing protection. In the 19th century, Charleston, South Carolina, had seven private fire companies. Today, tour guides point out clay or iron insignias (fireproof, of course) on the side of houses in Charleston and tell visitors that, according to local tradition, if a fire broke out all seven companies would show up, put out the fire, and the company that had insured the house would buy beer for the other fire companies. Logically, it does not make sense (it is economically inefficient) to have seven private firms providing the same service, so eventually fire protection became a public service.

A second critical economic role of government is to provide objective information. Market efficiency depends, in part, on having knowledgeable buyers and sellers. Information allows buyers and sellers to allocate their scarce resources to the purchase or production of goods and services that will provide the greatest utility. Often travelers in foreign country do not make the best choices due to lack of information about alternatives, prices, and differences in quality. In the United States, the Federal Trade Commission enforces many regulations requiring firms to provide accurate information on packaging and truth in advertising claims made by sellers.

Externalities, also called spillover effects, are costs or benefits not included in the market price. External costs or negative externalities occur when the production or consumption of a good inflicts a cost on someone other than the producer or consumer. Pollution is the most widely cited example of a negative externality. In many parts of the United States, consumers are warned not to eat fish from the local rivers because of high levels of mercury, a highly toxic element released into the air during the production of electricity using coal. Government is often asked to force power companies to capture pollutants or change production methods to reduce or eliminate contamination of their air or water. This process is called internalizing negative externalities, driving up the price of electricity but reducing the spillover effects.

A fourth role of government is to create and control monopolies. A MONOPOLY is a market in which there is only one producer, no close substitutes, and barriers to entry. Utility companies, including electricity, cable, water, and historically telephones, are usually monopolies. In most U.S. communities a private firm was given a franchise by the local government to build and operate the electrical system. Like fire protection mentioned earlier, it does not make sense to have multiple sets of power lines installed in a community. The utility was given a monopoly but agreed to be regulated by the government. In addition to utilities, governments create monopolies when they give patent rights to individuals and firms. PATENTS are a reward for innovation, allowing recipients to profit from creating new goods or services. In recent years, a major controversy has arisen regarding patent rights associated with DNA processing and technology, with firms claiming monopoly rights while scientists and competitors complain that this limits the ability of researchers to advance medical science.

Another role of government, guardian of efficiency, initially may seem a direct opposite of the previous role, creating and controlling monopolies, however, both are designed to provide greater output and lower costs, and reduce wastes. As guardian of efficiency, governments design and refine the "rules of the game," the game being market competition. The father of modern economic theory, Adam Smith, first articulated the idea of economic efficiency in his famous "invisible hand" analogy, suggesting that both buyers and sellers are guided by an invisible hand, self-interest, to maximize their well-being. This became known as LAISSEZ-FAIRE, literally, "let be free," a doctrine whose advocates, most notably the late Nobel Prize–winning economist Milton Friedman, argued that economic efficiency is maximized when markets are allowed to act freely without government control or intervention. Critics counter that economic efficiency depends on competition while businesses attempt to maximize profits, which is often achieved through reducing competition. ANTITRUST LAWS and enforcement are a major role for government as guardian of efficiency.

The ongoing healthcare reform debate is a classic example of the role of government as guardian of efficiency. It is an accepted fact that the United States spends more on healthcare (approximately 17 percent of GDP) than any other developed country in the world. Supporters of reform argue that the current system needs greater government regulation and public alternatives. Opponents argue this will reduce competition and increase government provision of healthcare at the expense of the private sector.

Last, the sixth economic role of government is to intervene in business cycles. In the 2008 recession, the federal government dramatically stepped into the marketplace, reducing INTEREST RATES (as part of MONETARY POLICY), guaranteeing loans, and increasing government spending (FISCAL POLICY), to offset reduced private sector spending (consumption spending and business investment). Until the GREAT DEPRESSION (1929–41), intervening in business cycles was not considered a logical or appropriate role for government. In the 1930s, the economic theories of John Maynard Keynes, called Keynesian economics, argued that the role of government is to stimulate the economy in times of a recession. (He also argued government should reduce spending and/or increase taxes during periods of economic expansion.)

In recent history, Somalia, Iraq, and Afghanistan have all experienced the chaos and anarchy associated with not having a government. When the United States overthrew the government of Saddam Hussein in Iraq, it initially became the de facto government. In addition to military forces, government administrators and technical experts were sent to try to restore public goods (water and electricity), manage the monetary system (retaining the Iraqi dinar as currency), and even-

tually facilitate the creation of a new government system.

government ethics

Government ethics may be broadly defined as a code—a compilation—of normative or described behavior of what is, by tradition, regulation and statute acceptable in the performance of the duties and tasks of government. Here we do not include codes of military ethics and justice. Some jurisdictions have separate bodies to review legislative, executive, and judicial staff. Others have one such body, usually administered under the executive branch, legislature, or office of the attorney general. Tyrannical and oligarchic governments often have codes of ethics that are ignored or rewritten to suit the needs of those in power.

Codified ethics derives from early Greek civilization. Aristotle in 350 B.C. considered a hierarchy of behaviors possible for mankind. His "Nicomachean Ethics" is an ideal of personal happiness achievable by seeking good and avoiding evil by habitual actions of character and virtue. Aristotle concluded that it was possible for politics to be a noble or higher pursuit. The English word *morals* is derived from the Latin word for custom extended to include COMMON LAW and culture. As such, though in common speech interrelated, morals are more loosely and culturally considered than the Aristotelian hierarchy of human potential. Value is a concept of relative importance. Therefore, some things and some human behavior may be more highly regarded. Varying theories and constructs of ethics, morals, and value have been promulgated over the centuries. Religious concepts of morality have in secular society evolved to codes of government ethics, which are not theoretical except broadly in terms of denouncing corruption and endorsing integrity. Government ethics codes are not only statutory but also normative in that they name or define acceptable behavior. They are practical in that they are the least of what is to be done, in practice.

Public trust in the processes of a democratic form of government demands transparency and freedom from undue influence of individuals or groups. It demands freedom from intimidation and has come to expect that issues such as campaign funding, lobbying, election fraud, freedom of information, postemployment use of information confidential to government, bribery, cost containment, financial contracts and acquisition, salary supplementation, and nepotism constitute areas of concern for government ethics. The proper use of convict labor may be included. The use of government property, acceptance of gifts, and abuse of power are all potentially covered in a government code of ethics as part of an attempt to ensure that public trust is not abused by the conduct of elected or appointed government employees. Democracy seeks to avoid anarchy and safeguard the public interest. While allowing the means for individuals to prosper, government is not to be a vehicle for personal or private gain. Governments have recognized the need to have oversight of the actions of personnel and to protect those who may wish to disclose impropriety as defined in a government codes of ethics.

Decorum in oversight has evolved to allow for review boards, or commissions of ethics. Municipalities, agencies, and state and federal government departments have ethics personnel. Appeals and disputes regarding conflict in attributing compliance may go before a board of commissioners. Members of the commissions are themselves scrutinized and held to a standard of impartiality, having been first evaluated for any criminal record or potential conflict of interest in their own backgrounds. Complaints are received confidentially by publicized means of petition. Review of disclosure forms for electoral candidates and lobbying groups are a part of the ethics board, or commission, review responsibility. Through its representatives, the commission itself may investigate apparent impropriety, such as information disclosed in public records or the media. The person initiating a complaint may have exposed himself to criticism and retaliation. Mindful of the potential threat, the complainant may have security by statutory protection under so-called WHISTLE-BLOWER laws. These laws vary and are still in flux. The ethics board or commission has

a responsibility to exercise prudence and act in a timely manner both to protect the accused from false claims and petty slander and to protect the citizenry. Codes of government ethics, being statutory, mandate administrative, investigational, and police powers. They include provisions for civil and criminal prosecution usually after referral to the state office of Attorney General, and they may lead to fines and incarceration for violation.

—Richard Fitzgerald, M.D.

Government National Mortgage Association
(Ginnie Mae)

The Government National Mortgage Association, better known as Ginnie Mae, is a government-owned CORPORATION that primarily provides INSURANCE for MORTGAGES originating through Federal Housing Administration (FHA) and Veterans Administration (VA) government-loan programs.

Ginnie Mae does not make mortgage LOANS; its mission is "to support expanded affordable housing in America by providing an efficient government-guaranteed secondary market vehicle linking the CAPITAL MARKETS with Federal housing markets." Ginnie Mae helps make mortgage-backed securities more attractive to investors, thereby increasing the availability of mortgage credit.

Ginnie Mae was created in 1968 as a wholly owned corporation within the Department of Housing and Urban Development (HUD). Its purpose is to serve low-to-moderate-income homebuyers. The National Housing Act was enacted on June 27, 1934, as one of several economic recovery measures during the GREAT DEPRESSION. It provided for the establishment of a Federal Housing Administration (FHA) to be headed by a federal housing administrator. Title II of the act provided for the insurance of home-mortgage loans made by private lenders as one of the FHA's principal functions.

Title III of the act provided for the chartering of national mortgage associations by the federal housing administrator. These associations were to be private corporations regulated by the administrator, and their chief purpose was to buy and sell the mortgages to be insured by FHA under Title II. Only one association was ever formed under this authority, the National Mortgage Association of Washington, which was created on February 10, 1938, as a subsidiary of the Reconstruction Finance Corporation, a government corporation. That same year the association's name was changed to the FEDERAL NATIONAL MORTGAGE ASSOCIATION (known as Fannie Mae). By revision of Title III in 1954, Fannie Mae was converted into a mixed-ownership corporation, its preferred stock to be held by the government and its COMMON STOCK to be privately held. By amendments made in 1968, the Federal National Mortgage Association was partitioned into two separate entities, one known as the Government National Mortgage Association (Ginnie Mae), the other, Federal National Mortgage Association. Ginnie Mae remained in the government, and Fannie Mae became privately owned by retiring the government-held stock. Ginnie Mae has operated as a wholly owned government association since the 1968 amendments.

Ginnie Mae issues securities that pass through payments of principal and interest received on a pool of federally insured mortgage loans. These pools of loans are originated by commercial banks, mortgage bankers, and other mortgage-lending institutions. Ginnie Mae dictates the specifications regarding which loans can be placed into the pool; does not purchase the loans from originators; and guarantees that payments will be made on a timely basis, reducing the risk to investors. Because most mortgages are repaid before their maturity (on average, Americans change homes every seven years), holders of Ginnie Mae securities recover most of their principle investment well before the scheduled maturities of the pool of loans.

In 2002 proposed legislation would have allowed Ginnie Mae to securitize conventional mortgage loans. SECURITIZATION is the process of aggregating a pool of debt instruments and issuing securities backed by the pool of loans. The legislation would have put Ginnie Mae in competition with Fannie Mae and Freddie Mac (the FEDERAL HOME LOAN MORTGAGE CORPORATION)

in the secondary mortgage-loan market, which went bankrupt in 2008 as a result of lax lending practices.

Further reading
Government National Mortgage Association Web site. Available online. URL: www.ginniemae.gov. Fernandez, Tommy. "Just Where Does the MBA Stand on GNMA Choice?" *The American Banker* (22 March 2002).

government-sponsored enterprises

Government-sponsored enterprises (GSEs) are government-created institutions designed to close perceived gaps in the country's capital markets for agriculture and housing. The major GSEs are the FEDERAL NATIONAL MORTGAGE ASSOCIATION (Fannie Mae), the FEDERAL HOME LOAN MORTGAGE CORPORATION (Freddie Mac), the FARM CREDIT SYSTEM, STUDENT LOAN MARKETING ASSOCIATION (Sallie Mae), and the FEDERAL HOME LOAN BANK SYSTEM. Most GSEs are WHOLESALERS in financial markets, buying securities from retail lenders and packaging them for resale to investors and INVESTMENT groups. The Farm Credit System (FCS) is an exception, in that it is a retail lender to agricultural and rural customers.

The need for GSEs grew out of the GREAT DEPRESSION. Over 10,000 banks failed during a two-year period, creating a credit crisis in the country. The 1934 National Housing Act established the Federal Housing Administration (FHA). Title III of the act provided for the chartering of national mortgage associations by the federal housing administrator. These associations were to be private CORPORATIONS regulated by the administrator, and their chief purpose was to buy and sell MORTGAGES to be insured by FHA under Title II. Only one association, Fannie Mae, was ever formed under this authority.

By revision of Title III in 1954, Fannie Mae was converted into a mixed-ownership corporation, its preferred stock to be held by the government and its common stock to be privately held. By amendments made in 1968, the Federal National Mortgage Association was partitioned into two separate entities, the GOVERNMENT NATIONAL

Mortgage Association (Ginnie Mae) and the Federal National Mortgage Association (Fannie Mae). Ginnie Mae remained in the government, and Fannie Mae became privately owned by retiring the government-held stock.

Freddie Mac, known as the smaller cousin of Fannie Mae, was established in 1970 to buy conventional (not federally insured) mortgage LOANS. In 1989 Freddie Mac became a private stockholder-owned corporation, but with a mixture of oversight. Freddie Mac's BOARD OF DIRECTORS includes 13 members elected by stockholders and five appointed by the president of the United States.

The Farm Credit System (FCS) was the first GSE, established under the Federal Farm Loan Act of 1916. The FCS was funded with government CAPITAL and tax-exempt BONDS to extend long-term loans to agriculture. Over the years, FCS has expanded and contracted with changes in the agricultural industry, but it continues to provide direct lending in rural areas of the country.

The Federal Home Loan Bank (FHLB) System includes 12 regional banks that provide loans ("advances") to retail financial lenders. While commercial banks make up the majority of FHLB System members, proposed changes in federal laws would expand credit to small community banks, allowing them to utilize new categories of collateral for loans and meet lesser standards for entry into the FHLB System. Private lenders are challenging these proposed changes as well as a new program that would allow direct lending through the System.

The fifth major GSE, Sallie Mae, was established in 1972 as a federally chartered, stockholder-owned corporation. Sallie Mae controls a variety of education-lending programs, the most widely known being the Student Loan Marketing Association (SLMA), from which Sallie Mae's name was derived. In 1997 it was reorganized with SLM Holding Company, and in 2000 it was renamed USA Education, Inc. Through a variety of subsidiaries, Sallie Mae is the leading student lending, servicing, and loan-guaranteeing organization in the country. Sallie Mae became a private company in 2004.

The major issue facing all GSEs is the implied federal guarantee of their securities. This decreases the perceived market RISK, reducing the cost of capital for GSEs. With lower-cost borrowing, GSEs can earn greater gross-PROFIT margins than competing lending institutions. This problem became front-page news in 2008, when the federal government bailed out and took over Freddie Mac and Fannie Mae.

A second issue is "mission creep," the expansion of GSEs beyond their original intent. Direct lending, on-line loan applications, home-mortgage INSURANCE, and other lending-related activities that are traditionally the domain of commercial, retail financial institutions are an increasing source of conflict between GSEs and the financial market.

Further reading
"Government-sponsored Enterprises." Available online. URL: www.aba.com; "About Us." Student Loan Marketing Corporation. Available online. URL: www.salliemae.com.

Gramm-Leach-Bliley Act (GLBA)

The Gramm-Leach-Bliley Act of 1999, also known as the Gramm-Leach-Bliley Financial Services Modernization Act, changed regulations regarding the merger, ownership, and operations of FINANCIAL INSTITUTIONS. The primary result of the act was to repeal portions of the Glass-Steagall Act of 1933, which had prohibited commercial banks from engaging in other financial services, specifically insurance and investment banking.

Glass-Steagall was enacted during the Great Depression as a response to the collapse of the banking system. Between 1929 and 1933, over 10,000 commercial banks (40 percent) failed, leaving depositors with nothing. (At the time, FEDERAL DEPOSIT INSURANCE CORPORATION (FDIC) insurance did not exist.) Commercial banks are defined as financial institutions that take deposits and make loans. Investment banks provide underwriting services, assisting companies with finding capital and short-term financing, and buy and sell financial securities. At the time, politicians and regulators, aiming to reestablish a sound banking system, prohibited commercial banks from engaging in what were perceived as riskier financing activities.

By the 1990s, many larger banks, using holding companies, had found ways around the restrictions imposed by Glass-Steagall, often having separate offices and personnel inside commercial banks where consumers could make stock market purchases and sales. GLBA sanctioned expansion and merger of commercial banks with other financial institutions. At the time, the largest merger was between Travelers Insurance and Citibank, creating Citicorp.

Numerous other mergers and acquisitions followed passage of GLBA with little fanfare. The financial crises of 2008 reignited discussion of Gramm-Leach-Bliley with Nobel Prize–winning economist Paul Krugman calling former senator Phil Gramm (also a Ph.D. economist) "the father of the financial crisis." The act had exempted CREDIT DEFAULT SWAPS from regulation and facilitated expansion of financial giants, contributing to the "too big to allow to fail" dilemma faced by the TREASURY DEPARTMENT and FEDERAL RESERVE in late 2008 and early 2009. As a candidate, President Obama argued GLBA led to deregulation that helped cause the crisis by allowing "the creation of giant financial supermarkets."

The act contained several other provisions including financial privacy, pretexting protection, and ATM rules.

Further reading
Gramm-Leach-Bliley: Summary of Provisions. Available online. URL: banking.senate.gov/conf/grmleach. htm. Accessed on May 4, 2010.

graphs
In business and economics, graphs are used to convey information and ideas quickly. The most frequently used types are line graphs, bar graphs, and pie charts. Typical line graphs include time-series and cause-and-effect relationship graphs. As a matter of convention, time-series graphs put time on the horizontal axis and whatever is being compared over time on the vertical axis.

Generally cause-and-effect relationship graphs show the dependent variable on the horizontal axis and the independent variable on the vertical axis, but not always so. The independent variable is the variable whose value is not determined by the value of other variables. The dependent variable is the variable whose value is determined by the value of the independent variable. For example, a demand curve shows the relationship between price and quantity demanded in a market in a period of time, ceteris paribus (other things being equal, unchanged). The amount of a product purchased depends on its price, which is the independent variable, determined by the business offering the good. Quantity demanded is the dependent variable, changing in response to changes in price.

In the example of a DEMAND curve, there is an inverse relationship between price and quantity demanded. As price rises, the quantity demanded decreases. As price decreases, the quantity demanded increases. (The degree to which quantity demanded responds to a price change is measured using the ELASTICITY OF DEMAND concept.) A direct, cause-and-effect relationship is one where a positive change in the independent variable causes a positive change in the dependent variable, and a decrease in the independent variable causes a decrease in the dependent variable. Two typical examples of direct relationships are supply curves and CONSUMPTION functions. In response to a higher price, producers will provide greater quantity. In response to an increase in INCOME, consumers will purchase more goods and services.

Graphs are used frequently by businesspeople and economists. Some students call economics courses "graphs and laughs." Others refer to economics as the "dismal science." Marketers use graphs to quickly display relationships like the growth in sales or market share over time. Unethical businesspeople use graphs to impress or "snow" consumers. Graphs are created using data, and the quality of the data used to create a graph determines the validity of the information or concept being portrayed. In statistics there is an old saying,

"Garbage in, garbage out." The same is true in the use of graphs.

gray markets

Gray (or parallel) markets are markets where legitimate (as opposed to counterfeit) trademarked goods are distributed and sold through unauthorized channels. Many U.S. manufacturers license their technology and BRANDS to companies in other countries. If there are significant differences in the price of domestically made goods and the same PRODUCT made under license by a foreign manufacturer, it can encourage the transshipment of the foreign-made product back into the U.S. market. For example, in the 1990s when the Mexican peso fell against the dollar (see PESO CRISIS), the price of consumer products like Colgate toothpaste made in Mexico was approximately one-third the price of the same product made in the United States. Similarly, Parker Pen authorized the PRODUCTION and sale of their pens to a Japanese manufacturer. If those pens are then shipped back into the U.S. market, they compete with the American-manufactured items. Most companies, in their CONTRACTS with international manufacturers, prohibit the shipment of products made under license back into the licensing company's home market, but it is debatable whether such actions violate U.S. importation, TRADEMARK, PATENT, or COPYRIGHT laws.

Sometimes consumer DEMAND creates gray markets. When Canon shifted supply of its copiers for the Russian market from factories in Japan to a company factory in China, sales plummeted. Canon dealers in Russia found gray marketers willing to ship them copiers made in Japan. Sometimes gray markets are created by company attempts at MARKET SEGMENTATION, in which marketers try to divide the total market into relatively homogeneous groups and charge a higher price to those groups who are willing and able to pay more for the product. Markets where the higher price is charged encourage ARBITRAGE, buying the product in the lower-priced market and reselling it in the higher-priced market.

With the speed and access of INTERNET communications, price differentials are quickly recognized, creating opportunities for gray marketers. Gray markets have even developed for computer chips, providing computer manufacturers alternatives to the authorized dealer when looking for components. Gray markets differ from markets for counterfeit products in the fact that they are made under license from the original company. Gray markets are not "black markets" because they are not trading illegal products. While price differences are the major factor in creating gray markets, customers concerned with service and warranties are not likely to purchase gray market products. Because these products are purchased through unauthorized marketing channels, service and warranties are difficult to obtain. One study found that gray markets benefit manufacturers because sales in those markets are mostly to price-sensitive customers who would not have purchased their product through the authorized and higher-priced channel.

Further reading
Champion, David. "The Bright Side of Gray Markets." *Harvard Business Review* 76, no. 5 (September–October 1998): 19.

Great Depression
The Great Depression (1929–41) was the most severe period of economic decline in the history of the United States. During the Great Depression, U.S. output declined by one-third, the unemployment rate reached 25 percent, the STOCK MARKET declined by 40 percent, and over 9,000 banks failed. The depression brought an end to the Roaring Twenties, a period of euphoria in the country marked by increasing output and INCOME, Federal Reserve management of the MONEY SUPPLY, and significant technological advances.

The causes of the depression are still being debated, and economists' lists of the contributing factors include

- TARIFFS
- overproduction
- the FEDERAL RESERVE SYSTEM
- the gold standard
- malinvestment

- rigid wages and prices
- distribution of WEALTH and power

During the economic boom of the 1920s, U.S. manufacturers significantly increased their export activity. Previously there was sufficient domestic DEMAND for new industrial output, and U.S. firms largely ignored EXPORTING. With the decline in 1929, Congress passed the infamous SMOOT-HAWLEY TARIFF ACT increasing tariffs an average of 60 percent. European countries and Canada quickly reciprocated causing a collapse in international trade.

Overproduction during the 1920s, both in industry and agriculture, resulted in declining prices. Declining prices are generally considered beneficial, reducing costs and controlling INFLATION. However, when price declines are widespread, DEFLATION occurs, and when deflation reaches a critical stage, it impacts financial markets, primarily banks. (At one point during the depression, prices fell 10 percent a year). Today many financial institutions make LOANS to businesses and deposit INSURANCE protects accounts, but in the 1920s, commercial banks almost exclusively provided business loans and FDIC insurance did not exist. When deflation occurs, the value of ASSETS decline. Eventually (as in Japan in the 1990s), banks have loans for which the collateral is worth less than the amount loaned; the result is bank failure.

In the early 1930s, over 9,000 U.S. banks failed, with depositors losing everything they had in the failed banks. Seeing their life savings disappear, many reacted by withdrawing any funds left in existing banks, contributing to a run on the BANKING SYSTEM. Future savings were also hoarded, buried in Mason jars, stuffed in mattresses—put anywhere but in banks. Savings are needed for INVESTMENT, but without funds being deposited in banks, banks cannot lend anything to businesses for investment and thus increase the supply of MONEY, leading to problems for the Federal Reserve, the nation's manager of MONETARY POLICY. In 1928 the Fed increased INTEREST RATES in order to discourage stock-market specu-

lation. When the stock market finally crashed in October 1929, panic struck. Banks raised their interest rates on business loans, further discouraging private investment. The Fed "tightening" of the money supply again in 1931 exacerbated the situation, which one economist described as a period of "collective insanity." There was no work, therefore there was no demand. Without market demand, there was no output and therefore no income.

The flow of output and income in an economic system requires money, which is not an asset but primarily a medium of exchange between producers and consumers and among traders in international transactions. During the Great Depression, the world was on the gold standard, and each country limited its money supply based on its gold reserves. In the United States, 1 ounce of gold equaled $20. Under the gold standard, a country with a trade surplus received gold and therefore could expand its money supply. A country with a trade deficit transferred gold to its trading partners, reducing its money supply and, in theory, correcting its trade imbalance through lower prices. Since gold was in relatively fixed supply, the world's money supply was more or less fixed. Thus monetary authorities had limited ability to increase the money supply when, during an economic downturn, an increase in the money supply could lower interest rates and stimulate economic activity.

With the booming economy of 1920s, the Fed allowed a 60 percent increase in the money supply, a decision that critics suggest abetted stock market speculation and contributed to the collapse in 1929. According to the Austrian school of economic theory, it also led to malinvestment—investments that were not justifiable at prevailing interest rates but were considered rational when interest rates declined. Monetary policy designed to stimulate investment is a temporary action, and when interest rates later rose, these investments were no longer profitable and therefore liquidated.

According to economists, rigid wages and prices contributed to the depression by not allowing markets to adjust. With the collapse of the stock market in 1929, consumers reduced their spending, causing a decrease in aggregate demand. Decreased spending along with flexible wages and prices would lower both, but businesses maintained prices in order to cover costs and workers resisted wage cuts, leading to both reduced sales and increased UNEMPLOYMENT.

Probably the most controversial theory regarding the causes of the Great Depression is the issue of wealth and power distribution. The 1920s saw the heyday of the industrial capitalists. Even with constraints imposed by the SHERMAN ANTITRUST ACT (1890) and the CLAYTON ANTITRUST ACT (1914), a relatively small number of individuals and companies controlled significant amounts of the country's wealth. Some economists suggest this contributed to the depression by concentrating demand in the hands of a small percentage of the population who, when the stock market crashed, pulled back their spending, furthering the decline. In addition, with a small number of large CORPORATIONS producing significant portions of the national output, the economy was adversely affected when a few of these companies declined.

As British economist John Maynard Keynes observed in 1930, the world was ". . . as capable as before of affording for every one a high standard of living. . . . But today we have involved ourselves in a colossal muddle, having blundered in the control of a delicate machine, the working of which we do not understand."

Further reading
Delong, J. Bradford. "The Great Crash and The Great Slump," UC-Berkeley. Available online. URL: econ161. berkeley.edu/TCEH/Slouch_Crash14.html. Accessed on June 17, 2009; Smiley, Gene. *Rethinking the Great Depression.* Chicago: I. R. Dee, 2002.

green cards
Green cards are immigrant VISAS giving foreigners permanent-resident status in the United States. Unlike visas, which are granted for a specific length of time to engage in specific business activities, green cards allow non-U.S. citizens to reside in the country indefinitely. Green-card status also allows individuals to become U.S. citizens after five years (three years if the immigrant acquired the green card through marriage to a citizen).

Most green cards, named such because of their color, are allocated based on the relationship of the applicant to U.S. citizens, but some are available based on business criteria. Employment-based green cards called First Preference Petition are issued to foreigners with extraordinary ability, including outstanding professors and researchers and certain executives and managers of MULTINATIONAL CORPORATIONS. Second Preference Petition cards are issued to members of professions holding advanced degrees and people of exceptional ability in the sciences, arts, and business. Third Preference Petition cards are available to skilled workers, professionals, and other workers, while Fourth Preference Petition cards are for special immigrants, including religious workers. Finally, Fifth Preference Petitions, known as million-dollar green cards, are available for people actively investing in a new business that will create at least 10 new full-time jobs for U.S. workers. The million-dollar requirement is reduced to half that amount for investment in low-population or high-unemployment areas of the country.

Green cards are difficult to obtain and often require hiring specialized legal assistance. Foreigners in the United States on visas are sometimes subject to different rules when applying for permanent-resident status. In the 1990s the United States created a lottery system for 55,000 green cards annually.

Further reading
U.S. Immigration and Naturalization Service Web site. Available online. URL: www.inscis.gov.

green marketing
Green marketing is the PRODUCTION, promotion, and reclamation of environmentally sensitive PRODUCTS. Green marketing includes a variety of activities and strategies, including recycling, pollution control and reduction, product development, POSITIONING, and reclamation systems.

The emergence and importance of green marketing in the United States is associated with a series of events over the last three decades of the 20th century. When Americans protested the use of pesticides on the first Earth Day in 1970, they sent a message to marketers that they wanted chemical-free food products. Earth Day influenced the 1970 formation of the ENVIRONMENTAL PROTECTION AGENCY. The Love Canal tragedy came to light in the late 1970s when Lois Gibbs documented diseases among residents in a housing development built on top of a toxic-waste dump. Three Mile Island, the 1979 nuclear-reactor crisis in Pennsylvania, galvanized environmentalist fears, and Exxon became a symbol of environmental irresponsibility with the Alaskan oil spill created by its ship, the *Exxon Valdez,* in 1989. The Brundtland Report (World Commission on Environment and Development, 1987), the Earth Summit in Rio (1992), and former vice president Al Gore's book *Earth in the Balance* (1993) added information and pressure to change business strategies.

Initially most American businesses responded to pressure from consumers and citizenry by instituting bottom-up pollution-prevention programs to reduce wastes and environmental pollutants. In the process many firms found environmental management could generate cost savings. Green-market concerns were framed in terms of risk reduction, reengineering, or cost cutting. In addition to companies, communities across the country initiated recycling programs to expand the supply of recyclable materials, sometimes beyond the industry capacity to use them in the production of new products.

Later some companies found green marketing could be used as a strategy to differentiate companies from their competitors. In the 1990s, whether through efforts to reduce pollution, increased use of renewable resources, donations to protect the rain forest, or new environmentally friendly products, American businesses began to develop green-marketing strategies. Most had to first overcome the problems of educating consumers about company products and green strategies, demonstrating tangible efforts and impacts and providing opportunities for choosing environmentally friendly products. The FEDERAL TRADE COMMISSION developed Guides for Use of Environmental Marketing Claims, providing green marketers with assistance in complying with truth-in-ADVERTISING regulations.

Early green-marketing efforts included organically grown produce, which some remember for being overpriced and of lower quality than nonorganic products. The utility industry is an often-cited example in green marketing. In the 1990s, many utilities, often under mandates from regulatory commissions, reluctantly developed sources of renewable energy, including solar, wind, and geothermal systems. Because these sources cost more to produce, companies charged a higher price. Consumers, who could not see the product, had to be shown the benefit of renewable energy sources and convinced the utility company was truly investing in environmentally friendly sources of energy. Consequently, green-marketing efforts by electric utilities have been only modestly successful.

In the late 1990s, the Green Gauge Report, conducted by Roper Starch Worldwide, reported that Americans' attitudes toward green marketing were changing. The report, which tracked Americans' environmental knowledge and concerns since 1990, showed the percentage in most environmentally dedicated groups, labeled the "True-Blue Greens," remained constant at 10 percent of the adult population. But the percentage of "Greenback Greens"—people willing to pay more for green products—had declined from 11 percent in 1990 to 5 percent in 1996. Some former Greenback Greens were now found in what Roper called the "Sprouts Group," people who still cared but were unwilling to pay more; this group represented 33 percent of adults. The third group, "Passive Grousers"—those who viewed the environment as someone else's problem—shrank from 24 percent to 15 percent in the 1990–96 period, but many of these consumers became "Basic Browns," or environmental deadbeats—people who did not care much, if at all, about the environment. This group grew from 28 percent to 37 percent.

Green marketing must appeal to consumers, but with increasing consumer apathy or indifference to environmental concerns, it has become less important among business concerns. Nevertheless, in a highly praised 1997 *Harvard Business Review* article, management professor Stuart Hart argues, "Rarely is greening linked to strategy or technology development, and as a result, most companies fail to recognize opportunities of potentially staggering proportions." Hart outlines a current strategy based on pollution prevention and product stewardship, leading to clean technology and a sustainability vision for future strategies. Interest in and growth of green marketing will likely move in cycles as world economic, political, and environmental conditions change.

Further reading

Hart, Stuart L. "Beyond Greening: Strategies for a Sustainable World." *Harvard Business Review* 75, no. 6 (January–February 1997): 66; Speer, Tibbett L. "Growing the Green Market." *American Demographics* 19, no. 8 (August 1997): 45–50.

Gresham's law

Gresham's law, named after 16th-century English businessman and royal adviser Sir Thomas Gresham, is the observation that when there are two forms of commodity MONEY that are legal tender, meaning they must be accepted as a means of payment, the higher valued form of money will disappear from circulation while the lower valued money will be used for making exchanges in a market. The shorthand version of Gresham's law is stated as "Bad money drives out good money."

The difference in value of two coins with the same nominal or face value can occur from a variety of circumstances. For example, in 1965 the U.S. government reduced the silver percentage in dimes, quarters, half-dollars, and dollar coins from 90 percent silver to 40 percent silver. The pre-1965 coins quickly disappeared from circulation, the 1965 coins being "bad" money, the 1964 and earlier coins being "good" money. In earlier times, when little paper currency existed, it was common for people to nick or scrape off gold or silver from coins, reducing the amount of precious metal while still maintaining the nominal face value.

At various times, the relative value of gold and silver has shifted, making one commodity money more valuable than the other. The more valuable metal quickly disappears from circulation. Similarly, when commodity monies have a face value less than the market value of the metal contained in them, entrepreneurial types will acquire and melt down the coins and sell the metal at market prices. In 2008, when copper prices rose dramatically, the *Wall Street Journal* reported a young man had a garage full of U.S. pennies. The government prohibits melting down U.S. coins but the young man held onto his collection, hoping at some point restrictions would be changed.

Since all paper currency in the United States is fiat money, not redeemable for gold or silver, it would be considered "bad" money. Before the creation of the FEDERAL RESERVE (1913) many paper currencies issued by state-chartered banks were used in market exchanges. During economic crises, the paper money issued by some banks was considered a better risk than others. Individuals would then hoard the paper money of financially sound banks and try to make exchanges with the less respected currency.

The existence of "legal tender" laws greatly influences Gresham's law. When governments declare certain paper money as legal tender, sellers must accept the money as payment. After the French Revolution (1789–99), authorities issued billions of livres' worth of paper currency. Gold and silver quickly disappeared from the marketplace. Livres were replaced with *mandats,* with fines and imprisonment decreed for anyone unwilling to accept them as payment. Napoléon Bonaparte restored order by declaring the government would only pay in coin and would not issue paper money.

Further reading

Train, John. *Famous Financial Fiascos.* New York: Random House, 1984.

gross domestic product

Gross domestic product (GDP) is the estimated MARKET VALUE (the price paid for goods and services) of all final goods and SERVICES produced in a country in a year. Generally, only those goods and services exchanged in markets for which there is taxable INCOME are included in GDP; most bartered services, illegal activities, household efforts, and in-kind transactions are not included. Some goods, particularly goods and services produced and sold to government, have no marketplace price. In this situation the cost to government is assumed to be the market value. For example, complex weapons systems only sold to the military are included in GDP at their cost.

Final goods and services are those that available to consumers. Since GDP is used to estimate the output of goods and services available to final consumers, primary goods such as raw materials and intermediary goods (which are used in the production of final goods) are not included in GDP. For example, few Americans buy wheat or flour; they purchase bread. Wheat is a primary PRODUCT, and flour is an intermediate product.

GDP can be calculated by either the sum of all expenditures for final goods and services or the sum of income received for the goods and services. These are known as the expenditures and income approaches, respectively. Recognizing in the CIRCULAR FLOW MODEL that businesses, households, and government are connected by flows of money, resources, and goods and services, the sum of expenditures for final goods and services will equal the income received for those products (with some statistical adjustment). Using the income approach, GDP equals the sum of wages, interest, rent, corporate PROFITS, capital CONSUMPTION allowance (the estimated value of DEPRECIATION of capital goods used in production), and indirect BUSINESS TAXES (taxes collected by businesses for government agencies), and net-factor income from abroad.

Using the expenditures approach, GDP equals the sum of consumption, INVESTMENT, and government spending, plus spending for exports minus spending for IMPORTS. Economics textbooks use the equation $GDP = C+I+G+(X-M)$ to show the expenditures approach. In the United States, consumption expenditures (C) represent approximately two-thirds of all spending. Changes in consumer spending can dramatically change GDP. Reports describing changes in consumer income, confidence, and credit levels are INDICATORS of likely changes in consumption spending. Investment spending (I), spending on capital goods, represents approximately 15 percent of U.S. GDP, but it is often the most volatile component of GDP. Business investment is made in anticipation of growing and changing DEMAND for consumer goods. Investment spending is also influenced by INTEREST RATES, the percentage of factory capacity currently being utilized, and changes in technology. Government spending (G) is that portion of government budgets used to purchase goods and services. The U.S. FEDERAL BUDGET is approximately $2 trillion, but transfer payments, redistribution of purchasing power from one group to another, is not a government expenditure. SOCIAL SECURITY and other government-sponsored WELFARE programs are subtracted from the budget to estimate government expenditures. Net trade (X-M) adds expenditures for exports and subtracts expenditures for imports from GDP. Since GDP measures the value of output in an economy, foreign purchases of U.S. output are part of GDP, but U.S. consumers' purchases of imports is not part of GDP. Net trade is influenced by EXCHANGE RATES, levels of income in other countries, barriers or reductions in TRADE BARRIERS, and consumer preferences.

In the United States, GDP is calculated quarterly by the Department of Commerce. Each quarter the department issues a preliminary estimate, followed by a first and then second revision for GDP. GDP and percentage changes in GDP are the most widely watched measures of economic performance, influencing American business and MONETARY POLICY.

GDP is also often used as a measure of the economic well-being of a country and its citizens. But since GDP is a measure of output in an economy, it does not include

- nonmarket activities
- black-market exchanges
- changes in the quality of goods and services over time
- distribution of income and goods and services
- depletion of natural resources
- environmental degradation
- distinction between the use of renewable and nonrenewable resources
- Composition of spending, i.e., spending on negative deterrence (defense and personal safety) versus positive benefits (such as recreation, culture, or education)

Advocates of sustainable development challenge the widespread acceptance of the idea that if GDP is growing, people are better off, and have offered a variety of alternatives to GDP to measure well-being in a society. The most widely quoted alternative is the Index of Sustainable Economic Welfare (ISEW). Created by former World Bank economists Herman Daly and John Cobb Jr., the ISEW adjusts GDP to account for environmental and social factors, including income distribution, value of household Labor, and environmental damage.

Further reading

Boyes, William J., and Michael Melvin. *Macroeconomics.* 7th ed. Boston: Houghton Mifflin, 2007; Folsom, W. Davis, and Rick Boulware. "Sustainable Development: Toward a Sustainable Environmental Index." Paper presented at the Mountain Plains Management Conference, Cedar City, Utah, October, 2000.

gross margin See INCOME STATEMENT, GROSS MARGIN.

Gross National Happiness (GNH)

Gross National Happiness (GNH) is an alternative measure of economic well-being. GNH challenges the traditional assumption that increasing GROSS DOMESTIC PRODUCT (GDP) and increasing per capita INCOMES improves the quality of citizens' lives. While GDP is a measure of the material output produced in an economy in a year, as first proposed in the 1970s by the king of Bhutan, GNH is based on four pillars: sustainable development,

environmental protection, cultural preservation, and good governance. Bhutan is a small, landlocked Buddhist kingdom in South Asia. One of the Buddhist precepts is the concept of a Middle Path, finding a balance between extremes. For Bhutan, an economic Middle Path weighs material needs against the impact on society and the environment. As reported in *National Geographic,*

> The Late Druk Gyalpo Jigme Dorji Wangchuck said that the goal of development is to make "the people prosperous and happy." The importance of "prosperity and happiness" was highlighted in his address on the occasion of Bhutan's admission to the United Nations in 1971. This vision was elaborated by the Fourth Druk Gyalpo Jigme Singye Wangchuck who declared in the first years of his reign that, "Our country's policy is to consolidate our sovereignty to achieve economic self-reliance, prosperity and happiness for our country and people." His Majesty's subsequent pronouncement that "Gross National Happiness is more important that Gross National Product" has captured the imagination of scholars and policy makers across the world. [In 2005–08, the king and his heir, against the wishes of many citizens, abdicated their authority, held national mock elections, and then real elections, creating a democratically elected government.]

Since the king of Bhutan's initial proposal, scholars and activists around the world have embraced and are attempting to quantify GNH. As stated on the Gross International Happiness (GIH) Web site:

> In order to develop real progress and sustainability and to effectively combat trends which compromise the planet's natural and human ecosystems, GIH aims to develop more appropriate and inclusive indicators which truly measure the quality of life within nations and organizations. . . . Rooted in Buddhist philosophy and values, GIH presents a radically different development paradigm, but one that holds a promise for achieving real sustainability. GIH aims to connect the international efforts which are tak-

ing place in the field of developing alternative development indicators, human economics and happiness psychology, so that individual efforts can benefit from each other and that collectively these efforts more strongly impact international development agenda's.

The Centre for Bhutan Studies expanded upon the king's four pillars, developing an elaborate set of indices, which combined result in an index of happiness. Some of the indices include Mental Health, Spirituality, Environmental Degradation, Ecological Knowledge, Afforestation, Education, Historical Literacy, Reciprocity, Basic Precepts, Family, and Living Standards.

Researchers around the world have also constructed happiness indices, most not as complex as the one used in Bhutan. For over 20 years, the University of Michigan's World Values Survey (WVS) has asked individuals around the world two questions: how happy are they, and how satisfied are they? The researchers labeled the combined responses to both questions "subjective well-being." Respondents use a scale including: 1. Very happy/satisfied 2. Rather happy/satisfied 3. Not very happy/satisfied 4. Not at all happy/satisfied. In surveys conducted from 1999 to 2002, people in Puerto Rico ranked the happiest, followed by citizens of Mexico, Denmark, Colombia, and Ireland. The United States ranked 15th out of 79 countries surveyed. Sixty-nine percent of Americans considered themselves happy, slightly higher than the world average of 65 percent.

The Gross National Happiness studies implicitly support the old maxim, "Money cannot buy you happiness." According to the Happiness Show, "Americans' personal income has increased 2½ times over the last 50 years, but their happiness level has remained the same, and Americans earning more than $10 million annually are only slightly happier than average Americans." Data from the World Database of Happiness show people in some European countries (Italy, Denmark, Spain, and France) are becoming happier while citizens of Portugal and Belgium report declines in happiness. In the United States, a *Wall Street*

Journal article reports, "In recent years, economists and psychologists have turned their attention to 'happiness research'—and the results are a little disturbing if your life's goals are a bigger paycheck and a fatter nest, money alone, it seems, just doesn't buy a whole lot of happiness. . . . Yes, if you live in poverty, more money can bolster your happiness. But once you're safe and warm and fed, it makes surprisingly little difference." The article goes on to report on research that found "that people with higher incomes tend to spend more time working, commuting and engaging in other obligatory nonwork activities, such as maintaining their homes. All of these are associated with lower happiness." Other findings of happiness that researchers include:

- People get more satisfaction and happiness from the anticipation of a purchase than from taking ownership of the item itself.
- Happiness is more likely if you earn more than $100,000 per year, attend religious services, and are a Republican.
- People who are more resilient are happier.
- Employees engaged in their work are happier.
- People measure themselves against their peers, and relative wealth is more important than absolute wealth.
- Physically active senior citizens are happier.

Further reading
Clements, Jonathan. "Money and Happiness: Here's Why You Won't Laugh All the Way to the Bank," *Wall Street Journal,* 16 August 2006; "The Smile Squad: Some of the Leading Happiness Researchers, and Their Findings," *Wall Street Journal,* 18–19 March 2006, P5; Happiness research Web sites. Available online. URL: www.grossnationalhappiness.com, www.thehappinessshow.com, www.grossinternationalhappiness.org. Accessed on January 31, 2009; Bhutan in *National Geographic.* Available online. URL: ngm.nationalgeographic.com/2008/03/bhutan/larmer-text. Accessed on January 31, 2009.

growth stocks
Growth stocks are COMMON STOCK equities in companies perceived by investors as having above-

average current- and projected-earnings growth. These stocks typically have very high price-earnings ratios and very low DIVIDEND yields; they have higher BETA COEFFICIENT ratios and are riskier INVESTMENTS, with greater upside and downside potential. The counter-investment strategy is value stocks. These stocks generally have low price-earnings ratios, higher dividend yields, and have a market capitalization (price times the number of shares outstanding) equal to or less than the value of the company's assets.

There are several ways a company can be a proven growth company, and several more in which it can be perceived by investors as having growth potential. If a company has an existing record of quarter-to-quarter (or year-to-year) above-average increases in sales, earnings, or gross PROFIT margins, investors will project these increases over many quarters or years and bid up the price of the stock well above current values in comparison to other investments. Companies without a verifiable record may project that their growth in sales or earnings will dramatically increase. They may also have investment analysts, bankers, or other promote their stock. Sometimes, because they are in the same industry or specific manufacturing or service category as other companies that have experienced superior growth in recent years, they feel they "deserve" a high price/earnings ratio or even a high price without any current earnings or substantial sales. Many U.S. DOT-COMS rationalized their high prices based on this reasoning.

The reward for investors in a company that is proven (or widely perceived) as a growth company is that the stock commands higher price/book, price/earnings, and price/sales ratios than its peers. The risk for investors in buying a growth stock is that the projection may be wrong, the premium paid for projected growth is withdrawn, and the stock falls substantially. More RISK is entailed buying smaller companies that have no current earnings or high debt.

Growth companies have arisen in many fields, from retailing to technology, tobacco to perfume. In some cases the company developed a concept or idea that set it apart from existing COMPETITION; or it became the most efficient and drove out or bought up the competition; or it invented an entire new field and was the first (or best of the first group of companies) to succeed in it, dominating the new industry. Examples of large, successful companies considered to be proven growth companies (i.e., those that have demonstrated above-average growth in sales and earnings over many years) are Intel, Microsoft, Philip Morris, and Walmart.

—Jerry and Jesse Rosenthal

guaranteed investment contract (guaranteed income contract)

A guaranteed investment contract (GIC), also referred to as a guaranteed income contract, is a CONTRACT between an INSURANCE company and a pension plan (i.e., 401(K) PLAN) or corporate PROFIT-sharing plan that guarantees a specific rate of return on the invested CAPITAL over the life of the agreement. The insurance company guarantees the rate of return and earns a profit by investing the funds in securities of similar DURATION (time to maturity) as the length of the agreement. For example, with a 10-year, 5-percent GIC, the pension plan will receive, on the employee's behalf, a 5-percent yield for 10 years. The insurance company will invest in BONDS, MORTGAGES or other debt securities that mature in 10 years. If the INVESTMENTS yield 7 percent, the insurance company profits by the spread, 2 percent between the guaranteed return and the yield.

The insurance company assumes all credit, market, and interest-rate RISKS. Credit or DEFAULT risk is the potential for a borrower to not repay their loan. Market or systematic risk is the risk associated with changing values in all securities in a class. STOCK MARKET risk is measured by the BETA COEFFICIENT, a statistical measure of the variability in a stock's price relative to the overall variability of stock-market prices. Interest-rate risk is the potential for fixed-interest-rate securities to decline in value if INTEREST RATES rise.

The term *guaranteed* refers to the rate of interest to be paid over the life of the contract, but it does not guarantee repayment of principal (the amount invested). Americans are used to FEDERAL DEPOSIT INSURANCE CORPORATION (FDIC) guarantees on bank deposits. The FDIC, a government-sponsored CORPORATION, guarantees depositors' savings should the bank fail. Insurance companies are not federally guaranteed. As a group, there have been relatively few defaults among GICs, and even when a GIC has failed, investors got most if not all of their principal returned.

As an investment in a RETIREMENT PLAN, GICs are referred to as stable-value ASSETS. GIC yields are almost always higher than money-market funds and similar to bond funds. Because investors are accepting a guaranteed rate, they are taking less risk than if they put their money in stock MUTUAL FUNDS. Stock mutual funds have historically generated higher yields than bonds or other fixed-income securities, but with greater variation in the short run. During the "go-go" years of the stock market during the mid-to-late 1990s, many employees removed their retirement investments from GICs and put them into stock mutual funds. With the decline of the stock market in early 2000 and again in 2008. GICs again became popular.

Further reading

Younkin, Timothy Owen. "Understanding GIC's." Available online. URL: www.timyounkin.com/articles/GIC.html. Accessed on June 17, 2009; "Stable Comeback." *Pensions and Investments* 30 (7 January 2002): 10.

harmonization

In general, harmonization means "to bring into common accord or agreement." In business, particularly international business, harmonization of laws, agreements, definitions, and specifications is an important consideration. Having common rules and specifications reduces uncertainty and reduces the problems businesspeople face when entering markets. Harmonization of rules and specifications increases both efficiency for business and market fairness, with each participant operating under the same standards.

Business literature includes many harmonization issues. For example, European and U.S. accounting systems still differ, adding to the difficulty in interpreting figures from one company to another. With the NORTH AMERICAN FREE TRADE AGREEMENT (NAFTA), the United States, Canada, and Mexico agreed to the NORTH AMERICAN INDUSTRIAL CLASSIFICATION SYSTEM (NAICS), defining products by the same classification system. NAICS is used in the HARMONIZED TARIFF SYSTEM (HTS), by which goods that are transformed from one product category to another are then subject to a different TARIFF classification.

As part of the WORLD TRADE ORGANIZATION, the United States agreed to harmonize its PATENT system with that of the EUROPEAN UNION (EU). Similarly, the EU harmonized taxation on inter-est INCOME in order to reduce the impetus for tax evasion. (A company or individual with interest income from several EU countries would rationally try to declare that income in the country with the lowest tax rate.)

The United Nations has helped to harmonize labeling and classification of products as a way to reduce miscommunication and misunderstanding of materials and chemicals. For example, in recent years the United States and the European Union have debated what criteria to use in defining organic foods. The International Standards Organization attempts to harmonize technical standards among global manufacturers, in the process increasing the substitutability of one firm's products for another, increasing market competition and reducing the need to produce different components and parts for each manufacturer.

Harmonization is a controversial issue in international business. Each company or country favors harmonization based on their own rules and specifications, which gives their firms a competitive advantage over other firms that would have to adjust to the new rules or standards.

Further reading

Leebron, David W. "Claims for Harmonization: A Theoretical Framework." *Canadian Business Law Journal* 27 (July 1996): 63; Lohr, Luanne. "Implications of Organic

Certification for Market Structure and Trade." *American Journal of Agricultural Economics* 80 (December 1998): 1,125.

Harmonized Tariff System

The Harmonized Tariff System (HTS) is an international system of numeric classification of PRODUCTS. With HTS, products are classified using a 6- to 10-digit number. The first six digits are standardized worldwide, while some governments use additional numbers to further distinguish products. Each nation applies its own TARIFF rates on products. HTS classification is important, because most countries apply different tariff rates for different categories of goods. For example, having a product classified as a component rather than a finished product may significantly reduce the tariff on imported goods.

Most tariffs are percentage rates applied ad valorem (according to value) of the imported product. Some prices are quoted CIF, meaning the price includes the cost of the goods, INSURANCE, and freight; while other goods are priced FOB (FREE ON BOARD), meaning cost of the goods and all transportation costs to the port of departure plus loading. Some tariffs are applied to the CIF value, while others are added to the FOB value for each HTS classification.

The U.S. INTERNATIONAL TRADE COMMISSION publishes the *Harmonized Tariff Schedule of the United States Annotated,* which provides categories and applicable rates for imported products.

Further reading

U.S. International Trade Commission Web site. Available online. URL: www.usitc.gov.

Hawthorne experiments

The Hawthorne experiments, conducted from 1924 to 1932, were designed to assess whether improvements in physical working conditions would increase employee productivity. Scientist Elton Mayo and his colleagues manipulated multiple aspects of the work environment for a selected group of workers at the Hawthorne Plant of the Western Electric Company and subsequently measured their productivity.

Six women who regularly assembled telecommunications relays from a number of small electronic parts were selected from the general population of workers at the plant. They began working in a special testing room where factors such as the level of lighting, workday length, and the number and duration of rest periods were each changed. Productivity then was measured in terms of the number of relays each woman assembled.

Results indicated that brighter light, shorter hours, and the addition of two rest periods during the day all increased productivity, theoretically by helping workers see and by preventing fatigue. But much to the researchers' surprise, productivity did not revert to lower levels when these changes were reversed. Rather, it climbed to an even higher level.

These unexpected results initially led Mayo and his colleagues to conclude that the workers became more productive simply because they were under observation. However, subsequent analyses of the testing situation revealed that several important social factors also differed markedly from the workers' previous environment, contributing to higher productivity. For example, the testing-room supervisor behaved in a friendlier fashion than did other company supervisors, and the testing personnel solicited participants' opinions about the upcoming changes as opposed to simply forcing new changes upon them.

Presumably these positive social conditions increased participants' self-esteem and made them feel like an important part of a team, unlike ASSEMBLY LINE workers. In essence, participating in the experiments led to more positive attitudes towards work in general and a higher level of commitment to working hard for the company. These factors, along with being under constant observation, help explain the high levels of productivity observed even after the changes were reversed.

Today, individuals who modify their behavior when they are being observed or when participating in research are said to exhibit the Hawthorne effect. This falls under the broader category of SOCIAL FACILITATION, which describes any behavioral changes that are due to the presence of other people or an audience.

The Hawthorne experiments were highly influential in expanding the scope of the field of INDUSTRIAL-ORGANIZATIONAL PSYCHOLOGY. The experiments led industrial-organizational psychologists to consider for the first time how social factors such as quality of supervision, informal groups, and employee satisfaction affect people's behavior in the business environment.

Further reading
Forsyth, Donelson R. *Group Dynamics*. 5th ed. Belmont, Calif.: Wadsworth Publishing, 2009; Mayo, Elton. *The Human Problems of an Industrial Civilization*. Cambridge, Mass.: Harvard University Press, 1933; ———. *The Social Problems of an Industrial Civilization*. Cambridge, Mass.: Harvard University Press, 1945.
—Elizabeth L. Cralley

health maintenance organization
A health maintenance organization (HMO) provides comprehensive health care to its members on the basis of a prepaid CONTRACT. HMOs function both as INSURANCE companies, collecting periodic premium payments; and as health-care providers, contracting with doctors and hospitals to provide services at predetermined rates. As such the HMO is an example of managed care, the goal of which is high-quality medical care at a reasonable cost.

HMOs are financed through a "capitated" system in which care is provided for each member at a fixed rate. In employer-supplied plans, this rate is paid by the employer through a contract with the HMO. Each member of an HMO selects a primary-care physician who is contracted to the plan, provides basic health care, and acts as a "gatekeeper" to specialists who may be consulted only on his or her referral. Sometimes, a small copay, or fee, is charged for each office visit. HMOs traditionally have stressed preventive health care, offering physicals and checkups at little or no extra cost as well as extra health and fitness programs or classes that address a variety of health concerns, such as helping members to lose weight or stop smoking.

There are currently several variants of the HMO scheme. In the classic HMO, the company owns most of its own facilities and hires all medical personnel. In a second type, the group-model HMO, the company contracts with a group of doctors who form their own professional CORPORATION. A more flexible variant of the second type, the individual-practice association, allows doctors in individual practices to form corporations with other doctors in their area to provide services to the HMO at predetermined fees. Point-of-service (POS) plans and preferred provider organizations (PPOs) are similar schemes that allow members to see doctors and use medical facilities outside of the network at an additional cost; they sometimes do not require a referral from the primary-care physician to see a specialist.

The industrialist Henry J. Kaiser created the prototype of the HMO when he teamed up with Dr. Sidney Garfield to provide a prepaid health plan to Kaiser's workers at the Grand Coulee Dam construction site in 1938. During World War II they offered a similar plan to 30,000 West Coast shipyard workers and their families. The popularity of the plan encouraged Kaiser and Garfield to offer it to the public after the war.

The postwar boom encouraged employers to offer health insurance as part of their EMPLOYEE BENEFITS package. Because of tax incentives (the premiums paid were tax deductible), most employers found traditional insurance supporting fee-per-service health care to be cost-effective. By the 1970s, though, rising health costs were becoming a burden for employers and the government. The Health Maintenance Organization Act of 1973 encouraged the creation of HMOs as a means of controlling medical costs. In the early 1970s, less than 3 percent of Americans were enrolled in an HMO, a number that rose to 30 percent by 1992. In the face of the economic stagnation and INFLATION of the late 1970s, many employers had to reduce benefits in traditional health plans and shift more of the burden of health-care costs to their employees, a situation that continued throughout the 1980s. But neither the increased reliance on HMOs and other types of managed-care plans nor the shifting of more costs to employees did much to rein in the spiraling health-care costs. Not only was there an increasing financial burden on employers, employees, and insurance companies, but an estimated 37 million Americans were uninsured or had lost their health insurance by the early 1990s. Health care became a major issue in the presidential campaign of 1992, but the Clinton administration's attempts at comprehensive health-care reform ended in a debacle that left managed care as the only viable alternative to the pay-per-service model. During the 1990s, employers moved rapidly away from traditional insurance to various kinds of managed care.

The proponents of HMOs, PPOs, and other kinds of managed care stress the plans' ability to contain costs while providing SERVICES like preventive medicine not usually associated with pay-per-service health care. They make the point that managed care is better able to prevent unnecessary medical procedures and to encourage more cost-effective alternatives to expensive procedures where appropriate. Opponents, on the other hand, have focused on what they see as compromises in the quality of care provided by such plans through practices such as subjecting physicians' requests for certain medical procedures to review by gatekeepers within the company (who are sometimes alleged not to be qualified to make major medical decisions) or giving doctors financial incentives and bonuses to choose less-expensive options.

Many of the more controversial aspects of managed-care plans have been addressed by legislation on the state and federal level and by numerous lawsuits. Some see a trend toward dismantling managed care, although a majority of insured Americans are still in managed-care plans. The 2008 Kaiser Family Foundation *Employer Health Benefits* study showed a continuing trend away from workers covered by traditional HMO (20%) to PPO networks (58%), and an increase in the number of workers (8%) enrolled in high-deductible health plans with a savings option (HDHP/SO). The latter probably reflects a response by employers to soaring healthcare costs. The Kaiser study reported a 119 percent increase in average single and family premiums since 1999, and a 117 percent increase in the average contribution workers made to their health coverage during the same period.

Further reading

Birenbaum, Arnold. *Wounded Profession: American Medicine Enters the Age of Managed Care.* Westport, Conn.: Praeger, 2002; Carlson Gail. "What Is a Health Maintenance Organization?" University of Missouri Extension Web site. Available online. URL: missourifamilies.org/features/healtharticles/health43.htm. Accessed on July 28, 2009; *Employer Health Benefits 2008.* Kaiser Family Foundation. Available online. URL: ehbs.kff.org/images/abstract/7791.pdf. Accessed on July 7, 2009; Enthoven, Allan C., and Laura A. Tollen. *Toward a 21st Century Health System.* San Francisco: John Wiley & Sons, 2004; Gustavson, Sandra G. "Health Insurance." In *Encyclopedia Americana.* International Ed. 2003; "Health Insurance Options." In *Encyclopedia of Business.* Edited by John G. Maurer, Joel M. Schulman, Marcia L. Ruwe, and Richard C. Becherer. New York: Gale Research, 1995; Kaiser Permanente History. Available online. URL: xnet.kp.org/newscenter/aboutkp/historyofkp.html. Accessed on July 7, 2009; Makoverb, Michael E. *Mismanaged Care.* New York: Prometheus Books, 1998; Smith, Richard Dean. *The Rise and Fall of Managed Care.* Lima, Ohio: Wyndham Hall Press, 2001.

—Andrew Kearns

hedge fund

A hedge fund in the United States is a private PARTNERSHIP that engages in a variety of high-risk INVESTMENT strategies for PROFIT. Investors should not think that a hedge fund provides them with protection against risk; in fact the opposite is true. Hedge funds operate under different rules from most MUTUAL FUNDS and engage in such activities as ARBITRAGE, investments in EMERGING MARKETS, SHORT SELLING, PROGRAM TRADING, swaps, and other financial investments.

Because they are private-investment partnerships, hedge funds in the United States are typically limited to 99 investors and a general partner. The general partner is paid a small management fee, usually 1 percent of ASSETS under MANAGEMENT, and given a significant share of the profits earned by the hedge fund, often 20 percent or more. Hedge funds are exempt from the Investment Company Act of 1940, meaning they not subject to the standard reporting requirements of CORPORATIONS or mutual funds. Taxation of hedge funds' profits is constantly changing.

At least 65 percent of the investors must be "accredited," meaning that each investor should have a net worth of at least $1 million and an INCOME of at least $200,000 in the previous year. Most hedge funds require a minimum investment of $25,000 or more and have lock-up periods (times during which investors cannot get their money back) of one year or more. The most famous hedge fund in the United States, Long Term Capital Management (LTCM), had a minimum investment of $5 million and a lock-up of two years.

As previously noted, hedge funds engage in high-RISK investment strategies, hoping to earn significant profits. One strategy, arbitrage, is the practice of buying a product at a low price in one market and selling it at a higher price in another market. Arbitrage is as old as trade. A basic business maxim is "buy low and sell high." Knowledgeable middlemen, knowing the prices of products in different parts of the world, would buy from producers in one region and sell to consumers or merchants in another region. One motivation for the exploration of the New World was the control of land-based trade by merchants in the Middle East. European businesspeople and monarchs knew that new DISTRIBUTION CHANNELS would reduce arbitrageurs' power. Hedge-fund managers are, typically, knowledgeable international traders who take advantage of price differentials, earning small profit margins on large sums of money. One of the most famous hedge-fund operators is George Soros, a Hungarian-born manager who made billions of dollars in currency and interest-rate markets in the United States.

A second hedge-fund strategy is investment in emerging markets. Often markets like Central European countries and Russia after the collapse of the Soviet Union offer tremendous profit opportunities for high-risk investors. Most small, individual investors do not have the time or knowledge to make investments in emerging markets.

Hedge funds also engage in short selling, the sale of borrowed securities, betting that the price of those shares will decline. If the share price does decline, the hedge fund repurchases the shares at the lower price, earning a profit on the difference.

Because they control significant sums of MONEY and additional borrowed funds based on their CAPITAL, hedge-fund managers can influence market prices through their buying and selling. Hedge funds often engage in program trading, the purchase and sale of large volumes of shares or other securities at preset prices. Computers are used to purchase and sell shares automatically, moving the hedge fund into and out of markets rapidly. Program trading was implicated in the massive 1987 sell-off of stock, when the Dow Jones Industrial Average declined over 500 points in one day.

Swaps are the exchange of securities with the agreement to repurchase them at some future time. Hedge funds engage in interest-rate and currency swaps, hoping to profit on changing market conditions. LTCM's demise came when the hedge fund bet that the spread between short-term and long-term INTEREST RATES would narrow. Instead the spread increased, and because the fund was highly leveraged, it lost billions of dollars.

Hedge funds control billions of dollars worth of assets and have significant influence on financial markets. They tend to profit during downturns in the economy and financial crises. Because they are exempt from SECURITIES AND EXCHANGE COMMISSION reporting requirements, there is relatively little information available about them.

Further reading
Baker Library Guide to Hedge Funds. Available online. URL: http://library.hbs.edu/guides/hedgefunds.htm.

hedging
Hedging is any business and INVESTMENT activity entered into to reduce RISK rather than to produce earnings. For example, a farmer makes a decision on how much wheat to plant. At the current price of wheat, he will make a good PROFIT, and if the price of wheat rises, it will be especially profitable, but if the price falls, it will be unprofitable. To hedge for

this uncertainty, he can enter into a FUTURES contract for wheat, which will be profitable to him if the price of wheat falls and unprofitable if the price rises. The risk of this futures CONTRACT offsets the risk of growing the wheat. In essence, the farmer has shifted the risk of the falling prices to the other person in the futures contract.

An investor must not think that a HEDGE FUND provides the investor any sort of protection against risk; in fact, the opposite is true. A hedge fund takes on risk by entering into contracts that hedge the risk for other businesses, so it would possibly be the other party in the contract with the farmer in the above example. If that is so, the investors in the hedge fund now have the risk of changes in wheat prices.

Hedging does not apply only to investment instruments; it should also be part of any sound BUSINESS PLAN. To hedge against bad economic times, a cruise-ship line can invest in a chain of movie theaters. During slow economic times, the cruise ships will lose money, but the movie theaters will make a profit, and vice versa. Each division serves as a hedge for the other.

Herfindahl Index (Herfindahl-Hirschman Index)

The Herfindahl Index, also referred to as the Herfindahl-Hirschman Index, is a measure of MARKET CONCENTRATION, the degree to which a few firms control the pricing and output in a market. In perfectly competitive markets there are many firms, and no one firm is large enough to influence the market outcome. In a MONOPOLY, however, there is only one firm, and its actions determine the market outcome.

Herfindahl Indices are most often associated with oligopolies, markets where there are only a few competitors. A market's Herfindahl Index is the sum of the squares of the market shares of each firm in the industry. For example, if there are only four firms in a market and two firms each have 30 percent of market sales, and the other two firms each have 20 percent of market sales, then the Herfindahl Index is:

$$30^2 + 30^2 + 20^2 + 20^2 = 2600$$

This market would be considered highly concentrated by the antitrust division of the U.S. Justice Department, which considers any market with a Herfindahl Index of less than 1800 to be competitive. When deciding whether to allow the merger or acquisition of companies, the Justice Department calculates the Herfindahl Index that would result if the merger or acquisition. One of the problems is defining the market in question. For example, the main competitors in the U.S. retail telecommunications market are the large telephone companies AT&T, Verizon, and Sprint, but consumers also use cellular phones and the INTERNET to communicate. If only these three large telephone companies are used to calculate the Herfindahl Index, it will be much higher than if the market is defined more broadly.

Before the development of the Herfindahl Index, the traditional measure of market concentration was the four-firm concentration ratio. This index was created by adding the market shares (percentage of market sales) of the four largest firms in the industry, a measurement that did not account for the size distribution of firms in the market.

See also OLIGOPOLY.

hierarchy of effects

The hierarchy of effects is a marketing model developed to improve the effectiveness of ADVERTISING that describes the stages of thought, emotion, and action that a consumer experiences when he or she purchases a product. Although the ideas behind this model have existed for many years, the modern term was coined by Kristian Palda in 1966 to describe the specific model developed by Robert J. Lavidge and Gary A. Steiner in 1961. Lavidge and Steiner suggest that a consumer transitions through seven steps when making the decision to purchase a product: (1) lack of awareness of the product; (2) awareness of the product; (3) knowledge of the product's attributes; (4) positive feelings about the product; (5) partiality toward the product over other substitute products; (6) belief that purchasing the product would be valuable; and (7) the actual purchase of the product. The consumer who experiences each of these steps moves through the "three functions of advertising." Becoming aware of the product and understanding what it has to offer involves the "information or ideas" or "cognition" function. Liking, and then preferring, the product involves the "attitudes or feelings" or "affect" function. Finally, desiring to purchase and then purchasing a product involves the "action" or "conation" function.

While the model demonstrates the steps a consumer takes when he or she first learns of a product and ultimately ends up purchasing it, every consumer does not experience each step and many consumers skip steps. For example, most consumers experience awareness and knowledge of a particular product, but fewer grow to like it, and even less go on to purchase it. Additionally, each consumer does not pass through every stage for each purchase he or she makes. As Lavidge and Steiner point out, a consumer who makes a fairly insignificant purchase impulsively is less likely to experience each stage than the consumer who conducts research and carefully considers making an important or expensive purchase.

Advertisers employ their understanding of this model when developing and evaluating advertisements. The first goal of advertising based upon this model is to catch consumers' attention and to develop their awareness of a particular brand. Advertisers may use creative advertisements or those that contrast heavily with others to attract attention. After initiating awareness, advertisers attempt to influence consumers to comprehend a product's uses by building up its positive qualities and distancing it from negative qualities. To persuade consumers to view a product positively, advertisers may try to assimilate their product into their consumers' values or beliefs or attempt to pique consumers' curiosity and willingness to learn more about a product. Emphasizing the entertainment aspect of a product and clarifying a product's use and value are advertising strategies meant to leave consumers with positive emotions toward a product. Finally, advertisers influence consumers to favor and then select a product by emphasizing creativity, consumer curiosity, and positive attitudes toward the product in their advertisements. If a consumer has previously developed negative attitudes or feelings toward a product, advertisers must first remove that negative emotion and then bring the consumer through the steps of the model.

The hierarchy of effects model has been studied and reformulated by many researchers. Throughout the 1960s and 1970s, several similar hierarchies were proposed based upon differing numbers of stages and ideas about the consumer. Recently, researchers have put forth several challenges and criticisms to the model. For example, Weilbacher argues that the hierarchy of effects model simply seems sensible but has never been proven. Further, the model is based upon theories of behaviorist psychology that have been dismissed by modern science. He also writes that many other factors go into a consumer's decision to purchase a product beyond the advertising alone. He argues that the model is too simplistic in that the competition of different brands within one product market is not addressed. Still others disagree with these criticisms, arguing that the model is applicable to more marketing concepts than simply advertising. Barry points out that it is the difficulty in measuring consumers' comprehension of information that has led to a lack of substantiation for the theory. He also writes that the model is sensible because it is based on logic.

While illustrating the flaws and weaknesses of the model, the arguments and criticisms of these and other authors also encourage continued research and study of the hierarchy of effects model, which improves the effectiveness of advertising (Barry, 2002). The ATTENTION, INTEREST, DESIRE, ACTION model (AIDA) incorporates a similar consumer decision-making process. The hierarchy of effects model continues to be an important influence on advertising and marketing for its "simplicity, intuitiveness, and logic" and as a basis for anticipating consumer actions, selecting marketing tactics, and educating.

Further reading
Barry, T. E. "The Development of the Hierarchy of Effects: An Historical Perspective." *Current Issues and*

Research in Advertising 10, no. 2 (1987): 251–295; ———.
"In Defense of the Hierarchy of Effects: A Rejoinder
to Weilbacher." *Journal of Advertising Research* 42, no.
3 (2002): 44–47; Bendixen, M. T. "Advertising Effects
and Effectiveness." *European Journal of Marketing* 27,
no. 10 (1993): 19–32; Lavidge, R. J., and G. A. Steiner.
"A Model for Predictive Measurements of Advertising
Effectiveness." *Journal of Marketing* 25, no. 6 (1961):
59–62; Smith, R. E., J. Chen, and X. Yang. "The Impact
of Advertising on the Hierarchy of Effects." *Journal of
Advertising* 37, no. 4 (2008): 47–61; Weilbacher, W. M.
Point of View: Does Advertising Cause a "Hierarchy of
Effects"? *Journal of Advertising Research* 41, no. 6 (2001):
19–26; ———. Weilbacher comments on "In Defense
of the Hierarchy of Effects." *Journal of Advertising
Research* 42, no. 3 (2002): 48–49.
— Mary Elizabeth Duncan and Rosa L. Cummings

hierarchy of needs   See MASLOW'S HIERARCHY
OF NEEDS.

Hofstede's dimensions

Hofstede's dimensions refer to a well-known study
of five dimensions of international cultural differences in work-related values. The five dimensions,
first published in 1980, include uncertainty avoidance, power distance, masculinity-femininity,
individualism-collectivism, and Confucian dynamism. Using existing survey data (sample size of
116,000) collected from a MULTINATIONAL CORPORATION, Hofstede, an IBM psychologist, developed
a score for each dimension for employees from 40
different countries.

Uncertainty avoidance refers to the levels of
people's comfort with ambiguity. Cultures with
high uncertainty avoidance prefer formal rules
and relationships, reducing uncertainty and anxiety, while cultures with low uncertainty avoidance
are more comfortable with lack of structure in
an organization. In countries with a high level of
uncertainty avoidance (such as Greece and Japan),
business environments tend to have formal rules
and procedures, and managers more often choose
low-risk alternatives. In countries with lower levels
of uncertainty avoidance (such as Denmark and
Great Britain), business activities are less struc-

tured and managers tend to take greater risks. The
United States ranks moderately low on Hofstede's
uncertainty avoidance scale.

Power distance refers to the extent to which
less powerful members of institutions accept and
expect that power will be distributed unequally.
In a workplace, inequality of power is normal,
as evidenced in hierarchical boss-subordinate
relationships. In Hofstede's study, Mexican and
Malaysian work environments had high power
distance, employees acknowledging the manager's
authority and seldom bypassing the chain of command. Austrian, Israeli, and Danish workplaces
exhibited lower power distance, while the United
States ranked in the middle.

Masculinity-femininity refers to the extent to
which society values assertiveness (masculinity)
versus caring (called femininity by Hofstede). In
this dimension, Hofstede evaluated expected gender roles in a culture. "Masculine" cultures tend to
have distinct expectations for males and females,
while "feminine" cultures have less-defined gender
roles. Japan and Austria rated high in masculinity,
while Denmark and Chile rated low. The United
States ranked in the middle on the masculinity-femininity scale.

Individualism-collectivism refers to the degree
to which ties among individuals are normally loose
rather than close. In more individualistic cultures,
all members of society are expected to look after
themselves and their immediate families. Collectivist cultures have stronger bonds beyond immediate families. The United States and Australia are
considered individualistic, while Indonesia and
Pakistan are considered collectivist cultures.

Confucian dynamism refers to the degree a
culture promotes ethics found in Confucian teachings, including thrift, perseverance, a sense of
shame, in addition to how it follows a hierarchy.
According to Hofstede, rapid ECONOMIC DEVELOPMENT in Asian countries is in part attributable to
this workplace cultural dimension.

Further reading
Deresky, Helen. *International Management.* 2d ed.
Reading, Mass.: Addison-Wesley, 1997; Hofstede, Geert.

Culture's Consequences: International Differences in Work-related Values. Newbury Park, Calif.: Sage Publishing, 1980.

holding company

A holding company is a CORPORATION that owns other companies or corporations. Holding companies typically own stock in or otherwise exercise managerial control over the companies they own; their controlling interest is usually at least 50 percent. For tax reasons, individuals sometimes create personal holding companies for their investments.

Holding companies are often created to separate a corporation's regulated and unregulated industries. For example, most PUBLIC UTILITIES in the United States are owned by holding companies. The utility part (an electrical or water supply company) operates as a regulated MONOPOLY, while the land development or other INVESTMENT part of the business operates as a regular corporation. Beginning in the 1960s, many U.S. banks created holding companies, which allowed them to expand over state lines and bypass laws limiting the number of bank branches allowed. Like utility companies, banks could also diversify into nonbanking activities, and holding-company status reduced some types of tax liability.

Further reading

Hamilton, Robert W. *The Law of Corporations in a Nutshell.* 5th ed. Eagan, Minn.: West Group, 2000; Kidwell, David S., David W. Blackwell, David A. Whidbee, and Richard L. Peterson. *Financial Institutions, Markets, and Money.* 10th ed. Hoboken, N.J.: John Wiley & Son, 2008.

home equity line of credit (HELOC)

A home equity line of credit (HELOC, pronounced "he loc") is a loan agreement set up as a line of credit with limits on the amount a homeowner can borrow over a specified period of time. It is a type of revolving credit tied to a homeowner's EQUITY in his or her house. Many lenders set the credit limit based on a percentage of the home equity by taking the appraised value and subtracting the balance owed on the primary MORTGAGE. HELOCs are an alternative to second mortgages where borrowers take out an additional loan against the value of their home.

HELOCs have advantages and disadvantages when compared to second mortgage loans. The first advantage is if the loan is secured against the homeowner's primary residence, the interest expense is likely to be deductible for federal income tax purposes on Schedule A, Itemized Deductions, and state income taxes. Automobile, credit card, and other personal loan interest costs are not deductible for individual taxpayers. A second advantage is that a line of credit provides ready access to borrowable funds, usually through preauthorized checks issued by the lender, but does not require the borrower to borrow any or all of the funds for which they have been approved.

Disadvantages associated with HELOCs include that interest charged is typically a variable rate, expenses are associated with setting up the line of credit, lenders use initial "teaser" rates, and using your home as collateral entails risk. Variable rates transfer interest rate risk from the lender to the borrower. HELOC loans are typically tied to the "prime rate," the rate charged to high-quality businesses for short, unsecured loans. If interest rates increase, the borrower's payments will increase. Of course, if interest rates decline payments will also decline. Also, HELOC loans typically adjust rapidly, month to month as market rates change. Usually, adjustable-rate (primary) mortgages (ARMs) change interest rates at most once a year.

Setting up a HELOC can be expensive, usually including an appraisal fee, application fee, upfront charges or "points" (with each point equal to 1 percent of the credit limit,) and closing costs, including fees for attorneys, title search, loan preparation, and filing. Some lenders also charge an annual membership or maintenance fee even if you do not access your line of credit.

A third disadvantage associated with HELOCs has been the practice of some lenders to offer temporarily low interest rates, often for a short period of time. When the initial discount rate ends, payments often jump rapidly, potentially putting borrowers at risk of default, which leads to the fourth disadvantage: Because the loan is secured by their home, borrowers could wind up in foreclosure. The FEDERAL RESERVE's "When Your Home Is on the Line" Web site also warns, "If you decide to apply for a home equity line of credit, look for the plan that best meets your particular needs. Read the credit agreement carefully, and examine the terms and conditions of various plans, including the annual percentage rate and the costs of establishing the plan. The APR for a home equity line is based on the interest rate alone and will not reflect the closing costs and other fees and charges, so you'll need to compare these costs, as well as the APRs, among lenders."

Despite these disadvantages, in the mid-2000s, with rapidly rising housing values, HELOCs became very popular. Economists referred to this as the "wealth effect." For example, if a homeowner put very little money down, say $10,000 on a home priced at $200,000, and found two years later that the house was worth 30 percent more, or $260,000, his net worth increased by 600 percent. Temptation and inducements from lenders encouraged many American homeowners to borrow and spend their newfound wealth. When the financial crisis hit in 2007, lenders cut or canceled unused credit lines and, with falling home prices, borrowers found themselves "upside down," owing more to lenders than their home was now worth. HELOCs contributed to increased foreclosures and walkaway borrowers. Lenders coined a new term, "jingle mail" for packages from borrowers in which were contained the keys to their house as they gave up trying to pay what they owed.

Further reading
Federal Reserve. "When Your Home Is on the Line." Available online. URL: www.federalreserve.gov/pubs/homeline/default.htm. Accessed on February 11, 2009.

human resources

The term *human resources* has two different meanings. It may refer to the people within an organization who are performing the work or it may refer to the human resources (HR) function—a collection of related activities that pertain to the manage-

ment of personnel within the organization. It is the second reference that is being discussed here.

The HR function has developed significantly in recent years. In many organizations today, human resources is considered an essential, strategic business function as well as an integral part of a company's administrative staff. This arm of the business is involved in ensuring that the employees accept responsibility; perform at high levels of efficiency; and make decisions within their area of responsibility, knowledge, and expertise. Senior MANAGEMENT expects HR to add unique, sustained value to the organization, thus helping the business improve its position over its competitors. Providing this competitive advantage helps the firm increase PROFITS, enhance CUSTOMER RELATIONS/SATISFACTION, and improve market share. Many HR functions work closely with management to help structure jobs so that the work is challenging and satisfying. HR also helps create the culture and shape the organization's management style.

Although HR professionals may place different emphases on core activities in accordance with the organization's current needs, there are five traditional HR activities: EMPLOYMENT, TRAINING AND DEVELOPMENT, COMPENSATION AND BENEFITS, employee and labor relations, and health and safety. These five activities comprise the HR function, although motivation, communication, and job and organization design are often delegated to HR. Following are brief definitions of the core areas.

1. Employment consists of recruiting and selection. Recruiting ensures a supply of qualified applicants from which the appropriate selection(s) of new hire(s) can be made. Often the process of socializing the new employee into the organization is a part of the employment process. Socializing reduces the potential of psychological shock the new employee may experience during the first few weeks or months of employment.

2. Training and development ensure that the organization has employees with the appropri-

ate knowledge, skills, and abilities to perform the necessary job duties. Training often has the connotation of learning specific job skills necessary to perform the current job. Development, however, has a longer-term focus to educate employees to perform future jobs that require higher knowledge, skills, and abilities.

3. Compensation and benefits comprise the total rewards package that an employee receives for performing the job. Compensation is considered direct pay, since it is the amount of money the employee receives. Benefits are indirect pay, since they are monetary equivalents that can be converted later into cash or cash equivalents. Benefits that are voluntarily offered by employers often include vacations, holidays, group INSURANCE (e.g., health and life insurance) and pension programs. Legally required benefits include SOCIAL SECURITY, UNEMPLOYMENT insurance, WORKERS' COMPENSATION, and in many cases time off to attend to family medical needs (see FAMILY AND MEDICAL LEAVE ACT). For every dollar paid in compensation, the CHAMBER OF COMMERCE estimates that 39–40 percent is spent for indirect compensation, leaving 60–61 percent for direct compensation. This is a composite average; individual companies and specific situations may vary considerably.

4. Employee relations is concerned with assuring that each employee is treated fairly, and if there is a concern or problem, those issues are addressed quickly. Employees are encouraged to discuss their concerns with either their supervisor or HR representative. The term *employee relations* is usually used when the organization's employees are not represented by a UNION. The term *labor relations* is used when specific employee groups are represented by a union. Individual union members are represented by a union representative called a union steward or committee person, although employees can still discuss issues with their supervisor or HR representative. When a union does represent groups of employees, the wages, hours, terms, and conditions of work are negotiated jointly by union and company representatives in a process called COLLECTIVE BARGAINING.

5. Health and safety standards ensure that employees work in an environment that is free from recognized hazards. Although safety and health activities are usually management-led, safety is everyone's responsibility. Safety committees are often established within each department to implement safety programs and assist in accident investigations. The Occupational Safety and Health Act (1970), a federal law, has many industry-specific safety regulations, but even when there are no specific guidelines, the act contains the General Duty Clause, which requires employers to conform to the law's intent of the law—safe and healthful working conditions.

See also OCCUPATIONAL HEALTH AND SAFETY ADMINISTRATION.

—John Abbott

identity theft

Identity theft occurs when someone steals your personal identification information, particularly your name, SOCIAL SECURITY number, or credit card number and uses that information to commit FRAUD or other crimes. The FEDERAL TRADE COMMISSION (FTC) estimates that 9 million Americans, approximately one in 15 adults, have their identities stolen each year. (Theft of children's identity is also a problem.) With identification information criminals can charge purchases to your credit cards, obtain loans in your name, rent apartments, open telephone or utility accounts, or obtain phony government documents and then default or commit other crimes, leaving you with the problems, tarnished credit history, and even the potential for false arrest.

The Federal Trade Commission is the primary government agency responsible for monitoring and addressing problems associated with identity theft. According to the FTC, the criminals use a variety of methods, including:

1. Dumpster Diving. Rummaging through trash looking for bills or other paper with your personal information on it.
2. Skimming. Stealing credit/debit card numbers by using a special storage device when processing your card.
3. Phishing. Pretending to be financial institutions or companies and sending spam or pop-up messages to get you to reveal your personal information.
4. Changing Your Address. Diverting your billing statements to another location by completing a "change of address" form.
5. "Old-Fashioned" Stealing. Stealing wallets and purses; mail, including bank and credit card statements; preapproved credit offers; and new checks or tax information. They steal personnel records from employers, or bribe employees who have access.
6. Pretexting. Using false pretenses to obtain your personal information from financial institutions, telephone companies, and other sources.

Unfortunately, most Americans find out their identity has been stolen only when a problem occurs. Bills for products or services you did not purchase, incorrect charges to credit cards, and denial of a loan or rental agreement are often how consumers find out there is a problem. To avoid these surprises, consumer advisers and the FTC recommend periodic review of your credit reports. An amendment to the FAIR CREDIT REPORTING ACT requires each of the three major credit reporting companies to provide consumers with a free copy of their report, at their request, once every 12 months. Though credit reports vary among the three companies, typically, if your identity has been stolen, the criminal will have engaged in enough fraudulent activity to show up on each of the reports. Consumer advisers recommend staggering your requests, obtaining a free report from one company every four months, and staggering requests to avoid having to pay for the report.

Early detection of identity theft will likely reduce the severity of the problem. The FTC recommends consumers who find their identity has been stolen should:

- File a police report. A theft report is needed to block fraudulent information from your credit report history and to place an extended fraud alert on your credit report
- Check all three of your credit reports.
- Place a fraud alert with the credit reporting agencies. An initial fraud alert stays on your credit report for 90 days. An extended alert lasts for seven years.
- Close accounts. Call and speak with someone in the security or fraud department of each company.
- Dispute any unauthorized charges
- File a complaint with the FTC, www.ftc.gov/bcp/ edu/microsties/idtheft/ 1-877-326-2502

Consumer advocates also warn identity theft victims to keep the original copy of all documents related to the theft, and copies of all reports and communications with the various agencies and companies.

Given the time and economic consequences of identity theft, how can Americans reduce the potential of becoming a victim? The FTC and consumer advocacy groups recommend individuals manage their personal information, including:

- Use a shredder to destroy old personal documents or any information containing your Social Security number, credit card number, or other personal information.
- Ask any business requesting your Social Security number to use some other form of identification.
- Deposit mail that contains your personal information such as credit card and mortgage payments directly in a U.S. Post Office mailbox.
- Avoid using easily predictable passwords on bank, phone, or credit card accounts

- Secure information in your home, especially if others have access to your home.
- Do not carry information with your Social Security number in your wallet or purse. (Medical insurance companies and universities are finally shifting away from using Social Security numbers as customer IDs.)
- Have a copy of credit card numbers and the companies' 800 numbers secured safely for emergencies.
- Never respond to online or telephone requests for your information. Phishing, seemingly legitimate requests from businesses and nonprofit groups consumers know, has become increasingly sophisticated.
- Keep up through news stories and consumer advocacy groups' reports on the latest identity theft scams.
- Update your computer virus protection regularly.
- Use a "wipe" utility program before discarding an old computer.

New methods of identity theft are constantly being created. Being aware of how information is stolen is the first step in protecting against identity theft. The Identity Theft Resource Center, a nonprofit organization based in San Diego, offers a variety of resources, including a breach list, scam alerts, lost or stolen wallet assistance, and medical identity theft.

The three major credit reporting companies are:

- Equifax, 1-800-685-1111 www.equifax.com
- Experian, 1-888-397-3742 www.experian.com
- Transunion, 1-800-916-8800 www.transunion. com

To obtain a free copy of your credit report contact Annual Credit Report, 1-877-322-8228, www. annualcreditreport.com. Note, many other credit information services will provide the same information but charge a fee. There are also identity theft reporting services that also charge a fee.

Further reading

Federal Trade Commission. "Identity Theft: What It's All About." Available online. URL: www.pueblo.gsa.gov/ cic_text/money/idtheftwhat/idtheftwhat.htm. Accessed on March 14, 2009; Federal Trade Commission. "Fighting

Back against Identity Theft: Deter, Detect, Defend." Available online. URL: www.ftc.gov/bcp/edu/pubs/consumer/idtheft/idt01.shtm. Accessed on March 14, 2009; Take the Federal Trade Commission's Identity Theft awareness quiz. Available online. URL: www.onguardonline.gov/games/id-theft-faceoff.aspx. Accessed on March 14, 2009; Identity Theft Resource Center. Available online. URL: www.idtheftcenter.org/.

import restraints

The United States, like many countries, uses a variety of methods to restrain IMPORTS into the country, including TARIFFS, quotas, tariff-rate quotas, and NONTARIFF BARRIERS. Tariffs are taxes or duties applied to imported products, paid by the importing company, increasing the cost of imported PRODUCTS. Quotas are limits on the number of units of a good that can be imported into the United States. Tariff-rate quotas allow a lower tariff rate on in-quota quantities of imports and a higher rate on over-quota levels of imports. Some imports are restrained through nontariff barriers, the rules and regulations with which imported products must comply. Nonconforming products are often banned from importation.

Many U.S. quotas were created to protect American agriculture. These quotas, mostly on animal feeds, dairy products, chocolate, cotton, peanuts, and selected syrups and sugars, are utilized to coordinate U.S. farming price-support programs. For example, the United States supports domestic sugar production by paying sugar producers prices significantly higher than world prices. In absence of import quotas, domestic sugar users, such as candy and soft-drink manufacturers, would purchase sugar on the world market instead of higher-priced domestic supplies. Some U.S. agricultural quotas are being "tariffed," converted into tariff-rate quotas, under the WORLD TRADE ORGANIZATION's Agreement on Agriculture.

Under the Trade Expansion Act of 1962, the United States authorized the president to "adjust imports" whenever necessary to the country's national security. Trade EMBARGOes, such as those against Iraq and Cuba, are conducted under this legislation. Narcotic drugs, "immoral" goods, and goods produced by forced, child-bonded, or convict labor are excluded from importation into the United States. Certain goods from the People's Republic of China have been banned based on these restrictions.

There are numerous nontariff barriers to imports into the United States. These barriers often arise out of state or federal health and safety concerns. Others are based on environmental, CONSUMER PROTECTION, product standards, and government procurement. Many nontariff barriers were created for legitimate consumer-protection reasons, but others are attempts by domestic producers to restrict COMPETITION. In addition to health and safety concerns, restrictions on imports are often justified based on saving domestic jobs, creating "fair trade," national defense interests, infant-industry arguments (protecting new domestic industries from established international competitors), and strategic trade-policy goals.

During the debates on the NORTH AMERICAN FREE TRADE AGREEMENT (NAFTA), then presidential candidate Ross Perot claimed NAFTA would create a "giant sucking sound," as U.S. jobs were drawn away to Mexico. Perot argued that Mexico's cheaper labor costs would cause the loss of millions of American jobs. Steel import restrictions are rationalized as being necessary so the United States will have a domestic source of steel in times of war. Countries sometimes justify protecting new industries, arguing the industries need time to become competitive with the rest of the world. In the mid-1980s, the United States negotiated voluntary import restrictions with Japanese automobile producers so that U.S. producers would have time to catch up to Japanese quality and technology.

Strategic trade policy is the use of trade restrictions or subsidies to allow domestic firms with decreasing costs per unit of output (ECONOMIES OF SCALE) to gain a larger share of the world market. Producers in many countries around the world argue they need access to the huge U.S. market in order to become large enough to effectively compete with giant U.S. CORPORATIONS.

Further reading

Boyes, William J., and Michael Melvin. *Microeconomics*. 7th ed. Boston: Houghton Mifflin, 2007; Folsom, Ralph H., and W. Davis Folsom. *Understanding NAFTA and Its International Business Implications*. New York: Mathew Irwin/Bender, 1996.

imports/exports

Imports are the goods produced in another country (foreign goods) that are brought into a home country (e.g., the United States) for sale. Exports are the goods produced by the home country (domestic goods) that are shipped to another country for sale. Thus one country's exports are another country's imports. Balance of trade occurs when a country's imports equal its exports.

A simplified explanation of why trade takes place is because the foreign country can produce a certain good cheaper than the importing country. The law of comparative advantage, however, states that the item will be made in a more expensive location as long as its relative cost of production is cheaper than in the importing country. For example, suppose a country could manufacture computers very efficiently and profitably but could less efficiently and profitably produce automobiles. If it did produce automobiles, though, they would be cheaper than those produced by its neighbor country. Yet in spite of the higher cost, it imports automobiles from its neighbors instead of moving workers and capital from its more profitable computer industry to produce domestic automobiles.

As demonstrated by the decline in the value of the U.S. dollar in 2008, imports and exports are sensitive to changes in currency exchange rates. With the decline in the dollar, foreign car imports declined and sales U.S. products abroad expanded. U.S. tourism abroad dropped significantly while foreign visitors to the United States grew. In many countries the value of exports and imports can equal or exceed a country's GROSS DOMESTIC PRODUCT (GDP). While trade represents approximately 6 percent of GDP in the United States, export income and competition from imported products contribute to the growth in the economy. Countries often attempt to maintain a positive trade balance in order to create and expand domestic jobs and income. The United States has run a significant (in 2008, more than $600 billion) current account deficit (the sum of merchandise, services, investment income, and unilateral transfers) since 1980.

The U.S. imports significantly more merchandise than it exports but exports more services than it imports. The United States perennially has a trade surplus in certain categories, including agricultural and technology products, and a trade deficit in energy and textile products. The major trading partners of the United States are Canada, Mexico, and Japan, with China becoming an increasingly important source of imports. Canada has long been the United States's leading trading partner, but trade with Mexico grew with the passage of the NORTH AMERICAN FREE TRADE AGREEMENT (NAFTA) in 1994.

income

The *Income* has many definitions, depending on the context in which it is used. Definitions of income can be separated into four categories: income related to personal taxes, business INCOME STATEMENTS; aggregate income in an economy; and money versus REAL INCOME.

In the U.S. personal-income tax system, the INTERNAL REVENUE SERVICE uses three definitions of income: total or gross income, adjusted gross income (AGI), and taxable income. Total income is, as the term suggests, money received by the taxpayer from all sources. For most U.S. taxpayers, total income is the sum of wage, salary, interest, and DIVIDEND income along with CAPITAL GAINS in a given year. Some taxpayers also have rents, royalties, distributions from INDIVIDUAL RETIREMENT ACCOUNTS (IRAs), refunds, alimony, business income, pensions, annuities, PARTNERSHIP income, and SOCIAL SECURITY benefits included in their total income.

Adjusted gross income is total income minus a variety of deductions, including IRA contributions, student-loan interest, medical savings-account deductions, moving expenses, self-employment tax, health Simplified Employee Pension (SEP) payments, and alimony payments. Taxable income is adjusted gross income minus tax credits, including standard or itemized deductions and personal exemption allowances. Taxable income is the net amount of total income subject to U.S. personal income taxes.

Business income statements, which can be quite complex, measure a firm's income for its accounting period. Businesses compare revenue with expenses and allowances for DEPRECIATION to develop a statement of the company's income.

While accountants calculate a company's income, the U.S. Department of Commerce estimates the country's aggregate income, the total value of all claims against output. Aggregate income (GROSS DOMESTIC PRODUCT [GDP]) equals the sum of wages, rents, dividends, and PROFITS less net-factor income from abroad, plus capital consumption allowance and indirect BUSINESS TAXES. National income is GDP minus factor income, CAPITAL consumption allowance and indirect business taxes. Personal income is national income adjusted for income that is received but not earned and earned but not yet received. Finally, disposable personal income is personal income minus personal-income taxes, or what people have available to spend or save.

Money income is income measured in dollars received in the current period of time, while real income is measured by the purchasing power of income received. Real income is money income adjusted for INFLATION. Economists use PRICE INDEXES such as the CONSUMER PRICE INDEX to compare the purchasing power of money income over time.

Further reading
Boyes, William, and Michael Melvin. *Macroeconomics.* 7th ed. Boston: Houghton Mifflin, 2007.

income elasticity of demand
Income elasticity of demand is the responsiveness of DEMAND for a good or service to changes in INCOME. As consumer income rises, the demand for most goods and SERVICES will increase. For

example, the demand for new cars and homes is quite sensitive to changes in income. Manufacturers of these PRODUCTS incorporate estimates of changing income when forecasting demand and making long-term planning decisions. Income elasticity of demand is calculated as follows:

$$E_y = \text{(\% change in demand for good X) /}$$
$$\text{(\% change in income)}$$

In the 1990s Americans' income rose steadily, and demand for most products also increased. If income rose 4 percent and demand for a product increased 6 percent, the income elasticity of demand would be .06/.04 = 1.5. If, as one source states, the income elasticity of demand for automobiles were 1.7, then with a 4 percent increase in income, demand would be expected to increase by 6.8 percent (.04 × 1.7). Similarly, when incomes declined in the 2008 recession, demand for new cars dropped precipitously, contributing to General Motors' and Chrysler's bankruptcies.

Economists call goods for which an increase in income results in an increase in demand "normal" goods. There are also goods for which an increase in income will result in a decrease in demand; economists call these "inferior" goods. The label has nothing to do with the quality of the product or service, just the fact that they have negative income elasticity. The classic "inferior" good is potatoes. However, as consumers' incomes rise, people substitute stuffing, gourmet rice, and other starches for potatoes. When consumers' incomes decline, they purchase more potatoes.

Another example comes from a very shrewd independent automobile mechanic. He observed that as the economy boomed, demand for his repair services declined, since people were buying new cars, trading in their "clunkers" and not creating work for him. But when the economy slowed, demand for his services increased as people held on to their cars longer.

Since income tends to change slowly, most managers do not consider income elasticity of demand in daily or operational plans but do incorporate the impact of changing incomes in their STRATEGIC

PLANNING. Some examples of estimated income elasticity include

movie tickets	3.4
foreign travel	3.1
wine	1.6
beef	0.5
beer	0.4
lard	−0.1

Further reading
Ruffin, Roy J., and Paul R. Gregory. *Principles of Economics.* 7th ed. Boston: Addison Wesley, 2001.

incomes policies   See WAGE AND PRICE CONTROLS.

income redistribution
Income redistribution is government action to transfer money and/or goods and SERVICES from some groups in a society to others. Income redistribution involves the transfer of money payments or goods and services with no requirement or expectation of exchange of RESOURCES or services by the recipients. In the United States, major income-redistribution programs include transfer-payment systems such as WELFARE, SOCIAL SECURITY, and UNEMPLOYMENT benefits; and transfer-in-kind programs such as food stamps, public housing, and medical care. Compared with most industrialized countries in the world, U.S. income-redistribution programs are quite modest, but they are a controversial part of U.S. public policy.

At the beginning of the 21st century, the fastest-growing income-redistribution programs in the United States were Medicare and Medicaid. Medicare subsidizes medical care for the elderly, while Medicaid provides health-care services for poorer Americans. However, the largest income-redistribution program in the United States is Social Security. When it was created, Social Security was intended to be a modest income INSURANCE program, by which workers paid into the program and later received benefits based on their contributions. Because of growth in the U.S. economy after World War II, there soon were many more workers

relative to beneficiaries, creating surpluses in the program. Congress then expanded the benefits and programs under Social Security well beyond its initial objective, and as a result, most retired Americans now get all they paid into Social Security plus interest within 3–4 years. Though most American retirees don't like the word, they are actually receiving welfare.

Today Social Security is an intergenerational income-transfer program, with current retirees being given money payments from current workers. Some analysts compare this system to a PONZI SCHEME, in which initial investors are paid with the funds collected from subsequent investors. The system works as long as there are new contributors to the system. With the ratio of retirees to workers increasing in the United States, officials anticipate problems with the Social Security program.

Further reading
Miller, Roger LeRoy. *Economics Today.* 15th ed. Boston: Addison Wesley, 2009.

income statement, gross margin
An income statement measures a firm's profitability (or lack thereof) for a period of time known as the accounting period, which can be monthly, quarterly, yearly, or any other length of time. If the accounting period coincides with the calendar year, the firm's INCOME is reported on a calendar-year basis. If the accounting period is a 12-month period of time other than the calendar year (say July 1–June 30), the income is reported on a FISCAL YEAR basis.

Because the income statement is one of the FINANCIAL STATEMENTS used to convey information about the firm to entities outside the firm, it must be constructed using the ACCRUAL BASIS and in accordance with GENERALLY ACCEPTED ACCOUNTING PRINCIPLES (GAAP).

An income statement consists of three major sections: revenues, expenses, and net income. Revenues are RESOURCES accruing to the firm as a result of the sale of goods and/or SERVICES, both for cash and on credit. Expenses are resources flowing out of the firm as a result of the revenue-earning process. Included in expenses are those that have been paid in cash and those that have not yet been paid but nonetheless were incurred during the accounting period being reported.

At the bottom of an income statement is the section stating net income. The difference between revenues and expenses is always called net income, both when there is a PROFIT and when there is a loss for the period. In corporate income statements, it is customary for the net income to be reported in total and per share. Earnings per share (EPS) is determined by dividing net income by the number of common shares outstanding.

Income statements are generally organized as multiple-step statements, as follows:

Revenues
Less: Cost of Goods Sold
Gross Margin
Less: Operating Expenses
Earnings before Interest and Taxes (EBIT)
Less: Interest Expense
Earnings before Taxes (EBT)
Less: Income Tax Expense
Net Income
EPS

The difference between revenues and COST OF GOODS SOLD is the gross margin—the excess (or mark-up) of a firm's prices for goods and services over their cost to the firm. A firm's gross margin is closely monitored and given a prominent place on the income statement. The gross margin must be sufficient to cover the firm's remaining expenses and to ultimately contribute to net income. If the gross margin is insufficient, the firm must raise prices (if possible), reduce expenses (including cost of goods sold), or implement some combination of these two. Gross margin is routinely expressed not only in dollars but as a percentage of sales. Firms in extremely competitive markets find it most useful to compare gross-margin ratios to monitor their profitability.

Cost of goods sold is a crucial element in the determination of a firm's gross margin. It is the most important and closely watched of all the expenses within a firm. While a firm has little,

if any, control over its revenues (a customer cannot be forced to buy), it does have control over its expenses. For this reason, cost of goods sold is separated from the other expenses and subtracted from revenues before the other expenses to determine the firm's gross margin.

Income statements, like all financial statements, are excellent tools of comparison among firms. Because revenues and expenses are reported on the accrual basis and statements must adhere to GAAP, the practice of accounting is standardized and interfirm and interindustry comparisons are possible.

See also FINANCIAL ACCOUNTING.

incorporation

Incorporation is the process of creating a CORPORATION. The rules on incorporating vary somewhat from state to state, with Delaware often perceived to be the most desirable state in which to incorporate because its fees tend to be low. The "articles of incorporation" typically create the company name, designate its corporate officers, identify its headquarters, indicate the amount of CAPITAL involved, and establish BYLAWS (rules of CORPORATE GOVERNANCE). A main reason for incorporating is to obtain "limited financial liability," which restricts, under most circumstances, owners' LIABILITY to their capital INVESTMENT. The two major reasons some businesses do not incorporate is its cost and being subject to corporate taxation.

To incorporate, generally a business organizer

- prepares articles of incorporation
- signs and authenticates the articles
- files the articles with the state's secretary of state and pays filing fees
- receives a "filed" copy of the articles from the secretary of state
- holds an organization meeting for the purpose of electing officers, adopting bylaws, and transacting other business

Although a corporation may do business in many states, usually the relationship among the corporation, its SHAREHOLDERS, and its managers is regulated by the state in which it was incorporated. The American Bar Association prepared a model statute that has been used by most states as the basis for their incorporation statutes.

Further reading
Hamilton, Robert W. *The Law of Corporations in a Nutshell.* 5th ed. Eagan, Minn.: West Group, 2000; Mallor, Jane P., A. James Barnes, Thomas Bowers, Michael J. Philips, and Arlen W. Langvardt. *Business Law: The Ethical, Global, and E-Commerce Environment.* 14th ed. Boston: McGraw-Hill, 2009.

independent contractors
Independent contractors are individuals or companies that provide SERVICES for consumers, businesses, or government. Most professionals are independent contractors, who are best defined by what they are not: employees. Independent contractors typically are paid by the task, while employees are paid by the hour. Independent contractors contract with the consumer or business to produce some result, while employees are told how to conduct their work. The distinction between independent contractors and employees has many legal, tax, and INSURANCE implications.

As cited in Mallor et al., U.S. courts use five factors in determining whether workers are independent contractors or employees. First is the degree of control exercised by the alleged employer. Does the employer determine when, where, what, and how a worker does their job? Independent contractors generally determine when and how work is done.

Second, what are the relative investments of the worker and alleged employer? If the worker provides equipment, transportation, and other ASSETS necessary to the task, they are more likely to be considered an independent contractor. In a factory where the company provides almost all of the materials and machinery needed to produce the products, workers are more likely to be considered employees. In the case described by *Mallor et al.,* topless dancers for the Circle C organization provided their own costumes and locks for their lockers, but Circle C provided the nightclub. The dancers' investments were relatively small compared to those of the business.

Third, to what degree does the alleged employer determine the workers' opportunities for PROFIT and loss? Independent contractors generally profit by their ability to gain CONTRACTS and complete their work. In the Circle C case, the dancers' initiative, hustle, and costumes significantly contributed to their income, but the club's ADVERTISING, location, aesthetics, and food and beverage service gave the club control over customer volume and therefore provided the dancers with opportunities for profit.

Fourth, what skills and initiative are required in performing the job? Most independent contractors provide a distinct skill that the consumer or business needs and wishes to hire for a specific purpose. Employees are generally trained to do tasks required by their employer.

Fifth, what is the permanency of the relationship between the worker and the alleged employer? Independent contractors generally have a short-term, task-specific relationship, while employees have a longer, hours-per-week commitment with the employer.

Independent contractors are typically liable for their work, while the consumer or business hiring them is generally not liable for the contractor's actions. There are exceptions to this distinction, such as when a firm hires an incompetent independent contractor or when the contractor is negligent in taking "special precautions needed to conduct certain highly dangerous or inherently dangerous activities."

Another important distinction between independent contractors and employees is eligibility for WORKERS' COMPENSATION and other benefits. Workers' compensation protects employees but not independent contractors against the risk of injury on the job. Many companies hire independent contractors in order to avoid the workers' compensation costs and liabilities. Independent contractors are also not eligible for a company's health-care program, RETIREMENT PLAN, vacation time, or other benefits. In the 1990s many companies reduced their number of employees, often rehiring laid-off workers, at a lower cost, as independent contractors. In the business world, these new independent contractors were called "corporate pilot fish."

Independent contractors are also treated differently under the federal tax code. Employees pay Federal Insurance Contributions Act (FICA) taxes based on wages, and their contributions are matched by their employers. Independent contractors are considered self-employers. If a contractor has employees, then he, she, or it could be a PROPRIETORSHIP, PARTNERSHIP, or CORPORATION. Many businesses prefer to classify workers as independent contractors in order to avoid the benefits and taxes paid on employees. The FAIR LABOR STANDARDS ACT (FLSA), passed in 1938 and amended many times since then, is a major labor-management law regulating wages and hours, child labor, equal pay and overtime pay, and employee-versus-independent contractor status.

Further reading

Mallor, Jane P., A. James Barnes, Thomas Bowers, Michael J. Philips, and Arlen W. Langvardt. *Business Law: The Ethical, Global, and E-Commerce Environment.* 14th ed. Boston: McGraw-Hill, 2009.

Index of Consumer Expectations

The Index of Consumer Expectations is a measure of how consumers view prospects for their financial situation and the general economy over the near term and long term. The index is part of the University of Michigan's monthly Surveys of Consumers. Created in 1946 by George Katona, the surveys document the importance of consumer spending and saving decisions as a major part of the national economy. Consumer spending represents two-thirds of GROSS DOMESTIC PRODUCT. Changes in consumer expectations influence spending decisions and have significant impact on the overall economy.

Each month a minimum of 500 telephone interviews are conducted by staff members at the University of Michigan survey center; the survey includes approximately 50 questions. One question consumers are asked is, "No one can say for sure, but what do you think will happened to INTEREST RATES for borrowing money during the next 12 months—will they go up, stay the same, or go down?" When consumers' responses are compared to the change in the prime rate (the interest rate charged by banks for short-term unsecured loans to top-quality commercial customers), consumer expectations change on average two quarters (six months) in advance of the change in the prime rate. Consumers generally anticipated interest rate changes six months in advance of the actual change.

Another question asked is, "How about people out of work during the coming 12 months—do you think that there will be more UNEMPLOYMENT than now, about the same, or less?" Survey results show consumers anticipate changes in the unemployment rate nine months in advance of the actual change. In a similar question about INFLATION, consumers predict changes in prices (as measured by the CONSUMER PRICE INDEX) by three months. Survey results also show consumers generally anticipate changes in home buying and vehicle sales by six months.

Business managers watch the Index of Consumer Expectations closely. Manufacturers of durable goods and housing-related products recognize the Index is an effective planning tool when making production decisions. Following the STOCK MARKET crash in October 1987, respondents to the survey displayed less panic than prognosticators on WALL STREET. Managers trusting the survey correctly concluded that stock-market fears would not greatly influence consumer-spending decisions. During the 2008–09 recession consumer expectations dropped dramatically as households feared rapidly rising unemployment rates.

The Index of Consumer Expectations is included in the Leading Indicator Composite Index published by the Department of Commerce. INDICATORS included in the Commerce Department index are based on their economic significance, statistical accuracy, consistency in timing the peaks and troughs of BUSINESS CYCLES, conformity to business expansions and contractions, consistency, and prompt availability. The Index of Consumer Expectations is the only consumer survey included in the composite index. Many other countries have developed consumer expectations indices based on the Index of Consumer Expectations model.

Further reading
Surveys of Consumers Web site. Available online. URL: www.sca.isr.umich.edu/main.php.

indicators

In the business world, economic indicators are measures associated with BUSINESS CYCLES. Business indicators are statistical measures used by individual firms or industry groups to measure and predict changes in business activity. There are three categories of indicators: leading, coincident, and lagging. Leading indicators change in advance of changes in real output—i.e., GROSS DOMESTIC PRODUCT (GDP). Coincident indicators change as real output changes following which lagging indicators will change.

The Department of Commerce index of leading indicators includes

- average workweek
- UNEMPLOYMENT claims
- manufacturers' new orders
- stock prices
- new plant and equipment orders

These statistical measures tend to move in advance of changes in the economy. Declining workweek hours, manufacturers' new orders, stock prices, and new plant and equipment orders tend to precede a decline in GDP. Unemployment claims tend to rise in advance of declining real output.

Coincident indicators include

- payroll EMPLOYMENT
- industrial production
- personal INCOME
- manufacturing and trade sales
- new building permits
- delivery times of goods
- interest-rate spread
- MONEY SUPPLY
- consumer expectations

Logically these indicators change at the same time as changes in real output. Some coincident indicators, such as payroll, personal income, and consumer expectations, affect primarily consumer spending; while other indicators, such as indus-trial PRODUCTION, trade sales, and delivery time of goods affect primarily business spending.

Lagging economic indicators include

- labor cost per unit of output
- inventories-to-sales ratio
- unemployment duration
- ratio of consumer credit to personal income
- outstanding commercial LOANS
- prime interest rate
- inflation rate for SERVICES

These indicators typically do not change until after real GDP has changed. Economists use lagging and leading indicators to distinguish the peaks and troughs in business cycles.

Major U.S. CORPORATIONS usually have a team of economists to analyze economic indicators and use these indicators to develop forecasts for future DEMAND for a company's products based on changes in real GDP. Many firms and industries develop customized sets of indicators for forecasting. For example, convenience-store operators know gasoline prices affect the demand for other PRODUCTS in their stores. Because the ELASTICITY OF DEMAND for gasoline is inelastic, or relatively unresponsive, consumers continue to purchase almost as much gasoline at a higher price as compared to when the price was lower. Higher prices reduce consumers' discretionary spending on candy, drinks, and other impulse purchases. Similarly, universities know changes in high-school graduation rates and federal loan and grant programs, as well as changes in the economy, affect demand for their services. One owner of a traditional men's clothing store noticed that demand for his products shifted depending on which business groups were doing well. At times he had many real-estate developers, other times business executives, lawyers, and doctors. He adjusted his MARKETING STRATEGY based on indicators predicting which segment of the market would continue to prosper.

Further reading
Boyes, William, and Michael Melvin. *Macroeconomics.* 7th ed. Boston: Houghton Mifflin, 2007.

individual retirement account

In 1974 the Employee Retirement Security Act created the individual retirement account (IRA), allowing eligible persons to establish their own tax-deferred retirement savings plans from which withdrawals can be made after age 70½. These so-called traditional IRAs offer an immediate tax benefit by deducting the allowed amount contributed from the annual taxable income, though there are some exceptions. When funds—principal and interest—are withdrawn, they are taxed. Early withdrawals, unless exempt, are subject to an additional 10 percent excise tax. The Roth IRA, established in 1998 and named for Delaware senator William Roth, does not offer investors an immediate tax write-off but allows them to make tax-free withdrawals after the mandatory age of 59½.

Contributions to IRAs can be made only from earned income, wages, salaries, and tips. Married couples who filed joint tax returns are excepted; even if one does not work, each may make a contribution for their "combined" income, with some limitations (see below). Annual contributions were originally limited to $2,000 per individual, but the Economic Growth and Tax Relief Reconciliation Act (EGTRRA) of 2001 increased the limit incrementally between 2002 and 2008, when it reached $5,000, or $6,000 for persons over 50. Since 2009 the contribution limit is indexed to the inflation rate, with the possibility of future increases in increments of $500.

A married couple's contributions to the traditional IRA may not be tax-deductible, depending on their enrollment in a qualified retirement plan and their modified adjusted gross income (AGI) level. A nonworking spouse's tax deduction is phased out if the working spouse is in a retirement plan and their joint AGI falls between $166,000 and $176,000 (filing jointly); the phase-out begins limiting the deduction starting at $166,000 and increases so that there is no deduction at $176,000 or more. Similarly, if the working spouse is in a retirement plan, his or her deduction is decreased once the AGI reaches $89,000, with total phase-out at $109,000. If neither is in a retirement plan, deductions are allowed, regardless of AGI. If both

work and are in retirement plans, deductions again are phased out from $89,000 to $109,000. The range is $55,000 to $65,000 for single filers. For a married person filing separately with a spouse who is covered by a retirement plan at work, a partial deduction is allowable for an AGI of up to $10,000.

Though tax deductions are not an option with Roth IRAs, a taxpayer's AGI can limit eligibility. For 2009, eligibility to contribute to a Roth is phased out between $166,000 and $176,000 for married couples filing jointly, between $105,000 and $120,000 for single filers, and between $0 and $10,000 for married couples filing individually. There are no longer required contributions after age 70½, but distributions to beneficiaries must begin from the Roth IRA after the death of the owner. "Unauthorized" withdrawals made before age 59½ incur a 10 percent tax, with the exception of distributions made

- to help pay the costs of a first-time home purchase (lifetime limit of $10,000)
- due to the disability of the IRA owner
- to a beneficiary or the estate of the IRA owner
- that represent a series of "substantially equal periodic payments" made over the life expectancy of the owner
- that are used to pay medical expenses not reimbursed and exceeding 7½ percent of the AGI
- that are used to pay medical insurance premiums after the owner has received unemployment compensation for more than 12 weeks
- that are used to pay for the qualified expenses of higher education for the IRA holder and/or eligible family members
- that are used to pay back taxes from an IRS levy against an IRA
- as a qualified reservist distribution
- as a qualified disaster recovery assistance distribution
- as a qualified recovery assistance distribution

Types of IRAs include the following:

1. A traditional or Roth Individual Retirement Account is set up through a bank, broker, or

mutual fund. Investments may be made in stocks, bonds, money market accounts, and certificates of deposit (CDs).

2. An Individual Retirement Annuity is the same as a traditional or Roth IRA, except that a life insurance company sets up the account through an annuity contract.

3. A group IRA, or Employer Association Trust Account, works like a traditional IRA but is run through an employer, union, or other employee association.

4. A Simplified Employee Pension (SEP-IRA) is a traditional IRA set up by a business for its employees. Employees must meet certain minimum eligibility requirements. The employer may contribute up to $49,000 (2009), or 25 percent of an employee's compensation annually to his/her IRA.

5. A Savings Incentive Match Plan for Employees IRA (SIMPLE-IRA) is a traditional IRA set up by a small employer for its eligible employees, who contribute to the plan through a salary reduction agreement. The employer also makes matching or nonelective contributions to the account. The contribution limit in 2008 was 3 percent of compensation up to $10,500, with an additional $2,500 for persons over 50.

6. A Spousal IRA is either a traditional or Roth IRA funded by a married taxpayer in the name of his or her non-working spouse. The couple must file a joint tax return in the year of the contribution. Contributions are limited to the lesser amount of $5,000 ($6,000 for persons over 50) or the total compensation of the working spouse. The phase-out limits for modified AGI listed above apply.

7. A Rollover (Conduit) IRA is a traditional IRA that receives a distribution from a qualified retirement plan. Distributions are not subject to any contribution limits and may be eligible for transfer into a new employer's qualified retirement plan.

8. An Inherited IRA is either a traditional or a Roth IRA acquired by the beneficiary of a deceased IRA owner. A spouse who inherits an IRA, may treat it as his or her own, making contributions or rolling it over into another retirement account. A nonspousal beneficiary may not make contributions to an inherited IRA, but may set up a trustee-to-trustee transfer for the account and to take distributions from it.

9. The Education IRA (EIRA) is now known as the Coverdell Education Savings Account. It is set up in the name of a beneficiary to pay for education in primary and secondary school and higher education. Contributions are not tax-deductible, but withdrawals are not taxed or penalized. Annual contribution limits are currently $2,000 per beneficiary.

10. In 2009, the Obama administration has proposed the Automatic IRA, for small businesses of 10 or more employees which do not now offer a retirement plan. Participation in the IRA would be required, and contributions would be made through payroll deductions.

Under certain conditions it is possible to transfer other retirement assets into traditional or Roth IRAs, or to convert traditional IRAs to Roth IRAs, provided that the modified AGI (married filing jointly) is less than $100,000. The amount converted, not including any distributions taken, is taxable, but if done properly, the conversion is not subject to the 10 percent early-withdrawal tax. The Tax Increase Prevention and Reconciliation (TIPRA) Act of 2005 set this limit to expire at the end of 2009; persons converting a traditional IRA to a Roth IRA in 2010 have the option of reporting the converted amount as taxable income over two years, 2011 and 2012.

Further reading
Internal Revenue Service. IRA Online Resource Guide. Available online. URL: www.irs.gov/retirement/article/0,,id=137320,00.html. Accessed on July 21, 2009; Internal Revenue Service. Individual Retirement Arrangements (Publication 590). Available online. URL: www.irs.gov/publications/p590/index.html. Accessed on July 21, 2009; Motley Fool Web site. All about IRAs. Available online. URL: www.fool.com/money/allaboutiras/allaboutiras01.htm; IRA glossary. URL: www. fool.

com/money/allaboutiras/allaboutirasglossary.htm. Accessed on July 21, 2009; Smart Money Web site. IRA information. Available online. URL: www.smart-money.com/personal-finance/retirement/spousal-iras-7956/. Accessed on July 21, 2009.

—Andrew Kearns

industrial-organizational psychology

The field of industrial-organizational (I/O) psychology includes the study of all aspects of human behavior in the business environment. Because people spend a considerable amount of time at work and often with other people, understanding work-related experiences and attitudes is critical for improving the overall quality of work life and employee performance within an organization. I/O psychologists study important organizational issues such as personnel selection, job-related training, employee PERFORMANCE APPRAISAL, group work, MANAGEMENT and LEADERSHIP quality, and general working conditions.

Personnel selection involves INTERVIEWING, selecting, and hiring job candidates who are suitably matched for particular jobs. Many organizations employ testing procedures to screen applicants beforehand, helping to ensure that an applicant has the necessary skills and abilities to perform a job before making any hiring decisions. I/O psychologists work to develop reliable and valid tests for job placements so that both the employer and the employee benefit from their use. In addition, I/O psychologists study the interview process itself, identifying variables that affect its success, such as the applicant's appearance and the interviewer's expectations.

I/O psychologists also study job-related training so employers know how and when to provide the necessary training for their employees. In addition, they work to ensure that additional training opportunities are provided, allowing employees to update and improve their job-related skills and knowledge.

Evaluation of employee performance is another critical concern. I/O psychologists review the procedures for performance evaluation and feedback, seeking to ensure that employees are evaluated fairly and accurately on job performance and not on extraneous or irrelevant factors. Ultimately performance evaluations feed into decisions about salary increases and promotions, both of which affect employees' satisfaction with their jobs and their commitment to the company.

I/O psychologists also study how groups function in the workplace, trying to increase productivity and decrease the occurrence of SOCIAL LOAFING. They seek to identify the variables that affect the quantity and quality of group work, such as feelings of cohesion, and assist in deciding whether particular projects are better suited for group work or for individual efforts.

Management and leadership quality have important effects on the business environment. I/O psychologists study how good managers motivate employees and make suggestions regarding what style of leadership is best suited for a given situation. Training can then be provided to enhance managers' leadership skills.

I/O psychologists are also interested in how the general working conditions in an organization affect employees and productivity. Safety on the job, exposure to workplace violence, general health concerns, absenteeism, and stress are all important concerns in the work environment. The HAWTHORNE EXPERIMENTS were highly influential in alerting I/O psychologists to social and physical factors that could affect worker productivity and satisfaction in general.

I/O psychology is a rapidly growing field. Ultimately research that helps organizations understand and improve their work environment can be of tremendous value in determining a company's success or failure.

See also SOCIAL FACILITATION.

Further reading

Schneider, Frank W., Jamie A. Gruman, and Larry M. Coutts, eds. *Applied Social Psychology: Understanding and Addressing Social and Practical Problems.* Thousand Oaks, Calif.: Sage, 2005; Schultz, Duane, and Sydney Ellen Schultz. *Psychology and Work Today.* 9th ed. Upper Saddle River, N.J.: Prentice Hall, 2006.

—Elizabeth L. Cralley

Industrial Workers of the World

The Industrial Workers of the World (IWW) was a major U.S. UNION during the early 20th century; today it is a small international union. Established in Chicago in 1905, the IWW (or "wobblies" as they came to be called) was one of the first industrial unions. These differed from CRAFT UNIONS in that industrial unions attempted to organize all workers in a factory or industry, while craft unions limited membership to workers with a particular skill. One IWW pamphlet stated, "The directory of unions of Chicago shows in 1903 a total of 56 different unions in the packing houses, divided up still more in 14 different trades unions of the AMERICAN FEDERATION OF LABOR. . . . What a horrible example of an army divided against itself in the face of a strong combination of employers."

The IWW defined itself as "One Big Union" undivided by sex, race, or skills. At the time this was a radical goal, earning IWW members labels as anarchists and socialists. Big Bill Haywood, leader of the Western Federation of Miners, stated at the 1905 meeting, "The aims and objects of this organization shall be to put the working-class in possession of the economic power, the means of life, in control of the machinery of production and distribution, without regard to the capitalist masters."

IWW membership probably never exceeded 10,000 people at any one time. Its leaders moved from one industrial conflict to another, and many were arrested frequently, often under anti-speech ordinances imposed to stifle union efforts. Joe Hill, an IWW organizer among western railroad workers, was accused of killing a grocer in Salt Lake City. Convicted and executed in 1915, he became famous to recent generations through a Joan Baez ballad.

Joe Hill was an African American. One of the IWW principles was the inclusion of workers from any race or nationality, a revolutionary practice at the time. When Big Bill Haywood was invited to speak to the Brotherhood of Timber Workers in Louisiana in 1912, he asked why there were no blacks present and was told it was illegal to have interracial meetings. Haywood argued, "If it is against the law, this is one time when the law should be broken," and blacks were invited to the convention.

With the outbreak of World War I, union activity declined, and the IWW diminished as an agent of change in the American labor movement. Today the IWW describes itself as "a union dedicated to organizing on the job, in our industries and in our communities both to win better conditions today and build a world without bosses, a world in which production and distribution are organized by workers ourselves to meet the needs of the entire population, not merely a handful of exploiters."

Further reading

Industrial Workers of the World Web site. Available online. URL: www.iww.org.

inflation

Inflation is a sustained rise in the average level of prices that causes a decrease in the PURCHASING power of a country's currency. By decreasing the purchasing power of money, inflation has what economists call redistributive effects. During periods of inflation, people who are on fixed INCOMES, such as pensioners, as well as holders of BONDS and other fixed-interest credit instruments are paid with MONEY that has lost part of its purchasing power. During the economic upheaval in 1990s Russia, retirees with fixed incomes saw their pensions become almost worthless as inflation eroded the purchasing power of their money.

People who borrow in advance of inflation pay back their LOANS with less valuable money. People who are able to increase their income equal to the increase in inflation do not lose their purchasing power. UNIONS frequently negotiate wage increases to protect their members' incomes. Often the owners of resources can increase the price of their resources to keep up with inflation.

Inflation is caused by an excess of DEMAND relative to SUPPLY, or a reduction in supply relative to demand. COST-PUSH INFLATION, sometimes called supply-shock or sellers' inflation, occurs when a decrease in supply of many or important resources causes an increase in the price of these resources resulting in price increases. The OPEC (ORGANIZATION OF PETROLEUM EXPORT- ING COUNTRIES) oil EMBARGO that caused huge increases in oil prices in the 1970s is an example of supply-shock inflation. Demand-pull inflation occurs when overall demand exceeds supply. One way to describe demand-pull inflation is "too many dollars chasing too few goods." "Too many dollars" in an economy is caused by an expansion- ary MONETARY POLICY or FISCAL POLICY, or some combination of both.

The most extreme example of demand-pull inflation occurred in Germany in the 1920s. At the end of World War I, the German economy was in a shambles. During the war the German government had issued bonds borrowing significant amounts from its citizens, and afterwards it was required to make reparation payments to the Allies. Having little economic activity to tax, the German gov- ernment literally cranked up the presses, printing deutsche marks. They paid off their debt, but in the process the currency became worthless as inflation increased 100 trillion times between 1914 and 1924. During the worst periods, German workers insisted on being paid twice a day so they could spend their money before it lost more of its purchasing power. One apocryphal story described a German consumer leaving a wheelbarrow full of money outside a bakery while making purchases in the store. Someone stole the wheelbarrow, dumping the money on the sidewalk. The deutsche mark became worthless during this period of hyperinflation.

Inflation in the United States is measured using three indexes: the GROSS DOMESTIC PRODUCT (GDP) DEFLATOR, the producer price index (PPI) and the CONSUMER PRICE INDEX (CPI). The GDP deflator measures price changes of all goods and SERVICES produced. The PPI measures changes in prices received by producers; inflation at the producer level usually precedes inflation at the consumer level. The CPI uses a "market basket" of typical goods and services purchased by house- holds in the United States to measure inflation at the consumer level. The CPI is the most widely watched and quoted measure of inflation and is used in making COST-OF-LIVING ADJUSTMENTS.

Further reading
Boyes, William, and Michael Melvin. *Macroeconomics.* 7th ed. Boston: Houghton Mifflin Company, 2007.

infomercials
Infomercials are program-length TV commercials, usually devoted solely to one product, that resem- ble regular programming; the name is derived from "information" and "commercials." Info- mercials are used to increase public awareness, develop brand-name recognition, and create a direct consumer response. They traditionally have been viewed with cynicism by the ADVERTISING industry. Early infomercials offering miracle prod- ucts and get-rich plans were sometimes accused of marketing PONZI SCHEMES. However, Microsoft's use of an infomercial to promote Windows 95 is credited with "legitimizing" this form of MARKET- ING COMMUNICATIONS.

Typical infomercials employ the television for- mat to demonstrate PRODUCTs and provide testi- monials. Often celebrities are used to bolster the credibility of marketers' claims.

Infomercials are expensive, costing on aver- age at least $300,000 to develop and more to air, depending on how often and in what time slots they will appear. On a per-minute basis, infomer- cials cost a fraction of the price of a 30-second tele- vision commercial.

Combined, infomercials and home-shopping networks (now called direct-response television) are big business in the United States, generating over $1.25 billion in revenue in 2000.

Further reading
Boone, Louis E., and David L. Kurtz. *Contemporary Marketing.* 14th ed. Cincinnati, Ohio: South-Western, 2009.

infrastructure
Infrastructure is man-made products services that facilitate production and distribution of other goods and services. The term was originally used to refer to the basic systems that support a commu- nity. Roads, bridges, railroad tracks, power lines, sewer systems, and water systems are considered

part of a community's infrastructure. Over time the phrase has expanded to include such things as postal and prison systems and the national defense system, but recently it has become widely used in the information technology industry, referring to the basic system of computing in general and to the INTERNET in particular.

In the United States, development of the railroads in the 1800s, the interstate highway system in the 1950s, and expansion of communication systems in the 1990s all were major infrastructure investments leading to economic growth. The decaying national infrastructure is a popular discussion topic in public-administration circles. This refers to the decay of the bridges, roads, and sewer systems on which communities depend. Often governments will defer improving infrastructure as a way to address a financial crisis, which could leave them in a situation of what is termed *hidden debt*. One government may have the exact same financial situation as one of its neighboring governments; however, it could be in serious hidden financial trouble because of decaying infrastructure that needs to be dealt with to keep the community viable. During economic declines, organizations such as school systems and businesses also defer infrastructure maintenance and replacement, hoping better ECONOMIC CONDITIONS or a crisis event will result in the needed resources to make infrastructure improvement. During economic expansions, managers are faced with the difficult choice of whether to increase output using existing technology, expanding work hours, or adding additional work shifts; or to replace existing CAPITAL with new technology. Often infrastructure constraints influence these business decisions.

—Mack Tennyson

initial public offering

"Going public" is when the stock of a closely held CORPORATION, PROPRIETORSHIP, or PARTNERSHIP is offered for sale to the public for the first time. This sale of formerly closely held shares is known as an initial public offering (IPO). IPOs are used to raise additional CAPITAL and result in publicly held corporations. In the late 1990s, initial public offerings of INTERNET companies dubbed DOTCOMS were compared to "feeding frenzies," with investors wildly bidding up the prices of new companies that had no earnings record and untested MANAGEMENT. Early investors in dot-com IPOs often "flipped" their shares, quickly selling them for a huge PROFIT. Insiders were prevented by SECURITIES AND EXCHANGE COMMISSION (SEC) rules forcing them to hold onto their shares for a period of time, usually six months. When the dot-com bubble burst in 2000, many SHAREHOLDERS watched as the value of their paper holdings disappeared.

injunctions

Injunctions are judicial orders to cease and desist from certain activities—for example, destroying documents relevant to litigation. Injunctions can also order persons and businesses to do certain acts, such as releasing documents. Injunctions can be "temporary" or "permanent," "preliminary" or "final," depending on the circumstances. Injunctions are considered a type of "equitable remedy" at law, meaning they can be fashioned to meet many judicial needs. They are available only when irreparable injury is likely to occur in absence of an injunction.

Failure to obey an injunction can lead to severe penalties, such as fines and penalties for being in contempt of court. For example, the TAFT-HARTLEY ACT allows the U.S. president to seek an injunction imposing a 60-day "cooling-off" period, delaying a UNION's strike in a labor dispute if the president determines the activity would harm national security or welfare.

Further reading
Dobbyn, John F. *Injunctions in a Nutshell.* Eagan, Minn.: West Group, 1974.

input-output (I/O)

In all businesses that produce a product or service there is an input-output process. This process includes all the resources needed to create the product or services that are then transformed into finished items that are sold in the marketplace. The process of taking the raw materials and other items necessary for production (inputs) and converting (transformation) them into finished goods and services (outputs) is an open, systematic approach to production. This process is often abbreviated as the I/O system.

Inputs in the I/O system include raw materials, technical information, financial resources, and people. Within the transformation process there are numerous subsystems. In a manufacturing environment raw materials are converted into a product by a production subsystem that includes all the equipment necessary to make the product. The building and the manufacturing equipment are maintained by a maintenance subsystem. Management, responsible for coordinating and controlling work, is another subsystem.

I/O systems are considered to be open systems if they are open to and respond to their outside environment. The environment is dynamic and, therefore, constantly changing. Open systems are constantly looking for changes in their environment (boundary spanning) and adapt to those impending changes. Forward-looking companies anticipated the growth of the Internet and electronic means of conducting business. They looked for changes in the legal and regulatory environment and were able to manage those changes through their adaptation subsystem. Closed systems rely on themselves and ignore their environment. These organizations are in an entropic state and will eventually collapse.

insider trading

Insider trading is the buying and selling of shares of stock in a CORPORATION by the company's managers, BOARD OF DIRECTORS, or other individuals with a financial interest in or knowledge of the company. Some insider trading is legal and closely watched in the marketplace, while other insider trading is illegal and closely scrutinized by securities-industry authorities. Managers, directors, and individuals who own 10 percent or more of a company's shares must disclose the purchase or sale of shares to the SECURITIES AND EXCHANGE COMMISSION (SEC) by the 10th of the month after their action. However, it is illegal for insiders to buy or sell stock based on their knowledge of material corporate developments that have not been made public. Material corporate developments may include MERGERS AND ACQUISITIONS, NEW PRODUCT DEVELOPMENT, divestitures, key personnel departures or appointments, and any other news that could affect the price of a company's stock.

In 1984 the Insiders Trading Sanctions Act imposed penalties of up to three times a trader's PROFITS on any trader who intentionally "tips" private market-sensitive information to a third party who then profits by trading based on that information. In 1988, incensed over continued insider-trading abuse on WALL STREET, Congress unanimously passed the Insider Trading and Securities Fraud Enforcement Act, extending penalties to employers or "controlling persons" who do not take steps to prevent illegal employee trading. Controlling persons are subject to civil penalties up to the greater of $1 million or three times the amount of illegal-trading profit. In addition to civil penalties, insider trading is subject to criminal prosecution, and professionals (accountants and lawyers) may be suspended or barred from practice.

Over the years, the SEC has been given increased power to oversee and curtail insider trading. One of the most notorious cases of insider trading involved Ivan Boesky, an arbitrageur who bought shares of stock in companies that were about to be taken over by another firm at an above-market price. Boesky learned in advance of these transactions through Dennis Levine, an investment banker, who worked in a company providing the financing for the takeovers. When confronted by the SEC in 1986, Boesky agreed to an out-of-court settlement banning him from securities trading, payment of a $100 million fine, and three years in jail.

Determining what is insider trading is generally based on the answers to three questions:

- Is the information public?
- Is the information material?
- Is there a fiduciary relationship?

Information is considered public when it has been distributed through the media, allowing the public to learn about it. Press releases, wire-service reports, and reports through business newspapers allow buyers and sellers in the STOCK MARKET to learn about and interpret information. If the public does not know about the information, it would be illegal to trade based on that information if it is significant enough to influence the stock's price.

What is and is not material information is a difficult question to answer. The SEC analyzes trading in stocks before and after important announcements. Using statistical variation from the norm, the commission looks for larger-than-normal trading activity just before a material event. After September 11, 2001, U.S. and global securities regulators analyzed stock and options trading in airline, INSURANCE, and financial stocks just prior to the attack. While trading volume was higher than normal, to date no known links have been made between terrorists and the individuals engaging in the stock-market transactions.

The third question of fiduciary relationship addresses whether or not an individual with information is an "insider." Any officer, director, or employee of a company is considered a "traditional insider," who must either make the information available to the public or refrain from trading or tipping other people who might trade. "Temporary insiders" include auditors, lawyers, brokers, and investment bankers who do not work for the company but often have access to sensitive, nonpublic information.

Possibly the most widely reported case of insider trading involved celebrity host and author Martha Stewart. In 2004, Stewart, a former stock broker and member of the board of directors of the NEW YORK STOCK EXCHANGE (NYSE), was found guilty of insider trading, selling less than 4,000 shares of ImClone stock based on information provided to her by ImClone CEO Samuel Waksal. The following day the firm's stock fell 18 percent. By selling in advance, Stewart avoided a loss of approximately $45,000, a minor sum for a multimillionaire. Initially, Stewart tried to ignore public uproar but, having been a member of the board of the NYSE, the argument that she did not know what she did was illegal insider trading did not have credibility. Stewart paid a fine and spent five months in a correctional institution.

As previously stated, insider trading can also be a legal activity watched closely by stock-market investors. For years investors have monitored the ratio of insider (officers and directors) sales to purchases of company stock, but like all investors, insiders have many reasons for buying and selling stock that don't rely solely on their perceptions of the company's future profitability. For example, in the late 1990s, Bill Gates, Microsoft's CHIEF EXECUTIVE OFFICER, announced that he would sell shares of his company over time, both to diversify his ASSETS and to finance the endowment he and his wife, Melinda, were establishing. Nevertheless, investors and financial news services often track insider-trading activity.

When insiders sell shares, stockholders worry that there is impending trouble ahead. But as managers of companies are increasingly offered STOCK OPTIONS, the reported statistics distort the reality of insider trading. Options are not included in purchases of shares, but sales based on the exercising of options are included in insider trading.

Further reading
Rosen, Robert C. "An Accountant's Guide to the SEC's New Insider Trading Regulations," *CPA Journal* 63 (February 1993): 67; Securities and Exchange Commission Web site. Available online. URL: www.sec.gov/answers/insider.htm. Accessed on June 17, 2009.

Institute for Supply Management
Formerly the National Association of Purchasing Managers, the Institute for Supply Management (ISM) is the leading professional organization of PURCHASING and supply-chain MANAGEMENT professionals; the organization changed its name in 2002. The ISM's mission is "to educate, develop, and advance the purchasing and supply management profession." Established in 1915, the association has over 40,000 members, provides a variety of publications, and offers seminars, conferences, and two certification programs: Certified

Purchasing Manager (CPM) and Accredited Purchasing Practitioner (APP).

The ISM is most noted for its Purchasing Managers' Indexes (PMI), which are based on surveys of purchasing managers around the country and recognized as important INDICATORS of economic activity. The PMIs include production, new orders and backlog of new orders, supplier, prices, inventories, new exports, and import of materials. Because purchasing managers are directly involved in production management and must order materials and supplies in advance of actual production activity, their assessments are good predictors of near-term manufacturing activity.

The ISM's standards of supply-management conduct provide a number of valuable insights into ethical conflicts in business. Some of their standards include

- perceived impropriety—avoid the intent and appearance of unethical or compromising conduct in relationships, actions, and communications
- CONFLICT OF INTEREST—avoid any personal business or professional activity that would create a conflict between personal interests and the interests of the employer
- personal INVESTMENT—ownership of stock by a supplier of goods or services, competitor, or customer should be reported to the employer for review and guidance to avoid the potential for impropriety
- issues of influence—avoid soliciting or accepting money, LOANS, credits, or preferential discounts, and the acceptance of gifts, entertainment, favors, or services from present or potential suppliers that might influence, or appear to influence, supply-management decisions
- confidential and proprietary information—handle confidential or proprietary information with due care and proper consideration of ethical and legal ramifications and governmental regulations.

Further reading
Institute for Supply Management Web site. Available online. URL: www.ism.ws.

Institute of Management Accountants

The Institute of Management Accountants (IMA) is "the leading professional organization devoted exclusively to MANAGERIAL ACCOUNTING and financial management." As set forth on its Web site its mission and vision statements, its goals are "to help members develop both personally and professionally, by means of education, certification, and association with other business professionals." Instrumental in shaping managerial accounting concepts and standards, the IMA also influences ethical practices and the development of ethical standards for practitioners.

The IMA offers certification: the CMA (Certified in Management Accounting). Earning and maintaining IMA certification tests individuals' competence and expertise in management accounting and financial management.

Further reading
Institute of Management Accountants Web site. Available online. URL: www.imanet.org.

institutional advertising

Institutional advertising, also called corporate advertising, is designed to promote the firm overall, not any one specific product or service. Institutional advertising is an extension of a firm's PUBLIC RELATIONS function. Typical institutional advertising activities include image advertising, event sponsorships, advocacy advertising, and cause-related advertising. Institutional advertising is often used to improve a firm's image in a community, and it may help a firm overcome consumer uncertainty or address community issues or questions.

Institutional advertising has been utilized as a tool to help companies establish or improve their images in a community since the 18th century. The Dutch East India Company is recorded as being the first company to use this advertising strategy. Well-known companies such AT&T, DuPont, General Electric, and Ford use institutional advertising to improve their images during uncertain times.

Local businesses often engage in institutional advertising. For example, a local community center received a grant to create a Computer Literacy Program for unemployed teenage mothers and senior citizens. Unfortunately, the grant did not include the cost for computer software and installation charges. The owner of a local computer company heard about the center's problems and donated the software and technical support to install the software at no charge. Mouse pads with the company's name and logo imprinted on them were donated as well. After talking with the program director about job placement for students who completed the program, the computer company's owner offered to hire a few of the students as interns with a possibility of becoming full-time employees.

The example above gave the firm a positive image, enhanced the public's perception, and raised awareness about its existence, products, and services. When a community has a sense of confidence in a company or organization, they will be more inclined to use its products, services, and recommend others to do likewise. But institutional advertising is controversial. Belch and Belch critique institutional advertising, suggesting:

- Consumers are not interested in this form of advertising
- Institutional advertising is a form of self-indulgence
- It suggests the firm is in trouble and needs to justify its existence
- It is a waste of money.

Institutional advertising will continue to be the vehicle that companies utilize to connect to the community in efforts to promote or refine their images.

Further reading

Belch, George E., and Michael A. Belch. *Advertising and Promotion: An Integrated Marketing Communications Perspective.* 7th ed. New York: McGraw-Hill, 2007; O'Neil, P. "Corporate Advertising." In *Encyclopedia of Advertising.* Vol. 1, pp. 397–402. New York: Fitzroy Dearborn, 2003; Sullivan, J. "What Are the Functions of Corporate Home Pages?" *Journal of World Business* 34, no. 2 (1999). Available online. URL: infotrac.galegroup.com.pallas2.tcl.sc.edu/itw/informark/. Accessed on June 29, 2009.

—Mary Dow

insurance

Insurance is an asset purchased by individuals and organizations to protect them from loss and provide them with a way to reduce the risk of exposure to possible injury or loss. There are three classifications of RISK—personal risk, property risk, and LIABILITY risk—and it is possible to be insured against all three types. Personal risk entails the loss of INCOME and/or ASSETS because the individual or organization can no longer work or operate. Property risk entails the loss of property (i.e., anything that an individual or organization owns). Liability risk entails the loss of assets or income due to an individual's or organization's NEGLIGENCE, as determined by law. Insurance transfers an individual's or an organization's risk to the insurer.

Insurance has been practiced in one form or another for thousands of years. In ancient Babylonian society, it was common for merchants to purchase bottomry CONTRACTS, or LOANS that did not have to be repaid if the purchased merchandise did not make it to its final destination. This evolved into a more sophisticated marine (shipping) insurance system. Modern marine insurance was introduced in Italy during the 13th century, when banks and merchants formed syndicates to protect themselves from shipping losses. In the 18th century a former coffeehouse named Lloyds developed into a major marine insurance group, and London developed into a center for marine insurance. The 18th century also introduced other types of insurance, including life, fire, and casualty insurance. The astronomer Edmond Halley made life insurance possible with the development of the first mortality table in 1683. The first insurance company in the United States was the Philadelphia Contribution, formed by Benjamin Franklin in 1752. The 1820s saw enormous growth in the insurance industry in the United States.

Today insurance is an international business dominated by huge companies. In the United States there are several thousand insurance companies employing millions of people. The insurance business uses statistical probabilities, usually in the form of actuarial tables, to determine if something or someone is insurable and to set premiums. The larger the number of individuals or organizations insured, the easier it is to set a reasonable premium. Higher premiums are assigned when an insurance company deems someone or something to be a larger risk. Some insurance companies then reinvest this premium money in revenue-producing projects, and for this reason some of the United States' largest institutional investors are insurance companies.

The McCarron-Ferguson Act (1945) left the regulation of U.S. insurance companies to the individual state, and for this reason insurance regulation is not as uniform as that in other industries. The McCarron-Ferguson Act affects Title 15, Chapter 20 (Regulation of Insurance) of the U.S. Code. It states that "the business of insurance, and every person engaged therein, shall be subject to the laws of the several States which relate to the regulation or taxation of such business" (U.S. Code Title 15, sec. 1012a). Some uniformity in state regulation does exist, however, due primarily to the National Association of Insurance Commissioners (NAIC), which works toward creating a uniform standard.

There are various types of insurance to protect against the three types of risk. To protect against personal risk, there is life insurance and health insurance, both of which most closely resemble the insurance model described above. Large groups of people contribute to a fund, and if an individual in that group is injured, gets sick, or dies, monetary relief is provided to him, her, or his/her beneficiaries.

Homeowners and commercial insurance are two types of protection against property risk, providing monetary relief if an individual or organization suffers accidental property loss; these types include fire and flood insurance. In many cases creditors require an individual or organization is required to obtain property insurance.

Liability insurance entails several types of insurance, including automobile, theft, and aviation, all of which may be legally required and will compensate others if personal negligence leads to their injury or loss. WORKERS' COMPENSATION is an additional type of liability insurance that protects employers from monetary loss in case of employee injury; it is mandatory for all employers to have workers' compensation insurance for all employees. Credit insurance and title insurance are two additional types of liability insurance that protect individuals and organizations from financial loss due to the negligence of others.

There is an additional type of insurance called "surety ship" that protects companies from losses due to their employees' dishonesty. Athletes' bodies, musicians' hands, and even weather for outdoor events are some examples of things that are currently being insured. As computers allow for the more accurate computation of risk, it will become possible for insurers to develop policies for almost anything.

Further reading
Vaughn, Emmett J., and Therese M. Vaughn. *Fundamentals of Risk and Insurance.* 9th ed. New York: Wiley, 2002.

—Joseph F. Klein

intellectual property
Intellectual property is a broad category of intangible property rights created by law. COPYRIGHTS, PATENTS and TRADEMARKS are examples of intellectual property.

Patents for inventions are adjudicated exclusively under federal and statutory law. A patent application results in a search of the "prior art" (state of knowledge) in the field. U.S. patent awards grant exclusive rights to make, use, and sell the invention for 21 years from the date of filing for the patent. In recent years patents for computer programs and "business methods" have grown in number.

Copyrights are likewise exclusively federal and statutory under U.S. law. Copyrights, such as the one on this book, last from the creation of a work to 70 years after the death of the author/creator. Copyrights protect the author/publisher from copying by others.

Trademarks and service marks are recognized under COMMON LAW by state registration and by federal registration. Trademarks and service marks are words and symbols that distinguish particular goods and SERVICES from others—Coca-Cola, for instance. Once registered and actively used, trademarks and service marks can be maintained indefinitely.

Other intellectual-property rights recognized in U.S. law and sometimes by international agreement include TRADE SECRETS, integrated circuits, industrial designs, and geographic indicators of origin like Kentucky bourbon and Mexican tequila.

See also WORLD INTELLECTUAL PROPERTY ORGANIZATION.

Further reading
Miller, Arthur R., and Michael H. Davis. *Intellectual Property—Patents, Copyrights and Trademarks in a Nutshell.* 6th ed. Eagan, Minn.: West Group, 2000.

Inter-American Development Bank
The Inter-American Development Bank (IDB) is a regional, multilateral development organization. Established in 1959 with 20 members, including the United States and 19 Caribbean and Latin American countries, the IDB's mission is to "promote and support development of the private sector and CAPITAL MARKETS in its Latin American and Caribbean member countries by investing, lending, innovating and leveraging RESOURCES."

IDB lending grew from $294 million in 1961 to $11 billion in 2008. Membership has also grown to 48 countries, 26 borrowing countries, and 20 non-borrowing countries. Initially the bank's lending focused on agriculture and INFRASTRUCTURE projects. Its current lending priorities include "poverty reduction, social equity, modernization, and the environment."

Within the IDB, two groups focus on private-sector lending. The Inter-American Investment Corporation (IIC) finances small- and medium-scale private enterprises, while the Multilateral Investment Fund (MIF) promotes INVESTMENT reforms and supports private-sector investment.

Headquartered in Washington, D.C., the IDB is largely funded by the United States and supports U.S. political agendas. When the IDB was created, most Latin American countries were controlled by dictators, some of whom were friendly to the United States and others hostile to U.S. interference and economic and domination. The IDB acts as a nongovernmental means of supporting political and economic change in the Caribbean and Latin America.

See also ECONOMIC DEVELOPMENT.

Further reading
Inter-American Development Bank Web site. Available online. URL: www.iadb.org.

interest
Interest is the fee charged to borrow assets. Interest is typically charged to borrow money but it is also charged to borrow shares of stock (selling short) and other assets. Interest is a payment for use of a RESOURCE. Like rent paid for use of a building or apartment, interest is the payment to rent money. The money lender is compensated for the use of his or her funds by payment of interest.

The practice of charging interest goes back to the creation of money. The Old Testament states:

If thou lend money to any of My people, even to the poor with thee, thou shalt not be to him as a creditor; neither shall ye lay upon him interest. (Exodus 22:24)

And if thy brother be waxen poor, and his means fail with thee; then thou shalt uphold him: as a stranger and a settler shall he live with thee. Take thou no interest of him or increase; but fear thy God; that thy brother may live with thee. Thou shalt not give him thy money upon interest, nor give him thy victuals for increase. (Leviticus, 25:35–37)

Thou shalt not lend upon interest to thy brother: interest of money, interest of victuals (food and supplies,) interest of any thing that is lent upon interest. Unto a foreigner thou mayest lend upon interest; but unto thy brother thou shalt not lend upon interest; that the LORD thy God may bless thee in all that thou puttest thy hand unto, in the land whither thou goest in to possess it. (Deuteronomy, 23:20–21)

The New Testament includes advice on interest and usury (the charging of excessive interest), stating: "Wherefore then gavest not thou my money into the bank, that at my coming I might have required mine own with usury?" (Luke 19:23). Finally the master said to him "Why then didn't you put my money on deposit, so that when I came back, I could have collected it with interest?'" (Luke 19:23). "Thou oughtest therefore to have put my money to the exchangers, and then at my coming I should have received mine own with usury" (Matthew 25:27).

In the Middle Ages, goldsmiths found they could issue IOUs for sums of gold stored with them by merchants. The merchants preferred carrying the IOUs to gold and when other merchants accepted these receipts as payment, they acted as money. The goldsmiths quickly figured out they could issue more receipts than they had gold and charge interest on these loans. Merchants borrowed the funds to expand their trading activities and therefore their profits. Thirteenth-century leading Catholic theologian St. Thomas Aquinas argued that interest was a double charge, first for the money and then for its use. Catholic Church prohibitions against usury were advocated into the 16th century. In the United States, usury laws were created and controlled by states and existed in many states until the inflation of the early 1980s, when limits on the rate of interest that could be charged were replaced by truth-in-lending laws.

Usury is also admonished by the Qur'an: "Those who charge usury are in the same position as those controlled by the devil's influence. This is because they claim that usury is the same as commerce. However, God permits commerce, and prohibits usury. Thus, whoever heeds this commandment from his Lord, and refrains from usury, he may keep his past earnings, and his judgment rests with God. As for those who persist in usury, they incur Hell, wherein they abide forever" (*Al-*

Baqarah 2:275.) Islamic banks avoid prohibitions against charging interest by taking an equity stake, often in the form of joint ventures, in business ventures, sharing the profits or losses but not charging a set interest rate for loaned capital.

interest rates

In economic theory, interest is what is paid to induce a person with MONEY to save it and invest it in long-term ASSETS rather than spend it or a payment by borrowers for the use of funds. The rate of interest is a product of the interaction between the DEMAND for CAPITAL and the SUPPLY of savings. A higher demand for capital relative to the supply for savings produces higher interest rates, and vice versa.

Economic theory also makes a distinction between real and nominal interest rates. A nominal rate is the rate stated in the loan agreement. Real rates are nominal rates minus the rate at which money is losing its value. Thus, a loan agreement may have a rate of 10 percent, but if money is losing its purchasing power at the rate of 1 percent per year, the real rate is only 9 percent. In a loan of $10,000, the borrower will pay the lender $1,000 at a nominal rate of 10 percent, but since the loan is being paid back using dollars that are 1-percent less valuable, the real cost of the loan to the borrower is only 9 percent. Therefore the interest rate of 10 percent can be considered to be made of two parts: the basic rate and a 1-percent adjustment for inflationary pressure.

Another important factor in the level of interest rates is RISK. If a particular loan has a higher risk, creditors will require a higher interest rate to induce them to make the loan. To continue the example started in the last paragraph, suppose that the risk-free interest rate is 6 percent. The closest thing to a risk-free rate is the loan of money to the federal government via the purchase of Treasury bills. The 10 percent nominal rate would then be a product of three things: (1) the risk-free rate of 6 percent, (2) a risk premium of 3 percent, and (3) an adjustment for inflationary pressure of 1 percent.

Interest rates are also viewed in terms of the loan's DURATION. Borrowing for up to a week is often referred to as the "overnight" rate. Short-term rates apply to LOANS intended to last up to a year, and long-term rates are for loans lasting over a year. In general, with longer-term loans, there is upward pressure on each of the three elements comprising the interest rate. The risk-free rate is higher, while the longer-term loan has more potential time for something to go wrong. Thus the risk premium is higher and inflationary pressure is more observable over a long period of time. Usually long-term debts have a higher interest rate, but there have been notable exceptions.

Rates are usually stated in terms of a percentage payable and as an annual percentage rate. This is true even if the borrowing is for shorter than a year. A 10-percent interest rate infers 10 percent a year. For example, if a loan was for $10,000 for six months, the interest cost would be $500 ($10,000 × 6/12).

The federal-funds rate is the rate that banks charge each other when they are making short-term loans to each other. The prime rate is the rate that banks charge their best customers for short-term loans.

In the 1970s, lenders were using hidden fees and weird calculations to calculate interest as a way of stating a low interest rate in order to induce someone to borrow from them; however, they then charged a higher interest rate. In response to this, the U.S. government passed a series of CONSUMER PROTECTION laws, including the Fair Credit Billing Act (1975) and the CONSUMER CREDIT PROTECTION ACT (1969). These laws allow lenders to continue their practices, but they must disclose what is termed the annual percentage rate (APR). In addition to standardizing the way that interest is calculated, the APR also considers all the hidden fees in the loan. Consequently, a lender may calculate interest and impose fees as it likes, but it must disclose the APR to its borrowers before they agree to the loan. The law specifies how the disclosure should be made; the simplest way is to ask the lender the APR on the loan and to compare this rate with the APRs quoted by other lenders.

Another issue relative to consumer interest rates is their duration. Some low rates are merely introductory and will adjust after a few months to more typical rates. As a result, a loan that was initially appealing may adjust to an unacceptable rate after the introductory period. The intent of most of these types of interest rates is to deceive unwary customers.

Introductory rates should not be confused with indexed or adjustable rates—that is, loans with flexible interest rates. In this case the interest rate is indexed to some rate not under the control of either the lender or the borrower, i.e., the prime rate. If an interest rate is stated as "two percentage points above prime," and the prime rate is 6 percent, then the loan rate is 8 percent. This allows the lender to reduce some of its risk in lending the money. For new loans, the interest rate for an adjustable-rate loan will be lower than the rate for a fixed-rate loan. This is because the lender in an adjustable-rate loan has shifted some of the risk of changing rates to the borrower. Usually the rate is subject to an annual "cap," or maximum that can be adjusted in one year, and a lifetime cap, over the life of the loan.

See also YIELD CURVE.

—Mack Tennyson

interlocking directorate

An interlocking directorate is a network of business leaders who are members of boards of directors of CORPORATIONS. Any situation in which a director sits on the board of two or more companies simultaneously creates an interlocking directorate. While interlocking directorates are most associated with Japanese business, they are a powerful force in U.S. business practices.

Individuals serving on more than one BOARD OF DIRECTORS provide an informal means of communication and facilitate the building of business relationships. The old saying "It's not what you know but who you know that counts" summarizes the benefits of interlocking directorates. Depending on how information and influence is used, interlocking directorates can aid small companies attempting to build strategic relationships or assist large companies in finding new sources of ideas, talents, or products.

Members of a corporate board of directors have a fiduciary responsibility to direct corporate policy in the best interest of the SHAREHOLDERS. Corporate ANNUAL REPORTS usually state directors' financial interests in the company but rarely state their other financial and managerial relationships. An individual who sits on the board of two companies has access to advance knowledge of what each company intends to do. In advising on policy, the board member is likely to use his or her inside information to guide business-strategy decisions, even without directly revealing the other company's plans. This could benefit either both companies the board member represents or one company at the expense of the other.

Research into the impact of interlocking directorates is limited by lack of information regarding the use of information to influence corporate policy. Studies suggest interlocking directorates

- have been responsible for rapid diffusion of POISON-PILL STRATEGIES
- influence corporate-structure decisions
- influence corporate acquisitions
- influence the decision to pursue ISO STANDARDS
- influence decisions on corporate charitable contributions

Further reading

"New Corporate Governance: The Role of Director Interlocks." Mind Theme. Available online. URL: www.mindtheme.com/knowledge/interlock.asp.

Internal Revenue Service

The Department of the Treasury is responsible for administering and enforcing the internal revenue laws of the United States. The Secretary of the Treasury has delegated most revenue functions and authority to the Commissioner of Internal Revenue, the CHIEF EXECUTIVE OFFICER of the Internal Revenue Service (IRS). The president of the United States appoints the commissioner to a renewable five-year term. The commissioner is responsible for overall planning, directing, and coordinating of IRS programs, as well as policy control. The IRS is one of about a dozen bureaus within the Depart-

ment of the Treasury, and with more than 100,000 employees, it is the second-largest federal government agency (after the Department of Defense).

The history of the IRS dates from President Abraham Lincoln and the Civil War. Congress created the office of Commissioner of Internal Revenue in 1862 and passed an income tax to pay expenses associated with the war: a 3-percent tax on INCOMES between $600 and $10,000 and 5 percent on incomes exceeding $10,000. This income tax was repealed 10 years later. The Wilson Tariff Act of 1894 revived the income tax, but the Supreme Court ruled it unconstitutional the next year. Early in the 20th century, Congress sought ratification of an amendment to allow the collection of a tax on income. Wyoming became the last state needed to ratify the amendment in 1913, and that year saw the introduction of a 1 percent tax on personal income greater than $3,000 and an additional surtax of 6 percent on incomes of more than $500,000. Later, the Revenue Act of 1918, in efforts to finance World War I, produced a top income-tax rate of 77 percent.

A reorganization of the IRS in 1952 replaced the patronage system—in which politicians had control of who was hired to do the agency's work—with independently hired professional career employees. A year later President Dwight D. Eisenhower changed the agency's name from the Bureau of Internal Revenue to the Internal Revenue Service.

The next major change for the system came in 1992, when taxpayers were allowed to file income tax returns electronically. Responding to a public outcry concerning a growing insensitivity on the part of the IRS and its possible abuse of power, Congress passed the Internal Revenue Service Restructuring and Reform Act in 1998, intended to protect taxpayer's rights. The act reorganized the IRS from a geographically based structure into four major operating divisions aligned according to types of taxpayers: the Wage and Investment Income Division, serving taxpayers who file individual and joint tax returns; the Small Business and Self-Employed Division, serving the approximately 45 million small businesses and self-employed taxpayers; the Large and Mid-Size Business Division, serving CORPORATIONS with ASSETS of more than $10 million; and the Tax Exempt and Government Entities Division, serving nonprofit charities and governmental entities. The 1998 act also set up a Taxpayer Advocate Service as an independent agency within the Internal Revenue Service to help resolve taxpayer problems.

In 1998 Congress also instituted a nine-member IRS Oversight Board, consisting of the secretary of the Treasury, the IRS commissioner, a representative of IRS employees, and six private-sector representatives; the president of the United States appoints all board members to five-year terms. The Oversight Board's duties are to review the IRS mission, strategic plans, operational functions, and processes; to review and approve the IRS budget; to recommend candidates for commissioner; and to ensure the proper treatment of taxpayers.

The IRS is an important component in the development of tax law. The IRS annually produces thousands of releases that explain and clarify tax law, including regulations, revenue rulings, letter rulings, revenue procedures, and technical advice memoranda. IRS publications, many of which are updated annually, are interpretations written in general terms using understandable language to provide guidance to the public. Although they do not bind the IRS and are not considered substantial authority, these publications can be very helpful for a taxpayer endeavoring to determine the best way to report a given transaction.

The IRS has the power to impose interest and penalties on taxpayers for noncompliance with tax law. Provisions such as the penalty for failure to pay a tax or file a return that is due, the NEGLIGENCE penalty for intentional disregard of rules and regulations ("substantial authority"), and various penalties for civil and criminal FRAUD serve as deterrents to taxpayer noncompliance.

Another deterrent to taxpayer noncompliance is the IRS audit process, which can take the form of correspondence audits, office audits, or field audits. While field examinations are common for business returns and complex individual returns, most returns are audited in an office audit. An audit notice indicating which items the IRS will examine and what information the taxpayer should bring are sent in advance. The IRS employee and the taxpayer and/or taxpayer's representative then meet at a nearby IRS office.

The IRS also has a computerized matching program through which the tax information filed on taxpayers' individual returns is compared with the information filed by payers or employers. Wages, interest, alimony, pensions, UNEMPLOYMENT compensation, SOCIAL SECURITY benefits, and other items of income are reported to the IRS by the payers. In addition, payees report deducted items, including state income taxes, local real-estate taxes, home MORTGAGE interest, etc. However, taxpayers who report only these items generally face a 100 percent audit rate.

Further reading

Internal Revenue Service Web site. Available online. URL: www.irs.gov/; Pope, Thomas R., Kenneth E. Anderson, and John L. Kramer. *Prentice Hall's Federal Taxation 2003*. Upper Saddle River, N.J.: Pearson Education, 2003; Nellen, Annette. *Tax Aspects of Business Transactions, A First Course*. Upper Saddle River, N.J.: Prentice Hall, 1999; Raabe, William A., Gerald E. Whittenburg, John C. Bost, and Debra L. Sanders. *West's Federal Tax Research*. Cincinnati, Ohio: South Western College Publishing, 2000; Tax History Project Web site. Available online. URL: www.taxhistory.org.

—Linda Bradley McKee and Stewart Curry

International Bank for Reconstruction and Development   See WORLD BANK.

International Brotherhood of Teamsters (Teamsters Union)

The International Brotherhood of Teamsters (IBT), also known as the Teamsters Union, is a major industrial UNION in the United States with a long and contentious history. Created in 1903, with Cornelius Shea elected as president, the Teamsters Union grew to represent over 1 million workers. Teamsters were men who drove horse-drawn wagons. The initial teamsters were quickly replaced with truck drivers, and the union expanded to represent different groups of transportation-related workers.

The Teamsters describe their goal as follows: "To make life better for Teamster members and their families—and for all working families—the Teamsters organize the unorganized, make workers' voices heard in all corridors of power, negotiate CONTRACTS that make the AMERICAN DREAM a reality for millions, protect workers' health and safety, and fight to keep jobs in North America."

After their initial meeting in 1903, the Teamsters met with considerable opposition, the bloodiest of which was a 100-day strike against Montgomery Ward in 1905, during which 21 lives were lost. The union has a long history of dissent and conflict both internally and externally. Local unions, opposed to national corruption and manipulation, have often seceded from the national union. The most famous Teamsters president was Jimmy Hoffa, who was elected in 1957 and disappeared in 1975.

With DEREGULATION of the trucking industry in the 1980s, Teamsters Union membership declined along with union membership in general in the United States. The 1997 United Parcel Service (UPS) strike brought a surprising resurgence in the Teamsters Union's influence as UPS management underestimated public and business support for UPS drivers. Businesses and consumers knew their UPS drivers by name, respected their fast and professional service, and supported union demands for increased EMPLOYMENT of full-time workers.

Further reading
International Brotherhood of Teamsters Web site. Available online. URL: www.teamster.org; Witwer, David. "Local Rank and File Militancy: The Battle for Teamster Union Reform in Philadelphia in the Early 1960s," *Labor History* 41, no. 3 (August 2000): 263.

International Energy Agency
The International Energy Agency (IEA) is an alliance of 28 nations created in the 1970s to ensure energy security for its members. The United States,

Japan, Korea, and most European countries are members of the IEA, which works in conjunction with the ORGANIZATION FOR ECONOMIC COOPERATION AND DEVELOPMENT (OECD). The IEA's objectives are

- to maintain and improve systems for coping with oil-supply disruptions
- to promote rational energy policies in a global context through cooperative relations with nonmember countries, industries, and international organizations
- to operate a permanent information system on the international oil market
- to improve the world's energy supply and demand structure by developing alternative energy sources and increasing the efficiency of energy use
- to assist in the integration of environmental and energy policies.

The IEA publishes the monthly *Oil Market Report* and the biannual *World Energy Outlook* and reports regularly on the energy policies of its member states and those of selected nonmembers.

Most of the IEA members are major oil-importing countries. As such, they oppose restrictions made on oil production, particularly the actions by the ORGANIZATION OF PETROLEUM EXPORTING COUNTRIES (OPEC) to reduce supplies and raise market prices. However, the IEA has no power to direct policies by member countries. Norway, an IEA member, changed from a net-importing country to the world's third-largest oil-exporting country. In 1998 and 2002, Norway reduced oil output along with OPEC countries in an effort to increase the world price of oil. The IEA reviewed Norway's actions but took no action.

Most industrial nations were caught by surprise during the energy crises in the 1970s. Working together through the IEA, member countries attempt to offset the market power of oil-exporting countries. One of the agreements among IEA members is to maintain a stockpile of oil to be released during emergencies. The United States maintains a stock of petroleum reserves in caverns in the western part of the country.

Further reading
International Energy Agency Web site. Available online. URL: www.iea.org.

International Labor Organization

The International Labor Organization (ILO) is a global international labor association with a primary goal of improving working conditions, living standards, and equitable treatment of workers in all nations. Most of the major industrialized countries in the world, including the United States, are members of the ILO, which was created in 1919 at the Versailles peace conference, ending World War I. The ILO's constitution is included in the Treaty of Versailles.

When it was created, the ILO's goals included humanitarian, political, and economic objectives; or, as its constitution states, "conditions of labor exist involving . . . injustice, hardship and privation to large numbers of people." The constitution also refers to "unrest so great that the peace and harmony of the world are imperiled." The ILO hoped to reduce worker-industrialization tension and in the process reduce social unrest. It further hoped to gain worldwide acceptance of basic rights and reforms, recognizing that countries where workers were exploited could produce goods more cheaply. Therefore, global acceptance of basic rights and working conditions would "level the playing field" in economic COMPETITION. At the Versailles peace conference, a fourth justification for creating the ILO emerged: "[U]niversal and lasting peace can be established only if it is based upon social justice."

Headquartered in Geneva, Switzerland, the ILO became a specialized agency of the United Nations in 1946. It issues conventions to recommend international labor standards when there is substantial agreement among members. It also issues recommendations in situations where the issue is complex or when there is not a consensus regarding proper labor practices. Member states are obliged to provide ANNUAL REPORTS to verify their compliance with ILO conventions they have ratified. The ILO's Committee of Experts on the Application of Conventions and Recommendations reviews submissions and compiles a "special list" of governments that have defaulted on their obligations to the ILO agreements. The list is then presented to the General Conference for review and approval. In 1974 the Soviet Union was included on the list for breach of the 1930 Convention Concerning Forced or Compulsory Labor. After considerable debate, the General Conference failed to adopt the committee's recommendations, leading to U.S. withdrawal from the ILO in 1977. The United States rejoined the organization in 1980.

In recent years the ILO has focused on human rights, stating as its strategic objectives to

- promote and realize standards and fundamental principles and rights at work
- create greater opportunities for women and men to secure decent EMPLOYMENT and INCOME
- enhance the coverage and effectiveness of social protection for all
- strengthen tripartism (government, labor, and industry cooperation) and social dialogue

In 1969 the ILO received the Nobel Peace Prize for its work.

Further reading
August, Ray. *International Business Law.* 2d ed. New York: Prentice Hall, 1997; International Labor Organization Web site. Available online. URL: www.ilo.org.

international management

International management is the process of applying MANAGEMENT concepts and techniques in a multinational, multicultural environment. Large, medium, and small firms are seeing increasingly more of their overall revenue coming from overseas markets. International management is changing rapidly, due in part to the fact that managers are increasing their contact with other countries as foreign INVESTMENT and trade are increasing and TRADE BARRIERS among countries continue to fall. Businesses are also depending more on international markets for larger percentages of their total revenues. Managers face challenges and problems in the economic, political, legal, technological, and cultural areas of doing business in a global environment.

A lack of ECONOMIC GROWTH in some countries makes it difficult for MULTINATIONAL CORPORATIONS to continue to do business there. Elements that contribute to the economic RISK of doing business globally include trade barriers, weak savings, inadequate INFRASTRUCTURE, and unavailable or unskilled labor force. Governments can mismanage their country's economy, or it can be hurt by global factors such as an increase in INTEREST RATES worldwide.

A country's political environment is very complex and can change rapidly; international managers must therefore be aware of the impact of both the existing situation and political changes on their business. Foreign firms doing business in a country can be harmed when its leaders interfere in their operations, taking over ASSETS, practicing policies and regulations that adversely affect foreign investors, and allowing political upheaval to disrupt foreign business. With such risks, government leaders at home may not encourage international trade and investment.

Legal issues affecting international management include determining which country's laws will govern expatriates, how INTELLECTUAL PROPERTY is protected, and how disputes are resolved. Managers must be aware of INTERNATIONAL LAW and extensions of home-country law, in addition to learning the host-country laws and regulations with which they must comply, including those relating to foreign investment, labor, and EMPLOYMENT. Other legal challenges include corrupt foreign governments, restrictive foreign bureaucracies, inefficient government controls, and PRIVATIZATION of state-run companies.

International managers face challenges in a rapidly changing technological environment. Increasing numbers of people now have access to the INTERNET and can obtain information more quickly than ever before. Security issues and E-COMMERCE pose additional challenges. Technology affects the number and nature of employees in international firms and also makes work more portable. Advances in telecommunications offer EMERGING MARKETS new opportunities to engage in international transactions.

The world's many cultural differences also affect managing in the international arena, and therefore it is vital for international managers to have an understanding of the impact of culture on behavior. Culture can affect managers' attitudes, business-government relations, how people think and behave, employees' work values and attitudes, and the local practices. Managers must be aware that different approaches may be necessary, depending on the country where business is being transacted. The success of the company and its employees depends on a thorough understanding of both the cultural differences and the similarities between the home and host countries.

Managing HUMAN RESOURCES across cultures is another challenge in international management. Processes for selecting, training, motivating, monitoring, and compensating foreign employees will differ by country. Specific approaches to labor relations in the international arena will also vary from country to country.

Further reading
Hodgetts, Richard M., and Fred Luthans. *International Management: Culture, Strategy, and Behavior.* 4th ed. New York: Irwin McGraw-Hill, 2000; Sullivan, Jeremiah J. *Exploring International Business Environments.* New York: Pearson Custom Publishing, 1999.

—Judy Mims

international marketing
International marketing is marketing products and SERVICES to customers outside a company's home country. It is important to both businesses and countries and involves a variety of strategy issues, laws, and other considerations.

International marketing is as old as civilization. Almost any issue of *National Geographic Magazine* will include a story about trade, whether it concerns an ancient sailing ship being raised from the ocean bottom or travel along centuries-old trails where merchants carried goods from one civilization to another. International trade exists and has existed for a variety of reasons, including access to products not available domestically, COMPARATIVE ADVANTAGE among producers in one country, foreign DEMAND, saturation of domestic demand, and technological advantage.

Historically the United States has not been a leader in international trade. As a colony it was subject to British laws requiring marketers to use British ships and requiring some products to be sold only to British merchants. With independence, U.S. producers focused mostly on meeting local demand. As the country grew and INFRASTRUCTURE expanded marketing opportunities, most U.S. manufacturers were content to work in domestic markets, while international trade was predominantly with Britain and later Canada. U.S. expansion into international markets grew rapidly after World War II, with the increasing dominance of American manufacturers and the growth of MULTINATIONAL CORPORATIONS. Today international trade represents a little more than 15 percent of U.S. GROSS DOMESTIC PRODUCT; most industrialized countries have a much higher percentage. While the U.S. percentage is small, on a dollar basis the United States is the largest trading country in the world, and U.S.-based companies dominate many international markets.

Companies expand into international markets either by careful analysis of the options and opportunities or almost by accident. Often international marketing begins with a request from a foreign company or a proposal from a foreign supplier. Many U.S. companies expanded internationally based on the MARSHALL PLAN programs for redeveloping Europe and Japan.

Many companies use MARKET RESEARCH to first assess opportunities when considering whether to expand into international markets. Market research is used to answer questions such as

- How is the social and cultural environment different?
- Are there infrastructure constraints?
- Who are the competitors and how competitive are they?
- Are there sufficient numbers of potential customers with sufficient purchasing power?

- What political and legal issues are likely to be a concern?
- What operating laws, standards, and taxes need to be considered?

Each of these questions needs to be analyzed carefully. Numerous articles describe INTERNATIONAL MANAGEMENT blunders—mistakes made by companies "going international." A classic example notes how Chevrolet marketed its Nova car in Spanish-speaking countries where *no va* means "no go." An Asian manufacturer shipped sandals to the Middle East with a tread pattern that closely resembled the Arabic word for Allah (god). Kodak attempted to sell their film in Japan by charging a lower price than Fuji, but later research revealed that Japanese film buyers perceived the lower price as meaning the PRODUCT was of lower quality.

Once international marketing opportunities have been identified, companies then address the question of how to expand internationally. The choices include EXPORTING, LICENSING, FRANCHISING, foreign direct INVESTMENT (FDI), JOINT VENTURES (JVs), and wholly owned subsidiaries. The choice will usually depend on a company's resources and willingness to take on RISK. Exporting—selling directly to a foreign buyer or to a middleman—requires little CAPITAL and, if managed properly, involves relatively little risk. Licensing—granting the right to a foreign producer to manufacturer a product for sale through foreign companies—also involves few resources and little risk. However, one risk is the potential creation of GRAY MARKETS, where licensed products made in other countries are returned into the company's domestic market, competing with domestically made products.

Franchising is a contractual agreement between a manufacturer or business-idea owner, the franchiser, and a WHOLESALER or retailer, the franchisee. It requires little capital on the part of the franchiser and relatively little risk. The franchiser sells to the franchisee the right to market its products or ideas, and to use its TRADEMARKS and BRANDS. The franchisee agrees to meet the franchiser's operating requirements, usually pays an initial fee for the franchise, and agrees to pay a percentage of sales to the franchiser. There is a potential risk if the franchisee harms the franchiser's reputation through shoddy products or dubious business practices.

Foreign direct investment (FDI) is the purchase of production, distribution, or retail facilities in another country. FDI requires capital, and because it generates physical ASSETS in another country, it creates greater risk. FDI also provides greater control and PROFIT potential than other less-risky international marketing options.

Joint ventures (JVs) are a popular method of expansion among U.S. companies; many U.S. companies first expanded into China and Mexico using JVs. Often the U.S. firm provided the capital and technology, while the Chinese or Mexican firm provided the contacts and distribution or retailing capability. Influence, connections, and relationships—called *guanxi* in China—are often as important as money in making business happen in international markets. Joint-venture agreements require capital and involve risk. There is an old saying that CONTRACTS are only as good as the people signing them. In many international markets, contracts are seen as establishing a relationship, not defining the terms and agreements of each party to a joint venture. Because of this, many U.S. businesses have been surprised or disappointed in their international joint ventures.

The last option for expanding internationally is the creation of a wholly owned subsidiary. Investment in foreign manufacturing or in an ASSEMBLY PLANT provides company control but requires investment capital and involve risk. Many companies create foreign operations as a means to overcome BARRIERS TO ENTRY. In the early 1900s, U.S. companies often created what were called "branch plants" in Canada as a way to sell goods there.

Basically, international markets are divided into three known spheres of influence in Europe, North America, and Asia, plus one unknown. The EUROPEAN UNION (EU) is called "fortress Europe." Companies wanting to market there often find it to their advantage to create manufacturing or assembly operations in one or more of the EU countries. North American international marketing is heavily influenced by the NORTH AMERICAN FREE TRADE AGREEMENT (NAFTA). Trade diversion, the shifting of production facilities in response to changes in international trade laws, grew with NAFTA's passage; other foreign companies frequently establish production facilities in North America in order to have access to the U.S. market. South Asia has historically been called "Japan Inc." dominated by Japanese multinational corporations. With the decline in the Japanese economy and the ascension of China to the WORLD TRADE ORGANIZATION (WTO) in 2001, Japanese dominance is being challenged by the relatively unknown, China.

While identifying opportunities for international marketing and deciding what type of international organization or option to use, marketers develop an international MARKETING STRATEGY, a firm's overall plan for selecting and meeting the needs of a target market. Marketing planning begins with comparing opportunities against the firm's resources, then developing objectives and mapping strategies, including tactical plans for implementation and control, to meet those objectives.

Marketing strategy includes decisions regarding product, promotion, pricing, and distribution (called the four Ps of marketing). When expanding into international markets, basic assumptions should be questioned and confirmed and minute details addressed. When considering product decisions, the easiest option would be to sell the same product in new markets. Depending on the country, marketers may need to change the size of the product, language, symbols, colors, and usually labeling. International marketers often hire labeling specialists to address the requirements of the country they are targeting. Since most of the rest of the world uses the metric system, weights and measures as well as container sizes probably will need to be changed. Packaging laws and environmental requirements can also necessitate product changes.

Pricing is a second strategy consideration. Logically marketers would like to charge a price similar to domestic prices but will consider adjusting prices based on consumer INCOMES in the new market. Other pricing factors need to be considered as well. For example, in many markets higher prices convey an image of better quality, so having the lowest or competitive price may not be the best strategy. Markups also vary from country to country, and the number of participants in the marketing chain may influence pricing decisions. For example, because lower incomes are normal in many South Asian countries, U.S. snack-food marketers reduced the size of their packages and then reduced prices.

As mentioned above, the number of participants in DISTRIBUTION CHANNELS may vary in international markets. Major retailers like Walmart will alter their distribution strategy depending on the country they are entering. In Canada, Walmart bought the Woolworth chain of stores but, rather than bring in its own distribution system, contracted with a Canadian-based company to distribute products to the stores. In many countries, distributors and their connections to government agencies require international marketers to hire local service providers. A fine line exists between hiring for distribution and customs services and paying bribes to get products into the market.

Promotion can be the most difficult challenge for international marketers. Symbols, colors, and expressions are all possible sources of confusion or misinterpretation, in addition to the obvious problem of language translation. Even in English-speaking countries, promotional messages need to be "translated." For example, in the United States to say people are "on the job" means they are there and actively working; in England the phrase refers to prostitution. There are many such "Englishes," and symbols also have many meanings. In Bali there is a lovely hotel called Hotel Swastika, bearing what Americans call the Nazi symbol—yet in Bali this symbol refers to the four forces on Earth. Color is another issue. While white is associated with purity and cleanliness in the United States, in many countries it is associated with death and funerals.

Even after addressing promotional message issues, international marketers have to consider media options. Newspaper, television, and radio options are likely to be different, and billboards and the use of premiums may not be allowed. Promotional specials may be regulated, and PERSONAL SELLING may be more important in some international markets. International marketing strategy is a classic example of Murphy's Law, "if it can go wrong, it will go wrong."

See also FOREIGN INVESTMENT.

Further reading
Folsom, Ralph H., and W. Davis Folsom. *Understanding NAFTA and Its International Business Implications.* New York: Matthew Bender/Irwin, 1996.

International Monetary Fund (IMF)

In 1945, 45 countries established the International Monetary Fund (IMF) to

1. promote international monetary cooperation
2. expand and balance international trade
3. promote currency-exchange stability
4. establish a system of international exchange payments
5. make resources available to assist countries having BALANCE OF PAYMENTS difficulties

There are now 185 member countries in the IMF. In contrast with the WORLD BANK, the IMF does not focus directly on development issues but is responsible for stabilizing the international monetary and financial system.

In its program called "Surveillance," the IMF each year evaluates each member country's exchange-rate policy within the overall framework of the member's economic policies. The IMF operates from the conviction that strong and consistent economic policies within a country will lead to stable EXCHANGE RATES and a growing and prosperous world economy.

In addition to the surveillance program, the IMF will extend credits and LOANS to a member country if it has balance-of-payment problems. It only extends such credits and loans to help a country bring about needed monetary and economic reform. In addition to this standard loan program, the IMF has a loan program designed to alleviate poverty and another designed to assist heavily indebted poor countries.

The IMF also has a training program to assist countries in stabilizing their economy and effecting ECONOMIC GROWTH. This includes giving technical assistance in such matters as FISCAL POLICY, MONETARY POLICY, and other macroeconomic efforts.

The IMF has been criticized on three fronts. Critics complain that because of the IMF, some poorer countries are indebted in such a way that they cannot possibly serve their citizens. In addition, the IMF stated purpose of advancing the global economy is opposed by many who think that a global economy damages such things as the ecology, worker rights, and national identity.

The IMF also receives a great deal of criticism from debtor nations who think the organization meddles in decisions to which the nations themselves have a national prerogative. For example, often the IMF will make a loan contingent on a country carrying out some economic reform. Such reforms, which critics call austerity programs, can cause economic suffering for the country's citizens and thus creates resentment against the IMF for dictating internal country economic policies.

Further reading
International Monetary Fund Web site. Available online. URL: www.imf.org.

—Mack Tennyson

International Organization for Standardization   See ISO STANDARDS.

International Trade Commission
The United States International Trade Commission, created by an act of Congress as the U.S. Tariff Commission in 1916, is an independent bipartisan commission that investigates matters of trade. The ITC conducts research and specialized studies of U.S. commercial and international trade policies and is charged with preparing reports analyzing international economics and foreign trade

for the executive and congressional branches of government, other government agencies, and the public. ITC activities include

- determining whether U.S. industries are materially harmed by IMPORTS priced at less than fair value or by subsidization
- directing actions against unfair trade practices such as TRADEMARK, PATENT, or COPYRIGHT infringement
- analyzing trade and TARIFF issues and monitoring import levels
- participating in the development of an international harmonized commodity code (Harmonized Tariff Schedule of the United States, or HARMONIZED TARIFF SYSTEM)
- making recommendations to the U.S. president regarding domestic industry injury determinations
- advising the president whether agricultural imports conflict with the U.S. Department of Agriculture's price-support programs

The ITC also advises the president regarding the probable economic impacts of proposed trade agreements with foreign countries.

The commissioners of the ITC are appointed by the president and confirmed by the U.S. Senate for nine-year terms. To increase its independence from the executive branch, no more than three commissioners may be from the same political party, and the ITC submits its budget directly to Congress, exempting it from review by the OFFICE OF MANAGEMENT AND BUDGET.

Further reading
U.S. International Trade Commission Web site. Available online. URL: www.usitc.gov.

Internet
The complex matrix of globally connected computer networks known today as the Internet is the product of past national-defense projects whose goals were to keep the United States ahead in the cold war's arms race. Following the 1957 launch of the Soviet Union's first satellite, Sputnik I, the U.S. Department of Defense (DoD) created

the Advanced Research Projects Agency (ARPA), which would develop a nationwide communications network to help protect the United States against nuclear attacks from space.

The 1960s saw the development of more advanced methods of data transfer, so that by 1969 the first wide-area computer communications network, called Advanced Research Projects Agency Net (ARPANET) was born. Through the 1970s, standards and protocols for communications were set in place, and the addition of England and Norway to the network made it truly global. Electronic mail (e-mail) became a reality, allowing computer users to send "instant" messages around the world.

By the 1980s, ARPANET was being used by universities and research institutions to share information, changing the network's functions from primarily military to educational uses. Also during this decade, the first news groups and on-line interactive games were created as the network continued to develop many useful applications. In 1990 a faster network called NFSNet, allowing more users to get connected to the growing network, replaced ARPANET.

This growth in the number of users throughout the 1980s, thanks mainly to the availability of desktop computers during this period, led inevitably to the network's commercialization by 1994. With more than 3 million Web locations or hosts connected, on-line retailers, banks, and entrepreneurial businesses were established daily, and by 1995 the U.S. government had handed control of the network over to private organizations. The WORLD WIDE WEB (WWW) was born out of this growth, as privatization and the development and standardization of a hypertext computer language allowed users to "browse" the network quickly and efficiently.

Business interest in the Internet first began when companies created network "browsers," computer programs that allowed users to move among the Internet's "Web site pages" easily. Then, coupled with the greater availability of desktop computers, businesses offering dial-up connections began to sell their SERVICES, facilitating the

Internet's expansion. By 2008 there were over 1.6 billion Internet host sites.

During the 1990s, as more hosts and users became connected, businesses began researching how they could use the Internet for both the transfer of information in and between markets, as well as for direct commerce. Scores of companies, called DOT-COMS (referring to their Internet address endings of *.com*), sprung up seemingly overnight, selling everything imaginable to "online customers." The excitement over the potential of a new global market that was opening up to businesses of every size and geographic location created an electronic commerce (E-COMMERCE) frenzy. It was not long before the new market was flooded with competitors. However, by 2000, when on-line shopping had become less novel, many of the dot-coms suffered decreasing PROFITS or ceased to exist altogether, creating what was called the "dot-com burnout" and a market crash.

In spite of the failures of many eager E-BUSINESSES, the Internet has continued to be a source of high profits for the firms who established themselves on the Internet early and were able to set themselves apart from their competitors. The Internet has also created new markets, specifically in ADVERTISING and communication. Advertisers understand that with more and more people becoming "connected" to the vast network, there will be greater potential to reach them with their messages.

In areas of communication, the early 2000s have seen the creation of handheld computers that allow users to receive e-mail messages almost anywhere on the planet. A further development in creating a "wireless" Internet is removing more geographical and physical barriers to the network.

—Daniel P. Whicker

Internet Fraud Complaint Center

The Internet Fraud Complaint Center (IFCC) is an organization that takes Internet FRAUD complaints from consumers and reports cases to authorities for investigation. The IFCC is a joint project between the National White Collar Crime Center and the Federal Bureau of Investigation (FBI).

The center maintains a database tracking Internet fraud complaints and biannually publishes and publicizes INTERNET fraud activities.

In 2008 the highest percentage of complaints was nondelivery of merchandise or payment (32.9 percent) and auction fraud (25.5 percent). Internet auction fraud, the misrepresentation of products for sale through on-line auctions, has been the number-one type of Internet fraud since the creation of such auctions. Often, the fraud involves the sale of name-brand merchandise, which when received is a "knockoff" (an illegally produced copy of inferior quality), like the $15 Rolex watches and $25 Gucci bags Americans have purchased abroad on the street or in flea markets. In 2008 on-line auction fraud cost consumers an estimated $265 million. The major on-line auction companies have attempted to reduce this problem through buyer-rating surveys and increased policing of their auction services, but it remains a major problem.

In 2001 the IFCC ranked an Internet version of the "Nigerian money-order scam" as its third most frequent complaint. In the Nigerian money-order scheme (named after the 1980s letter scams frequently starting from Nigeria), the solicitor claims to be a Nigerian government official or widow of an official with access to an unclaimed bank account with a huge amount of money. The solicitation offers a percentage of the funds if the recipient will help transfer them to a U.S. bank account—the recipient's account. After getting the account information, the defrauder takes the money. A variation on the Nigerian money-order fraud involves a Russian claiming a loved one died in the World Trade Center after depositing millions that must now be claimed.

Internet fraud tends to be similar to other consumer fraud. In addition to the top three categories, other types of reported Internet fraud involve Internet access services, information adult services, computer equipment/software, work-at-home offers, advance-fee loans, credit-card issuing, and business opportunities/franchises.

Other groups also track Internet fraud, including the Department of Justice and the National Fraud Information Center. In addition to the kinds of Internet fraud already mentioned, the Department of Justice scrutinizes market-manipulation schemes. In this type of fraud, criminals use investment chat rooms to "pump" up interest and speculation in a stock and then sell their shares before the company whose shares are being touted refutes the false rumors. A variation in this scheme involves selling a company's stock short and then disseminating negative false information, driving the stock price down.

Further reading
"Internet Fraud." Available online. URL: www.fbi.gov/majcases/fraud/internetschemes.htm; Internet Fraud Complaint Center. Available online. URL: www.ic3.gov/; Internet Fraud Watch. Available online. URL: www.fraud.org/internet/intinfo.htm.

Internet marketing

Internet marketing is the use of the INTERNET to promote, distribute, and price goods and SERVICES for target audiences. While uses of the Internet are constantly changing, several successful Internet marketing models are evolving to facilitate E-COMMERCE and E-BUSINESS.

First, the Internet as a means of promotion is clearly established. Early Internet marketers had dreams of putting up a site on the WORLD WIDE WEB and drawing customers from around the world. In many ways, it was like the production mentality of the AMERICAN INDUSTRIAL REVOLUTION: build it and they will come. The implosion of the DOT-COMS industry in 2000 brought marketers and investors back to reality, but the use of the Internet to promote goods and services is still expanding daily. Early Internet marketers often created what were known as "billboards" a Web page listing the phone number and address of the company and its logo. These were quickly replaced by informational sites that allowed consumers to access a wide array of information about the company, thus saving time and personnel for marketers. Since the goals of promotion are typically to inform, persuade, and/or remind consumers about a company, Internet marketers quickly learned to use the new medium in such a way that consumers could gather helpful information for their purchase decisions.

Some Internet marketers found they could do more than just promote their PRODUCTS; they could also take and confirm orders, and even deliver products electronically. The airline, hotel, and auto-rental industries quickly developed the capability to make reservations over the Internet. In the process, distribution systems changed. Travel agents and other service-industry intermediaries are disappearing as Internet direct sales are expanding. Automobile manufacturers have also been tempted to use the Internet for DIRECT MARKETING, but to date, having established distribution relationships with car dealerships, most have opted to direct Internet customers to retail outlets.

One of the Internet's most amazing uses is on-line auctions. eBay and other Web auction systems are dramatically changing a wide variety of markets. The market prices for antiques and collectibles have plummeted with expanded market access through the Internet. In addition, Internet auction sites are important sources of market price information, reducing the ARBITRAGE possibilities used by many retail antique dealers. While some auction systems like Priceline.com have not been fully accepted by consumers, businesses are expanding their use of Internet auctions both to sell excess inventory and to purchase standardized products.

Another use of the Internet is the expansion of specialty merchants on-line. Several years ago, one merchant created a Web business solely for marketing hot sauces. Amazon.com started as a new-book retailer, holding minimal inventory but using relationships with major publishers to quickly fulfill Internet orders. Comparison-shopping Web sites expanded, allowing consumers to search multiple Web merchants for the best price for the product or service they desired.

Pricing strategy using the Internet is just beginning to evolve. Airlines are now ADVERTISING discount rates for Internet users both on their own sites and through group sites. Orbitz.com, created by airline companies, competes with other discount-pricing sites. Hotel and auto-rental companies have been slow to recognize the Internet as a distinct market segment and a way to discount services.

Some products and services like software and information can be delivered over the Internet. Relatively few firms are making a PROFIT using the Internet for delivery, but products such as antivirus software, information distributors such as the *Wall Street Journal,* and agencies such as the INTERNAL REVENUE SERVICE are using the Internet to reach consumers. Access to secondary data, whether from government or private sources, is one of the major products available through the Internet. This information access is allowing entrepreneurs throughout the world to compete in major markets like the United States. For example, data processing and accounting services for U.S. firms are now being subcontracted to Indian businesses.

One of the visions of Internet marketing was a global marketplace in which a small entrepreneur with the right strategy could compete with the multinational giants. To some degree this is possible, but like BRANDS in a store, name recognition, preference, and loyalty is an evolving trend on the Internet. Major Internet marketers are buying up failing competitors' domain names (their identifying Web address), increasing their market dominance. International trade restrictions are to some degree limiting global COMPETITION. Because Internet markets are changing so rapidly, global trade agreements regarding Internet marketing lag behind market advances.

Establishing and maintaining loyal Internet customers is a challenge for many marketers. With a click consumers can move from one competitor to the next. Contests, newsletters, and frequent-user programs are all being tested to increase Internet customer loyalty. Many different models are being used in Internet marketing, as evidenced in the wide variety of hotel Web sites. Some are "designer" sites—i.e., "come look and see how fabulous your stay will be with us" sites. Another group of sites will be more direct—"Let us take your order." A third group of sites will display everything there is to do and see in or know about the cities or areas where the hotels are located.

One successful Internet marketing strategy is target e-mail. By using opt-in e-mail distribution lists, lists of e-mail recipients who have agreed to receive marketing messages, marketers are quickly and efficiently communicating with target audiences. For example, one car dealership purchased an e-mail list for consumers in its geographic area and sent a message to 20,000 addresses, offering a price reduction to anyone who responded and offering a contest for a free car. Recipients enthusiastically entered the contest, forwarded the e-mail solicitation to friends, and generated more than enough new customers to justify the cost.

Like most marketing methods, Internet marketing is not without controversy and concern. The two major issues are PRIVACY and spam (junk e-mails and ads). Most ethical marketers reframe from spam, and most Internet marketers have established and posted clearly stated privacy policies. Other Internet marketing issues include "cyber hustlers," "cyber squatters," and "typo squatters." Cyber hustlers are marketers who legally purchase rights to domain names that are not renewed. Like TRADEMARKS, domain names have value and are obtained on a first come, first served basis. In the United States domain names are registered through domain registry companies, licensed by the government to allocate specific Web addresses. If a company does not renew its domain name, it gives up its rights to the name, which then goes back into the available domain-name pool. Cyber squatters purchase potentially popular domain names and sell them to late-entry marketers. For example, an entrepreneur who learned about the new South Carolina lottery registered a number of logical domain names for the new program. Typo squatters register domain names that misspell or approximate a popular domain name, hoping to sell them to businesses at a profit. For example, one typo squatter registered amaza.com.

According to Net Solutions, the first domain registry company in the United States, in November 1999 the U.S. Court of Appeals (Ninth Circuit) ruled that the company had "no responsibility or duty to police the rights of trademark owners concerning domain names." Questions about domain-name disputes are referred to www.domainmagistrate.com., which lists the new Uniform Domain Name Resolution Policy (UDRP). The site also suggests that viewers go the U.S. Patent and Trademark Office site (www.uspto.gov) to see if the domain name in which they are interested is similar to a trademark registered with the office.

The WORLD INTELLECTUAL PROPERTY ORGANIZATION (WIPO), one of a number of organizations handling domain-name disputes, reports increasing disagreement between cyber hustlers and previous owners of domain names. WIPO has no specific measure to address the problem, and instead the disputes have been referred to the UDRP.

Three of the many newer Internet marketing strategies are customization of Web sites, use of pop-up promotions, and viral marketing. Web sites can be customized based on viewers' past visits or current movement within a site. For example, Amazon.com welcomes returning visitors. Pop-up promotions appear on computer screens after viewers visit particular sites. Pop-ups are considered annoying and force viewers to have to close the ad on their screen. Viral marketing is e-mail messages sent to groups asking recipients to forward the message to others. With relatively low entry costs, the Internet will continue to evolve and become an important part of almost any organization's MARKETING STRATEGY.

Further reading
Wilson Internet. Available online. URL: www.wilsonweb.com.

Internet surveys
Internet surveys provide an efficient and inexpensive means of collecting marketing information from a large number of people. Internet surveys are often used to collect demographic information and viewer opinions regarding products, services, or core issues. Researchers may either post SURVEYS on Web sites or e-mail them to potential respondents. However, there are both advantages

and disadvantages to the use of INTERNET and e-mail surveys.

Perhaps the most important benefit of using Internet or e-mail surveys is that both types of surveys are inexpensive. Without printing, paper, and mailing expenses, these surveys typically are more cost-efficient than their traditional paper counterparts, MAIL SURVEYS. In addition, Internet and e-mail surveys can reach a very large and potentially diverse group of people who otherwise might not be accessible for survey research. For example, Internet or e-mail surveys may be the best way to reach people with specific characteristics or backgrounds, such as highly intelligent members of the population, people with unusual illnesses, or people from different countries. The use of these types of surveys also allows researchers to collect information around the clock, as the respondents choose when they wish to complete the survey.

However, Internet and e-mail surveys do have disadvantages. Although they allow researchers to reach unique groups of people, the typical Internet sample is not representative of the general public. For instance, Internet samples are restricted to people who have Internet access. To the extent that some people either cannot afford computer access or tend not to use the Internet, such as people from lower socioeconomic levels and the elderly population, certain groups may be excluded from an Internet sample.

In addition, Internet and e-mail surveys offer researchers less control over who completes the survey. Several potential participants may use the same e-mail address, and any one participant may use multiple computers. Technical variation in computers, monitors, browsers, and Internet connections also may affect responses to any given survey. Research suggests that there is a high attrition rate for Internet surveys, which means that although many participants may start the survey, many do not complete it. Finally, there is typically no opportunity for participants to ask the researcher any questions, as they might in a TELEPHONE SURVEYS or PERSONAL-INTERVIEW SURVEYS.

There also are important considerations for researchers when choosing between Internet and e-mail surveys. Although e-mail surveys tend to be simple to construct and easy to distribute, there may be limited formatting options. Many standard QUESTIONNAIRE-layout techniques, such as tables and GRAPHS, either cannot be created in an attractive format or viewed properly as an attachment file. E-mail surveys are also restricted to people with e-mail accounts, the currency of which must be updated frequently. On the other hand, while Internet surveys usually require more time during the construction phase, they may save time at a later point if the data can be directed automatically into an electronic database.

In general, Internet and e-mail surveys are applicable in many areas of research. Businesses that make use of these means of collecting information can use the data to better target marketing promotions, improve product quality, and test new product ideas.

Further reading

Dillman, Don A., Jolene D. Smyth, and Leah Melani Christian. *Internet, Mail, and Mixed-Mode Surveys: The Tailored Design Method.* Hoboken, N.J.: John Wiley and Sons, 2008.

—Elizabeth L. Cralley

internships

Business internships are opportunities for students to experience working in a company or industry; they can be paid or unpaid, part-time or full-time, and can last a semester, a summer, or a year. Because schools and businesses define internship programs differently, it is important for students considering internships to carefully consider the expectations and benefits of internships at their institutions.

For students, internships provide

- a great way to learn about a career direction before leaving school
- a way to differentiate oneself from students who do not have relevant work experience
- job opportunities
- opportunities to explore specialized business professions

Business internship programs have become popular in the United States; over 40,000 internship opportunities are available annually. Especially in times of low unemployment, businesses are eager to have the added help of interns and also benefit by bringing in people with fresh ideas and new skills, in addition to considering and recruiting future employees. Many companies compete to recruit summer interns from prestigious schools and professional programs.

A good internship program should include

- meaningful work
- projects that can be completed in the time of the internship
- broad exposure for the intern within the organization
- time set aside to learn about the company in general
- the expectation that the intern will present the results of his or her project

Some industries have been accused of exploiting interns, using them for low- or no-cost labor. The U.S. DEPARTMENT OF LABOR's Wage and Hour Division provides guidelines distinguishing interns from employees.

Further reading
Ryan, Cathy, and Roberta H. Krapels. "Organizations and Internships," *Business Communication Quarterly* 60, no. 4 (December 1997): 126–132.

Interstate Commerce Commission

The Interstate Commerce Commission (ICC) was established in 1887 to regulate surface transportation in the United States as a response to market manipulation and control of railroads during the AMERICAN INDUSTRIAL REVOLUTION. The ICC was the first regulatory commission in U.S. history, but from 1887 until 1906 it had little control over the transportation industry. Vague wording in the initial legislation and lack of enforcement power limited the commission's effectiveness.

With the passage of the Hepburn Act in 1906, the ICC's functions and power grew, giving the commission control over interstate railroads, trucking, bus lines, freight forwarders, water carriers, oil pipelines, transportation brokers, and express agencies. The ICC was allowed to set prices for interstate transportation and, like public utility commissions, to determine fair rates of return for industry firms. In the 1950s and 1960s, the ICC oversaw the consolidation of railroad systems and enforcement of desegregation in public-transportation systems.

Beginning in the 1970s, government regulation of interstate transportation declined. With the Motor Carrier Act of 1980, the ICC's control over the trucking industry was diminished, and subsequent legislation reduced its control over railroads, bus lines, and other transportation markets. The ICC's decline was one of the first steps in the movement away from government regulation of business. The commission was eliminated in 1995, and some ICC functions were conveyed to the DEPARTMENT OF TRANSPORTATION, while others were transferred to the newly created National Surface Transportation Board.

Further reading
Records of the Interstate Commerce Commission. Available online. URL: www.archives.gov/.

interviewing

Interviewing job candidates is an important part of any business organization's efforts to succeed and prosper. From an employer's perspective, numerous issues and legal concerns are involved in business interviewing. From a job candidate's perspective, interviewing is a skill that can be developed for successful hiring.

Well before interviews take place, managers must address a variety of questions. Who will participate in the hiring process? Who has the authority to make the final decision? Companies then conduct a job analysis, addressing the questions of what activities, tasks, and responsibilities are involved in the job to be filled. For unique, new positions in a company, job analysis can be a detailed process. For companies hiring additional people to do a common task, job analysis is standardized.

From the job analysis, job descriptions and a statement of job qualifications are written. Most companies first advertise the new position within the organization but will also look at outside applicants. Before interviewing candidates, companies screen applications and creates a list of top candidates to interview. Major companies are often flooded with applications and use computerized software designed to pick out key words in applicants' résumés as an initial basis of screening.

When interviewing is scheduled, managers need to decide whether to use structured or unstructured interviews; most prefer unstructured interviews, asking candidates about a variety of subjects. Sometimes candidates are asked to demonstrate their ability in an area related to the job description. Candidates for sales positions should anticipate being asked to make an on-the-spot sales presentation. MANAGEMENT candidates should anticipate being given hypothetical situations. Unstructured interviews will often put candidates in different situations, including group interviews, one-on-one conversations, and discussions over meals.

In structured interviews, each candidate is asked the same predetermined questions. Well-developed questions help managers gain insight into a candidate's capability. Many public organizations, using teams of staff members not used to interviewing, will employ structured interviews, which provide an advantage in comparing candidates. Often when a group is involved in interviewing, rating forms are used to evaluate each candidate's response to specific questions. Structured interviews have the potential disadvantage of not probing or drawing out unique qualities during the interview process, but they help the interviewing team to avoid asking inappropriate questions.

Numerous federal laws impact business interviewing. The CIVIL RIGHTS ACT of 1964 prohibits discrimination based on race, color, religion, national origin, or gender. The Age Discrimination in Employment Act (1967) prohibits discrimination against people ages 40–70. The AMERICANS WITH DISABILITIES ACT (1990) prohibits discrimi-

nation based on handicaps or disabilities, either mental or physical.

These laws and others lead to a list of "do not ask" questions during the interviewing process, including

- *religion.* Candidates should not be asked about their religious beliefs or whether the work schedule would interfere with their religious activities.
- *sex and marital status.* Sex is obvious, but a common mistake is asking candidates about their marital status, including questions about whether their spouses work, their children, or whether a woman would prefer to be addressed as Ms., Mrs., or Miss.
- *age.* Candidates may be asked whether they are a minor or over 70, because special laws affect those people. Otherwise candidates should not be asked their age or date of birth.
- *nationality and race.* Questions or comments about race, color, or national origin should not be asked of the applicant or his/her spouse. Candidates can be asked if they are U.S. citizens, but not whether they, their parents, or their spouses are naturalized or native-born citizens. Applicants who are not citizens may be asked if they have the proper VISAS to work in the United States.
- *physical characteristics.* Questions related to disabilities, handicaps, or health problems should be avoided. Candidates can be asked if they are capable of performing tasks stated in the job description.
- *bankruptcy or garnishments* (directed payments from wages to a creditor). Generally, these questions should be avoided because the U.S. bankruptcy code prohibits discrimination against people who have filed for bankruptcy.
- *arrests and convictions.* Questions about past arrests are not legal. Candidates can be asked about past convictions.

From a job candidate's perspective, interviewing can be an intimidating experience. Numerous interviewing "tips" articles provide ideas and guidelines when preparing for a job interview. The first step is to learn about the company; like the

Boy Scout motto, "be prepared." Applicants should use the INTERNET, local newspapers, CHAMBER OF COMMERCE, or stockbrokers to learn basic information such as the number of employees, history of the company, major products, and competitors.

The second step is dressing appropriately; there is only one chance to make a first impression. What is appropriate dress for an interview will vary depending on the organization, the region of the country, and the type of position for which one is interviewing. One salesman tells the story of wearing a conservative suit for the interview, which went well. He was invited to the second round of interviews, but as he only owned one quality suit, he went to the local men's clothing store and bought a second suit on credit. After the second interview went well, he was invited for a third set of interviews at the regional office. After buying another suit on credit, he got the job. Afterwards his new manager confided that they almost did not hire him because he dressed too well, and they thought he was too affluent to work hard in sales.

Common advice for job candidates in an interview is to answer one question at a time and take time answering questions. One should also be prepared to talk about past employment and to stress the positive aspects of those jobs. Other advice is to ask questions, make good eye contact, and avoid telling jokes. A common technique interviewers use is to tell a slightly off-colored or inappropriate joke and watch the candidate's response. Job candidates should think of an interview as an opportunity to sell themselves.

Common questions asked in business interviews include

- What is your greatest strength?
- What is your greatest weakness?
- What makes you different from other candidates with similar background and education?
- If you were hiring someone for this position, what qualities would you look for?
- Are you more comfortable working alone or as part of a team?
- Describe one of your experiences working in a team.

- Why are you leaving your current position?
- Describe a situation where something went wrong and how you handled the situation.

Further reading

Churchill, Gilbert A., Neil M. Ford, and Orville C. Walker. *Sales Force Management*. Boston: Irwin McGraw-Hill, 1999.

inventory control

Inventory control is the management of raw materials, work in process, and final goods. Inventory control attempts to minimize costs while avoiding production stoppages, the cost of idle workers, and the potential for lost sales due to not having sufficient PRODUCT available to meet market DEMAND. In many business environments, inventory control is a complex, dynamic process that requires continual oversight and decision making.

Logistics management specialist Jeroen P. Van den Berg divides inventory control into two parts: planning and control. In his article Van den Berg states "Planning refers to MANAGEMENT decisions that affect the intermediate term (one or multiple months), such as inventory management and storage location assignment. Control refers to the operational decisions that affect the short term (hours, day) such as routing, sequencing, scheduling and order-batching." Adjusting final goods inventory to meet anticipated changes in demand would be part of inventory planning, while changes in raw materials and work-in-progress levels would be part of inventory control.

One method of assessing inventory control is called materials-requirements planning (MRP) and materials-resource planning (MRPII). MRP is an operational planning system in which, by looking at the end product and working backward, all the labor, materials, and other RESOURCES needed to produce the product are determined. Computer models are used to assess the complex relationships among the production processes, including timing, energy requirements, machine and worker-production capacities, and shipping and handling. MRPII takes the resource requirements estimated from MRP, analyzes the production costs at various levels of output, and coordinates resource controls with estimated market demand.

In the 1970s many companies shifted emphasis from PRODUCTION improvement to inventory reduction. MRP and MRPII led to the concept of just-in-time (JIT) inventory minimization. In Japan the Toyota Production System, "kanban," or time-based management, called for eliminating inventories, with suppliers delivering materials and components, sometimes within 30 minutes of when the inputs were needed for production. The system saved money for Toyota, but as correspondent Roger Schreffler states, "The savings realized through kanban, however, aren't necessarily passed on to Japanese suppliers. In fact, much of the cost for ensuring on-time delivery of precise quantities of components and materials falls directly on the suppliers' shoulders." JIT inventory-control systems work better when suppliers and customers are in close proximity, but as Toyota learned in the 1990s, such systems create risks. When Toyota's only brake-part supplier's factory burned, its ASSEMBLY PLANT had only a few hours' worth of parts to use, and production stopped. Other suppliers quickly created alternative sources of parts, but Toyota lost millions of dollars' worth of production.

In the United States, Dell Computer Corporation and Walmart are recognized leaders in inventory control. In the 1980s Walmart developed an often-copied electronic sales, ordering, and warehousing system. Scanning systems constantly transmit sales from each store to Walmart headquarters in Bentonville, Arkansas. Reorders based on sales are automatically transmitted to vendors, who then ship to Walmart's distribution centers. Distribution centers are expected to maintain no inventory but instead constantly coordinate shipments from vendors to individual stores. As an old saying goes, "Nothing gets sold in the warehouse." A story in the *Wall Street Journal* about sales on September 11, 2001, provides insights into both American CONSUMER BEHAVIOR and Walmart's inventory-control system. The article reported that during the morning of September 11, sales of all

goods plummeted as Americans were transfixed to their television screens. In the afternoon sales of water, batteries, canned goods, and ammunition skyrocketed. By evening, sales of American flags had exhausted stores' inventories.

Dell Computer Corporation is another example of the importance of inventory control. Relatively few Dell customers realize the company does not produce computers or computer parts. Instead, when customers go on-line and order a Dell computer, their orders automatically send other orders to Dell suppliers to produce and send the needed components. By maintaining no inventory, Dell reduces their costs, allowing them to adjust for market conditions and also to avoid inventory obsolescence.

Without such methods, many companies wind up with products or components that are out-of-date. Managing inventory has been critical to minimizing costs of production, especially in the personal computer market, when the "state of the art" technology was being replaced every 12–18 months.

See also MASS CUSTOMIZATION.

Further reading
Schreffler, Roger. "Kanban Isn't Perfect—Really!" *Chilton's Distribution,* August 1987; Stoner, James, and R. Edward Freeman. *Management.* 5th ed. Upper Saddle River, N.J.: Prentice Hall, 1992; Van den Berg, Jeroen P. "A Literature on Planning and Control of Warehousing Systems." *IIE Transactions,* August 1999.

investment

Investment can refer to either economic investment or financial investment. Economic investment is the purchase of new productive ASSETS—buildings, equipment, computers, etc.—that are used to produce goods and SERVICES. Financial investment is the use of CAPITAL (MONEY) to generate hoped-for PROFITS. Financial investment includes the purchase of shares of stock in a company, other securities, or assets with the goal of selling them at a higher price.

Economic investment is part of aggregate expenditures in an economy. In NATIONAL INCOME ACCOUNTING, aggregate expenditures are the sum of CONSUMPTION, investment, government, and net trade spending for final goods and services in an economy in a year. In the U.S. economy, investment spending represents approximately 17 percent of total spending annually, but it is the most volatile component of aggregate expenditures. Business managers determine economic investment. The decision whether or not to invest in new productive assets is primarily influenced by expected profits. Managers make their best projections of future sales of output from the new investments and compare expected sales with estimated COSTS. Like the oracles in ancient societies, managers seek out "divine wisdom" when making investment decisions.

In addition to being influenced by expected profits, economic investment decisions are also affected by changes in technology, capacity utilization, and the cost of borrowing. Often managers will replace existing equipment, even though the existing equipment is fully operational. If new technology can result in a better-quality product, managers are forced to purchase the new equipment in order to remain competitive. Capacity utilization is the percentage of existing productive capacity that is currently being used. The Department of Commerce maintains an overall capacity utilization rate for U.S. manufacturers; generally 85-percent capacity utilization is considered close to full capacity. If, when operating at full capacity, managers think DEMAND for their PRODUCTS will continue to grow, they will decide to invest in new productive capacity. New investment is also influenced by INTEREST RATES, or the cost of borrowing. As interest rates decline, the cost of new productive assets decreases, stimulating additional investment spending.

As stated earlier, financial investment is the use of money to generate hoped-for profits. Financial investment can lead to economic investment, but not necessarily. Often people will say, "I invested in a new car." Almost always this is an incorrect use of the term *investment*. If someone bought a car for use in his or her business, say for delivery of goods to customers, then yes, it would be an economic investment. But most often when people

purchase a car, it is what economists call durable consumer expenditure, the purchase of a product for personal benefits with an expected use life of more than one year. An example of a financial investment would be a person who bought an antique car with the expectation of selling it for a profit.

Financial investment decisions involve a comparison of RISKS versus returns. Returns are expected profits, often expressed by a percentage return on investment (ROI). Risks can include DEFAULT, exchange, INFLATION, interest-rate, liquidity, and political risks. Default risk is the likelihood that the borrower will not repay the loan. Exchange risk is the potential for losses due to an unfavorable change in EXCHANGE RATES. Inflation risk is the potential loss if the value of the asset or money loses value due to increased inflation. Interest-rate risk is the potential decreased value of a fixed-rate debt like a bond, due to rising interest rates. Liquidity risk is the potential problem of not being able to find a buyer for the investment. Owners of small businesses and obscure investments often face liquidity risks. Political risk is the potential for nationalization (takeover) of investments by a government or the potential for political instability causing a decrease in value of an investment. For example, the major unresolved issue in the long-standing U.S. EMBARGO of Cuba has been the 1960s nationalization of businesses by the Castro government.

Financial investment can also take place through either direct or portfolio investments. DIRECT INVESTMENT is the purchase of a business or assets by an investor; portfolio investment is the purchase of securities representing an ownership (EQUITY) interest in an enterprise. Direct investment generally involves a long-term commitment of resources, while portfolio investment can be sold quickly in STOCK MARKETS. Stock markets are exchanges, which facilitate the transfer of financial investments.

Investment can also refer to INVESTMENT CLUBS, INVESTMENT BANKING, and investment grade. Investment clubs are groups that pool their funds and analyze investment choices before allocating the club's money. Investment bankers are FINANCIAL INTERMEDIARIES assist in merger acquisitions, offer securities brokerage services, and who help CORPORATIONS and governments raise capital through UNDERWRITING and distributing new securities. Investment grade refers to BONDS issued by corporations that are rated above a specified level by bond-rating agencies.

investment banking (I-banking)

Investment banking, also called I-banking, refers to the financial services provided by investment bankers. Until 1933, commercial banks participated in activities that are now purely investment-banking activities, such as UNDERWRITING. The 1929 STOCK MARKET crash and the resulting GREAT DEPRESSION led U.S. lawmakers to pass several laws between 1933 and 1940 that aimed to regulate the securities industry, since bankers and financial institutions were perceived as having created the crash and depression. Laws aimed at regulating the securities industry included the Glass-Steagall Act of 1933, the Securities Act of 1933, and the Securities Exchange Act of 1934.

The term INVESTMENT BANKER was created in 1933 when the Glass-Stegall Act prohibited commercial bankers (i.e., those whose functions included making LOANS and accepting deposits) from participating in risk-taking activities such as underwriting and dealing in corporate securities and certain governmental securities. The act also aimed to encourage the stability of commercial banks in that entities that pursued underwriting and dealing in securities were considered investment bankers and could not offer services such as providing loans or accepting deposits. Conversely, entities that provided loans and accepted deposits were commercial bankers and could not underwrite or deal in securities. Thus, after 1933 the financial-services industry was divided into investment banking and commercial banking.

Investment bankers are not investors or bankers. Rather, they are firms that provide a wide range of financial services, including underwriting and distributing new securities issues to help CORPORATIONS and governments raise CAPITAL

or obtain financing, MERGERS AND ACQUISITIONS services, and wholesale and retail broker services.

Corporations and government entities sometimes issue securities such as stocks, BONDS, and OPTIONS in order to raise capital or funds for their operations. Investment bankers act as FINANCIAL INTERMEDIARIES between the investing public and corporate and government securities issuers. Generally investment bankers buy new securities issued by a corporation or a government entity and resell those securities to the public. Firm-commitment underwriting refers to the practice of investment bankers purchasing new issues of securities (purchase price) and reselling those securities at a higher price than the purchase price. The investment bankers' PROFIT is the spread (or the difference) between the purchase price and the selling price of the securities. Investment bankers may also sell new securities issues on a "best effort" basis, which refers to the practice of their marketing and selling new securities issues on a commission basis rather than underwriting.

Investment bankers may assist businesses with mergers, acquisitions, and divestitures—for instance, identifying possible merger opportunities, negotiating the purchase of another business, and structuring the purchase. Investment bankers may also offer wholesale and retail broker services to assist institutional investors, such as entities that manage large groups of funds like pension funds or MUTUAL FUNDS, in buying or selling securities for their portfolios; retail brokerage services for individuals who are interested in creating and managing their individual investment portfolios; and private, brokerage and money-management services for very wealthy individuals.

There are three major categories of investment bankers based on the types of service they offer and where they offer those services: full service, regional, and boutiques. Full-service investment bankers are large organizations that operate on a global basis and offer a full range of investment banking services. Some full-service investment bankers are known as "super-bulge" bracket firms because they have major market share in the industry and relationships with most of the leading corporations. Goldman Sachs and Merrill Lynch are examples of super-bulge bracket firms.

Regional investment bankers are those investment bankers that operate in a particular region or city. Boutiques are investment bankers that specialize in a particular function of investment banking, such as advising on mergers and acquisitions.

The Securities Act of 1933 regulates public offerings of securities and requires full disclosure of information with regard to new security issues. Under this act, issuers of new securities are required to file a "registration statement" with the SECURITIES AND EXCHANGE COMMISSION (SEC) and receive approval from the SEC before the securities can be sold. Issuers are also required to furnish prospective investors with a PROSPECTUS, which is typically incorporated into the registration statement. Criminal and civil penalties will be imposed for false or misleading statements in the registration statement or prospectus, or for noncompliance with the registration and prospectus requirements. Thus, before an investment banker can sell new issues of securities, it must ensure that the new securities issues have been properly registered with and approved by the SEC.

The Securities Exchange Act of 1934 regulates secondary trading of securities listed on national securities exchanges and securities that are traded over-the counter and therefore not listed. This act requires disclosure of information on securities traded on national securities exchanges and over the counter. Further, representations of securities must be accurate.

See also BANKING SYSTEM.

Further reading

Downes, John, and Jordan Elliot Goodman. *Finance and Investment Handbook*. 3d ed. New York: Barron's, 1990; Gitman, Lawrence J. *Principles of Managerial Finance*. 6th ed. New York: HarperCollins, 1991; Hayes, Samuel L., and Philip M. Hubbard. *Investment Banking: A Tale of Three Cities*. Boston: Harvard Business School Press, 1990; Kessler, Robert A. "The Effect of the Securities Laws upon the Small Business," *The Practical Lawyer,* 1 September 1982: 11. Reprinted in Larry D. Sonderquist, et al. *Corporations and Other Business Organizations: Cases, Materials, Problems*. 5th ed. New York: LEXIS Publishing, 2001.

—Gayatri Gupta

investment clubs

Investment clubs are a popular way for Americans to learn about and become involved in STOCK MARKET investing. In an investment club, members agree to contribute a set amount of MONEY each month, often $50; review and evaluate stock choices; and make INVESTMENT decisions based on member voting.

Many Americans, especially before 1990, had little involvement in the stock market. Until then, stock-market investing could only be done through brokerage houses, which provided investment management and advice but also charged significant fees for purchases and sales of stock. In addition, until the 1990s, most American workers were part of defined-benefit rather than defined-contribution RETIREMENT PLANS. In a defined-benefit plan, a worker's retirement pay is a percentage of his or her pay. In a defined-contribution plan, workers contribute a set percentage of their pay into a retirement plan, which is usually matched by their employer, but each worker determines how the funds are invested. The movement away from expensive, full-service brokers and the increase in worker-controlled retirement investment contributed significantly to the growth of investment clubs.

The National Association of Investment Clubs, later renamed the National Association of Investors Corporation, was established in 1951. Interest in investment clubs grew rapidly in the 1990s, and, by 1998 there were over 36,000 NAIC clubs with 600,000 members.

In the early 2000s, the organization was the subject of a Senate Finance Committee inquiry regarding not-for-profit organizations. The committee referred the organization to both the INTERNAL REVENUE SERVICE and the SECURITIES AND EXCHANGE COMMISSION, suggesting NAIC had violated its tax-exempt status. An investigative television news story and a 2007 *Wall Street Journal* article included allegations of excessive executive compensation and mismanagement. As a result of these problems, many local and national volunteers have resigned from BetterInvesting (NAIC) and membership has fallen from a high of over 400,000 in 1999 to official estimates of approximately 100,000 in summer 2007.

There is also a World Federation of Investors.

Further reading
National Association of Investment Clubs Web site. Available online. URL: better-investing.org.

investment fraud
Many years ago the police officers who arrested bank robber Willie Sutton asked him why he always robbed banks. Sutton reportedly replied, "Because that is where the money is." Today, with a majority of Americans responsible for their own investment/retirement decisions, the opportunities for stealing people's money are many. In 2008 investment adviser Bernard Madoff was finally exposed in the largest PONZI SCHEME in history. A Ponzi scheme, named after Charles Ponzi, is an investment fraud in which investors are usually promised extraordinarily high rates of return. Initial investors are paid off with the funds of subsequent investors. Word quickly spreads and new investors, "pigeons," flock to the scheming promoter, sometimes begging to be taken on as an investment client. Madoff used this technique for over a decade with one variation. He did not promise or deliver extremely high rates of return but, instead, reported consistent, better-than-average returns during a period of market VOLATILITY.

A second type of investment fraud involves boiler rooms, TELEMARKETING criminals who call potential investors promoting the stocks of little-known companies, assuring investors that the stock price will rise rapidly. The SECURITIES AND EXCHANGE COMMISSION (SEC) describes a typical boiler room operation as:

> The brokers sat "cheek by jowl" in a room the size of a basketball court. All of their desks were lined up side by side in rows. The firm held mandatory sales meetings every morning at 8:30 a.m. at which time sales techniques were demonstrated and scripts for the firm's "house stock" . . . were distributed. Brokers were expected to follow the scripts and only give customers the information they contained. Brokers were discouraged from doing any outside research, and were told to rely on the firm's research and representations. . . . After the morning sales meeting, brokers were expected to spend the entire day (except for a lunch break) on the telephone. The firm expected a high volume of sales, and if brokers did not stay on the phone, they were fired.

Boiler room operators hold large quantities of the stock they are promoting, often in collusion with the owners of the company, and engage in what is called "pump and dump," pushing up the stock price and then selling their shares to naive or uninformed investors. Boiler room operators also promote exotic offshore investments, "risk-free returns," and "big money returns working from your home computer." To help investors avoid being take advantage of, the SEC created a list of "Ten Questions to Ask About Any Investment Opportunity."

1. Is the investment registered with the SEC and the state securities agency?
2. Is the person recommending this investment registered with the state securities agency? Is there a record of any complaints about this person?
3. How does this investment match the investor's investment objectives?
4. Where is the company incorporated? How can the investor obtain the latest reports that have been filed on this company?
5. What are the costs to buy, hold, and sell this investment? How easily can I sell?
6. Who is managing the investment? What experience do they have?
7. What is the risk that I could lose the money I invest?
8. What return can I expect on my money? When?

9. How long has the company been in business? Are they making money, and if so, how? What is their product or service? What other companies are in this business?

10. How can I get more information about this investment, such as audited financial statements?

While the Internet is a powerful tool for consumers and investors providing vast amounts of easily accessed information, it is also a common tool used in investment fraud. The SEC warns investors to be cautious in using information found on the Internet for investing decisions, particularly online investment newsletters, bulletin boards, and e-mail spam, in stating:

Online investment newsletters: Many offer investors seemingly unbiased information free of charge about featured companies or recommending "stock picks of the month." While legitimate online newsletters can help investors gather valuable information, others are fraud. Some companies pay the people who write online newsletters cash or securities to "tout" or recommend their stocks. While this isn't illegal, the federal securities laws require the newsletters to disclose who paid them, the amount, and the type of payment. But criminals fail to do so. Be suspicious of newsletters that do not specifically disclose these items: who paid them, the amount, and the type of payment. The following examples raise red flags because they do not contain specific information:

"From time to time, XYZ Newsletter may receive compensation from companies we write about."

"From time to time, XYZ Newsletter or its officers, directors, or staff may hold stock in some of the companies we write about."

"XYZ Newsletter receives fees from the companies we write about in our newsletter."

Online bulletin boards: Whether newsgroups, usenet, or web-based bulletin boards—have become an increasingly popular forum for investors to share information. Bulletin boards typically feature "threads" made up of numerous messages on various investment opportunities.

While some messages may be true, many turn out to be bogus—or even scams. Fraudsters often pump up a company or pretend to reveal "inside" information about upcoming announcements, new products, or lucrative contracts.

E-mail spam: Because junk e-mail is so cheap and easy to create, fraudsters increasingly use it to find investors for bogus investment schemes or to spread false information about a company. Spam allows the unscrupulous to target many more potential investors than cold calling or mass mailing.

While the Internet is widely used by criminals, it can also be used to avoid investment fraud. The SEC suggests investors start their research with the SEC's EDGAR database, where all U.S. companies with 500 or more investors and $10 million in net assets, and companies listed on any of the major stock exchanges, are required to submit audited financial statements. When considering investing in small, unregistered companies, the SEC candidly states, "The difference between investing in companies that register with the SEC and those that don't is like the difference between driving on a clear sunny day and driving at night without your headlights. You're asking for serious losses if you invest in small, thinly-traded companies that aren't widely known just by following the signs you read on Internet bulletin boards or online newsletters."

The Internet can also be used to check the disciplinary history of the broker or firm that's touting the stock, through the Financial Industry Regulatory Association's (FINRA) broker check Web site. In 2009 the SEC provided a sampling of recent cases in which it took action to fight Internet fraud:

Francis A. Tribble and Sloane Fitzgerald, Inc. sent more than six million unsolicited e-mails, built bogus Web sites, and distributed an online newsletter over a 10-month period to promote two small, thinly traded "microcap" companies. Their massive spamming campaign triggered the largest number of complaints to the SEC's online Enforcement Complaint Center.

Charles O. Huttoe and 12 other defendants secretly distributed to friends and family nearly 42 million shares of Systems of Excellence Inc., known by its ticker symbol "SEXI." Huttoe drove up the price of SEXI shares through false press releases claiming nonexistent multimillion dollar sales, an acquisition that had not occurred, and revenue projections that had no basis in reality. He also bribed codefendant SGA Goldstar to tout SEXI to subscribers of SGA Goldstar's online "Whisper Stocks" newsletter. Both Huttoe and Theodore R. Melcher, Jr., author of the online newsletter, were sentenced to federal prison.

Matthew Bowin recruited investors for his company, Interactive Products and Services, in a direct public offering done entirely over the Internet. He raised $190,000 from 150 investors. But instead of using the money to build the company, Bowin pocketed the proceeds and bought groceries and stereo equipment. He was convicted of 54 felony counts and sentenced to 10 years in jail.

IVT Systems solicited investments to finance the construction of an ethanol plant in the Dominican Republic. The Internet solicitations promised a return of 50 percent or more with no reasonable basis for the prediction. Its literature contained lies about contracts with well-known companies and omitted other important information for investors.

Gene Block and Renate Haag were caught offering "prime bank" securities, a type of security that doesn't exist. They collected over $3.5 million by promising to double investors' money in four months. The SEC has frozen their assets and stopped them from continuing their fraud.

Daniel Odulo was stopped from soliciting investors for a proposed eel farm. Odulo promised investors a "whopping 20% return," claiming that the investment was "low risk."

Further reading
Securities and Exchange Commission Web site. Available online. URL: www.sec.gov.

invitation to bid   See REQUEST FOR PROPOSAL, INVITATION TO BID.

ISO standards
The International Organization for Standardization (ISO) is a nongovernmental worldwide federation whose mission is to promote the development of standardization (have weights, measures, etc., conform to a standard). The ISO believes standardization facilitates the international exchange of goods and SERVICES; its efforts result in international agreements reducing or eliminating technical barriers to global trade. For example, through the ISO a uniform thickness of 0.76 millimeters was agreed on for credit, debit, and phone cards. This has created greater efficiency for both consumers and businesses as CREDIT CARDS can be used in almost any country in the world, in part because the size of cards were standardized.

The ISO includes national standards bodies from 130 countries, each of which has one organization representing it in the ISO. The U.S. representative is the American National Standards Institute (ANSI), a private, nonprofit organization, which administers and coordinates U.S. private-sector voluntary standardization. ANSI was founded by five engineering societies and three governmental agencies in 1918. Its goal is to "enhance global competitiveness of U.S. businesses and American quality of life by promoting voluntary consensus standards and conformity assessment systems."

International standardization began in electromagnetics with the creation of the International Electrotechnical Commission (IEC) in 1906. The International Federation of the National Standardizing Associations (ISA), emphasizing mechanical engineering standards, was set up in 1926. The ISA effort ceased with the beginning of World War II and was replaced by the ISO in 1947.

The acronym ISO is, in itself, a standardization. In English the organization's initials would be IOS, but in French, the other standard language of the ISO, its initials would be OIN (from Organization International de Normalization). Instead, ISO, which comes from the Greek *isos,* meaning "equal," is the group's global acronym.

A few years ago not many people had ever heard of the ISO. Today, trade liberalization, GLOBALIZATION, interconnections among market sectors, worldwide communications systems, global standards for emerging technologies, and the needs of developing countries for INFRASTRUCTURE standardization all contribute to the expanding need for technology standards. As a result, the ISO's role is growing rapidly.

Within industries, suppliers, users, and sometimes governments participate in the process of defining standards. The ISO's goals are to "facilitate trade and TECHNOLOGY TRANSFER through:

- Enhanced product quality and reliability
- Reduced waste
- Greater compatibility and interoperability of goods and services
- Simplification for improved usability
- Reduction of the number of models
- Increased distribution efficiency and ease of maintenance."

The process of creating ISO standards involves thousands of people, including ISO committees, representatives of industries, research institutes, government authorities, consumer groups, and international organizations. The need for a standard is usually proposed by an industry sector, which communicates their need to their national member body (ANSI in the United States), which then proposes study of the issue to the ISO. Once accepted for evaluation, the first phase involves definition of the technical scope of the future standard.

Over 30,000 experts participate in ISO-sponsored meetings annually. The organization's members group themselves into standards committees, and the views of all interest groups are solicited. Groups within the ISO negotiate the detailed specifications within a standard. During the final phase, a draft international standard must be approved by three-fourths of all voting members. By the year 2009, there were over 17,500 international standards.

As their goals suggest, the ISO is primarily a business organization. Standardization reduces the cost of doing business. For example, anyone who has worked on both an American-made and a foreign-made car knows two sets of wrenches are required. Similarly, anyone who has traveled

abroad knows U.S.-made appliances cannot be used in most foreign electrical systems. Standardization eliminates such problems. The ISO facilitated the creation of standards for:

- film-speed code
- freight container sizes
- paper sizes
- symbols for automatic controls
- codes for country names, currencies, and languages

In the last decade, two of the ISO's major efforts were ISO 9000, which provides a framework for quality management and quality assurance; and ISO 14000, which provides a framework for environmental management. First adopted by European manufacturers in the 1990s, ISO 9000 standards of quality assurance have become widely accepted and are often a condition for doing business with companies. To become ISO 9000-certified, a company must conduct an on-site audit, including inspection, to ensure that documented quality procedures are in place and that all employees understand and follow those procedures. Once certified, a company is periodically audited to verify it is in compliance with ISO standards.

The ISO 9000 series standards include nine principles of quality management.

- customer focus
- LEADERSHIP
- involvement of people
- process approach
- system approach to MANAGEMENT
- continual improvement
- factual approach to decision making
- mutually beneficial supplier relationships

The ISO 14000 series, first published in 1996, is a result of the ISO's focus on sustainable development. The 14000 series has 21 published standards, including an audit of a firm's environmental management system; monitoring and measuring environmental performance of its activities, PRODUCTs, and services; and LIFE CYCLE assessment. Both the 9000 and 14000 series are in the process of being reviewed and revised, reflecting changing technology and lessons learned in QUALITY CONTROL and environmental management.

The ISO is headquartered in Geneva, Switzerland, which is also the headquarters of the WORLD TRADE ORGANIZATION (WTO). It is "building a strategic partnership" with the WTO, providing technical agreements to support WTO trade agreements. The ISO also maintains ISONET, the ISO Information Network, a global network of national standards information centers.

Further reading

Boone, Louis E., and David L. Kurtz. *Contemporary Marketing.* 14th ed. Fort Worth: South-Western, 2009; International Organization for Standardization Web site. Available online. URL: www.iso.ch.

job satisfaction

Job satisfaction has to do with employees' attitudes towards and liking for their work. Measures of job satisfaction are often used to predict how long employees will continue working for a particular company, as well as their level of ORGANIZATIONAL COMMITMENT. Variables affecting job satisfaction typically include both organizational and personal factors.

There are numerous organizational factors that affect job satisfaction. First, the structure of the company's reward system—the means through which employees earn promotions, salary increases, or other rewards—is important in determining satisfaction. Reward structures that hinder professional development or provide little recognition for employees' contributions to company success lead to lower levels of satisfaction. On the other hand, reward structures that provide reasonable and adequate opportunities for employees' contributions to be recognized and rewarded are associated with more positive attitudes about the job.

Both the actual and perceived quality of the supervision at work also affect job satisfaction. Competent supervisors who treat employees with respect and consider the needs and interests of the employees when they make decisions tend to foster high levels of job satisfaction on the part of the company's employees. Company executives who are flexible and recognize when a particular situation calls for them to change their tactics tend to provide the most effective LEADERSHIP. Sometimes a leader may need to be autocratic when directing employees in order to accomplish a task or resolve a problem. However, at other times the key to success may involve a democratic approach, with employees participating in decision making and helping to shape outcomes. Unfortunately, some leaders are rigid about their preferred approach and may miss opportunities for more successful interactions with employees. Poor leadership or supervision is associated with low levels of job satisfaction and higher levels of job turnover, which may ultimately cost the company in terms of money and reputation.

The specific characteristics of the job also affect satisfaction. Jobs that allow workers to use a variety of skills and see tasks through to completion are associated with higher levels of job satisfaction. Higher job satisfaction is also related to perceiving importance in the work, having a sense of autonomy on the job, and receiving feedback. Monotonous and hectic tasks and those assignments that do not stimulate employees are all related to lower levels of job satisfaction. Employees in these types of positions, such as people who work on ASSEMBLY LINES in factories, report higher levels of psychological distress and tend to have a high number of absences from work. High-quality supervision is especially important in these types of jobs, as it can help increase productivity and satisfaction when workers perceive that their contributions are valued. The HAWTHORNE EXPERIMENTS demonstrated positive effects on productivity when management simply showed an interest in their factory workers.

Many personal factors also affect job satisfaction—for example, higher levels of status and SENIORITY. Employees who have been with a company for longer periods of time typically tend to have seniority and are more satisfied than are newer employees. In addition, when the responsibilities of a particular job are well matched to the employee's personal interests, job satisfaction tends to increase. Finally, job satisfaction is linked to employees' personal satisfaction with life outside work. People who are happy in their personal lives tend to have more positive attitudes toward work than those who are unhappy.

There are many ways a company may try to increase job satisfaction for its employees. For example, rewarding an employee with a deserved raise in a timely fashion or amending a job description so that it more closely matches the employee's interests will likely increase satisfaction both at work and at home. Given that job satisfaction is such an important aspect of working life, leaders who carefully consider how their decisions affect both the company and its employees should promote the success of both.

See also EMPLOYEE MOTIVATION.

Further reading
Baron, Robert A., Donn Byrne, and Nyla R. Branscombe. *Social Psychology*. 11th ed. Boston: Allyn and Bacon, 2006; Schneider, Frank W., Jamie A. Gruman, and Larry M. Coutts, eds. *Applied Social Psychology: Understanding and Addressing Social and Practical Problems*. Thousand Oaks, Calif.: Sage, 2005.

—Elizabeth L. Cralley

joint venture

A joint venture is the combined effort of two or more business entities for a limited purpose. Joint ventures are frequently established for coordinated research, international expansion, and specialized PRODUCTION. Creating a joint venture involves both legal and strategic MANAGEMENT implications.

In the United States, joint venture agreements are similar to PARTNERSHIPS. Generally partnership law applies to joint ventures, including personal LIABILITY for its debts and treatment for federal income-tax purposes. The most significant difference between a joint venture and a partnership is that participants in a joint venture usually have less implied and apparent authority than partners, because of the limited nature of the joint-venture activity. For example, a joint venture among pharmaceutical companies to conduct research would limit the actions and decision-making authority of managers to research-related activities, and not include marketing or production decisions.

Joint ventures are also scrutinized under ANTITRUST LAW. Joint ventures, by definition, involve integration of resources between or among firms. Joint ventures hope to yield improved efficiencies through collective effort, more than could be achieved by any one firm. While a joint sales agency created to fix prices would be illegal, a joint research and development venture is more likely be legal. In 1984 Congress passed the National Cooperative Research Act (NCRA), requiring firms contemplating a joint RESEARCH AND DEVELOPMENT venture to notify the Department of Justice and the FEDERAL TRADE COMMISSION in advance. The act limited the antitrust liability of firms engaged in joint research and development ventures. The act was later amended to include joint production ventures as well.

Joint ventures often enter into strategic management decisions when they are used or considered in international expansion. Frequently U.S. businesses expanding abroad will choose to form joint-venture agreements with host-country firms. After the passage of the NORTH AMERICAN FREE TRADE AGREEMENT (NAFTA) in 1994, many U.S. firms entered Mexican markets through joint ventures. Walmart partnered with Cifra, a chain of discount stores in Mexico, which provided knowledge of local markets, customs, rules, and regulations, as well as an existing distribution system. Walmart provided financial RESOURCES, buying power, and systems management experience and efficiency. Some U.S. firms entered Mexico through joint-venture agreements and then bought out their partner or expanded on their own.

Management specialists caution companies entering into joint ventures to carefully define the rights and responsibilities of each participant and to develop a working relationship before entering into a joint venture. In the 1990s, many U.S. firms rushed into joint ventures as a means to enter the Chinese market, only to be disappointed with the results.

Further reading

Mallor, Jane P., A. James Barnes, Thomas Bowers, Michael J. Philips, and Arlen W. Langvardt. *Business Law: The Ethical, Global, and E-Commerce Environment.* 14th ed. Boston: McGraw-Hill, 2009.

Jones Act (Merchant Marine Act)

The Jones Act (officially named the Merchant Marine Act of 1920) and related statutes require that vessels used to transport passengers and cargo between U.S. ports be owned by U.S. citizens, built in U.S. shipyards, and manned by crews of U.S. citizens. According to the wording of the act, its purpose "is to maintain reliable domestic shipping services and to ensure the existence of a domestic maritime industry available and subject to national control in time of need." The Jones Act is also known as the "cabotage" law. Cabotage, from the old French word for "cape," means navigation along a coastline and now refers to all navigation within a country's waters. Most major maritime countries have cabotage laws similar to the Jones Act.

Enacted after World War I, the Jones Act, like other industry-protection laws, reduces market competition in the name of national security. When World War II began, the existing shipping industry and ship-building INFRASTRUCTURE became the basis for naval military resources. More recently, during the 1990 Gulf War, the U.S.

military chartered domestic cargo ships and tankers from the "Jones Act fleet" and used American merchant seaman to supply U.S. forces in the Middle East.

One question associated with the Jones Act is: What is a vessel? According to the Louisiana Workers' Compensation corporation Jones Act case history defines a vessel as "a structure designed for and being used for the transportation of passengers, cargo, or equipment across navigable waters." Determining what constitutes a Jones Act vessel has significant implications. The act's critics contend the United States' fleet of vessels is miniscule, and it is unrealistic to think the Jones Act is helping to protect national security in an emergency. The Jones Act Reform Coalition claims, ". . . the United States today has no more than 128 privately owned vessels over 1,000 tons in domestic service . . . all but 33 of these vessels are tankers or tub-barge combinations carrying liquid bulk cargoes." The act's supporters contend the United States has "more than 44,000 vessels in the U.S. Jones Act fleet." Both sides agree that foreign-flagged vessels transport 97 percent of all cargoes moving into and out of American ports.

Critics argue the act has not worked and has increased the cost of goods to consumers. They use examples like the reduction in U.S.-flagged tankers bringing oil from the Caribbean as a major factor in raising the cost of transportation of fuel oil to the Northeast. Other critics point out the act does not allow foreign-flagged shippers to stop in Hawaii on their way to the West Coast, forcing goods to go to the West Coast and then back to Hawaii. One University of Hawaii economist estimated abolishing the Jones Act shipping rules would save $500 to $600 per Hawaiian household. The act also prevents foreign-flagged cruise ships from operating in the Hawaiian Islands unless they add one foreign stop to the cruise itinerary—a difficult requirement, given how far Hawaii is from any other foreign port of call. Yet cruise companies are adding foreign destinations because it is cheaper than complying with U.S. merchant laws that would force them to hire U.S. crews and conform to U.S. environmental and labor laws.

Supporters of the Jones Act, such as Representative Neil Abercrombie, contend that "the dependability of Hawaii's maritime links to the mainland would vanish . . . Our now-dependable shipping would be under the control of whatever foreign government was most willing to subsidize its shipping. We could find Hawaii-mainland shipping routes under the control of a hostile nation."

As Representative Abercrombie suggests, many foreign governments are actively involved in subsidizing shipbuilding and shipping. Shipping is part of international trade infrastructure and almost always the cheapest form of bulk transportation. Countries that have access to international shipping have a COMPARATIVE ADVANTAGE over those that do no shipping. Shipbuilding is labor-intensive, creating thousands of jobs, and many countries subsidize shipbuilding as a means to ECONOMIC DEVELOPMENT. In the United States, one controversial "boondoggle," according to Arizona senator John McCain, was the proposal supported by Mississippi senator Trent Lott for the U.S. Navy to take over the CONTRACT for cruise ships being built in Mississippi boatyards.

Further reading

Dicus, Howard. "Rough Sailing for Shipping. Cloudy Future for Jones Act," *Pacific Business News,* 26 October 2001; "Jones Act Heightens Supply Risk," *LatAm Energy,* December 1, 2000; "The Jones Act: Fact and Fiction," Maritime Cabotage Task Force. Available online. URL: www.mctf.com.; Louisiana Workers' Compensation Corporation Web site. Available online. URL: www.LWCC.com/articles_legal.cfm?A=76&C=3. Accessed on June 2, 2003.

jumbo mortgage

A jumbo mortgage is a MORTGAGE with a loan amount above the industry-standard definition of conventional or "conforming loan" limits. In the United States, the conforming loan standard is set by the FEDERAL NATIONAL MORTGAGE ASSOCIATION (Fannie Mae) and the FEDERAL HOME LOAN MORTGAGE CORPORATION (Freddie Mac), until 2008 the two largest secondary mortgage market buyers. Since banks and mortgage brokers keep only a small portion of the loans they initiate in their portfolio of assets, most of the mortgage loans they make must meet Fannie and Freddie standards in order to be resold in the secondary market. As of 2009, the limit, for single-family units, was $417,000, or $625,500 in Alaska, Hawaii, Guam, and the U.S. Virgin Islands. (In 2008 as part of an economic stimulus package, President George W. Bush included a temporary increase in the conforming limit to $729,500 for the rest of that year.)

Other large investors, such as REAL ESTATE INVESTMENT TRUSTS (REITs), insurance companies, and banks purchase and hold jumbo mortgage loans. The interest rate charged on a jumbo mortgage is typically greater than is normal for conforming mortgages, and they vary depending on property types and mortgage amount. Historically, the rate on jumbo mortgages was about 0.3 percent higher than the rate on conforming mortgages. During the financial crisis in 2008–09 the differential rose to approximately 1.5 percent, reflecting the greater risk associated with these loans, the difficulty and added time needed to sell luxury housing, and the reluctance of lenders to make loans on higher-priced homes. Even before the financial crisis, most lenders required at least 5 percent down payment for a jumbo mortgage. Because the loans are large, jumbo lenders frequently offer only variable loan programs to jumbo clients, shifting interest rate risk to the borrower. It can be more expensive to refinance jumbo loans due to the higher closing costs and more limited choices of funding.

Until the housing market crash in 2007, in many areas of the country housing prices frequently rose above conforming limits, creating a large increase in the demand for jumbo loans. New loan programs began to be offered, including 40- or even 50-year amortization, or interest-only mortgages. These loans allowed the borrower to pay the mortgage over a longer period of time, or to defer any repayment of principal, thus reducing their current monthly payment. During the hey day of the housing boom, 80/20 and 80/15 jumbo loan programs became very popular with new home purchasers, where the homebuyer borrowed 80 percent using a jumbo first mortgage and then borrowed an additional 20 or 15 percent with a second mortgage. This allowed borrowers to avoid very expensive private mortgage insurance (PMI) required by most lenders to protect them from mortgage default.

In 2009 President Obama's housing stability plan excluded jumbo mortgage borrowers from nearly all of the government's bailout provisions. This forced buyers of high-priced homes to put up a greater percentage of the home price in order to get financing, with some lenders requiring up to 30 percent down payment. Other lenders are charging jumbo mortgage borrowers upfront origination fees of up to 5 percent of the loan. Tight financing resulted in reduced sales in affluent residential communities, further lowering housing prices. In 2009, nationwide, approximately 4 percent of all borrowers had jumbo mortgages, but the percentage varied significantly by region with much higher percentages in California and New York.

Further reading
Federal Home Loan Mortgage Corporation (Freddie Mac) Web site. Available online. URL: www.freddiemac.com; Timiraos, Nick. "Jumbo Mortgages, Jumbo Headaches," *Wall Street Journal,* 24 February 2009, D1.

just cause (sufficient cause)
Just cause is the dismissal or termination of an employee with good reason. Just-cause dismissal (also referred to as sufficient cause) can be based on any of four reasons: unsatisfactory performance, lack of qualifications, changed requirements for the job, or misconduct.

Unsatisfactory performance is failure to do the job as expected. It can include excessive absenteeism, tardiness, or failure to meet the job requirements. Human Resource professor Gary Dessler adds unsatisfactory performance can also be claimed when an employee displays an "adverse attitude toward the company, supervisor, or fellow employees."

Lack of qualification for a position exists when an employee diligently attempts to perform the job but is unable to do so. Changed job requirements as a basis for dismissal occurs when the needed tasks change or are eliminated. Workers who become unemployed due to changing job requirements are referred to as structurally unemployed.

Misconduct, which is usually defined as deliberate violation of the employer's rules, can include theft and insubordination. Insubordination is often used as a basis for just-cause dismissal of employees. Author Gary Dessler lists a variety of employee actions that can be labeled as insubordination:

- direct disregard for the employer's authority
- refusal to follow a supervisor's orders
- deliberate defiance of clearly stated company rules and policies
- public criticism of the employer
- blatant disregard for the supervisor's reasonable instructions
- disregard for the organizational chain of command
- participation in efforts to undermine and remove the supervisor

Just-cause dismissal contrasts with WRONGFUL DISCHARGE, dismissal that does not comply with laws or contractual arrangements between the employer and employee. Union CONTRACTS state the procedures and bases for employee dismissal in great detail. In nonunion workplaces, employee manuals, employment contracts, and promises between the employer and employee define just-cause dismissal. WHISTLE-BLOWER laws protect employees from wrongful discharge, but workers who engage in whistle-blowing often are dismissed, suffer ruined reputations, and spend years attempting to gain redress in the legal system.

Just-cause dismissal also contrasts with EMPLOYMENT (or termination) at will, a common legal doctrine in the United States, allowing either employers or employees to terminate a work agreement for any reason. State and federal laws vary, limiting termination-at-will doctrine in many situations.

Further reading

Dessler, Gary. *Human Resource Management*. 11th ed. Upper Saddle River, N.J.: Prentice Hall, 2007.

just-in-time production

Just-in-time production (JIT) is a MANAGEMENT philosophy that embraces eliminating all waste and continually upgrading and improving PRODUCTION processes. The basic concept of JIT is that materials and supplies are replenished exactly when they are needed rather than too early or too late, thus ensuring an efficient flow of production. JIT reduces the cost of having expensive materials sitting idle while waiting for production and eliminates the cost of having expensive equipment sitting idle while waiting for materials. It also reduces or eliminates related production costs such as scrap materials, defective PRODUCTS, unnecessary inventory, and wasted space, so that a company expends the least amount of RESOURCES—including materials, personnel, and facilities—to produce its final products. While traditional companies focus more on planning than control, expending tremendous time and energy planning inventory level, materials and parts shipments, production schedules, etc., a just-in-time company emphasizes control more than planning by developing flexible, fast operations and processes that enable quick response to changing market conditions.

The Toyota Motor Company developed the just-in-time production strategy in Japan in the mid-1970s. The Japanese approach to JIT is to make products "flow like water" through a company. JIT readily exposes problems common in traditional companies, such as defective parts, lost orders, late shipments, and an over-reliance on overtime, by eliminating the excessive inventory levels and management practices used to compensate for these problems. The Japanese compare inventory to a lake, and these types of problems to boulders beneath its surface. As the "water" (inventory) recedes, the "boulders" (problems) are exposed and "removed," or resolved. By reducing inventory to minimal levels, a JIT company achieves a constant work pace with products "flowing" through the production facility. Using the JIT philosophy,

Toyota reduced the time required to produce an automobile from 15 days to 1 day.

While JIT emphasizes the importance of reducing material inventories to support the concept of "the right parts, at the right place, at the right time," it is more than just an approach to dealing with materials. Just-in-time production affects all aspects of a company's operations, from product design and manufacturing operations to parts-suppliers and CUSTOMER RELATIONS. A JIT production environment requires a company to develop close relationships with selected vendors who participate in the design process and will ensure consistently high quality and on-time delivery of materials. JIT product engineering and design emphasizes standardization and continuous process improvements. The just-in-time production philosophy also changes the role of the labor force and of management. JIT strives to develop flexible, broadly skilled workers who are capable of solving production problems and initiating process improvements. In a non-JIT environment, management typically makes all production-related decisions. In a JIT production environment, teams comprised of workers and management make decisions jointly through consensus. Eliminating many of the status symbols traditionally reserved for management such as the executive dining room, reserved parking places, and executive bonuses creates a less adversarial relationship between workers and management, enhancing cooperation.

The just-in-time production concept, or management philosophy, is very much a part of the competitive strategy of most large companies today. Often referred to by other names such as "continuous flow manufacturing," "stockless production," "cellular manufacturing," or "lean production," JIT simplifies production and lowers costs, giving JIT companies a competitive edge. Current management literature suggests that implementing JIT offers many advantages to companies, including

- maintaining minimum inventory levels
- establishing customer order-driven production planning and scheduling

- purchasing materials in small-lot sizes only when required
- performing simple, quick, and inexpensive machine setups
- developing a flexible, multiskilled, and empowered workforce
- creating a flexible manufacturing system that quickly adapts to changing market conditions
- improving and maintaining product quality
- developing time- and cost-effective preventive maintenance
- promoting continuous process improvements
- improving worker morale
- reducing labor, material, and overhead costs

In spite of the obvious advantages of just-in-time production, many U.S. manufacturers have still not adopted a JIT philosophy. The dominant reason is that JIT requires an overall change in CORPORATE CULTURE at every level of an orga-nization. JIT demands new types of relation-ships with suppliers, customers, and employees that render traditional methods and processes obsolete. Additionally, implementing JIT requires an ongoing commitment to continuous improve-ment, not only in a company's products but also in its processes.

Further reading

American Production & Inventory Control Society, Incorporated. *Just-In-Time Reprints, Articles Selected by the Just-In-Time Committee of the APICS Curricula & Certification Council.* Alexandria, Va.: APICS, 1998; Monden, Yasuhiro. *Toyota Production System, An Inte-grated Approach to Just-in-Time.* 3d ed. Norcross, Ga.: Engineering & Management Press, 1998; Wheatley, Malcolm. *Understanding Just in Time.* Business Success Series. Hauppauge, N.Y.: Barron's Educational Series, 1997.

—Karen S. Groves

Keogh plan

A Keogh plan is a tax-deferred savings vehicle serving as a RETIREMENT PLAN for unincorporated businesses, usually small businesses or people who are self-employed. Keogh plans (which are also sometimes called "qualified plans" or "H.R. 10" plans) were named after New York Representative Eugene James Keogh and were first introduced in the 1960s. Keogh plans offer significant benefits over traditional INDIVIDUAL RETIREMENT ACCOUNTS (IRAs) and 401(K) PLANS for self-employed individuals and their employees. Like traditional IRAs and 401(k)s, Keogh plans allow for contributions to a retirement account, and the employee's contribution is pretax, which reduces his or her taxable INCOME. This MONEY can be invested, and the interest from INVESTMENTS is tax-free until the money is withdrawn from the plan. There is an additional tax advantage to employers who receive a "dollar for dollar" tax write-off for any money contributed to an employee's plan.

The chief advantage of a Keogh plan over traditional retirement accounts is the fact that it is possible to contribute more money annually. The amount of contribution possible depends on the Keogh plan chosen, but in 2009 it was generally a maximum of $49,000 per year. However, this changes often due to legislation and INFLATION.

There are two different Keogh plan options: the defined-benefit plan, and the defined-contribution plan. The defined-benefit plan is set up to give individuals a desired income upon retirement. There is a complex actuarial formula that is created individually for each employee to reach this income level, which cannot be more than the lesser of 100 percent of the employee's average compensation for the three highest consecutive calendar years, or $135,000 of income per year.

The more common defined-contribution plan allows for a maximum contribution of 100 percent of the employee's actual compensation, or $49,000. With defined-contribution plans, there are several ways that the money can be contributed. The most popular is the PROFIT SHARING plan, which allows employers to contribute up to 25 percent of all compensation per year to all participants in the plan. The employer also has the discretion to contribute nothing. Another option is a money-purchase plan in which the employer is required to contribute a set percentage of the employee's compensation regardless of whether the company makes a profit or not. It is also possible to combine the profit-sharing and money-purchase options so that a portion is at the discretion of the employer and a portion is set. One important note is that if a self-employed individual has a net loss for any year, that individual cannot contribute to his or her plan but may still contribute to his or her employee's plan.

Because Keogh plans are so complicated, it is usually necessary to have a retirement specialist set them up. Such specialists are a good source for more detailed information regarding Keogh plans. Details about the most current versions of Keogh plans can be found on the Internal Revenue Services Web site in Publication 560, available in PDF format on the INTERNET at www.irs.gov/pub/irs-pdf/p560.pdf; the information is in the section entitled "Qualified Plans."

—Joseph F. Klein

Keynesian economics

Keynesian (pronounced Canes-e-an) economics refers to the macroeconomic theories of John Maynard Keynes (1883–1946), considered by many to be the greatest economist of the 20th century. Lord Keynes, knighted for his work on behalf of Great Britain, developed much of the framework of modern macroeconomic theory.

Keynesian economics focuses on aggregate expenditures rather than aggregate SUPPLY in an economy. Aggregate expenditures are divided into four categories: CONSUMPTION, INVESTMENT, government, and net trade. In the Keynesian economics income-expenditures model, the price level is assumed to be fixed, and changes in aggregate expenditures determine the EQUILIBRIUM level of output. Later economists relaxed the assumption of fixed prices, arguing that as an economy approaches a full-EMPLOYMENT level of output, increases in aggregate expenditures will increase both INCOME and prices.

The Keynesian model challenged the prevailing classical theory, which suggested that an economy was always at or near a full-employment level of output and that adjustments in prices and wages would alleviate any temporary surpluses or shortages in the market.

Focusing on aggregate expenditures, the Keynesian economic model suggests that any source of expenditure stimulates output, income, and employment. Developed in the 1930s during the height of the GREAT DEPRESSION, Keynesian economics supported government intervention into the marketplace during periods of insufficient private-sector DEMAND. Keynesian economic thinking was consistent with the efforts of Franklin Roosevelt's "New Deal" programs, creating huge increases in government spending. (In Keynesian economics, when an economy is at or above a full-employment level of output, it is logical for government to reduce spending and/or increase taxes as a means of reducing inflationary pressure.)

Keynesian economics focuses on short-run adjustments in aggregate expenditures and income. In possibly his most famous quip, Keynes justified his approach by saying, "In the long run we are all dead."

Monetarists challenge Keynesian economic theory regarding the role and importance of INTEREST RATES. In Keynesian theory, changes in interest rates affect overall aggregate expenditures by changing levels of investment. Monetarists suggest changes in interest rates have a greater impact in an economy.

Further reading

Boyes, William, and Michael Melvin. *Macroeconomics*. 7th ed. Boston: Houghton Mifflin, 2007.

know-how

Know-how is valuable business knowledge; it may or may not be a trade secret, and may or may not be patentable. Know-how often refers to technical, scientific, or engineering fields. An engineer who specialized in industrial coatings once said, "I am more than willing to show my ideas and inventions to potential partners and investors. They could try to steal my ideas, but they do not have the know-how that comes from experience to make these things work without me." Know-how can also be more general in character, encompassing marketing and MANAGEMENT skills as well as simple business advice.

Legal protection for know-how is limited. Unlike PATENTS, TRADEMARKS, and COPYRIGHTS, individuals cannot obtain exclusive rights to know-how by registration. Knowledge is a public good; once it is made available to others, it can generally be used by anyone and is nearly impossible to retrieve. Because know-how is so difficult to protect, preserving its confidentiality is often an important business strategy. If competitors gain access to critical knowledge about a firm's production or operations, the firm loses some of its competitive advantage. For example, one of Walmart's secrets of success is its inventory management system. When Amazon.com hired away some of Walmart's inventory-management executives, Walmart sued, claiming loss of company know-how. Similarly, one of the best-kept business secrets is the Coca- Cola formula. Only a few people in the company know the formula, a necessary precaution to prevent loss of this critical knowledge.

Protecting business know-how is usually done through confidentiality CONTRACTS, civil law, and use of trade-secret law. It is often difficult to sue for the loss of know-how, so employers' best efforts focus on protecting knowledge. In the United States, the ECONOMIC ESPIONAGE ACT (1996) created criminal penalties for misappropriation of financial, business, scientific, technical, economic, or engineering information whose owner has taken reasonable measures to keep it secret and whose "independent economic value derives from being closely held." MARKET INTELLIGENCE experts advise that people are the sources of information, and the best protection of know-how is clear instructions to company personnel.

knowledge management

Knowledge management (KM) is a business activity through which organizations generate value utilizing their explicit and tacit intellectual assets. This is accomplished through the dissemination and utilization of knowledge. The practice of KM involves combining explicit assets (information technologies) with tacit assets (competencies and experiences possessed by employees).

In one form or another, knowledge management has been around for as long as people have been conducting business. Elements of KM exist in all work environments. SENIORITY systems explic-itly place a value on the knowledge gained over time by employees who have worked longer in the organization. Companies often have someone who is known and deferred to for his or her knowledge of company history. In many societies, philosophers, priests, teachers, and politicians act as the source of knowledge for their organization. In the 1990s, KM became popular among "new economy" companies, where the rapid pace of technology led to almost continual improvement of software, computer, and electronic technology. Firms that did not retain their RESEARCH AND DEVELOPMENT personnel quickly lost their knowledge base and competitive advantage.

Knowledge management helps organizations gain knowledge from its own experiences and the experiences of its employees. This knowledge is then merged into the organizational structure and existing technology, which in turn produces new knowledge, continuing the organization's evolution.

Many companies have attempted to formulate explicit knowledge-management programs. In any organization it is difficult to determine what is known and who knows it. MARKET INTELLIGENCE professionals recommend determining what information is most valuable and deciding who should have access to that information. KM professionals attempt to determine where information is gathered and coordinate access to that knowledge in order to achieve company goals. With today's electronic information systems, many professionals are experiencing information overload. Effective DATABASE MANAGEMENT systems allow managers to access explicit information as needed and combine tacit knowledge to explore new opportunities, address problems, and achieve objectives.

Further reading

Hallriegel, D., S. E. Jackson, and J. W. Slocum, Jr. *Management: A Competency-Based Approach.* 9th ed. Cincinnati, Ohio: South-Western Publishing, 2002; McFarland, Dalton E. *Management and Society.* Upper Saddle River, N.J.: Prentice Hall, 1982.

—R. Joseph Harold

Kondratev waves

Kondratev waves are 50-year periods of expansion and contraction in Western countries during the period from 1790 to 1940. These long-term BUSINESS CYCLES were first observed and analyzed by the Russian economist and statistician Nikolay Kondratev.

Kondratev's analysis showed three cycles.

1. 1792–1815
2. 1850–1896
3. 1896–1940

The third cycle included expansion from 1896 to 1920 and then contraction from 1920 to 1940, the period of Joseph Stalin's rule over the Soviet Union. This did not endear Kondratev to Russian leaders, and in 1928 he was dismissed from his post as director of the Institute for the Study of Business. He was later arrested, imprisoned, and received a death sentence.

Business-cycle scholars have studied Kondratev's work and developed a variety of hypotheses regarding these long-term waves, but no general consensus explanation has developed.

Kyoto Protocol (Kyoto Accord, Climate Change Treaty)

The Kyoto Protocol is a treaty intended to reduce the impact of human activity on the earth's environment. The focus of the treaty is global warming, but it also contains goals to reduce poverty and shepherd water RESOURCES. It is also called the Kyoto Accord or the Climate Change Treaty. This agreement was signed on December 11, 1997, in Kyoto, Japan, and was ratified by 160 countries by September 2002, the time of the United Nations World Summit on Sustainable Development in Johannesburg, South Africa. The Kyoto Protocol is significant for its emphasis on economic development in a manner that can be sustained by the planet's resources.

The Kyoto Protocol sets targets to reduce greenhouse gas emissions 8 percent below 1990 levels in the EUROPEAN UNION and 6 percent in Japan. Less-developed countries are not obligated to limit their emissions under the agreement. Under the Clinton administration, the United States agreed to a 7 percent reduction below 1990 levels, but the second Bush administration argued that this target would curtail its economy too much and withdrew from negotiations in March 2001.

History

The United Nations Framework Convention on Climate Change (UNFCCC) resulted in the creation of the Kyoto Protocol. In 1974 an English atmospheric scientist, Brian Gardiner, hypothesized that the earth's stratosphere was developing a hole in it due to chlorofluorocarbons (CFCs), chemicals found in refrigerants and aerosol propellants and fossil fuel emissions. The decade from 1970 to 1980 saw an increased awareness in the damage to the earth's stratosphere, as the "hole" in the ozone layer over Antarctica grew.

The Kyoto Protocol evolved out of many earlier steps.

- Vienna Protocol (1981). This summit was convened to acknowledge and discuss the problem with the ozone layer, and it organized a working group.
- MONTREAL PROTOCOL (1987). This measure identified offending chemicals by name and stipulated that industrial activities continue on the condition that industry produce fewer CFCs. The Montreal Protocol added halon (an ingredient in fire extinguishers) to the list of offending chemicals.
- London Amendment to the Montreal Protocol (1990). The London Amendment mandated complete phase-out of the production of chemicals degrading the atmosphere (CFCs, halon, carbon tetrachloride by 2000, and methyl chloroform by the year 2005). This was a more aggressive approach, in place of reductions in production levels.
- The Copenhagen Agreement (1992). This was significant for its establishment of a WORLD BANK fund to assist EMERGING MARKETS in seeking alternatives to CFCs. The fund's contributors were developed countries such as United States.

In 1997 the Kyoto Protocol set the following environmental goals: to slow the rate at which emissions are accumulating in the earth's atmosphere, to decrease the world's reliance on fossil fuel, to stop deforestation, and to explore renewable energy more actively. Industrialized nations argue that too drastic a reduction in the rate of increase in emissions will stagnate the world economy. Environmentalists counter that all nations enjoy the benefit of the clean air, therefore all must join in the effort to end global warming.

Participants in the Debate Over the Kyoto Protocol

Scientists, on whose work legislators rely but whose word is sometimes disputed, play an important role in defining environmental problems. Participants in the Kyoto Protocol who are held accountable for environmental degradation challenge the credibility of scientific data or deny the environmental problem altogether. Lawmakers who do not understand or trust data they are being given, however good that data may be, postpone decisive action. With each environmental summit called by the United Nations, countries review new developments from scientific research (either privately funded or government-funded) and revisit questions on pollution costs.

Members of industry, whose PRODUCTION processes create harmful emissions, argue that the cost of providing their communities with goods and services will go up if the standards of the Kyoto Protocol are enforced. The threat of putting employees out of work leads to some vociferous arguments against environmental standards that are seen as too harsh. The biggest consumers of fossil fuels are power plants, energy-intensive industries, and motorized vehicles. History shows that an industry or a utility, left on its own, is very slow to change its manufacturing practices if it must incur a cost.

Southern countries (Australia and New Zealand) whose land mass is closest to the Antarctic, where the ozone hole is located, suffer higher rates of skin cancer due to exposure to too much ultraviolet light. (Australia did not ratify the Kyoto Protocol, although it was to be permitted to increase its levels of emissions to +8 percent of the 1990 levels.)

Developing countries (e.g., India, Thailand) need to develop INFRASTRUCTURES, generate electricity, and grow economically to catch up to a STANDARD OF LIVING more like that of industrialized nations. The social agenda of the Kyoto Protocol is complex because there must be increased productivity to raise developing nations out of poverty. That is why the developing countries have no emissions caps set in their portion of the agreement, something the developed nations perceive as unfair COMPETITION. A long-standing struggle between industrialized nations and developing nations concerns the proposition that the most-polluting nations should own the biggest share of the cost.

The emissions of developed countries (European Union, United States, and Japan) constitute the bulk of the problem plaguing the environment. These nations wish to continue to grow and also retain a competitive presence in the world economy. In 2002 California's emissions equaled Germany's, at 12 percent of the world's output. The United States' emissions contribution was 36 percent of the world's output.

The withdrawal of the United States from the Kyoto Protocol has drawn criticism from most quarters, especially U.S. environmentalists. Their skepticism comes from doubt regarding the United States' ability to control its level of greenhouse emissions by government programs inside the country. The Kyoto Protocol contains numerous compliance-related elements, such as reporting requirements and an expert-review process to assess implementation and identify potential cases of noncompliance.

To satisfy critics, the United States opted in 2001 to allocate money to research on advanced energy technology and research on climate change. Under the second Bush administration, the Office of Energy Efficiency and Renewable Energy had its budget increased by $1.2 billion. Its mission has been to investigate the use of wind power, solar power, and renewable energy.

The Kyoto Protocol strives for reduction in the rate of growth of emissions so that all countries can continue to have clean, healthy air without making the problem of global warming worse. The protocol also addresses the need for people to rise from poverty in developing nations. It presses for respect for the environment while achieving sustainable development so that the earth's resources are not exhausted prematurely. The levels of emissions prescribed in the treaty, tolerable to the environment if not world governments, are set to allow the world's rate of ECONOMIC GROWTH to continue, even if more slowly. As long as there are industries, utilities, and cars serving people, greenhouse gasses will persist.

Further reading

Buchanan, Rob. "1984: The Sky Is Falling," *Outside Magazine* 27, no. 10 (October 2002): 114; Department of Energy Office of Energy Efficiency and Renewable Energy Web site. Available online. URL: www.eren.doe.gov. Accessed on November 15, 2002; "Kyoto Protocol," Washington, D.C.: Congressional Quarterly Press, 2001; *Federal Regulatory Directory, 9/E.* Washington, D.C.: Congressional Quarterly Press, 1999; Harvard University International Environmental Policy Reference Guide. Available online. URL: environment.harvard.edu/guides/intenvpol/indexes/treaties/FCCC.html. Accessed on November 15, 2002; "Kyoto Conference/Protocol." In *International Encyclopedia of Environmental Politics.* Edited by John Barry and E. Gene Frankland. London, New York: Routledge, 2002; United National Framework Convention on Climate Change: Kyoto Protocol Text from the UNFCCC. Available online. URL: unfccc.int/resource/convkp.html. Accessed on November 18, 2002; "Global Warming," Environmental Protection Agency. Available online. URL: yosemite.epa.gov/oar/globalwarming.nsf/content/index.html. Accessed on November 17, 2002; United Nations Environment Programme. Available online. URL: www.unep.ch/ozone/vienna.shtml. Accessed on November 15, 2002.

—Dominique Winn